INDEPENDENT
HISTORICAL SOCIETIES

INDEPENDENT
HISTORICAL SOCIETIES

*An enquiry into their research and
publication functions and their
financial future*

BY

WALTER MUIR WHITEHILL

The Boston Athenæum · 1962

Distributed by Harvard University Press

THE STINEHOUR PRESS · LUNENBURG · VERMONT

To

Waldo Gifford Leland

CONTENTS

Preface

FEW books of American history are published today without some expression of the author's gratitude to one of the older state historical societies for assistance or for permission to publish manuscripts in their possession. The holdings of these societies turn up with remarkable frequency in the Franklin and Jefferson papers, and others of the great editorial projects inspired by the National Historical Publications Commission. The editors of *The Papers of James Madison,* for example, obtained copies of documents from fifty-five historical societies and fifty-three privately supported college libraries, yet, according to Dr. Ralph L. Ketcham, "the three largest providers have been the Pennsylvania, New-York, and Massachusetts Historical Societies, each of which had over one hundred Madison items." Dr. Ketcham goes on to remark: "After visiting scores of both public and private manuscript depositories, I have no hesitation in saying that insofar as protection from the elements, prevention of theft, and care in arrangement are concerned, the advantage over the years lies overwhelmingly with the private societies."

Professor Merrill Jensen of the University of Wisconsin wrote in 1955 to Dr. Stephen T. Riley, director of the Massachusetts Historical Society, to ask permission to reproduce manuscripts in a volume of American Colonial Documents, 1607–1776, which he edited for the series of *English Historical Documents* published by the Oxford

University Press. In his letter Professor Jensen observed: "When I came to sorting out the documents according to sources in which I found them, I discovered that the Massachusetts Historical Society wins by many lengths! It is not flattery but a simple statement of fact that the Massachusetts Historical Society has published more of what I consider to be the basic documents for early American history than any other society in the country. I must confess, however, that I didn't realize it until I had compiled my volume."

For periods ranging from 100 to 170 years, these societies, chiefly located along the Atlantic seaboard, have, as their chief reason for existence, collected, preserved, made available to scholars, and published source materials of American history. They have done so, without fanfare, from private funds that are astonishingly small for the results achieved. Their quiet work, which is not dramatic or spectacular in terms of news releases, is as little understood by the man in the street as what goes on in a scientific laboratory. Things of the mind do not lend themselves to sensational pronouncements. The opening paragraph of Dr. R. W. G. Vail's 1959 Director's Report of the New-York Historical Society is a case in point:

Every now and then the unique importance of our collection is emphasized when an item of some distinction is rediscovered by an expert and heralded to the scholarly world as an important find even though its possession was no surprise to us. This last year a historian from one of our neighboring universities "discovered" in our manuscript collection the original manuscript of paper Number 64 of *The Federalist* in the handwriting of John Jay, thus presumably proving that he was its author. Since we had had this significant document filed for years with our other Jay papers there did not seem to be too much reason to get excited about it, though it did make a good newspaper story throughout the country.

Until the last quarter of the nineteenth century, these old eastern state historical societies did their work virtually unaided by other than private funds. In the twentieth century other organizations entered the field of American history. Certain university libraries, of which Virginia and Yale are conspicuous examples, and others founded by great private collectors like John Carter Brown, William

L. Clements, and Henry E. Huntington, besides numerous historical museums and restorations, among which Colonial Williamsburg holds first place, have all made contributions as extensive as they are varied. The federal government, particularly through the establishment of the National Archives, and various enlightened states that have placed their own archives in good order or appropriated generously for their own historical societies, have eased the path of the historian. These newer allies have not, however, supplanted the older historical societies, which continue to collect manuscripts, set them in order and make them freely available to scholars, and to publish important collections of documents, journals, and monographs of professional value that have frequently an even wider general interest.

The financial resources of the independent historical societies are disparate in size, but almost invariably inadequate to the work in hand. Their expenditures are microscopic in comparison with those of scientific institutions. In recent years large sums have been made available for various efforts to popularize American history, but precious little has been directed towards the institutions that, at no expense to the taxpayer, have gathered and care for the basic sources. Never forget that without the essential manuscripts of American history there would be nothing to popularize; that without the continued work of the major independent historical societies there could be no Colonial Williamsburg, no *American Heritage*.

Many of the older societies have used their wits in imaginative ways to gain the support necessary for their activities. Their continued existence demonstrates that where ideas exist, money somehow gets found for useful enterprises. Nevertheless all independent historical societies spend too much of their time piecing their rags together. Because of the widespread nature of this financial crisis, the Massachusetts Historical Society, the American Antiquarian Society, the Historical Society of Pennsylvania, and the Virginia Historical Society joined informally in 1958 to seek foundation support for a study of the problem. The Council on Library Re-

sources, Inc., a subsidiary of the Ford Foundation, recognizing that
a genuine library problem is involved, made a grant for such a
study. In this I have been engaged, full time from the autumn of
1959 to October 1960, thanks to the willingness of the Trustees of
the Boston Athenæum to release me from my normal duties for
this period, and part time since.

Between October 1959 and June 1960 I traveled through three
quarters of the fifty states, visiting historical societies and as many
other institutions of allied interest as time permitted.   Wherever I
went I was impressed by the community of interests and feeling on
the part of those societies responsible for major manuscript collections, by their devotion to what they are doing as hewers of wood
and drawers of water in the cause of American history, and, in almost all cases, by the utter inadequacy of their financial resources.
I have never spent nine pleasanter or more profitable months. No
two societies are exactly alike or ever will be. Their principles, resources, and aspirations could never be adequately reduced to punch
cards or expressed in statistical tables. But through visiting them I
came to know an extraordinary number of highly intelligent, energetic, and amiable people, many of whom I already regard as valued
friends.

With the prosperity of the 1950s, many cities in the United States
are fast losing their distinctive characteristics through the blight of
speculative redevelopment. New airports, civic centers, and housing
projects in which gaunt boxlike forms rise from a sea of parked cars
are making many American cities look like each other or like some
in the Netherlands and Israel. Even in unregenerate areas, haphazard
demolition to create parking lots makes many city blocks as un-
attractive as a smile that is short of teeth. The approaches to cities are
often disfigured by miles of used car lots, made glittering by ropes of
electric bulbs or, even worse, by the dumps of rusting carcasses of
automobiles that are past resale. Most interstate highways have a
monotony of outlook, for only the most mountainous terrain resists
the leveling jaw of the bulldozer, and the restaurants along them
achieve a wearisome mediocrity of victuals from coast to coast.

Good guide books are scarce. With only the uncritical and strongly commercial assistance of *This Week in Demopolis*, thoughtfully provided in hotel bedrooms along with the Gideon Bible (and in some regions the *Book of Mormon*), the traveling foreigner, or even a footloose New Englander, might easily be misled into thinking that large areas of the United States were uniformly dull or monotonous. He might also fail to discover that many of the disagreeable qualities once found by Sinclair Lewis in Main Street have, in the past generation, moved east to Madison Avenue, to the great improvement of their former habitat.

Mercifully all regions have their share of opposite-minded persons who cultivate the arts, enjoy good conversation, food, and drink, and cherish the characteristics of building and scene that differentiate their county from the next. A large proportion of these have some connection with historical societies, libraries, or the history departments of universities. At no point in my travels did I fail to encounter someone of this temperament. In fact I found so many, and through their guidance developed an enthusiasm for so many places in the United States, that I am here reduced to collective thanks for friendly assistance generously given wherever I went.

The great variety of historical activity that I encountered proved particularly interesting because of the heterodox sequence of events in my own life over the past thirty-five years. For ten years after graduation from Harvard in 1926 I was immersed in the Spanish middle ages, working chiefly in architectural history and paleography, with the British Museum, the Courtauld Institute of the University of London, and the Institut d'Estudis Catalans in Barcelona as my chief bases. During these years I came to know a number of libraries, archives, and museums in the British Isles, Spain, and France, as well as the techniques of research in a field where documents are scarce and one must extract all possible meaning from those that have survived.

During six years as assistant director of the Peabody Museum of Salem, a post that I took in 1936, originally with the thought of having something to do for the duration of the Spanish Civil War, I became so much involved with American history that I have never returned to Spain or the middle ages. There I became familiar with the mixture of administrative, curatorial, and editorial work that is inevitable in a historical museum with a small staff. I hung exhibitions, cleaned out storage cases, arranged and catalogued many thousands of manuscripts, edited publications, and with a group of friends launched in 1941 *The American Neptune, A Quarterly Journal of Maritime History.*

At the Office of Naval Records and Library, Navy Department, from 1942 to 1946, I was chiefly concerned with the current operational records of World War II. In Spain I had had to scratch hard to find pertinent documents. In Washington, where mailbags full arrived several times a day under Marine guard, the problem was to get masses of papers under lock and key and reduce them as rapidly as possible to an order suitable for current as well as historical reference. During these years I observed some of the problems of recording "oral history," became familiar with the bowels of the National Archives, and came to know Fleet Admiral Ernest J. King, whose biography I wrote after the war. That book, like all pieces of contemporary history, involved a selection of sources that was quite the opposite of the technique that one would follow in the middle ages. In compensation, it was a great advantage to have my subject at hand, willing and ready to answer questions.

Since 1946, as director and librarian of the Boston Athenæum, a proprietary library founded in 1807 that promotes in its own curious way the functions of research and pleasant general reading, I have seen something of the problems of an old institution chiefly dependent upon endowment, during inflationary times. As part-time senior tutor of Lowell House from 1952 to 1956 and lecturer on history, Harvard University, 1956–57, I had a chance to try my hand at teaching undergraduates. Since 1946 I have also been closely involved in the affairs of the Massachusetts Historical Society, the Colonial Society of Massachusetts, the American Antiquarian Society, the Institute of Early American History and Culture at Williamsburg, and have served on the boards of the *New England Quarterly*, the *William and Mary Quarterly*, and the Adams and Franklin papers. As a trustee of one college, four museums, the National Trust for Historic Preservation, and a number of corporations that own historic sites on a beat extending from Vermont to Virginia, I have had a chance to learn something about historic preservation and education, in addition to the writing of history, which I conceive to be my profession.

This curious muddle of occupations, brought about in part by the circumstances of the Spanish Civil War and World War II, has been helpful in this study, for there are few activities of any historical society with which I had not had some previous acquaintance. For example, I have had a particular interest in observing the relationship between officers and members of the professional staffs of historical societies, for, while in one capacity I am responsible to the Trustees of the Boston Athenæum, in others I sit on the boards of a number of institutions.

While the announced purpose of this study is "the research and publication functions and the financial future of the independent historical societies," I have not confined my visits to privately supported state historical societies or my inquiries and comments to research, publications, and finances. Within the limits of the year available, I tried to get as clear a picture as I could of related activities in many parts of the country. As this provides a background for the situation of the independent historical societies, I have included much of it, although without claim to completeness or exhaustive treatment.

"Surveys" have become a national pastime. I eschew the word in connection with this study because of an item on the front page of the *Los Angeles Times* of 12 March 1960, headed "Trash Collection Survey Start Expected April 1," which states:

An over-all survey of refuse collection and disposal problems within the city of Los Angeles by nationally known research organizations may begin by April 1. That was indicated yesterday as members of the City Council's Public Works

Committee and other city officials met with representatives of Black and Veatch, Kansas City consulting firm, and Refuse Research Associates of San Diego, and agreed to terms of a contract by which the two firms will undertake the survey as a joint venture.

Lest there be any confusion in the reader's mind between historical and trash collection, I avoid the official phraseology and form of a "survey" as consistently as I can.

The first ten chapters describe the principal independent historical societies with historical background designed to suggest the manner in which they became what they are. Other organizations, save the State Historical Society of Wisconsin, which is treated in some detail as the prototype of the publicly supported society, are described more briefly with greater emphasis on their present activities. The final chapters consist of general observations and conclusions derived from the facts set forth earlier in the book.

Current information has been derived from personal observation, from conversation with or letters from the heads of organizations, or from published reports. Footnotes have been kept to a minimum. When a historical sketch of a society, or something else that is worth reading for its own sake, exists, I have given a reference. I have not done so when the note would only permit the reader to verify the accuracy of my transcription.

Where detailed histories do not exist, I have made constant use of *American Historical Societies, 1790–1860* by Dr. Leslie W. Dunlap, now director of libraries at the State University of Iowa. This valuable book, privately printed at Madison, Wisconsin, in 1944, not only gives brief sketches of individual societies, but discusses the nature of their activities. Within the period that it covers, I have mined many facts from it; as it has an excellent index, I have not given references for these. I am indebted to Dr. Dunlap for the gift of a copy, as I am to Mrs. Mary Givens Bryan, Director, Georgia Department of Archives and History, for a copy of the *1957 State Records Committee Reports* of the Society of American Archivists, which contains her highly useful comparative study of state and

U. S. territorial laws governing state archives. This has been another highly useful reference work.

I owe sincere thanks to the Council on Library Resources, Inc., for the opportunity to make this study and to the Trustees of the Boston Athenæum for the year they have allowed me for travel and writing—a kind of sabbatical leave that normally is restricted to university faculties. I am deeply grateful also to Mrs. Wendell D. Garrett for keeping my office in operation during my absence, as well as unearthing numerous useful facts, and to Miss Evelyn M. Coker for typing the final draft of the manuscript.

While so many friends have contributed to the making of this book that their help must be acknowledged in general terms, I must particularly thank Julian P. Boyd and Lyman H. Butterfield for constant encouragement and stimulating suggestions, and give myself the pleasure of dedicating this book to Waldo G. Leland, who fifty years ago probably knew more about American historical societies than I know now.

The preface and the first fourteen chapters that follow were completed at Starksboro, Vermont, in September 1960. I returned to the Boston Athenæum at the expiration of my year's leave of absence on 1 October 1960, foolishly confident that in the coming months I would find time for the remainder. I now wish that I had remained in Vermont until Thanksgiving. During the winter that followed I was asked to speak to various historical societies that I had previously visited. As these addresses frequently had to be printed, their preparation took time set aside for the writing of later chapters. Their publication has, however, given some advance circulation to the findings contained in this book. Thus in addition to "Celebration versus Celebration" for the Virginia Historical Society in May 1960 (*Virginia Magazine of History and Biography*, LXVIII [July 1960], 259–270), I spoke in December 1960 to the Historical and Philosophical Society of Ohio (*Bulletin*, XIX [January 1961], 3–20), and the Society of American Archivists (*The American Archivist*, XXIV [April 1961], 133–139), in February 1961 to the New-York

Historical Society (*Quarterly*, XLV [October 1961], 346–363) and the Missouri Historical Society, in March to the South Carolina Historical Society, and in April to the Maryland Historical Society (*Maryland Historical Magazine*, LVI [December 1961], 321–334). Unanticipated crises in historic preservation in Boston, combined with the extraordinary variety of inquiries of an unrelated sort that occur every day in the Athenæum, have made the final chapters go at a snail's pace. The 150th anniversary of the American Antiquarian Society, one of the sponsoring institutions of this study, makes October 1962 an inescapable publication date, for the society wishes to use this book as the theme for a two-day conference on the role of independent historical societies to commemorate that occasion. Where I have had continued association with a society or when the information has readily come to hand, I have inserted in the earlier chapters references to significant events of 1961 or the early months of 1962, but the majority of facts and figures offered date from my visits of 1959–60.

WALTER MUIR WHITEHILL

Boston Athenæum
28 May 1962

INDEPENDENT
HISTORICAL SOCIETIES

Chapter I

THE MASSACHUSETTS HISTORICAL SOCIETY

There is nothing like having a *good repository*, and keeping a *good lookout*, not waiting at home for things to fall into the lap, but prowling about like a wolf for the prey.

— REV. JEREMY BELKNAP, 1795

T HE Massachusetts Historical Society,[1] the first in the United States, was founded during President Washington's first term. Thomas Jefferson was in the White House, however, before it had any company. Its founder, the Reverend Jeremy Belknap (1744-98), had become minister of the Federal Street Church in Boston in 1787, after serving in Dover, New Hampshire, for twenty years. During his earlier pastorate Belknap began his *History of New Hampshire*, a work to which William Cullen Bryant later attributed "the high merit of being the first to make American history attractive." The first volume appeared in 1784; the third and last in 1792, five years after its author's return to Boston.

At that period the study and writing of modern history was the private affair of learned men. It was not an academic discipline and did not begin to become one for half a century. The writers and

---

1. The only recent historical sketches are Stephen T. Riley, *The Massachusetts Historical Society, 1791–1959* (Boston, 1959) and Stewart Mitchell, "Historical Sketch," *Handbook of the Massachusetts Historical Society, 1791–1948* (Boston, 1949), pp. 1–14. Statements and quotations in this chapter not otherwise documented are derived from these.

well-wishers of American history were clergymen, lawyers, public figures, booksellers, and merchants, rather than professors. When Jared Sparks was appointed McLean Professor of Ancient and Modern History at Harvard College in 1838, he was, according to Samuel Eliot Morison, "probably the first professor of civil history in any American university."[2]

In the summer of 1774, Dr. Belknap's friend Ebenezer Hazard, a New York bookseller, later postmaster general of the Confederation, issued a circular stating that he was compiling five volumes of *American State Papers*, containing "every important public Paper (such as Royal Grants, Acts of Parliament, &c. &c.) relating to America, of which either the original, or authentic Copies can be procured" from the voyages of the Cabots "down to the present time" and requesting "Gentlemen who are possessed of proper Materials for the Purpose . . . to favour him with the Use of them." The idea, although admirable, never came to complete fruition. The Continental Congress approved the project by formal resolution in 1778, but subscriptions came so slowly that publication began only in 1792 and ended two years later with the second volume, which only reached the year 1664. Perhaps the most significant result of Hazard's proposals was the testimonial elicited from Thomas Jefferson:

I learn with great satisfaction that you are about committing to the Press the valuable Historical and State Papers you have been so long collecting. Time and accident are committing daily havoc on the originals deposited in our public offices; the late war has done the work of centuries in this business; the lost cannot be recovered; but let us save what remains; not by vaults and locks, which fence them from the public eye and use in consigning them to the waste of time, but by such a multiplication of Copies as shall place them beyond the reach of accident.[3]

An acquaintance of Hazard's, a New York merchant, John Pintard (1759–1844), who possessed a valuable library of American

2. Samuel Eliot Morison, *Development of Harvard University, 1869–1929* (Cambridge, 1930), p. 152.

3. Lyman H. Butterfield, "Draper's Predecessors and Contemporaries," *Four Essays Commemorating The Draper Centennial* (Madison, 1954), pp. 2–4. Thomas Jefferson's letter is reproduced in Hampton L. Carson, *A History of the Historical Society of Pennsylvania* (Philadelphia, 1940), I, facing 158.

history, while visiting Boston in August 1789, called on Dr. Belknap and mentioned his dream of founding a society of antiquaries,[4] inspired at least in name by the Society of Antiquaries of London. This idea matured more rapidly in Boston than in New York, for Pintard's first attempt to carry it out in his own city fell by the wayside. On 26 August 1790 Pintard wrote to Thomas Jefferson:

In behalf of the trustees of the American Museum, belonging to the St. Tammanys Society in this city, I take the liberty to request, in case there should appear any supernumerary papers, Gazettes, &c. in your Department, not worth the trouble and expence of removal to Philadelphia, that you would be pleased to deposit them in the Museum where they will be carefully preserved and tend to form a collection which will always be open to the curious.

The object of this institution is to collect and preserve whatever relates to our Country in art or nature, as well as every material which may serve to perpetuate the Memorial of national events and history. A small fund is appropriated to support this design which is yet in its infancy, but we rely chiefly on what may be obtained by donations. The plan is a patriotic one and if prosecuted may prove a public benefit by affording a safe deposit for many fugitive tracts which surviving the purpose of a day, are generally afterwards consigned to oblivion tho' ever so important in themselves, as useful to illustrate the manners of the times.[5]

This museum, conceived by Pintard on a high level, degenerated under the guidance of others into a collection of curiosities and odd-

4. This visit, like other details of the founding of the Massachusetts Historical Society, is reflected in the pleasant correspondence between Belknap and Hazard, published in Massachusetts Historical Society *Collections*, 5th ser., III (1877). On 10 August 1789 Belknap wrote (p. 157) that Pintard had called: "he seems to have a literary taste, is very loquacious and unreserved. Do give me his character." On 27 August Hazard (p. 162) described him as "a lively, chearful man, who appears to me not to want understanding as much as he does solidity" and as "a singular mixture of heterogeneous particles." On 3 September (p. 164) Belknap wrote: "Pintard has written me a letter, and sent me some books. I must correspond with him." Hazard, on 5 September (p. 165), reports that "Mr. Pintard has mentioned to me his thoughts about an American Antiquarian Society. I am pleased with it." That Pintard was subsequently very helpful with the distribution of the *History of New Hampshire* is seen from Belknap's letter of 8 May 1792 (p. 293): "he was very friendly to me. He was my bookseller in New York, and paid me immediately for the whole parcel of the 1st and 2d volumes which I sent him, taking the distribution entirely to himself." See also James Grant Wilson, *John Pintard, Founder of the New York Historical Society* (New York, 1902); Walter Muir Whitehill, "John Pintard's 'Antiquarian Society'," *The New-York Historical Society Quarterly* XLV (1961), 346-363.

5. I owe the text of this letter to Julian P. Boyd, editor of *The Papers of Thomas Jefferson*. Pintard was for a time Grand Sachem of the St. Tammany Society.

ments; indeed in the next century its collection passed into the hands of P. T. Barnum.[6] But the idea of a society of antiquaries soon took hold in Boston. Dr. Belknap in the course of preparing his *History of New Hampshire* had frequently been in need of manuscript sources that were privately owned and not always accessible. In addition he often received requests for the use of manuscripts in his possession. Why not, indeed, establish a convenient centre where books and documents would be available to those who needed them?

To this end Dr. Belknap summoned four friends, two clerical and two lay—the Reverend John Eliot (1754–1813) of the New North Church, the Reverend Peter Thacher (1752–1802) of the Brattle Street Church, the distinguished Boston lawyer William Tudor (1750–1819), and James Winthrop (1752–1821), sometime librarian of Harvard College and later a judge of the Court of Common Pleas for Middlesex County. These five met on 26 August 1790, probably at Dr. Belknap's house, to discuss such a possibility.

The following day, Belknap, who never let grass grow between his feet, drew up a momentous document entitled "Plan of an Antiquarian Society"[7] in which he proposed:

A Society to be formed consisting of not more than *Seven at first* for the purpose of collecting, preserving and communicating the Antiquities of America.

Admissions to be made in such manner as the associated shall judge proper, the number of members to be limited.

Each Member to pay [blank] at his admission and [blank] yearly, this and other money to be applied to promoting the objects of the Society.

Each Member on his admission shall engage to use his utmost endeavours to collect and communicate to the Society—Manuscripts, printed books and pamphlets, historical facts, biographical anecdotes, observations in natural history, spe-

6. I. N. Phelps Stokes, *The Iconography of Manhattan Island* (New York, 1928), VI, 47–48, states that Pintard was working out the idea of such a museum as early as August 1789; that it was established in June 1790, but soon fell into the hands of Gardiner Baker who ran a "Menage" for wild animals and birds, which was the first zoological garden in the country. After various changes of hands P. T. Barnum bought it in 1841. It was destroyed by fire in 1865. This clearly was not the fulfillment of Pintard's idea.

7. Reproduced in facsimile in M.H.S. *Collections*, 5th ser., III, opposite 231.

cimens of natural and artificial curiosities and any other matters which may elucidate the natural and political history of America from the earliest times to the
present day. . . .

Letters shall be written to Gentlemen in each of the United States requesting
them to form similar societies and a correspondence shall be kept up between them
for the purpose of communicating discoveries to each other.

Each Society through the United States shall be desired from time to time to
publish such of their communications as they may judge proper, and all publications shall be made on paper and in pages of the same size, that they may be bound
together, and each society so publishing shall be desired to send gratuitously to
each of the other Societies one dozen copies at least of each publication.

Quarterly meetings to be held for the purpose of communicating, and in this
State the quarterly meetings shall be held on the days next following those appointed for the meetings of the American Academy of Arts and Sciences.[8]

When the Society's funds can afford it salaries shall be granted to the Secretaries
and other Officers.

The news of this meeting and plan was conveyed in confidence to
Hazard in a letter that Belknap wrote on the afternoon of 27 August:

When Mr. Pintard was here, he strongly urged the forming a Society of American
Antiquarians. Several other gentlemen have occasionally spoken to me on the
same subject. Yesterday I was in company where it was again mentioned, and it
was wished that a beginning could be made. This morning I have written something, and communicated it to the gentlemen who spoke of it. How it will issue,
time must determine. If it should come to any thing, you shall hear farther.[9]

A letter of 14 September suggests that the lawyer William Tudor
had been full of enthusiasm, but was now dragging his heels.

No more as yet about the Antiquarian Society. The gentleman who seemed so
zealous, as I wrote you has been ever since overwhelmed with business in the
Supreme Court, and I have not once seen him, for I seldom attend courts of any
kind.[10]

---

8. They still are, although both organizations now meet monthly from October
to May. The academy meets on second Wednesday evenings; the society on second
Thursday afternoons. A small number of gentlemen still follow each other about
in this way. The American Academy of Arts and Sciences was founded in Boston in
in 1780 by John Adams; its treasurer today is his great-great-great-grandson Thomas
Boylston Adams, president of the Massachusetts Historical Society.

9. M.H.S. *Collections*, 5th ser., III, 231.

10. M.H.S. *Collections*, 5th ser., III, 233.

Ebenezer Hazard replied on 8 October 1790: "I like Pintard's idea of a Society of American Antiquarians, but where will you find a sufficiency of members of suitable abilities and leisure?"[11]

Julian P. Boyd, who 144 years later described Jeremy Belknap's prospectus as "a charter of the historical society movement," observed that "In this provision for the exchange of multiple copies, and in Hazard's remark concerning men of 'suitable abilities and leisure', we have an indication of the nature of the early historical societies. They were to be academies for the exchange of facts and ideas among recognized men of learning; Belknap's prospectus called for a membership of seven but this was soon extended to thirty."[12]

The immediate solution for finding suitable members was for each of the founders to invite one friend each to join in the organization of what seemed on second thought more appropriate to call "The Historical Society." Thus Dr. William Baylies (1744–1826), the Reverend James Freeman (1759–1833) of King's Chapel, George Richards Minot (1758–1802), historian of Massachusetts and of Shays' Rebellion, James Sullivan (1744–1808), historian of the District of Maine and later Governor of Massachusetts, and Thomas Wallcut (1758–1840), an eccentric bachelor book collector, became part of the new enterprise. Eight of these ten "original members"— Minot was ill and Baylies out of town—met on 24 January 1791 at William Tudor's house in Court Street to organize a society whose aims were thus set forth:

The preservation of books, pamphlets, manuscripts and records, containing historical facts, biographical anecdotes, temporary projects, and beneficial speculations, conduces to mark the genius, delineate the manners, and trace the progress of society in the United States, and must always have a useful tendency to rescue the true history of this country from the ravages of time and the effects of ignorance and neglect.

11. M.H.S. *Collections*, 5th ser., III, 237.
12. "State and Local Historical Societies in the United States," *American Historical Review* XL (1934–35), 17.

A collection of observations and descriptions in natural history and topography, together with specimens of natural and artificial curiosities, and a selection of every thing which can improve and promote the historical knowledge of our country, either in a physical or political view, has long been considered as a desideratum; and, as such a plan can be best executed by a society whose sole and special care shall be confined to the above objects, we, the subscribers, do agree to form such an institution, and to associate for the above purposes.

Dr. Belknap was not a man to draft a dignified and resonant statement and sit back, waiting for nature to take its course. He was aware that before "books, pamphlets, manuscripts and records" could be preserved they must be collected. His energetic theory of seeking them out was summarized in a letter, often subsequently quoted, of 19 February 1791 to Ebenezer Hazard, who was to be the first corresponding member of the new society:

We intend to be an *active*, not a *passive*, literary body; not to lie waiting, like a bed of oysters, for the tide (of communication) to flow in upon us, but to *seek* and *find*, to *preserve* and *communicate*, literary intelligence, especially in the historical way.[13]

And again in 1795, in anticipation of scrounging documents from John Hancock and Samuel Adams, Belknap wrote to Hazard: "There is nothing like having a *good repository*, and keeping a *good lookout*, not waiting at home for things to fall into the lap, but prowling about like a wolf for the prey."[14] Stephen T. Riley, the present director of the society, whose skill and energy as a collector would have won the commendation of Dr. Belknap, has thus described the founder's activity:

Rare books and manuscripts were easily come by. Very little competition for them existed in those early years, and volumes that would now cause considerable stir in any auction of Americana were quietly given to the Library. Fortunately Dr. Belknap believed in the direct approach. He badgered Paul Revere into writing an account of his famous ride for the Society's archives, journeyed to Lebanon, Connecticut, to pick up the manuscripts collected by Governor Jonathan Trumbull, selected suitable manuscripts and books from the papers of the late

13. M.H.S. *Collections*, 5th ser., III, 245.
14. M.H.S. *Collections*, 5th ser., III, 356–357.

Governor John Hancock, and speculated about what might be forthcoming when Samuel Adams' "head was laid." Unfortunately Dr. Belknap predeceased Adams; otherwise Adams' papers might be in the Society today instead of in New York City.

Publications were undertaken with the same promptness and energy as collecting. Although Boston Federalists never saw fit to elect Thomas Jefferson to corresponding membership, they followed his principle of saving what remains of historical documents, "not by vaults and locks . . . but by such a multiplication of Copies as shall place them beyond the reach of accident." During the society's first year an arrangement was made with Dr. Belknap's printer son, Joseph, to issue a weekly newspaper, *The American Apollo*, in which a separately paged section would be provided for the society's publication. The first issue appeared on 6 January 1792. In the course of thirty-nine numbers, 208 pages of the first volume of the society's *Collections* appeared, including such documents as Francis Higginson's *New-Englands Plantation* (1630), Morrell's *Nova-Anglia* (1625), Gookin's "Indians in New England" (1674), extracts from *New Englands First Fruits* (1643), and a Roger Williams letter of 1670. As *The American Apollo* did not prove a financial success, other means were found of printing the *Collections*. Volumes two and three (1793, 1794) were issued in monthly parts: four and five (1795, 1798) in quarterly. Thereafter the *Collections* appeared in volumes without an attempt at serialization.

When the society was incorporated in 1794 its name was definitely established as the Massachusetts Historical Society. The date of its foundation was a matter of less definite agreement. The founders regarded the meeting called by Dr. Belknap on 26 August 1790 as the beginning of the society; hence the first bookplate, printed in the summer of 1791, states unequivocally "This Book is the property of the Historical Society, Established in Boston, 1790." At a later time it was concluded that Monday, 24 January 1791, was the time of birth. According to this theory, the society was planned in August, but first set up the following January. This makes as little sense as a woman lying about her age, but the date 1791 has been generally accepted within and without the society.

The society's first home was the library room of the Massachusetts Bank in Hamilton Place. It then passed a couple of years in the north-west corner of the attic of Faneuil Hall,

> Undaunted by proximity
> Of sausage on the rack[15]

in the butcher stalls on the ground floor of this combined market house and meeting hall. Although from 1794 to 1833 the society occupied a room over the arch in the centre of Charles Bulfinch's elegant new Tontine Crescent, in what is now Franklin Street, its officers and members continue to this day to visit the stalls of Faneuil Hall to replenish their larders. In 1833 the society bought the second story of the building of the Provident Institution for Savings in Tremont Street, overlooking King's Chapel Burying Ground. This was a considerable convenience to an organization in which everything was accomplished by the voluntary work of members, for James Savage, treasurer of the society from 1820 to 1839 and its president from 1841 to 1855, was an officer of the bank. For two decades, one may suppose, Savage would receive deposits on the ground floor; then, when banking business slackened, he might nip upstairs for a bit of historical editing. The society bought out the bank in 1856 and pulled down the building in 1872 to replace it with a new one. In 1899 it moved to its present home at 1154 Boylston Street, overlooking the Fenway.

In a sketch of the society published in 1959, Stephen T. Riley wrote:

The manuscript collection of the Society is its chief attraction. Of the 1,500 or so scholars who visit the Society each year perhaps 8 out of every 10 do so to investigate its rich manuscript holdings. This constant mining of our collection for historical information shows little evidence of exhausting the main supply, which is

15. Francis W. Hatch, "Beef before Baubles," quoted in Walter Muir White-hill, *Boston: A Topographical History* (Cambridge, 1959), pp. 43–44.

constantly being replenished. . . . In addition to the Adams Papers, which are now being edited by this Society, the great editions of the writings of such outstanding figures in our history as Calhoun, Clay, Franklin, Jefferson, Marshall, Theodore Roosevelt, and Washington, which have been or are now being edited, would be sadly incomplete if they did not include our holdings. Several years ago a search for papers relating to the ratification of the Federal Constitution and the First Congress revealed that the Massachusetts Historical Society held the largest number outside the Library of Congress. . . . The importance of the collection may best be suggested by pointing out that of 112 eminent Americans, from earliest to recent times and in every field of endeavor, whose papers the National Historical Publications Commission has recommended for publication, almost one third are represented in the Massachusetts Historical Society by either the principal collection of their surviving papers or by significant bodies of correspondence.

This great accumulation of historical manuscripts was not a happy accident. As we have seen, the founders worked tirelessly to attract important bodies of papers to their rooms. With the passing of the founders, the initial enthusiasm diminished somewhat, but manuscripts still continued to come in as gifts. By 1844 the Society could report 100 volumes of bound manuscripts including the papers of Belknap, William Heath, Thomas Hollis, James Otis, William Pepperrell, and Israel Williams. The greatest single gift to come to the Society in these early years was the manuscript journal of Governor John Winthrop kept from the time of his departure from England in the *Arbella* in 1630 until his death in 1649. Of outstanding importance, too, was the receipt of the original manuscript of George Washington's Newburgh Address of March 15, 1783. . . .

With the close of the Civil War, the Council called upon the Members of the Society to collect manuscripts and printed works relating to that conflict. This was done with considerable success as our collection of Civil War manuscripts indicates. About this time the great Samuel Sewall diary came to the Society as the gift of various Members. . . .

Three major collections came to the Society at the end of the nineteenth century. In 1885 Francis Parkman began to place in the Library the holdings of original papers and transcripts which he had collected for his historical works. Thirteen years later Thomas Jefferson Coolidge presented to us the second greatest collection of Thomas Jefferson papers in existence. . . . In 1905 the Winthrop family papers were given to the Society by the estate of Robert C. Winthrop, Jr. This added to our holdings what might be called the greatest single collection of American colonial manuscripts known.

During ₁the last half century₁ the Society acquired such important collections as the Atkinson, Bellows, Dana, Everett, Lee, Livingston, Long, Minot, Morse, Paine, Quincy, Rhodes, Saltonstall, Sedgwick, Ward, and Warren papers. Logbooks of such historic ships as the *Columbia* were secured and rich autograph collections placed on our shelves. Perhaps the highest point in our collecting history was reached in May, 1956, when gifts of the Adams family papers and the Paul Revere papers were simultaneously announced to the Society. Since then other collections have been received, ranging in time from early colonial days to the middle 1950's.

The society's feeling of responsibility to make these holdings widely available to scholars has been shown by the publication of 228 volumes, exclusive of extensive photostat and microfilm series, picture books, pamphlets, and ephemeral material, during the past 171 years.[16] The first series of ten volumes of the *Collections* was completed in 1809, the second in 1823, the third in 1849, the fourth in 1871, the fifth in 1888, the sixth in 1899, the seventh in 1915. At that point a numbering by series was abandoned and the next volume designated as LXXI.

The thirty volumes of the first three series contained miscellaneous documents, with the exception of volumes V and VI of the second series, which were devoted to a text of William Hubbard's "General History of New England" (1620–80). Although there are three miscellaneous volumes in the fourth series, the *Collections* for the past hundred years have consisted of larger segments of documents, in which related papers might occupy from one to four volumes. The newly rediscovered text of Governor William Bradford's "Of Plimoth Plantation" was first printed in full in 1856 as volume III of the fourth series; single volumes of Hinckley and Mather papers and two volumes each of Winthrop and Aspinwall papers completed that series. The fifth series included three volumes of the Sewall diary, two volumes each of Belknap and Trumbull papers, one of Heath papers, and the third and fourth volumes of the

16. Stewart Mitchell, *Massachusetts Historical Society, Handbook of the Publications and Photostats, 1792–1935* (Boston, 1937), contains a detailed analysis of the contents of *Collections* and *Proceedings*. Appleton P. C. Griffin, in his tediously complete "Bibliography of American Historical Societies," *Annual Report of the American Historical Association for the Year 1905* II, 345–439, lists 702 publications of the society before 1905. Griffin, however, listed even pamphlets and reprints.

Winthrop papers. In the sixth and seventh series were published two additional volumes each of Winthrop, Trumbull, and Heath papers, another Belknap, two each of the Sewall letter book, the Belcher, Bowdoin-Temple papers, and the Cotton Mather diary, single volumes of Pepperrell and Jefferson papers, a Calendar of the Pickering papers, and two volumes on the Commerce of Rhode Island. Volumes LXXI to LXXIX have included one of Copley-Pelham papers, two of Warren-Adams letters, letters to Jasper Mauduit, reference works on Massachusetts Broadsides, 1639–1800, the Numismatics of Massachusetts, Massachusetts Privateers of the Revolution, the John D. Long papers (1838–1915), and the Logs of the *Columbia* (1787–92). Selections from the papers of Robert Treat Paine and of the Saltonstall family are now in preparation for the *Collections*.

In 1859 the society embarked also on the publication of *Proceedings*, containing papers read at meetings. Volume III (1855–58) was the first to appear, as volumes I and II were reserved for retroactive publication of the records of meetings from 1791 to 1855. The *Proceedings* have appeared every few years during the past century. Volume LXXII is now in press. General indices, by groups of twenty volumes, were published in 1887, 1909, and 1937.

In addition to the long runs of *Collections* and *Proceedings*, the Massachusetts Historical Society has, within the present century, issued a substantial number of other publications. John Langdon Sibley, librarian of Harvard College, published between 1873 and 1885 three volumes of *Biographical Sketches of Graduates of Harvard University*, which contained lives of graduates from the Class of 1642 to that of 1689. On his death in 1885, Sibley left to the Massachusetts Historical Society, of which he had been a resident member since 1846, a bequest of $161,169.33 to carry on the preparation and publication of his series. The terms of the bequest, which was subject to a life interest of his widow, specified that one quarter of the income must annually be added to the principal until the year 2002; they further permitted any funds not needed for the *Biographical Sketches* to be used for additions to the library or for the general purposes of the society. Although Mrs. Sibley died in 1902, thirty years passed before the right means of continuing the *Biographical Sketches* was discovered. Finally, in the euphoria of the 1930 tercentenary, Samuel Eliot Morison had the happy thought of engaging Dr. Clifford K. Shipton, then a promising young colonial historian, now the director of the American Antiquarian Society, to try his hand at continuing "Sibley" on a part-time basis. Thus a fourth volume, covering the Classes of 1690–1700, appeared in 1933, forty-eight years after the third. Few books sound duller or prove to be more exciting than the eight volumes by which Dr. Shipton has carried Sibley's *Biographical Sketches* through the Class of 1745. He is a meticulous scholar, familiar with all possible documentary sources; he also has a sense of humor, a sense of perspective, and knows how to write. Thus he has brought back to life hundreds of obscure eighteenth-century Harvard graduates, as well as brilliantly reappraising the well-known figures, in so vivid a manner that his volumes have no air of antiquarian piety. They are not only valuable works of reference for the colonial historian; they are enchanting reading for amusement.[17]

One cannot claim as much for the thirty-six volumes of the *Journals of the House of Representatives of Massachusetts* (1715–80) that the society has wearily been publishing since 1919. Volume XXIV, part 1, which appeared in 1961, records the deliberations of the House through 31 December 1757. The original printings of the journals are scarce; at best a very few copies have survived, at worst only one. They are useful to specialists in colonial history. Today they would be thought a good subject for some microform; forty years ago reprinting in letterpress seemed the only solution. Since 1951, with volume XXVI, the *Journals* have been reproduced from the originals in offset by the Meriden Gravure Company, with superior

17. *Sibley*, XII, Mr. Shipton's ninth volume, will be issued by the time the present volume appears. To make this remarkable work more widely known to general readers, the Harvard University Press will publish in 1963 a one-volume selection of these biographies.

results at reduced cost. As the society has a fund of $25,000 given in 1927–28 by William Bradford Homer Dowse, the income of which is designated for this purpose, and as the Commonwealth of Massachusetts buys a supply of each volume, the project will continue at the rate of one a year until the terminal date of 1780 is reached.

Five volumes of *Winthrop Papers*, covering the years 1498 to 1649, were published between 1929 and 1947. Others, continuing the chronological presentation of this great collection of correspondence of Governor John Winthrop (1588–1649), John Winthrop Jr. (1606–76), and their descendants down to the year 1850, are in preparation.

Special publications have included *The Education of Henry Adams*, whose substantial royalties have belied Worthington C. Ford's comment on the financial failure of *The American Apollo*: "The wholesome lesson was early learned, that the society must support its publications and could not hope to derive any profit from them."[18] The *Education*, like *Mont-Saint Michel and Chartres*, the autobiography of Charles Francis Adams (1835–1915), the correspondence of William Hickling Prescott, and certain other special publications were sold by Houghton Mifflin Company.

Profit in publications over the years has been rare and somewhat accidental; the guiding motive has always been "a multiplication of copies" of useful documents. In the past decade two new types of ephemeral publications for wide distribution have been inaugurated. The *M.H.S. Miscellany* is an occasional publication that permits the prompt printing of useful documents and lists that might be of general interest. The fifth number (December 1958) contained a brief listing of the society's manuscript collections that was, through the kindness of the National Historical Publications Commission, a preprint of one section of the commission's *Guide to Archives and Manuscripts in the United States*.

18. Worthington C. Ford, "The Massachusetts Historical Society," *Annual Report of the American Historical Association for the Year 1912*, pp. 217–223. Future quotations from Ford, except where otherwise attributed, are from this address.

An offset picture book has been issued each May since 1954 in connection with a temporary exhibition and reception for friends of the society. By this means good reproductions of portraits, prints, maps, and drawings in the society's possession have been made widely available at low prices. In 1958, a year in advance of the centenary of the death of William Hickling Prescott, a picture book was devoted to him, with an introductory essay by Samuel Eliot Morison, in order to anticipate the numerous frantic requests for information that are received from journalists and the general public when they are suddenly seized with anniversary-consciousness. This little book was soon translated into Spanish by the United States Information Service and distributed by that agency in South America. In 1959 the picture book was devoted to the history of the society, with a sketch by the present director from whom I have quoted; in 1960 the subject was Thomas Jefferson's architectural drawings, with an introduction by Professor Frederick D. Nichols of the University of Virginia. A second and enlarged edition, to which Professor Nichols added a complete list of Jefferson's architectural drawings, has been issued as a joint publication of the society, the University of Virginia Press, and the Thomas Jefferson Memorial Foundation.

The evolution of the library of the Massachusetts Historical Society is best summarized in reports of the library committee, consisting of L. H. Butterfield, Chairman, Keyes DeWitt Metcalf, and Henry L. Seaver, submitted to the council in February and March 1958, which established the current acquisition policy.

When housed in an attic room of Faneuil Hall in the 1790's, the library consisted of 225 books and 500 pamphlets. By 1860 there were 8,000 books and 13,000 pamphlets. In the flush times following the Civil War the collection of printed materials quietly but relentlessly doubled, redoubled, and nearly redoubled again, until, when the present building was occupied in 1897, it amounted to perhaps 150,000 titles, supported by a vast assemblage of early newspapers and by some of our most extensive and valuable collections of original manuscripts. . . . In short, the library had by 1900 become one of the great repositories of printed and manuscript records relating to the history of the Commonwealth, the region, and the the nation.

In the present century the growth of the Society's collections has continued along similar lines but with some shifts in emphasis. Early American imprints and newspapers had become rare and costly and could no longer be acquired, by either gift or purchase, in large lots. Some notable private libraries have been added, such as that of Henry Adams relating to general and architectural history and that of Francis Russell Hart relating to the Caribbean area, but the rate of growth in the book collections has generally slackened. The Librarian estimates that there are now perhaps 300,000 separate titles in the catalogue, not counting some thousands of broadsides, many hundreds of bound volumes of newspapers, and uncounted maps and prints.

While the greatest riches of the society are in its manuscripts, the library contains in early printed items outstanding collections of Cambridge and Boston imprints, books relating to the New England Indian wars, Indian captivities and treaties, early printed laws of the Massachusetts Bay and Plymouth colonies, the writings of the Mathers, and Massachusetts broadsides. The society is today, as the library committee points out,

a research library with a national and to some extent an international constituency. Relatively few of its members make much use of its facilities, but scholars—from young hopefuls to accomplished veterans—have beaten a path to our door. When they have found their way to the reading room, have found a space to work there, and have signed the register, they may use what they wish, subject only to regulations for safeguarding valuable materials. They seldom go away disappointed; they pay no fees; and the Society's compensation is ordinarily limited to acknowledgments in prefaces and footnotes. It asks and expects no more....

The first and overwhelming impression the Society makes upon a thoughtful observer is the great wealth of its resources for historical research. These are beyond all appraisal, to say nothing of replacement. The second impression is the poverty of the Society's means for maintaining and servicing these splendid holdings. To process and catalogue its acquisitions, to keep its collections in order and in repair, and to serve them to readers, the Society employs a staff of five and a janitor. The result is that there are heavy arrearages in all routine library operations except in the cataloging of manuscripts, a task which the librarian himself performs in addition to his duties as a reference librarian and as administrator of the Society.

Lack of hands, lack of space, and lack of funds for acquisitions, cataloguing, and binding have led in the past to improvisations of a vexing sort that are only now beginning to be ameliorated. The library committee reports of 1958 recommended a drastic weeding operation, a vigorous house-cleaning operation on collections retained, an accelerated binding program, additional help for the librarian, an improved reading room, and the creation of a permanent fund for the enlargement, improvement, and maintenance of the library collections. In the past four years progress has been made along all these lines. The conversion of Ellis Hall, on the ground floor, from a museum to a handsome and well-appointed reading room, opened for use on 13 October 1960, is the most visible result, although a library fund of over $50,000 has been created by the sale of duplicates and irrelevant books. Another consequence has has been the adoption of an acquisition policy for printed books that the present director has thus summarized:

Instead of continuing to collect on a wide scale the Society has now wisely decided to build to its strength and concentrate its efforts on acquiring all materials printed in Massachusetts through the year 1825. It also seeks to acquire early items relating to Massachusetts that have been printed elsewhere and the important basic materials on Massachusetts and New England history after 1825. Since it is necessary that the Library possess the working tools essential for the use of these basic materials by researchers and staff and for meeting the needs of its editors, the Society is attempting to build up two other categories: a strong bibliographical section and a solid collection of pertinent secondary works—local and national history, including the publications of other historical societies, and biography.

The Massachusetts Historical Society has always been a small body, relying on the industry and generosity of its members. The original limit of thirty on resident membership was raised to sixty in 1794 and to one hundred in 1857. As the society received its first endowment fund in 1854, it is evident that collecting and publishing were done by devoted members who were not only expected to but *did* work. It had, for example, no paid librarian until 1918. The formidable Samuel Abbott Green, M.D., sometime mayor of Boston, became a resident member of the society as well as its cabinet keeper in 1860. In 1868 he assumed the duties of librarian on a voluntary basis and died in office half a century later on 5 December 1918.

Allan Forbes, president of the State Street Trust Company and treasurer of the society, delighted to recall how he had been summarily ejected from 1154 Boylston Street early in this century by Dr. Green, when, as a young man, he had had the temerity to solicit some business for his bank. Samuel Eliot Morison as a graduate student at Harvard as late as 1910 was not permitted by Dr. Green to use the society's card catalogues.

Until 1889, when Charles Card Smith was appointed, the society had no regular editor. Smith retired in 1907. Worthington C. Ford, who served as editor from 1909 to 1929, brought to the post a new professional competence derived from his broad experience as chief of the division of manuscripts of the Library of Congress, as well as from other posts in the Boston Public Library and the Department of State. However resolutely Dr. Green might individually play the ogre, the society had always had generous intentions. The presence of Ford helped to ease the transition from the era of the amateur scholar to that of the professional historian.

In the first eighty years of the society's life, American history had been the province of gentlemen like Bancroft, Prescott, and Parkman, whose activities were known and admired in all historical societies. In the last quarter of the nineteenth century as American history became an academic discipline in the hands of younger men, trained in the seminars of German and American universities, members of historical societies and of university faculties sometimes failed to see their common interests and became peevishly critical of each other. In retrospect it becomes readily understandable. Elderly men who had devoted time, thought, and money to the preservation of historical sources inevitably had a proprietary feeling towards their collections; to them a newly engrossed PH.D. diploma might have been written in Tibetan. The new professionals perhaps a bit arrogantly took their welcome for granted and did not always avail themselves of the small routine courtesies that open many doors throughout the world. Some of the frictions of the time may have been comparable to those that hinder easy harmony between scientists and humanists today. The best physicists are often men of remarkable general cultivation, with a broad knowledge of the arts. Yet there are many younger scientists who by dint of concentration on a single speciality have become as single-minded in learning as Jehovah's Witnesses have in religion. Not all householders welcome *The Watchtower* when it is offered at their doors; no more did some late nineteenth-century historical societies necessarily welcome the unsolicited admonitions and demands of the new professionals.

In 1893 the council of the Massachusetts Historical Society brought this situation to the attention of their fellow members in the annual report.

While it is our duty to see to the careful preservation of our possessions, while we must safeguard their use with such precautions as may insure their safety, our policy as to the manuscripts in our hands should be thoroughly generous. This only will secure the continued reception by us of valuable manuscripts. The rooms of this Society are not now the only possible place of deposit for family papers and historical material. Testators and donors can find other repositories and will do so, if we do not let our light shine before men.

Nevertheless Dr. Green continued his role of growling Cerberus. Seventeen years later in 1910, after observing that the society's chief function was the preservation of historical documents, the council remarked:

It is generally admitted that the relations of the Society, not only to the outside public but to scholars, are far from what they should be, and demand a radical improvement. To accumulate and bury was never the intention of the founders of the Society. To collect and to hold rigidly for the use of the Society would be a suicidal act. The book or the manuscript which enters the doors of this Society has been lost to investigators, on the double plea that it was a private society, and that its collections should be held for the use of its members or its own publications. The Society has lost by cultivating such an impression, and, by what is probably an unconscious narrowness of policy, permitting that impression to become general. ... Your Council believes in perfect freedom in the use of the Society's accumulations and in giving every facility to those who come to consult them. In this way only can ... the proper functions of the Society be fulfilled.

The presence of Ford did much to implement this policy. In a paper on the society, read at the 1912 meeting of the American Historical Association, he emphasized the importance of publishing.

He pointed out that the society had in recent times narrowly restricted its collecting of printed books, relying upon Harvard College, the Boston Public Library, the Boston Athenæum, the John Carter Brown Library, and the American Antiquarian Society for certain rare printed material, rather than seeking to duplicate what was available there, for the "books could not have been purchased without crippling the publishing activity of the society." As a sequel to this refutation of the old-time collector's desire to maintain exclusive and proprietary rights over rarities, Ford went on to say of the society:

It seeks not to accumulate, but to advance the study and use of material—to serve as an active influence, not as a burial place of accumulation. Here the earnest investigator should be welcome, for what is here is intended to be used.

Last month a gentleman came in, a stranger, and with the air of proper timidity which marks those who ask in expectation of being denied. His question was, "What are the restrictions and what are the privileges in making researches here?" My reply was, "There are no restrictions and there are all privileges." I saw him blink, as if I had tapped him lightly between the eyes; but he soon caught my meaning, explained his wants, and in 10 minutes had the pleasure of making some unexpectedly rich discoveries of material on his subject. My point is this: In nine cases out of ten the inquirer does not know what he wants; no catalogue will help him; no general phrases will satisfy him. He must dig out his facts as he goes along. To question him closely, suspiciously, and with jealousy, is the wrong tack; invite his confidence, put him in touch with what may help him, and leave the rest to his industry and judgment. This is especially true with pamphlet and with manuscript material.

In an address at the centennial observance of the New Hampshire Historical Society in 1923, Worthington C. Ford gave a classic definition of the purpose of a historical society.

Before the writer of history can exist the material he needs must be placed at his service. In that sentence the functions of a historical society are summarized. It collects and makes available the records of the past; it encourages the investigator and writer of history by offering these records in a form fitted for his purpose.[19]

19. *Addresses delivered at the observance of the Centennial of the New Hampshire Historical Society, September 27, 1923* (Concord, 1923), pp. 57–58.

In performing this role of hewer of wood and drawer of water for the scholar, it is obvious that a historical society must look beyond its own possessions to comparable and related material elsewhere. Manuscripts are by their nature unique; those that belong together are often widely scattered for accidental reasons that cannot now be remedied. Even with printed books, where a reasonable number of copies once existed, only a single example may have survived. The location of the products of the seventeenth-century Cambridge press is a case in point. The only known copy of the 1648 laws of the Massachusetts Bay Colony is in the Huntington Library; other unique survivals are to be found in several other libraries. In such a field it is evident that, even with an aggressive policy of collecting and unlimited funds, no single library could assemble, in original form, all the material that a scholar might need. Consequently there exists a need for the assembly of useful reproductions.

An attempt toward the solution of this problem was made by the Massachusetts Historical Society's two series of Photostat Americana. In the first of these, issued under Ford's editorship in the decade immediately following World War I, 261 titles of carefully chosen imprints, ranging from the discovery of America to the close of the Revolution, were reproduced for eleven subscribing libraries. These were the Massachusetts, New York, and Wisconsin historical societies, the American Antiquarian Society, the Library of Congress, the New York Public Library, Yale University, and the John Carter Brown, William L. Clements, Henry E. Huntington, and Newberry libraries, thus scattering copies throughout the United States. The second series of 169 numbers brought the total of titles reproduced to 430.

Between 1915 and 1933 the society similarly reproduced five colonial newspapers, *The Georgia Gazette*, 1763–73, *The Domestic Intelligence*, 1679–80, *The Boston News-Letter*, 1704–76, *The New-England Courant*, 1721–26, and, in collaboration with the Virginia Historical Society, *The Virginia Gazette*, 1736–80. These were produced in somewhat larger quantity, *The Virginia Gazette*, for example, going to twenty-three subscribing libraries. In addition photostats were produced of George Washington's Ledger A, from the original in the Library of Congress, of the records of the West Parish of Barnstable, Massachusetts, of Pierre d'Ailly's *Imago Mundi* with annotations by Christopher Columbus, and, in collaboration with the Rhode Island Historical Society, of the letters and papers of Roger Williams, 1629–82.

With the coming of World War II large-scale photostatic under-takings became impossible; by the end of the war it was clear that microphotography offered a more economical and manageable solution for the dissemination of historical sources. During the 1950s the society devoted considerable effort to the preparation and distribution of a microfilm edition of the Adams papers. In 1905 the three surviving sons of Charles Francis Adams (1807–86) and one of his grandsons had established the Adams Manuscript Trust in order to provide for the proper care and use of the public and private papers of President John Adams, his son President John Quincy Adams, his grandson Charles Francis Adams, together with the papers of their wives and children. Before the trust was established, the Adams papers had been, in 1902, moved from Quincy to a separate room in the Massachusetts Historical Society, where they were housed apart from the society's manuscripts. They were not open to the public, but remained in the control of the trust.

Most members of the Adams family had been people of strong ideas and convictions, addicted to diaries and letter writing and averse to throwing papers away. Thus there had accumulated in the library of the family house at Quincy a unique body of documents, highly significant for the history of the United States and fascinating for their depiction of individuals who for four generations had been involved in a remarkable variety of public and private enterprises. The family had a strong sense of historical and archival responsi-bility. The elder Charles Francis Adams had edited the works of his grandfather, John Adams, and the diary of his father, John Quincy Adams. His sons, Charles Francis Adams II, president of the Massachusetts Historical Society from 1895 to 1915, Henry Adams, and Brooks Adams were all productive and imaginative historians, although not always in agreement with each other's theories. As their lives had taken them away from Quincy, they were concerned about the safety of the family papers. They were aware that they should be preserved and eventually published, although no one of them wished to do the job himself. The magnitude of the collection defied ordinary approaches. While they could not readily hit upon a plan, they were in full agreement that the papers should be kept together; that they should not be divided as if they were dining chairs or other private property; and above all that they should not be dispersed for anyone's personal profit. The trust was therefore established to provide a breathing spell, during which the physical safety of the collection would be assured.

The Adams trustees were receptive to sensible proposals about the use of the papers. After the arrival of Worthington C. Ford in 1909 serious publication plans were considered. Ford, for example, edited seven volumes of the papers of John Quincy Adams that were published commercially by the Macmillan Company before World War I, and, after his retirement from the society in 1929, edited two volumes of the *Letters of Henry Adams: 1858–1918*. Such ventures as these were, however, like trying to demolish a mountain with a single pick, shovel, and wheelbarrow. Charles Francis Adams II died in 1915; his brother Henry in 1918, and Brooks, the youngest, in 1927. With the disappearance of the three historian brothers, Henry Adams II, a deaf bachelor son of Charles Francis II, became the trustee most closely responsible for the family papers. Henry Adams II was keenly interested in the collection, although often depressed by the problems imposed by its size and diversity. He would work by the hour in the Adams Room at the society, wearing a black alpaca coat, as he sought to locate some reference needed by a scholar. Immensely helpful to serious inquirers who presented their requests in a civil manner, in particular to Samuel Flagg Bemis, whose studies of John Quincy Adams greatly interested him, Mr.

Adams bristled with annoyance at uncivil inquirers, who invoked "rights" that he did not feel they possessed.

Upon the death of Henry Adams II in 1950, his nephew, Thomas Boylston Adams, who succeeded him as the active trustee, immediately created an advisory committee of scholars, sought their advice about the correct handling of the Adams papers, and, when he received it, acted promptly and decisively. It was agreed that the papers should be microfilmed, with copies made available on a subscription basis to libraries throughout the country. Dr. Vernon D. Tate, then director of libraries at the Massachusetts Institute of Technology, now librarian of the United States Naval Academy, prepared a tentative plan for the filming. The American Philosophical Society and the American Academy of Arts and Sciences made contributions that covered the purchase of the necessary microfilm equipment and the issuing of a prospectus. A subscription price of $3,000 per set was established, largely by divination, as no one could make any firm advance estimate of the number of items to be filmed. Part I, consisting of 88 reels of 35mm film, was distributed in 1954; part IV, which brought the total reels to 608 (27,464 feet of film in all), was completed in 1959. Forty-five sets (including those required for copyright purposes) were, in the end, needed. The receipts of $120,000 from subscriptions made the project self-liquidating so far as materials and photographic expenses were concerned; they did not, however, reimburse the society for the considerable amount of time spent by members of its staff in arranging the papers for filming. The subscription price was raised on 1 January 1961 to $4,500 per set.

The Adams papers were given to the Massachusetts Historical Society in 1956 on the termination of the family trust. Two years earlier, while the microfilming was still in its early stages, the Belknap Press of Harvard University Press offered to print and publish, at its expense, a selective edition of some seventy-five volumes of the Adams papers, provided the society would undertake the editing. Such a task would have been beyond the current resources of the society, but through the interest of Roy E. Larsen, who was both president of Time, Inc., and chairman of the visiting committee of the Harvard University Press, a solution was found. Time, Inc., agreed to give $250,000 to the Massachusetts Historical Society, payable over a ten-year period, in return for the advance serialization rights for *Life* magazine of the Adams volumes that were to be published by the Belknap Press.

The society was thus able in 1954 to persuade Dr. Lyman H. Butterfield, director of the Institute of Early American History and Culture, Williamsburg, Virginia, to join its staff as editor-in-chief of the Adams papers. His experience as associate editor of *The Papers of Thomas Jefferson* and his keen personal interest in the Adams family made him the ideal person to reduce this great mountain of manuscripts to editable order. The papers owned by the society have now been arranged, copies assembled of other Adams documents owned elsewhere, control files to facilitate their use created, and a substantial amount of transcription and editing accomplished. The existence of the microfilm edition of all the Adams papers owned by the society makes possible a selective edition in letterpress—a fortunate providence when one considers that the edition is not of the writings of a single man, like Franklin or Jefferson, but of several generations of an articulate family. Diaries, family correspondence, public papers, and legal documents will be published in separate series. Although uniform in appearance, the size of the edition and the publishing treatment will vary from volume to volume. Some groups of volumes will have a broad general interest and be printed in substantial quantity; others will be issued in numbers designed only to meet the demands of libraries and specialists.

The publication of the four volumes of the *Diary and Autobiography of John Adams* by the Belknap Press of Harvard University Press on 22 September 1961 attracted national attention to the project.[20] The President of the United States addressed a luncheon in

20. *The Adams Papers, A Ceremony Held at the Massachusetts Historical Society on September 22, 1961, Marking the Publication of the Diary and Autobiography of John*

Washington on 3 October in honor of the work, sponsored by the *Washington Post*, the American Historical Association, the Library of Congress, the National Archives, the National Historical Publications Commission, and the Belknap Press.[21] The reception and sales of the work so far exceeded those normally anticipated for a rigorously scholarly work costing $30 as to set a new standard in the publications of historical societies. In the April 1962 issue of the *William and Mary Quarterly*, Professor Bernard Bailyn observed:[22]

If by now there remains any large number of literate adults in the United States unaware of the fact that the first volumes of *The Adams Papers* have been published, it is not the fault of *Life* magazine, the Harvard University Press, or the book review editors of the country.

Two volumes of family correspondence are scheduled for publication in the spring of 1963, while two volumes of the diary of Charles Francis Adams, now being edited by Professor and Mrs. David Donald[23] will appear in the autumn of that year.

Adams (Boston, 1962), a preprint from volume LXXIII of the society's *Proceedings*, contains the addresses given by Samuel F. Bemis, Paul H. Buck, Julian P. Boyd, and others on this occasion, which was attended by more than four hundred members and guests.

21. *The Adams Papers, Remarks by Julian P. Boyd, Editor, The Papers of Thomas Jefferson, Thomas B. Adams, President, The Massachusetts Historical Society, L. H. Butterfield, Editor, The Adams Papers, The President of the United States, J. R. Wiggins, Editor, The Washington Post, Presiding* (Cambridge, 1962) records the addresses at the special *Washington Post* Book Luncheon at the Statler-Hilton on 3 October 1961, which was attended by 600 guests.

22. Bernard Bailyn, "Butterfield's Adams: Notes for a Sketch," *William and Mary Quarterly* XIX (1962), 238–256. Other important reviews are by Edmund S. Morgan in the *New England Quarterly* XXXIV (1961), 518–529, Adrienne Koch in *The New York Times Book Review* and Henry Steele Commager in the *New York Herald Tribune*, both of 24 September 1961.

23. Mr. Butterfield's designation as editor-in-chief reflected the hope that it might be possible to have certain segments of *The Adams Papers* edited, under his general direction, by other scholars. Thus while he and his assistant editor, Wendell D. Garrett, are at work on the family correspondence, Professor and Mrs. Donald are simultaneously editing the Charles Francis Adams diary. Similarly two volumes of the legal papers of John Adams are currently being prepared for publication, under a grant to the Harvard Law School from the Cromwell Foundation, by two young legal historians, L. Kinvin Wroth and Hiller Zobel, with Professor Mark DeWolfe Howe as consulting editor. These projects lend some support to President

The papers of General Henry Knox (1750–1806), deposited in the Massachusetts Historical Society by the New England Historic Genealogical Society, have since been microfilmed, under the technical supervision of the Microreproduction Laboratory of the Massachusetts Institute of Technology, in fifty-five reels. These are offered for sale, with an index volume, at $375 a set. This, like other photoreproduction projects of the society, is on a nonprofit basis.

The reader will have noted from the preceding pages that the manuscript collections and publications of the Massachusetts Historical Society have not been rigidly confined to the geographical limits of Massachusetts. Nevertheless the circular of 1 November 1791 stating the professed design of the society as "to collect, preserve and communicate, materials for a complete history of this country, and accounts of all valuable efforts of human ingenuity and industry, from the beginning of its settlement" somewhat staggers the imagination, until one recalls that the "complete history of this country" to Dr. Belknap's contemporaries meant less than two centuries of only the thirteen colonies. Time and experience have produced a soberer limitation of interest, while the establishment of specialized institutions in Massachusetts has relieved the society from any sense of responsibility for some activities that in 1791 seemed appropriate.

Any interest in natural history or in the "specimens of natural and artificial curiosities" that were considered essential in the cabinet of an eighteenth-century amateur was abandoned soon after the organization of the Boston Society of Natural History in 1830. The Massachusetts Historical Society still has a cabinet keeper,[24] whose

Kennedy's remark at the Washington luncheon on 3 October 1961: "I have no doubt that Lyman Butterfield and Thomas Adams are breathing heavy sighs of relief—four volumes out and only eighty or a hundred more to go. Obviously the worst is over."

24. When Edward P. Hamilton, succeeding me in that office a few years ago, was unable to locate a giant clam, whose gift was noted in the early records, he formally accused me of having eaten it. See *Proceedings*, LXXI (1953–57), 522, and the index entry (556): "Whitehill, Walter Muir, putative appetite."

responsibilities are confined to the care of a superb series of portraits and historical objects.

The society does not today maintain a museum as such; its paintings and historical objects are used as house decoration, shown in temporary exhibitions each spring, or lent to other institutions. Its paintings include works by Blackburn, Blyth, Copley, Harding, Malbone, Smibert, and Stuart; portraits of Increase Mather, Peter Faneuil, Samuel Sewall, Thomas Hutchinson, Daniel Boone; the pictures of Lafayette by Joseph Boze and of Washington by Joseph Wright that were purchased at the sale of Thomas Jefferson's collection, and many others of comparable interest. Among the historical objects are matrices of Benjamin Franklin's type, the gorget worn by Washington when he served as aide-de-camp to Braddock, the crossed swords of William Prescott and John Linzee that hung in William Hickling Prescott's library, the pen with which Abraham Lincoln signed the Emancipation Proclamation. Some of the society's best silver is on display at the Museum of Fine Arts; some of its paintings, and Shem Drowne's Indian archer weather vane, have traveled widely in exhibitions of early American art. To arrange these pictures and memorabilia in any meaningful public display would require space, time, and money that the society cannot contemplate sparing for the purpose.

The society's single-minded concentration on its manuscripts and publications is part of a general pattern by which numerous Massachusetts institutions informally but effectively delimit their fields of activity so as to apply their resources economically and without competition. The Massachusetts Historical Society has never become involved in the preservation of historic buildings or in the affairs of county and local historical societies throughout the state, as these activities have been for more than half a century the specific provinces of other organizations. The Society for the Preservation of New England Antiquities, founded in 1910 by William Sumner Appleton, has from private funds acquired and maintained some fifty properties in various parts of New England. Monuments like the Old South Meeting House, the Old Corner Book Store, the Paul Revere and Hichborn houses in Boston, Craigie House in Cambridge, Gore Place in Waltham, John Greenleaf Whittier's birthplace in Haverhill, are, in addition, preserved by independent charitable corporations organized for the purpose. The Bay State Historical League since 1903 has endeavored to further co-operation between town historical societies in Massachusetts.[25]

Some Massachusetts historical organizations owe their foundation to ancient squabbles long since forgotten. As Stewart Mitchell once observed: "The New England Historic Genealogical Society and the Prince Society were organized in 1845 and 1858, respectively, by men who were annoyed because they had not been elected Members of the Massachusetts Historical Society.[26] In 1892, the Colonial Society of Massachusetts began its creditable career because of a personal feud between Henry Herbert Edes and Samuel Abbott Green." As time has passed, these personal animosities have been long since forgotten, while the institutions that sprang from them have made useful contributions to many aspects of New England history. Over the past 117 years the New England Historic Genealogical Society has developed a superb library of 220,000 volumes in its speciality; at 9 Ashburton Place the genealogist is as happily satisfied as the historian at 1154 Boylston Street. When the Prince Society, after eighty-six years of life, concluded that a publishing society "on the mutual principle" had become an anomaly, it dissolved, giving the small balance in its treasury to the Massachusetts Historical Society as a publication fund.

The Colonial Society of Massachusetts has been for seventy years a publishing organization, devoting the income from its funds,

25. For details of foundation, see Nathaniel T. Kidder, "Bay State Historical League," *Annual Report of the American Historical Association for the Year 1916*, I, 222–230.

26. Details of nineteenth-century antiquarian squabbles, involving some self-important and not always very well-educated people, are delightfully revived by George G. Wolkins, "The Prince Society," M.H.S. *Proceedings*, LXVI (1936–41), 223–254.

which now have a book value of over a third of a million dollars, to the printing of documents and monographs on the seventeenth- and eighteenth-century history of the Plymouth and Massachusetts Bay Colonies. During this time it has issued forty-one stout volumes of publications, as well as subsidizing the *New England Quarterly*, of which it has been copublisher since 1945. When in 1928 Samuel Eliot Morison, Arthur M. Schlesinger, and other members of the Massachusetts Historical Society and of the Colonial Society established the *New England Quarterly*, they were acting as individuals. The magazine they founded, however, has served many useful functions for both societies.

Any animosity that may have existed between the two organizations vanished when H. H. Edes, the founder of the Colonial Society, was elected to the Massachusetts Historical Society in 1911. Mr. Edes had a flair for recognizing historical talent and bringing it into the society; an outstanding example of his instinct led to the election of Samuel Eliot Morison when still a graduate student, without a single publication to his credit. The Colonial Society has always tried to follow that principle; in consequence many of its members, elected young, have subsequently become members of the Massachusetts Historical Society, to such an extent that today the membership lists of the two are very similar in content.

For its first sixty-two years the Colonial Society had its headquarters in its editor's hat and held its meetings at members' houses or at the Club of Odd Volumes. Consequently any manuscripts or records that came its way were promptly turned over to the Massachusetts Historical Society. In 1954 it received, by gift of Mrs. Llewellyn Howland, a fine Bulfinch house at 87 Mount Vernon Street, with an endowment fund that would permit its maintenance without strain on the publication funds. Francis Parkman's study from 50 Chestnut Street has been reconstructed on the top floor of that house, because space was available there for it, although Parkman's letters written to his family from the Oregon Trail, which turned up in a desk drawer during the installation, were promptly and properly sent to the Massachusetts Historical Society to rejoin other Parkman manuscripts.

No formal link exists between any of these societies, the American Antiquarian Society in Worcester, the Boston Athenæum, the Bostonian Society, such a county organization as the Essex Institute, or a centre of maritime history like the Peabody Museum of Salem. Yet through a series of personal ties, centering upon the Saturday luncheons of the Club of Odd Volumes, and by a quite haphazard series of intertwining directorates, the Massachusetts Historical Society is closely linked to their activities. To give a few examples of the same dogs wearing different collars: the president of the Massachusetts Historical Society was until recently a vice-president of the Colonial Society, the president of the Boston Athenæum is president of the American Antiquarian Society, and has been in the past treasurer of the Society for the Preservation of New England Antiquities and on the council of the Massachusetts Historical Society. The director of the Boston Athenæum is recording secretary of the Massachusetts Historical Society, editor of the Colonial Society, a council member of the American Antiquarian Society, and secretary of the Peabody Museum of Salem. The director of the American Antiquarian Society is Sibley Editor of the Massachusetts Historical Society, keeper of the Harvard University Archives, and president of the Colonial Society. The directors of the Harvard University Press and Library are or have been members of the council of the Massachusetts Historical Society, and so on endlessly. It is reminiscent of the Soldier's Chorus in *Faust*, where the same few soldiers march on and off the stage to create the illusion of an army. Nevertheless it agrees with the Boston temperament, and it seems to work.

The resident membership of the Massachusetts Historical Society, increased to 100 in 1857, is limited today to 150, with allowance for not more than 100 corresponding and 10 honorary members. Only here and in the American Antiquarian Society and the Colonial Society of Massachusetts has the early tradition of the closed academy survived. The provision of the bylaws that "in the election of members, which shall be by secret vote, the law and custom of our forefathers shall be observed, by taking the question with Indian corn and beans; the corn expressing *Yeas*, and the beans *Nays*," is still punctiliously observed. After a harangue on the merits of a candidate, which is often in the mock-heroic tone customary to public orators at the older British universities, the recording and corresponding secretaries leave their places at the right and left hand of the president in the Dowse library and circulate mahogany ballot boxes, containing corn and black beans. The absolute secrecy of the vote is open to question. I have heard a teller, observing a bean on its way to the hole, remark in a stentorian whisper: "You're putting in a black ball," at which the elderly voter, whose eyes were not of the keenest, retrieved his vote with a grateful: "I didn't intend to."

There are no dues, but members are carefully chosen, not only for their historical accomplishments or interests, but with a definite view to what they will contribute to the society in scholarly work, in manuscripts, or in money. Membership brings only the privilege of working or giving, for the society's collections are freely open to any sober, literate, and well-behaved person who wishes to use them. Worthington C. Ford wrote in 1912:

Membership is a recognition of whatever quality may advance the study of history; and the list of members since 1791 indicates with what care that necessary feature of the society has been safeguarded. Some changes in the quality of this membership it would be interesting to study, for they would mark the changes that have occurred in historical study and writing in more than a century. For example, in the first ten years of the society 58 members were elected, and of these just one-third were clergymen; in the last ten years [1902–1912], of 59 members elected only 1 was a clergyman. There are at present 5 of that profession in the full hundred members. The cause is not far to seek. In the first 10 years there was chosen no representative from Harvard College or from any institution of learning in Massachusetts. At present more than one-fourth (29) of the total resident membership is actively or passively (emeritus) connected with such institutions. The trained and specialized historical worker has taken the place of those who engaged in the writing of history as a secondary occupation.

Today more than half of the total membership consists of members of university faculties or of the staffs of libraries or learned institutions. In the corresponding membership the proportion is two to one. In 1960 of the 139 resident members, fifty were from the faculties of Harvard, Boston University, M.I.T., Amherst, Williams, and Smith; six were schoolmasters; fifteen were from libraries or museums. There were eleven lawyers, five clergymen, four doctors of medicine, two artists, two senators, one editor, one architect, one retired diplomat, but thirty-eight men engaged in business or banking. This proportion led President Thomas Boylston Adams to remark at the 1958 annual meeting:

This Society from its inception has been a bridge between the world of commerce and the world of the mind. We have never failed to number among our Members prominent historians and men prominent in business life—merchants they used to be called. More than once we have combined the two in one person. This is one of our more important functions. Men come here from both sides of the Charles to civilize and be civilized. Their urbanity is such they do not fail to recognize their need to help each other. And so our meetings seem each year to be better attended and ever more amusing and instructive.[27]

Subsequent deaths and elections have caused no visible change in the pattern.

The society receives no public support; its operation is from the income of endowment and from private gifts. With the exception of the Sibley Fund, previously mentioned, whose principal now amounts to $335,336.48, the William Crowninshield Endicott bequest of $100,000, the Stewart Mitchell Fund (a bequest of $50,000 from Mrs. Georgine Holmes Thomas that has now, by reinvestment of income, reached $100,000), and Grenville Howland Norcross's bequest of $50,000, most funds received by the society have been of modest size. But even small gifts in sufficient number make themselves felt. When John Adams became president of the society in 1950 he undertook by no stronger solicitation than the writing of

27. The society meets in the Dowse Library. For details, see my "The Centenary of the Dowse Library," M.H.S. *Proceedings*, LXXI (1953–57), 167–178.

personal letters to create a new endowment fund; a decade later this has passed the $100,000 mark; similarly between December 1959 and the autumn of 1960 a fund of $35,000 for an improved reading room and other arrangements that will increase the convenience of scholars using the library was raised by his son and successor. On 30 June 1961 the market value of the society's investments was $3,291,583.01; the income available for restricted and unrestricted purposes, after certain obligatory transfers of income to capital, was $96,997.[28] Of this sum $76,897 was spent for general and administrative expenses; the remainder was transferred to restricted income fund balances designed chiefly to meet the cost of publications. To this should be added the $25,000 received annually for ten years from Time, Inc., toward the expense of the Adams papers editorial office.

The staff of the society has never been large. Upon Ford's retirement in 1929, he was succeeded by Stewart Mitchell, a Harvard PH.D. in history and managing editor of the *New England Quarterly* (1928–37). When Julius H. Tuttle, who had become the society's first paid librarian after the death of Dr. Green, retired in 1934 Allyn Bailey Forbes took over that post. Editor Mitchell and Librarian Forbes reigned as joint consuls, without too clear definition of authority. In 1939 Mitchell resigned the editorship and Forbes was named director, carrying responsibility for both the library and editorial work. Upon Forbes's sudden death in 1947, Stewart Mitchell returned to the society as director. While he retained personal charge of the editing, he promoted to librarian Stephen T. Riley, a PH.D. from Clark University, who had worked closely for some years with Forbes. In 1957, upon Stewart Mitchell's second and final retirement, Dr. Riley became director, while Dr. Malcolm

28. The total income from investments of $109,122 (before the obligatory transfer of $12,126 to the principal of certain funds) represents an increase of 43.8% over the $75,861 of 1957. While some of this was due to additions to principal, the greater part was the result of the investment skill of the society's treasurer, Mr. John Bryant Paine Jr., who is the chairman of the finance committee which includes President Adams and two former treasurers of Harvard College, Messrs. Henry Lee Shattuck and William Henry Claflin.

Freiberg, a colonial historian with a special interest in Governor Thomas Hutchinson, came to the society as editor. Dr. John D. Cushing, also trained at Clark, became assistant librarian in September 1960. These three men, all with professional training in history, are, with the help of Warren Gage Wheeler, assistant librarian of many years standing, a cataloguer, a manuscript repairer, one secretary, and a janitor, responsible for the current activities of the society. In the Adams papers office Dr. Butterfield, editor-in-chief, and Wendell D. Garrett, assistant editor, have one additional hand engaged in transcription and editing.

Of the society's future role, Dr. Riley has recently written:

After an existence of more than a century and a half the Society finds itself in a position greatly changed from 1791. It is now only one of a group of specialized libraries and museums in Metropolitan Boston. Many of the functions that are ordinarily discharged by historical societies in other parts of the country have been assumed in this area by neighboring institutions. In Boston alone there is a genealogical society; a great public library and a famous proprietary library, both with important special collections; a society devoted to New England antiquities and the preservation of historic houses; a magnificent museum with rich holdings of American paintings, silver, and furniture; a society with a museum devoted to the history of the City of Boston; and a half-dozen other learned societies. Within a a forty-five mile radius, there are such well known libraries as Harvard's Houghton and Widener, the John Carter Brown, the American Antiquarian Society, and the Essex Institute and the Peabody Museum of Salem. In this setting the Society feels that it can make its greatest contribution by continuing to serve as a research institution devoting its attention to the collection of historical manuscripts and books in its special field, bringing minds capable of exploiting and interpreting these primary sources into contact with them, and publishing or arranging the publication of the results. It does not and should not compete with the long-established programs of nearby institutions. Nor does it or should it pursue a program of popular education, with such attendant features as news stories, lecture series, and radio broadcasts. It will concentrate rather on furthering the kind of basic research that leads to a deeper and truer understanding of our past.

Chapter II

THE NEW-YORK
HISTORICAL SOCIETY

Without the aid of original records and authentic documents, history
will be nothing more than a well-combined series of ingenious conjectures and amusing fables.—*Address to the Public, The New-York
Historical Society*, 1805

JOHN PINTARD'S[1] dream began to come true on 20 November 1804 at a meeting which he summarized in the following
simple minutes: "The following Persons viz: Egbert Benson, Dewitt Clinton, Revd. William Linn, Revd. Samuel Miller, Revd.
John N. Abeel, Revd. John M. Mason, Doctor David Hosack,
Anthony Bleeker, Samuel Bayard, Peter Stuyvesant and John Pintard, being assembled in the Picture Room of the City Hall of the
City of New York, agreed to form themselves into a Society the
principal design of which should be to collect and preserve whatever
may relate to the natural, civil or ecclesiastical History of the United
States in general and of this State in particular and appointed Mr.
Benson, Doctor Miller and Mr. Pintard a Committee to prepare and
report a draft of a Constitution. The meeting then adjourned until
Monday evening the 10th of December next."

1. In the spring of 1792, Pintard had failed in business as a result of having endorsed
notes of nearly $1,000,000 for William Duer. Belknap and Hazard were genuinely
distressed by their friend's loss of fortune; see M.H.S. *Collections*, 5th ser., III, 290,
293, 295. He spent thirteen months in a debtor's prison before going through bank-
ruptcy.

At this later date, when ten additional members had been rounded up, a constitution was adopted, naming the new organization the New York Historical Society,[2] setting forth its object in terms identical to the "principal design" indicated above, and providing for resident members living within the state, who were to pay a $10 admission fee and $2 annually, and honorary members, residing elsewhere, for whom dues were optional. No limit was set upon the number of members. Meetings were to be held quarterly. At a third meeting on 14 January 1805 officers were elected, the Honorable Egbert Benson (1746–1833), a judge of the New York Supreme Court and former member of the Continental and United States Congresses, becoming president. John Pintard, whose idea it had all been, was elected recording secretary, a post that he was to hold until 1819 when he turned treasurer.

Equipped with a constitution and officers, the new society now circulated among prospective members and donors and caused to be printed in the *New-York Herald* of 13 February 1805 and other newspapers an address to the public. This remarkable document stated the need for such a society, indicating that

to rescue from the dust and obscurity of private repositories such important documents, as are liable to be lost or destroyed by the indifference or neglect of those into whose hands they may have fallen, will be a primary object of our attention, . . . for without the aid of original records and authentic documents, history will be nothing more than a well-combined series of ingenious conjectures and amusing fables. . . .

Not aspiring to the higher walks of general science, we shall confine the range of our exertions to the humble task of collecting and preserving whatever may be useful to others in the different branches of historical inquiry. We feel encouraged to follow this path by the honourable example of the Massachusetts Society, whose labours will abridge those of the future historian, and furnish a thousand lights to guide him through the dubious track of unrecorded time. Without aiming to be rivals, we shall be happy to co-operate with that laudable institution in pursuing

2. Information in this chapter not otherwise acknowledged is derived from R. W. G. Vail, *Knickerbocker Birthday. A Sesqui-Centennial History of The New-York Historical Society, 1804–1954* (New York, 1954).

the objects of our common researchers; satisfied if, in the end, our efforts shall be attended with equal success.

Our inquiries are not limited to a single State or district, but extend to the whole Continent; and it will be our business to diffuse the information we may collect in such manner as will best conduce to general instruction. As soon as our collection shall be sufficient to form a volume, and the funds of the Society will admit, we shall commence publication, that we may better secure our treasures by means of the press, from the corrosions of time and the power of accident.

There follows an amazingly thorough list of the subjects upon which manuscripts, books, and pamphlets are solicited: orations, sermons, and poems upon any public occasion; legal and diplomatic records; ecclesiastical documents from all denominations; narratives of missionaries, Indian wars, the adventures and sufferings of captives, voyagers, and travelers; minutes and proceedings of societies for the abolition of slavery and transactions of political, literary, and scientific societies; accounts of universities and schools; topographical descriptions and maps; statistical tables of diseases, births, deaths, population, meteorological observations; accounts of exports, imports, and the progress of manufactures and commerce; magazines, reviews, and newspapers, especially those prior to 1783; biographical memoirs; and accounts of any state, city, town, or district. A questionnaire of twenty-three items was appended, requesting specific information about first settlers, occupations, fortifications, commerce, manufacturers, houses, militia, territorial disputes, Indian tribes and place names, ecclesiastical history, schools, early printers and booksellers, libraries, laws, epidemics, and much else, including:

18. Can you furnish any information concerning the *progress of luxury?* Do you possess any records or anecdotes respecting the introduction of the most conspicuous articles of elegant indulgence, such as *wheel-carriages,* &c. &c.?

19. Can you give any information which will throw light upon the state of *morals* in our country, at different periods, such as the comparative frequency of *drunkenness, gaming, duelling, suicide, conjugal infidelity, prostitution,* &c. &c.?

In April 1805, 500 copies of this comprehensive appeal were printed, together with the constitution, bylaws, and list of officers, to stimulate the campaign for members and materials. Although various gifts to the library were received, only one new member was added— an early and sad commentary on the effectiveness of direct-mail circularization.

Although he was not well off, John Pintard was a skillful and inveterate book collector who had gathered a substantial library on American history. He realized that the society's library would develop more rapidly if it had a properly balanced foundation. As he could not afford to give his own books, he offered in the spring of 1807 to sell them to the society at cost. By the autumn of 1809 sufficient funds had been assembled to purchase the collection. On 10 January 1809, however, Francis B. Winthrop had given a collection of twenty-two books and sixty-one sermons, including works of such rarity that the society was encouraged to petition for an act of incorporation. By the Legislature's act of 10 February 1809, "the New-York Historical Society" was incorporated for a term of fifteen years. As the hyphen thus crept into the name by legislative act, it has been scrupulously retained ever since!

R.W. G. Vail, director of the New-York Historical Society from 1944 to 1960, opens a chapter, "Elegant Dinners and Eloquent Diners," of his sesquicentennial history of the society with a significant comment:

The natives of New Amsterdam have always been famous for their enjoyment of oratory and ample provender, when properly washed down with a goodly beaker of Holland gin. It is therefore but natural that their descendants should also take pleasure in learning, set forth with taste and eloquence, and that they should then sojourn to a nearby hostelry to enjoy the fruits of the forest, the field, and the vine and to vie with one another in the drinking of patriotic and graceful toasts until their elocution and madeira should be exhausted.

Although resources were short and John Pintard had not yet been paid for his library, the 200th anniversary of Captain Henry Hudson's discovery of the region was an opportunity that could not be missed. On 4 September 1809 the Reverend Samuel Miller delivered a suitable commemorative address at a meeting of the society in the Courtroom of Federal Hall in Wall Street. After the discourse, when the ladies had been sent home, the members with ten invited guests adjourned to the City Hotel, where they conducted a little routine business that included the nomination of Oliver Wolcott and Washington Irving to membership. At four o'clock they settled down to the real business of the day, an elegant dinner "consisting of a variety of shell and other fish, with which our waters abound, wild pigeons and succotash, the favorite dish of the season, with the different meats introduced into the country by the European settlers." When adequately nourished, they fell to the drinking of thirty-one toasts to such varied personages and institutions as Christopher Columbus, Queen Isabella, John and Sebastian Cabot, John Verrazano, Henry Hudson, all the Governors of Colony and State, Richard Hakluyt and Samuel Purchas, Jeremy Belknap and George R. Minot, the United States of America, the State of New York, the Massachusetts Historical Society "which set the honorable example of collecting and preserving what relates to the history of our country," and Our Forefathers. After the thirty-first the governor and mayor went home, while the more stalwart diners continued with a profusion of volunteer toasts. As compensation for the ladies, who had been packed off to dine at home, John Pintard concluded this memorable dinner with a final toast:

The American Fair, without whose endearing society this Western World, the rich inheritance from our enterprising Ancestors, would still be a wilderness indeed.

This fine day eventually led to the publication, in 1811, of the society's first volume of *Collections*, which contained Dr. Miller's discourse, journals of Verrazano and Hudson, documents on New York under the Dutch extracted from the second volume of Ebenezer Hazard's *Historical Collections*, and the previously unpublished laws established by the Duke of York in 1664/65 for the government of New York.

After roosting in temporary quarters in the old City (Federal) Hall, the society in the autumn of 1809 secured more commodious space in Government House at the foot of Bowling Green, which had been intended originally for President Washington's occupancy. Its first meeting was held there eleven days after the Hudson celebration. Another campaign for gifts that autumn produced books and manuscripts in gratifying number, but so little money that the society turned to the State for help . In March 1810 De Witt Clinton tacked onto a Senate bill concerning a lottery to raise money "for the exterpation of Wolves & Panthers" as well as for Union College and the New York City Board of Health, a rider to provide funds for the society. On the twenty-second he happily wrote Pintard "that the bill for endowing the Historical Society, and killing the wolves and panthers, passed the Senate this morning without opposition." Alas, twelve days later S. L. Mitchell wrote from Albany: "I have the mortification to inform you that the bill from the Senate for the destruction of wild beasts, and for the encouragement of history, was this day debated and finally rejected."

Although financial problems remained as acute as ever , the annual meeting of the society on 6 December 1810 was a genial occasion in honor of St. Nicholas, whose feast it was. After an address by Hugh Williamson on the benefits of civil history, the society dined at the Washington Hotel, where, under Dutch flags, they drank seventeen regular toasts, beginning with "Sancte Claus, goed heylig man!" and three volunteer toasts. This proved so congenial that a St. Nicholas Day celebration has continued annually to the present, with a few lapses.

De Witt Clinton continued his efforts to obtain State support for the society, finally securing the passage of a bill on 15 April 1814 granting the right to raise, by means of a lottery, the sum of $12,000 for its benefit. In happy anticipation of this windfall, the society imprudently borrowed money to buy books and manuscripts, to pay for the second volume of its *Collections* and for the publication of the first catalogue of its library. This had been undertaken by the Reverend Timothy Alden, who while its librarian in 1808–09 had compiled a catalogue of the Massachusetts Historical Society and who offered to perform a similar service for the younger organization while staying in New York. The catalogue made more readily available the 5,000 books and pamphlets, the numerous newspaper files, maps, prints, and manuscripts that had been acquired. So much had come in that space in Government House was inadequate. Finally in 1816, after three years of negotiation, Pintard obtained from the city space in the Old Alms House in City Hall Park for the extremely modest "yearly rent of one peppercorn, if lawfully demanded." At the first meeting held there on 9 July 1816, Pintard was able to report the important gift of the Revolutionary War papers of General Horatio Gates, which have been of great utility ever since.

With space available, and the eventual expectation of lottery money, the society expanded its horizons. Meetings began to be held monthly. In February 1817 committees were appointed for the collecting of zoology, botany and vegetable physiology, mineralogy and fossils, coins and medals, manuscripts, and books. Cases were built for the display of such objects, and lectures given in the natural sciences. Specimens poured in, including the herbarium of Dr. Samuel Bard. As this department eventually became so large that it tended to overshadow the chief purposes of the society, it was wisely decided in 1829 to turn over the natural history collection to the Lyceum of Natural History.

The Massachusetts Historical Society waited until 1918 before employing a paid librarian; the New-York Historical Society on 8 September 1818 engaged Stephen B. Hutchings, "a young man of probity and well known to some members" as sublibrarian at the munificent salary of $100 a year.

For all this activity, finances still continued precarious. The anticipated State aid was long in coming; finally in the summer of 1823 the society was able to sell its interest in the lottery for $8,000 and thus pay some of its debts. But early in 1824 it was ascertained that a debt of nearly $10,000 remained with no obvious means of repayment. A regime of strict economy was inaugurated; the sublibrarian was sent away and the library closed, but still the nightmare continued. To raise their spirits, the members held a meeting on 17 August 1824 at which they elected General Lafayette, who had arrived in New York two days earlier, and his son, George Washington Lafayette, honorary members. The new members courteously appeared the next afternoon to accept their enlistment aboard what was apparently a sinking ship.

The suicidal proposal of selling the library to pay the society's debts, when made early in 1825, raised a commotion within and without. Poor John Pintard, to whom the society owed $3,000, was so disillusioned by this turn of events that he never attended a meeting after January 1825, although he nominally held office as treasurer through 1827. As Dr. Vail has remarked, "A newer element was taking over the running of the Society; a group more interested in an honorable settlement of its finances than in the preservation of its great library. The Society's situation was indeed desperate."

The society was apparently split in two. Dr. David Hosack, the president, resigned during the meeting of 14 June 1825 when the sale of the library was moved. Vice-president John Trumbull took the chair, but also resigned and left the meeting when the motion was carried. The situation was so charged with feeling that no further action was taken and no meeting was held for over a year. Meanwhile the fifteen-year act of incorporation expired. Governor Clinton, in his message to the Legislature in 1826, recommended that "the resuscitation of this society, and a liberal provision for its extended usefulness are measures worthy of your adoption." This procured the renewal of the charter, but funds were only obtained in 1827 through the effective lobbying at Albany of Frederic De Peyster Jr., the society's corresponding secretary. Thanks to a bill passed on 1 March 1827, the society received $5,000, provided it could find a way to pay off its indebtedness of $7,500. This State grant saved the library, and the society finally balanced its accounts by the ungenerous policy of not paying its founder, John Pintard, $1,400 that he claimed for books that he had paid for personally. Dr. Vail notes: "The Society, which now consisted of 230 active and 181 honorary members, sent its formal thanks to Governor De Witt Clinton, the Legislature, and Mr. De Peyster, and the entire Legislature was elected to honorary membership in the Society. But nobody thanked Mr. Pintard."

During the presidency of Chancellor James Kent, 1828 to 1831, the society's affairs were placed on a more orderly basis. James Delafield, who succeeded Pintard as treasurer, not only rounded up the dues of delinquent members, but straightened out the library, with the aid of his son and daughter. During this cleanup the natural history specimens were disposed of. A collection of books and $300 in cash, received in 1832 from the estate of Isaiah Thomas, founder of the American Antiquarian Society, offered an encouraging instance of friendliness between institutions; it was also the New-York Historical Society's first legacy. Seventeen years passed before another was received.

The society had its ups and downs during the 1830s and 1840s. It was forced to move its quarters three times. It relapsed into debt, locking up shop entirely on occasions when there was no money to pay a librarian. But the inauguration of a series of paid historical lectures in 1838 provided some immediate financial relief, as well as setting a pattern that proved congenial during coming decades. As Dr. Vail has pointed out, residents of New York have, or had, a seemingly limitless capacity for oratory and provender. Philip Hone noted in his diary of a special meeting of the society on 15 June 1838 for members of the Court of Errors, "I never saw a finer dinner or drank better wine." The semicentennial of Washington's inauguration in 1839 was celebrated with a two-hour discourse by John Quincy Adams; at the fortieth anniversary of the society five years later John Romeyn Brodhead, historical agent of the State of New York for collecting materials in the archives of England, France, and Holland,[3] gave an oration. Both celebrations concluded with monumental dinners. The fortieth anniversary dinner, thanks to plentiful

3. The society in 1838 had suggested to the Legislature that funds be appropriated for copying and publishing documents from European archives on the early history

sherry, madeira, hock, and champagne, lasted until one-thirty in the morning, and led the committee on arrangements to "regret their inability to present a more full report of the speeches delivered," because of their reliance "upon notes taken at the time, which are frequently and necessarily imperfect."

Lectures in 1841 by the archaeologists John L. Stephens and Frederick Catherwood and Jared Sparks's series on the American Revolution were so successful as to furnish the means by which, in the elegant language of the minutes for 4 January 1842, "The pecuniary embarrassments of the Society have been removed." The adoption of George Folsom's suggestion of 4 October 1842 that "refreshments should be furnished . . . and that strangers should be invited to be present at the regular meetings" brought a marked increase in attendance. By November 1846 ladies, who had previously been packed home before the food appeared, were allowed to stay for refreshments after lectures. This became standard practice. With the passage of time, the ladies often proved more attentive than their husbands and fathers. Mrs. William Ray Smith has recorded her girlhood recollections of this situation.

When I was growing up, I often went with my father to the lectures. . . . They were attended by a very few old gentlemen, who all went to sleep in the course of the lectures[4] (which I found very interesting) and I happened to catch the lecturer's eye as he glanced over his audience. Without changing his "lecturing voice," he said "As you are the only person awake in the room, with your kind permission I will omit the next ten pages," which he did, and concluded rather abruptly.

---

of the State. $4,000 was appropriated in 1839, and Brodhead employed by the State to carry out the plan. From this suggestion of the society eventually resulted E. B. O'Callaghan's four-volume *Documentary History of the State of New York* and fifteen-volume *Documents Relative to the Colonial History of the State of New York* and the beginning of a long series of historical publications by the State of New York that continue to the present day.

4. This is not a unique peculiarity of the New-York Historical Society. Even during the best papers delivered in the Dowse Library, some member of the Massachusetts Historical Society is certain to be asleep, thanks to a combination of afternoon sun and comfortable chairs. When I once, in the course of a paper, quoted John Brown of Osawatomie's four-letter opinion of Wendell Phillips, I was diverted to observe the speed with which the sleepers awoke.

After the lectures we used to go down to the basement and sit on tombstones and marble sarcophagi and partake of what my father always called "a light collation." This consisted of the very best water-cress and lobster sandwich I ever ate, and cups of very hot, very strong chicken bouillon. All the old gentlemen, refreshed by their naps, became very lively—and a good time was had by all!

A turning point was reached in mid-century. On 7 January 1851 it was announced by President Luther Bradish and his colleagues that the society was "in a condition of prosperity in all respects never before attained." This time prosperity remained permanent, for, as Dr. Vail has remarked, "the Society never again spent money it did not already have in the bank." Since 1841 the society had roosted with New York University in Washington Square. A $5,000 bequest of Miss Elizabeth Demilt received in 1849 was placed in a building fund, which by 1853 had grown to $35,000. With this money in hand, a site was purchased at the southeast corner of Second Avenue and 11th Street, where on 17 October 1855 a cornerstone was laid. Additional funds were raised as the work progressed. On 3 November 1857 the society dedicated the first building that it had ever owned—a handsome structure costing nearly $85,000, with a lecture room seating 600 on the first floor. Above was the tall white and gold library, with books on the main floor, maps, engravings, and newspaper files in the first gallery, and pictures in the second. A medal was struck in commemoration of the opening, bearing the head of John Pintard and a view of the building.

During the previous fifty-three years, the society had received numerous historical portraits, which merited proper exhibition. As New York had never previously had an adequate gallery for displaying works of art, the new building attracted to the society a considerable number of paintings, sculptures, and archaeological and ethnological specimens, domestic and foreign. While many of these acquisitions had artistic merit, their range was so great that they could hardly be considered appropriate for a historical society whose field was less than the entire universe. The collection of the New York Gallery of Fine Arts, which included works of Cole, Durand, Flagg, Mount, and Trumbull, as well as European paintings, was given in the spring of 1858. James Lenox in the same year gave thir-teen marble bas-reliefs from the palace of Sardanapalus in Nineveh, c. 650 B.C., which had been heavily on the hands of Henry Stevens of London for some time past. Although the ownership of these massive sculptures, which could only be matched in the British Museum and the Louvre, added to the contemporary prestige of the society, they were placed in the basement, for that was the only part of the building with a floor strong enough to hold them. This excursion into the ancient past inspired the *purchase* for $60,000 of Dr. Henry Abbott's collection of 1,100 Egyptian antiquities, includ-ing three great mummified bulls! These, Dr. Vail heartlessly obser-ved, "may have been sacred bulls to the Egyptians . . .but they have always been white elephants to us—but how the public loved them!" A more plausible acquisition, at one fifteenth the cost, were Audubon's original water colors of American birds, purchased from his widow in 1862. The income of the society's third legacy, a bequest of $10,000 from Seth Grosvenor received in 1859, helped with the current expenses of the new building. Encouraged by this, the society proposed to expand its art collection "with a view to pro-viding a public gallery of art in this city." It proposed such a build-ing in Central Park, securing in 1868, by act of the Legislature, a site covering 81st to 84th Streets, 300 feet west of Fifth Avenue. Although grandiose plans were drawn and an effort made in 1870 to secure funds for carrying them out, the cost was so great that the society finally abandoned the scheme. The city then built the Metropolitan Museum of Art on this site, at an initial cost of a million dollars, although the society clung to its European art and ancient antiquities for more than half a century after the opening of the Metropolitan in 1872.

The new prosperity of the society pleased some New Yorkers more than others. George Templeton Strong "looked through the premises" on 3 May 1858, noting in his diary:

The Historical Society owns some nice books. My life membership is not absolute-ly valueless. The prosperity of that institution shows what activity and loud bray-ing can do. Its corporate functions are not exalted. Its office is to collect and preserve books and MSS illustrative of our brief and barren history. That is all. The lectures and "papers" it generates so abundantly I set down as equal to zero; an estimate more charitable than accurate, for they are properly affected with a negative sign, as gaseous secretions of vanity and dilettantism.

Strong's private comment is harsh, yet it cannot be denied that the society had a weakness for celebrations and public events, and, in its desire for public approbation, a habit of sailing before the wind, from whatever quarter it might be blowing. At the time Strong wrote, the society had published ten volumes of *Collections*, while the Massachusetts Historical Society had issued thirty-four. But in 1858 a fund had been established for the publication of materials on American history which was eventually to improve the output. There was some delay in building the fund to a point that permitted the beginning of publication. At the meeting of 5 June 1866, John R. Brodhead

moved that the Strawberry entertainment be dispensed with, and that its cost be appropriated to the Publication Fund; and Mr. Edward Bill moved, as a substitute, that none but subscribers to that Fund be allowed to taste the strawberries and cream. Neither of these propositions was seconded, and the former was received by members of the Society with the most significant demonstrations of disapprobation.

In spite of the loss of this motion, the first volume in the Publication Fund Series appeared in 1868. Eighty other volumes have followed, including numerous Revolutionary documents, the papers of Silas Deane and Cadwallader Colden, seventeen volumes of *Abstracts of Wills on File in the Surrogate's Office, City of New York, 1665–1801*, the diary of William Dunlap, letter books and order books of Admiral Lord Rodney, four volumes of letters of John Pintard to his daughter, and others on the arts and crafts in New York, on the exhibitions of the National Academy of Design, the American Academy of Fine Arts, and American Art Union, and on the Supreme Court of Judicature of the Province of New York, 1691–1704.

From the income of a revolving fund endowed by John Divine Jones in 1874 and 1878, thirteen volumes have been published.

Several deal with Revolutionary subjects; others with the work of such American painters as John Ramage, Gilbert Stuart, John Wesley Jarvis, and Edward Greene Malbone.

The building that had seemed so spacious in 1857 was already crowded by the early 1870s. In 1885 a conditional gift of $100,000 toward a new building was offered by Mrs. Robert L. Stuart, provided an additional $150,000 were raised. In 1889 the building fund had reached $250,000, but as the site purchased in 1891 on Central Park West, between 76th and 77th Streets, cost $286,500 there was considerable delay in construction. Ground was broken in 1902. Through the insistent urgings of the nonagenarian Henry Dexter, president of the American News Company, who implemented his admonitions with gifts totaling a quarter of a million dollars, the central pavilion of the present building was completed in 1908 at a cost of $421,150, exclusive of land. The move from Second Avenue to Central Park West was a formidable problem for a staff consisting only of the librarian, Robert H. Kelby, two assistants, and a janitor. The building was too small from the start. By 1913 it was so overcrowded that there began to be talk of completing it by adding two wings along 76th and 77th Streets.

There had been some heartening additions to endowment funds, the largest of which was $607,000, received in 1911 from the sale of real estate bequeathed by the Misses Cornelia Beekman DePeyster and Catherine Augusta DePeyster, but two decades were to pass before the society felt justified in enlarging its building. That possibility came through a spectacular and unexpected windfall. It had been known for some time that the Misses Elizabeth Gardiner Thompson and Mary Gardiner Thompson and their brother, Charles Griswold Thompson, had drawn identical wills, leaving each other a life interest in their property, and that on the death of the last survivor, after specific bequests had been paid, the residue of the survivor's estate was to be equally divided among six New York institutions, of which the New-York Historical Society was one. Miss Elizabeth died in 1913, the brother in 1919, while Miss Mary

Gardiner Thompson reached the age of ninety-one, dying only in 1935. The society's one sixth of the residue amounted to $4,633,915.92!

The Thompson bequest almost immediately made possible great changes in the housing and operation of the society. The much-needed wings were promptly added, the building in its present form being reopened on 29 March 1939. Even after this expense, $3,077,-769.44 of the bequest remained for endowment. Dr. Vail has thus described the staff situation:

Up to 1917, there were but two professional members of the Library staff, the Librarian and Assistant Librarian who doubled as cataloguer, bookkeeper, museum curator, and editor, and eight members of the building staff. That year five more assistants were added to the professional staff, . . . we hired a bookkeeper and three years later a firm of certified public accountants . . . was employed to audit the Society's books.

At that time the librarian was Robert Hendre Kelby, who retired in 1921, after fifty-three years service. His successor, Alexander J. Wall, had come to work in 1898 at the age of fourteen. When he became librarian, he had been with the society for twenty-three years and was to serve it for another twenty-three, until his death in 1944. In 1937 his title was changed to director. Mr. Wall was a society-educated man, who knew the collections as only one who had lived with them all his life could. He helped move them from Second Avenue in 1908; he had an active part in planning the new wings, with particular reference to their lighting and use. For many years he edited the society's publications, and in 1917 he started *The New-York Historical Society Quarterly*, which is now in its forty-sixth volume. In 1942 he began to conduct a course, "Resources and Methods of an American Historical Society," planned jointly by the graduate history faculty of Columbia University and the society, which was designed to produce closer co-operation with academic faculties and graduate students. It is nevertheless widely believed in Cambridge, Massachusetts, that a professor of history in Harvard University who wished to consult a manuscript in the New-York Historical Society, was, during Mr. Wall's regime, turned away disconsolate because he had failed to provide himself with a suitable letter of introduction.

After the receipt of the Thompson bequest, Dr. Vail writes:

The Society went to work immediately to build up an adequate staff by the addition of a Librarian (Mr. Wall having become Director), an Editor, Art and Museum Curators, and a Supervisor of Education and Public Relations; a Bibliographer, a Reference Librarian, and Curators of Manuscripts, Newspapers, Map and Prints; as well as additional accessionists, cataloguers, reading-room and museum assistants, including museum and picture frame restorers. The photographic staff of two was adequate but we added to our bindery and maintenance staffs until we had a total of 48 employees in 1938 and later nearly the 75 employees deemed necessary for the proper operation of the completed building.

Mr. Wall's successor as director, Dr. Robert William Glenroie Vail, had a distinguished professional background. A graduate of Cornell in the class of 1914, he attended the Library School of the New York Public Library, where he came in contact with that remarkable bibliographer, Wilberforce Eames. After service in the New York Public Library, the Minnesota Historical Society, and the Roosevelt Memorial Association, Dr. Vail became editor of Sabin's *Dictionary of Books on American History*, which he brought to completion in 1936 by editing the last nine volumes of the twenty-nine volume work. He then became librarian of the American Antiquarian Society and remained in Worcester until 1940, when he went to Albany as State Librarian. Through his wide acquaintance with institutions, historians, and bibliographers, Dr. Vail was able to diminish the parochial quality of the New-York Historical Society and to bring it in more intimate relation with scholarly projects elsewhere. Upon Dr. Vail's retirement on 1 April 1960, he was succeeded by Dr. James J. Heslin, previously associate director and librarian, who not only is the holder of a Boston University PH.D. in American history, but has had professional library training at Columbia University.

Membership in the New-York Historical Society, unlike its Massachusetts counterpart, has never been limited in number. In its early years the society was constantly scratching about for new members or trying to persuade existing ones to pay their dues. Increases in number were proudly noted. During the presidency of Peter Gerard Stuyvesant, 1836–39, 215 were added. In 1883 there were nearly 2,000 members in all classes.

The office of president seems to have been esteemed for reasons not strictly historical in character, if one reads between the lines in Dr. Vail's history. Witness the occasion when the hard-working and faithful Frederic De Peyster, who had saved the society in 1827 by his successful lobbying for funds at Albany and was its eleventh president from 1864 to 1866, was dumped out in 1867 by members who wished "a man of greater political distinction to bring prestige to our deliberations." The successful candidate, Hamilton Fish, who was elected without his knowledge or consent, resigned two years later to become Secretary of State. Augustus Schell, elected the fourteenth president in 1872, was not re-elected in 1873 because De Peyster's friends returned him to the office, which he held until his death in 1882. Augustus Schell, who had shown his displeasure by remaining away from the society during the nine years of De Peyster's second term, was once again elected president in 1883. He died in office fourteen months later, seemingly unmollified, for, although very well off, he left the society only $5,000 in his will.

The comic but harrassing efforts of a female member to take over the management are divertingly described in an incident that Dr. Vail has dubbed "Mrs. Van Rensselaer's War." Mrs. John King Van Rensselaer, who "decided to torpedo the Society," carried on hostilities from 1915 to 1920. Among other things, she fired

a barrage of critical letters to the President of the Society in which she suggested changes which were clearly impossible to carry out until the building could be completed and the endowment increased. She called for a vigorous campaign for the collecting of the furnishings and heirlooms of the old New York families when it was obvious that there would be no present place to display or even to store them. Pointing out that, in ancient times, the king had to have a Queen Consort, she suggested that the President come and see her in order to hear her views for the Society's improvement and threatened that she and her friends would deflect their activities elsewhere if the Society did not adopt their suggestions. She further proposed that various old families be invited to endow individual rooms and put up memorial windows to their New York ancestors, forgetting that there was no place for such rooms or windows. Later on, she threatened that, if the President did not appoint her and two of her friends a committee to have a series of teas in our building, she would play a practical joke on the Society that would make it ridiculous.

After wasting a great deal of everyone's time and temper for a period of years, Mrs. Van Rensselaer's attempt to take over control was roundly defeated at the annual meeting of 6 January 1920. The incident had shown, however, the risk of harm that might be done by a self-seeking member who packed a business meeting with cronies. Consequently the bylaws were revised to transfer the management of the society from members in a meeting to an executive committee. In 1947 further revisions were made which placed responsibility entirely in the hands of a board of trustees, thus assuring stable administration of a sort compatible with the present financial situation of the society and preventing any recurrence of "raids" similar to "Mrs. Van Rensselaer's War." It should be noted that among the present trustees are Thomas Winthrop Streeter, treasurer since 1948, a former president of the American Antiquarian Society, and Frederick B. Adams Jr., director of the Pierpont Morgan Library.

The 1961 annual report indicates that at the end of that year the society had 13 honorary members, 20 patrons ($5,000 each), 15 fellows ($1,000 each), 158 life members ($100 each), 491 annual members ($10 annually), and 142 associate members, a total of 837. The members' dues of $5,300 provide an insignificant portion of the annual income of $414,149.36; thus the size of the membership is today financially immaterial.

The New-York Historical Society receives no public funds; it is supported entirely from private gifts and bequests. Its investments, as of 31 December 1961, show a book value of $7,963,714.75 and an approximate market value of $12,695,303.41. Old institutions are sometimes hampered by ancient provisions restricting the use of their funds to semiobsolete purposes. This society is fortunate not only in the size of its endowment but the amount of it that is unrestricted. Endowment and memorial funds without restriction (excluding any portion invested in the museum) total $4,014,702.66; special funds whose use is governed by provisions of the gifts amount to only $1,068,389.64.

Of the unrestricted funds, eleven are nineteenth-century bequests, totaling $44,300; the remainder have been received in the present century. The enormous Thompson bequest accounts for the lion's share; the De Peyster bequest of $607,271.43 was also substantial. It is noteworthy, however, that there have been five gifts or bequests ranging from $20,000 to $100,000 within the twentieth century, but more than thirty of $10,000 or less.

In the special funds more than half of the $1,068,389.64 has been derived from three bequests, all recent and for useful purposes: that by James B. Wilbur (1935) of $100,000 for the purchase of books, manuscripts, and prints; that of Mrs. John Jay Watson (1958) of $150,000 for the purchase of American historical paintings; and that of Mrs. Lathrop C. Harper (1958) of $441,095.29 for the purchase of books.

The provision of funds for acquisitions is not only fortunate but necessary when one considers the size and scope of the library. In round numbers, the New-York Historical Society today owns 500,000 books, 18,000 broadsides (3,000 of which antedate 1800), 3,000 manuscript and printed maps, 1,200 atlases, 35,000 prints (drawings, caricatures, portraits), 150,000 photographs, and 750,000 manuscripts. The original field of the society was defined in its constitution as "the natural, civil, literary, and ecclesiastical history of the United States in general, and of this State in particular." In 1804, when Lewis and Clark had not yet crossed the continent and when libraries and learned institutions were few in number even in the most settled parts of the country, this was a reasonable aspiration. Although the passage of time constantly reduced the practicability of this original purpose, collections continued to be assembled on so broad a basis that there has often been uncertainty as to whether, as Lawrence C. Wroth has put it, "the Society was a state historical society with New York as its main reason for being or something quite different, that is, an institute of American history situated in New York."

To resolve this problem, the trustees of the society in 1956 requested Mr. Wroth, librarian of the John Carter Brown Library, to survey the library and make recommendations about future policy. He pointed out that since 1804 many other institutions have developed and carried out collecting policies duplicated by the society and that if it continued to make all of American history its field, the final result would be a mediocre collection. He recommended instead building on the fields in which the library was already strong. On the basis of Mr. Wroth's report, the library committee prepared a study of future acquisition policies. By approving this study, the board of trustees, on 27 May 1959, in effect endorsed the view that their institution was a State historical society located in New York, but that the society's strong collections of various special fields of United States history other than New York would be recognized by continuing acquisitions in those fields, under certain limits.

The manuscript collection is the heart of the library. In 1813, when the Reverend Timothy Alden's catalogue was published, fifty-one manuscripts were listed. It now consists of over 300,000 single manuscripts and more than 3,500 bound volumes. Among these are papers of the colonial and Revolutionary period, account books, diaries, journals, and letters of New York and early New Yorkers. The largest collection relating to one subject is that of the American Fur Company, containing 131 volumes and more than 18,000 separate manuscripts. In 1941 a ninety-six-page *Survey of The Manuscript Collections in The New-York Historical Society* was issued, which serves as a convenient guide. Since the appearance of that list, many additions have been received, of which the business, family, and personal papers of James, Gerard, James W., and other members of the Beekman family are of particular interest. From them Philip

L. White drew material for his *The Beekmans of New York in Politics and Commerce, 1647–1877* and the three-volume edition of *The Beekman Mercantile Papers, 1746–1799*, which were published by the society in 1956. Sir Richard Pares in the *English Historical Review* of January 1958 characterized these volumes as "the largest single contribution to early American business history in twenty years, and a considerable contribution to New York political history."

Planning began in 1958 on a joint research and publishing project between the society and New York University for an edition of the papers of Albert Gallatin, the second Secretary of the Treasury of the United States and the ninth president of the society. Under this co-operative arrangement, the society makes available all the Gallatin material in its possession—some eighty-two boxes and twenty-one volumes of manuscripts, amounting to some 20,000 pieces—while the university provides the research and editorial staff for the production of the volumes. The editor will be Professor Bayrd Still, chairman of the department of history at New York University, while the society will be represented on the board of the project by its director, Dr. Heslin, and by Trustees Lucius Wilmerding and Frederick B. Adams Jr. The president of New York University will act as chairman, with the president of the New-York Historical Society as vice-chairman.

The manuscript collection, which is particularly cohesive, is enriched almost equally by gift and by purchase. In the future it is proposed that only material be bought which has special relevance to subjects already represented in the collection.

The library contains complete runs of New York City directories, business directories, and guides. There are indexes to vital records, wills, newspaper records, as well as early reports of New York City religious, benevolent, charitable, social, and fraternal organizations. There are partial files of early city departmental records, together with printed records of the common council, the board of aldermen, and such like. Added to the maps, atlases, and prints, this collection of New York City material through the nineteenth century is most comprehensive. Sets of official documents of colonial and state legislative journals, laws, and executive documents, regional, county, city, and town guides and directories, and the publications of colleges, universities, and local historical societies comprise a cross section of the New York State records in the library. Every town, city, and county history of New York State that can be procured has a place in the library. County histories of the New England states, New Jersey, Pennsylvania, and the old northwest are included in the future acquisition policy; beyond these regions the society only proposes now to have a good history of each state. The library has a large collection of collective and family genealogies, to which only New York City and State families are to be added in the future. The policy of the New York Public Library is to acquire a copy of every printed genealogy relating to families in the United States, as well as to some in Britain and Canada. This policy, added to the existence in the city of the New York Genealogical and Biographical Society Library, makes any wider collecting of family histories by the New-York Historical Society superfluous.

The society's collection of eighteenth-century newspapers is the fourth largest in the country. It collects United States newspapers through 1820, with particular emphasis on the eastern seaboard, and attempts to obtain New York State newspapers of the nineteenth century, especially for the early years of communities. Outside of New York State, newspaper collecting is chiefly confined to the early period. Where exceptions exist, the material has generally come by gift. The society has been successful, however, in exchanging out-of-state later nineteenth-century newspapers for New York State ones of a similar period. The newspaper collection is constantly used and is, in every sense, active. It is worth noting that, except for sporadic collecting by the New York State Library at Albany, there appears to be little planned collecting by other institutions of nineteenth-century New York State newspapers.

There are important collections of political caricatures and posters to 1910, steamboats to 1920, eighteenth- and nineteenth-century maps of New York and the eastern seaboard, state and county atlases, views of New York City and State and of cities outside the State before 1850. The society continues to add to these as it does to its holdings of portraits, photographs, and lithographs of New Yorkers and of national figures.

The society will continue to add primary material to its already strong collections concerning slavery, United States naval and military history through 1898, the Civil War, travels in the United States prior to 1850, and the circus, but will purchase only selected secondary works of particular importance in those fields. It will add to its collection of American Indian captivities only when primary material is available. It will make no additions to its existing collections concerning the early southwest exploration period, the eighteenth century in Florida, the California Gold Rush, sheet music and songsters, trials in the United States up to 1860, and Latin America, which consists chiefly of general histories of the Spanish exploration period. To its collections of American drama to 1860 and American fiction, poetry, and belles-lettres to 1850, it will add only material of special interest relating to New York City and New York State, up to and including 1900.

The library in 1961 had a total annual attendance of 5,532. It should be noted that nonmembers outnumber members in a ratio of 6.6 to 1. Qualified researchers are permitted to use source material upon presentation of suitable credentials and a reasonable explanation of their need to do so. For the use of manuscripts or other rare material, the permission of the director, librarian, or curator of the collection is required. The society's manuscripts are not for genealogical use per se. As a rule undergraduates are not allowed to use the collections, although this restriction is waived in the case of a serious student who demonstrates that he has used all available secondary material on his subject. In so far as possible, consistent with the responsibility for safe preservation of sources, the society welcomes serious readers. For those unable to come in person, there are facilities for photographic reproduction. Over 1,200 inquiries by mail are received during the average year from all parts of the United States, as well as from foreign countries. The library has a staff of eighteen, usually recruited from library schools in the area or from the history departments of graduate schools of neighboring universities.

The total attendance at the New-York Historical Society during 1961 was 80,165, an average of 246 visitors for each of the 326 days on which the building was open.[5] Of this number, 5,532 were users of the library, as we have seen. There was an educational attendance of 11,464 at programs offered for schools. After deducting these figures, it will be seen that more than 60,000 people are annually drawn to the building by the extensive and varied exhibitions that the society offers. On the first floor are rooms for changing exhibitions, as well as the Port of New York Gallery, exhibitions of military and naval history, and a nearly complete collection of Rogers groups. On the second floor are a series of New York History Galleries, which tell the story of New York and Manhattan Island chronologically from Indian times through the Federal period. On the same floor are collections of English Staffordshire ware, American glass, the Prentis collection of colonial New England furnishings, including three period rooms, two rooms from Mount Pleasant, the home of the Beekman family from 1764 to 1874, early American toys, and the Audubon Gallery, which contains a selection from the society's collection of 460 of the 500 original watercolor drawings by John James Audubon of the birds of America. On the third floor is the Bella C. Landauer collection of American business, industrial, and advertising history, and exhibitions of early American arts and crafts and costumes. The fourth floor, of skylighted picture galleries, is given over to the society's very extensive collection of paintings, which includes 1,143 American portraits, many of which are of remarkable distinction. The painting galleries exhibit Dutch and English colonial New York portraits, distinguish-

5. The building was open on Sundays, but closed during the month of August and on New Year's Day, Memorial Day, 4 July, Labor Day, Thanksgiving, Christmas, 24 and 31 December, and half days 23 and 30 December.

ed national figures of the American Revolution, portraits of presidents and statesmen, of American artists and men of letters, as well as American landscape and genre paintings, nineteenth-century portraits, and eighteenth- and nineteenth-century portrait miniatures. Objects from the collections of American furniture, silver, and sculpture are interspersed through the portrait gallery, just as numerous prints, maps, and drawings are exhibited in corridors throughout the building. In the basement are galleries containing carriages and volunteer fire department equipment.

In 1936, when plans for the completion of the building were under way, the Egyptian collection, the Nineveh marbles, and small but choice groups of pre-Columbian Central and South American Indians artifacts and weapons and implements of Plains Indians were lent to the Brooklyn Museum, which purchased the greater part of them in 1948.[6] Thus the bulkiest aberrations of nineteenth-century collecting enthusiasm have passed into useful and more appropriate hands, while the society has, from their sale, an Abbott-Lenox Fund of $110,000, the income of which is available for the purchase of more suitable museum accessions.

The basis of the society's paintings and sculpture rests upon four collections, that of the New York Gallery of Fine Arts (including the Luman Reed collection), received in 1858, 433 paintings given by Thomas J. Bryan in 1867, 181 from the estate of Louis Durr, received in 1882, and the Robert L. Stuart collection of 243 pictures, deposited by the New York Public Library in 1944. The Bryan, Durr, and Stuart paintings represent the taste of nineteenth-century American merchant-collectors prior to the establishment of public

6. In 1941, five years after the Egyptian collection went to Brooklyn, Park Commissioner Robert Moses, in a report to the mayor in which he denounced various New York institutions as "musty" and "sacred" and stated that they "must let down the bars for the great masses of the people," criticized the duplication of Egyptology in the American, Metropolitan, and Brooklyn Museums, *and* the New-York Historical Society! In reply Mr. Wall very properly pointed out that the Pharoahs had left 170 Central Park West, which was a private institution, open free to the public, to which thousands of visitors, ranging from scholars to school children, came every month.

art museums. While the American paintings received in this way are largely on exhibition, the majority of the six hundred or more European pictures, representing almost every school of art, are in storage.

The Department of the Museum has a staff of six, that is to say a curator, assistant curator, painting restorer, museum restorer, and two assistants. In addition to the care of the collections and the permanent installations, they are responsible for temporary exhibitions, such as those of 1961: *A Nation Divided, 1861–62*; *John Hill, Master of Aquatint*; and *American Portraits by Enit Kaufman*.

An Editorial Department of two is responsible for the *Quarterly* and for the society's publications.[7] In 1959, for example, there appeared the three volumes of *Supreme Court of Judicature of the Province of New York 1691–1704*, by Paul M. Hamlin and the society's editor, Charles E. Baker. This consisted of an introductory volume of nearly 500 pages on the establishment of the court, its personnel, the jury system, and court procedure; a second of 386 pages containing the annotated minutes of the court; and a final volume of 500 pages providing a biographical dictionary, glossary, sources, and indexes of cases by plaintiff and defendant, of persons, places, and subject matter. In that year the *Quarterly* consisted of 484 pages, containing nineteen articles and sixty-three book reviews. Eight of the articles and thirty-five of the reviews were by members of the staff.

For more than twenty years the society has conducted an educational program, under the direction of a supervisor of education, directed primarily for New York City school children of the fifth grade and above. Arrangements are made for visits of school groups; four circulating loan exhibitions are extensively used in New York City high schools; film programs, story hours, theatrical programs, and puppet shows are offered from time to time. In addition the Education Department arranges free public lectures relating to

7. In addition to publications previously mentioned in the course of the chapter, one should note the appearance in 1957 of *The New-York Historical Society's Dictionary of Artists in America 1564–1860*, by George C. Groce and David Wallace, published by the Yale University Press.

American history and art, gallery talks on weekend afternoons, and provides guided tours for clubs, colleges, and other groups. Free public concerts are presented on Sunday afternoons during the winter.

A Department of Public Relations and a Photographic Department serve both the society and the public.

The New-York Historical Society, although supported entirely from private funds, not only offers to scholars the rich accumulations of its library, manuscript, and portrait collections, which contain much early material of significance beyond the borders of New York, but also provides exhibitions, lectures, and other educational services to a wide audience in New York City. It should be noted that the society could not have assumed these public functions without detriment to its service to scholarship until the receipt of the Thompson bequest a quarter of a century ago made possible both the provision of adequate gallery space and the employment of a technically qualified staff. It might also be observed that the Thompson bequest came from wills drawn in 1907, a time when the society was still jammed into its old quarters downtown on Second Avenue; that it represented not a specific enthusiasm for any one of the society's activities, past or present, but a general regard for the society as one of the useful institutions of New York City.[8]

No institution ever has all the space or the money that it needs. Nevertheless the New-York Historical Society is in a more fortunate position towards the future, as to buildings, resources, and staff, than any other of the privately supported state historical societies.

8. The other recipients of one sixth of the residuary estate of the survivor were the New York Association for Improving the Condition of the Poor, the Children's Aid Society, the Society of the New York Hospital, the Presbyterian Hospital, and Columbia University.

Chapter III

THE AMERICAN
ANTIQUARIAN SOCIETY

Any to whom the Library and Cabinet of this Society may be useful, will not greatly regret the distance which separates them from
the objects of their pursuit, if they can but eventually obtain in one
place, what, otherwise, they would have to seek in many.
                                        —ISAIAH THOMAS, 1814

TO American historians the names of John Carter Brown, Henry E. Huntington, J. Pierpont Morgan, and William L. Clements signify men made rich by business who subsequently assembled great libraries that they housed and endowed for the good of learning. The third historical society to be founded in the United States was the work of such a man, Isaiah Thomas (1749–1831), who had by his own efforts become the chief printer-publisher-bookseller of the young United States. The great library that he established in 1812 does not bear his name; it is known as the American Antiquarian Society.[1]

Isaiah Thomas[2] began printing before he could read. At the age of six, in the Boston shop of Zechariah Fowle to whom he was apprenticed, he set up from a copy a broadside ballad, *The Lawyer's Pedigree*,

---

1. Clarence S. Brigham, *Fifty Years of Collecting Americana for the Library of the American Antiquarian Society* (Worcester, 1958); Clifford K. Shipton, "The American Antiquarian Society," *William and Mary Quarterly*, 3rd ser., II (1945), 164–172.
2. Clifford K. Shipton, *Isaiah Thomas, Printer, Patriot and Philanthropist 1749–1831* (Rochester, N. Y., 1948).

Tune, Our Polly is a sad Slut. At sixteen he ran away from his shift-less master to Halifax, where he did most of the work on the *Halifax Gazette*, until the jibes against the Stamp Act that he insinuated into this official organ of the provincial government made him unwelcome in Nova Scotia. After picaresque adventures between Maine and South Carolina, which included the unhappy acquisition of a wife of dubious virtue, Thomas returned to Boston in the spring of 1770, where he soon set up a newspaper. *The Massachusetts Spy*, which first appeared on 7 March 1771, made him even more obnoxious to constituted authority than he had been in Halifax. So vigorously did he advocate the cause of revolution that by the spring of 1775 he thought it wise to decamp. On the night of 16 April, with the aid of General Joseph Warren and Captain Timothy Bigelow, he ferried his press and types across the Charles River from Boston to Charlestown and sent them off by wagon to Worcester, forty miles inland. Two nights later the twenty-six-year-old printer assisted Paul Revere and members of the Committee of Safety to alarm the Middlesex countryside that British troops were on the way to Lexington and Concord. On the nineteenth of April, according to one of his friends, he joined the minute men in sniping at those troops from behind stone walls; on the twentieth he followed his printing equipment to Worcester, where he set up shop. There he remained for fifty-six years, to create the principal printing and publishing business in the country, which eventually included newspapers, a paper mill, bindery, and bookstores.

With prosperity Isaiah Thomas became stylish. He was the first resident of Worcester to boast a carriage for pleasure, with colored coachman in livery. With leisure he also became a collector and scholar. Having accumulated a considerable library illustrative of his craft, he wrote and published the first history of American printing. He was elected to the Massachusetts Historical Society in 1811, the New-York Historical Society in 1813, and the American Philosophical Society in 1816. Dartmouth College made him an honorary Master of Arts in 1814, while Alleghany College, of

which the Reverend Timothy Alden had become president, awarded him an LL.D. in 1818.

In 1812, when he had already retired from business, Thomas pe-
titioned the Massachusetts Legislature for permission to establish a
society to which he proposed to transfer his library. Thus on 24
October 1812 the American Antiquarian Society was incorporated.[3]
At the first meeting of the new organization, held at the Exchange
Coffee House in Boston on 19 November 1812, Thomas was elected
president; at the second, on 3 February 1813, he announced the gift
of his library.

The purposes of the new organization were even broader than
those of its two predecessors, for Thomas stated that "the chief
objects of this society will be American Antiquities, natural, artificial
and literary; not, however, excluding those of other countries."
Worcester logically enough became the headquarters of the American Antiquarian Society. For one thing, Thomas lived there; for
another, it was considered safer than a coastal town, which was
exposed to enemy invasion. The War of 1812 was in progress.
Joseph Peabody, the principal merchant of Salem, had already
bought a farm in Danvers, five miles away, to protect his goods
from possible bombardment. As Thomas said,

For the better preservation from the destruction so often experienced in large
towns and cities by fire, as well as from the ravages of any enemy, to which sea-
ports in particular are so much exposed in time of war, it is universally agreed that
for a place of deposit for articles intended to be preserved for ages, and of which
many, if destroyed or carried away, could never be replaced by others of the like
kind, an inland situation is to be preferred; this consideration alone was judged
sufficient for placing the Library and Museum of this Society forty miles distant
from the nearest branch of the sea, in the town of Worcester, Massachusetts.

The earliest bylaws provided for three meetings a year, in Worcester in September and in Boston in December and June. The annual meeting in December, at which a "public oration" was enjoined,

3. For the early years, see *Proceedings of the American Antiquarian Society 1812–1849*
(Worcester, 1912).

became an occasion of some ceremony. The society would march in procession, sometimes escorted by the gaudily attired Ancient and Honorable Artillery Company, from the Exchange Coffee House to King's Chapel, where after suitable religious exercises the address was given. In 1816, when the Reverend William Bentley was the speaker, the meeting opened with the resounding metrical version of the seventy-ninth Psalm that is still today a moving part of Harvard Commencement.

> Let children hear the mighty deeds,
> Which God perform'd of old;
> Which in our younger years we saw,
> And which our fathers told.

A newspaper announcement of the first anniversary meeting in 1813 notes that "pews are appropriated for the Ladies who may honor the Society with attendance." It also corrected a misapprehension that somehow had got abroad. "The report of a Contribution at Church is unfounded. None is expected." By 1831 meetings of the society had become semiannual, but the practice of holding one in Boston has remained. Today the society meets at the Club of Odd Volumes in Boston on the third Wednesday of April and at its own building in Worcester on the third Wednesday of October.

Isaiah Thomas's *An Account of the American Antiquarian Society*, which was its first publication, issued in November 1813, refers in such detail to the Society of Antiquaries of London as to make it clear that that organization served as his inspiration in other respects than name. Indeed the designation of the new society's first serial Publication, *Archaeologia Americana*, is an obvious derivation from *Archaeologia* which the London body had been publishing since 1770.

The objects that the American Antiquarian Society wished to collect were, according to Thomas:

books of every description including pamphlets and magazines, especially those which were early printed either in South or in North America; files of Newspapers of former times, or of the present day . . . specimens, with written accounts respecting them, of fossils, handicrafts of the Aborigines, &c. Manuscripts, ancient and modern, on interesting subjects, particularly those which give accounts of remarkable events, discoveries, or the description of any part of the continent, or the islands in the American seas; maps, charts, &c.

The society's aspiration to be American in the widest sense is indicated by the provision of the bylaws that "it shall be the duty of the Council to enquire concerning the character of persons living outside the Commonwealth proper to be elected honorary members, particularly in Spanish America." The three fields of enquiry specifically suggested by the Reverend William Jenks in his oration at the anniversary meeting in October 1813 were the ancient Indian nations of our continent, the "Western Mounds of Earth," and the early European settlements. In 1814 Thomas proposed "to have a suitable number of respectable and useful members in all the principal cities and towns in the United States, and some in the interiour of every state" and to enlarge the number of counsellors from seven to perhaps thirty in order to have representatives of all states on the governing body. Recognizing the difficulty of assembling such a group with any regularity, he suggested the appointment of subcouncils of five, one in Boston and one in Worcester, that, by monthly meetings, would accomplish the society's routine business.

The minutes of the 29 June 1815 meeting give evidence of the interest of at least some of the more distant members.

Several communications from members residing in various parts of the United States were read, among which was one "concerning the Primitive Inhabitants of North America," from Moses Fisk, Esqr., of Hilham, State of Tennessee.

A communication from William Sheldon, Esq., of the Island of Jamaica, containing some particulars respecting the ancient state, and the antiquities of the Island of Jamaica, was laid before the Society.

In 1816 Charles Wilkins of Lexington, Kentucky, generously attempted to send the society a "dessicated mummy" unearthed a couple of years before on his property near Mammoth Cave by workmen digging for saltpeter. Unhappily Nahum Ward, who was entrusted with its delivery, absconded and exhibited the mummy hither and yon to gaping crowds for his own profit. Although the society eventually retrieved the gift, which Ward had touted as "one of the greatest curiosities ever exhibited in the American world," it did not give unanimous satisfaction to the members, for Benjamin Russell, one of the original incorporators, wrote thus to Thomas:

Very few people attend to see the skeleton, and those who do universally express their disgust at it. For myself, I cannot perceive how the cause of science, history or antiquarianism is to be benefited by the preservation of those dried up particles. I have seen a dead cat, which accidentally was inclosed in an oven, and found some months afterwards in as good a state of mummy preservation as this skeleton. The best thing in my opinion which could be done with it would be to give it to some anatomical school or bury it in the cemetery.

Russell's suggestions were not followed, but the mummy was, after being shown at the Centennial Exhibition in Philadelphia in 1876, given to the Smithsonian Institution, which wanted it. After sixty years, the society had begun to narrow its field.

Leslie W. Dunlap, in his *American Historical Societies, 1790–1860*, well observed that "Emerson's remark, 'An institution is the lengthened shadow of one man' is probably truer of the American Antiquarian Society than of any other early historical association." Isaiah Thomas continued to serve as president until his death in 1831. Unlike some presidents, who occupy the chair on ceremonial occasions and leave the work to others, Thomas constantly served the society that he had founded in a remarkable variety of ways. His diaries[4] are dull reading on the whole, involving, as they do, taking physick, killing pigs, and buying hay. They give, however, some hint of his constant devotion to the American Antiquarian Society.

On 11 November 1814 he records:

Purchased the Remains of old Library of the Mathers which had belonged to Drs. Increase, Cotton and Samuel. This is unquestionably the oldest in New England. The Remains are between 600 and 700 Vols. Worked hard all day with Lawrence [his coachman] and other assistance in packing and removing it.

On the twenty-eighth, when the books were safely in Worcester:

4. *Transactions and Collections of the American Antiquarian Society*, IX–X (1909).

Have been engaged in taking a Catalogue and putting the books in order of the Mather Library for the last 8 days, have not been abroad for the last six days.

It was not necessary to go abroad, for at this period Thomas cared for the society's library in his own house. He skipped a bank meeting the next day to continue his cataloguing, and the day after Christmas reported:

Still at work on the Mather Library—very assiduously—have been only to bank and to Church for a month past. Have got through with the bound books—now engaged on the MSS.

The society still has the seventy-five-page folio catalogue that Thomas compiled, in which, opposite each entry, he noted the price that he paid to the seller, Mrs. Hannah Mather Crocker, a granddaughter of Cotton Mather.

In mid-January 1815 Thomas spent three days with the council revising bylaws. A year later he cooked up a scheme for a lottery with a grand prize of $25,000; the public was to buy $110,000 worth of tickets, and, after prizes were paid, the society would receive $30,000. As the Legislature disapproved, Thomas eventually provided the society with a building at his own expense. In the spring of 1817 he offered to contribute the site, 150,000 bricks, and $2,000. Ground was broken on 31 May 1819. On 9 August 1820 he notes in his diary:

Settled with the Master Workmen for building the American Antiquarian Society Library. This building cost, the mere building cost, without Land, or fences, or fixing the grounds, &c 6752 dollars 84 cents. The building only.—Extra Labour on the Cellar, 11 dollars in all 6763 dollars 84 cents.

A week later, "began to remove the American Antiquarian Library from my house to the New Edifice for the Library—4 or 5 members attended all day." This labor continued until the twenty-fourth, when the fine new building was publicly dedicated. As a final touch, one might note that on 23 June 1828, Thomas, aged seventy-nine, "Cut the Grass at A.A.S. Library."

In assisting the American Antiquarian Society towards its goal of "collecting and preserving every variety of book, pamphlet and manuscript that might be valuable in illustrating any and all parts of American history," Isaiah Thomas gave it between seven and eight thousand books and more than $20,000. With a founder who was learned, generous, and indefatigable, and who also had time and money to spare, the society's first nineteen years were considerably less accidented than the comparable period in the life of the New-York Historical Society. He not only contributed liberally himself; he expected every member to give some article of value to the society's collections at least once a year.

With Isaiah Thomas's death there was no interruption in the growth of the library, thanks to the energetic activity of Christopher Columbus Baldwin, who became librarian on 1 April 1832 at a salary of $600 a year. Baldwin was familiar with the scene. He was a member of the Harvard Class of 1823 who, upon being rusticated in May of his senior year because of an outstanding Harvard riot, came to Worcester to study law. From 1826 until the spring of 1830, when he temporarily moved elsewhere, Baldwin served first as assistant librarian and then as librarian and cabinet keeper of the society on a volunteer basis. The newspaper collection became one of his first interests, for he noted in his diary[5] on 10 July 1832:

This day I have shelves erected in the chamber of the north wing of Antiquarian Hall for the reception of newspapers. The shelves are put up, and I load them with six hundred volumes of papers, which comprise about half of our collection of that kind of reading.

It is one of the chief sources of my trouble (being happy enough in all other respects) that only a part of the members of the Council of the Society are willing to increase the numbers of our newspapers. Since I have been here, I have been unwearied in my pains to get good files of papers from all parts of the country. I have made arrangements with some forty or fifty individuals from different sections of the U. S. to procure for me ancient as well as modern sets and to preserve all those that they now subscribe for. In this way the collection must become exceedingly valuable. I suffer no traveller to visit me without enlisting him in my cause, and giving him directions how to find them and how to send them to me. Though I may fail of getting as many as I wish, I am sure that I shall entitle myself to the gratitude of future antiquaries.

5. *Transactions and Collections of the American Antiquarian Society*, VIII (1901).

When in Boston on 28 December 1831, before formally taking office, Baldwin tried to persuade the proprietor of the Tremont House to turn over his files of current newspapers to the American Antiquarian Society, and Dr. Seth Bass, librarian of the Boston Athenæum, "to use his influence for the purpose of giving our Library their duplicate pamphlets." The latter effort bore fruit, for in January 1834 Baldwin was at the Athenæum, happily rooting among 10,000 duplicate pamphlets, "laying in a disorderly heap." He obtained other duplicates from the Massachusetts Historical Society, although his greatest haul was from the private library of one of its founders, the eccentric Thomas Wallcut. While the donor was generously disposed, his possessions were inaccessibly stored in the garret of an oil store in India Street. Baldwin went there on Saturday morning, 2 August 1834, to find considerable confusion.

They were put in ancient trunks, bureaus, and chests, baskets, tea chests and old drawers, and presented a very odd appearance. Mr. Wallcut told me that I might take all the pamphlets and newspapers I could find and all books that treated of American history, and that I might make use of any of the boxes containing them. I went immediately to work putting them in order for transporting to Worcester. Everything was covered with venerable dust, and as I was under a slated roof and the thermometer at ninety-three, I had a pretty hot time of it. Nothing but a love of such work would inspire any man to labor in such a place. The value of the rarities I found, however, soon made me forget the heat, and I have never seen such happy moments. Everything I opened discovered to my eye some unexpected treasure. Great numbers of the productions of our early authors were turned up at every turn. I could hardly persuade myself that it was not all a dream, and I applied myself with all industry to packing, lest capricious fortune should snatch something from my hands. I worked from 8 in the morning until half past two in a heat and dust and stench of oil that would have been intolerable in any other circumstances. When I came out to go to dinner I could but just crawl. Yet at three o'clock I returned to it again and labored until night.

On Monday morning, Baldwin was up at four, even though he could not gain access to the marvelous garret until seven. Renewing his labors "with fresh fury" he unearthed the forty-first year of Cotton Mather's diary. After seven hours of this, the heat became so intolerable that he knocked off and escorted a visitor from Georgia to the Athenæum, the Massachusetts Historical Society, Faneuil Hall Market, and the State House. Although the temperature stayed at ninety-three, Baldwin put in full days on Tuesday and Wednesday. On Thursday he loaded 4,476 pounds of books, pamphlets, and manuscripts onto the wagon that was to convey them to Worcester. It was an imposing sight, equal in dimensions to a load of hay.

Baldwin was more than a little downcast to find the council of the society less enthusiastic about his two-and-a-quarter-ton haul. "They did not so much as utter a single note of gratitude" at their 27 August meeting, although Samuel Jennison, who was not present that evening, expressed himself warmly in favor of the gift.

It was some comfort to me to know that no one knew so much of their worth as I did myself, for no one had examined them. I had the horrors for a few days, but ultimately recovered.

Baldwin was right, for the Wallcut books are today regarded by the society as one of the most important collections of Americana acquired by the library in the nineteenth century. It was some consolation that by 1 February 1835, Frederick W. Paine, one of the doubting members of the council, was turning up every afternoon to help Baldwin arrange the Wallcut gift for binding; "instead of being a pamphlet hater as he was a few months ago, he has now become a pamphlet hunter."

Like Isaiah Thomas, Baldwin was ready to undertake anything that might prove useful to the American Antiquarian Society. He commemorated the anniversary of the Battle of Lexington in 1834 by drinking a glass of wine by himself before spending the afternoon planting trees around the Antiquarian Hall.

I have now planted all I designed to in the beginning. I have set out, perhaps, five hundred of different kinds. I have dug them up in the woods and brought them on my back without the assistance of even a boy, except for two days' work of one man, and he was engaged a part of the time in other business. They will afford a comfortable shade for my successor, if I should not live to enjoy it myself.

It was, alas, Samuel Foster Haven, librarian from 1838 to 1881, who enjoyed the shade of the pines, for in the following summer Christopher Columbus Baldwin set out for Ohio to examine Indian mounds and was killed by the overturning of a stagecoach near Norwich, Ohio, on 20 August 1835. This was a sad day for the American Antiquarian Society; one cannot help speculating over what this gifted and energetic thirty-five-year-old librarian might have done during the next forty years.

The visit to the Indian mounds of Ohio which led to Baldwin's death represented a phase of the society's preoccupation with archaeological matters. In a period when the country was only partially explored, there was always the hope of something world-shaking over the next hill. Bernard De Voto once traced the westward elusiveness of the Welsh Indians, the supposed descendants of Prince Medoc, a legendary Welsh predecessor of Columbus. The locale in which these Welsh-speaking aborigines were last reported moved from the Alleghanies through the Rockies, always just ahead of the advancing frontier. The visions of the Vermont prophet Joseph Smith, which led to the publication of the *Book of Mormon*, convinced many thousand Americans of a tie between the North American continent and the Lost Tribes of Israel. However evanescent these transoceanic links might be, the Ohio mounds were impressive monuments, inviting speculation and warranting investigation.

The *Transactions and Collections* of the American Antiquarian Society, designated as *Archaeologia Americana*, in emulation of the publication of the Society of Antiquaries of London, first appeared in 1820. Volume 1 is concerned entirely with matters distant from Worcester in time and space. Opening with Hennepin's account of the discovery of the Mississippi, it includes Caleb Atwater's "Description of the Antiquities Discovered in Ohio and other Western States," Moses Fiske's "Conjectures Respecting the Ancient Inhabitants of North America," the Reverend Timothy Alden's "Antiquities and Curiosities of Western Pennsylvania," accounts of caves in Kentucky and Indiana, and of "the Caraibs, who inhabited the

Antilles." Albert Gallatin's "A synopsis of the Indian tribes of North America" and Daniel Gookin's "An historical account of the doings and sufferings of the Christian Indians of New England" appeared in the second volume, published in 1836. The society's publications thereafter moved forward into the colonial period. Although Increase A. Lapham's 1850 investigation of Indian mounds in Wisconsin was financed by the society, his report was published by the Smithsonian Institution. In the remaining volumes of the series—the twelfth and last appeared in 1911—Indians were crowded out by the 1628–30 records of the Massachusetts Bay Company, a second edition of Isaiah Thomas's *History of Printing in America*, the 1638–41 notebook of the Boston lawyer Thomas Lechford, French and Indian War papers of Sir William Johnson and Colonel John Bradstreet, as well as the diaries of Isaiah Thomas and Christopher Columbus Baldwin.

Proceedings first appeared in 1843; from 1849 they have been published regularly twice each year, to form an annual volume. In this long series have appeared many historical monographs, originally read at meetings, and bibliographies of American newspapers, almanacs, periodicals, cookbooks, and of individual authors and localities. The catholicity of subject matter in the *Proceedings* reflects the spirit of an early statement of the society:

The history that is hereafter to be written is not to be merely the history of government and of politics, but the history of man in all his relations and interests, the history of science, of art, of religion, of social and domestic life.

Christopher Columbus Baldwin's premature death fortunately set no precedent for the librarians of the American Antiquarian Society, for his successor, Samuel Foster Haven, held office for forty-three years, a tenure surpassed in the present century by Clarence Saunders Brigham's fifty-one years of active service. The quality of the library today is largely due to policies of collecting consistently followed over a long period by a small number of people who knew what they were doing. During Haven's regime the library increased considerably. In 1843 it contained 16,000 volumes, while in 1859 the number had risen to more than 27,000. In 1853 a brick and stone library replaced the original Antiquarian Hall, built by Isaiah Thomas in 1820. This was enlarged in 1877 and in turn replaced in 1910 by the present library, which was the gift of the society's president, Stephen Salisbury of Worcester. With two subsequent stack additions of 1924 and 1950, the 1910 library still affords admirable and congenial lodging for the society.

A visitor entering the 1853 building, which fronted on Lincoln Square, would immediately be confronted by an overpowering copy of Michelangelo's colossal statue of Moses and would find in the reading room a copy of Michelangelo's Christ. Indian, Icelandic, and Hawaiian artifacts and relics from Yucatán, including a vast plaster reproduction of the temple at Labna, testified to the society's early and universal interest in antiquities. In spite of C. C. Baldwin's diary entry remarking that it was absurd "to pile up old bureaus and chests, and stuff them with old coats and hats and high-heeled shoes," the American Antiquarian Society accumulated a staggering variety of objects, as well as printed matter, during the nineteenth century. Believing the continent to be its field, it had looked with tolerance if not favor upon whatever "might be valuable in illustrating any and all parts of American history." Perishable ethnological material was mercifully sent to the Peabody Museum, Harvard University, in 1886, to be followed nine years later by a large part of the remaining archaeological and ethnological collections.

When Clarence S. Brigham became librarian in 1908, he introduced a rigorous delimitation of fields of interest and had the grandmother of all house cleanings. Moses retired to the County Court House; Our Lord to the Worcester Art Museum, where He was eventually discarded with other plaster casts; the façade of the Yucatán temple to the Smithsonian Institution. Antiquities and curiosities were ruthlessly dispatched, museum functions discontinued as such, and only those objects of historical association retained that had some germane relation to the books and manuscripts, or that served as house decoration. In the librarian's report for 1842,

S. F. Haven had observed: "It is somewhat difficult to preserve the proper distinction between the true nature of this institution, as one of a literary character, intended for scientific uses and the gratification of enlightened curiosity, and a mere museum of articles for idle and unprofitable inspection." This dilemma was definitively resolved sixty-six years later; since 1908 there has been no question that the American Antiquarian Society is completely a research library, where only "enlightened" curiosity is permitted.

Clarence S. Brigham became librarian of the American Antiquarian Society at the age of thirty and made it his life work. He was a graduate of Brown University in the Class of 1899 who had spent a year as an assistant in the Brown University Library and eight as librarian of the Rhode Island Historical Society. In 1930 when the office of director was created for him, Robert W. G. Vail became librarian. Dr. Brigham continued as director until October 1959, when he was succeeded by Clifford Kenyon Shipton, who had come to the society twenty years before when Dr. Vail resigned to become State Librarian at Albany. From 1955 until 1959 Clarence Brigham was also president of the American Antiquarian Society.

Upon his arrival in 1908, the library contained about 99,000 volumes. Ninety-six years of collecting had produced important collections of early American newspapers and imprints, and fair collections of early schoolbooks and psalmody. A great part of the library consisted of miscellaneous books, many of which were in foreign languages or on irrelevant subjects that had no bearing upon American history. Not only did Clarence Brigham sweep out inappropriate objects in preparation for the move to the present building in 1910; he limited the fields of interest of the library to areas in which it was already particularly strong. His book, *Fifty Years of Collecting Americana for the Library of The American Antiquarian Society, 1908–1958*, briefly outlines the manner in which, by building upon these strengths, he achieved a collection of national usefulness within a limited field of American history. Today the library contains some 600,000 titles, plus an additional 500,000 manuscripts, maps, broadsides, and prints.

Isaiah Thomas's gifts had included half a dozen long files of eighteenth-century newspapers and many single issues of papers from the Atlantic States and the middle west. There were, in spite of C. C. Baldwin's brief efforts in the 1830s to establish a current flow, only a few files of major newspapers through the Civil War period and only a scattering of small town papers after 1810. In 1908 the newspaper collection consisted of approximately 6,000 volumes, of which 1,500 had been published before 1865. The new policy involved the goal of acquiring all American newspapers prior to 1821, even in single issues; long files of important city newspapers from 1821 to 1870 and short files of ones that were either rare or particularly desirable for historical study; after 1870 only newspapers of a few leading cities and all Worcester files. By 1917, 5,000 volumes and 200,000 separate issues had been added. Among the long runs were such papers as the Reading, Pennsylvania, *Adler* (1796–1913), Carlisle, Pennsylvania, *Gazette* (1787–1817), Alexandria, Virginia, *Gazette* (1800–1910), *Missouri Gazette* (1809–18), Lexington, Kentucky, *Reporter* (1808–20), *Arkansas Gazette* (1820–49), *Connecticut Journal* (1770–1839), *Newport Mercury* (1801–75), *Providence Gazette* (1780–1825), *Washington Globe* (1832–63), *San Francisco Herald* (1851–61), Napa, California, *Reporter* (1852–98), *Wisconsin State Journal* (1842–48). In the 1940s, as syndicated material, national news, and advertisements led to a great similarity between contents of city newspapers throughout the country, the society sharply reduced its acquisition and binding of current city papers outside New England. Today, with microfilm available, only the *New York Times*, the Worcester newspapers, and four other New England papers are currently preserved and bound. Today the newspaper collection numbers about 22,000 volumes, with nearly a million separate issues shelved in manila envelopes. It occupies six floors in three bookstacks that contain close to five miles of shelving.

Clarence Brigham became not only an aggressive collector of

American newspapers but their chief bibliographer. He began publishing in the society's *Proceedings* in 1913 a bibliography covering the years 1690 to 1820, which caused him to travel widely throughout the United States in search of data. Of this he has written:

The plan of publication was to write a brief historical account of each newspaper, followed by a checklist of all files located. The decision was made to limit the final date to the year 1820, partly because this was the date chosen by Evans for the final year of his great *American Bibliography*, also because it covered the beginnings of printing in the middle West, but chiefly because the bibliography had to stop somewhere and to extend it into later decades might cause the entire undertaking to fall under its own weight. Incidentally, it was the choosing of this final date which caused the editors of the *Union List of Newspapers*, published in 1937, to begin their massive checklist with the year 1821.

After the publication of the eighteenth and final installment in the April 1927 *Proceedings*, Mr. Brigham began a thorough revision and amplification that culminated in 1947 in two quarto volumes totaling 1,508 pages, that are the standard work on American newspapers through 1820. The statistical conclusions of this book's introduction warrant summary quotation for their indication of the paramount character of the American Antiquarian Society's newspaper collection.

In the period from 1690 to 1820, there were 2120 different newspapers published. Of this total the six New England States had 447 papers, the six Middle Atlantic States from New York to Maryland had 1023 papers, the ten Southern States from Virginia to Louisiana had 425 papers, and the seven Western States had 225 papers. The city which from the beginning to 1820 had the most newspapers was New York with 138, followed by Philadelphia with 107, and Boston with 73. The six largest collections of newspapers before 1820 are in the American Antiquarian Society which has 1496 titles, the Library of Congress with 936 titles, Harvard with 732 titles, the New-York Historical Society with 634 titles, the New York Public Library with 480 titles, and the Wisconsin Historical Society with 415 titles.

The second field chosen for concentrated expansion was that of American imprints to 1820. In ninety-six years of collecting, the society had, by 1908, acquired about 5,000, chiefly an inheritance from the libraries of the Mathers, Isaiah Thomas, Thomas Wallcut, and the Reverend William Bentley of Salem. Today there are 50,000, which is about half of the total number known to have been published. These are made accessible by a catalogue of some half a million cards, in 322 trays, which includes, in addition to main entries for author, subject, and title, a chronological and a geographical catalogue, as well as entries for printers, booksellers, and publishers.

Existing collections of genealogy, local history, psalmody, early schoolbooks, United States documents, and almanacs were notably increased. New collections of American literature, maps, book catalogues, song books, sheet music, lithography, bookplates, colonial currency, cookbooks, Hawaiiana, music, railroads, and western narratives were established and built to major dimensions. In such minor ephemeral fields as valentines, stereoscopic views, lottery tickets, miniature books, awards of merit, watch papers, and watermarked paper, useful holdings were assembled that have sometimes proved to be unequaled.[6]

As bibliographies appear, Dr. Brigham has always enjoyed the game of checking the American Antiquarian Society's relative strength in the field covered. With Lyle H. Wright's *American Fiction*, covering all novels produced in this country from 1774 to 1850, there are 2,772 entries, of which the society has 2,110, Yale 1,977, the Library of Congress and New York Public Library nearly 1,100 each, and Harvard 876. In Mr. Wright's second volume, dealing with adult fiction from 1851 to 1875, the society has about 62% of the 2,832 entries. Through the gift in 1948 of Donald McKay Frost's collection of close to 5,000 titles of early Western narratives, the society's western collection came to have somewhat over 70% of the titles listed in the 1937 edition of the Wagner-Camp bibliography, *The Plains and the Rockies*.

While the active collecting of the American Antiquarian Society

6. Mr. Shipton's report at the 1960 annual meeting, published in *Proceedings*, LXX (1960), 353–370, includes an admirably realistic appraisal of the society's major collections, with an indication of its future policy regarding acquisitions.

has been chiefly in printed material, it has nevertheless acquired by gift a respectable number of manuscripts. It does not attempt to compete with the great manuscript depositories or the important State collections, for the society believes that local manuscripts belong in their own region. It has, however, some 198 collections, occupying 1,320 feet of shelving and containing about half a million pieces, which have been reported to the National Historical Publications Commission's *Guide to Archives and Manuscripts in the United States.* Isaiah Thomas's acquisition of the Mather papers became the cornerstone of the collection. As Dr. Shipton has observed:

For lack of a better regional depository, the American Antiquarian Society has gathered in the family correspondence and institutional records of Worcester County. Its collection of colonial manuscript diaries, chiefly of New England origin, is the largest, and is the outcome of an interest in almanacs and an attempt to carry on the Forbes bibliography. In the field of printing and graphic arts, the collection of manuscripts does invade the national field, and includes such material as the papers of Isaiah Thomas and Matthew Carey, and the firms of McCarty and Davis, West, Richardson and Lord, Lee and Shepard, and D. C. Heath.

In the twentieth century the American Antiquarian Society has made remarkable contributions to bibliographical knowledge and to the wide dissemination of scholarly sources. C. C. Baldwin, who dreamed the year before he was killed of compiling a *Bibliotheca Americana* on the model of Robert Watts's *Bibliotheca Britannica*, would have delighted in the accomplishments of those who followed him. The *Proceedings* are rich in bibliographical material. Dr. Brigham, in addition to his *History and Bibliography of American Newspapers, 1690–1820*, published in 1954, after thirty years of study, the standard work on *Paul Revere's Engravings*, in which all of Revere's work in that field is not only thoroughly described but reproduced in exact size in collotype. The work contains 139 reproductions, five of which are, as originally issued, in color. R. W. G. Vail edited the last nine volumes of Sabin's *Dictionary of Books relating to America* during his years as librarian in the 1930s. Clifford K. Shipton in 1955 added a thirteenth volume to Charles Evans's *American*

Bibliography, completing that work through the year 1800, while in 1959 the society published with the co-operation of the Virginia Bibliographical Society a cumulative index to the thirteen volumes of Evans, prepared by one of its members, Mr. Roger Bristol of the University of Virginia.

The American Antiquarian Society's most extensive contribution to scholarly work in early American history is *Early American Imprints, 1639–1800*, edited by Dr. Shipton, which is a microprint edition of every extant book, pamphlet, and broadside printed in what is now the United States from 1639 to the end of the year 1800. Keyed to Evans's *American Bibliography*, it not only reprints in full the texts of more than 30,000 titles, but includes all of Dr. Shipton's very substantial revisions of Charles Evan's pioneering effort. The work, which is sponsored by the Committee on Documentary Reproduction of the American Historical Association, is published by the American Antiquarian Society by the Readex Microprint process, which offered a factor of edition savings superior to any of the other microreproduction processes. Its cards are issued in boxes of a size and shape to facilitate shelving like books. The final group is scheduled for delivery by 30 June 1963. The subscription price of $8,000 begins to seem reasonable when one remembers that *Early American Imprints* furnishes usable reproductions of works seldom if ever to be readily found in the book trade, at a cost of scarcely more than 25c each.

The availability of *Early American Imprints* to any library (or individual) in possession of $8,000 is capable of changing the whole direction of the teaching and writing of colonial history. Until it appeared, research in that field could only be satisfactorily carried out in a small number of institutions in the northeastern United States, because of the scarcity of many imprints before 1800. Hundreds of them exist in unique copies. Cambridge seventeenth-century imprints come on the market so seldom that not even the richest new library, with the most aggressive collecting policy, could hope to build up a collection that would adequately serve the purposes of a colonial historian specializing in a seventeenth-century Massachusetts Bay subject. Because of this distribution of research material, many young scholars whose doctoral dissertations have been in the colonial field have, on accepting positions in distant universities, been forced to shift their research to more modern fields. With *Early American Imprints* available in their university libraries, it becomes possible for them to continue their work in colonial history in termtime, even though they may wish in summers to return to the sources of the originals.

Dr. Shipton is now engaged in extending the principle of micro-print publication to colonial newspapers, which are not included in *Early American Imprints*. With the editorial assistance of Mr. Ebenezer Gay, executive officer of the Boston Athenæum, the American Antiquarian Society is now issuing runs of such newspapers for particularly important periods, which may be purchased in small and relatively inexpensive groups.

The American Antiquarian Society had, and still has, a small membership, restricted in numbers and chosen for a devotion to history, combined with a willingness to work and to contribute. The attempt in the earliest years to achieve wide geographical distribution encumbered the membership list with useless though ornamental names. Most of these were eventually dropped, and in 1831 the membership was fixed at 140; today it is 225. As Dr. Shipton said in his April 1960 report, his first as director:[7]

In the early years of our Society, representation on the Council was on a geographical basis, and dozens of men in distant states were elected only on their reputations. In 1831 the membership list was revised to drop uninterested members and to obtain a more workable concentration. After this reorganization seven per cent of the membership lived in Worcester and sixty per cent in New England. The local concentration gradually increased until the beginning of Mr. Brigham's administration, when twenty-three per cent of the membership was from Worcester and seventy-three per cent from New England. During the past fifty

---

7. Mr. Shipton continued to carry on the librarian's duties as well until July 1960 when Marcus Allen McCorison took over that post, which he now holds.

years there has been a steady spreading out of the membership, so that today twelve per cent are local and fifty-five per cent from New England.

No single type predominates in the membership. There are professors of history, librarians, bibliographers, collectors, authors, business and professional men. The Worcester members make themselves responsible for the greater part of the administration of the society's financial and business arrangements, but more distant members, as in the case of Mr. Bristol and the Evans index, participate very actively in scholarly projects. Even the Californians and others almost as distantly situated turn up with gratifying regularity at the semiannual meetings, which are valuable opportunities for the exchange of ideas and projects.

As at the Massachusetts Historical Society, members pay no dues. Those who are able to do so, however, make frequent and generous contributions towards current expenses and the purchase of books. Indeed much of the collecting of the past fifty years has been made possible by such gifts from members. The sum of $25,748.13 received in this way during the year ending 30 September 1960 is indicative of the helpful spirit of the membership. The investments of the society on 30 September 1961 had a book value of $1,180,301 and a market value of $2,816,890. From them, income of $89,978.96 was received, which, with gifts of $12,101.54 and over $11,000 from the sale of publications, brought the total income for the year to $113,465.06. General operating expenses for the year were $91,610.97 with the additional expenditure of $26,067.23 for the purchase of books and equipment, and for publishing.

The American Antiquarian Society runs on a frugal basis, with high return in additions to the library and in scholarly work for every dollar expended. It has always been shorthanded and constantly has to raise money for purchases of books and any special undertaking that cannot be made self-liquidating. Its Worcester officers and members in the present century deserve high commendation for their disinterested support of a national organization that maintains rigid scholarly standards. Many of them are business and professional men, with numerous more localized interests, which they meticulously refrain from entangling with the purposes and policies of this society. In other regions efforts are sometimes made by historical societies to gain the support of local industry by popularizing the approach, or slanting the activity of the society towards business history, or something that might be thought to prove sympathetic to the industrialist. It is greatly to the credit of the American Antiquarian Society and the leaders of the Worcester community that they have long understood each other and worked profitably together, without a hint of such obvious and spurious ingratiation. The society receives helpful support from the local scene because its Worcester members realize that its uncompromising contributions to learning do credit to their city.

The present status and purposes of the American Antiquarian Society are admirably and concisely summarized in two paragraphs of Dr. Shipton's April 1960 report:

Of recent years we have elected no one simply to confer an honor upon him; we choose our members from the group interested in coöperating in the work which has occupied us for nearly a century and a half. The founders of the American Antiquarian Society were men who had participated in the establishment of the United States and, believing that its democracy was the wave of the future and the hope of mankind, were determined to preserve the record of its organization and growth in order that less fortunate peoples might follow in their footsteps. The Puritans had been content to found the City upon a Hill to serve as a beacon for mankind; our founders were shrewd business men determined to package and to distribute aggressively their wares. The American Academy of Arts and Sciences had been founded for the same purpose, among others, but to the disgust of our founders it had confined its activities to the reading of papers and to communication among the members. The American Antiquarian Society, on the other hand, has always been devoted to the collection, preservation, and processing for utilization of the records of our past. It is the processing activity which marks us off to such a degree from our sister institutions, and it is this which employs the larger part of the time of our staff. Corn in an Iowa field does nothing for the breakfast tables of the world until it is processed and distributed, and ideas affect only the originators until they are disseminated. The processing of historical materials involves collection, the compilation of catalogues and bibliographies, and the distribution of the processed documents in print or microprint form. This is precisely the work which Isaiah Thomas began with his bibliography of pre-Revolutionary imprints.

Since Thomas's day our goal has been narrowed, our purposes sharpened, and our energies canalized. In our early years we assumed that the term Antiquarian covered the fields which are today called history, anthropology, archaeology, ethnology, and ethnography. Indeed, our founders, still having time on their hands, proposed that the Society should, in addition, concern itself with all that man and nature have done anywhere. For the academies founded in the several preceding centuries, this was a perfectly reasonable goal, but by 1812 the world had begun an expansion of human knowledge which can be compared only to an explosion. In this explosion the American Antiquarian Society was blown aimlessly about. When Justin Winsor, one of our most faithful members, was presiding at the organization of the American Historical Association in 1884, he justified his divided attention by pointing out that we, in trying to do too much, had become provincial. The Historical Association exists to serve a profession which did not exist when we were founded. Twenty other national organizations and a thousand regional societies now exist to explore aspects or regions within our original sphere of activity. Yet so skillful has been the retreat of the American Antiquarian Society to our core function that these daughter societies of ours to a great extent rely on us to preserve the record of the beginning of work in their respective fields.

─◄☼► ─◄☼► ─◄☼► ─◄☼► ─◄☼► ─◄☼► ─◄☼►

Chapter IV

THE NEW ENGLAND STATES

Now there are diversities of gifts, but the same spirit.—I *Corinthians* 12:4

MORE than three decades after the foundation of the Massachusetts Historical Society, three other New England states in close succession began to establish similar organizations. Maine and Rhode Island did so in 1822, New Hampshire in 1823. A Connecticut Historical Society, incorporated in 1825, died of inertia after four meetings and was resuscitated in 1839. In Vermont a society was founded in 1838. During the nineteenth century these five New England societies followed the familiar pattern of collecting and publishing, with Maine the most productive of publications. Today they have diverged more markedly in their interests. Connecticut, after a fumbling start, is now the best endowed and most active of the five, with New Hampshire as a likely second. Those societies receive annual legislative grants of $1,000 and $500, respectively, which may be considered tokens of recognition rather than instances of public support. In Rhode Island and Maine, while both City and State make annual grants of more respectable size, the majority of operating expenses are met from private sources. In Vermont alone, where the society has the smallest endowment of the five, the State appropriates a sum that provides a major element of support. In Vermont also, which is the least heavily populated of the New England states, the historical society has the largest number of members; only there do receipts from membership provide a significant part of the annual income. All five welcome historians on serious business, but have a considerable number of genealogists among their library clientele. Connecticut is today the most active both in publications and museum displays, having both the largest resources and the most recent building. The manner in which these five societies have become what they are will be clearer if their development is outlined individually.

MAINE

The district of Maine was separated from Massachusetts and became a state in 1820. Two years later on 5 February 1822 the Legislature passed a bill incorporating the Maine Historical Society,[1] whose duty was "to collect and preserve, as far as the state of their funds will admit, whatever, in their opinion, may tend to explain and and illustrate any department of civil, ecclesiastical and natural history, especially of this State and of the United States." The terms are familiar, save for the realistic Maine qualification "so far as their funds will permit." With a later start and smaller resources than the older societies, Maine's sights were set more narrowly on the State rather than the national scene. Thanks to the existence of the Portland Society of Natural History that phase of activity eventually went by the board.

At the first annual meeting, held in Portland on 11 April 1822, Governor Albion K. Parris was elected president; other offices were were filled by a lawyer, the Chief Justice of Maine, and a Portland clergyman. For nearly sixty years the Maine Historical Society was based at Bowdoin College in Brunswick, with professors of that institution—Henry Wadsworth Longfellow among them—serving as its librarians. Meetings were held sometimes at the college and sometimes in Portland, the largest city, or Augusta, the State capital. In 1881 the society moved permanently to Portland, occupying

1. Marian Bradford Rowe, *History of the Maine Historical Society*, reprinted from *The New England Social Studies Bulletin* (October 1953).

rooms provided by the city government. With this change of locale, Hubbard W. Bryant, an antiquarian bookseller, became librarian. During the next twenty-five years he bestirred himself more actively than had his academic predecessors in the cataloguing of books and manuscripts, the collecting of newspapers, and the maintenance of scrapbooks of clippings. When the Portland Public Library occupied its new building, given by Hon. James Phinney Baxter, in 1889, the Maine Historical Society was given the use of rooms there.

By bequest of Mrs. Anne Longfellow Pierce, a younger sister of Henry Wadsworth Longfellow, the society came into possession of the handsome house on Congress Street, built in 1785 by their maternal grandfather, General Peleg Wadsworth, in which the poet had lived as a boy and young man. The bequest, which included the complete furnishings of the house, required that the lower front rooms be reserved for family belongings and that the society construct a library building on the land behind. Thus a fireproof structure with three tiers of bookstacks, a reading room on the first floor, auditorium on the second, with basement areas for newspaper and map collections, came to be dedicated on 22 February 1907, the centennial of Longfellow's birth. The poet's nephew, Alexander Wadsworth Longfellow of Boston, was the supervising architect. This building was enlarged in 1951 by the addition of a new air-conditioned bookstack.

The Wadsworth House, entirely furnished with contemporary effects of the Wadsworth and Longfellow families, is open to visitors on payment of 50c. The society's building, situated in the garden, is a commodious and agreeable working library intended for serious use, although some visitors wander on from the house to inspect the portraits and historical objects that decorate the reading room, corridors, and working areas. In recent years junk has been eliminated, and the pictures and objects attractively although simply displayed. There being no space for rotating exhibitions upon special themes, such museum collections as the society has retained are placed in appropriate permanent locations. A small number of ship pictures and nautical instruments are used, for example, to decorate the map and chart room in the basement. The society's premises thus consist of a library on the one hand and a historic house on the other, both located on the same property in what has become the business centre of Portland.

When the society moved to Portland its library contained approximately 11,000 volumes; today the number is 34,879. A collection of Civil War books owned by the Maine Commandery of the Loyal Legion was added in 1910, while in 1922 the library was substantially increased when the Maine Genealogical Society merged with the Maine Historical Society. This alliance has given a marked genealogical character to the use of the library, which is encouraged by the provision on microfilm of census records and York deeds and probate records. In this direction, the society has co-operated with the extensive microfilming operations of the Genealogical Society of the Church of Jesus Christ of Latter-day Saints in Salt Lake City.

The manuscript collections include papers of Governor William King, General Henry Knox, and Sir William Pepperrell, and documents dealing with the Northeastern Boundary, the Kennebec Purchase, and the Pejepscott Purchase. The J. S. H. Fogg Autograph Collection contains, among other things, a complete set of the signers of the Declaration of Independence and a set of letters of Presidents of the United States. Although no separate guide to the collection has been issued, the society's manuscript holdings are recorded in the three volumes of Elizabeth Ring's *A Reference List of Manuscripts Relating to the History of Maine*, published by the University of Maine.[2]

The Maine Historical Society began in 1831 to issue *Collections*, containing both documents and papers read at meetings. Nine volumes were published by 1887; a tenth, consisting of a general index to this series, appeared in 1891. A second series of ten volumes, entitled *Collections and Proceedings*, was published between 1890 and

2. *The Maine Bulletin*, XLI, 1 (August 1938); XLII, 1 (August 1939); XLIII, 8 (February 1941), as *University of Maine Studies*, 2nd ser, no. 45.

1899, while two volumes of a third series appeared in 1904 and 1906. The society in 1836 persuaded the State to appropriate funds for copying documents in British archives concerning the early history of Maine. Dr. Leonard Woods, formerly president of Bowdoin College, who was in Europe, took charge of the project. From this resulted twenty-four volumes of a *Documentary History of Maine*, published by the society between 1869 and 1916. Richard Hakluyt's "Discourse on Western Planting" of 1584 was issued as volume II in 1877, the Trelawney papers in 1884 as volume III; three volumes of the Baxter manuscripts, edited by Hon. James Phinney Baxter, followed. Much of the publishing energy of the society was due to the interest of Mr. Baxter, who was its president from 1891 to 1921. Besides editing nineteen volumes of the *Documentary History* series, he spent great personal effort unearthing additional sources of early Maine history in English archives and libraries. Some of his discoveries in this area led to his three-volume work, *Sir Ferdinando Gorges and his Province of Maine*, published by the Prince Society in 1890. He was a corresponding member of the Massachusetts Historical Society, a member of the American Antiquarian Society, and from 1901 to 1921 president of the New England Historic Genealogical Society in Boston. After Mr. Baxter's death in 1921, at the age of ninety, publishing activity diminished. Since that time, the society's publications have been restricted to four substantial volumes of *Maine Province and Court Records*, the first edited in 1928 by Charles F. Libby, the second and third by Professor Robert E. Moody of Boston University, and the fourth in 1958 by Dr. Neal W. Allen Jr. The society issues no serial publication beyond a *News-Letter*.

The Maine Historical Society originally limited its membership to 100, but the number was increased to 200 in 1910, to 400 in 1914, and to an optimistic 1,000 in 1922. There are at present in the vicinity of 700 members. The annual dues of $3 a year were raised to $4 in January 1960. Beyond attendance at the annual meeting, the principal privilege of membership is the right to enter the bookstacks and take out books for home use. During the year ending in June 1960,

2,311 members and 1,627 nonmembers used the library for reading and research.

In its early years the Maine Historical Society was entirely dependent upon the annual assessments from members for its support, but in 1849 it was granted half a township by the State, the sale of which produced $6,000. This was the beginning of an endowment fund. As of 31 May 1959 the society had capital assets of $242,064.94, which produced an income of $9,655.74. The State annually gives $2,750 and the City of Portland $1,000, both without restrictions of any kind. Dues (at the $3 rate) produced $1,988 and admissions of visitors to the Wadsworth-Longfellow House $4,034, although more than half of the latter sum was required for upkeep and attendants. The society's total income for the year 1958–59 was $19,769.80; its expenses $17,421.

From these figures it will be seen that the society, in order to remain solvent, restricts its operations to a modest scale. Since 1914 it has always had a female librarian with professional training. The present incumbent, Miss Marion Bradford Rowe, a graduate of Colby College and Simmons College Library School, came to the society in 1935 as an assistant, succeeding to the librarianship in 1943. With two assistant librarians, Miss Rowe today carries out the work of the society.

The society very rightly wishes to maintain the scholarly standards of its documentary publications in the *Maine Province and Court Records*. These have a limited market, largely because of the high price that is considered necessary to recover costs from one volume before proceeding to another. The production of volume IV, for example, cost $8,384.42. Even with gifts of $2,500 towards this, a retail price of $18 was set, which gravely restricts sales to libraries and a small number of individuals. This is a pity, for colonial court records can be fascinating reading for other than legal historians.

The Maine Historical Society maintains its old learned tradition within the limits of its resources. It has cultivated no arts of public address nor painted its face in an attempt to draw attention to itself.

It is a quiet and respectworthy institution, attending to its business without clamor. With its present resources it is doing everything that it can. One hopes that in the future it will build upon existing strengths, rather than attempting to change its nature, for with a modest increase in funds and the enlistment of an enthusiastic editor its publication program could be revivified and accelerated.[3]

RHODE ISLAND

The Rhode Island Historical Society was founded in June 1822 "for the purpose of procuring and preserving whatever relates to the topography, antiquities, and natural civil and ecclesiastical history of this State." As was inevitable at the time, the wild animals and fishes are still in the purpose, but in this instance the scope was restricted to the narrow confines of the smallest state in the Union.

The original plan was to establish two cabinets, one in Newport and one in Providence. Thus for its first twenty-two years the possessions of the Rhode Island Historical Society were divided between a room in the Redwood Library in Newport and another in the Providence Library Company. In 1844 they were brought together in the society's first building, the Cabinet at 68 Waterman Street, Providence, on the campus of Brown University, designed by the Rhode Island builder, James C. Bucklin. There they remained until 1942, when the society moved a short distance to the John Brown House at 52 Power Street.

This superb three-story brick house, built in 1786, excited the admiration of the young John Quincy Adams, who wrote in his diary on 9 September 1789: "We only saw the outside of it, which is the most magnificent and elegant private mansion that I have ever seen on this continent." There have been larger ones since, but few any handsomer. It was given to the society by John Nicholas Brown,

---

3. The publication of *Letters of General Peleg Wadsworth to His Son John Student at Harvard College, 1796–1798*, a 44-page pamphlet admirably printed by the Anthoensen Press, the appearance of an equally well designed current list of members, and the inauguration of a multilithed *News-Letter* in the course of 1961 are all useful steps in this direction.

who has been active over many years in preserving the historical
and architectural character of the hill upon which Brown University is situated. The society's acceptance of the house involved both
a chance to improve its own location and to further the architectural preservation of an important area in the city. The ground
floor was set aside for a meeting room and the display of some of the
fine Rhode Island furniture owned by the society. The library took
over the upper floors, while offices and a few exhibition rooms were
improvised out of bathrooms, pantries, and the like.

According to a folder issued by the society, "the library contains
one of the largest genealogical collections in New England." It is
also rich in other aspects of Rhode Island history, including imprints
beginning with the products of James Franklin's press at Newport
in 1727. It contains a notable collection of newspapers, among them
the complete file of the *Providence Gazette*, begun in 1762, which
has been microfilmed and widely distributed. The Rhode Island
State Library turns newspaper files over to the society rather than keeping them. For the past two years, an annual State appropriation of
$6,000 has permitted the society to microfilm certain later news-
papers of the pulp period, both in the interest of preservation and
conserving space.

The manuscript collection covers a wide variety of Rhode Island
subjects. The Foster, Ward, and Hopkins papers are rich in eighteenth-century material. The maritime history of the State is represented in the Nightingale-Jenckes, the Champlin, and Obadiah
Brown papers; business history in the Almy and Brown papers,
which are the earliest records of an American textile manufactory,
and the papers of the Builders Iron Foundry.

The early volumes of the society's *Collections* differed from those
of other institutions by each treating of a single theme rather than
containing a miscellaneous variety of documents. Volume I (1827)
was devoted to a reprint of Roger Williams's *A Key into the Language
of America*; volume II (1835) to Samuel Gorton's *Simplicity's Defence
against Seven-Headed Policy*, an account of the persecution of War-

wick settlers by Massachusetts, first printed in London in 1646; volume III (1835) to Elisha R. Porter's *The Early History of Narragansett*; volume IV (1838) to a reprint of John Callender's 1739 *An Historical Discourse on the Civil and Religious Affairs of the Colony of Rhode Island*. After the appearance of volume V (1843), William R. Staples's *The Annals of the Town of Providence from the First Settlement to the Organization of the City Government (1832)*, publication ceased for more than twenty years. Between 1867 and 1902 five more volumes were issued, after which the *Collections* became a quarterly publication rather than a series of books. During the 1920s and 1930s of the present century, the society issued a number of separate books, such as Howard M. Chapin's *Rhode Island Privateers in King George's War, 1739–1748*, *The Letter Book of James Browne of Providence, Merchant, 1735–1738*, and the letter book and correspondence of Esek Hopkins. In 1952 it published Bernhard Knollenberg's *Correspondence of Governor Samuel Ward, May 1775–March 1776*, to which Clifford P. Monahon, the present director of the society, added a genealogy of the Ward Family.

In 1942 a quarterly entitled *Rhode Island History* began to appear. It is a modest venture, often of thirty-two pages, but attractively presented, and designed to combine historical accuracy with a certain popular interest. Contributions on Rhode Island themes by scholars from other regions frequently appear; the April 1959 issue, for example, contains an article by George A. Billias, Assistant Professor of History at the University of Maine on General John Glover's role in the Battle of Rhode Island, and one on an aspect of King Philip's War by Douglas Edward Leach, Assistant Professor of History at Vanderbilt University. The number also gives a brief account of the 137th annual meeting and one installment in a seemingly endless serial catalogue of the society's furniture collection, compiled by Ralph E. Carpenter Jr.[4]

The director of the society at the time of the move to the John

4. Wendell D. Garrett of the Massachusetts Historical Society is now preparing a catalogue of the furniture in the Rhode Island Historical Society for publication as a book.

Brown House was the late William Greene Roelker, who had retired from business in middle life and taken some graduate work in history at Harvard before assuming his duties. Clifford P. Monahon, a teacher who had spent a year at the Columbia University Library School before becoming librarian some sixteen years ago, became director upon Mr. Roelker's death in 1953. Mr. Roelker's aim was to enlarge the activities of the society and to expand its membership. On his arrival there were 500 members; there are today 1,850. Dues of active members are $5; of contributing, $10; of sustaining, $25 per year. Life membership is set at $250. In addition there is a student-teacher category at $3 that does not include a subscription to *Rhode Island History*. For the year ending 30 June 1958, members' dues produced an income of $9,665. As *Rhode Island History* costs about $2 per subscription to produce, some financial benefit is received from increases in membership.

The society receives annual grants of $2,000 from the City of Providence and $8,500 from the State of Rhode Island, without restriction as to use. This State appropriation is a general one, without reference to grants that may be made for microfilming newspapers, or other specific projects. From an endowment somewhat in excess of $200,000, investment income of $10,638.76 was received. The total income of the year was $35,883.92; the expenses $34,767.58. It will thus be seen that the support of the Rhode Island Historical Society is tripartite; public funds, private endowment, and membership dues figuring in roughly similar proportions.

In its attempt to be all things to all men, the society is doing what it can in a variety of directions. It maintains a scholarly library, although three quarters of its use is by genealogists. It attempts to exhibit some fine furniture and objects, yet lacks the space to do so extensively. It preserves a superb historic house, yet by housing its library and museum therein detracts from the beauty of the house. It has partially discarded its former wardrobe, but not quite completed a new one. To do so satisfactorily will require larger funds and a supplementary building to house library and museum activities.

NEW HAMPSHIRE

The 200th anniversary of the first settlement of the Piscataqua region led to the foundation of the New Hampshire Historical Society in 1823.[5] From a meeting convened at Portsmouth on 20 May developed an organization that was incorporated on 13 June 1823. On the same day William Plumer of Epping, a man of marked historical interests, formerly a United States Senator and four times Governor of New Hampshire, was chosen president. A young Concord printer and bookseller, Jacob Bailey Moore, was the society's first librarian. He had already published *Collections, Topographical, Historical, and Biographical, relating principally to New Hampshire*; in their preparation he had had the collaboration of the Concord druggist-antiquarian-genealogist, John Farmer, whose diligent activities were to inspire the society in future years.

The preparation of publications, rather than the assembly of a library, was the society's first effort. In 1824 it issued a volume of *Collections*, followed by others in 1827, 1832, 1834, and 1837. Eventually a room was secured in the State House, and then rented quarters outside. Finally in 1869, the society bought the building of its former landlord, the Merrimack County Bank, at 214 North Main Street, Concord.

Edward Tuck, a New Hampshireman who had gone to France as a consul in the 1860s, become a banker, and spent his life in Paris, provided the society with its present home in Concord near the State House. This granite building of massive construction, rich in marble and bronze decoration, was designed by Guy Lowell of Bos-

5. *Dedication of the Building of the New Hampshire Historical Society* (Concord, 1912), which includes, among other things, a spirited address (pp. 65–72) by Charles Francis Adams, cursing out "those female sentimentalists" who had prevented the Boston Athenæum from abandoning 10½ Beacon Street and moving to a new building a dozen years earlier; *Addresses Delivered at the Observance of the Centennial of the New Hampshire Historical Society, September 27, 1923* (Concord, 1923); *The New Hampshire Historical Society* (Concord, 1940).

ton. The cornerstone was laid on 9 June 1909; the building dedicated on 23 November 1911. While the severe functionalist might deplore the magnificence of the marble staircase and the domed rotunda, there could be no question about the handsomeness of the reading room or the utility of the bookstacks and meeting room. Mr. Tuck's gift was a mark of affection for his native state from one who had lived most of his adult life in Europe. It was in the tradition of Joshua Bates, the Massachusetts boy who had become a partner in Baring Brothers and who more than half a century before had put the infant Boston Public Library upon its feet. Upon moving into the new building, the society had Guy Lowell remodel its old one in North Main Street for museum purposes. For some forty years both were maintained for their different functions.

Ten volumes of *Collections* were issued in the course of the nineteenth century, nine miscellaneous in content, the tenth (1893) containing a list of documents in the Public Record Office relating to the Province of New Hampshire. Five volumes of *Proceedings*, covering the years 1872 to 1912, were published. In 1915, after a hiatus of twenty-two years, the *Collections* were resumed in the form of volumes upon single subjects. *The Indian Stream Republic and Luther Parker*, edited by Professor Grant Showerman of the University of Wisconsin, appeared in 1915 as volume XI. In 1928, Otis G. Hammond, the director of the society, edited volume XII, *The Utah Expedition 1857–1858, Letters of Captain Jesse A. Gove, 10th Inf., U.S.A., of Concord, N.H.* Mr. Hammond also edited the very creditable three-volume edition of the *Letters and Papers of Major-General John Sullivan, Continental Army* that appeared between 1930 and 1939 as volumes XIII–XV. This edition included not only the 500 letters of General Sullivan owned by the society, but the texts of any others that could be procured elsewhere. No subsequent volumes of *Collections* have been published.

The New Hampshire Historical Society's library contains today some 80,000 volumes, including extensive runs of New Hampshire newspapers to 1890. It is rich in New Hampshire imprints, pamphlets, and broadsides, manuscript and engraved maps of towns, annual reports of towns, cities, and counties, and much other material relating to the State. Family and local histories and vital records of the New England states are segregated in rooms on the second floor for the use of genealogists.

The manuscript collection abounds with the papers of residents of New Hampshire and other New Englanders from the colonial period onward. John Langdon, Richard Waldron, John Farmer, Jeremiah Mason, General John Stark, Governor Jonathan Belcher, John Wentworth, President Franklin Pierce, William E. Chandler, John P. Hale, George H. Moses, Charles S. Mellen, and John W. Weeks are among the figures represented. An extensive body of Daniel Webster papers is one of three principal groups of material relating to that statesman, the others being at Dartmouth College and the Massachusetts Historical Society.

As the State of New Hampshire has no archival program, provincial records and maps, although under the legal authority of the Secretary of State, have long been in the custody of the New Hampshire Historical Society. These public records include 450 volumes and 55 boxes of the early archives, the original documents in 30,000 cases of colonial courts of law, and of 4,000 estates in the colonial probate court, the first hundred volumes of records of deeds prior to the establishment of separate counties in 1771. The society also houses in its stacks 400 volumes of original records of New Hampshire towns and more than 300 volumes of church records. The State, by way of stingy compensation, grants the society $500 a year, which is more than spent in providing suitable folders and filing cases for the colonial court records.

In the 1940s, the New Hampshire Historical Society, like other organizations relying chiefly on private endowment, began to feel pinched. Its director, Elmer M. Hunt, who, like William G. Roelker in Rhode Island, had taken over his post after retiring from a business career, began an effort to increase both popular interest and membership in the society. In this change of direction, publications became more popular in character. *Historical New Hampshire*, an occasional illustrated leaflet-magazine, first appeared in November 1944. Mr. Hunt drew upon his personal interest in typography for the reproduction of a number of New Hampshire maps, broadsides, and views, whose distribution tended to increase general interest in the society. On his retirement, he was succeeded by Philip N. Guyol, the author of a history of New Hampshire in World War II and a former editor of the Macmillan Company, who became director on 1 January 1956.

The museum in the old building in North Main Street had become overcrowded. To reduce the expense of maintaining two separate establishments, the old building was sold late in 1952 and its contents stored in the basement of the library, pending the future construction of a new museum wing.

Early in Mr. Guyol's administration, Katherine Prentis Murphy of New York City, an indefatigable collector of early American furniture, who, with her brother Edmund Astley Prentis, had in 1951 given three period rooms to the New-York Historical Society, proposed a comparable gift in New Hampshire. As Mrs. Murphy had spent her entire married life in Concord, she developed a considerable interest in the New Hampshire Historical Society. In 1958 the furnishings of a parlor, dining room, bedroom, and kitchen, intended to suggest the home of a prosperous New England merchant of about 1730, were given to the society by Mrs. Murphy and her brother, in memory of her husband, David Edward Murphy of Concord. A large proportion of the furniture had been found in New Hampshire, and much of it is thought to have been made there. To house this collection properly, the society cleared several rooms on the second floor, which had previously been jammed with a jittery miscellany of historical objects, and created by the use of old paneling a suitable setting for the Prentis Collection. Thus, by giving up a major part of the available exhibition space to one type of thing, that one has been done superlatively well. It is hoped that the interest aroused by this first-rate exhibition of one early phase of

New Hampshire history will lead eventually to the construction of a museum wing in the rear of the present building. Fortunately Mr. Tuck's generosity of half a century ago provided land adequate for such future expansion.

The Prentis Collection is regarded as one phase of a future museum of New Hampshire history rather than as the beginning of extended collecting in the field of decorative arts. The society wishes to place major emphasis on the presentation of the economic and industrial history of the State, when space for adequate exhibition is obtained.

There are six classes of membership: active at $5, sustaining at $10, contributing at $25, corporate at $50, institutional at $100, and and life upon one payment of $250. In July 1960 there were 1,070 members. Dues amounted to $4,613 for the calendar year 1959, although the society hopes in coming years to increase that amount substantially by adding to the membership, particularly in the corporate and institutional classes. Today the lion's share of the society's basic annual income of approximately $50,000 comes from investments that have a book value of $556,542.29 and a market value, as of 31 December 1959, of $874,783.37.

The present trustees of the society are fortunately aware that living within one's income does not necessarily encourage further gifts and that finding funds for one specific and desirable purpose often produces the means of accomplishing others. In January 1960 the trustees budgeted some $6,000 over the anticipated income of $50,000, relying upon the current gifts of friends to cover this deficit.

The society is still shorthanded. The library and research activities are well housed in the 1911 building, although any museum development must await an addition. Publications are in process of change. *Historical New Hampshire* was enlarged to a new format with volume XIII in December 1957. While it now appears annually, it is hoped that it may before long be expanded into a quarterly journal. Book publication was resumed in 1958 with William Robinson Brown's *Our Forest Heritage* and continued in 1959 by Elwin L. Page's *Judicial Beginnings in New Hampshire, 1640–1700.* The latter volume is a remarkable evidence of the spirit that now prevails in the New Hampshire Historical Society, for its author, associate justice of the Supreme Court of New Hampshire from 1934 to 1946 and now first vice-president of the society, works regularly in the basement as a volunteer member of the staff. Over a number of years Judge Page has been refiling and placing in order the thousands of cases of colonial court records. He has used them as the basis of this book, which is not only an admirable piece of colonial legal history but uncommonly good reading into the bargain. When this kind of thing occurs in one area within a society, there is reason to believe that similar intelligent activity will develop in others. Where ideas exist, the means usually get found.

CONNECTICUT

Although the Connecticut Historical Society[6] got off to a slow and fumbling start, it has made up for it in later years. It was incorporated by the General Assembly of Connecticut in May 1825 on the petition of thirty-one citizens of Hartford. At the first meeting on 30 May 1825, in the State House at Hartford, the poet John Trumbull, author of *M'Fingal*, was elected president. After four meetings within the year, Judge Trumbull moved to Detroit, and nothing more happened for fourteen years. A group of the original incorporators, with additions, procured in 1839 a renewal of the original charter and set to work. Late in December 1843 the Connecticut Historical Society moved into the partially completed Wadsworth Athenaeum where it remained for more than a century.

Thompson R. Harlow, the society's present director, thus describes the energetic campaign of collecting that the society undertook on its second start:

Committees were appointed to ask particular items from specific persons. For example, two members were instructed to call upon Mr. Timothy Woodbridge

6. [Thompson R. Harlow], *125 Years of The Connecticut Historical Society, 1825–1950* (Hartford, 1951).

to request deposit in the archives of the Society of papers relating to the Gore Company. The Corresponding Secretary was asked to write all publishers of periodicals in the State requesting them to save copies of their publications and upon completion of a volume to present them to the Society. Busts of eminent persons were requested, and calls were made upon newspaper publishers with a view toward securing back files of their papers. Ex-Governors were asked to donate portraits of themselves, and any and all manuscript records of their public service, and writers of historical subjects were "waited upon" for copies and contributions to the Society. How successful this campaign was is apparent upon only a fleeting examination of the Society today, for almost every request met with immediate response.

In fact it was so successful that, after moving into the new rooms in the Wadsworth Athenaeum, the Society decided it needed someone to arrange and care for its treasures. The committee appointed to look into the matter did not seek a librarian or curator (there was no such thing as special training in these fields then), but they sought a man who had plenty of books to add to the Society's growing library. He, as luck would have it, had been Corresponding Secretary of the Society in 1825, but in the meantime had left East Windsor for Mattapoisett, Mass., where annually he expended most of his salary in buying books for his private library. This man, the Rev. Thomas Robbins, needed little urging to agree to come to the Society at $600 a year with the understanding that his library would become the property of the Society upon his death.

This good arrangement lasted until 1856. The most extended term of any librarian was that of Albert Carlos Bates, who took office in 1893 and held it until succeeded by Mr. Harlow in 1940.

The first volume of *Collections* appeared in 1860; a hundred years later the thirtieth was in preparation. Towards the publication of this series, the State of Connecticut contributes $1,000 annually, the only public support received by the society. The series has included rolls of Connecticut men in the French and Indian Wars and the Revolution, correspondence of the unlovely Silas Deane, papers of such Governors of the Colony of Connecticut as Jonathan Law (1741–50), Roger Wolcott (1750–54), Thomas Fitch (1754–66), and William Pitkin (1766–69), as well as five volumes of the papers of the early nineteenth-century Governor John Cotton Smith.

For many years in the present century, the Connecticut Historical

Society's quarters in the Wadsworth Athenaeum were woefully inadequate. In 1950 the problem was solved by the purchase of a large private house at 1 Elizabeth Street in the western part of Hartford, which was pleasantly situated in eight acres of landscaped grounds. The house was of massive construction and no particular architectural distinction. It could, therefore, be remodeled with impunity. By the addition of a substantial bookstack and meeting room it adapted itself readily to the use of a library and museum.

The library contains 70,000 volumes, dealing with New England and the regions of Connecticut migration and emigration, and more than a million manuscripts. It includes the best extant collection of eighteenth-century Connecticut imprints and newspapers, among them virtually complete files of the *Hartford Courant* from 1764, the *Hartford Times* from 1817, and publishers' files of the *New London Gazette* from 1763, the *Middlesex Gazette* from 1785, and the *American Mercury* from 1784. The genealogical collection is described as "justly famous for its completeness of printed records and for its manuscripts compiled by such eminent genealogists as Homer W. Brainard, Mrs. Edna Minor Rogers and Charles L. N. Camp." In Mr. Harlow's summary of resources for the student of history,

The historical manuscripts comprise an excellent record of Connecticut from the early 17th century. Of particular significance are a shorthand account of Thomas Hooker's sermons, and thousands of letters, diaries and account books of Oliver Wolcott, Jeremiah Wadsworth, William Samuel Johnson, Samuel Colt and Lydia Sigourney. Specific items include Nathan Hale's diary, the contract between Lafayette and Silas Deane under which Lafayette served the Revolutionary forces, the Windsor Law Book, containing the first codification of Connecticut laws and session acts from 1651–1708, and a report and survey of the defences of New Haven Harbor by Major General Steuben in 1779.

The map collection includes several unique items and many rarities. Abel Buell's *Chart of Saybrook Barr* 1771 is the earliest line engraving of any consequence in Connecticut. The same engraver's *Map of the United States*, 1783 is the first map of the new republic by a native.

In the museum are examples of the work of such Connecticut cabinetmakers as Aaron and Eliphalet Chapin, Isaac Tryon, Benjamin Burnham, and Brewster Dayton, silver, pewter, glass, china, paintings by Richard Jennys, Joseph Steward, Ralph Earl, John Trumbull, Samuel F. B. Morse, and others, as well as hundreds of views of Connecticut scenes, prints, miniatures, and silhouettes. Pleasantly arranged galleries furnish good space for both permanent and rotating exhibitions. The museum attracts an audience that might not be inclined to work in the library.

Regular meetings on the first Tuesday of each month from October through May, with speakers often drawn from the neighboring faculties of Trinity College or Yale University, attract members from all corners of Connecticut. Although these have been open to the public, the size of some audiences has suggested the possible necessity of limiting the attendance to members.

The Connecticut Historical Society Bulletin, in its twenty-fifth volume in 1960, is a thin quarterly, usually of thirty-two pages, combining a few historical articles with a bit of membership information and a "Genealogical Department." The society has in recent years undertaken the publication of certain books on historical subjects whose interest is too limited for commercial publication, when a subsidy has been provided by the author. As an example, Melancthon W. Jacobus's *The Connecticut River Steamboat Story* was published in this way in 1956. By December 1959 it had met expenses; the author and the society were sharing profits evenly, with only seventy copies remaining in stock. By this means a number of worth-while books have been placed in circulation. During the last ten years the society has published fifteen books with gross sales of almost $28,000.

Three classes of annual membership exist: associate, for non-residents, at $3, active at $5, and contributing at $15. In 1961 there were 1,414 members, the highest number in the history of the society. Increases in number are sought by active means. In his 1959 annual report, Mr. Harlow observed:

It is essential that we have a large membership, for their interest is reflected in the growth of the Library and the Museum—an intangible support that cannot be measured in dollars. Memberships, though, should contribute to the overall operation of the Society and obviously as presently set up, receipts from dues are of no assistance.

Certainly at the present rate, members represent an intangible rather than a financial asset, for in the year 1961 their dues of $5,345.25 were almost eaten up by the expense of preparing and distributing the *Bulletin*. The total endowment, as of May 1961, with a book value of $1,338,217, produced income of $97,740.32.

The Connecticut Historical Society has been singularly successful in supplementing its income from endowment by current gifts and grants, which over the previous ten years have averaged between twenty and twenty-five thousand dollars annually. The year ending 30 April 1960 was singularly fruitful in this direction, for there were received during it gifts for current projects of $55,495.74, a grant of $1,000, and gifts and bequests to endowment of $109,350.12. The following year $47,789.33 was added to endowment. Local Hartford foundations have in recent years been helpful in assisting in the accomplishment of specific projects. In 1959 a grant of $5,000 from the Ensworth Charitable Foundation permitted the society to complete its files of Hartford newspapers with microfilm and to obtain much-needed museum storage facilities, while $8,750 from the Hartford Foundation for Public Giving made possible the restoration of forty-six paintings.

In January 1960 an agreement was reached with the City of Hartford whereby the Connecticut Historical Society would operate the old State House, in which its first meeting had been held on 30 May 1825, as a public museum. Although restoration and furnishing are still under way, the State House was opened to visitors on 2 January 1961.[7]

Of the five organizations considered in this chapter, the Connecticut Historical Society today is in the most fortunate situation. It has

7. The society's report for the year ending 30 April 1961 shows a city appropriation of $15,000 for the operation of the State House. During the four months in which the building was opened, admission fees amounted to $247.35, with expenses of $6,893.92.

an adequate building, adapted to its varied present needs; it also has the largest annual income, all but a token $1,000 of which is derived from private sources. It has, in addition, succeeded in convincing general local charitable foundations that the specific projects of a historical society may be appropriate recipients of their assistance.

VERMONT

The Vermont Legislature on 5 November 1838 approved an act to incorporate the Vermont Historical and Antiquarian Society—later shortened to Vermont Historical Society[8]—"for the purpose of collecting and preserving materials for the civil and natural history of the State of Vermont." A meeting of the society, however, was not held until 15 October 1840. The founder was Henry Stevens, father of the Vermont-London bookseller of the same name. The elder Stevens, although he had had few advantages of education, had vowed on his seventeenth birthday to collect a thousand volumes of newspapers before he reached the age of sixty. For this object he "spared no pains, lived poor and worked hard," although he was fearful of being considered "the greatest fool that lived in America during the Nineteenth Century." Stevens, who was chosen president and librarian at the first meeting, was at first permitted to keep the library of the society with his own belongings in his home at Barnet. Dr. Richard G. Wood, the present director, in a sketch of the society, has thus referred to its modest beginnings:

The Society did not gain a home until ten years after its founding when space was granted it in the second State House [at Montpelier]. When the State House burned in 1857 and the Legislature saved its one hundred spit boxes, without which (presumably) the process of lawmaking would have been retarded, the Vermont Historical Society lost everything except the portrait of George Washington. Thus, a century ago the Society had to start all over again.

After the rebuilding of the State House, the society was assigned

8. Richard G. Wood, *The Vermont Historical Society: A Status Report*, reprinted from *The New England Social Studies Bulletin* (October 1957).

quarters there, which it occupied until 1918 when it moved next door into the new State Library and Supreme Court Building. After more than forty years there, it recently moved to larger quarters on the first floor of the old National Life Insurance building on the other side of the State House.

The first recorded publication, an address by J. D. Butler before an annual meeting on 16 October 1846, is entitled *Deficiencies in our history*. Among other deficiencies the speaker notes that of the society to publish. Addresses and an occasional pamphlet of *Proceedings* appeared every now and then, but it was 1870 before a series of *Collections* was undertaken. It is natural that this society should have done less with learned publications than others, for Vermont is a rural state with a small population, more of which, it is proudly claimed, are cows than people. One tends to think of Maine and Vermont together, yet the records of their history are very different. Fishermen and explorers were messing about the coast of Maine from the beginning of American history, while the recorded story of Vermont begins in the eighteenth century.

The progress of the Vermont Historical Society was slow. The first State appropriation to be received was in 1896, when $100 was was given for the cataloguing of books. In more recent times that has changed, for today Vermont, alone of the New England states, makes an appropriation of significance to its historical society.

Today there is a library of 30,000 volumes, consisting chiefly of a reference collection on Vermont subjects, including the history of the State, imprints, and books by Vermont authors, and a genealogical library. The latter section, comprising some 800 volumes, represents a co-operative effort with the Society of Colonial Dames, which purchases genealogical books, to which it retains title, although it places them in the custody of the Vermont Historical Society. Newspapers are within the province of the nearby State Library, while the photostat and microfilm equipment of the Public Records Commission, in the same building, are available to the society.

The manuscript collection consists of some 700 journals, account books, and other bound volumes, 61 filing case drawers, 59 manuscript boxes, 140 document boxes, and 65 cartons of papers, dating from 1740 to 1950 and relating chiefly to Vermont. Among the personal papers are those of Royall Tyler, playwright, novelist, and the first Chief Justice of Vermont, of James Whitelaw, early surveyor general and pioneer, of Zadock Thompson, naturalist and mathematician, and of Senator Justin S. Morrill. Business papers include records of milldam, scale, and furnace companies, lumbering operations on the Connecticut River, and account books of general stores.

The museum collections range from the Stephen Daye press through Indian artifacts, a diorama of Dewey's victory at Manila Bay, to the stuffed skin of the last panther killed in the State. Some 7,000 school children a year come to view these varied specimens. Most of the objects are good.

Outside of Montpelier, the society opens to visitors during the summer months the Kent Tavern in Calais, which was bequeathed to it in 1944, with an endowment fund. Dr. Wood thus describes the building:

Opened as a hotel in 1837 by Abdiel Kent, this structure was constructed from hand-hewn timbers from the forest, lumber from the family sawmill, and hand-made nails from the family smithy. The granite came from Barre, and Abdiel could haul only one stone a day with his Morgans on a thirty-five mile round trip. The wallpaper, however, came from Boston. This building had become a tavern by 1847, but by 1860 much of its space had become filled by Kent's own family, which numbered thirteen.

Regular serial publications are the quarterly *Vermont History*[9] and a monthly *News and Notes*; both have a predominantly popular appeal. A number of town histories have been published in recent decades, of which Ernest L. Bogart's *Peacham: Story of a Vermont Hill Town* is an outstanding example. The society maintains a book-stall at which it offers for sale a wide variety of current books on Vermont subjects, seldom seen together in one place. From sales on

9. Beginning in 1962, *Vermont History* has appeared in an improved format, printed by the Stinehour Press of Lunenburg, Vermont.

the spot and mail orders received from the distribution of an annual book list a modest profit is made. In 1959 it was close to $600.

Although Vermont is the most thinly populated of the New England states, the Vermont Historical Society outdoes all others in the size of its membership. When the late Professor Arthur W. Peach became director in 1950 he found 900 members on the rolls. When a poet who is also a skillful lecturer and a convincing talker puts boundless energy into an enterprise he is apt to be successful. Largely because of his personal popularity throughout the State, Dr. Peach, by the time of his death in 1956, had raised the membership to more than 3,500. While this was excellent public relations, it was less realistic economy, for with a $3 membership fee the society lost money on each member.

After some careful cost accounting, which indicated that a subscription to *Vermont History* and to *News and Notes* cost $3.20 to distribute, the lowest class of dues was increased on 1 May 1957 to $5. Some numerical loss resulted, but with the compensation of greater solvency. Even at the increased rate, there were on 1 October 1959 2,851 members, which still far surpasses any other New England state. Of these 2,275 were active members at $5; 409 were sustaining at $10; 26 institutional and 24 contributing at $25, while there were 117 life members who had made a single payment of $150.

Receipts from dues for the fiscal year ending 30 June 1959 were $16,416.83, again the largest in any of the five societies considered in this chapter. From the income of private endowment $7,947.19 was received; $23,000 from State appropriation. The total receipts for the year were $49,130.19; the expenditures $45,931.59, of which $9,061.16 was spent on the two serial publications sent to members.

Upon Dr. Peach's death, he was succeeded as director by an outlander from New Hampshire, Dr. Richard G. Wood, a graduate of Dartmouth College and a Harvard PH.D. in history, who, after teaching at the Massachusetts Institute of Technology and the University of Maine, had spent fourteen years on the staff of the National

Archives. The Vermont Historical Society is fortunate in having a director of such professional experience who is temperamentally congenial to the character of the State.

In normal Vermont fashion, the society operates on a modest scale, but for an organization that has adopted the slogan "History is for every man" it has done a creditable job of living up to its principles. Its two publications are of genuine interest to several thousand people, while at the annual meeting each July the Eastern Star caters, with plenty to eat.

Chapter V

THE HISTORICAL SOCIETY

OF PENNSYLVANIA

How can the Historian himself perform his task with honor and credit if the materials for his work are not collected and preserved for him, before all-devouring time has blotted from the memory of men those interesting details, which alone can give the key to the true causes of public events?

—PETER S. DU PONCEAU, 1815

BY the establishment of the American Philosophical Society in 1743, Benjamin Franklin made Philadelphia the seat of the first learned society in British North America. That historical societies were founded in Massachusetts, New York, Maine, Rhode Island, and New Hampshire prior to any such move in Pennsylvania may have been due to an expectation of action by the Philosophical Society. At least Ebenezer Hazard had such a thought when he wrote Jeremy Belknap on 14 January 1791 from Philadelphia:

You ask me if an Antiquarian Society cannot be established here. Perhaps it might, and perhaps the thing might be considered as falling within the Philosophical Society's department.[1]

The idea eventually occurred to others, for on 17 March 1815 the American Philosophical Society, which had previously worked chiefly in the physical and mathematical sciences, added to its six existing committees a seventh, "of History, Moral Science, and Gen-

1. M.H.S. *Collections*, 5th ser., III, 242.

eral Literature." Peter S. Du Ponceau (1760–1844), a brilliant Frenchman who had come to America in 1777 as Baron Steuben's aide and had naturalized himself in Philadelphia as a lawyer, was charged with producing a plan of operations. Although a public appeal for information on the history of the State produced few results, Du Ponceau carried on for several years an extensive correspondence in search of historical sources. In spite of his considerable personal exertions, the committee had ceased to function by 1820.

There are several versions of the events that led to the founding of the Historical Society of Pennsylvania.[2] One would offer the New-York Historical Society as the inspiration. Another suggests that an annual dinner of "The Sons of New England" caused a Philadelphian to propose a comparable organization to be called "The Sons of the Soil"! Whatever its ancestry may have been, a meeting was held on 2 December 1824 at the house of Thomas I. Wharton, at which it was agreed that "it is expedient to form a Society for the purpose of elucidating the history of Pennsylvania." Several organizational meetings followed. William Rawle was elected president on 28 February 1825. A constitution of the Historical Society of Pennsylvania was approved by the Attorney General on 27 January 1826, and an act of incorporation signed by the Governor the following June.

The new organization, after meeting briefly in the quarters of the Phrenological Society in Carpenter's Court, rented a room in the summer of 1825 on the second floor of the American Philosophical Society, which also served as landlord to the Athenæum of Phila-

2. Hampton L. Carson, *A History of The Historical Society of Pennsylvania* (Philadelphia, 1940), 2 vols., is the most detailed account of any historical society to have been published. It cannot be considered a model for others to follow because of its discursive and uncritical nature. Mr. Carson, who was president of the society from 1921 until his death in 1929, devotes more space to the personalities of the presidents and officers than to the historical activities of the society. He wrote from long personal knowledge and with deep affection, reticence, and a profound respect for both constituted authority and property. One is inevitably reminded of Lord Dunsany's character "who in the end never died, but passed away at his residence." Although his volumes are valuable for reference, they are heavy sledding if read consecutively.

delphia. Committees were appointed on the national origin, biography of early settlers, biographical notices of distinguished persons, Indians, population, provincial government, juridical, literary, and medical history, and the progress of agriculture, manufactures, and commerce. A circular was distributed indicating the types of material desired by the new society for its library and cabinet. Volume I, part I, of a series of *Memoirs* appeared in 1826, to be followed the next year by part 2. The original hope that comparable volumes would appear at six-month intervals was not sustained. The two parts of volume II were published in 1827 and 1830, while the fourteenth, and last, of the series appeared in 1895.

Handsomely bound copies of the *Memoirs* sent to Granville Penn in England led to the gift of a portrait in armor of his grandfather, William Penn. The association thus established with the Penn family resulted eventually in further gifts of relics of the founder of Pennsylvania, including the wampum belt given him by the Indians.

Peter S. Du Ponceau, who had succeeded to the presidency of the society in 1837, following the death of William Rawle, reviewed the accomplishments of a dozen years in an inaugural address. Among them he notes that "in conjunction with the American Philosophical Society, we have prevailed on the Legislature of Pennsylvania, to publish at their expense, the Provincial Records deposited at Harrisburg, and thus made the State an associate in our labours." This action led eventually to the printing by the State of sixteen volumes of *Colonial Records* and the twelve volumes of the first series of *Pennsylvania Archives*.

The Historical Society of Pennsylvania was not conceived in terms of a learned academy of limited membership. William Rawle, its first president, in commenting on the earlier failure of the history committee of the American Philosophical Society, had attributed its difficulties to the fact that its members were drawn only from the severely restricted ranks of the older scientific body. Because of this, he observed, "fewer interests are therefore combined, and the public looks on them with indifference." Now the membership of the

American Philosophical Society and of its Boston counterpart, the American Academy of Arts and Sciences, was restricted on the basis of supposed services to learning. Jeremy Belknap planned the Massachusetts Historical Society in similar terms, as a small group whose members were chosen on the basis of their proved or potential services to history, whether as scholars, collectors, or contributors. Some of the founders of the Historical Society of Pennsylvania, however, had notions of a more meaningless restriction, based upon the accident of birth. The rejected earlier name, "Sons of the Soil," suggests an organization like the Native Sons of Kansas City, where the circumstance of being born within a specific geographical area alone makes one eligible to be counted among the sheep rather than the goats. William Rawle would have none of this. He notes that, when asked if he would accept the office of President,

As I had by this time understood that it was intended to be confined to *natives of* Pennsylvania I objected to its being placed on such a narrow basis but professed my willingness to accept the station if it was enlarged to all *residents in* Pennsylvania. [italics mine]

Although his view prevailed, the original constitution of the Historical Society still provided that no person shall be eligible for contributing membership (those residing in the city of Philadelphia or the state of Pennsylvania within ten miles of the city) or corresponding membership (those living in any other part of Pennsylvania) "unless he be a native of Pennsylvania, or shall have been *domiciliated there for a space of ten years.*" While the State of Maine wisely protects the economic interests of its coastal citizens by restricting the right to set lobster pots to residents of some years standing, one may doubt if the mere fact of having lived in the Commonwealth of Pennsylvania for ten years would have an appreciable effect upon a man's historical competence. There was, however, a provision for honorary membership, open to persons residing in any part of America, including "females."

Within the limits of Pennsylvania residents, however, the society by no means wished to appeal only to specialists. Du Ponceau urged that the *Memoirs* be made interesting to the general reader and that "for that purpose they should have a literary, and if I may so speak a *popular* character, by which means they will be more generally read, and more extensively diffused."

In spite of these generous aspirations, the society was at a low ebb in the late 1830s. In March 1838 it had but fifty-three members, fifty having resigned and twenty-two died; it even reached the all-time low of twenty-four during that year. Meetings would be attended by six members, while twelve was considered a crowd. An anonymous letter in the *National Gazette* of 20 July 1841, signed "Eheu" contrasted the "sluggishness" of Philadelphia with "the spirit of historical research that animates the New Yorker." It continued:

We have a Historical Society that does little, a Historical Committee of the Philosophical Society, which does less, and a William Penn Society, or something of the sort that does nothing. Thus with the necessary material for vigorously carrying on the siege, all hands lie down in the trenches and go to sleep! This state of things is discreditable to Philadelphia.

Stung by this reproach, eight members of the council met the following day: the "scurrilous paragraph" laid before them "became, justly, the subject of severe animadversion." After Du Ponceau's death in 1844, his will, written five years earlier, proved to contain a bequest to the society of $200 and books, with the admonition:

The Historical Society of Pennsylvania is in danger of perishing for want of support. . . . I recommend to them to increase the number of their members, and, perhaps, to raise the annual subscription to five dollars. I would also recommend to them to apply for aid to the Legislature.

Somehow the crisis was weathered. The society moved to a new room at 115 South Sixth Street in the spring of 1844; three years later it migrated to the third floor of the newly completed Athenæum in Washington Square, where it remained for twenty-five years. With new quarters, members and possessions slowly increased. On leaving the American Philosophical Society in 1844, the librarian reported that he had had to transport "about sixty books and some unopened boxes of public documents," while in 1849 there were 1,761 volumes, which were listed in a thirty-six-page printed catalogue. In 1846 there were 162 contributing members, but in 1850 290. In 1854 the number had risen to 402, while the library had increased to 3,500 books and 100 volumes of manuscripts.

Through the 1840s and 1850s there were rather indecisive experiments with the form of publications. A quarterly *Bulletin* was tried in 1845 and abandoned in 1847. Volume IV, part 2, of *Memoirs* appeared in 1850, ten years after part 1. A solitary volume of *Collections* was published in 1853, although the *Memoirs* were resumed when Winthrop Sargent's great edition of the journals of the Braddock expedition of 1755 were published on the centenary as volume V. The printing of this important work, which was the most ambitious the society had undertaken, had been made possible by the establishment in 1854 of a publication fund. Subscribers of $20 to that fund were entitled for life to a copy of each future book published from it. By April 1856 it had grown to $10,800.

In February 1860 Joseph R. Ingersoll, formerly Minister to the Court of St. James's, was elected president of the society; although re-elected in February 1861, he failed to put in an appearance until March 1861, when he delivered a fluent though absurd inaugural address, in which he alleged that "the wide range of the annals of the human race" was the society's "pasture and hunting ground," that "all the arts and all the sciences are within its scope." A month later, President Ingersoll took the chair at the 8 April 1861 meeting, suspended the regular order of business, and introduced the Reverend Philip Schaff, who read a paper on the "History of Involuntary Servitude among the nations of Asia and Europe," remaining in the moral stratosphere without reference to current national crises. During the eight years of his presidency, Mr. Ingersoll, perhaps fortunately, turned up at but eleven meetings of the society and two of the executive committee. While waiting for him first to appear after his election in 1860, this committee, which was the governing body of the society, fell into a state of desuetudinous languor. In May and June, Townsend Ward, the librarian, constituted a meeting all by himself. From March to December 1861 its meetings were completely suspended, but in February 1862 Vice-president B. H. Coates, one of the founders of 1824, took the helm and prevented the society from going on the rocks. In a revision of the constitution and bylaws under his urging all restrictions upon membership of residence or sex were eliminated.

With someone steering once again, gifts and members increased rapidly. Ebenezer Hazard's son Samuel, who had published the *Register of Pennsylvania* from 1826 to 1835, became librarian and reclassified the books. In February 1863 he reported 6,980 volumes by actual count. Although well qualified for his duties, Samuel Hazard was too old and weary to continue. His successor, Samuel Leiper Taylor, an aggressive lawyer with fluency in jargon that would do credit to a contemporary behavioral scientist, devoted his energies to another reclassification, which concluded with a division of Oikeigraphy, "deeming this *coined* word, the etymology of which, *oikeios* pertaining to home and *grapho* I write, a better title than Local History." Had Mr. Taylor's ideas obtained general acceptance, we might today have an American Oikeigraphical Association. That we do not is due to his faulty judgment in reading a lengthy report to the seventeen members present at the January 1865 meeting, in which he described himself as "no musty Dry-as-dust, hardly breathing, buried deep under fathoms of obstruction; no cringing sycophant, bowing at the shrines of fashion." At the February 1865 meeting 145 members turned up and voted him out of office. Mr. Taylor's subsequent charges of unfair methods and "politics" in his defeat were vehement. The incident oddly resembles more modern squabbles involving academic and institutional tenure.

By the death of Dr. George W. Fahnestock in December 1868 the society received the bequest of his great collection of pamphlets, numbering according to estimate 70,000 items. This gift aggravated housing problems, for the 11,483 books and 12,910 pamphlets that the society owned in January 1869, exclusive of the new bequest, were closely huddled together in the third floor rooms in the Athenæum. New quarters became essential. These were procured by taking a ten-year lease on a detached two-story structure on Spruce Street between 8th and 9th, on the grounds of the Pennsylvania Hospital. This "Picture Building," so called from its construction in 1816 to house a painting by Benjamin West, was remodeled to accommodate the growing library of the Historical Society, which formally took possession of its new quarters on 11 March 1872.

The centennial year of 1876, which brought so much of the United States to Philadelphia, thus found the Historical Society of Pennsylvania better housed and more usefully employed than at any previous time in its career. A great body of Penn papers were acquired in 1873 by subscriptions of members after three years of negotiation with British dealers. Two volumes of the long promised *Correspondence between William Penn and James Logan,* from documents in the Logan family, appeared in 1870–72 as volumes IX and X of the *Memoirs.* In 1875 the settlement of the estate of Henry D. Gilpin, who had died fifteen years earlier, brought the society the sum of nearly $60,000.

Among the centennial visitors to Philadelphia were a body of the new-style librarians, who, during a three-day conference at the Historical Society of Pennsylvania early in October 1876, founded the American Library Association. Although the Boston Public Library, which was the first of the great tax-supported institutions of the kind, had opened less than twenty-five years before, similar libraries had been springing up like the crop sowed by Cadmus. With them was developing a new professional approach to the care and use of books. As Justin Winsor, the greatest instigator of all this, remarked in the address that he gave upon his election to the presidency of the new association, "The day is passed when librarianships should be filled with teachers who have failed in enforcing discipline, or with clergymen whose only merit is that bronchitis was a demerit in their original calling."

The early years of any successful professional movement are marked by the presence of a small number of able men who establish standards as they go along in their several organizations. The Historical Society of Pennsylvania was fortunate in having Frederick D. Stone, who was such a man, as its librarian from 1877 to 1897. He became a member of the society in 1863, while still in his early twenties. Four years later he was entrusted with the first attempt at the classification of its manuscripts, engravings, and broadsides. In the decade prior to his appointment as librarian, he had prepared for the press five volumes of *Memoirs* and in countlesss other ways had grown into the possessor of remarkable knowledge concerning the society. Until his death in 1897, Stone was the unifying element in the society's activities. As Mr. Carson well put it:

He knew what the Society had, and also what it needed. He knew not only the names and positions of the books, but their contents as well. . . . He knew the deficiencies of this library as a well informed commander knows the weakness of a brigade. He was ever alert to strengthen it by repeated acquisitions. . . . By twenty years of incessant toil, he built up a great department of manuscript and printed material of such exceeding richness as to lay the lasting foundations for the study of history in the United States. . . . The donors felt that in hands like his [their gifts] were not only safe, but would be useful. The Tower collection of colonial laws, the Dreer collection of manuscripts, the Peters papers, the Wayne papers, the McKean papers, the Pemberton papers, the Buchanan papers, the Tilghman papers, the Hollingsworth papers, the Baker collection of the portraits of Washington, to say nothing of a thousand special gifts of books, of pictures, of relics, became the property of the Society largely because of the surpassing fitness of its librarian for his office. . . . In time, in the estimation of scholars, he became indistinguishable from all that made the Society useful as an institution.

While Frederick D. Stone was the tireless helper of other scholars, he found time for historical writing of his own. At the request of Justin Winsor, he contributed chapters on "The Founding of Pennsylvania" and "The Struggle for the Delaware" to the *Narrative and Critical History of America*. Long after Stone's death, Dr. Ellis P. Oberholtzer wrote of him:

He was the nearest thing to a painstaking, qualified, accurate authority on Pennsylvania history that we have ever had there, was he not? He was a lover of truth and knew where to find it. He was a good librarian, but he had scholarly historical interests of an unusual kind into the bargain. Since he was viewed with faith and confidence the Society and the library also came to command respect as it did not have this in the public estimation before.

Stone's most permanent claim to national remembrance is as the first editor of the *Pennsylvania Magazine of History and Biography*, which began publication in 1877. The society's first half century of publication had progressed by fits and starts. With the quarterly, designed "to foster and develop the interest that has been awakened in historical matters, and to furnish the means of inter-communication between those of kindred tastes," a medium was found that simultaneously solved the society's publishing problems and proved of immeasurable benefit to historical studies far beyond Pennsylvania. The *Pennsylvania Magazine of History and Biography* is in 1962 in its eighty-sixth year of continuous publication. It was the first general historical quarterly of its type; it established a pattern that in later years has been widely emulated by other historical societies in the twentieth century, just as the *Collections* of the Massachusetts Historical Society furnished a model that was generally followed by others in the nineteenth. It continues to be a first-rate scholarly journal, printing sound readable articles.[3]

While the old Picture Building was an attractive enough place for visitors interested in American history, it proved entirely inadequate for the research library that was growing under Stone's guidance. In 1883 the society consequently bought the house of General Robert Patterson at 13th and Locust Streets, which stood in a lot of 120 by 125 feet. The house, originally built in 1832, was remodeled to

3. When Miss Lois V. Given, associated with the *Pennsylvania Magazine* since 1947, was in January 1962 appointed editor to serve jointly with Nicholas B. Wainwright, her first act was to print in the current issue a resounding affirmation entitled "Upholding a Tradition" in which she stated: "From its outset, the *Pennsylvania Magazine* has been essentially a scholarly publication. To our knowledge, no serious suggestion to change it to any other kind of periodical has ever been made." This admirable statement of policy is further mentioned in chapter XXIII.

provide exhibition and reading rooms, fireproof housing for the library, and an auditorium. Two thirds of the cost of $96,318 was met by individual private subscriptions. At the inauguration of the building on 18 March 1884, Professor John B. McMaster, in the course of a congratulatory address, remarked of the pleasantness of the surroundings:

Not many years since an Historical Society was commonly believed to differ little from a dime museum. People believed its quarters to be a dingy room in an attic, and its treasures bullets from Bunker Hill and guns from Yorktown, arrowheads from Tippecanoe, books nobody ever read, and portraits, as like as two peas, of gentlemen in small clothes with red curtains tastefully draped behind them and cannon and flags beyond. That there was anything lively and human about such societies was doubted. But this, most happily, is so no longer.

McMaster spoke of the sources of history, of the pamphlets, letters, journals, and newspapers of the past, and of the duty of gathering

material for an honest history of the present, such as will show up fairly both sides of every controversy in politics, every discussion in morals, every great movement in social science, the condition of the laborer, the state of the arts, the life and manners of the time.

In this direction he outlined the functions of historical societies throughout the country, by saying,

Each one should be a storehouse for that carefully-sifted material by which alone posterity can see us as we are. A century hence this will be precisely the most difficult kind of knowledge to acquire. Newspapers will not furnish it, for they are not reliable. Letters will not contain it, for they are too hastily written to be of much value, and too numerous to be preserved.

It was, incidentally, Professor McMaster who, with Frederick D. Stone, edited in 1888 the great *Pennsylvania and the Federal Constitution, 1787–88,* which was an outstanding contribution by the society to the historical literature of the time.

Libraries never stay within their bounds for long. Five years after the opening of the new quarters, a fireproof building was added along the 13th Street frontage, as a gift from John Jordan Jr., who had in 1841 subscribed towards the purchase of the first bookcase needed by the society. Soon after the turn of the century, plans were undertaken that led to the eventual replacement of the Patterson house by a modern building of fireproof construction. To this undertaking the Commonwealth of Pennsylvania contributed $150,000. The present four-story building was formally opened in the spring of 1910.

Today the library activity of the Historical Society of Pennsylvania constitutes its pre-eminent function. While it has remarkable collections of portraits and historical objects, these are incidental to its purpose of maintaining one of the great historical research libraries of the country, which contains something over half a million books, pamphlets, newspapers, and broadsides. Among the great rarities are books and pamphlets from the library of Benjamin Franklin; Pennsylvania imprints of the eighteenth century from the presses of the Bradfords, Franklin, Keimer, Saur, Robert Bell, Aitken, Cist, Carey, and others; the Cassel collection of Pennsylvania German imprints; the Baker collection of Washingtoniana; the Charlemagne Tower collection of colonial laws, representing nearly all the British colonies in North America from Nova Scotia to Bermuda. It has outstanding collections of early Philadelphia imprints, of printed works to do with the history of Pennsylvania, and of prints and maps of the state. The newspaper collection of 5,377 volumes is remarkably rich for the middle states, including at least one Philadelphia newspaper for each year from 1720 to the present. To make these widely available, the society has issued microfilm reproductions of the *Pennsylvania Gazette*, 1728–89, and a broken run from 1790 to 1815; the *Pennsylvania Journal*, 1742–93; the *Pennsylvania Chronicle*, 1767–74; the *Pennsylvania Packet*, 1771–90; the *New York Journal*, 1766–76; the *Wochentlichte Philadelphische Staatsbote*, 1763–79; and two of Christopher Saur's newspapers, *Hoch-Deutsch Pensylvanische Geschicht-Schreiber*, 1739–1745, and *Pensylvanische Berichte*, 1745–62.

When the second edition of the *Guide to the Manuscript Collections of the Historical Society of Pennsylvania* appeared in 1949, it stated that "some 4,000,000 items are to be found in 1,609 collections," and that whereas in 1940 only 30% of the manuscripts were arranged for ready use by students, in 1949 98% were in that order. The collections deal primarily with Philadelphia and with Pennsylvania, although because of Pennsylvania's importance to the United States, there is much of national interest. The 25,000 Penn manuscripts, including journals and letters of Admiral Sir William Penn, letters and diaries of William Penn the Founder, and the important letter books of later proprietors, cover the period 1629–1834. There are extensive collections of the Logan, Norris, Shippen, and Pemberton families, 25,000 items of the papers of Pennsylvania's only president, James Buchanan, 6,500 of General Anthony Wayne, 60 volumes and 20,000 additional items of Jay Cooke, the financier of the Civil War. As an example of the richness in the early national scene, one might note nearly 400 letters of George Washington, including his first survey and his last letter, and 150 letters from John Adams to his friend Francis Adrian van der Kemp.

The Historical Society of Pennsylvania was instrumental in securing the passage of an Act of 8 March 1860 requiring the registration of marriages, births, and deaths, which is the fundamental Pennsylvania statutory regulation concerning vital statistics. In 1892 certain members of the society organized the Genealogical Society of Pennsylvania as an auxiliary body to be devoted to the collection of genealogical information. With resources of its own, this group has assembled extensive collections of copies and photostats of official records containing vital statistics, which, by original agreement, belong to the Historical Society of Pennsylvania. Since 1956 the reading room of the Genealogical Society has been consolidated with that of the Historical Society.

While the *Pennsylvania Magazine of History and Biography* remains the great contribution of the society to historical publishing, a variety of books, not in series, are issued from time to time. During the 1930s, when Julian P. Boyd was librarian and editor, there were a number of developments in this area, ranging from a magnificent edition of *Indian Treaties printed by Benjamin Franklin* to a new pamphlet series entitled *Narratives and Documents*, to make available in separate form some of the more important documentary materials published in the *Pennsylvania Magazine*. *Oliver Evans, A Chronicle of Early American Engineering*, by Greville and Dorothy Bathe, was published in 1935; Lawrence Henry Gipson's *Lewis Evans* in 1939; Philip S. Klein's *Pennsylvania Politics, 1817–1832, A Game Without Rules* in 1940.

Dr. Boyd's years in Philadelphia resulted in the superb *Statement of Policy by The Historical Society of Pennsylvania*, prepared by a Committee on Objectives that included himself and his successor, R. Norris Williams 2nd, the present director of the society. Published in the April 1940 issue of the *Pennsylvania Magazine*, this eleven-page "declaration of faith and purpose" is grounded upon certain compelling assumptions.

It implies a belief in the value and dignity of the incomparable story of America, a delight in its variant voices from all lands blending into a common voice of hope and promise. It means a deep concern for the life of the people as well as a desire to record the actions of their leaders. It means that here in Pennsylvania—from the beginning the most cosmopolitan and democratic of all the States—history concerns itself with the Finns and Swedes, the Dutch and English, the Scots-Irish and Germans, the Negroes and Slavs, without regard to their status, their beliefs, their color, their accent. It means a broad and intelligent interest in the fundamental unit in society, the family, and not a mere concern for the compilation of genealogical tables. In the explicit statement concerning new instruments for reproducing and collecting historical records, it means a desire for the increased usefulness of its collections and for the manifold benefits that flow from a knowledge and understanding of backgrounds. This is, indeed, a formal abandonment of the warehouse theory of custodianship; it substitutes therefor a trusteeship, to be justified only in terms of increased accessibility and increased usefulness.

Two important publications issued through Mr. Williams's particular efforts afford examples of the desire to make the society's great resources of material more readily available to those who need them: these are the previously mentioned 1949 edition of the *Guide to the Manuscript Collections* and a magnificent cumulative index to the first seventy-five volumes of the *Pennsylvania Magazine of History and Biography*, prepared and printed at a cost in excess of $100,000. These are instances of generous service to learning, in which there is not the slightest possibility of recovering the costs.

Philadelphia in the Romantic Age of Lithography, by Nicholas B. Wainwright, the society's editor, which appeared in 1958, furnishes an admirable example of how a historical society, by the use of excellent illustrations and good typography, may make a scholarly publication palatable and saleable to a general audience. Basically Mr. Wainwright was preparing an essay on Philadelphia lithographers with a catalogue, highly useful for reference, of the fine collection of their works that is owned by the society. The lithographs themselves, when well reproduced, provided such a varied and engaging picture of Philadelphia life in the nineteenth century that the edition of 1,500 copies was entirely sold within four weeks of publication. It should be noted that in the same year Mr. Wainwright received a special citation, never before presented, from the Society of American Historians "for the high standard of scholarship and readability" which the *Pennsylvania Magazine of History and Biography* has sustained under his editorship.

Although the Commonwealth of Pennsylvania contributed generously, more than half a century ago, towards the Historical Society of Pennsylvania's present building, that sum was the only public money ever received. The society today receives no public funds from state or city. Its current income, which is grossly inadequate in relation to its responsibilities to scholarship, is derived from endowment, the dues of members, and the sales of publications. There are approximately 2,300 members, 300 of whom are life members. From the remaining 2,000, who pay annual dues of $10, $20,000 a year is derived, against which must be charged the cost of furnishing them with subscriptions to the magazine. Income from investments, which on 31 December 1958 had a book value of $2,276,946.10 and a market value of $2,638,327.59, is slightly in excess of $100,000. The total income from all sources in 1958 was $134,497.56; the total expenditure $125,773.84, of which $113,606.64 represented the normal operating expenses, and the remainder the appropriations made for the publication of the *Pennsylvania Magazine* and such unpleasant necessities as "New parapet on roof, $4,230.00."

The Historical Society of Pennsylvania stays within its income only by being understaffed, by paying the staff that it has less than it would wish, and by publishing fewer books than it should. It needs money with which to increase salaries in general; it needs specifically a curator of rare books, a curator of prints, and more stenographic help to relieve an overburdened staff. However acutely its officers may feel that in these respects the Historical Society of Pennsylvania is only just holding its ground, it moves forward in a statesmanlike and imaginative manner where plans to advance historical scholarship are concerned. The discussions now under way between the society and the Library Company of Philadelphia are a case in point.

Philadelphians, like Bostonians, enjoy doing business with themselves in different capacities. When Peter S. Du Ponceau died in 1844 he was simultaneously president of the American Philosophical Society, the Historical Society of Pennsylvania, and the Athenæum of Philadelphia, all three of which were then housed under the same roof. The Library Company of Philadelphia being, at the time, just across 5th Street, one had four libraries within a few steps of each other. The Historical Society and the Athenæum moved away in the 1840s, although the Library Company remained in 5th Street until the late 1870s when it accepted a great new neoclassical structure at Broad and Christian Streets, provided under the will of Dr. James Rush and named the Ridgway Building in graceful acknowledgment of the fact that Dr. Rush's fortune had come from his father-in-law, Jacob Ridgway. At the time this seemed to be an admirable move, for the Ridgway Building was ample in size, monumental in appearance, and accompanied by some $300,000 for its maintenance and the purchase of books.

Forward-looking persons who try to place institutions in sites that anticipate the future growth of a city sometimes guess wrong. Dr. Rush's death-bed admonition to his executor to build the library that he was providing at Broad and Christian Streets is a conspicuous example of the futility of attempted divination. That location was remote from the normal beat of most users of the Library Company in the 1870s; so remote, in fact, that it was determined to build a supplementary library for current reading at the corner of Locust and Juniper Streets. Thus from 1880 onwards the possessions of the Library Company were divided between two buildings.

With the establishment of the Free Library in 1894, the unique usefulness of the Library Company to citizens of Philadelphia was diminished. The Ridgway Building was remote; its approaches and surroundings became grubbier by the year; its rich treasures were gradually forgotten by all but a handful of scholars. The depression of the early 1930s diminished the Library Company's income to a point that in 1940 required the abandonment and demolition of the Locust Street library and the consolidation of all the books in the Ridgway Building. The site of the Locust Street library became a parking lot.

The supposed mission of the Library Company was ambivalent and confusing. On the one hand it attempted to provide current fiction and other light reading for its stockholders; on the other it possessed the rich accumulation of two centuries of collecting that was invaluable for scholarly research. The second aspect has been admirably described in a recent publication of the library.[4]

The collection of the Library Company reflects a unique picture of American life. Franklin's first electrical experiments, which were performed in its rooms, are recalled in its rich collection of scientific books. Its fascinating old works on natural history came over from England in the same boxes with seeds for James Logan and John Bartram. Logan's brother and two of his grandchildren, and Benjamin Rush

---

4. *Why the Library Company Should Move, A Description of the Library stressing its Fundamental Values and the Reasons why the Ridgway Building can no longer be considered an Adequate or Safe Home* (Philadelphia, 1960).

and his son James were physicians. Their interests remain on our shelves in a re-markable group of medical books. The Company's members were active in politics and its rooms on the second-floor of Carpenters' Hall were open to the members of the Continental Congress which met downstairs. Impressive rows of political pamphlets and broadsides issued from the time of the Stamp Act to the establishment of the Constitution survive from those days. Philadelphians founded insurance companies, banks, railroads, philanthropic institutions, abolition socie-ties, churches, schools and colleges. Many of the earliest printed records of these endeavors are among the library's holdings. With Philadelphia pioneering west-ward across the continent, a surprising number of accounts of expeditions gravita-ted to our library. The Civil War brought in an outpouring of books, pamphlets, broadsides, prints, photographs and memorabilia of all kinds.

Here then are the records, the raw material of history. This material is further enhanced because thousands of the books belonged to William Penn, James Logan, Benjamin Franklin, Benjamin Rush and John Dickinson, others to Isaac Norris, William Byrd of Westover, and Thomas Jefferson. They were given to us, many of them, by civic-minded Logans, Biddles, Vauxes, Ingersolls and Leas. They were used by the Founding Fathers of the nation, by writers like James Fenimore Coop-er. Poor artisans and wealthy merchants turned to our library for ideas, education, and relaxation.

From 1943 to 1955 the Free Library of Philadelphia became the cor-porate librarian of the Company, responsible for the administration of the library in return for a fee. This interim time-marking counsel of desperation was ended after a surprising and wholly delightful improvement in the Library Company's fortunes from a most unlikely source. In 1952, by building a four-story parking garage on the site of the former Locust Street branch, the income of the Library Company improved to a state where its directors were once more able to make their own plans for the future, with an assurance of the means to carry them out. One hears great lamentations about the congestion of traffic in American cities; the Library Company was fortunately able to turn that nuisance into channels that benefit learning. With funds once more in hand, the Library Company sought the advice of eminent librarians from other cities who were unanimous in agreeing that its greatest strength lay in its rare books and manuscripts, and that its greatest contribution would be as a scholarly research library, with special emphasis upon American history and culture. Edwin Wolf 2nd, formerly with the rare-book firm of Rosenbach, who had made a preliminary survey of the over-crowded shelves in the Ridgway Building, was engaged as librarian. Like Frederick D. Stone in an earlier generation, Mr. Wolf has proved to be a librarian who knows not only the names and positions of books, but their contents as well, for he writes history as ably as he compiles bibliographies. As a result of his inspired work of dis-covery, recataloguing, reshelving, and rehabilitation, 50,000 rare books and pamphlets have been rescued from the Augean general stacks of the Ridgway Building and segregated in a temporarily rehabilitated area in one wing. While this work of revivification has had no official connection with the Historical Society of Penn-sylvania, it should be noted that Nicholas B. Wainwright, editor of the *Pennsylvania Magazine of History and Biography* at the society, is also president of the Library Company of Philadelphia. Seldom in the history of American libraries can there have been a happier, more harmonious, or more fruitful relationship between the president of a board and the librarian who carries out its policies.

In the autumn of 1959 Mr. Wolf's recataloguing had reached a point where he had run out of respectable shelf space. Either the Library Company would be forced to rehabilitate another section of the Ridgway Building, which would be throwing good money after bad, or take steps to move to more suitable permanent quarters. Once again the directors consulted outside librarians and scholars—the directors of the American Antiquarian Society and the Boston Athenæum; the Pierpont Morgan, John Carter Brown, Houghton, Huntington, and Clements libraries; and editors of the Franklin, Jefferson, Adams, and Walpole papers—concerning the most desir-able of three possible locations for a new building that would bring the Library Company closer to another similar institution, that would make possible the construction of modern, air-conditioned stacks for its rare books, and that would place it in an area "physically and psychologically accessible to local and out-of-town scholars."

Ten of the eleven persons consulted favored a location next to the Historical Society of Pennsylvania, with close ties between the two institutions in the handling of their collections. The directors of the Library Company approved early in November 1959; the shareholders concurred at the annual meeting on 2 May 1960. The way is therefore clear for detailed planning. It can be hoped that in the near future the Historical Society of Pennsylvania and the Library Company of Philadelphia, whose great scholarly resources would so admirably complement one another, will once again be neighbors, although on a far more intimate footing than they were when across 5th Street from one another in the 1840s. Of this plan Julian P. Boyd has written:

The suggestion that the Library Company and the Historical Society could share such facilities as exhibition space, photographic laboratories, and, I presume, auditorium and conference rooms is to me a remarkable evidence of wise planning and intelligent economy. But, beyond the area of what might be called good cultural housekeeping, the idea that one institution might be given custody of rare books and the other that of manuscripts strikes me as being nothing less than library statesmanship. This would indeed present a unique and shining example for libraries and historical societies to try to emulate.

Chapter VI

THE VIRGINIA
HISTORICAL SOCIETY

The historical society has to determine what its function is as an educational institution and not scatter its shot too much.
— WILLIAM M. E. RACHAL, 1954

THE foundation of a historical society in Virginia is cred-
ited to a native of New Hampshire, who was a graduate of
Phillips Exeter Academy and of Dartmouth College. Jonathan Peter Cushing (1793–1835) went south soon after leaving Dartmouth in 1817 because of delicate health, with the intention of
practicing law in Charleston. Instead he became a teacher in Virginia, first as a tutor at Hampden-Sydney College, then as Professor
of Chemistry and Natural Philosophy. In 1821 he became president
of that college, an office that he held until his premature death at the
age of forty-two.

On 29 December 1831 Dr. Cushing brought together a small
group in the hall of the House of Delegates in Richmond to organize the Virginia Historical and Philosophical Society.[1] Chief Justice John Marshall was elected president, while John Floyd, then
Governor of Virginia, and Cushing became vice-presidents. An
address to the public, published in October 1832, indicated the new
society's interest not only in historical sources but in zoology, bota-

1. [William G. Stanard], "History of the Virginia Historical Society," *Virginia
Magazine of History and Biography* XXXIX (1931), 292–362.

ny, geology, chemistry, mineralogy, and "natural, mental or moral philosophy." Efforts were promptly made to collect manuscripts or, where the original documents could not be procured, as in the case of the journal kept by William Byrd while running the dividing line, to have them copied. The society was incorporated by the General Assembly on 10 March 1834.

A volume of *Collections,* containing an address by Jonathan P. Cushing and the text of a memoir by Colonel John Stuart of Greenbrier concerning the Indian Wars and other occurrences in western Virginia before and during the American Revolution, was issued in the spring of 1833. This proved to be the only volume in the series, for between 1835 and 1837 the society's publications[2] appeared in the pages of the *Southern Literary Messenger.* After the annual meeting of 20 February 1838, the society became inactive for nearly a decade. The reason for this sudden and complete collapse is unknown; perhaps Dr. Cushing's untimely death in 1835 had left the society without a pilot.

The society's possessions and its corporate existence were somehow preserved through these lean years. An effort to move the base of operations to the University of Virginia was defeated in 1846; early in the following year a resuscitation was achieved in Richmond, at which time the organization's name was unofficially shortened to the Virginia Historical Society. Rooms were obtained in a new building at Franklin and 12th Streets, overlooking Capitol Square and the Governor's garden, which remained the society's home until 1852 when the city provided rent-free quarters in the Athenæum Building. From 1848 William Maxwell, secretary of the society, issued quarterly *The Virginia Historical Register, and Literary Advertiser* under his own imprint "to furnish the Virginia Historical Society . . . with a convenient organ with its members and the Public." After the appearance of six volumes, Mr. Maxwell

2. Clayton Torrance, *et al.,* "The Semi-Centennial of the Virginia Magazine of History and Biography," *Virginia Magazine of History and Biography* LI (1943), 217–282, contains a bibliography of the society's publications to that date.

discontinued publication of the *Historical Register*, as it was commonly called, with the October 1853 issue. The next year it was replaced
by *The Virginia Historical Reporter conducted by the Executive Committee of the Virginia Historical Society*, which, through 1860, afforded
means for publishing the proceedings of annual meetings and
addresses.

An endowment fund begun in the early 1850s had by careful
saving and hard work reached the sum of $4,614.50 in 1861. With
the outbreak of war the state and city bonds in which this fund had
been invested were at once sold and the proceeds lent to the Confederate Government. Wartime exigencies of space forced the
Virginia Historical Society to shift quarters and store its possessions
where it could. Fortunately some of them survived the great fire of
April 1865 that destroyed so much of Richmond, but the society
emerged from four years of war without funds and without quarters. From January 1866 onwards, the executive committee met
occasionally in an effort to bring together the scattered fragments.
With a population containing a high proportion of widows and
children, whose personal resources had vanished along the same
road as the society's, there was small prospect of financial support
from the local scene, however much good will there might be. In
the spring of 1868, the Massachusetts Historical Society showed its
friendship and its confidence in the future of the Virginia Historical
Society by sending to its colleagues in Richmond the original manuscript of a narrative of Bacon's Rebellion and a number of volumes
of its own publications. In the same spirit W. W. Corcoran of
Washington gave $100, while other gifts were received from John
William Wallace, president of the Historical Society of Pennsylvania, from W. W. Galt of Washington, and James T. Suttor of New
York.

Regular meetings were resumed in 1870. Hugh Blair Grigsby
was elected president; a committee was appointed to consider the
publication of a periodical; and $500 was raised towards the replac-
ing of the lost endowment. By act of the General Assembly on 11

July 1870 the name "Virginia Historical Society" became the legal title of the organization, thus regularizing a usage that had been common for the previous twenty-two years. From this revival the Virginia Historical Society was once more in regular operation, although gravely hindered for more than twenty years by lack of funds and adequate quarters. The papers of Alexander Spotswood, Lieutenant-Governor of Virginia, 1710–22, were purchased in 1873. Thus in difficult times the society reaffirmed its responsibility for preserving the sources of the early history of Virginia. Although numerous Confederate books and pamphlets were acquired, the society wisely steered away from relics and objects of purely sentimental interest by advising would-be donors to give such objects to the Confederate Museum.

Under the direction of Robert Alonzo Brock, who was elected corresponding secretary in 1875, a remarkable resurgence of publications occurred. Eleven volumes of a new series of *Collections*, containing documents of high importance for Virginia history of the seventeenth and eighteenth century, were edited by him in the decade following 1882. In that year Brock published the first volume of the Spotswood letters, which had been bought in 1873; the second volume appeared in 1885. *The Official Records of Robert Dinwiddie, Lieutenant-Governor of the Colony of Virginia, 1751–1758*, the originals of which had been given to the society in 1881 by W. W. Corcoran with $500 to aid in their publication, followed in two volumes, issued in 1883 and 1884. Then came in 1886 and 1887 two volumes of miscellaneous documents relating to Huguenot emigration to Virginia and other subjects, and in 1888 and 1889 two volumes of *Abstract of the Proceedings of the Virginia Company of London, 1619–1624*. The two-volume *History of the Federal Convention of 1788, with some account of the Eminent Virginians of that era who were members of the body*, by Hugh Blair Grigsby, who had continued in the presidency of the society until his death in 1881, appeared in 1890 and 1891. The eleventh and final volume of this new series of *Collections* contained a group of papers relating to various aspects of

Virginia history that had been prepared for the annual meeting of 21–22 December 1891, at the suggestion of Dr. Lyon G. Tyler, as a means of popularizing the activities of the Virginia Historical Society.

These eleven volumes appearing in the course of ten years would, in quality as well as quantity, represent a distinguished accomplishment for any historical society; in the light of postwar conditions in Virginia they are even more remarkable. Although R. A. Brock was clearly responsible for them, he was in 1892 unceremoniously dumped out of office in a palace revolution, the motives of which are not clear at this distance of time. That it was something of a fracas may be gathered from blank pages in the society's record book, where the account of the annual meeting of 22 December 1892 should have been entered. From newspaper reports it appears that Brock failed of re-election by a single vote, while Joseph Bryan became president in place of William Wirt Henry.

Whatever the motives of this change may have been, the society replaced one able scholar with another, for Brock's successor as corresponding secretary and librarian was Philip Alexander Bruce, the future author of the *Economic History of Virginia in the Seventeenth Century, Institutional History of Virginia in the Seventeenth Century, Social Life in Virginia in the Seventeenth Century, History of the University of Virginia 1819–1919,* and *The Virginia Plutarch.* Bruce soon shifted the form of the Virginia Historical Society's publications from volumes of *Collections* to a quarterly magazine of the pattern established fifteen years earlier by the Historical Society of Pennsylvania. The first issue of *The Virginia Magazine of History and Biography* appeared in July 1893. While each number contained certain pages of proceedings and a genealogical section, the *Magazine* was remarkable for its richness in documentary publications of lasting value. It very early received high commendation from Edward Channing, Worthington C. Ford, James Schouler, John Fiske, and Theodore Roosevelt. When Mr. Bruce retired from office in 1898 to devote his time to his own writing, William G. Stannard became editor of the *Magazine* and continued in that post for thirty-five years. *The Virginia Magazine of History and Biography*, like its Pennsylvania prototype, has proved to be a permanent and substantial contribution to historical literature, for volume LXX is being published in the course of 1962. Since 1954 it has been ably edited by Mr. William M. E. Rachal.

A temporary solution to the housing problem was achieved in 1879 when the Virginia Historical Society accepted the offer of the Westmoreland Club in Richmond to provide space for its books, manuscripts, and portraits. While this arrangement got the society in out of the rain for thirteen years, it had its obvious disadvantages, for the occupation of rooms in a private social club necessarily made the library practically inaccessible to the general membership. In 1892 Mrs. John Stewart and her daughters offered the society the use of a three-story brick house at 707 East Franklin Street that had been the wartime Richmond home of General Robert E. Lee and his family. Although Mrs. Stewart's original proposal had been a ten-year lease, during which time she would pay all taxes, she altered it to an outright gift, with the sole condition that if the house ceased to be used by the society it should revert to her heirs. When the society took possession in April 1893, the eight large and four small rooms of the Lee House, as it was generally called, offered more than ample space for its possessions. There it remained for over sixty-five years, with overcrowding increasing in proportion to the steady growth of the collections.

After thirty-one years at 707 East Franklin Street, when things had become uncomfortably tight, Mr. and Mrs. Alexander W. Weddell made a singular and generous proposal. They were in 1924 in the process of building Virginia House[3] at 4301 Sulgrave Road in the new Windsor Farms section overlooking the James River, west of Richmond. The Weddells had bought in England an immense amount of building material obtained after the demolition of Warwick Priory, which they were incorporating into a great new Tudor house of considerable charm. This they proposed upon its

3. Alexander W. Weddell, *A Description of Virginia House* (Richmond, 1947).

completion to share with the Virginia Historical Society. The suggestion was appealing, but in the end was rejected as impracticable. Even with new space in Virginia House, the society would have been obliged to retain the Lee House for many of its collections. The society's endowment at this time was under $30,000. The expense of caring for two separate installations, several miles apart, would have been too great for such slender resources, while the Weddells began to see the problems that might arise from the generous attempt to share a part of their house and grounds with a public organization. The difficulty was solved by withdrawing their original proposal and instead conveying Virginia House to the Virginia Historical Society on 31 May 1929, retaining only a life tenure for themselves. Thus the property would eventually come to the society, with a substantial endowment, for occupancy after their deaths.

Although the society remained in the Lee House, to which a fireproof wing for the library and picture storage was added in 1934, Virginia House was in May 1929 the scene of a great public loan exhibition of colonial portraits illustrative of Virginia history, which brought together for the first time many pictures that had never been previously seen. Mr. Weddell participated actively in the assembly of the exhibition and edited the 556-page *Memorial Volume of Virginia Historical Portraiture* that the society published in 1930 as a permanent record of the exhibition. While he was long absent from Richmond in service as Ambassador to Argentina and Spain from 1933 to 1942, his interest in the society's affairs was unfailing. In 1945, upon his retirement from the foreign service, he prepared another publication, *Portraiture in the Virginia Historical Society*.

Virginia House became the property of the Virginia Historical Society far sooner than anyone would have wished or anticipated, due to the tragic death of both Mr. and Mrs. Weddell in a wreck on the Missouri Pacific Railroad on New Year's Day 1948. With the house and gardens were received funds more than adequate for their upkeep, which greatly strengthened the society's general financial situation. At the end of 1961 the Virginia Historical Society's investments had a book value of $1,479,834.36 and a market value of $3,513,208.65. Of this endowment more than 88% was received from the Weddell bequests.

Virginia House is today regularly open to visitors. It is a fine building in itself, superbly furnished and admirably fitted for certain types of gatherings of the society. It is a valuable reminder of the England that seventeenth-century settlers of the New World left behind them. No other historical society in the United States enjoys a setting better suited to the handsome reception of its guests. Yet Virginia House is an appropriate possession for the society solely because its generous builders bequeathed with it funds more than adequate for its upkeep. Otherwise it would have been a most unsuitable white elephant. As it is, less than one quarter of the income received from the Weddells is annually required for the maintenance of their house; the remainder is of great service to the general purposes of the society.

The Weddell bequest was, however, far from solving all problems of its recipient. While Virginia House is extremely attractive to the casual visitor, it in no way relieved extreme overcrowding at the Lee House, where the chief research activities were carried out. It bore little relation to the announced purposes of the Virginia Historical Society, which are:

1. To collect, preserve, and make available to students and scholars the diverse materials which might permit a thorough study of the history of Virginia.

2. To publish documentary materials, monographic studies, biographical compilations, bibliographical lists, and indexes that might facilitate the study of Virginia history.

3. To sponsor lectures that might stimulate interest in Virginia history.

4. To encourage research projects and programs that might promote Virginia historical scholarship.

5. To collect, maintain, and exhibit a representative collection of Virginia historical portraiture.

The society's acceptance in 1946 of the Confederate Memorial Institute, popularly known as Battle Abbey,[4] at 428 North Boulevard in Richmond had added still another handsome amenity that, while of interest to the casual visitor, was equally peripheral to these fundamental scholarly purposes. This institution owed its being to the generous sentiment of Charles Broadway Rouse, a native of Winchester and sometime private soldier of the Army of Northern Virginia, who, having later prospered in the ready-made clothing business, wished to establish a permanent memorial to the Confederate cause. In 1896 he offered to give $100,000 for such a building, provided that the people of the whole south raise a like sum. Richmond was chosen as the ideal location. Mr. Rouse's lofty aspiration was not reflected in the activities of certain persons who undertook to handle the money raising. In fact the early years of the Confederate Memorial Association offer a classical example of the way in which skulduggery may enter into popular appeals for memorial, sentimental, or patriotic purposes. Due to these misfortunes, the laying of a cornerstone was deferred until 20 May 1912, while Battle Abbey was only finally completed after World War I.

It was a handsome limestone building, placed in grounds occupying two city blocks that were superbly planted with *allées* of magnolias and great mounds of box. It contained three lofty exhibition rooms. To the right of the entrance was a moving display of massed Confederate battle flags;[5] to the left a gallery of dramatic mural paintings of the four seasons of the armed forces of the Confederacy by Charles Hoffbauer. Dead ahead a third exhibition room offered an undistinguished series of military portraits, seemingly painted in boot blacking, from photographs, that only a relative of a subject could even tolerate, plus a collection of Civil War weapons. Battle

4. George L. Christian, *Sketch of the Origin and Erection of the Confederate Memorial Institute at Richmond, Virginia* (Richmond, n.d.); Robert L. Scribner, "Born of Battle," *Virginia Cavalcade* III, 3 (Winter 1953), pp. 24–32, reprinted in *American Heritage* V, 3 (Spring 1954), pp. 32–40.
5. *The Returned Battleflags of the Virginia Regiments in the War between the States* (Richmond, n.d.).

Abbey, save for the portraits, was a first-rate although static commemorative monument of one moment in the three and a half centuries of Virginia's history. When Douglas Southall Freeman first took me there in the spring of 1946, I was greatly moved by the place; such was his enthusiasm that I have ever since had a special affection for it.

By the time of my first visit, the generation that had built Battle Abbey had largely followed the Confederate veterans that it commemorated, and the future of the building was precarious. Aided by Dr. Freeman's eloquence, the Virginia Historical Society was shortly after induced to absorb the Confederate Memorial Institute which owned the building. By a merger completed on 30 August 1946, all assets of the association were transferred to the society. Since that date the Commonwealth of Virginia has continued the annual grant of $3,000 that it formerly made to the association for the upkeep of the building, in return for free admission of school children. I could fully appreciate the willingness of the Virginia Historical Society to ensure the proper preservation of this handsome and touching memorial. Nevertheless its acceptance involved still another problem in real estate maintenance that was peripheral to the main purposes of the society.

Thus in the mid-fifties the Virginia Historical Society possessed three properties of very different character in widely separated parts of Richmond, no one of which was in any way suitable for the present accommodation of its research and publication functions, let alone their future growth and expansion. It was in the situation of being real-estate-poor, for admission fees paid by visitors produced scarcely a third of the annual cost of maintaining and insuring the three properties.

The solution achieved was admirable in its simplicity. To provide adequate stack space and reading rooms for the library and manuscript collections, as well as working areas for the staff, a new wing was added in the rear of Battle Abbey. The Lee House was given to the Confederate Memorial Literary Society, the owner of the White

House of the Confederacy, which has reopened it. This transfer was completed in the spring of 1959. Eppa Hunton IV, chairman of the building committee, reported to the annual meeting of the society in January 1959:

As the project has progressed, we have been impressed more and more by the wisdom of the Executive Committee's decision to incorporate the old Battle Abbey building and the new structure into one edifice.

The old building, with its handsome entrance hall and exhibit galleries and its commodious storage areas, could hardly be duplicated under present conditions at a cost of less than $1,000,000. But the total cost of revamping the structure and adding 30,000 square feet of new construction on the rear will barely exceed $550,000. Thus, with a relatively modest expenditure, the Society has obtained a headquarters and library building, fireproof and air-conditioned throughout and containing a total of 60,000 square feet of usable space, that has a replacement value in excess of $1,500,000. The building is surrounded, moreover, by seven and one-half acres of beautifully landscaped grounds, owned in fee simple by the Society.

The establishment of our headquarters within these premises infuses life into a fabric which was in danger of being merely the mausoleum of a lost cause. The memory of our dignified and valiant Confederates, in whose honor the building was originally conceived, could not be more effectively served and kept alive than through the operations of the Virginia Historical Society. This does not imply that the Civil War will become our major field of interest. But the fact remains that the history of Virginia and that of the Confederacy are uniquely and inextricably intertwined. Indeed, the history of Virginia, from the date of its settlement in 1607, is a heritage which we share with the South in particular, as well as with the entire United States.

The building is ideally adapted for the work—present and future—of a serious historical society. Architecturally it harmonizes inconspicuously on the exterior with the older structure that it enlarges. This in 1960 is a conspicuous achievement, for many architects of the day appear to design their buildings with indifference to, if not actually defiant disregard of, their surroundings. Often in their attempts to attract attention to their work they resemble the small boy who thumbs his nose, wiggles his ears, and sticks out his tongue simultaneously. The Irish poet Stephen Rynne remarked that he could not praise a new church in Cork because of "its sin against architectural charity in striking such a discordant note with its neighbor." Here that sin has been skillfully and gracefully avoided on the exterior. Within, the new wing is functional in the truest sense, for it has been designed with its use in mind, and executed in the simplest, most serviceable and economical of materials. Nothing has been squandered on bronze and marble, for the existing entrance to Battle Abbey provided all the monumentality that anyone could require.

Formerly the visitor came to Battle Abbey, spent an hour at most in reflective contemplation of the battle flags and the murals, and went away again. Today the front rooms have lost none of their old nostalgic quality, although they are considerably cleaner and handsomer; the back room contains fine Virginia portraits of an earlier period, and, most important of all, it leads to a well-designed library and manuscript room, where the serious worker may happily pass as many hours, days, or weeks as he can spare in the company of the true treasures of the Virginia Historical Society.

The construction of this admirable building was accomplished through a grant of $200,000 from the Old Dominion Foundation and the raising of close to twice that sum from members and friends of the society. It has not only provided the best working quarters of any privately supported state historical society in the country; it has also consolidated the property of the Virginia Historical Society by reducing the number of its establishments from three to two, with consequent economies in operation.

The manuscript collection of the Virginia Historical Society contains approximately 500,000 items, running from 1607 to the present, that relate chiefly to Virginia and the south. The papers of prominent colonial leaders in Virginia include those of the two William Byrds, Chief Justice Paul Carrington, and Lieutenant Governors Robert Dinwiddie and Alexander Spotswood. Among the political leaders of the Revolution and the early years of the Federal Government, Thomas Jefferson, Francis Lightfoot Lee, Richard Henry Lee,

William Lee, James Madison, John Marshall, James Monroe, John Randolph of Roanoke, and George Washington are substantially represented in the collection. There are holdings, significant both in size and importance, of the papers of Robert E. Lee and Matthew Fontaine Maury, as well as colonial records of the General Court of Virginia, the Council of Virginia, and the House of Burgesses. A curator of manuscripts is in charge of the collection.

The library contains approximately 100,000 printed books and pamphlets, concentrated chiefly on the history of Virginia, that of the Confederate States of America, and English local history. Within the major fields of interest are sizable collections of early Virginia imprints, Confederate imprints, English county histories, and architectural treatises that are believed to have influenced taste in colonial Virginia. There are some 500 bound volumes of Virginia newspapers and over 10,000 unbound issues, including the only surviving copies of the *Virginia Gazette*, Virginia's first newspaper, covering the first four years of publication, 1736–40. In collecting newspapers, the society concentrates on eighteenth- and nineteenth-century Virginia issues of the period prior to the introduction of wood pulp paper stock; other institutional libraries throughout the State have assumed the responsibility, on a co-operative basis, for preserving twentieth-century files of the newspapers published in their respective areas.

A map collection of over 5,000 items includes good examples of the early Virginia cartographic landmarks (Ferrar, Fry and Jefferson, Henry, and Madison) and the original manuscript maps of the Virginia counties prepared by the Confederate Corps of Engineers. The print and photograph collection contains some 20,000 items, all focused on Virginia, with unintended emphasis on portraiture and architecture. Among the 300 broadsides are unique examples of eighteenth- and early nineteenth-century Virginia imprints, as well as otherwise unrecorded Confederate imprints. A music collection of 500 titles is weak save in materials on the Confederacy. Among the 2,500 examples of obsolete paper currency are important holdings of eighteenth-century Virginia notes and exceptionally fine assemblages of Confederate and Confederate State notes and bonds. The society also collects printed ephemera of a local nature.

A curator of rare books and a cataloger of printed books, both with graduate degrees in library science, are responsible for the care of the library, while an editor, with graduate work and teaching experience in American history, deals with the society's publications.

Although the *Virginia Magazine of History and Biography* has been for the past seventy years the society's principal vehicle for publication, several books have been issued since World War II. These are George MacLaren Brydon's *Virginia's mother church and the political conditions under which it grew* (1947); Ralph T. Whitelaw's *Virginia's Eastern Shore* (1951); *The Spanish Jesuit Mission in Virginia* (1953); Marshall W. Fishwick's *General Lee's photographer, the life and work of Michael Miley* (1954); Richard L. Morton's edition (1956) of *The present state of Virginia* by Hugh Jones; and Laura Polanyi Striker's edition (1957) of Henry Wharton's *The life of John Smith, English soldier*. Between 1953 and 1959 Frank E. Vandiver edited three volumes of the proceedings of the Confederate Congress from 7 December 1863 to 18 March 1865, which the society published as volumes L–LII (and last) of the *Southern Historical Society Papers*. *Colonial Virginia*, by Professor Richard L. Morton of the College of William and Mary, was published in November 1960. In 1961 the society issued Angus James Johnston II's *Virginia Railroads in the Civil War* as well as two volumes in a new series of Virginia Historical Documents: *The Poems of Charles Hansford*, edited by James A. Servies and Carl R. Dolmetsch, and *Four Years in the Confederate Artillery: The Diary of Private Henry Robinson Berkeley*, edited by William H. Runge. *William Fitzhugh and His Chesapeake World: 1676–1701*, a study by Dr. Richard Beale Davis of the University of Tennessee, based on the letter books of a leading planter of colonial Virginia, is scheduled to appear in the autumn of 1962.

Although visitors are welcome at Virginia House and in the exhibition rooms at Battle Abbey, and many come, the society does not attempt to maintain a museum as such, nor does it seek to attract crowds for their own sake. It prefers to concentrate its efforts upon making its resources available to those who have serious need of them. Some 1,200 researchers, on the average, turn up in person during the course of a calendar year to examine the collection of source materials, while an equal number of written requests for information of a serious nature are received during the same period of time. The library is open, without charge, to anyone who professes to be engaged in historical research, but casual browsers and "junior historians" are discouraged, whenever possible, from using the collections. The main users of the manuscript collection consist of professional historians, graduate students, popular historical writers, and, of course, genealogists; over 60% of the persons who appear in the society's search room are from outside Virginia.

At a 1954 conference sponsored by the American Association for State and Local History, Mr. William M. E. Rachal, editor of the Virginia Historical Society, made, during the discussion following a paper, this comment,[6] which summarizes succinctly the theory of operation of other societies than his own:

We, like every other historical society, unless it be one of those midwestern ones that tap the public treasury, have limited resources, and we are faced with this problem: at what level should we operate as an educational institution? We decided that our function was to serve at the top level, i.e. to supply the source materials. For that reason we decided that the funds we have for publication will be used for source materials. Every day we get quite a volume of mail reading, "I am in the fifth grade and I am writing to you for a picture of your state flag," or "Will you send me everything you have on Thomas Jefferson? We are studying him in the fourth grade." We have a form letter that tells the writers that we do not have anything for them. I think that the historical society has to determine what its function is as an educational institution and not scatter its shot too much. For that reason we collect source material. We would rather pay $1,500 for one rare source book than buy fifteen hundred general books at a dollar apiece. And if we have a $1,500 book, then we are not particularly anxious to have the junior high school students prepare their papers in our library. We don't throw them out; we try to be as nice to them as we can, but we are not encouraging them to come down there. We

6. James H. Rodabaugh, *The Present World of History* (Madison, Wis., 1959), p. 18.

would rather have one university professor stay fifteen days in our library than one junior high school pupil stay fifteen minutes.

In the president's report for 1959, Dr. Wyndham B. Blanton wrote with respect to the future only a few days before his death on 6 January 1960:

We find ourselves today as Emerson in 1822 found the then new quarters of the Boston Athenæum, "royally fitted up for elegance and comfort." This is a pleasing situation but one not devoid of danger. A state of serene satisfaction can paralyze activity. The urge to bivouac even when marching orders are in hand can be a temptation. As far as your officers are concerned I assure you no sit-down program is contemplated.

The Virginia Historical Society exists for the purpose of discovering, acquiring, preserving and disseminating historical knowledge about Virginia. The renovation of Battle Abbey and the erection and occupation of a new library puts us well on the road to the realization of one of these goals. . . .

As is well known our present holdings consist of approximately 100,000 printed books, 500,000 manuscripts, 25,000 newspapers, and a great mass of cognate material. This is impressive but it represents by no means an exhaustive collection of Virginiana. And so we must continue to expand our collections. At the same time it is well to remember that the unrestrained acquisitive instinct may easily assume Gargantuan proportions. Without willingness to be selective and to expand primarily in depth, without determined courage in culling, hungry book shelves, display cases, and archives may soon cease to reflect that spirit of specialized excellence to which we aspire. There can be little disagreement with the idea that there should also continue to exist areas of emphasis within the framework of this general program. There are lists detailing what we *have* in the way of valuable manuscript and printed books. I know of no list which reflects what we *have not*.

In the matter of printed books there is room for considerable selective expansion. Briefly stated our present needs lie in the direction of more seventeenth-century tracts of Virginia interest, eighteenth-century Virginia imprints, Confederate imprints, American Colonial histories, English local source materials, additional bibliographical and other reference works, items in such specialized fields as seventeenth- and eighteenth-century prints and engravings of Virginia interest, books on cookery, farming, and sports, sheet music, Virginia newspapers prior to 1890, maps, and ephemerae, such as broadsides, invitations, programs and so forth.

The need for expanding our manuscript collections is even more urgent. It is later than most of us realize, and now is the time, if ever, to enlarge it with original material and with photocopies of original material, such as family and personal papers (letters, diaries, letter books, account books). Obviously many manuscripts dealing with Virginia and important to us are already permanently resident in other historical libraries. Funds must be made available for microfilming and photographing this type of material. . . .

With our growth the making available and the dissemination of historical knowledge relating to Virginia has become increasingly important. But the temptation to overzealousness may lead to a hydra-headed program, the very mention of which raises the blood pressure of our professional friends who envision split level activities and the popularization of history at the expense of scholarship. It should be understood that we take our stand for scholarship, now as always. To this end basic research is fundamental. We seek to promote it with every means at our disposal. It is not enough to furnish serious students with comfortable and efficient working conditions. To satisfy their real needs, it is our responsibility to fill as rapidly as possible those lacunae in our collection already alluded to.

While the Virginia Historical Society has no formal or official relationship with neighboring universities and colleges, it is bound to them by many personal ties. Among the present members of its executive committee are Dr. Earl G. Swem, librarian-emeritus of the College of William and Mary, whose *Virginia Historical Index* is one of the most monumental works of scholarly reference of our time, and Francis L. Berkeley Jr., keeper of manuscripts at the University of Virginia. The president of Hampden-Sydney College and members of the board of visitors of the College of William and Mary, the University of Virginia, and the Medical College of Virginia are among other members of the executive committee today; a similar representation has prevailed throughout the society's history. The present director, Mr. John Melville Jennings, who was a student of Dr. Swem's, came to the society as librarian in 1948 after service as curator of rare books and manuscripts at the College of William and Mary. In recent years the society has published books by professors of history at the College of William and Mary and at Washington and Lee University. It is, moreover, committed to publishing others by faculty members of the University of Virginia and the College of William and Mary whenever the dilatory authors submit their completed manuscripts.

A grant made by the society to Mr. Berkeley for a preliminary exploration of British manuscript repositories for early sources relating to the history of Virginia was the beginning of the Virginia Colonial Records Project, which has brought to this country in the form of microfilm a vast amount of new source material that will be of value to a distant future. Although originally conceived as a preparation for the 350th anniversary of the Jamestown landings, this project still continues. Julian P. Boyd, in appraising Virginia's historical activities in 1957, observed that "one of its most inspiring, most useful, and most enduring accomplishments will very likely turn out to be the gathering of the vast historical records that will help us to understand as well as to commemorate."[7] This project is under the joint sponsorship of the University of Virginia, the Virginia State Library, and the Virginia Historical Society; Mr. Jennings, the director, represents the society on its four-member guiding committee. In another major scholarly enterprise, Mr. Rachal, the society's editor, represents the University of Virginia on the editorial board of *The Papers of James Madison*.

Although the Virginia Historical Society has a membership of over 2,000, members have in recent years proved an expensive luxury rather than a source of financial support. As of 30 June 1960, there were 1,702 annual members at $10; 31 annual supporting at $25; 5 annual sustaining at $50; and 317 life members who had made a single payment of $100. The total, including honorary members and libraries, was 2,354. During the five-year period 1954–58, the annual average income from dues was only $10,944, while the average annual disbursements for members in defraying the cost of their subscriptions to the *Virginia Magazine*, postage, meetings, and entertainments came to $20,058.49. Thus every member added increased the drain upon endowment income by a sum roughly equivalent to the dues that he paid!

To remedy this pointless situation, the lowest annual dues were

7. Julian P. Boyd, "A New Guide to the Indispensable Sources of Virginia History," *William and Mary Quarterly*, 3rd ser., XV (1958), 3–13.

raised from $5 to $10, effective 1 July 1959. In the year that followed, all annual members were billed at the new rate: 83% paid without comment or protest, 7.6% resigned, and 9.4% had not been heard from. Some of the latter were expected to pay, and others to be dropped as delinquent. While the number of resignations was greater than in previous years, they were offset by an almost equal number of new elections. As of 31 December 1961 there were 2,366 members.

The only public support received by the Virginia Historical Society is the yearly appropriation of $3,000 from the Commonwealth of Virginia towards the upkeep of Battle Abbey. Of the estimated income of $178,613.76 in the 1962 budget, $100,000 is derived from endowment, of which, as has previously been noted, the greatest part came from the gifts of Mr. and Mrs. Alexander W. Weddell. For general operating expenses $28,220 was allocated; $37,165 for buildings and grounds; $40,242 for the library; $10,228 for the museum; and $30,984 for publications. This division includes the salaries for the various departments.

The Virginia Historical Society weathered difficult storms during its first fifty years; indeed it is only within the past fifteen years that it came into possession of any substantial endowment. Almost all of that came from a husband and wife who were singularly devoted to its serious purposes. Today it has highly commodious quarters for its library, an imaginative and energetic staff, and friends who add superbly to its manuscript resources. Early in 1960 a member of the Lee family presented, without fanfare of trumpets, a group of "family papers," which included some twenty George Washington holographs, a score of letters writtten to Washington by Jacky Custis, letters written by or to Anne Hill (Carter) Lee, letters of both "Lighthorse" and "Blackhorse" Harry Lee, over 120 Robert E. Lee holographs to his wife and to his son Rooney, and even a letter or two written by William Byrd to John Custis.

These things have occurred because the society, even in its leanest years, devoted such means as it had to the collection, preservation, and dissemination of the sources of Virginia history. While it is better off today than it has ever been before, it will need additional support in the future to maintain its scholarly usefuness. The fact that it has been able within very recent years to achieve its present building with the aid of the Old Dominion Foundation and a relatively small number of private supporters indicates that an independent historical society can obtain needed support without lowering its sights from its scholarly functions.

Chapter VII

THE MIDDLE STATES

I have observed, in regard to all the literary and scientific societies
with which I have ever been connected, that, however numerous
the members, some dozen or two of them performed almost all the
work.   —REV. SAMUEL MILLER, 1845

NEW JERSEY, Maryland, and Delaware, although they
were settled early, were slow in forming historical societies
to collect and preserve the records of their rich and varied
colonial history. They were preceded by Ohio in 1831 and Georgia
in 1839 in the establishment of organizations that have usefully
continued to the present day, and which will be described in a later
chapter. The Maryland Historical Society was only founded in 1844;
that in New Jersey the following year, while Delaware was, as Leslie W. Dunlap has pointed out, the only state east of Texas that had
not established such an organization by the outbreak of the Civil
War.

NEW JERSEY

The Reverend Samuel Miller (1769–1850) of the Wall Street Presbyterian Church in New York City had, at the age of thirty-five,
joined John Pintard in the establishment of the New-York Historical
Society, of which he was corresponding secretary from 1805 to 1813.
Forty years later, as one of the founders of the New Jersey Historical
Society, he offered the new organization the practical observation
that heads this chapter. It was based upon experience, for after four

decades the New York body had still not struggled out of the woods although it was nearing open country.

Appleton P. C. Griffin's *Bibliography of American Historical Societies* begins its listing of the publications of the New Jersey Historical Society with a *Constitution and by-laws, with the circular of the executive committee*, printed at Newark in 1818. This seems to have been a false alarm, for the society claims today that it was founded by twenty men who gathered at Trenton on 13 January 1845, in spite of a raging blizzard. Its announced objects were "to discover, procure and preserve whatever related to any department of the history of New Jersey, natural, civil, literary or ecclesiastical; and generally of other portions of the United States." Dr. Miller proposed, in an address delivered at a meeting in Princeton on 4 September 1845, that a history of each town and county in New Jersey should be written. While meetings were early held in various parts of the State, the society's library was, from June 1847, located in the building of the Newark Library Association, notwithstanding objections voiced by members from other regions. By 1860 the collection amounted to some 2,500 volumes and 3,500 pamphlets. Committees were appointed within the first decade to obtain vital statistics and personal biographical information from distinguished citizens of the State. While gravestone inscriptions antedating 1800 were copied in five towns, the attempt to collect personal narratives—an early anticipation of present-day enthusiasm for "oral history"—came to very little for "want of co-operation on the part of those who alone possessed the requisite information."

Dr. Miller's observation about a small number of members performing almost all the work was conspicuously borne out in the New Jersey Historical Society. During the first four decades, it was a single man, William A. Whitehead, corresponding secretary from 1845 to 1884, who was responsible for its most permanent achievements. In 1845 Whitehead inaugurated the *Proceedings*; the following year his *East Jersey under the proprietary governments* was published as the first volume of a series of *Collections*. He eventually wrote or edited five of the first seven volumes of these. As in Rhode Island, the *Collections* consisted of entire volumes on separate subjects rather than containing groups of miscellaneous documents.

Volume V (1858), *An analytical index to the colonial documents of New Jersey, in the state-paper offices of England*, compiled by Henry Stevens and edited by Whitehead, represents an important instance of private enterprise where public support was not forthcoming. The New-York Historical Society had been successful in persuading its state government to undertake the search for pertinent documents in British archives. As the New Jersey Assembly not only turned down a similar proposal in 1843 and 1845, but in 1850 rebuked the New Jersey Historical Society for making a third request, funds for the project were obtained by private subscription. The 1,800 cards prepared by Henry Stevens describing New Jersey documents from 1664 to 1775, which were received in Newark in September 1851, caused the Legislature to change its mind and appropriate $500 for buying copies of the index if it should be published! Other volumes in the *Collections* were *The life of William Alexander, Earl of Sterling*; *The provincial courts of New Jersey*; *The papers of Lewis Morris, governor of the province of New Jersey, from 1738 to 1746*; *Records of the town of Newark, N.J., from its settlement in 1666 to its incorporation as a city in 1836*; and *The Constitution and government of the province and State of New Jersey, with biographical sketches of the governors from 1776 to 1845*. The twelfth and latest volume in the *Collections* is *Juet's Journal, The Voyage of the* Half Moon *from 4 April to 7 November 1609*, edited by Robert M. Lunny, with an introduction by John T. Cunningham, which was published in 1959 on the 350th anniversary of Henry Hudson's third voyage.

William A. Whitehead also inaugurated in 1880, and edited the first eight volumes of, the important series of documents known under the general title of *New Jersey Archives*. His successor, William Nelson, who served into the present century, was also a prolific writer, who edited the next sixteen volumes of the series, as well as the *Proceedings* for thirty years. The forty-two volumes of the first series of *New Jersey Archives* include ten (with a general index) of colonial documents from 1631 to 1776, eleven of abstracts from American newspapers relating to New Jersey from 1704 to 1775, six of the Journal of the Governor and Council, 1682–1775, as well as numerous abstracts of wills and early vital records. Five volumes of a second series have carried the extracts from newspapers relating to the State through the year 1782.

The intelligent industry of Whitehead and Nelson thus gave the nineteenth-century output of the New Jersey Historical Society a distinguished position in documentary publication. Leslie W. Dunlap, after remarking that American historical societies—of which there had been sixty-five established—published more than 500 separate works before the Civil War, thus analyzed their origin:

This activity was participated in by all except ten short-lived organizations. However, in no field was the dominance of large institutions more apparent, for ten societies issued about three-fourths of the titles. Five of the ten, the American Antiquarian Society, and the state associations of Massachusetts, New York, Pennsylvania, and Maryland, published more than the total of the other fifty. Less than a fourth of all the publications contain more than eighty pages, and these came from seventeen organizations. The institutions in Boston, New York, Newark, and Philadelphia issued at least two-thirds of the longer works.

Although the New Jersey Historical Society continued to publish very actively during the remainder of the nineteenth century, the pre-eminent position that it held before 1860 has not been maintained in more modern times. Its *Proceedings* continue today as a quarterly magazine of New Jersey history, although with such features as an "Antiquer's Attic" and a "Genealogist's Corner"; volume LXIX appeared in 1961. Since 1958 it has been supplemented by the *New Jersey Messenger*, a four-page periodical designed "to provide a newsy contact with the members, informing them of current historical events and activities, with small articles and other tid-bits of New Jersey historical interest."

Since 1931 the New Jersey Historical Society has been installed in an attractive fireproof building at 230 Broadway in Newark, designed to accommodate its library and museum. The library, which claims to be the best single collection devoted exclusively to the history of the State, consists of some 30,000 bound volumes, which include many early New Jersey imprints, plus bound volumes of newspapers, and some thousands of reels of microfilm. The 80,000 manuscripts have been described in *A Guide to the Manuscripts Collection of the New Jersey Historical Society*, published in 1957. This was the work of Mr. Fred Shelley, then librarian, who has since become head of the Presidential Papers Section in the Manuscript Division of the Library of Congress.

A substantial part of the building is given over to the museum, whose collections illustrate the history of New Jersey from the earliest settlement to the present. Exhibits range from fine eighteenth-century furniture in period rooms of 1775 to the varnished wainscoting of a kitchen of 1875 in the Victorian Gallery, in which a long-suffering housewife bends over a well-blacked coal range. In addition to permanent displays of paintings and decorative arts, maps and prints, New Jersey transportation by land, water, and sea, various temporary exhibitions are arranged from time to time. An attractive group of snow scenes by George Henry Durrie, lent by Mr. and Mrs. P. H. B. Frelinghuysen of Morristown in the winter of 1959, showed the immense superiority of Durrie's oils to the popular lithographs made from them by Currier and Ives. In the spring and summer of 1960 a loan exhibition "The Thoroughbred Horse of New Jersey," cosponsored by the Thoroughbred Horse Breeders' Association of New Jersey, was shown not only at the society's building but at Garden State Park and Monmouth Park. It was estimated that at Monmouth Park this pictorial review of the history of thoroughbred breeding and racing in New Jersey was visited by 40,000 persons. A sixteen-page offset picture book, with text prepared by Peter Cole and Ronald C. Weyer, was published in connection with the exhibition. In the winter of 1960–61 an exhibition of "Early Maps of North America," was sponsored by C. S. Hammond and Company, map makers of Maplewood, New Jersey, to commemorate their sixtieth anniversary, with a distinguished selection of maps, charts, and globes lent by the Library of Congress, the American Geographical Society, the libraries of Rutgers and Yale, the New York and Newark Public libraries, the New-York Historical Society, and several distinguished private collectors. An attractive volume, *Early Maps of North America*, by Robert M. Lunny, with illustrations by the Meriden Gravure Company, was published as a permanent record of the exhibition. Also in 1961 the Historic Publishing Company of Montclair reproduced a full-size color facsimile of the 1778 Faden map of New Jersey from the original in the society's Ely collection. The publishers bore all expenses of production (from color separations made in Italy) and promotion, and pay a royalty to the society on copies sold. Miss Mary Bartlett Cowdrey, who joined the staff in November 1960 as curator of prints and drawings, is working on a projected publication of early New Jersey views in prints, water colors, and drawings, which will appear in connection with the New Jersey tercentenary in 1964.

A recent booklet entitled *Your New Jersey Historical Society*, which bears the mark of the professional fund-raiser, contains the following statement on the future of the society by the present director, Mr. Robert M. Lunny:

At some point in the life of a historical society a decision must be made as to its future course. It could on the one hand direct all its energies toward establishing a great research library. Research must always remain a central function of the historical society.

Or it could decide to establish itself as a popular force in the community, meeting in a variety of ways the constantly growing taste for history. Not only the historical researcher and the genealogist, but the school child and his teacher, the casual museum visitor, the housewife, the patriotic society and other groups, the collector of decorative arts, the business man, and the industrial firm—all should find in this type society something of value to themselves and to the community.

This latter decision has been chosen by this Society as the better if the harder course.

The society is consequently attempting a program that is very broad for the extent of its present resources, in the hope that new activities will bring new support. Although volunteers, encouraged by a state-wide woman's branch, give valuable help, these varied efforts place a considerable burden on the small professional staff. The tenth annual New Jersey Historical Conference, held at the Cherry Hill Inn, Delaware Township, near Haddonfield, on 18 and 19 June 1960, which I attended, gave a most agreeable opportunity to inspect the historic sites of Burlington and Mt. Holly and to meet the active members of local historical societies. Such peripatetic meetings, however pleasant they may be for those who come, place a heavy burden on the few people responsible for the efficient arrangements.

Essay contests in local history for students in high and junior high schools, public, parochial, and private, throughout the State, with thirty-five prizes, whose winners "will be given an all-expense, three-day trip by motor bus throughout the state to visit its historical and other interesting spots" involve a considerable administrative load, coupled with the risk of boredom for those who have to read the submissions. Similar problems are inherent in contests for school class groups announced in this wise:

SO YOU'RE GOING TO VISIT THE NEW JERSEY HISTORICAL SOCIETY?

Your teacher has made an appointment for you to visit the Museum of the New Jersey Historical Society in the near future. We are looking forward to seeing you and want you to enjoy your visit to our Museum as much as possible.

We have a surprise for you. The Society is running a contest, really two contests, for each school class that visits us. The one contest is for those of you who like to write. You can write an original little essay on a story in New Jersey history based on something you see when you come to the Museum. Write clearly and hand your essay to your teacher, who will send it in for you.

The other contest is for those of you who like to draw. You may paint or draw a poster or picture on some scene in New Jersey history suggested by something you will see in our Museum. The paper may be any size but not larger than 10 inches by 16 inches, folded once. This your teacher will send in for you.

The prizes for the best essay and the best picture from your class will be a book on New Jersey history for each winner. There is a gift for your class, too. A selection of essays and posters will be shown in the spring.

Such contests involve a great deal of work; there exists also the possibility that those on whom so much effort is lavished may not respond to it. The June 1960 meeting at Haddonfield, at which Frederick L. Rath Jr., vice-director of the New York State Historical Association, read a paper entitled "Two Cheers for History Junior Style," was to include the first "junior conference." Through failure of the schools to co-operate, the only "junior historian" present was one highly intelligent small boy, the son of an officer of a local historical society.

A European tour for members of the New Jersey Historical Society is projected for the summer of 1962. One hundred and and thirty-four members can be accommodated in a chartered jet plane. Sixty of these will stay at Attingham Park for the first week and visit English country houses on a tour planned by Sir George Trevelyan of the Shropshire Adult College. Others on the flight will travel independently during the twenty-seven days before the return flight. A visit to Jersey is included.

The industry, the scholarly resources, and the housing of the New Jersey Historical Society are far superior to its financial situation. In 1959 the book value of its investments was only $121,877. For the year 1960 dues from 1,562 members amounted to $11,643; donations $1,252, while $6,040 was raised by an annual dinner at which the price of tickets was substantially above the cost of victuals consumed. The publication of the *Proceedings* cost $5,554; their sale brought in $5,459. The total income for 1960 was $35,120; the expenses $48,174; the operating deficit $13,054. Thus, even with some gains on changes of investments, the surplus, which stood at $478,796 at the beginning of 1960, had been reduced twelve months later to $467,028. The society has too little money, but is spending some of what it has in the hope of attracting more. An encouraging note is found in the 1960 report of the board of trustees.

At the February meeting of the Board of Trustees a simple announcement was made of a "Plan for Expanded Activity" for the Society, calling for contributions totalling $100,000 for a variety of special purposes. Before summer this fund had

grown in donations and pledges to $40,000. None of this amount, given so gener-
ously, is to cover operating expenses of our Society. It is all to go to forwarding
our work of creating greater interest in New Jersey and its history.

One gift made in support of this plan will provide for the publication of Miss Bartlett Cowdrey's work on early New Jersey views.

The size and geographical location of New Jersey present a difficult problem for a historical society. Many of its residents gravitate
more regularly and readily into Philadelphia and New York than to
Newark. Modern transportation makes it easy to pass through the
State without a pause. Although I have traversed the New Jersey
Turnpike on dozens of occasions, with perhaps a detour to Princeton, I had never seen the extraordinarily interesting monuments of
Burlington and Mt. Holly until the New Jersey Historical Conference of June 1960 took me there by deliberate prearrangement.
Most New Yorkers, who waste interminable hours getting about
Manhattan Island, would no more think of going to see an admir-
able temporary exhibit that might be on view in Newark than they
would contemplate going to Brooklyn. In Texas or Vermont, for
example, there is a historical cohesiveness lacking in New Jersey.
This is not the fault of the society; it is mainly a matter of geography.

In spite of this inherent disadvantage, efforts are being made, particularly by the woman's branch, to increase the membership. In
1960 a generous friend offered to match the total amount of dues
collected from new members acquired during the year, up to
$5,000, and to continue the gift in future years. In 1960 there were
497 associate members at $5; 589 contributing at $10; 201 family at
$15; 115 sustaining at $25; 9 supporting at $100; 33 institutional at
$100 or more, as well as 99 life members who had made one pay-
ment of $250, and 11 patrons who had given $1,000 or more. The
net increase over the preceding year, spurred by the incentive of
matching gifts, was just over 25%. Even so the sum received for
dues showed an increase of only $1,520 over 1959, while the opera-
ting deficit increased in the same period by $5,068.

The society grievously needs money for its central purposes. The

1958 report of the library committee contains the pathetic comment:

> We operate on the pitiful budget of $750 for the purchase of books and MSS. while sales of rare items flash by out of our reach. Meanwhile, we do what we can with the book sale and hope for more benefactors of great (or even moderate) wealth. At the moment we are in acute need of a book truck and would settle for that.

The expansion of the society's activities, in spite of such a situation in the library, is apparently due to a comprehensible unwillingness to refuse any reasonable show of historic interest. Thus what shot exists is rather widely scattered. Energy and good will abound among the officers, staff, and members of the society. A recent remark of the director's: "I know there is grave danger in evaporating if you try to pour yourself in all directions at once" raises hope for the future.

MARYLAND

The Maryland Historical Society was established at a meeting in Baltimore on 27 January 1844. As Brantz Mayer, one of its founders, had previously corresponded widely with existing organizations in other states, a constitution and bylaws were adopted at the first meeting. An act of incorporation was approved on 8 March 1844. During the earliest years, meetings were held in the rooms of the Maryland Colonization Society on Fayette Street. Then in 1848 a group of citizens subscribed $45,000 for the construction of an Athenaeum, at St. Paul and Saratoga Streets, to house the Maryland Historical Society, the Library Company of Baltimore, and the Mercantile Library, with the provision that if any tenant moved or suspended operations, its share of the building would pass to those that remained. A consolidation with the Library Company in 1858 increased the library of the Maryland Historical Society by some 11,000 volumes. Eventually the society became the sole occupant of the Athenaeum, which remained its home until 1919.

The organization had elements that were not strictly historical. Monthly soirees were held. As in the Athenaeum of Philadelphia, a

chess room was provided for the daily use of members, while newspapers were made available in a periodical room. An art gallery of
copies of European masterpieces was added "for the improvement of
the taste of the public in regard to Art, as well as the occupation and
amusement of its idle hours." This preceded the New-York Historical Society's excursion into the fine arts.

In spite of these extraneous activities, historical publishing began
promptly and was continued extensively. Brantz Mayer's edition of
the *Journal of Charles Carroll of Carrollton during his visit to Canada in
1776, as one of the Commissioners from Congress* was issued in 1845 and
reprinted in 1876 as part of the centennial observances. Papers read
at meetings were published as separate pamphlets, rather than as part
of a numbered series of *Proceedings*. In lieu of *Collections*, the Maryland Historical Society issued between 1867 and 1901 thirty-seven
volumes of what were known as "Fund Publications," from the
interest on a fund of $20,000 given by George Peabody. These
included documentary works like the Calvert papers and monographs on a variety of Maryland subjects. George Peabody had
besides in 1853 given the Maryland Historical Society a collection of
abstracts, prepared by Henry Stevens, of documents relating to
Maryland history in British archives.

Very early the State Legislature deposited with the society the
Maryland Proprietary and State papers from 1637 to 1776. These
remained in Baltimore until the founding in 1933 of the Hall of
Records at the capital, Annapolis. In 1882, under a contract from the
State, the society began the publication of the nearly seventy volumes of the *Archives of Maryland* series, which continues today under
an annual $5,000 State appropriation for the purpose. Dr. Elizabeth
Merritt, working on a part-time basis, today ably edits this distinguished series from photostats supplied by the Hall of Records.
The society publishes the volumes in an edition of 400 copies;
after distribution by the State to libraries of history in this country
and abroad, about half the edition remains with the society for sale.
This series, unequaled, unless it be in Pennsylvania, both in com-

prehensiveness and scholarship, reflects great credit upon the society and its editors, past and present.

The quarterly *Maryland Historical Magazine*, which began publication in 1906, is now edited by Professor Richard Walsh of the history department of Georgetown University. Since 1943 it has been supplemented by a four-page quarterly news bulletin, *Maryland History Notes*. Since 1953 four books in a series entitled *Studies in Maryland History* have appeared. These are *His Lordship's Patronage: Offices of Profit in Colonial Maryland*, by Donnell M. Owings; *Baltimore as Seen by Visitors, 1783–1860*, by Raphael Semmes; *The Dulanys of Maryland*, by Aubrey C. Land; and *William Buckland, 1734–1774, Architect of Virginia and Maryland*, by Rosamond Randall Beirne and John Henry Scarff. The late director, Mr. James W. Foster, whose death on 30 April 1962 is a grievous loss, interested a few members in giving money to launch the series. The books have each been published in an edition of 500 copies and have in the end paid their way, income after costs being used to create a revolving fund. Under contract from the State, the society assembles World War II records and has published four volumes of *Maryland in World War II* as well as the histories of two older Maryland regiments. Among its occasional publications are *My Maryland*, a school history, taken over from Ginn & Co., revised, and offered to schools at modest cost, of which 21,000 copies have been sold since 1955; popular pamphlets; circulars describing portions of the collections; and catalogues of exhibitions.

The Maryland Historical Society moved in 1919 to its present quarters at 201 West Monument Street, Baltimore. These consist of a large house, built in 1847 by Enoch Pratt, which Mrs. H. Irvine Keyser gave as a memorial to her husband, with the addition of a fireproof wing containing a portrait gallery, library stack, and reading room. The last, by the shuffling of furniture, doubles as a meeting room.

The library contains 60,000 bound volumes, chiefly on the history of Maryland and the early United States, a large pamphlet collection, files of bound newspapers, including nearly all Baltimore papers from 1773 on, and an extensive collection of prints, maps, architectural drawings, Maryland imprints, sheet music, and broadsides.

The rich manuscript collection includes 1,300 papers of the Lords Baltimore, among which are the "Instructions to the Colonists" of 1633 and the Act of Toleration of 1649; the papers of Charles Carroll of Carrollton and his cousin, Charles Carroll, Barrister; those of General Mordecai Gist, General Otho Holland Williams, and of such Maryland families as the Bordleys, Dulanys, Goldsboroughs, Howards, Keys, Latrobes, Lloyds, McKims, Ridgelys, and others. In the winter of 1959–60, through the energetic exertions of its president, director, board, and many friends, the society was able to purchase the Benjamin Henry Latrobe collection of 8,800 letters, 310 paintings and drawings, and 14 diaries. Latrobe's sketches give a graphic picture of the United States between 1796 and 1820. Not only are his papers of high architectural importance, but they contain much material of general historical significance. The effort devoted to this acquisition does great credit to the society;[1] it is hoped that the Latrobe papers may be published in accordance with the recommendation of the National Historical Publications Commission.

Parts of the collection of 450 portraits and 250 miniatures are shown in the portrait gallery of the wing added by Mrs. Keyser, while the large rooms of the original Pratt House are chiefly devoted to museum exhibition. The society owns fine examples of Baltimore and Annapolis furniture, and much silver, china, porcelain and glass, as well as costumes, clocks, quilts, and textiles. Certain rooms have been set aside for family possessions. The Patterson-Bonaparte room contains belongings of Betsy Patterson who married Jerome Bonaparte in 1803, of their son Jerome, and their grandson Charles Joseph

1. *Maryland History Notes* XIX, 3 (November 1961), p. 12, contains the welcome announcement of the purchase of an additional group of Latrobe papers which further strengthens the society's holdings.

Bonaparte, who was not only Theodore Roosevelt's Secretary of the Navy and Attorney-General but H. L. Mencken's especial bête noire. Some rooms contain possessions of the Key and the Cohen families, while others simulate domestic life of various periods. A maritime history section contains, besides ship portraits of Baltimore interest, the collection of carvings from and half-models of Chesapeake Bay watercraft gathered by Lieutenant Commander M. V. Brewington, U.S.N.R.(ret.), formerly of Cambridge, Maryland, now assistant director of the Peabody Museum of Salem. The Pratt House, although handsome in itself, is not ideally adapted for museum use, nor is it big enough. Because of the society's wish to encourage mass visits of school groups, and also on account of a shortage of staff to protect the objects, some of the exhibition rooms when no guide is available must be seen through a glass panel in the door. This feature, combined with overcrowding, in some instances makes the museum confusing.

A recent fund-raising or member-getting pamphlet entitled *Treasure House of Maryland* opens with a statement by Senator George L. Radcliffe, the president of the society since 1939: "The day when historical societies limited their functions to the storing of books, documents and heirlooms is over. Today, the activities of the Maryland Historical Society are varied and its influence reaches into many parts of the world." In accordance with this theory, during the past two decades a considerable effort has been exerted to increase the membership and broaden the popular appeal of the Maryland Historical Society. The following instances of "calls for service" listed in this pamphlet suggest that because of the desire to be helpful much time is spent satisfying public curiosity in one direction or another:

Every day a stream of questions pours into the Soicety. Recently answers have been found to these, among many others:

How many Marylanders died in World War II?

How many Marylanders received the Medal of Honor in the last war?

What was the dollar value of war contracts held by Maryland manufacturers in World War II?

What agency has supervision over the Mason and Dixon line stone markers?
What part did Francis Hopkinson play in designing the U. S. flag?
What is the history of the village of Port Tobacco, Charles County?
Are there visible evidences of two immigrations of French into Maryland?
What was the population of Annapolis at the outbreak of the Revolution?
Will you outline a tour of historic points in Baltimore for a civic group?

The Society broadcast 24 radio talks during last year, published four numbers of its magazine and four of its bulletin, prepared three books for publication, held 42 meetings of its own and 34 meetings of other groups. It conducted more than 100 tours of school pupils and other groups and furnished professional or technical information to countless individuals, business and civic organizations.

In line with this catholicity of interest announced by the president, the addresses given at the monthly evening meetings have not always been confined to subjects strictly relating to Maryland history. Public figures sometimes substitute for historians. Joint meetings with the English Speaking Union have led to such addresses as Sir Josiah Wedgwood's "The Wedgwood Story," illustrated by motion pictures, and "The Australian Scene," by Air Vice-Marshal Sir Robert George, K.C.M.G., retiring Governor of South Australia. A series of afternoon illustrated lectures for members has dealt not only with "John Frederick Amelung, Maryland's Pioneer Glassmaker" and "John Needles, Baltimore Cabinetmaker" but with "Loom and Needle in North Africa" and "Underwater Exploration of Shipwrecks." From a desire to meet public taste on its own level, the society accepted some years ago several trolley cars; these for the present require storage elsewhere.

Another recent booklet describing the society, entitled *Guardian of Our Heritage*, makes the following statement about the future:

Since we believe that the foundations upon which our nation is built are grounded in experience, we seek to preserve the good in our way of life. Furthermore, because our heritage in Maryland has a character and richness that make for sane living and sound citizenship, we are eager that its essentials be handed down to oncoming generations. Through an agency like the Maryland Historical Society we can help to perpetuate the principles and atmosphere that have been characteristic of our history. We can thereby make a worthwhile contribution to the future of our country.

One often wonders what the adman would do without the word "heritage."

Membership in the Maryland Historical Society has fluctuated considerably over the past three decades. At the end of 1929 there were 1,315 members who paid $6,228 in dues. After five years of depression there was a drop of one third in number to 961, but only a decrease of one quarter in revenue, for in 1934 dues payments amounted to $4,872, which suggests that in bad times those who pay the least drop off first. In 1939 1,163 members paid $5,015. Four years later the number had increased by only 75, but through later campaigning in years when dues were still $5 as many as 3,500 members were at one time on the books. The lowest rate is now $8, with the usual classes of membership at larger sums. On this basis in 1959 the dues of 2,989 members produced $26,509.50. As the current cost of furnishing each member with the *Maryland Historical Magazine* and *Maryland History Notes* is $4.46, the increase of the minimum rate from $5 to $8 was clearly indicated.

In 1956 the endowment of the Maryland Historical Society had a book value of $482,789 and produced an income of $26,385. In 1959, thanks to gifts, legacies, and gains realized on the sale of securities, the book value had increased to $801,308 and the income to $38,730. The bequest of Miss Elizabeth Chew Williams, which was paid in the late summer of 1960, increased the endowment principal by $200,000. The 1959 income, of which membership dues represented a little over one third, was $76,509.22; expenditures of $87,339.84 were incurred with the knowledge that income from the Williams estate would ultimately become available for use. In 1961 the future of the Maryland Historical Society looked bright. Substantial bequests that were promised, or that were held in trust during the lifetime of surviving beneficiaries, seemed likely to augment the financial resources in the predictable future. The society had raised a very large sum of money for the purchase of the Latrobe papers. Professor K. R. Greenfield, chairman of the publications committee, had recommended that a full-time professional curator of manuscripts be appointed, as a necessary preliminary to the preparation of a printed guide to that part of the library, and proposed the creation of a seminar in Maryland history, modeled on the advanced seminar in history in use at Johns Hopkins. The director, Mr. Foster, had begun his 1959 report with the observation that the size of the staff was for the first time in his experience "nearly adequate to the current load the Society attempts to carry" and that there was also a high level of competency.

The death on 28 June 1961 of Mr. John L. Thomas brought the Maryland Historical Society more than $200,000 from his own estate and more than $2,000,000 from the estate of his elder brother, William S. Thomas, in which he had had a life interest. This large sum was, however, by the will of the elder Thomas, restricted to the construction and maintenance of a building to be known as the Thomas and Hugg Memorial. Fortunately the society had an already cleared site on Park Avenue, adjacent to the Keyser Memorial, well suited to the construction of a building that would contain, in addition to the much-needed manuscripts division of the library, exhibition rooms and an auditorium. In the autumn of 1961 the firm of Meyer and Ayers were preparing plans for a building to harmonize felicitously with the Pratt House, the Keyser Memorial, and the region in general. When considerable work had already been completed on these plans, the council, at the insistence of President Radcliffe, shifted the proposed location to a site on Monument Street west of the Pratt House, even though this would involve the demolition of several nineteenth-century houses that formed a useful and pleasing architectural element in the region. The first of the announced reasons for the change was that "the Monument Street site is in keeping with the size and importance of the gift."[2] The

2. *Maryland History Notes* XIX, 4 (February 1962), p. 15. In October and December 1961 I went to Baltimore and spent many hours with the president, director, and various officers of the society discussing the plans for the new building. The other reasons given for the Monument Street site—"(2) it will provide centralization of work areas and control of public spaces, affording efficient operation, and (3) an appropriate building here will be in harmony with the Keyser Memorial and benefi-

spectacle of a historical society unnecessarily demolishing its own surroundings, when an equally suitable site was available around the corner, disgusted historic preservationists who cared for the traditional character of the Mount Vernon Place area. The National Trust for Historic Preservation in the April 1962 issue of *Preservation News* publicly inquired "Who guards the guards?" in a note that stated:

At the request of concerned members of the National Trust in Maryland and members of the Maryland Historical Society, the Trust informed its Maryland membership of the proposed demolition of three houses by the Maryland Historical Society. It was reported that "in proposing a valuable and important addition to its distinguished headquarters on West Monument Street in Baltimore, the Society is planning to raze three early houses facing that street and invade the small but distinguished town garden maintained for the Society by the Garden Club. To the rear of the lot is ample enough ground to build the needed addition, making it in every way a fitting and becoming extension of the original headquarters building." Maryland members were encouraged to express their opinions to Senator George L. Radcliffe, president of the Society, for consideration.[3]

Even more unfortunate for the future of the society was the resignation of its director, Mr. James W. Foster, followed within a few weeks by his death on 30 April 1962. Thus at a critical moment in its history, when decisions of the utmost importance must be made, the Maryland Historical Society has lost its pilot.[4]

─────────

cial to the surrounding area in which the Society is deeply interested"—do not accord with the facts as I saw them on the spot at that time.

3. On 12 March 1962, as a trustee of the National Trust for Historic Preservation, I sent a formal letter to Senator Radcliffe, protesting against the demolition of houses involved in the choice of the Monument Street site and summarizing the views that I had presented to him in person on 31 October and 14 December 1961. I have received no reply.

4. The council contains regrettably few members with professional experience in history, and its age average is high. The president, who has served since 1939, will be 85 on 22 August 1962.

DELAWARE

The Historical Society of Delaware, the last State society to be established in the east, was organized on 31 May 1864.[5] The object of the society was succinctly stated as "the elucidation of History, particularly such portions as may refer to this State." Its inspiration was the Historical Society of Pennsylvania, which sent a delegation, headed by the Hon. John M. Read, a former Chief Justice of that State whose historical activity reached back forty years to the foundation of the Philadelphia society, to the inaugural meeting at Wilmington. Colonel J. Ross Snowden, who delivered the address on that occasion, gave the newly organized society copies of the agreement of 10 May 1732 between Lord Baltimore and the Penns and of the commissions given and reports made by the commissioners to mark out the lines between Maryland and Pennsylvania, and the lower counties on the Delaware River. Other friends soon gave books, manuscripts, portraits, and relics, while the New Hampshire Historical Society and the State Historical Society of Iowa promptly sent copies of their own publications.

From 1872 the society had quarters in the Masonic Temple on Market Street above 8th in Wilmington, and from 1878 to 1916 in the attractive but tiny eighteenth-century First Presbyterian Church,[6] also in Market Street. Soon after the superb Town Hall in Wilmington, built in 1798 from plans of the French refugee Peter Bauduy, was vacated by the city authorities in 1916, the society bought it for $90,517.50, of which two thirds was borrowed on mortgage. As the building was in need of restoration, for which no funds were immediately available, it was from 1917 to 1926 rented to the Ameri-

5. *Proceedings of the Inaugural Meeting of the Historical Society of Delaware, held at Wilmington, 31st May 1864, together with the Constitution and By-Laws then adopted* (Wilmington, 1864); *Catalogue of the Historical Society of Delaware, with a History, Constitution, and By-Laws* (Wilmington, 1871).

6. This church, the Old Town Hall, and the Old Swedes Church are the only three public buildings in Wilmington built before 1800. The Presbyterian Church, shortly after the Historical Society of Delaware vacated it, was moved to a new location and now houses the Colonial Dames.

can Red Cross.[7] The society's records and museum objects were placed in storage, where they remained until 1927 when the restoration of the Old Town Hall was completed. The fine rooms on the first two floors of the building are used for museum purposes, and the attic for storage. A small fireproof wing houses the library and manuscript collection.

Between 1879 and 1922 the Historical Society of Delaware issued sixty-seven publications. While many of these were pamphlets of addresses or monographs, the series included such documents as *Minutes of the Council of Delaware State, 1776–92* (1887), *Records of Holy Trinity (Old Swedes) 1697–1810* (1890), *Letters of James A. Bayard, 1802–14* (1901), *Records of Welsh Tract Baptist Meeting, 1701–1828* (1904), and *Journal and Order Book of Captain Robert Kirkwood, Delaware Regiment, Continental Line* (1910). Three numbers of a new series were published between 1927 and 1941, as well as George H. Ryden's edition of *Letters to and from Caesar Rodney* (1933), Christopher L. Ward's *Delaware Continentals* (1941), Robert G. Caldwell's *Penitentiary Movement in Delaware, 1776–1829* (1946), and Albert Cook Myers's edition of *Walter Wharton's Land Survey Register 1675–1679* (1955).

Beginning in January 1946, *Delaware History* has been published semiannually. Volumes I and II, consisting of two parts each, coincided with the years 1946 and 1947. Since 1948 the practice has been followed of forming a volume of four parts, issued during the course of two years. *Delaware History* is a serious historical periodical, devoted to the publication of sound research and of a few documents; it reflects great credit upon the society.

The printed books in the library of the Historical Society of Delaware chiefly concern the history of the State, although the *New Jersey Archives* and comparable sets for Maryland and Pennsylvania are owned. The collection includes Delaware imprints, almanacs, biographies, genealogies, directories, maps, court records, legal jour-

7. *The Old Town Hall Wilmington Delaware, Its History and the Plan for its Restoration and Use* (Wilmington, 1920).

nals, and calendars of wills. Delaware newspapers published before 1821 are collected whenever possible. Microfilm copies of all extant newspapers of this period not owned by the society were obtained between 1951 and 1956.

The Historical Society of Delaware receives an annual grant of $1,000 from the State Legislature. Its private income in 1959 was $21,048.32, of which $12,092.22 came from endowment and $7,615 from the dues of members. Both figures have improved steadily over the past seven years, for in 1953 endowment income was $8,420 and dues $5,520. In 1957 there were 595 annual members at $5; 207 contributing at $10; 57 sustaining at $25; 6 patrons and 2 business members at $100, while 15 life members had made a single payment of $1,000.

The staff of the society consists of an executive secretary, Mrs. H. Clay Reed, the wife of a faculty member at the University of Delaware, a librarian, and an assistant editor. Now and then Hagley Fellows from the University of Delaware lend a hand with exhibits for brief periods.

The Old Town Hall is an important historic monument, whose rooms are somewhat overcrowded by exhibition cases. It is visited by about 6,000 persons a year, apart from scholars using the library. Temporary exhibits of timely interest are frequently arranged, even though that can only be accomplished by displacing something from its permanent position. In time snatched from other duties, Mrs. Reed has been accomplishing a major reorganization of objects in storage and back stock of publications. The society is shorthanded and short of space, but it makes the most of what it has and, in its publication program, sets its sights high. Every dollar spent accomplishes a useful purpose; one could wish that there were more to spend, and hope that in the future there may be.

DISTRICT OF COLUMBIA

An American Historical Society, with Peter Force as its leading spirit, was organized in Washington on 12 October 1835. Its announced scope was national, according to Leslie W. Dunlap's account of it. John Quincy Adams was its president. Twice it held annual meetings in the Hall of Representatives and printed the lectures given at them in 1836 by Lewis Cass and in 1837 by Levi Woodbury. In 1839 it issued a single volume of *Transactions*, consisting chiefly of a reprint of thirteen of Peter Force's *Tracts*, and, seemingly, died of the effort.

More than half a century later the Columbia Historical Society was founded with more modest aspirations. Incorporated in 1894, its objects were "the collection, preservation and diffusion of knowledge about the history, biography, geography and topography of the District of Columbia, national history and biography, and in general, the transaction of any business pertinent to an historical society at the National Capital." For more than sixty years the society maintained headquarters in its officers' hats and devoted all its efforts to the publication of annual volumes of *Records*, which contained the proceedings of its monthly meetings. This series is a mine of information about the history of the District of Columbia. While some of the papers are of an amateurish, discursive reminiscence, others are of high quality, for the Columbia Historical Society has drawn to its ranks not only "old inhabitants" but scholars of distinction from the Smithsonian Institution, the Library of Congress, the National Archives, and the Carnegie Institution. A cumulative *Index to Volumes 1–48/49*, compiled by Maud Burr Morris and Laurence F. Schmeckebier, and an *Analytical Index* to the first twenty volumes, prepared by Louis D. Scisco, greatly enhance the usefulness of the more than fifty volumes of the *Records of the Columbia Historical Society*.

On the death of Mrs. Christian Heurich on 24 January 1956, the society came into possession of a very large house at 1307 New Hampshire Avenue, N.W., built by her late husband in 1892. Christian Heurich, born in Germany in 1842, turned up in Washington at the age of thirty where he established a successful brewery, producing a light Pilsen-type "Senate Beer." In twenty years he prospered to an extent that permitted the building of this miniature fortress, designed by John Granville Meyers. It is a typical "brewer's castle" of the kind dear to the German immigrant who has prospered: solid in the extreme, paneled in exuberantly carved woodwork, full of outsize furniture, and decorated with such sympathetic mottoes as "Ein guter Trunk macht Alte junge." Christian Heurich, following the formula of "Practice moderation and drink Heurich beer," lived long to enjoy his castle, for he died only on 7 March 1945 at the age of 102. As he had been a member of the Columbia Historical Society for more than forty years, his widow gave the house to the society, retaining a life interest in it.

Although the house was given without endowment for maintenance, the society obtains some revenue by furnishing office space to the American Peace Society and the National Genealogical Society. Under the presidency of Major General U. S. Grant 3rd, it has appealed for gifts to an endowment fund, which at present approaches $30,000.[8] The Columbia Historical Society receives no public support. Its operating income of some $10,000 a year comes from dues and contributions. Its affairs are cared for by its executive secretary, Mr. David J. Guy, a retired engineer, while certain of its officers, as volunteers, work over its small library, manuscript and photograph collections, and continue to edit its *Records*. As an example of one phase of American taste at the end of the nineteenth century, the Heurich House is worth preserving. Whether it will ultimately assist or hinder the Columbia Historical Society in its principal business, which should be the continuation of its extensive series of *Records*, remains to be seen.

8. *The Washington Post*, 13 October 1959, D14, contained a full-page advertisement of The Hecht Co., complete with photographs of General Grant and the Christian Heurich Memorial Mansion, saluting the Columbia Historical Society on its 65th birthday. Among the objects shown in Hecht's department store at an "exciting Washington historical exhibition" were "a piece of the fabled cherry tree chopped down by George Washington." One hopes that this was one of the objects lent "by private individuals in who [sic] the traditions of our community are deeply steeped," rather than anything from the *Schatzkammer* of the Heurich House.

Chapter VIII

THE SOUTHEASTERN STATES

It must be the key idea of all hands that we will make the best of
what we have.   —ADMIRAL ERNEST J. KING, 1941

PRIVATELY supported State historical societies in Georgia
and South Carolina, founded respectively in 1839 and 1855,
with creditable records of preserving sources and of publication, exist today in Savannah and Charleston. Although a society
was established in Florida in 1856 it proved impermanent; the
present Florida Historical Society, which is primarily a publishing
organization, closely associated with the university at Gainesville, is
a twentieth-century creation in its present form. Historical activities
in North Carolina, Alabama, and Mississippi are today the responsibility of State agencies, although privately supported societies were
started in those states before the Civil War. The Historical Society
of Mississippi had a singularly inglorious career, for not long after
its foundation in 1858 it was discovered that only three members
had paid the reasonable dues of $1; it therefore gave up the ghost in
discouragement.

GEORGIA

A circular issued at Savannah on 26 June 1839 in the name of the
library committee of the Georgia Historical Society solicited, in the
most systematic detail, "contributions of books, manuscripts, pamphlets, newspapers, and every thing which can elucidate the history

of America generally, as well as Georgia in particular." This was the result of a meeting held on the previous 24 May, which had been inspired by the versatile William Bacon Stevens, physician, historian, and, at a later date, Episcopal Bishop of Pennsylvania, and Israel K. Tefft, a native of Rhode Island settled in Savannah, who was a passionate collector of colonial and Revolutionary autographs and documents. The Georgia Historical Society[1] was incorporated on 19 December 1839. Within a year it had issued its first volume of *Collections*; a second followed in 1842 and part of a third in 1848. In 1841 the society requested William Bacon Stevens to undertake the writing of a new history of Georgia; this task occupied him for more than fifteen years. The first volume was published in New York in New York in 1847 and the second in Philadelphia in 1859.

The Georgia Historical Society doubled the size of its library in 1847 by the acquisition of 2,500 books, obtained through a merger with the Savannah Library Society; the following year it built "a small but beautiful Gothic hall" on Bryan Street, Savannah, at a cost of $6,000.

Under the inspiration of its presidents, the Right Reverend Stephen Elliot and George Wymberly Jones De Renne, the Georgia Historical Society resumed its activities more rapidly after the Civil War than had been possible in Richmond. Mr. De Renne, when living before the war at Wormsloe plantation, had assembled a substantial library and had published a historical series of Wormsloe Quartos in very limited editions for private distribution. In 1871, while living in Savannah, he procured for the Georgia Historical Society transcripts from the British Colonial Office of letters of General James Oglethorpe to the Trustees of the Colony of Georgia between 1735 and 1744, and of letters from Sir James Wright, the last Royal Governor of the province, describing local events of the

---

1. Lilla M. Hawes, "A Profile of the Georgia Historical Society," *The Georgia Historical Quarterly* XXXVI (1952), 132–136; Charles C. Jones Jr., *The Georgia Historical Society: Its Founders, Patrons, and Friends. Anniversary Address delivered in Hodgson Hall On the 14th of February, 1881* (Savannah, 1881).

American Revolution from the Loyalist point of view. These were published by the society in a volume of *Collections* in 1873, which Mr. De Renne paid for, as well as the next volume, that of 1878, which contained "The Dead Towns of Georgia," by Charles C. Jones Jr.

An even more remarkable piece of good fortune was the gift of a new building to replace the smaller hall of 1847. Hodgson Hall,[2] the present home of the society at 501 Whitaker Street, Savannah, was built in memory of William B. Hodgson by his widow and her sister, Miss Mary Telfair. This building, designed by Detlef Lienau of New York City, was dedicated on 14 February 1876. On the ground floor was a spacious meeting room; above was a two-story galleried library of considerable architectural charm, capable of housing some 20,000 volumes. At the time it was "thought to surpass any Library Room in the Southern States."

Although shortage of funds always hampered the society's activities, publications continued within the limits of available resources. Volumes v to ix of the *Collections* appeared between 1901 and 1916, containing a good number of eighteenth-century documents. Dr. J. Franklin Jameson, in an address given before the society on its seventy-fifth anniversary in 1914,[3] observed:

In the seventy five years of its existence it has kept brightly alive the love of history in its constituency, it has collected an invaluable library, it has issued volumes of Collections whose superior worth has been recognized by scholars in every part of the country. Its first volume, published in 1840 by Dr. William B. Stevens, took rank at once with the best of its class. It chose from the beginning the right path, in composing its volumes mainly of those original and contemporary materials whose value is permanent and secure. Its editions of the letters of Oglethorpe and Montiano and Wright, of James Habersham and Joseph Clay, are alone sufficient to confer distinction upon such a society.

In spite of this analysis by one of the most judicious and critical professional historians, certain faculty members of the University of

2. *Proceedings of the Dedication of Hodgson Hall, by the Georgia Historical Society, on occasion of its thirty-seventh anniversary, February 14, 1876* (Savannah, 1876).
3. *The History of Historical Societies* (Savannah, [1914]).

of Georgia at Athens decided that the society was a moribund Savannah conspiracy. They therefore orgainized a rival Georgia Historical Association, based at the University, which began a publication of its own. This competition from Athens woke up Savannah. In 1920 the society and the association were amalgamated and joined forces in the publication of *The Georgia Historical Quarterly.* Professor E. Merton Coulter, who had joined the faculty of the University of Georgia in that year, became the editor of the periodical and has continued in that capacity for forty years. The *Quarterly,* which represents a happy instance of the merger of the older amateur and the newer professional approaches to American history, is, according to its imprint, "edited and published at the University of Georgia, Athens, by the Georgia Historical Society, Savannah." More than forty volumes have now appeared through Professor Coulter's voluntary devotion.

Issues of *The Georgia Historical Quarterly* often contain, in addition to scholarly articles, the texts of documents, which are subsequently reprinted in book form. Thus the society has been able to issue, as Volumes x to xiii of its *Collections, Proceedings and minutes of the Governor and Council of Georgia, 1774–1775, 1779–1780* (1952); *Papers of James Jackson, 1781–1798* (1955); *Papers of Lachlan McIntosh, 1774–1799* (1957); and *The Letter book of Thomas Rasberry* (*Savannah merchant*), *1758–1761* (1959).

The library in 1960 contained 9,914 catalogued books and as many more besides. The printed books, which deal chiefly with the history of Georgia, contain many rarities, while the collection of Savannah newspapers extends, with some gaps, from the first one published— *The Georgia Gazette* of 7 April 1763—to the present. Although the director has had professional library training and holds a certificate in administration of archives, she works entirely alone, save for occasional clerical help. When one realizes that on an average more than a thousand persons a year come to consult manuscripts or early Savannah newspapers, and that she annually furnishes information in response to queries by letter or telephone from an even larger number, it is remarkable that she has found the time to catalogue so much of the library.

Late one evening in August 1959, for example, J.-J. de Pury of Neuchâtel, Switzerland, turned up in Savannah by air. With six hours to spare the following day, he hoped to locate the site of a Carolina ghost town, Purisburg (or Purrysburg) on the Savannah River, which had been founded in 1733 by Swiss settlers led by Jean-Pierre Pury, once mayor of Boudry. Monsieur Pury was short both of time and of precise geographical information. According to the account "A la recherche de Purisburg en Amérique" that he published in the *Feuille d'avis de Neuchâtel* of 29 and 30 October 1959, he set out on foot at 7 a.m. to explore Savannah.

Rentré à l'hotel, je trouvai le tenacier du kiosque à journaux qui époussetait nonchalamment ses livres. "Savez-vous, lui demandai-je, quelle est la personne de Savannah qui connait le mieux l'histoire de la région?" "C'est Mme Hawes, la directrice de la Société d'histoire de Georgie", me répondit-il.

In a quarter of an hour he was in Hodgson Hall. Mrs. Hawes dropped everything; drove him upriver to the site of the vanished town, now marked only by a stone cross; brought him back to the society and produced both eighteenth- and twentieth-century maps and surveys of the region, which were in due course photographed and forwarded to Neuchâtel, where they proved of great interest to the compatriots of the early Swiss settlers. Such mornings as this retard the process of cataloguing.

In an account of the society, published in *The Georgia Historical Quarterly* for June 1952, Mrs. Hawes gave the following summary of outstanding items in the manuscript collection:

Among these, for the Colonial period, are the account books of George Galphin (Indian trader at Silver Bluff), lists of presents given to the Indians by the Trustees of the colony, records of Midway Church and Savannah port records. Representative of the Revolutionary period are the journals of the Georgia Council of Safety and Executive Council, minutes of the Royal Governor and Council of Georgia, papers of General Lachlan McIntosh, Samuel Elbert, Anthony Wayne, Nathanael Greene and the diary of the Rev. John Joachim Zubly, first minister of the Independent Presbyterian Church. Of the post-Revolutionary period, we have papers of James Jackson, order book of Gen. John Twiggs, papers of Benjamin Hawkins (Indian agent), militia papers of Burke and Liberty counties. Of the early 19th Century, there are minute books and account books of the Savannah Free School and Savannah Anti-Duelling Association; papers of Thomas A. Burke of Athens, papers of William Jones of Augusta and Goshen, the Bull-Murrow family of Augusta. Papers of local military companies are those of the Irish Jasper Greens, the Chatham Artillery, the Republican Blues and the Georgia Hussars. There are many early land grants and deeds and a large collection of Confederate States Army muster rolls and payrolls, records of extinct Savannah business firms, personal diaries, census records, land lottery records, plantation records, personal account books and private letters.

Hodgson Hall is now used not only by the Georgia Historical Society but as a library for the nearby Armstrong College of Savannah. In return for this use, the City of Savannah pays the society an annual sum of $3,000. This in theory counts as dues for all students in the college, although they are not listed on the membership rolls and do not receive the *Quarterly*; in practice it amounts to rent for the use of part of the building. The college pays all expenses of light, heat, and janitor service, while the society is responsible for repairs and capital improvements.

Total annual income for the year 1959 was $7,044.75 of which the $3,000 received for the use of Hodgson Hall was a substantial part. The only other sources of revenue were $569.75 from sales of publications and contributions, and $3,475 from membership dues. In that year there were 401 regular members and 107 institutional members at $5; 75 contributing at $10; 3 sustaining at $25; and 1 life member who had paid $100. As the estimated expense of printing and mailing the *Quarterly* and of sending meeting notices to members was $2.34 each, any increase in membership produces some financial benefit.

That useful scholarly activity is carried out on such a budget is due entirely to the disinterested devotion of the editor and the director. For forty years Professor Coulter has worked entirely without compensation; he is strongly suspected of incurring a number of expenses on the society's behalf for which he asks no reimbursement. The singularly efficient and versatile director works a forty-hour week at a token salary; this labor of affection is possible because she is the wife of the president of Armstrong College. Were she to become weary of well-doing, she could not be replaced by a person of equal professional competence without a drastic increase in salary. Moreover, the use of Hodgson Hall as the college library provides an essential element in the society's budget.

The Georgia Historical Society, like those in Massachusetts, New York, Pennsylvania, and Virginia, focuses its activity on the preservation and dissemination of source materials. The modest scale upon which it operates is due to its complete lack of endowment. That it continues with energy and cheerfulness after 123 years is a striking instance of Fleet Admiral King's concept of making the best of what one has, a principle that was of paramount importance to the short-handed United States Navy in the undeclared Atlantic war of 1941.

Each dollar spent in Savannah brings an extraordinarily high return; if more were available one could confidently predict a comparable increase in scholarly production. While the situation is precarious, the society has valuable assets in the richness of its manuscript collection, the charm of its building, and the devotion of those who serve it. It has excellent relations not only with the University of Georgia in Athens but with the State Department of Archives and History in Atlanta, whose energetic and able director, Mrs. Mary Givens Bryan, assists it in many ways. The former president, Mr. Walter C. Hartridge, his successor, Mr. Herman W. Coolidge, and and other well-wishers hope that residents of Savannah will become more fully aware of the esteem in which the Georgia Historical Society is held by scholars in many parts of the country and will be induced for the honor of their city to provide more generous support for its activities. With increased funds, publications projects could be undertaken that would inject new life and new purpose into this venerable and respectworthy organization.

SOUTH CAROLINA

The South Carolina Historical Society was organized in Charleston on 19 May 1855 and incorporated on 20 December 1856. Although it was the first organization formed for the express purpose of promoting the study of South Carolina history, unsuccessful efforts had been made as early as 1827 to secure copies of South Carolina records from British archives, and the Charleston Library Society had in 1833 appointed a historical committee to collect documents relative to the history of the State. The late Dr. J. H. Easterby, formerly director of the South Carolina Archives Department, in his admirable pamphlet, *The Study of South Carolina History*,[4] pointed out that although the South Carolina Historical Society arrived on the scene relatively late it has proved to be permanent.

It was not one of the first historical societies organized in the United States. Actually, it ranks forty-ninth, in the order of time, among the sixty-five societies established prior to the year 1861. It is, however, one of only thirty-two in the country at large and one of only five in the southern states which have survived and are active at the present time.

Its founders and leaders were professional men, coming more largely from academic life than would have been the case in a society founded earlier in the century. Frederick Adolphus Porcher, who delivered the inaugural address on 28 June 1855, had recently been appointed professor of history and belles-lettres in the College of Charleston. Among his associates were a private school teacher, William James Rivers; Bartholomew R. Carroll, also a teacher, who had earlier edited *Historical Collections*; Doctors James Moultrie and John Edwards Holbrook, physicians and teachers in the Medical College; and Dr. Lingard A. Frampton, a book collector who later became librarian of the College of Charleston. The purpose of the society, according to Porcher, was "to collect information respecting

4. *Bulletins of the Historical Commission of South Carolina*, no. 13 (Columbia, 1951). Many of the details of this account of the South Carolina Historical Society have been derived from Dr. Easterby's pamphlet.

every portion of our State, to preserve it, and when deemed advisable to publish it."

For four years after its incorporation, the South Carolina Historical Society received public encouragement in the form of an annual grant of $500 from the General Assembly. The papers of Henry Laurens, which are today the chief jewel of the manuscript collection, were received as early as 9 September 1856. They proved to contain "besides the Tower Narrative and accompanying documents, . . . a complete set of the Letter Books . . . affording, among many original letters, several from Washington, Adams, Franklin, Lafayette, De Estaing and Burke, together with a large private correspondence." Efforts were promptly made to obtain transcripts and calendars of English records. Henry Laurens's narrative of his capture and confinement in the Tower of London, 1780–82, and a calendar of papers in the State Paper Office, London, relating to South Carolina between 1629 and 1748 were included in a first volume of *Collections*, published in 1857. The continuation of the calendar through 1774, together with the 1775 Journal of the South Carolina Council of Safety, and documents relating to the Huguenot settlement in Abbeville District, appeared in a second volume the following year. A third in 1859 contained the Journal of the Second Council of Safety and further lists and abstracts of British documents.

The papers of General Thomas Pinckney soon joined those of Henry Laurens. By May 1860 the manuscript collection had grown to a size that warranted the society being granted the use of a room in the State records building at Charleston, a superb structure designed by Robert Mills and completed in 1827. Because this was one of the first efforts at fireproof construction in the United States, it has always been called by Charlestonians "the Fireproof Building."

The sixth anniversary meeting of the South Carolina Historical Society was held "at a time," as William J. Rivers later recalled, "when the reverberations of the guns in the opening bombardment of Fort Sumter had scarcely died away on the ruffled waters of our harbor." The war caused a fourteen-year hiatus in activity. No further meetings were held until 10 July 1873, when Professor Porcher was elected president. After an unsuccessful attempt at revival, he wrote despairingly:

Our Historical Society is very feeble and has published nothing since the War except an anniversary address occasionally. We printed three volumes before the War but the third was deposited in the Room belonging to the Society and left there during the War. When I returned to Charleston I found the room in occupation of negroes and the whole edition besides several other publications lost. . . . Before the War the state gave us the moderate sum we had asked for. Since then we have not felt inclined to petition the legislature for its bounty and we have few men whose means enable them to be literary patrons.

Of the postwar period, Dr. Easterby wrote:

The Society, however, did not give up the struggle as did most of those in other southern states. Perhaps it may best be said of its activities during the last thirty years of the century that they declined quantitatively but that, thanks largely to the leadership of a few of the founders, they were continued at a fairly high level of quality. Reorganization was accomplished in 1875. Permission to use the room in the Fireproof Building was not renewed; but space was found in the quarters of the Charleston Library Society, and some additional manuscripts were acquired. A grant of $300.00 from the state in 1884 made it possible to issue volume four of the *Collections*.

This contained the report of the committee appointed by the General Assembly of South Carolina in 1740 on the St. Augustine Expedition under General Oglethorpe, a memoir of General Christopher Gadsden, a study of colonial education in the State, and two anniversary addresses. A fifth volume edited by Langdon Cheves, appearing in 1897, contained the texts of papers of Anthony Ashley Cooper, first Earl of Shaftesbury, which had been obtained from the Public Record Office through the efforts of William A. Courtenay, Mayor of Charleston.

Well before the appearance of the Shaftesbury papers, the efforts of Mayor Courtenay, in co-operation with the historical society, to obtain transcripts of South Carolina records from England, had led to the appropriation of $4,000 by the General Assembly on 23 December 1891 and the establishment of a commission that on 27

December 1894 became a permanent State agency, known as the Historical Commission of the State of South Carolina. This body, which is today responsible for the magnificent work of the South Carolina Archives Department, is reasonably considered to be the first archival agency created in the southern states.

Although the work of documentary publication passed to the state-supported historical commission—and it should be noted parenthetically that the documentary publications of the South Carolina Archives Department are among the most distinguished in the United States—the South Carolina Historical Society undertook a quarterly that in 1962 is in its sixty-third volume. The inspiration was the *Virginia Magazine of History and Biography*. Mr. A. S. Salley Jr., the secretary and treasurer, who had previously succeeded in raising the membership of the society from 60 to 300, became editor of *The South Carolina Historical and Genealogical Magazine*, whose first number appeared in January 1900.

When the duties of the historical commission were enlarged in 1905 to include "the care and custody of all the official archives of the State not now in current use," Mr. Salley was appointed its secretary, although he continued to edit the *Historical Magazine* until 1909, when Miss Mabel Louise Webber took over. The society continued to occupy space with the Charleston Library Society, moving with them into their new building in 1914. Although legacies totaling $30,000 provided some slight relief from financial strain, the society was gravely restricted during the 1920s and 1930s by lack of space and funds. Its one room was so completely filled that gifts or deposits of large collections of manuscripts were necessarily refused for want of space. There was thus little incentive to collect, even if anyone had had the time or money to attempt to do so. The historical society did what it could, but no institution in South Carolina systematically approached the problem of preserving private manuscripts.

The result [Dr. Easterby observed] was the wholesale pillaging of the state by representatives of institutions in other parts of the country. Employing the argument that South Carolina repositories were unable to provide for additional manuscripts and that they would be more effectively used in the great research centers, they induced many families to part with papers that were becoming a burden as spacious old houses were replaced by small modern apartments. The result is that today the printed inventories of the Wisconsin State Historical Society, the Library of Congress, Duke University, the University of North Carolina, and the Historical Society of Pennsylvania read like dictionaries of South Carolina biography. In some instances the owners of these papers are not without blame; cases might be cited in which local repositories were looked upon with contempt, and it was thought a distinction to have one's family records in an institution of national renown.

In the years between the two world wars, the publishing activities of the South Carolina Historical Society were carried on under grave difficulties. Concerning these, Dr. Easterby wrote:

South Carolina will always owe a debt of gratitude to Mabel Louise Webber and a few faithful contributors who persisted, in the face of serious obstacles, in publishing the *South Carolina Historical and Genealogical Magazine*; but it must be regretted that it was compelled to devote so much space to genealogical materials. At the conclusion of its thirtieth volume, its publication committee reminded its readers that it had already remained active through "a period far exceeding the life of any monthly, quarterly or annual periodical published in this state," but an accompanying analysis of its 7,615 pages showed that 1,048, or about one seventh, had been devoted to genealogy. Some 4,118 pages contained documentary materials and 1,459 indexes and other matter. Only 990 pages were devoted to essays and other interpretative articles, and of these 747 were written by one contributor, the indefatigable Henry A. M. Smith. Among the documents printed there was much significant material, but little applied to the period subsequent to the Revolution.

Twenty years ago the tide began to turn. In 1943 the South Carolina Historical Society was granted a thirty-year lease of two floors in the Fireproof Building at the nominal rental of $1 a year. With space available, the society began to take such active steps in seeking manuscript collections that it today possesses something like triple its 1940 holdings. Among papers added in recent times have been the Langdon Cheves, the R. F. W. Allston, the Arnoldus Van der Horst, the Henry W. Conner, and the Joseph W. Barnwell collections.

Occupancy of the Fireproof Building is in itself an asset because of the architectural distinction of the structure. Its architect, Robert Mills, thus described it in 1826 in his *Statistics of South Carolina*:

It is designed in the simple Greek Doric Style, without any ornament, except that afforded by the porticoes which face each front. These porticoes are each composed of four massy columns, three and a half feet in diameter, raised on an arcade, the columns rise the whole height of the building (comprising two stories) surmounted by their entablature, and crowned with a pediment, which extending across the building, meet together in the middle; the remaining part of the building, on each side constitutes wings to the center, falling below the apex of the pediment; the front of these offices is 66 feet; and in breadth 46 feet, besides the porticoes which project about 12, and extend in front 33 feet each. They are communicated with from the street by a double flight of stone steps at both ends. The basement porticoes, cornice, etc. are of stone. The walls are of brick, stuccoed in imitation of the same.

The rooms for offices are vaulted in brick, and the roof covered with copper so as to render the building secure from fire. As a further guard the sashes and frames are all of iron with the shutters.

Each front presents two doors of entrance which lead into corridors communicating with the several offices. The number of distinct apartments in the several stories includes twenty-four, besides the staircase and passages.

The interior stair-steps are of stone, rising from the basement story to the third floor, and lighted by a skylight.

Although exterior maintenance of the Fireproof Building is provided by the county in return for the annual rent of $1, the society is responsible for interior repairs. It has gradually been endeavoring to restore the original attractiveness of the building.

An information leaflet issued in 1947 by the South Carolina Historical Society states that "its annual income from all sources has seldom reached the sum of $3,000." A considerable change has occurred since, for in 1959 total receipts were $10,547.50, of which $1,195 (11%) came from endowment, $7,477.09 (71%) from membership dues, and the remainder from gifts, sales of publications, and the proceeds of Charleston tours and other activities organized on behalf of the society. In 1959 there were 1,315 members who received the *Magazine*; libraries paid $5 and individuals $6. Here membership represents a substantial element of support, for the publishing costs in 1958 were $3,100 and the receipts from dues $7,477.09.

Although the society is understaffed and runs on a narrow margin, it is in able and professionally competent hands. Professor Charles L. Anger, head of the history department at the Citadel, has been its president. The secretary-archivist, Mrs. Granville T. Prior, the widow of Professor Anger's predecessor at the Citadel, is a competent scholar in her own right. With only a little more assistance than Mrs. Hawes in Savannah, Mrs. Prior attends very ably to the daily work of the society, in addition to editing *The South Carolina Historical Magazine*. Its title has within the decade dropped the *and Genealogical*, with corresponding change in content. The South Caroline Historical Society has greatly strengthened its position in the last two decades; nevertheless, like its counterpart in Georgia, it is in dire need of increased support, for too much depends upon the devoted industry of a few able people. In Charleston, as in Savannah, additional income would unquestionably be prudently and usefully spent to the benefit of learning and the honor of the community. The society is, for example, deeply interested in publication projects that are at present hampered by insufficient funds.

South Carolina, like Massachusetts, has a variety of privately supported institutions that today informally divide their fields of activities harmoniously. The South Carolina Historical Society does not emphasize newspaper collections because its neighbor, the Charleston Library Society, possesses rich holdings of early South Carolina newspapers. The Charleston Museum, under the directorship of Mr. E. Milby Burton, is active in popular historical and scientific exhibiting, while Mr. Burton himself has made distinguished studies on the decorative arts in Charleston. The South Carolina Art Association not only maintains an art gallery, but actively defends architectural and historical monuments.

In 1930, when historical activity in Charleston was at a low ebb, a group of history teachers throughout the State, led by the late Professor Robert L. Meriwether of the University of South Carolina at Columbia, founded the South Carolina Historical Association. The new organization had no intention of maintaining premises or assembling collections; it was rather designed to promote an annual meeting at which professional teachers and scholars, with some admixture of laymen, would join in a program of carefully prepared papers.

Ever since the establishment of the American Historical Association in 1884 regional replicas of it were frequently being established. They represented, in general, the professional approach to history. Their members were more often scholars and teachers rather than amateurs and collectors. In general they had no truck with antiquarianism or genealogy, being rather concerned with the interpretation of history. The phrase "historical association" came to connote such an organization, deriving its inspiration from the Amercan Historical Association, just as the phrase "historical society" usually implied a descent from the movement that began in Massachusetts in 1791. I recall no conscious statement that has been made on this point; nevertheless "association" seems to have had an informal semantic implication.

The South Carolina Historical Association has met annually for the past thirty years; from the papers read at these gatherings an annual pamphlet of *Proceedings* has been edited. Dr. Easterby observed that of the seventy-five articles that appeared in the first nineteen issues "many are good, several are indifferent, and a few are poor," but that forty-six of them are devoted to South Carolina subjects: "taken together they constitute an important contribution, and it is not unlikely that they have had the effect of greatly improving the quality of historical scholarship in the state." The association has a few more than one hundred members, who contribute dues of $4 and receive the *Proceedings*. Some eighty libraries throughout the country subscribe at $2. There is no office, for the secretary-treasurer—at present Robert S. Lambert of Clemson College—conducts association business through the clerical staff of his own academic institution. The only real expense is the publication of the *Proceedings*, and an average annual income of about $600 usually takes care of that.

Several of the founders of the association were not only members, but ardent supporters of the older society. Dr. Easterby, as one who valued his connection with both, believed "that the leaders in the new organization would have gladly suggested a union with the old, had they felt that the conservative men who were then directing the policies of the Society would have had the slightest interest in their plan." In Georgia a similar association had, after a brief career, merged with the older society. Although that did not occur in South Carolina, relations are entirely harmonious today.

Professor Meriwether was a man of energy and organizational resource. In 1940 he founded the University South Caroliniana Society at Columbia, to provide a means of preserving historical manuscripts under the wing of the university at which he taught. At this time, as has been previously noted, many South Carolina personal and family manuscripts were leaving the State for want of a depository within it. While the State Archives Department has always had full authority to accept or collect private papers, its director at that time so zealously confined himself to official records as to show actual hostility to the offer of private papers. The South Carolina Historical Society, before it was able to lease the Fireproof Building, was forced to refuse many for want of space. The University South Caroliniana Society was an invention of Professor Meriwether's to attract to the university library a large dues-paying membership from all parts of the State that would potentially both give books and manuscripts and provide funds for their purchase. In the neighborhood of 500 persons were eventually attracted to this "friends of the library" type of organization, which has become a valuable mainstay of the South Caroliniana Library, now housed in the handsome 1840 South Carolina College Library building on the campus at Columbia. The University South Caroliniana Society is the only group in the State with ready funds for the purchase of manuscripts; it has not only proved its value in saving sources but has done some useful publishing. It complements rather than competes with the South Carolina Historical Society, for Professor Meriwether gained general acceptance for the view that upcountry manuscripts should be preserved, whenever possible, in the South Caroliniana Library at Columbia, and low-country material in the South Carolina Historical Society in Charleston.

Professor Meriwether's last contribution to South Carolina history was the editorial project for *The Papers of John C. Calhoun*, as part of the national program recommended by the National Historical Publications Commission. Having been by arrangement with the University of South Carolina relieved from half his teaching load, he established an editorial office in the South Caroliniana Library with part-time assistants provided by the State Archives Department. Through the University of South Carolina Press, provision was made for publication from an appropriation of the Archives Department. Although Professor Meriwether's sudden death on 24 August 1958 was a major blow to the Calhoun project, arrangements were soon made for Dr. W. Edwin Hemphill, formerly of the Virginia State Library, to join the staff of the South Carolina Archives Department, giving half his time to editing State records and half to Calhoun. Volume 1 appeared in 1959, and others will follow in due course.

The frequent appearance of the name of Dr. J. Harold Easterby in recent pages is indicative of his invaluable ubiquity in all matters of historical moment in South Carolina, whether publicly or privately supported. Originally a professor of history at the College of Charleston, he made the South Carolina Archives Department one of the best administered in the country. The publication of a new series of the colonial records and of the State records of South Carolina represented his enlightened activity on one front; the opening of a new archives building in Columbia on 19 April 1960 was evidence of another aspect. His untimely death on 29 December 1960 was a grievous loss to his State and his profession. At once an able scholar and an able public official, his disinterested assistance was of value wherever history was concerned. In some states private institutions and State officials have little in common. It was fortunate for the South Carolina Historical Society that they ordered these things better in Columbia.

FLORIDA

The activities of historical societies in Florida, although intermittent, have included two remarkable examples of the fruitful collaboration of private collectors and professional historians in the twentieth century. A Historical Society of Florida, established at St. Augustine in 1856, had a better record of ambition than accomplishment. Its objectives were, in the fulsome and imprecise language of its chief organizer, George R. Fairbanks:

To explore the field of Florida history, to seek and gather up the ancient chronicles in which its annals are contained, to retain the legendary lore which may yet throw light upon the past, to trace its monuments and remains, to elucidate what has been written, to disprove the false and support the true, to do justice to the men who have figured in the olden time, to keep and preserve all that is known in trust for those who are to come after us, to increase and extend the knowledge of our history, and to teach our children that first essential, the history of our State, are objects well worthy of our best efforts. To accomplish these ends, we have organized the Historical Society of Florida.

While plans were made for the assembly of a library and the publication of manuscripts relating to the history of the State, little was accomplished. The society lapsed into inactivity, which continued until its reorganization in 1902 under the title of the Florida Historical Society. While the resuscitated body really made a fresh start, it had some personal continuity with the 1856 effort, for George R. Fairbanks was elected to the presidency in 1902.

Notwithstanding its incorporation in 1905, the present activity of the Florida Historical Society only began after World War I. A quarterly journal, started in 1908, suspended publication after six issues and was only revived in 1924 when Julien C. Yonge of Pensacola, a private collector of material on Florida history, became its editor. A serious illness while an undergraduate at Auburn University having prevented Mr. Yonge from undertaking a professional career, he devoted his efforts from 1900 onwards to collecting Floridiana, which eventually filled the old carriage rooms and stable of his father's house in Pensacola. For thirty-one years he edited *The Florida Historical Quarterly* and played a major role not only in its development but that of the Florida Historical Society which published it.

With great generosity, Julien C. Yonge and his sister gave the great historical library that he had assembled to the University of Florida in 1943. He was persuaded with some difficulty to come from Pensacola to Gainesville as director of the P. K. Yonge Library of Florida History named in honor of his father. There he worked in close and harmonious relationship for fifteen years with Dr. Rembert W. Patrick, now the Julien C. Yonge Graduate Research Professor of History, and other members of the history department, until 1959 when upon his retirement he returned home to Pensacola. Although Professor Patrick became editor of the *Quarterly* in 1955, Mr. Yonge prepared the index to its first thirty-five volumes, which was published in 1958, and planned and edited the Pensacola Quadricentennial Issue of January-April 1959. There can be few instances of finer or more useful devotion to the history of a State than that of this selfless collector and editor, who died in 1962.

At various times in its career the Florida Historical Society has had its headquarters in St. Augustine, in the Jacksonville Public Library, and at the University of Florida at Gainesville, where it is now. Its resources in books and manuscripts, received entirely by gift, are limited. It owns, among other things, the letter book of Florida's Civil War Governor Milton, the Greenslade papers, relating to the second Spanish period (1783–1821) in Florida, and groups of private letters and diaries. Neither the manuscripts nor the 5,000 volumes of printed books are catalogued. The university supplies 1,500 square feet of space for the society's library and office; furnishes light, heat, and telephone, and pays the salary of a secretary, who keeps the library open and attends to bookkeeping, billing, and the clerical work of the society.

In reply to my query about the Florida Historical Society's staff, its training and recruitment, Professor Patrick wrote me: "We must be unique in the United States. We have no problems, because we have no staff. The University of Florida supplies a secretary." This simplicity is achieved because the society concentrates its efforts in two useful directions: the encouragement of State agencies and the publication of the *Quarterly*. On the first point, Professor Patrick states:

Perhaps the greatest achievement of the Society has been in stimulating state agencies (University of Florida, Florida State Library at Tallahassee, and the Florida State University at Tallahassee) to do something about collecting and preserving Floridiana (books, pamphlets, pictures, diaries, letters, maps, newspapers, manuscripts). In 1940, for example, the University of Florida had nothing more than a few books on Florida. Today the University has a multi-million dollar collection, and there are smaller but valuable collections in the State Library and the Florida State University Library. The reason for this growth lies in the fact that the university has supplied salary and travel expense for a collector, takes care of the collected sources, and will buy material, though 95 per cent has come from gifts. And the present Editor of *The Florida Historical Quarterly* has done the work for the University—so there is a conflict of interest.

Although the society has investments of $5,600, which it regards as an endowment fund, its major source of income is its 800 members, most of whom pay $5 annually, although a few pay $10 or $25. There are sixteen life members who have paid $100. Two hundred libraries subscribe to the *Quarterly* at $5 a year. No officer receives any salary or expense money. Two assistant professors of history help Dr. Patrick in editing the *Quarterly*, all voluntarily. As the university provides quarters and clerical assistance, all receipts are devoted to publishing and to research grants. One hundred and twenty-five exchange subscriptions are given to the University of Florida Library in appreciation of space and assistance provided the society.

Income and expenses average $7,000 a year. The annual net loss of

$1,000 from membership fees over the cost of publishing the *Quarterly* is made up by gifts. For the past five years one individual has given $1,000 each year. In 1960 a similar sum was received to support a research grant. The *Quarterly* publishes an average of 400 pages a year. Although its editors are professional historians, they recognize that 95% of its readers are laymen. They therefore strive to maintain a balance between serious scholarly contributions to Florida history and some of the lighter reminiscent type of articles that prove of broader interest to the general reader.

Although the Florida State Historical Society no longer exists, its activities in collecting and publishing historical sources in the 1920s deserve mention.[5] This was the personal creation in 1921 of Colonel John B. Stetson Jr. of Philadelphia, arising from his enthusiasm over the history of Florida in the Spanish period. With the assistance of Dr. James Alexander Robertson of Washington, D. C., and Miss Irene A. Wright, who had long worked in the Archivo General de Indias at Seville, Colonel Stetson assembled, at a personal cost of half a million dollars, a great collection of photostats of materials relating to Florida in Spanish archives and, to a more limited extent, in French and English archives. The 300 individuals and libraries that became members of the Florida State Historical Society, which was based at DeLand, Florida, were essentially subscribers to publications, of which eleven were issued before 1933. These handsome limited editions of historical sources, designed by Carl Purington Rollins of the Yale University Press, were so attractive to collectors of fine printing as well as to libraries, that they rapidly went out of print. Typographically they were as fine as any work ever issued by an American historical society, while their contents made available important documents in the early history of Florida.

The European collecting activities of the Florida State Historical Society produced copies of more than 7,000 documents, which,

5. Charles W. Arnade, *Florida History in Spanish Archives, Reproductions at the University of Florida* (n.p., n.d.), an address given at the annual meeting of the Florida Historical Society on 15 April 1955, reprinted from the *Florida Historical Quarterly*.

because of the verbosity of the Spanish notarial mind, totaled about 130,000 sheets of photostats. As the work was entirely financed by Colonel Stetson, his severe financial losses in the 1929 stock market debacle put an end to it. Although copying in Spain was suspended before completion, the body of material assembled represented the best source available in the United States for the study of Spanish Florida from the first settlement to the American period.

No publications were issued after 1933, and the Florida State Historical Society ceased to exist except in name. Although it theoretically became a part of the Florida Historical Society in 1939, the great collection of photostats had been placed by Colonel Stetson on sealed loan in the Library of Congress. There the documents remained, unavailable to scholars, until 1954, when, after extended negotiation by Professor Patrick, they were obtained, partly through the gift of Colonel Stetson and partly by purchase, for the P. K. Yonge Library of Florida History at the University of Florida.

Thus the principal assembly of sources of Florida History within the State is due to a combination of the activities of private collectors and professional historians, interwoven in an uncommon pattern involving two independent historical societies and a State university. The unusual elements involved are hardly likely to be duplicated elsewhere, but the end achieved serves the good of learning. It is fortunate that devoted and energetic individuals have bestirred themselves, for, although St. Augustine was founded decades before Jamestown or Plymouth, Florida is still young so far as any historical consciousness or cohesiveness is concerned. Of the almost five million people now in the State, more than two million have been added within the last decade. Thus Florida has not yet acquired the settled population that is interested in history. When that interest develops, there will be gratitude for what has been assembled at Gainesville in recent decades, thanks to the Florida Historical Society.

Chapter IX

INDEPENDENT SOCIETIES IN
MIDDLE WESTERN CITIES

The funds which we have raised from many sources represent an
unusual record of achievement, and a certain amount of this effort
is very healthy for any organization. However, there is a point of no
return in such endeavors, and that point is reached when so much
effort is spent on raising money that the essential and learned purposes for which the organization was created, suffer.
—CHARLES VAN RAVENSWAAY, 1959

WEST of the Alleghanies, State historical societies are
customarily supported chiefly by public appropriations.
In certain large cities in the Ohio and Mississippi valleys
and along the Great Lakes, however, independent historical societies
exist, the richness of whose manuscript holdings gives their collections a more than parochial importance. These are sometimes older
than the publicly supported groups based at the State capital. Because of their age and the nature of their interests, their present
problems resemble those of the independent societies of the Atlantic
seaboard. They will be here described in manner similar to that given
to independent State societies in the preceding chapters, while reference to their corresponding publicly supported neighbors will be
deferred until a later chapter.

HISTORICAL AND PHILOSOPHICAL
SOCIETY OF OHIO

In New England one established a historical society and then sought
incorporation when the organization was safely under way. The

reverse might happen west of the Alleghanies, where the legislative act sometimes preceded reality. This occurred in Ohio, where an act to incorporate the Historical Society of Ohio was approved on 1 February 1822, but nothing happened. A second attempt by the Ohio General Assembly took, for the Historical and Philosophical Society of Ohio,[1] incorporated on 11 February 1831, not only met in the Court House at Columbus on 21 December 1831, but is still in existence. For a time meetings were held regularly at the capital of the State, but in the 1840s it became apparent that the requisite interest was lacking in Columbus. At the annual meeting of 1844, which followed a three-year lapse, delinquent membership dues for the previous four years were forgiven. Nevertheless another lapse followed, for at the next meeting, which did not occur until 23 December 1848, there was no quorum. Assembling the day after Christmas, the society reached an important decision.

The disadvantages of the location at Columbus having now become fully apparent, it was resolved to change the place of meeting for the transaction of business, to remove the books and archives to the more populous city of Cincinnati, and to unite it with the Historical Society of that place.

It was soundly reasoned that the inhabitants of a prosperous commercial river city were likely to prove more useful neighbors than the politicians of the centrally located State capital. Indeed what publishing the society did had moved to Cincinnati well before the formal change of locale. Volume I, part 1 of a series of *Transactions*, had been printed at Columbus in 1838, but part 2 appeared at Cincinnati the following year, as did Jacob Burnet's 500-page *Notes on the early settlement of the Northwestern Territory* in 1847.

A Cincinnati Historical Society had been founded in the summer of 1844, under the presidency of the Reverend James Handasyd Perkins (1810–49), a Unitarian clergyman from Boston, whose son,

1. Virginius C. Hall, "Historical and Philosophical Society of Ohio: A Short History," and other articles in *Bulletin of the Historical and Philosophical Society of Ohio* XIV, 2 (April 1956); Alice Palo Hook, "The Historical Society Library," *Special Libraries* L (1950), 114–118.

Charles Elliott Perkins, was later to become the builder and president of the Chicago, Burlington and Quincy Railroad. To this society S. P. Hildreth of Marietta had presented the manuscript of his *Pioneer History: being an account of the first examinations of the Ohio Valley, and the early settlement of the Northwest Territory*, which was printed the following year as its first major publication. The two societies merged in February 1849, retaining the name of the older one. Thus Hildreth's second volume, *Biographical and historical memoirs of the early pioneer settlers of Ohio*, appeared in 1852 as a publication of the Historical and Philosophical Society of Ohio.

After this spurt of publishing energy, activity subsided for two decades. From 1852 the society had rooms in the Cincinnati College building, but during the Civil War its belongings were in storage and it ceased to meet. When it was revived in 1868, only four active members remained, but during the 1870s and 1880s fresh progress was made. Publication was resumed in 1873 with the *Journal and letters of Colonel John May, of Boston, relative to two journeys to the Ohio country in 1788 and 1789*, while in 1885 were issued two volumes of Eugene F. Bliss's translation from the German of the *Diary of David Zeisberger, a Moravian missionary among the Indians of Ohio*. In 1885 the society reached the point of buying its first permanent home, a house (now demolished) in Garfield Place, which it occupied for sixteen years.

At the end of the century a decision of great importance to the future was taken. The agreement concluded with the University of Cincinnati on 10 November 1899, whereby the Historical and Philosophical Society of Ohio was granted occupancy of space in the new university library, was equivalent to an affirmation of the scholarly and professional interests of the tenant. When the society moved into its new quarters in the Van Wormer Library in November 1901 it brought with it 16,696 bound volumes and 64,016 pamphlets. Upon the completion of a new university library building in 1930, the society moved there, where it now occupies two floors of the bookstack in addition to a reading room of its own.

Like most organizations of early foundation, the Historical and Philosophical Society of Ohio had envisioned a very broad field of collecting. "Everything relating to the history and antiquities of America, more especially to the State of Ohio" became a greater impossibility with the passage of each decade. The establishment at Columbus in 1885 of the Ohio State Archaeological and Historical Society, which is today one of the most liberally supported and best managed of the State historical agencies, made it even more desirable for the older society to limit its field to a part of Ohio. At the present time its constitution states that:

The object of this Society shall be to institute and encourage historical inquiry and to collect and preserve historical material relating to the State of Ohio, and the Ohio River and its tributaries, with particular reference to the Miami Purchase, Southwestern Ohio, south of Columbus, west of the Scioto River, east of Indiana and north of Kentucky, and to spread historical information, especially concerning (firstly) Southwestern Ohio and (secondly) the old Northwest Territory of the United States.

This is a reasonable and realistic aspiration.

The library conforms closely to that limitation today, for in 1944, following a survey by K. D. Metcalf, then director of the Harvard University Libraries, the collecting range of the library was carefully defined and extraneous material withdrawn. There have been kept until now some 34,500 printed books with particular emphasis on early politics, biography, travel, and county and local histories, plus about 28,000 pamphlets. The most frequently consulted source in the library is the newspaper collection, for, beginning with the *Centinel of the North-Western Territory*, 1793–95, there are extensive files of Cincinnati newspapers through the year 1930, as well as files of certain papers printed in other Ohio cities and towns prior to 1865. German-language newspapers for the years 1843–52 and 1874–1939 abound.

The manuscript collection, which is estimated at over 100,000 items and volumes, from 1765 to the present, relates chiefly to the Ohio valley. It contains papers of political, military, social, economic, business, artistic, and personal character. The Torrence collection contains 2,056 letters and 115 documents between 1790 and 1857 on the settlement of Cincinnati and vicinity. Among the papers of the Ohio lawyer Rufus King (1817–91) are 115 letters of the earlier Rufus King who was a delegate to the Continental Congress. The papers of John Johnston (1775–1861) include some 222 letters on Indian affairs in Ohio, while those of the sculptor Hiram Powers (1805–73) throw light upon his work and upon his relations with Cincinnatians. The correspondence on political and social themes of William Greene (1797–1883) of Rhode Island and Ohio includes letters of Dr. Frederick Roelker (1809–81) bearing upon early Cincinnati and local German politics of the mid-century. To these and other sizable personal collections have been added numerous early church and cemetery records, journals and diaries of early settlers, Civil War correspondence, business records, and the minutes of societies, clubs, and institutions. There are also some 1,600 maps, numerous broadsides, cartoons, prints, and photographs, including an extensive holding of Cincinnati views and pictures of river steamboats. Probably the handsomest of the local topographical items are five water colors of scenes in downtown Cincinnati in 1835 by John Casper Wild, which offer a moving reminder of the lost architectural attractions of the city.

The society's long-standing location in the university library makes it extremely convenient for scholars but somewhat inaccessible to the casual visitor. Since 1947 the latter difficulty has been admirably solved by a series of annual exhibitions held each spring at the Taft Museum. That delightful institution, in which European paintings and Chinese porcelains of great distinction are permanently shown in the finest surviving early nineteenth-century house in Cincinnati, has made its temporary exhibition galleries available to the Historical and Philosophical Society of Ohio each May and June for the past fourteen years. Thus many of the paintings, prints, and photographs from the society's working collection are annually exhibited in surroundings that show them off to advantage.

These spring exhibitions have been useful in enlarging the general membership, as distinct from the smaller core of serious workers who have long appreciated the society's scholarly resources. Two meetings are held each year, the annual meeting in December and one at the opening of the spring exhibition. In 1941 there were but 76 members; in 1952 there were 779; in 1960 there were 1,250. Individual membership is $10 per year, and life membership involves a single payment of $100. Of the $36,900.85 spent by the society in 1959, $13,390 was received from membership dues, and $24,329.61 from the income of investments having a book value of $242,428.96 and a market value of $737,497.

A quarterly publication, issued from 1906 to 1923, was the means of disseminating the texts of numerous items from the rare book and manuscript collections. After this was given up, the practice of publishing books from time to time was resumed. Thus the *Correspondence of John Cleves Symmes* was published in 1926; *Some Considerations on . . . the French Settling Colonies on the Mississippi* in 1928; Josiah Morrow's *History of the Sycamore Associated Reformed Church* in 1930; *Colonel A. W. Gilbert*, edited by William E. and Ophia D. Smith, in 1934; *Courses of the Ohio River*, edited by Beverly W. Bond Jr., in 1942; Robert L. Black's *The Centenary of the Cincinnati Observatory* in 1944; William E. and Ophia D. Smith's *The Buckeye Titan* in 1943; and *Intimate Letters of John Cleves Symmes*, edited by Beverly W. Bond Jr., in 1957. A *Bulletin*, first issued in 1943 as a four-page leaflet, has grown to a quarterly whose issues now normally consist of eighty pages. Volume XVIII appeared during 1960.

The principal achievement of the Historical and Philosophical Society of Ohio in the present century has been its library, which since 1947 has been in the charge of Mrs. Alice P. Hook, an intelligent and energetic professional librarian. There has been less continuity in the directorship of the society. During 1959 and 1960 Mr. Herbert F. Koch, a retired professor of business administration at the university, served as director to assist the society until a permanent appointment could be made. Mr. Koch, recording secretary from

1944 to 1951 and a trustee from 1951 to 1959, has been a devoted friend of the society and has given much time to spreading the news of its activities in Cincinnati. In October 1960 Dr. Louis Leonard Tucker, a PH.D. in American history of the University of Washington and from 1958 to 1960 a Fellow of the Institute of Early American History and Culture at Williamsburg, Virginia, became director.

The course upon which the Historical and Philosophical Society of Ohio is now traveling is realistic and useful. Additional staff and endowment are the major needs. Although the arrival of Dr. Tucker represents a step in the right direction, the society is still badly in need of additional staff. In regard to endowment, there is reason to hope that under the presidency of Mr. Lucien Wulsin, who is active in most of the artistic and musical enterprises of Cincinnati, private gifts towards that end may soon be forthcoming.

While this book was in press, the society announced that it expected two years hence to move to new quarters in a three-story wing that is to be added to the Cincinnati Art Museum. This will provide increased space for the society's library and book stacks, a handsome room given, in memory of his parents, by Cornelius J. Hauck to house and display the rare books and manuscripts that he has collected, and a small lecture hall seating 150. The latter will be shared, like the present museum auditorium, by the historical society and the art museum. The society's quarters will have an independent entrance and parking lot. While there have been substantial advantages to having the books of the Historical and Philosophical Society of Ohio under the roof of a larger general library, space at the University of Cincinnati has become crowded. What there is has been accessible only by a tortuous route that has effectively concealed the society's existence from casual visitors. So far as quiet work is concerned, this is a blessing. It is equally disadvantageous to any attempt to make the society more widely known in the city. One hopes that the new and attractive quarters will prove the first step in a chain of events that will culminate in a substantial increase in endowment. Residents of Cincinnati generously support art and music; there is every reason why they should be similarly generous to the Historical and Philosophical Society of Ohio.

WESTERN RESERVE HISTORICAL SOCIETY

The oldest cultural organization in Cleveland is the Western Reserve Historical Society, founded in 1867. Although originally established (under the name of Western Reserve and Northern Ohio Historical Society) to collect and preserve material relating to that portion of northeastern Ohio which was originally the Western Reserve of Connecticut, the society today possesses manuscripts that are of more than regional significance. Whittlesey's *Early history of Cleveland*, although published privately in 1867, had the patronage of the society, which in 1871 issued the *Journal of Capt. William Trent, from Logstown to Pickawillany, 1752 . . . with letters of Governor Robert Dinwiddie*, edited by its secretary, A. T. Goodman. The Western Reserve Historical Society has, throughout the years, been more distinguished for collecting than publishing. Its series of numbered *Tracts*, which began in 1870, although numerous, consisted chiefly of thin pamphlets. While the translation of a German work on the history of Sandusky has recently been successfully issued in continuation of the numbered series, the only current serial publication is a monthly four-page *Historical Society News* that has appeared during the past sixteen years.

The manuscript collection of approximately 1,000,000 pieces between 1750 and the present relates chiefly to Ohio, but contains much of wider interest. The Shaker material assembled by Wallace H. Cathcart, for example, which consists of 6,000 volumes, 384 hymnals, 125 feet of documents, and 28 letter files, includes the records of nineteen Shaker communities in eight states, beginning in 1776. For the Civil War period, the William P. Palmer collection covers both sides and includes letters and papers on slavery, abolition, the Underground Railway, and various campaigns, while the society also owns papers of the Confederate Braxton Bragg of Louisiana and

Texas and the Union officer Franz Sigel of Missouri and New York. Many important documents are included in the letters of signers of the Declaration of Independence and the Presidents of the United States, which are on permanent exhibition in a special gallery.

Individual collections of political significance include the 90,000 letters of Elisha Whittlesey, the papers of Senator Theodore E. Burton of Ohio, Ambassador Myron T. Herrick, Warner M. Batemen Sr., and others. Military papers relate to the French and Indian War, the Revolution, and the War of 1812, and the records of the Connecticut Land Company, besides extensive collections of other papers, provide sources for the early history of the Western Reserve. Records of business houses and associations; materials on railroad, canal, and lake transportation; local township and church records; unpublished genealogies; and other manuscripts make collections of wide interest.

The printed books also contain much material useful for research. While particularly rich in nineteenth-century Americana, there are specialized groups dealing with local history, genealogy, Mormonism, the history of costumes, Lincoln and the Civil War, New England history, the War of 1812, the Shakers, early Ohio laws, arctic exploration, the Lewis and Clark expedition, and Napoleon Bonaparte. The 25,000 bound volumes of newspapers are of especial value for Civil War research, as they include some 22,000 issues of papers published in the Confederate States.

Although the resources of the library attract historians in many fields, the Western Reserve Historical Society, and its present director, Mr. Meredith B. Colket Jr., formerly of the National Archives, have a special interest in genealogy. Much effort is spent on the perfecting of indexes of value to genealogists.

The Western Reserve Historical Society is very handsomely housed in a unique manner that combines historic preservation and practical utility. For some years it occupied two very large detached private houses on East Boulevard, near the art museum and Western Reserve University. One of these had been built by Mrs. John Hay;

the other was the former home of Mrs. Leonard C. Hanna. One housed the library; the other a museum. Both buildings were good examples of Cleveland taste in a Renaissance mood in the early years of the twentieth century that, while worth preserving, would not have survived save for adaptation to other uses. In 1959–60 these two houses were joined by a connecting wing, built at the cost of a million dollars, raised by fairly large gifts from private sources. This recent addition contains exhibition galleries, library reading room, and bookstacks. Architecturally it is a skillful piece of work in that it brings two separate houses into common use, without swearing at either one. While the bookstacks are completely utilitarian, the façade, courtyard, and public rooms of the new wing are suggestive of the Florentine Renaissance inspiration of the earlier construction. While this was desirable to create an impression of unity, it resulted in somewhat greater cost than was entailed in the Virginia Historical Society's comparable addition to Battle Abbey.

A part of the new wing and one of the houses are now used for museum purposes. Among the exhibits a log cabin shows the possessions of a frontier family before the invention of the sawmill, and objects used by early settlers of the Western Reserve and by the Amish and Shakers contrast with furniture, silver, glass, and pottery representing a more luxurious state of society. Tract number 24, issued in October 1874, reported the gift by W. P. Fogg of bricks from Babylon, Nineveh, and the Arch of Ctesiphon, and other objects from the Near East. Most historical societies have by now narrowed the scope of their possessions to at least the national scene. Not so the Western Reserve Historical Society. Not only are an Egyptian mummy and pre-Inca Peruvian pottery still on display, but in the new wing two galleries especially designed around great panels of French scenic wallpaper are devoted to a Napoleonic collection that includes pictures, furniture, documents, books, and personal objects belonging to, or concerning, the emperor.

Emphasis on the museum is part of the Western Reserve Historical Society's attempt to attract popular interest. The April 1960 issue of *The Historical Society News* describes the Charles G. King costume collection in the library as "the best examples of beautifully illustrated and authoritative writings on native dress and customs of peoples in all parts of the world," which is "widely used by designers, art students, little theatre groups and other persons seeking accurate information on the subject." It announces an exhibition of "gowns worn by fashionable women in the 1890's," arranged to mark the opening of the current opera season; a program of color slides on Amish life on 17 April; a "genealogical workshop" on 20 April; a puppet show for children entitled "Heels to Wheels to Automobiles" produced by the Junior League Puppet Workshop on the 23rd; and on Sunday, 8 May, "color slides of the Swiss Alps and the fairy tale castles of Bavaria and France" by Mr. Julius Czapko, a former member of the Cleveland Orchestra.

The society's present annual income of $94,000 is derived from three sources; endowment which produces $57,000; a County grant of $25,000; and $12,000 from membership dues. In addition to its headquarters in Cleveland, the society owns three other properties: Lawnfield, the home of President James A. Garfield at Mentor, which is maintained by the affiliated Lake County Historical Society; Shandy Hall, near Unionville, Ashtabula County; and the Jonathan Hale Homestead near Peninsula, a pioneer house which is now being developed as a farm museum. The staff of twenty-six, a number of whom are persons of long service, includes the director, a genealogist, a cataloguer, two library assistants, an editor, six guards, and three cleaning women.

CHICAGO HISTORICAL SOCIETY

An Antiquarian and Historical Society of Illinois, founded at Vandalia in 1827, and an Illinois Literary and Historical Society, established at Upper Alton in 1843, both proved impermanent, while the present publicly supported Illinois State Historical Society, with headquarters at Springfield, dates only from the year 1899. The

Chicago Historical Society, founded in 1856, is the oldest significant body of the kind in the State of Illinois; it is not only privately supported, but is among independent historical societies second only to the New-York Historical Society in the size of its endowment. The account of its first 100 years was cheerfully and impressionistically sketched by its director, Paul M. Angle, in *The Chicago Historical Society, 1855–1956, An Unconventional Chronicle*.

From this diverting book, the main lines upon which the society developed are easily seen. There was, as in most cases, an indefatigable collector, in this instance the Reverend William Barry, a Unitarian clergyman, who served as recording secretary and librarian for the first decade. His activities produced a library that required housing, which was acquired in 1868 in the form of a handsome two-story brick and stone building at the corner of Ontario and Dearborn Streets. This, at its dedication, was with reason referred to as the beginning of "a great public library," for the Chicago Historical Society antedated the Newberry, the John Crerar, the Chicago Public, and the University of Chicago libraries. Even after these institutions were founded, the paramount interest of the Chicago Historical Society continued to be its library. Only after more than sixty years was there a change of emphasis.

The great fire of October 1871 swept away building and contents. In a few hours it had a more devastating effect than four years of war had achieved with the southern historical societies. Only in 1874 was a revival attempted, with the encouragement of the prospect of an eventual $60,000 from the estate of Henry D. Gilpin of Philadelphia, one of the benefactors of the Historical Society of Pennsylvania. As the society's only surviving assets were the subscriptions of $300 each received from early life members, which continued to draw interest, it was in 1876 proposed that annual members, whose yearly dues had been the remarkably high sum of $25, be asked to "submit to an assessment of Fifty Dollars each for the entire interregnum of five years." This proved difficult to collect in most cases, but somehow between August and October 1877 a modest one-story building was achieved on the old site. While this was a poor substitute for what had been lost in the fire, it served as a rallying point and housed the society until it was replaced by a substantial Romanesque library in 1896.

History of Illinois from 1778 to 1833; and Life and times of Ninian Edwards, written by Ninian W. Edwards at the request of the society and published at Springfield in 1870, was the chief work produced before the fire. Although four volumes of *Collections* were issued between 1882 and 1890, most of the nineteenth-century publications of the Chicago Historical Society were relatively brief addresses, memorials, or records of meetings.

Mr. Angle reports two conspicuous examples of disharmony between officers and staff. Albert D. Hager, whose energetic begging from the moment of his appointment as secretary and librarian in 1876 had been instrumental in the restoration of the library, was sacked in 1887 after disagreements with the president, Edward G. Mason. The eminent bibliographer Charles Evans, who took the post in 1896, was dismissed in 1901 because of some conflict with the executive committee. While the reasons for this have long been forgotten, along with the executive committee, the *American Bibliography*, which began to appear a few years later, has given the name of Charles Evans a permanent place in American historiography.

In the spring of 1920 the Chicago Historical Society took a step which permanently changed the character of its activities. Mr. Angle thus describes it:

For fifty years Charles F. Gunther, candy manufacturer, alderman and trustee of the Chicago Historical Society, had been amassing an enormous collection of art treasures, rare books and prints, manuscripts, and historic objects. He stopped at nothing, even bringing Libby Prison from Richmond to Chicago. The private museum he maintained in his place of business had become one of the sights of the city, attracting thousands of visitors annually. Gunther died on February 10, 1920. Six weeks later—on March 26—the *Daily News* reported that the Gunther collection would go to the Historical Society.

The agreement to purchase the Gunther collection for $150,000 effectively put the Chicago Historical Society, hitherto chiefly a library, into the museum business. Miss Caroline McIlvaine, the society's librarian, was quoted by the *Daily News* as stating that "the Americana in the collection is the greatest Americanization force that can be assembled merely as propaganda." Raising the money was slow business, but in the autumn of 1923, after some concessions in price had been made by the Gunther estate, the society came to own the collection, which it had no space to exhibit.

Charles B. Pike, who was elected president in November 1927, set his heart upon the construction of a million-dollar museum of American history in Lincoln Park; in spite of the depression he achieved his goal, for the society's present building was opened to the public in November 1932. It is a handsome brick and marble structure, equipped with exhibition galleries, an auditorium, and classrooms, as well as commodious housing for the library. Its galleries were designed for an exhibition of American history from Columbus up, based upon the varied objects in the Gunther collection. To provide a permanent background for the museum, the architects painstakingly copied and adapted historic interiors from many parts of the country. This costly eclecticism causes the visitor to proceed from the Foyer of Independence Hall in Philadelphia into a considerably enlarged but unmistakable copy of the stair hall of the Lee Mansion in Marblehead, Massachusetts. The Senate chamber of Congress Hall, Philadelphia, is reproduced elsewhere, while visiting Bostonians were apt to be startled by a life-size replica of the Paul Revere House, accurately copied from that building as it was restored by Joseph Everett Chandler early in the present century.[2] John Robinson Hall in the Peabody Museum of Salem was meticulously reproduced, even though the original of that room had been cobbled together out of offices, closets, and corridors only a few years earlier. Although much of the museum deals with the United States in general, one gets closer to home with the replicas of the Lincoln parlor in Spring-

2. In 1961 the Paul Revere House replica was being demolished to make way for a more appropriate exhibit.

field and the room in which he died in Washington, the simulations of nineteenth-century dentist's office, drugstore, and pioneer interiors, and numerous dioramas depicting events in the life of Lincoln and of the history of Chicago.

The financial picture was gloomy upon completion of the building; expenses mounted as income from investments and membership fell. Nevertheless President Pike was undaunted. His generous devotion to the society continued until his death in April 1941; through the gifts of his widow and his brother, Eugene R. Pike, of Mrs. Joseph M. Cudahy and others, the Chicago Historical Society today has not only its building but gross assets with a book value of $5,163,132.35.

The building, although constructed by private funds, is, being in Lincoln Park, upon city-owned land that is leased to the society in perpetuity. In consequence of this, the society receives $25,000 annually from the Chicago Park District, which is a portion of the museum tax that is levied and divided among the various institutions whose buildings are located in city parks. This is the only public support received. Of the budget for the fiscal year ending 30 June 1960 of $311,850, some $19,000 is received from the 1,983 members (of which $8,000 represents income from the investment of life membership fees), and $11,000 is derived from admission fees, sales, and other miscellaneous sources. The remainder—more than four fifths of the total—is supplied from the income of endowment. It should be noted that the bulk of this endowment is less than twenty-five years old, and that much of it has come in large gifts. Membership is thus chiefly useful for maintenance of public interest, and of gifts in kind; it does not today represent an important element in financial support. Thus, unlike the Art Institute of Chicago, which places great store on the size of its membership, the Chicago Historical Society indulges only in low-pressure solicitation by mail.

Emphasis in the library is placed upon the City of Chicago, the State of Illinois, and the Old Northwest Territory, although special holdings concerning the Civil War, the history of sports, and the print, map, and broadside collections extend far beyond this area. The Chicago collection is rich in directories; business, club, and church histories; scrapbooks and commercial catalogues. It contains material on Chicago criminals, labor unions, and ship disasters on the Great Lakes. It has the best file of Chicago newspapers of any institution in the region.

The manuscript collection[3] contains material relating to fur-trading enterprises on the Great Lakes and in the Mississippi valley; the Flower family papers concerning the early English settlements in the State; the papers of Ninian Edwards, Elisha Kent Kane, E. S. and Louis Kimberly, and William Butler dealing with Illinois politics; the Hardin papers which cover Mormon as well as political activities in Illinois; and manuscripts of Chicago interest relating to the Haymarket Riot, the University of Chicago Settlement House in the the stockyards area, and the Agnes Nestor papers which relate to women in the labor force. It includes a set of signers of the Declaration of Independence, and letters of the presidents, with groups of Washington, Jackson, Lincoln, and Grant letters.

The library is open to high school students. It is used largely by them, by undergraduates, by radio, TV, and advertising people, by publishers, and avocational historians, but no genealogists. It answers many phone inquiries and furnishes numerous illustrations for reproduction. Mr. Angle characterizes it as "a scholarly library not much used by scholars, but extensively used by people with a commercial interest in history." This is in line with the "bus and trolley car audience" to which the society today makes its chief appeal through its museum.

Mr. Angle tells the diverting story of how Sally Rand's ostrich fans almost became an "attraction" in the museum. In 1943 her press agent had the notion of offering the fans to the Chicago Historical Society as a memento of the Century of Progress Exposition. Mr.

---

3. Margaret Scriven, "Chicago Historical Society," *Illinois Libraries* XL, 4 (April 1958), pp. 287–288. This "manuscript issue" describes the manuscript collections of Illinois libraries.

L. Hubbard Shattuck, Mr. Angle's predecessor as director, seemingly found the idea captivating for he was quoted by the *Herald American* of 9 May 1943 as saying: "These fans made history. They represented one phase of American life, and help to round out the picture for the ages. It means we are trying to get a broader view. Things we have overlooked in the past are now becoming recognized as having a place in the historical picture of the world." When the trustees of the society firmly concluded they did not want the fans, Sally Rand vented her annoyance in an interview by Jerry Thorp of the *Daily News*:

"What is of historical interest from this dizzy decade?" the fiery-eyed dancer continued. "If I hadda museum I'd have a flagpole that a flagpole sitter sat on. I'd have a goldfish that one of the college boys swallowed. . . . But maybe I don't know what is of historical interest," she pondered. "I've never been to a historical museum."

Then brightly: "Have you?"

"No."

"No—of course not. And neither has anyone else I know"...

"I wonder," she meditated, "what that outfit would have done if Eve had offered them her fig leaf?"

Newspapers throughout the country thoroughly enjoyed this contretemps. Of the deluge of publicity received by the Chicago Historical Society, Mr. Angle offers as "the pithiest, and funniest, comment" that of David V. Felts in the Decatur *Herald*:

It is true, of course, that nobody was interested in seeing Sally's fans, even in 1933. They tried to see Sally and the fans were always in the way.

During the year ending 30 June 1959 there were 188,384 visitors, of whom 120,491 were children and students. Saturday morning lectures presented on 23 Saturdays of the school year brought 9,256 school children. Other programs on 21 Wednesdays of the school year were attended by 12,910, while Summer Fun programs, during the vacation, attracted 12,977. Teachers brought 34,168 students to tour the museum, of whom 14,806 were given 631 guided tours and specially scheduled gallery talks. To teachers calling in person 914 sets of educational materials were given; 790 were sent in reply to telephone requests, and 923 in response to requests by mail.

For the eleventh year a photographic competition, Chicagoland-in-Pictures, was held with the co-operation of the Chicago Area Camera Clubs Association with prizes for outstanding local views. From these submissions 1,021 prints were added to the society's permanent collection. Since the beginning of this project 7,146 photographs of present or future historical significance have been obtained.

The only current publication is a pocket-size quarterly, *Chicago History*, strongly reminiscent of *The Month at Goodspeed's*, which has been issued for many years by Goodspeed's Book Shop in Boston. Like its prototype, it is attractive and pleasant to read, but entirely popular in its appeal. This little quarterly is in a sense symbolic of the last forty years of the Chicago Historical Society. By acquiring the Gunther collection and shifting its emphasis to museum exhibition, the society has come to appeal largely to a popular and commercial audience. It has been successful in the transformation, through the generosity of certain large donors. It carries out its exhibiting and educational activities admirably and spends the greater part of its substantial income in doing so. Its library, although constantly replenished by new sources, has not generated any particular scholarly activity from within. That the Georgia Historical Society, which operates on less than 3% of the Chicago Historical Society's current budget, publishes far more is an evidence both of the great expense of popularization and of the difficulty of maintaining research and publication functions once an institution has wholeheartedly embraced the theory of popular appeal.

MISSOURI HISTORICAL SOCIETY

In Missouri as in Ohio, the principal city proved to be a more propitious location for a historical society than the capital of the State. The Historical and Philosophical Society of Ohio soon moved from

Columbus to Cincinnati. Without regard to, or more likely without knowledge of, that experience, the Missouri Historical and Philosophical Society established itself in the capital and soon died. Organized in the Senate chamber at Jefferson City on 14 December 1844, that society anticipated support from the State. Its twenty-nine-page *Annals* issued in 1848—the first of three publications—stated: "It is appropriate that the Historical and Philosophical Society of the State should be located at the seat of government, and that the public authorities, and citizens from every county, should aid in carrying it into successful operation." Seemingly this view was not shared, for the present State Historical Society of Missouri, based at today's capital, Columbia, only claims to have been founded in 1898. The privately supported Missouri Historical Society, established at Saint Louis in 1866, has over ninety-six years developed a research library of high scholarly importance.

In collecting, the Missouri Historical Society recognized that the history of Saint Louis and of Missouri were inextricably entwined with that of the Louisiana Territory and of the Mississippi valley in general. Its library is therefore of broad usefulness. It contains about 100,000 catalogued titles of books, pamphlets, and periodicals, and the usual body of works remaining to be catalogued. Possessed of significant holdings of historical journals, Missouri and national magazines, it also owns adequate general research collections on each state and territory; American travel books; genealogies, particularly of the south; studies of Indians, and State publications. There are 2,000 bound volumes of newspapers and a sizable group of broken volumes and short runs; although most are from Missouri, there are significant files published in New Mexico, Kansas, Kentucky, Virginia, Washington, D. C., and New York.

The manuscript collection contains something over 1,000,000 items, chiefly relating to Missouri and the west. The more important holdings deal with such subjects and figures as Thomas Jefferson, Missouri's colonial archives and some early State archival material, Aaron Burr, Lewis and Clark, George Rogers Clark, the Mexican War, the Civil War, colonial business and commerce in the Missouri area, the Women's Suffrage Movement, the Russian Revolution, and the American fur trade. Smaller but significant collections centre about Walt Whitman, Eugene Field, Kate Chopin, and other literary figures.

There are as well 200,000 prints, photographs, and early advertising pieces, with emphasis on topographical and architectural views, steamboats, and river traffic. Within the museum there are almost 400 oil paintings, among which are portraits of William Clark, Generals Fremont, Grant, and Kearny, and other such persons, painted by Chester Harding, George C. Bingham, Carl Wimar, Sarah Peale, and others. Major museum collections deal with the American Indian, the westward expansion, costumes, business and industry, and transportation. Since 1927 items used by General Charles A. Lindbergh on his "Spirit of St. Louis" flight and trophies and gifts received by him have been a popular attraction. Within the limits imposed by the unhandy architectural confinement of the galleries, the exhibits are well arranged.

The Missouri Historical Society is housed in the Jefferson Memorial Building, a permanent survivor of the exposition, in Forest Park, Saint Louis. The monumental dignity of this building replete with bronze and marble is equaled by its inconvenience, for it is divided into two separate sections by a great open peristyle. Thus, to go from the second floor of one wing to the other, one must go down stairs, out of doors, and up again, or in foul weather continue below to the basement, where there is the only interior connection between the two wings. The Jefferson Memorial Building is owned by the City, which maintains the exterior and provides heat, water, and electricity, as well as furnishing one guard on a twenty-four-hour basis. To aid in the educational program, the Saint Louis Board of Education gives $1,000 and the Board of Co-operating Superintendents, St. Louis County, $2,000 annually. Otherwise the Missouri Historical Society depends entirely upon private support.

Its endowment has always been notoriously inadequate; until the end of World War II its membership was small. Today the society is extremely active. Between 1946 and 1960 its annual income more than sextupled from $20,000 to over $133,000; its members increased from 500 to almost 4,000 individuals, paying $10, and over 100 corporate members with dues (based on the number of employees) ranging from $100 to $500 each. This is a conspicuous example of what can be accomplished by organized imaginative energy. This change coincides precisely with the directorship of Charles van Ravenswaay, a man who has shown unique skill in attracting wide popular support without ever losing sight of the serious purposes for which the society exists. All too often successful organization becomes a fascinating game in itself that eventually beclouds the reason for which it was undertaken; that this is not the case in Saint Louis does honor to Mr. van Ravenswaay's sense of proportion, quite as much as the increase in activities does credit to his unflagging energy and ability to inspire others.

In stating that the present purpose of the society is "to use history as a vital force in shaping and enriching the cultural and intellectual life of this region," he makes the following comments:

We are concerned with the whole history; architecture and the decorative arts of this region; the printed and written record of man's experiences and thoughts; music; and the pictorial record of the past. We are not specialists. We do not cater to any small group.

This program has expanded since World War II because of the pressure of public interest, and because of our conviction that we cannot meet our intellectual and moral responsibilities unless the Society uses its own collections for the widest public good. We could not have developed such a broad program without this public interest, or without our very diversified museum and library collection.

To fulfill our purposes we have expanded not only our in-the-building program, but we provide many field services such as: historic preservation advice and direction throughout Missouri and Illinois; chairmanship of the St. Louis Mayor's Bicentennial Planning Committee and of the St. Louis County Historic Buildings Commission, as well as many other field services; projects with business, industry, the schools, and other groups.

The character of Saint Louis has played an important part in the revival of the Missouri Historical Society. It is a large and rich city whose inhabitants are susceptible to the arts; they are, moreover, energetic and seem to enjoy public occasions, especially when these are not dull. In contrast to Bostonians, who abominate publicity, give an almost clandestine quality to their good works, and loathe being in a crowd, residents of Saint Louis cheerfully enter into group activities if they are properly presented and serve a desirable purpose. Thus the women's association of the Missouri Historical Society, an auxiliary organized to expand services and increase interest and support, has been highly successful not only in increasing membership but in raising substantial sums by imaginative means.

Since 1954 they have staffed and operated a country store in one room of the Jefferson Memorial Building. The sale of stone-ground flour, herbs, Christmas cards, and other irresistible knickknacks has permitted the women's association to make an annual gift of $6,000 to $8,000 a year to the society. The Flea Market, a glorified rummage sale of monumental proportions, netted in the year 1958–59 in excess of $30,000, which provided funds for the skillful rehabilitation of the costume room in the museum. Thus a formerly dreary portion of the basement of the Jefferson Memorial Building has become a smartly attractive asset.

A recent membership drive, carried on by the women's association, of a magnitude that could only be considered once every five years or so, practically doubled the size of the society. At a minimum of $10, 1,935 members were obtained for net costs of $4,552.84, which do not take into account the immense amount of time and effort expended by members of the association, staff of the society, and countless volunteers. Thus Mr. van Ravenswaay's report of June 1959 gives the following statistics of membership changes:

Total active members, May 1, 1958	2,023
Members gained during the year	2,059
	4,082
Memberships lost (death, 25; resigned, 43; non-payment, 96)	−148
	3,934
Members reinstated, 21; gained by transfer, 12	33
	3,967

The receipts from individual membership during the fiscal year ending 1 May 1960 were $33,707, which contrast with the $1,600 received from similar sources in 1945. Even more significant is the $23,730 received from corporate membership, a class that has proved more successful in Saint Louis than most other cities. The extent to which the Missouri Historical Society depends upon current hard work will be appreciated when one notes that out of $133,395.26 received in the fiscal year ending in May 1960, only $26,865.28 was derived from endowment.

The extent and variety of the activity necessary to support life places a considerable burden upon the modest staff. The museum is in the charge of a full-time curator. In the library, a part-time librarian and assistant librarian and a full-time reference librarian cope with cataloguing and more than 2,000 reference requests, a half of which were represented by research workers who came in person. The manuscript room, which is staffed by two full-time librarians, had 456 personal visits of research workers, in addition to those that also used printed books. The manuscripts of the Missouri Historical Society attract many professional historians, besides the large number of persons who have a commercial interest in history. To compensate to some extent for the heavy demands of the latter group, a service charge of $2 a day has been imposed for nonmembers and of $2 per hour for staff research.

A full-time curator and an assistant curator are occupied with the Pictorial Department, where so many pictures are supplied for commercial use that a modest net profit is made. It is hoped that in time this income will more than support the costs of the department. A grant of $3,000 from the Pitzman Trust of Saint Louis has made possible the provision of a full-time staff member to deal with the Mississippi River collection. This curator has, among other things, obtained new material for the museum exhibit and library collections, given many talks to children and special groups, and written articles on the subject.

Mrs. Dana O. Jensen, as part-time editor since September 1949, has transformed the society's *Bulletin* from an inconsequential publication to a highly respectable historical quarterly, devoting much of its space to scholarly articles and significant documents. New letters of Walt Whitman to members of his family, recently acquired by the society, were, for example, edited for the January 1960 *Bulletin* by Professor Edwin Haviland Miller of Simmons College, whose forthcoming edition of the Whitman correspondence is to be published by the New York University Press. Although the society has published no books in recent years, the *Bulletin* in its present form of quarterly issues of about 100 pages of text, with eight pages of illustrations, represents a useful contribution to historical literature.

An Educational Department, with a staff of three full-time members, who are assisted by volunteers during rush periods, dealt with a total of 26,974; 4,374 during the summer of 1958 and 22,600 in the course of the school year 1958–59. Groups attended from Saint Louis public schools and from other parts of Missouri and Illinois, including special groups of blind, deaf, gifted, and retarded children. During the summer of 1958 the department began to experiment with adult classes, which had an average attendance of 100 at each session.

With present limitations in gallery space, educational attendance has already reached a maximum. Any expansion must await reconstruction and enlargement of the building. The greater part of the cost of the Educational Department is met by the $3,000 annually received from the Saint Louis Board of Education and the Saint Louis County Schools, and from an annual Famous-Barr Grant of $8,000.

A membership secretary and a bookkeeper handle the multifarious details of clerical work connected with the expanding membership. With the assistance of funds provided by the women's association, the part-time staff member who handles publicity has assumed the additional work of co-ordinating special events. This is a step forward, for, as Mr. van Ravenswaay observed in his 1959 report:

Much of the economic health of the Society depends upon a continuous and changing pattern of special events, all of which represent endless details. It is not fair to expect the Women's Association, the director, or other staff members to handle many of these.

In addition more assistance is urgently needed in the library and the museum to handle the new demands that come from increased use. New members generate calls for additional service, thus increasing the expense of operation.

The achievement of the Missouri Historical Society in recent years has been remarkable, but it raises a problem of general application. Any institution, if it is to do its job properly, must have a staff that cares more about the job than their own personal convenience; that does not quit on the whistle of union working hours. Any privately supported society that is truly successful must be in the charge of someone who makes it his life, who cares more deeply for the institution than for his personal professional advancement. Nevertheless, with the money that readily flows to skating rinks, scientific libraries, and the like, there appears to be something wrong with the distribution of support in the United States. This is expressed in another way in the concluding paragraph of Mr. van Ravenswaay's 1959 report, when he writes:

The funds which we have raised from many sources represent an unusual record of achievement, and a certain amount of this effort is very healthy for any organization. However, there is a point of no return in such endeavors, and that point is reached when so much effort is spent on raising money that the essential and learned purposes for which the organization was created, suffer. That point has been reached. While we must continue our essential money-raising projects for many reasons, we must also find a long-range solution to our financial needs which will provide a certain assured income each year. Either income from taxation, or income from endowment would seem to be the two obvious answers. There may be others. But whatever the answer is, the problem should be carefully studied, and a long-range plan developed to achieve it.

Mr. van Ravenswaay's resignation early in 1962 to accept the presidency of Old Sturbridge Village suggests (at least to an observer halfway across the continent) that the Missouri Historical Society must have failed to develop the long-range plan for stable financial support that he so cogently urged in 1959. The future of the society will depend upon the possibility of finding a successor who is able to maintain the delicate balance between scholarly endeavor and popular activity that Mr. van Ravenswaay created during his years in Saint Louis. Regrettably, such men are in extremely short supply.

THE FILSON CLUB

A Kentucky Historical Society incorporated on 1 February 1838 held its first meeting at Louisville in the following month. It seems to have moved by fits and starts, for it was reorganized at Frankfort, the State capital, in 1878. The present Kentucky State Historical Society at Frankfort dates from still another reorganization in 1896. Louisville, like Cincinnati, Cleveland, Chicago, and Saint Louis, proved to have a climate propitious to private historical enterprise. The Filson Club, named in honor of John Filson, was organized there in 1884 on the centenary of the publication of his pioneer history, *The Discovery, Purchase and Settlement of Kentucke*. Colonel Reuben T. Durrett, a journalist and lawyer with a keen interest in Kentucky history, brought nine friends together at his home in Louisville and founded the Filson Club[4] as an association to collect and preserve Kentucky history. Colonel Durrett was president from the beginning until his death, at the age of eighty-nine, in 1913. For these twenty-nine years meetings were held in the library of his house; a paper was read; an open discussion followed; and the evenings concluded pleasantly over crab-apple cider and Filson Club cigars. Membership was carefully limited, and attendance at meetings confined to members and invited guests.

During Colonel Durrett's lifetime the Filson Club prepared and issued no fewer than twenty-six substantial publications on Kentucky history. Although these were all published in limited editions, any copies not subscribed for by members or exchanged with other historical societies were for sale. In this first period, the Filson Club somewhat resembled the Club of Odd Volumes, founded in Boston

---

4. Otto A. Rothert, "A History of the Filson Club, 1884–1934," *The Filson Club History Quarterly* VIII (1934), 139–168; Richard H. Hill, Dorothy Thomas Cullen, and Mabel Clare Weaks, "*The Filson Club's Seventy-fifth Anniversary,*" *ibid.*, XXXIII (1959), 187–256.

in 1887, which for a number of years was a small band of sociable collectors without premises, but which, nevertheless, published by subscription a considerable number of books of typographical and bibliographical interest.

As sometimes happens in informal organizations centered about a single person, the belongings of Colonel Durrett and the Filson Club became inextricably entangled without clear marks of ownership by the one or the other. During his final illness meetings were suspended; after his death, unknown to the members of the club, his executors sold Colonel Durrett's library to the University of Chicago. Thus, for lack of adequate identification, much material gathered by the club in its early years migrated from Louisville to Chicago. R. C. Ballard Thruston gathered up what remained and transferred it to his office, where, at his own expense and with careful markings, he housed the club's books, documents, and other belongings until 1929. In this period meetings were transferred to the Louisville Free Public Library, and nine more publications were issued.

In 1926 the Filson Club, in conjunction with the History Department of the University of Louisville, began the publication of *The History Quarterly*, with Robert S. Cotterill as managing editor. In 1929 the name was changed to *The History Quarterly of the Filson Club*, and beginning with volume IV in 1930 it reached its present form, *The Filson Club History Quarterly*. Since 1928 it has been edited by the secretary of the club. Its thirty-fourth volume appeared in the course of 1960.

During the 1920s the Filson Club began its metamorphosis into a broader type of historical society. Mr. Thruston in 1919 promised to give the club his own historical library and collections, with an endowment fund of $50,000, provided a building with at least one fireproof room be procured. A drive for funds in 1926 led to the purchase and remodeling of two houses at 118 West Breckinridge Street, Louisville, which were occupied in June 1929. At this juncture, Mr. Thruston not only fulfilled his offer of 1919 but gave the club an additional $50,000 of securities as an emergency fund. They were well chosen, for a golden anniversary sketch of 1934 notes: "None of these securities, it may be well to add, have ever defaulted in any way." Until his death in 1946, Mr. Thruston continued to be the constant friend and benefactor of the club. When anything was needed for which there was insufficient money in the treasury, he happily provided it.

In 1929 the club adopted a new constitution and bylaws which completed its transformation. Membership became open to anyone interested in Kentucky history, subject only to a formal proposal. In spite of depression and war it has shown a steady increase from 242 in 1929 to 526 in 1936 and 803 in 1946. In 1959 there were 59 endowment members who had paid $1,000; 684 life members who had paid $100; and 1,023 annual members at $5.

With the occupation of its own building, the club secured a curator; it has since had a small professional staff. The present curator, Mrs. Dorothy Thomas Cullen, a trained librarian, has held office since 1952. With the help of Miss Evelyn R. Dale as assistant curator, Mrs. Cullen is responsible for the library and research problems. An archivist, Miss Mabel C. Weaks, formerly of the State Historical Society of Wisconsin and the New York Public Library, deals with the manuscript collection, while Richard H. Hill, the secretary of the club, edits the *Quarterly* and arranges the monthly meetings.

The library, which had its foundation in the 5,467 books and pamphlets given by Mr. Thruston, now contains some 26,000 volumes on Kentucky history and related subjects. Appropriately it begins with two copies of Filson's history and two copies of the first edition *Map of Kentucke*, published at Philadelphia in 1784. It contains county histories, abstracts of county records, publications of the State Legislature, compilations of laws and court actions, the Kentucky Geological Survey, church histories, biographies, genealogies, literary works by Kentucky authors, and books about the State. Early newspapers of pre-Civil War Kentucky, including files of Frankfort and Louisville papers, form an important part of the collection. Miss Mary Verhoeff, first vice-president of the club and chairman of its library committee, has actively added photostats and microfilms of pertinent newspapers where the originals could not be procured. Similarly microfilm has been extensively used to secure copies of pertinent doctoral dissertations, official county records, and books that could not be readily available otherwise.

The manuscript collection has been assembled not only by gift but by purchase, through a Historical Acquisition Fund of $25,000 provided by Mr. Thurston in 1935. By this means the club has been able to buy numerous groups of family papers, as well as field notes of eighteenth-century land surveys, Ohio Canal Company documents, and Shaker manuscripts. The Club actively seeks any manuscripts of Kentucky interest that become available; it is equally anxious that its resources be used by scholars.

As of 31 October 1959 the Filson Club had invested funds with a book value of $547,649.73, which produced income of $32,616.82. Membership dues and subscriptions to the *History Quarterly* brought in $10,220. The total receipts were $44,871.12; the expenses $39,332.02.

The success of the Filson Club's collecting is shown by the fact that, after twenty-five years in its building, it became necessary in 1954 to construct an addition that doubled the stack space and added new offices and workrooms. Although it celebrated its seventy-fifth anniversary in 1959, the club is notable for having in the past thirty years—which have had their share of financial and military disturbances—achieved such progress in housing, endowment, collecting, and publication, entirely from private sources. Even with the latest addition space is somewhat short, and salaries are lower than anyone would wish. Nevertheless from endowment of relatively recent date and the receipts from membership, the Filson Club accomplishes a very creditable amount in collecting, preserving, and publishing materials on the history of Kentucky.

Chapter X

CALIFORNIA AND HAWAII

> Oh! California,
>   That's the land for me!
> I'm off for Californi-a
> With my washbowl on my knee.
> —*Anonymous Salem Forty-niner*

IN its present form the California Historical Society[1] is only some forty years old. This lively and imaginative organization is, however, the latest in a series of reincarnations that have had little beyond the name in common with one another. A ghostlike reference of 1887 to the incorporation in 1852 of a Historical Society of the State of California is unconfirmed, either by records in the State offices at Sacramento or evidence of any activity. This remark, which is attributed to John T. Doyle, a San Francisco lawyer who often performed legal services for the Roman Catholic Church in California, suggests that the society sprang from "the desire of the immigrants of English stock to preserve the materials for the history of the Spanish antecedents," inasmuch as "with respect to its social life, California, after its acquisition by the United States, became in a certain sense the heir to two civilizations." Whatever the accomplishments, if any, of this society, they have not survived.

Doyle was successful in persuading the reverend faculty of Santa Clara College to organize in the summer of 1870 a California His-

---

1. "The California Historical Society: Past—Present—Future," the manuscript of an address by George L. Harding, President (1958–60), furnished me by the society, summarizes the history of the preceding organizations.

torical Society "to collect, preserve, and from time to time make public the interesting records of our early Colonial history." This body, which according to the 1872 San Francisco directory was incorporated on 14 July 1870, had twenty-five members, and held its annual meeting at the college on commencement day, published two important works. Four volumes of Father Francisco Palou's *Noticias de la Nueva California*, with an introduction by Doyle, were printed in 1874 in an edition of 100 copies at the expense of Joseph A. Donohoe. Although a second publication, *Reglamento General para el Gobierno de la Provincia de Californias, aprobado por S. M. en el Real orden de Octubre de 1781*, was subsequently printed in an edition of 150, the activities of this society were small in size and never widely known.

In 1886 Edward S. Holden, who had recently become president of the University of California, was inspired by the operations of the Historical Society of Wisconsin to propose a similar organization in San Francisco. Although this movement began in complete ignorance of earlier activity, the survivors of the 1870 society soon came into camp harmoniously. Doyle, for example, contributed a "History of the Pious Fund of California" to the single volume of *Papers of the California Historical Society* that was published in 1887. This third incarnation throve until 1893 and then sickened. Through the influence of its secretary, Colonel A. S. Hubbard, a genealogically-minded lawyer who was the founder of the Sons of the American Revolution, it joined in 1902 with the California Genealogical Society, organized in 1898, to form a California Historic-Genealogical Society.

The San Francisco fire of 18 April 1906 completely destroyed the property, collections, and library of the combined organizations. When revival was attempted in 1908, genealogical interest so far predominated that the name of California Genealogical Society was resumed and purely historical concerns went by the board. Thus, as George L. Harding has put it, in 1908 "the California Historical Society in its third incarnation appears to be dead and buried in a pauper's grave," although Colonel Hubbard had managed to save its corporate records, including the certificate of incorporation dated 6 March 1886.

So matters rested until 1922 when, under the impetus of C. Templeton Crocker, an avid collector of western Americana, and Henry R. Wagner, whose bibliographical and cartographical studies have become the foundation of much of modern western history, the California Historical Society was revived. Although surviving members of the earlier organization were notified of plans, the steps taken in the spring of 1922 represented a fresh start. There were, for example, no preoccupations with family history, that field being left to the California Genealogical Society, which today has its library in the De-Young Building in San Francisco. Nor was there any close tie with historians at the University of California across the bay or with the faculties of other academic institutions. The present California Historical Society is largely the work of business and professional men whose enthusiasm for collecting sources of California history has often led them to writing scholarly works.

San Francisco and Boston have more things in common than a vested interest in neighboring oceans. A Bostonian walking along a Montgomery Street sidewalk passes total strangers who bear a marked similarity to individuals who might, 3,000 miles away, be emerging from doorways in State and Devonshire Streets. San Francisco and Berkeley, like Boston and Cambridge, have their own habits. Although both San Francisco Bay and the Charles River are spanned by bridges, there are, both in California and Massachusetts, men who sustain a marked devotion to history with only occasional crossing of the water that separates them from the neighboring universities. Thus the California Historical Society like that of Massachusetts maintains a strong tradition of work in history by men of other professions, as one may note from the numerous works of Henry R. Wagner or from Carl I. Wheat's monumental study of western cartography. Similarly the California Historical Society is, alone among those of western states, entirely privately supported.

Article 1, paragraph 1, of the bylaws of the society declares that "its object shall be to collect, preserve, and diffuse information relating to the history of California and the American west." Diffusion began at the earliest possible moment, for the publication of the *California Historical Society Quarterly* has been a major activity continuously since 1922. The forty-one volumes that have appeared by 1962 represent a substantial historical contribution; they are also attractive to read both because of the nature of their contents and because of the high standards of typography that prevail in San Francisco. Of all journals issued by State historical societies today, this one is the most pleasing to the eye.

Immediately after the meeting of 27 March 1922, which is considered the beginning date of the society in its present form, room 508 in the Wells Fargo Express Building at 85 Second Street was rented, and Miss Dorothy H. Huggins, who had been Henry R. Wagner's secretary, was hired as corresponding secretary. President C. Templeton Crocker rented the adjoining room, placing in it his large and valuable collection of books, manuscripts, and documents pertaining to California history. Thus through his generosity, the society had available from the beginning for its editorial work and for its visitors and students an important research collection. Five years later the society moved to rooms at 609 Sutter Street, and from 1938 to 1956 shared quarters with the Society of California Pioneers at 456 McAllister Street, opposite the City Hall. During this period, collections grew to such an extent that it became apparent that Pioneer Hall could not long continue to house the activities of both its occupants.

After a good deal of house hunting, the California Historical Society agreed in June 1956 to buy for $75,000 the Whittier mansion at 2090 Jackson Street. This very large red sandstone house, on the northeast corner of Jackson and Laguna Streets, had been built between 1894 and 1896 by William Frank Whittier, a Maine man who had prospered as an early San Francisco paint dealer and capitalist. Designed, on a generous scale, by Edward R. Swain, it was one of the first town houses to be built entirely of stone on a steel framework. The public rooms on the first floor were handsomely paneled in oak, mahogany, or Tamano wood, with German silver fittings. The records of the San Francisco Water Department show that late in 1894 service was connected in the thirty-room house for use in "3 wash trays, 15 wash basins, 6 baths, and 10 water closets." In addition to this profusion of plumbing, adequate even by 1956 standards, the house offered 3,500 square feet of usable space on each of three floors, exclusive of a 36 x 54 foot ballroom in the basement, where the hill fell away. As one of the few great nineteenth-century San Francisco houses that had survived alike the 1906 earthquake and fire, and subsequent demolition, or conversion into apartments, the building was regarded by architects as worthy of preservation for its own sake. It also was not difficult to convert to institutional uses.

The ballroom serves, without change, for meetings. The public rooms on the first floor have been restored to a semblance of their original appearance; by the use of temporary screens they can be converted into a gallery for exhibitions of graphic material, without detriment to their appearance. The sitting rooms and bedrooms on the second floor have been converted to library use, while an editorial office, board room, and additional library storage are available on the third floor. Offices have been contrived out of the service wing.

The new house was occupied in the winter of 1956–57. It is a handsome building and a good rallying point. The library, which is on freestanding steel shelving that can eventually be dismantled and used elsewhere, is already crowded. It occupies a crazy pattern of bedrooms, dressing rooms, and onetime bathrooms, and only a dozen readers can be accommodated simultaneously. All this will soon be solved, for in 1962 the society acquired, with funds given by Mr. Walter L. Schubert, another large house, formerly the home of Mrs. Adolph Uhl, which abuts the garden of the Whittier mansion. Schubert Hall, as the new property is called, will furnish good space for reading rooms, stacks, and staff offices.

The Templeton Crocker collection is the foundation upon which the library of 14,000 books has been built. That collection's weakness in California county histories and city and county directories has been remedied, largely since 1949, so that the present holdings place the California Historical Society today in fourth rank, following the Bancroft, Huntington, and California State libraries. In the past decade the collections of five deceased members and the California sections of the early libraries of Faxon D. Atherton and General Ralph Kirkham have been added to the Crocker nucleus. To increase previous strength in the fields of travel narratives and early imprints purchases over the past five years have been concentrated in these areas. From shortage of staff, there has been no formal cataloguing in recent years, although Mr. James De T. Abajian, who has been librarian since 1950, has the books logically arranged and is able, by use of a keen memory, to turn things up with facility.

While the periodical collection of 1,800 titles (ranging from individual issues to long runs) contains a number of great rarities, its acquisition has been haphazard, and complicated both by the lack of an exchange program and by the misplaced generosity of interested members. The California newspaper collection of 109 bound volumes and some 6,000 separate issues has been limited to rarities; few additions are made by purchase. The titles and holdings of each paper have been listed, with duplicate cards placed within the union list held by the California State Library. About 50,000 ephemeral items, such as trade cards and catalogues, business photographs, billheads, calendars, and broadsides, as well as programs, menus, invitations, announcements, and the like, are filed geographically and indexed carefully. Since 1955, when business (associate) memberships in the society were established, considerable attention has been given to the ephemeral collection, and some business ephemera have been bought. The best body of theatrical material in the State is held by the library of the California Historical Society.

The manuscript collection contains over 130,000 items, mainly of the nineteenth and twentieth centuries, relating chiefly to California. It includes the 1774 *Diario* of Governor Diego Rivera y Moncada; papers of such pre-Gold Rush merchants as William D. M. Howard,

William Heath Davis, William E. P. Hartwell, and Jacob Leese; ships logs, diaries, and records of the Gold Rush; papers of New England companies organized for emigration; and two volumes and one hundred pieces concerning the San Francisco Committee of Vigilance. There are substantial quantities of the papers of Joseph L. Folsom, collector of customs at San Francisco; of Andrew Smith Hillidie, engineer, inventor, builder of suspension bridges and the city cable-car system; of Senator Milton Slocum Latham and Mayor Adolph Sutro; business records of several San Francisco firms, notably the Alaska Commercial Company, 1868–1918, the Crim Real Estate Company, 1846–1904, and Spreckels Enterprises, 1868–1918, representing the sugar, transportation, and other business interests of John D. and Adolph B. Spreckels.

In iconographic materials there are some 40,000 photographs and drawings, arranged geographically, as well as perhaps 15,000 indexed entries to book, serial, and ephemeral publications containing illustrations, as well as 6,000 film and glass photograph negatives. Twelve thousand photographs of portraits are arranged by subject.

Although the California Historical Society has a keen interest in illustrative material, it has been firm in refusing to accept any but the most remarkable and pertinent museum-type display items. Basically it confines its collecting to books, manuscripts, ephemera, paintings, prints, and photographs. Although it does not maintain a museum as such, its iconographic and ephemeral collections lend themselves readily to special exhibitions. While collecting over the past forty years has often been sadly hampered by lack of funds, of space, and of time to search for possible material in private hands, carefully defined limits have been maintained, as well as strict conditions governing the acceptance of gifts. Mr. Abajian, the librarian, and Mrs. Jean Martin, the curator, have shown great wisdom in such buying as they have done, and skill in building upon strengths in their search to attract gifts. Both library and exhibit materials have been handled intelligently with regard to their preservation and use. There have never been enough hands to catalogue books and manuscripts in an orthodox manner. Mr. Abajian has, however, improvised temporary arrangements that permit him to give excellent service to those who seek information from the collection. Among these is a card index of facts furnished in response to inquiries, reference to which may often save considerable time in answering questions of a recurring nature.

Most of the problems of the California Historical Society arise from its youth and from the necessity of raising money for every step taken. In forty years it has progressed from a rented office with the borrowed library of its president next door to a substantial organization, owning a handsome building that is well filled with significant historical sources. While achieving this considerable feat, without public help of any kind, it has consistently published its *Quarterly*. Until 1960 everything had to be accomplished without the benefit of endowment, which was so small as to be negligible. From 1922 until 1959 the society subsisted on membership dues and on gifts, usually of a specific and limited nature, designed to meet a particular emergency, a year-end deficit, or the purchase of some special item for the collections. Of total operating expenditures of $70,026.53 in the calendar year 1959, only $241.03 was met by income from endowment. Towards the end of 1959 about $95,000 in endowment funds were secured, on some $87,000 of which the interest could be immediately used for general purposes. Thus in preparing the 1960 budget, at least $3,700 additional could be counted on, the possibility of which provided for a number of improvements in operations. On the death of a devoted member early in 1960, the society received a residuary bequest, subject to the life interest of an aged sister, that will in the predictable future increase the endowment funds to something in excess of half a million dollars. Even when that occurs, the society will still be underendowed in relation to older institutions elsewhere, but the prospect is pleasing by comparison with earlier years. The beginning of an endowment fund is one of the major accomplishments of the presidency from 1958 to 1960 of George L. Harding, who, in addition to a full business career in the Pacific Telephone Company, has found time to write the biography of California's first printer Zamorano and to set the society on a useful path to the future.

A total income of $80,673.59 was received in 1959, of which $13,000 was a capital contribution to pay off the mortgage on the society's house. As $52,571.51 of the remaining $67,673.59 came from membership dues, it will be seen that the membership supplied some 80% of the operating income. At the end of 1955 there were 1,537 members; four years later their number had risen, by 43%, to 2,685. Their financial usefulness is due to the realistic rate of $15 for active membership, which is paid by the great majority. Thirty-four student members are enrolled at $5 so long as they continue to be registered in a school or college. Otherwise everyone pays a sum that not only fully covers the cost of their subscription to the *Quarterly* but provides needed revenue for general operations. Active and student members' dues brought in nearly $31,500 in 1959. $9,195 was received from sustaining members at $25; $5,900 from patron members and $6,000 from associate members (business corporations) at $100 annually.

Contributions for the General Fund for 1959, which is another way of describing the current deficit, were $7,981.72. In 1958 approximately $12,000 had been required for the purpose. With income from endowment entering the picture, it is hoped that future budgets will be balanced without recourse to such desperate year-end solicitation. Trustees, past and present, have been exceedingly generous in meeting operating deficits. It is hoped that, as a balanced budget becomes a great likelihood, their interest may continue in help for specific purposes that are carefully planned. No city or State appropriations have been received, anticipated, or required. The grant of approximately $15,000 from a local San Francisco foundation of unrestricted field towards the preparation and publication of a cumulative index to the first thirty-eight volumes of the *California Historical Society Quarterly* is the only substantial gift of its kind, although several family foundations have made grants, usually of less than $1,000, for general operating expenses or for modest special projects.

The record of publications by the California Historical Society is remarkably distinguished for an organization that has had to pay as it went. The *Quarterly*, which has a unique place among journals of and about the west, is, in addition, the society's major means of contact with members living at some distance from the San Francisco Bay area. Since it began in 1922, its contributors have been divided about equally between academic and nonacademic historians. The nonacademic group have contributed important original material and penetrating analyses in their reconstructions of California's past; as historians and historiographers they were very seldom amateurs, at least not for long. In spite of a few lapses into antiquarianism, the caliber of articles has generally been high. In recent years articles are almost as often concerned with the twentieth as with earlier centuries. Since they deal quite as frequently with art, architectural, economic, social, intellectual, and business history as with political history, and more often than with tiresome reminiscence, the *Quarterly* is today more successful than in the past both in reaching generally informed nonspecialist readers, and in stimulating the specialists.

In addition to forty-one volumes of the *Quarterly*, monthly *Notes* have been issued since 1948, as well as thirty-two special publications, eighteen pamphlets, and three guide books. Standards of editing and typography have been high. Among the special publications are Henry R. Wagner's *Spanish Voyages to the Northwest Coast of America in the Sixteenth Century* (1929); *The Topographical Report of Lieutenant George H. Derby* (1933), with notes by Francis P. Farquhar, the present president of the society; Oscar O. Winther's *The Story of San José, 1769–1861* (1935); Henry R. Wagner's *Juan Rodriquez Cabrillo, Discoverer of the Coast* (1941); and *Jedidiah Smith and his Maps of the American West* (1954), by Dale L. Morgan and Carl I. Wheat. Cheek by jowl with such products of scholarly research have appeared a series of more popular Christmas books in which recollections of the season in earlier stages of California life have been presented in engaging typographical dress. Keepsakes are issued now and then to sustain the interest of members; in 1959 there was sent to all members a reproduction of an 1857 lithographic view of Los Angeles drawn by Kuchel and Dresel and printed by Britton and Rey, famous collaborators in the history of print making.

A series of paperback guide books to significant areas of California accessible to large numbers of Californians and visitors from elsewhere was inaugurated in 1958. The first was Oscar Lewis's *Fabulous San Simeon*, an account of the history of the San Simeon Ranch and a guide to the artistic accumulations of William Randolph Hearst that are on display there. W. W. Robinson's *Los Angeles from the days of the Pueblo* followed in 1959 and George R. Stewart's *Donner Pass* in 1960. These guides, written by authorities of national stature, who are paid customary royalties, appear under the society's imprint in editions in the tens of thousands; they are widely distributed through commercial publishing channels so as to reach the traveling audience for which they prove particularly useful. Other volumes are in prospect in this experiment in wide diffusion of accurate information on California history.

Publications not only pay their way but add a modest profit to the revolving publication fund. On 1 January 1959 it stood at $15,658.53, with a beginning inventory of $11,008.32 in books. During the year $13,387.42 was received from sales; $14,003.25 was expended for new titles; $4,688.63 for editorial, selling, and shipping expenses, and for royalties to authors. The net gain for the year proved to be $805.40, for on 31 December 1959 the fund amounted to $16,463.93, with an ending inventory of $17,118.18. This is a creditable example of noncommercial publishing on a shoestring that deserves study and emulation.

Aside from its own headquarters, the society has not entered the historic preservation field. To the present time it has been reluctant to engage in public and political activity in connection with historical preservation projects. When called up, as it sometimes is, by the State Park Commission or the State Division of Beaches and Parks, it lends a hand with the placing of historic markers, although it has no official tie to either public agency.

Mr. Donald C. Biggs, the present director, in a memorandum to me, noted:

In addition to this sampling of our activities and services, we—to put it bluntly— sell soup. At least we provide it to those members who want twice or three times a year to take the *romerías* to various historic California spots—trips of two days usually, planned to the last detail with all the imagination we have.[2] Comfort and quality have throughout been high; prices are medium. All transportation, meals, tours, and activities are planned by our staff. In addition to bringing new members into the Society, these *romerías* carry the Society to various parts of California, particularly to members living in distant spots who do not get to San Francisco frequently or ever. Since several hundred members on such a tour is not an uncommon number, this activity evidently does satisfy a need.

The program of the 1959 Fall *Romería* to Santa Barbara and San Simeon on 28 and 29 November suggests a dizzying complication of administrative arrangements. For Southern California members, chartered Gray Line buses would leave the Biltmore Hotel in Los Angeles on the 28th at 9 a.m. Northern Californian travelers were offered a choice of reserved sleeper or chair car accommodations on the Southern Pacific's *Streamliner Lark* leaving San Francisco on the 27th at 9 p.m., with alternative boardings at Oakland, Palo Alto, and San Jose, or a chartered Pacific Airlines Martinliner leaving San Francisco International Airport on the 28th at 9 a.m. All this is just to get the pilgrims *to* Santa Barbara; once there an equally intricate series of tours, bus transfers, and box lunches was offered.

A benefit tour to the Hakone Japanese Garden on Sunday, 8 May 1960, where multicolored paper carp flying in the brilliant spring sunshine gave pleasure to many visitors, raised $2,200 and provided a remarkable instance of the esteem in which the society is held by various religious groups. Through the courtesy of Father Gerald Geary, the Sacred Heart Church provided parking for the visitors,

2. The members going on a *romería* do not subsist literally upon soup, for the announcement of the spring 1960 expedition to the Mother Lode dangles the prospect of *crabe aux champignons* in Mokelumne Hill and prime ribs in Grass Valley.

while Japanese tea and cookies were served in cups lent by the Japanese Buddhist and the Chinese Methodist Churches! While all this is, for the visitors, in the best light-hearted spirit of San Francisco, it takes arranging behind the scenes.[3]

The society's house is a pleasant background for members' meetings, chamber music concerts, and receptions, as well as a useful place for serious work. At a dinner held there on 28 September 1959, the first annual Henry R. Wagner Memorial Award was presented to the author of the work published within the preceding two years in the field of California history, cartography, or bibliography which the Awards Committee deemed most worthy of recognition. The judges in this case were George P. Hammond of the Bancroft Library, Glenn S. Dumke, and Thomas W. Streeter of Morristown, New Jersey; the recipient was Carl I. Wheat in recognition of the first two volumes of his *Mapping the Transmississippi West, 1540–1861,* which when completed will run to five large folio volumes. Book auctions of duplicate and out-of-field material from the library are held from time to time; these are good fun and bring in some cash that is used for accessions.

The house serves admirably for this kind of purpose. The library is best adapted to the scholar who knows exactly what he wants. It cannot, with limited staff and space, do so well for visitors with only a general interest in history, yet these are attracted in increasing numbers by the growth in membership. Like Mr. Charles van Ravenswaay in Saint Louis, the energetic and imaginative director Mr. Donald C. Biggs, who came to the society in February 1958 from the faculty of San Francisco State College, has to act as if he had the numerous feet and hands of the god Siva. Mr. Biggs would like to do more for the member with only general interest, for persons at a distance who send inquiries by mail, and for the teachers of California history in

3. *California Historical Society Notes* for April 1960 announces events on thirteen out of the thirty days of the month: three dedications of markers, one breakfast, three luncheons, four dinners, a society meeting, a *romería,* a book auction, and the opening of an exhibition, as well as two Junior League meetings at the mansion. The directorship is no place for a lazy man!

the schools, yet he wisely refrains from embarking prematurely upon such extensions lest the society run the risk of jeopardizing its other activities, "no single one of which," he modestly alleges, "is as good as it might be." Such a statement is in pleasing contrast to what one often hears from energetic directors. It is evidence of the realism and of the passion for quality that have characterized the California Historical Society. The record of the past forty years in San Francisco offers conclusive proof that the independent historical society as a type, even though its origins go back to the eighteenth century, is not dead yet, provided its officers and staff have standards, imaginative energy, and a clear picture of what they are trying to accomplish.

HAWAII

Twenty-one charter members established the Hawaiian Historical Society on 11 January 1892 for the collection, study, and preservation of material pertaining to the history of Hawaii. Articles of incorporation of May 1924 which extended the field of coverage to "Hawaii, Polynesia and the Pacific Area" provided a more accurate description of the society's interests, for, from the beginning, its library had included not only imprints and manuscripts originating in Hawaii, but the works of circumnavigators, sailors, missionaries, traders, and settlers throughout the Pacific. The Hawaiian Historical Society today defines its objects as the collection, preservation, and study of material pertaining to this broader ocean-wide area; the compiling of catalogues and indexes of these holdings; the preparation and distribution of papers relating to this area; and the cultivation among citizens of Hawaii of an interest in and knowledge of the history of the Pacific. The membership, today in the vicinity of 300, includes descendants of the original Hawaiians, of the early American pioneers, traders, and missionaries, and of the later immigrating groups of Portuguese, Chinese, and Japanese.

The library consists today of 6,358 volumes, 2,789 pamphlets, and four filing drawers of manuscripts. The bases of the collection were early newspapers and periodicals printed in English, Hawaiian, and Portuguese; the literature of Anglican, Congregational, Episcopal, Mormon, and Roman Catholic churches to which Adventists and Buddhists have subsequently been added; and reports of government officials, educators, agriculturalists, scientists, and commercial groups. Texts, documents, and grammars of the various Polynesian dialects, as well as of Micronesian and Melanesian groups, have been included, while voyages and narratives of explorers, missionaries, and settlers throughout the entire Pacific have always been well represented. Complete files of the quarterlies of the California, Oregon, and Washington historical societies, and the Pacific coast branch of the American Historical Association are on the shelves. With the increasing interlacing of the histories of the peoples of the Pacific, the society's coverage is being increased through the assistance of the South Pacific Commission and the Office of the High Commissioner of the Trust Territory of Pacific Islands.

Manuscripts, which relate chiefly to the Hawaiian Islands and Polynesia between 1828 and 1912, include the papers or journals of several missionaries, such as Hiram Bingham Jr., Sereno Edwards Bishop, Samuel Northrup Castle, and Titus Coan; the records of consuls, merchants, officials of the Hawaiian kingdom, two kings, and of Henry Obookiah, a Hawaiian who was a pupil at a mission school in Connecticut. The books and manuscripts in the library record historical events from the beginning of the Hawaiian kingdom through the years of change to Provisional Government, Republic, Territory, and State of Hawaii.

The Hawaiian Historical Society has a highly creditable record of publication. Since 1892 it has issued sixty-seven annual reports, each containing one or more studies on some historical or ethnological theme, twenty-one papers, five reprints, and three genealogies. Able scholars from other parts of the United States have published useful articles in the annual reports, which contain material of wide interest.

Since 1950, the society has been part owner and joint occupant with the Hawaiian Mission Children's Society of a new building, known as the Mission Historical Library, at 560 Kawaiahao Street, Honolulu. Previously it housed its collections for twenty-one years with the Honolulu Library and Reading Room Association, and for thirty-eight years in the Library of Hawaii.

The Hawaiian Historical Society receives no public support. Its normal operational expenses are barely covered by a small income from endowment and the dues of its members, who pay $5 for annual membership, $10 for contributing, $25 for sustaining, or $100 for life membership. Its publication costs are normally met by special grants or gifts. Its staff consists of a half-time librarian, Mrs. Willowdean C. Handy, who copes with cataloguing and research, acts as assistant treasurer and corresponding secretary, and keeps the reading room open five days a week. Several meetings are held each year, at which the serious papers published in the annual reports are read. The lengthy and valuable list of the publications of the Hawaiian Historical Society is yet another example of the intelligent application of limited resources.

Chapter XI

DRAPER IN WISCONSIN

Such activities merely indicated that Lyman Draper was a typical
American promoter. Although neither his manner nor his physique
conformed to the sterotype of the "booster," his spirit was that of an
optimist and an enthusiast for Wisconsin's future. He was a believer
in publicity, and missed no opportunity to advertise himself, the
Historical Society, the city of Madison, and the state of Wisconsin.
—WILLIAM B. HESSELTINE, 1954

THE American has a natural inclination to attempt to
prove that he is as good—if not better—than other people.
Even if his surroundings are obviously rude and his resources
meagre, he will claim that he likes them that way, or even that they
have, by their nature or because of his own effort, some considerable
superiority to what is accepted elsewhere. So it came about that in
the Mississippi valley historical societies were formed before there
was any considerable body of history to record. In the autumn of
1849, less than eight months after the establishment of Minnesota
Territory, when most of the area still belonged to the Indians, the
fifth act of the Territorial Legislature was the incorporation of a
Minnesota Historical Society. This cheerful anachronism, comparable to the notion of establishing historical societies in Virginia in
1607 or in Massachusetts in 1620, occurred at a time when the 5,000
white inhabitants of Minnesota were confined to a small wedge
between the St. Croix and Mississippi rivers. At the society's first
annual meeting in 1850, a clerical speaker, drawing upon the accomplishment motif, observed: "You have been organized at a most

favorable period. On the bluff where we are assembled, there are temples of religion and education . . . yet around us, the skin-lodges of the Dakotas are still visible. . . . The scalp-dance is yet enacted within our hearing, and not a year rolls by, but the soil of Minnesota is reddened with Ojibwa and Dakota blood."[1]

In such surroundings the man of leisure and property, who had been the mainstay of historical societies in the east, was conspicuously lacking. If support were to be found, the only source was the State. While State governments had, during the first half of the nineteenth century, occasionally appropriated modest sums for archival investigation in England or other historical projects, there was no tradition of continued and systematic public assistance. Now and then politicians might sympathetically toss a life line; normally historical societies had, by their own efforts, to swim or sink. Thus, as has been noted in preceding chapters, historical societies founded at an early date in some southern and western states had brief lives.

Such a false start was made in Wisconsin during the first State constitutional convention in 1846, when twelve men went through the motions of organizing a historical society to no effect. Another attempt, made in 1849, produced better results, although it was only with the election of Lyman Copeland Draper (1815–91) as corresponding secretary in 1854 that the real career of the State Historical Society of Wisconsin began. To this incurable romantic of humble origins, who had first-rate energy and a second-rate education, the development of the state-supported historical society in the middle west owes more than to any other single person. Draper's life, as his biographer Professor William B. Hesseltine[2] indicates, was an odd muddle of patriotism, scalp-hunting, self-justification, Baptist theology, spiritualism, promotion, thwarted ambition to write best sellers, autograph dealing, speculation in mining stocks, and hypochondria. As a boy of seventeen in Lockport, New York, he wrote historical

1. Mary Wheelhouse Berthel and Harold Dean Cater, "The Minnesota Historical Society: Highlights of a Century,"*Minnesota History* xxx (1949), 293–294.
2. *Pioneer's Mission, The Story of Lyman Copeland Draper* (Madison, 1954).

articles for the *Rochester Gem* and pestered the aged James Madison in search of material.

At seventeen this precocious lad went to work for Peter A. Remsen, a forty-seven-year-old Mobile cotton dealer who was married to one of Draper's cousins. Lydia Remsen, who was twenty-five years younger than her husband but only four years older than her cousin Lyman, lived on a farm in Alexander, New York, while her husband attended to his business in Alabama. It was an odd arrangement all around but a fortunate one for young Lyman Draper, for after a winter of clerking in Mobile he was sent by Remsen to Granville Literary and Theological Institution, to get what education that newly founded Ohio Baptist college could provide. After two years of schooling at Granville, Draper transferred to the Hudson River Seminary at Stockport, across the river from Albany, New York. All the while he had a passionate interest in the adventures of frontiersmen and in tales of Revolutionary soldiers, which he nourished by writing letters requesting information from anyone he was able to wheedle into correspondence. As he came to believe that "very much precious historical incident must still be treasured up in the memory of aged Western Pioneers, which would perish with them if not quickly rescued," he convinced himself of his Christian duty to undertake such work.

The idea had occurred to others earlier. In 1825 John F. Watson of Germantown[3] had urged the newly founded Historical Society of Pennsylvania to appoint a committee

to rescue from oblivion, the facts of personal prowess, achievements, or sufferings, by officers and soldiers of the Revolutionary War—I believe the recitals of many brave men, now going down to the Tomb,—of what they saw, or heard, or sustained, in that momentous struggle which set us free, would form a fund of anecdotes and of individual history, well deserving of our preservation. Many Privates "unknown to fame" peculiarly distinguished by their actions, would thus receive their just memorial. . . .

If the Pioneers still alive in some of the interior settlements would set down

3. Hampton L. Carson, *A History of The Historical Society of Pennsylvania* (Philadelphia, 1940), I, 110–112.

the difficulties they encountered—the state of the Woods, marshes, country &c—anecdotes of themselves and neighbours—amusing or interesting facts of their aboriginal neighbors . . . very many facts might be elicited, which would furnish to future generations the themes of many interesting Stories.

Although this proposal for the collection of popular and heroic anecdotes of personal prowess met with no interest in Philadelphia, a similar passion, independently achieved, became the dominant motive of Lyman Draper's life. The manner in which he gratified this curiosity, like most things that he did, was unusual.

From the autumn of 1838 until the spring of 1852 he was mostly employed as the manager of Peter Remsen's northern properties and as companion, confidant, and piano teacher to his cousin Lydia, who did not accompany her husband to Mobile. With this as his livelihood, Lyman Draper was able to borrow time for the investigation of the human drama in the lives of the pioneers of the old southwest, the border region between the Alleghanies and the Mississippi. In an effort to rescue the scanty record of the accomplishment of this "remarkable band of worthies," as he was pleased to call them, and to establish the distinction of the borderers who had made the west, Draper journeyed thousands of miles during the 1840s, interviewing survivors and begging documents from descendants who were the more ready to give them because of his grandiose plans for a series of books that would rescue the memory of their ancestors from oblivion. Draper was a born collector, with no aptitude for writing. Whenever he drove himself to write, he would take sick after achieving a few lines of club-footed grandiloquence. On recovery he would return to collecting with an eagerness comparable to that of the hypothetical graduate student in Samuel Eliot Morison's *History as a Literary Art*, who happily abandons his thesis, after two lame sentences, to return to the Widener stacks in search of a missing fact.

The unexpected death of Peter Remsen in the spring of 1852 precipitated a crisis in Lyman Draper's life. At the age of thirty-six, with a great mass of historical manuscripts as his chief asset, he had to

find a new livelihood. Friends held out hope of public employment
in the new State of Wisconsin. On ascertaining that there was a Baptist church in Madison, he moved there in October 1852, taking
Lydia Remsen and her adopted daughter with him. Although the
State librarianship, for which he had hoped, was not available, the
new historical society offered possibilities. Draper became a member on 19 January 1853 and was promptly elected to the executive
committee.

In a short time Lyman Draper and his friend Judge Charles Larrabee were seized with the notion of obtaining a charter from the
State Legislature by which fourteen incorporators would "be constituted and created a body politic and corporate" under the name of
the State Historical Society of Wisconsin. Professor Hesseltine thus
describes the drafting of this document:

Paragraph 2 of the proposed charter was a medley of the phraseology of Larrabee
the lawyer and Draper the romantic historian. The object of the Society, wrote
Charles, "shall be to collect, embody, arrange, and preserve in authentic form a
library of books, pamphlets, maps, charts, manuscripts, papers, paintings, statuary
and other materials, illustrative of the history of the State." That was the judge in
solemn mood. Then Lyman added: "to secure from oblivion the memory of its
early pioneers, and to obtain and preserve narratives of their exploits, perils and
hardy adventures."[4]

Remembering the interests of Governor Farwell and James Doty and Morgan
Martin and Cyrus Woodman, the two authors added another clause: "to exhibit
faithfully the antiquities and the past and present condition and resources of
Wisconsin." The Society could promote the study of history by lectures, and
"diffuse and publish information relating to the description and history of the
State."

The act chartering the society was duly signed by the governor on 4
March 1853. On 4 September of the same year Lyman Draper and
Lydia Remsen were married, and on 18 January 1854 he was elected
corresponding secretary of the State Historical Society.

4. Save for the substitution of "rescue" for "secure," this grandiloquent phrase of
Draper's was included verbatim in an 1868 amendment to the charter of the Minnesota Historical Society; see Lucile Kane, "Collecting Policies of the Minnesota Historical Society: 1849–1952," *The American Archivist* XVI (1953), 128.

The charter provided for active members at $1 a year, life members at $20, and honorary members chosen "from persons in every part of the world, distinguished for their literary or scientific attainments and known especially as friends or promoters of American history." As dues were clearly not going to buy a collection and pay a secretary, who needed a salary, the Legislature was induced to appropriate $500 for the society. This success led Draper to claim that "in a few years, as a result, we *must* necessarily have the best Historical Library in the North West extant."

As Professor Hesseltine has observed,

The legislative appropriation was only the initial step in the building of the Historical Society. Draper had other ideas. A vain little man himself, avid for praise and recognition, he understood well how to appeal to the vanity of others. Already he had built a great collection by flattering old pioneers and their descendants. He had told them how important their contributions, or their ancestors', had been; men had told him their stories, and given him their papers or access to them because he promised to rescue their memories from oblivion and set straight the historical record of their services. Knowing well that few men could resist appeals which carry honor and praise and publicity, he planned to build the Historical Society's library as he had built his own.

Draper thus got printed some certificates of election to honorary membership, which included a list of objects desired by the society; he fed names of everyone he had ever heard of anywhere to the executive committee for election, and mailed out the notifications as fast as he could fill in the blanks. Thus Francis Parkman, William H. Seward, Washington Irving, Charles Francis Adams, William H. Prescott, Salmon P. Chase, and the King of Denmark were among those who soon found themselves honorary members of the State Historical Society of Wisconsin. "The list of those who might be presumed to be friends of American history," Professor Hesseltine observes, "—geologists, autograph collectors, publishers, educators, army officers, and ministers of the gospel—was curtailed only by the limited acquaintance of the executive committeemen. In the first month Draper mailed out six hundred certificates of membership."

The returns were gratifying. Prescott sent his volumes on Mexico and Peru; Charles Francis Adams his ten-volume edition of the works of John Adams. By 10 April, 600 books and pamphlets had been received. Draper then procured from the Legislature copies of State reports and promotion pamphlets which he shipped off to the international library exchange conducted in Paris by his French counterpart in learned promotion, the ex-mountebank Alexandre Vattemare.[5] Thomas Sully of Philadelphia, on receiving his notice of election, inquired what portrait he might paint for the society and was informed that a copy of Stuart's Washington would be highly acceptable. Robert M. Sully of Richmond not only copied the portraits of Black Hawk and Tecumseh's brother that he had made for the Virginia Historical Society, but threw in a spurious portrait of Pocahontas and suggested moving to Madison. Draper's happy anticipation of an artist in residence was frustrated, for although Sully set out the next year from Virginia, while visiting Buffalo en route he was most unfortunately taken drunk and died. By the summer of 1854 so many gifts had been received that the State Historical Society of Wisconsin was able to set up shop in the basement of the new Baptist church in Madison. This arrangement, concentrating as it did his two principal interests under one roof, was highly convenient for Draper.

At the end of 1854 the society reported an income of $552.52; $500 from the Legislature and $52.52 from dues and gifts. The annual meeting of 2 January 1855 voted commendation to Draper and set out to get him a salary, which he needed. In March the Legislature appropriated $500 for this purpose, in addition to a similar sum previously voted for the purchase of books. Volume 1 of a series of *Reports and Collections*, which appeared in the summer of 1855, gave evidence of such industry that Draper's friends sponsored a bill to raise his salary to $1,000. While it was under discussion, the copying by Wisconsin newspapers of stories planted in New York and Chica-

5, For an example of the nature of Vattemare's activities, see my *Boston Public Library, A Centenary History.*

go papers, lauding both the society and Draper, proved so effectively that they were advertising their State, that the salary increase was obtained without difficulty.

Draper organized a Society of Wisconsin Pioneers, summoning old settlers to a handsome dinner in February 1856 at which he induced them to reminisce for the historical society's archives and publications. The following year he even cajoled the railroads into offering reduced fares to the gathering. Early in 1857 he wrote a forty-eight-page pamphlet, entitled *Madison, the Capital of Wisconsin: Its Growth, Progress, Condition, Wants and Capabilities*, of which a delighted city council printed 10,000 copies. At the same time he was compiling *The Wisconsin State Directory*. Such publications, "designed," as Draper said, "to show the wonderful advance the great North-West in general, and Wisconsin in particular, are making in all the elements of greatness and prosperity," furnish adequate justification for Professor Hesseltine's characterization (printed at the head of this chapter) of Draper as "a typical American promoter." A single sentence of Draper's—

Madison may have her share of croakers who can never rise above their own narrow contracted view, but she will nevertheless continue on the high road to prosperity, and take her appropriate place in the first rank of the beautiful cities of the land.

would entitle him to permanent honor among boosters and boasters.

Rather than get on with his historical writing, which always made him sick, Draper turned to Democratic politics as a means of supplementing his salary. In November 1857 he narrowly won election as State superintendent of public instruction. For two years he energetically attacked the duties of that post in addition to those of the historical society, until he was turned out of office because of the partisan and sectarian coloring of his educational activities. After his defeat in the 1859 election, Draper no longer enjoyed the adulation of his neighbors that had brightened his earlier years in Wisconsin. Although in discouragement he thought of going to Mississippi or Tennessee, his post with the historical society still offered a better livelihood than he could conjure up elsewhere. Even that came under fire, for a Senate committee began to growl over the discovery that, although the society's charter contained no mention of State aid, the Legislature had in six years appropriated $12,613.64 for its support and that the State printer had done more than $20,000 worth of work on its *Collections*, including editions in Norwegian and German. Save for the elimination of funds for printing, this crisis passed. So, by a narrow margin, did an attempt to turn Draper out of the secretaryship, but few newspapers any longer troubled to print the stories of his and the society's accomplishments that he indefatigably supplied. While autograph dealing began to alleviate his finances, a mail-order course of medication for sexual debility that he took did not restore his health to a point where he could contemplate writing the great historical narratives for which he had collected such vast resources.

The outbreak of the Civil War inspired Draper to seek an army paymaster's billet from which he could "collect and preserve from personal observation" the record of the exploits of "our gallant Wisconsin troops," with a view to eventual publication of a history of the State in the war, complete with biographies of everybody and his brother. Although this aspiration came to nothing, Draper turned the war to the historical society's benefit by collecting flags, cannon balls, Confederate money, diaries, journals, and battlefield souvenirs. In 1863 the Legislature halved his salary.

In spite of Draper's personal disappointments, the State Historical Society grew steadily. When in January 1866 it abandoned the basement of the Baptist church for the entire second floor of the south wing of the new State capitol, it possessed 43,400 books, newspapers that filled seventy-seven feet of shelving, and numerous portraits. Early the next year the Legislature restored Draper's $1,000 salary, while publication was resumed in 1868. He had convinced the politicians that a volume of *Reports and Collections* would "bear upon its face the evidence that ours is a *live* Society . . . garnering and preserving the past and passing history of our portion of the Great Republic." Through the 1870s Draper nursed the Legislature into increasing appropriations for books, staff, and publications, always accompanying his pleas by statistical comparisons of accomplishments. It had taken the Massachusetts Historical Society eighty years to acquire 50,000 volumes; he had done it in eighteen, not of course drawing attention to the disappointing quantity of theology, natural history, and science contained in the 4,812 volumes of the Tank collection, which was the largest single gift that had been received. Such assertions as "we may justly challenge a comparison with the most successful Historical Societies and State Libraries of the country" heartened the vanity and increased the liberality of politicians. There were nevertheless setbacks which caused Draper to say, "I am quite sensitive in my nature and cannot consent to fill a place where I must *fight* for my reputation."

Such a necessity arose soon after an apparent triumph. At the 1877 annual meeting, Draper proudly called attention to the society's growth during the previous decade. The library had burst the seams of its rooms in the capitol; with 70,000 books it had spilled into corridors and had recently invaded two tower rooms. Such growth, Draper glowingly announced "will be regarded as alike creditable to the management of the Society, and the enlightened liberality of the legislature of the State . . . There is nowhere on record an instance of public assistance, to the same extent, to any similar association in this or any other country." Yet in two months Senator David E. Welch of Milwaukee was noisily "investigating" the affairs of the State Historical Society. The State had spent more than $11,000 for the society the previous year—and since 1854 more than $127,779.79 —yet it had, Welch claimed, "no control over the management nor even a shadow of a control over the expenditures made almost solely by the Corresponding Secretary." He questioned the propriety of the corresponding secretary being "a well-known collector of precisely such articles and books as are wanted and desired for a historical society." Although the Senator gave Draper an unconfortable time, the Legislature in due course passed the bill for the society's appropriation as usual. It was just as well that Welch had not looked into the society's binding fund, where Draper's bookkeeping was of an unorthodox nature.

In 1882, armed with statistics to prove that its library ranked third in size among the seventy-seven historical societies in the country, Draper lobbied for a separate building for the State Historical Society. He got instead more room in the capitol. He dreamed also of an endowment, so that the society might "eventually become independent, and be no longer a public pauper—and possibly escape becoming the receptacle, by party legislation, for broken down politicians." Although neither a building nor an endowment materialized in Draper's lifetime, he had, before his retirement in 1887, built the library to 110,000 volumes. He also chose as his successor a Massachusetts-born journalist, Reuben Gold Thwaites, whose combination of scholarly and administrative abilities contributed markedly to the successful development of the society during the next quarter century.

Lyman Draper, while an avid collector for the State Historical Society, always retained his great assembly of frontier manuscripts as working capital for the great books that he was always going to write. They represented also a resource for his autograph dealing. His original intention had been to bequeath them to a historian who would complete his work. As he never found the ideal recipient, in the end he willed the papers to the society. After his death on 27 August 1891, the society thus received 2,546 volumes, and manuscripts, bound and unbound, to make 478 volumes, which have been its greatest treasure ever since.[6]

---

6. Alice E. Smith, "The Draper Manuscripts," in Donald R. McNeil, ed., *The American Collector: Four Essays Commemorating The Draper Centennial of The State Historical Society of Wisconsin* (Madison, 1954), pp. 45–61. In 1906 the society published a *Descriptive List* as a general guide to the Draper collection, three volumes of calendars (1915, 1925, 1929), and five volumes of selections from the manuscripts themselves (1905–17). In 1948 the microfilming of the entire collection was undertaken. Positive films are available at $1,500 for the complete set and at corresponding prices based upon length for any one of the fifty series that comprise the collection.

In reviewing Lyman Draper's thirty-three years as the builder of the State Historical Society of Wisconsin one notes certain elements in his character and behavior that became accentuated through the constant necessity of wheedling funds from the Legislature. He was an energetic man with a passion for history, whose efforts in collecting manuscripts have given him greater posthumous fame than the books he wished to write. But the necessity of selling his wares to an audience that did not share his knowledge caused him constantly to strive for effect, to make boastful pronouncements, to sing his own praises in press releases, and otherwise indulge in activities that denied him any reputation for modesty, or reticence. His excursions into promoting the State of Wisconsin similarly cast doubt upon his critical faculties, for success in the literature of promotion requires not only a glib tongue but convenient moments of temporary blindness and deafness. From his early excursion into politics and later unsuccessful attempt to secure Federal appointment as commissioner of pensions or of Indian tribes, one cannot escape the impression that, much as Lyman Draper did for the State Historical Society, he was first of all working for his own advantage and would not have hesitated to decamp rapidly had a better opportunity been offered elsewhere. One blames him less for this seeming fickleness in view of the tendency of the Legislature to blow hot and cold in rapid succession; to praise one moment and investigate the next.

Something of the problem that Draper faced is reflected in remarks made by Reuben Gold Thwaites at the American Historical Association meeting of 1909.[7] In commenting on a paper by Worthington C. Ford, Thwaites pointed out an essential difference between the eastern organizations and western historical societies dependent upon State appropriations.

In order to secure political support it seems essential, at least in the earlier years of the society, to produce publications having a quasi popular character. When it is remembered that legislators and public officials seek these books for free distribu-

7. *Annual Report of the American Historical Association for the year 1909* (Washington, 1911), pp. 307–309.

tion to constituents, and often regard their popularity as their only excuse for being, one may hardly blame the society management for desiring to make the volumes, or at least part of them, readable by men of average interest and intelligence. This is one quite sufficient reason why so much interest is paid in many States to the narrative side of history—for the story of the pioneers always appeals strongly to the "general reader."

After a society has become firmly established as a State institution, a necessary adjunct of the State's educational machinery, then it becomes possible to maintain publications of a more scientific character. For instance, if I may mention my own State, in Wisconsin we are at last able to devote our collections entirely to the presentation of documentary material, and our proceedings to the usual administrative reports, monographs, pioneer recollections, and such other matter as is presented at the annual meeting. This sharp difference, in which we follow quite closely the custom of Mr. Ford's own Massachusetts society, would not have been thought possible a dozen years ago [i.e. 1897].

Continuing in an apologetic vein about the "wretched slop work job" of State printers and the lack of funds for really competent editors, Thwaites paid tribute to Draper as a rarity.

A literary hermit, caring little for even what most of us deem the necessities of cultured existence, buoyed by unquenchable enthusiasm, ever toiling for the one great end, he continued to struggle through life on a salary less than a drygoods clerk can now earn. Herein lies the real secret of the Wisconsin society. He starved himself that the institution might live. But such men seldom appear on this earth. It takes money successfully to run historical societies. Legislatures, and the public at large that they represent, require coddling if their support is to be obtained.

Lyman Draper coddled so well that the pattern he established was followed in Iowa, then in Kansas, and at last in so many other states that the idea of publicly supported State historical societies has become standard, save along the Atlantic seaboard. His lifelong passion for tales of frontier exploits was ideally suited to the coddling process; without him in Wisconsin at that one particular moment the notion of public support might not have developed so early. Yet public support has its hazards, for some or all of the less attractive aspects of Lyman Draper's career may well reproduce themselves at any time or in any place where a historical society undertakes to coddle politicians.

In the era of Reuben Gold Thwaites, the State Historical Society of Wisconsin, while remaining in Madison, moved from the orbit of the capitol to that of the university. Though the distance was slight in hundreds of yards, spiritually it marked a shift from the amateur to the professional approach to American history. In 1893 the society formally announced the opening of the Draper collection of manuscripts. In the same year Frederick Jackson Turner of the University of Wisconsin presented at a meeting of the American Historical Association his "Significance of the Frontier in American History." It would be pleasant to think that Draper, the old collector, and Turner, the young historian, had enjoyed each other's company in Madison, but such does not seem to have been the case. Professor Hesseltine reports only a single meeting between them, that might be considered an allegory of the misunderstandings between the old and the new practitioners of history.

The young instructor made his way to 333 West Washington Street and spent several hours in Draper's dark and littered "den" while the old man talked of Boone, and Kenton, and Brady, and Sumter, and Clark, and showed the youth the collections he had made during half a century. But Turner's young energy had no sympathy for the old man's puttering methods, and the academic historian found no common ground with the antiquarian. He left in disgust. "He is a peculiar man," he asserted. "The truth is he is a great procrastinator and will hardly come to *any* conclusion. I shall not hunt after him."

Thwaites, by contrast, was anything but a procrastinator, as the quantity and quality of his own scholarly work testifies. The seventy-three volumes of *Jesuit Relations and Allied Documents* that he published between 1896 and 1901, his eight-volume edition of the *Original Journals of the Lewis and Clark Expedition*, his *Early Western Travels* series, and countless other volumes of historical editing and writing did credit not only to Thwaites but to the society that he administered.

The building that Draper had so ardently desired was built through Thwaites's efforts between 1895 and 1900, at State and Park Streets, with grants totaling $620,000 from the State Legislature. Although erected for the society, it was for more than fifty years jointly occupied with the library of the University of Wisconsin, which paid rent and furnished electricity and heat. The two libraries followed a co-operative policy in the purchase of books to avoid duplication. As it was thus impossible for any member of the University of Wisconsin during the first half of the nineteenth century to seek a book without entering the premises of the State Historical Society, in Wisconsin a more intimate relation between professional scholars and the society developed than in other states. Thwaites consciously sought to promote this intimacy by his own scholarly work and by such acts as setting aside a seminar room for Turner's use.

The State Street building would have merited all of Draper's superlatives. It was the finest and the largest possessed by any historical society in 1900; it offered, moreover, a conspicuous example of the advantage of legislative support when properly channeled. On moving in, the historical society brought there a library of over 100,000 volumes and a similar number of pamphlets, built from scratch since 1854, almost entirely by Draper's efforts. As all learning had been taken as its field, it was a general library, although history was naturally its strongest area. From 1900, by agreement with the university, the society's field of collecting was narrowed to history, particularly that of Wisconsin, America, England, and Latin America, although most of the older general material was still retained. Under the direction of Thwaites and his successors Milo M. Quaife (1914–20), Joseph Shafer (1920–41), and Edward P. Alexander (1941–46), the library more than tripled in size. Between 1900 and 1943 it grew from 100,000 to 328,000 volumes, by an average annual increase of 4,000 volumes, fairly evenly divided between gifts and purchases.

While the collection of Americana continued even in the depression, English and Latin American history were only superficially treated. The newspaper collection had overflowed its space to such an extent that there was no way to shelve the normal annual addition of 1,000 volumes of bound newspapers. Thus in the 1940s the field of collecting was limited to America north of the Rio Grande, and microfilm was resorted to as a solution for the space problem in the great newspaper collection. Even with this limitation, it will be seen that the Wisconsin library covers a far broader field than is general in a State historical society. Most of the older societies had begun with national, if not universal, ambitions, but had pulled in their horns as a result of growing realism. The State Historical Society of Wisconsin, because of its close association with the university, had had reason to attempt the continued coverage of the national scene.

Even the most spacious libraries seldom remain convenient for more than a generation. A new stack wing was added in 1911–14; by 1925 another was needed but not built. In the 1940s the once adequate building had become a nightmare. A pamphlet of 1945, *Building Needs of the Wisconsin State Historical Society*, offered a cogent statement of the library problem, although with an eye to popular appeal and legislative sympathy its cover showed a mass of school children, packed in like New York subway riders. A caption described this photograph thus:

Santa Claus and his friends reach the Museum during the Christmas Party of 1944. More than a thousand children attended the affair despite a raging blizzard, and the line of children of which this is the head stretched from the Museum across Park Street to Music Hall. These children are some of the citizens of Wisconsin whom the Society is trying to serve with a woefully inadequate and antiquated building.

A solution was found in the 1950s by the construction of a new university library across the way. The historical society building was remodeled to provide museum galleries on the first as well as the third floor, while the library had room to expand into the area occupied for so many years by university books.

The contents of the manuscript collection were summarized in 1906 in a *Descriptive List*, which was the first guide solely devoted to manuscripts to be issued by an American historical society. This contained a survey of the nearly 500 volumes of papers relating to the history of the first American west collected by Lyman Draper. A *Guide to Manuscripts of the Wisconsin Historical Society*, edited by Dr. Alice E. Smith in 1944, listed (exclusive of the Draper papers)

802 collections which amounted to some 720,000 unbound pieces and 2,500 volumes. In her preface, Dr. Smith states:

In these manuscripts gathered so carefully through the first nine decades of the state's existence, lies the story of the region that is now Wisconsin. Among them are the correspondence and diaries and account books of explorers and missionaries, of attorneys, farmers, merchants and scientists; they include the records of temperance and antislavery societies, of churches, banks, and cooperatives; they tell of the building of roads and harbors, of the establishment of homes, the founding of social institutions, and the development of the commonwealth. The numerous collections of personal papers of public officials—governors, judges, legislators, and members of Congress—are admirably supplemented by records from the offices of the governor and secretary of state and other state departments, transferred to the Society by virtue of its position as legal custodian of the state's non-current archives.

While the society's primary task is the collecting of records on the history of Wisconsin, such papers as the John R. Commons collection relating to the history of labor and socialism in the United States go far beyond the State boundaries, as do the Draper papers and photocopies of French and British documents dealing with the early history of the region that is now Wisconsin.

The phenomenal rate of growth of the collection is indicated by *Supplement Number One* to the *Guide*, edited by Josephine L. Harper and Sharon C. Smith in 1957. This volume, of almost the size of the original, lists 702 organized and 89 unprocessed collections that were acquired in thirteen years. Reflected in this supplement were records acquired through the Labor History Project, initiated in 1947 to develop representative records of labor organizations, and the Medical History Project of 1951, which was concerned with the history of medicine and dentistry in Wisconsin. Unlike the original *Guide*, the supplement describes no State archives material, for when a public records program was established by the Legislature in 1947, a separate archives division was created within the society to collect, administer, and service government records within the State. At this point, many official papers were transferred from the manuscript section to the new archives division, where they properly belonged.

The recent experience of the archives division furnishes an example of the backing and filling that may occur in a society dependent upon public support. In the *Proceedings 1957–1958* the archivist, Dr. Jesse E. Boel reported:

At the last session of the legislature, the statutory functions of the Committee on Public Records and its staff were transferred from the State Historical Society to the Bureau of Purchases in the Executive Department. The State archives were, however, left under the custody of the State Historical Society, without staff to handle the work. Under an informal agreement between the Executive Office, the Division of Purchases, and the director of the State Historical Society it was agreed that the staff of the Committee on Public Records would be available to the director of the Society to handle the work of the division of State archives in the same manner as before its transfer to the Bureau of Purchases.

Another transfer in 1960 restored the *status quo ante*.

During the years from 1946 to 1958, under the directorship of Dr. Clifford L. Lord, now dean of the College of General Studies, Columbia University, the activities of the State Historical Society of Wisconsin were greatly expanded in an extraordinary number of directions. The extent of this expansion is reflected in the State appropriation, which was $84,531 in 1945–46 and $487,361.16 in 1958–59. Moreover, in recent years the society has attracted current private gifts to supplement its legislative appropriation. The treasurer's report as of 30 June 1959 showed a private endowment income of $28,467.75 derived from a capital of $637,434.63 (mostly received thirty or more years ago); receipts during the year of $49,764.59 from the operation of historic sites, of $101,299.16 from special projects (of which $52,830.70 was credit to the publication fund), and current gifts and foundation grants of $17,863.73. Current receipts from all sources, public and private, during the year 1958–59 were therefore in the vicinity of $635,000.

In this period of expansion, an effort was made to broaden the base of collecting policies by exploring the manuscripts of the then fashionable "common man."[8] The collection was also greatly enlarged by two groups of papers that are not of specifically Wisconsin content. In the winter of 1951 the McCormick collection of 1,000,000 items, plus 30,000 books and pamphlets formerly known as the Collections of the McCormick Historical Association of Chicago, arrived, complete with Dr. Herbert A. Kellar, who had been assembling it since 1915 for the McCormick family. This collection, based upon the personal papers of Cyrus Hall McCormick, the inventor of the reaper, which includes the papers of his children and McCormick Company records from 1849 to 1902, was the gift of Anita McCormick Blaine, the last surviving child of the inventor. The family's object had been to gather in one place everything that could be found about C. H. McCormick and his family, and to set this family in its natural background of time and place. Dr. Kellar's interest in agricultural history is reflected by groups of papers, of which many come from Virginia, that throw light on farming before and after the invention of the reaper, while the varied interests of members of the family cause the collection to offer a remarkable cross section of life in the United States. Since Dr. Kellar's sudden death in 1955, the collection has been in the care of his widow. Although it forms a part of the maps and manuscript section of the research division of the society, it is housed in separate rooms.

Dr. Lord's report for 1957–58, his last before leaving the society, summarizes another bulky accession, national in scope.

Here the Mass Communications History Center, formally inaugurated with a notable symposium and banquet address on Founders Day, has received the papers, in whole or in part, of movie magnates Harry and Roy Aitken of Waukesha; onetime Secretary of Commerce Herbert Hoover (copies); commentators Robert S. Allen, Gunnar Back, Rev. R. R. Brown, W. R. G. Baker, Dr. W. W. Bauer, Cecil Brown, Charles Butterfield, Charles C. Collingwood, Henry Cassidy, Alex Dreier, John Gunther, Qunicy Howe, founding father Hans V. Kaltenborn, Fulton Lewis, Jr., Clifton Utley, and the humorous commentator, Clarence Kemp (Uncle Ezra); cartoonists Carl Anderson, Fontaine Fox, Frank King, H. T.

8. Donald R. McNeil, "The Wisconsin Experiments," in *The American Collector*, pp. 36–44.

Webster, and Gluyas Williams; reporters Albert Crockett, Joseph C. Harsch, Louis P. Lochner; public relations experts Lemuel Boulware, A. C. Nielson, Anthony Marshall, Daniel Starch; newsletter authors Willard and Austin Kiplinger and Percival Whaley; pioneers Patt Barnes, Donald de Neuf, Victor Diehm, Joseph Herold, Malcolm P. Hanson, Lester W. Lindow and the pioneer radio station WHA (Madison); engineers C. J. Jansky, Jr., and Scott Helt; executives Edward R. Hitz and Rogan Jones.

Pledged are the papers of other outstanding personalities such as Bruce Barton, Wade Barnes, Albert Lasker, William T. Evjue, Merrill Mueller, John Daly, Ned Calmer, Helen Zotos, Marguerite Higgins, Edward P. Morgan, John Fischer; and the records of WWJ. This project enjoys cordial support of the University which has promised special travel allotments to selected faculty members to help the Society collect materials in this field. The project has attracted national attention, has been featured in appropriate trade organs, and is at the moment the prototype of a radio-television Hall of Fame and museum projected by the industry. If ultimately established elsewhere, the latter will lack the great supporting research library in American and Canadian history which Madison has to offer.

This down-to-the-minute extension of Lyman Draper's preoccupation with "passing history," like other projects in the collection of contemporary sources, raises problems of housing and handling, for the space gained by the departure of the university library half a dozen years ago is rapidly being filled by new accessions. In 1959, for example, the archives of the National Broadcasting Company began to arrive in Madison.

In the 1958–59 report, Donald R. McNeil, who served as acting director pending the arrival of Dr. Leslie H. Fishel Jr., the present incumbent, points out that the 2,500,000 mark has been passed in manuscripts, with well over 1,500,000 acquired since 1948.

The congestion continues and will probably get worse. More collections will soon have to be placed in the basement, the corridors, the offices, and the aisles in the stack. Workspace is deplorably inadequate. We have closed four museum galleries in the last two and one-half years; we have our manuscript librarians processing materials in the stacks because the workrooms are full; we have shifted and hauled and consolidated as each new space crisis has arisen.

The State Historical Society of Wisconsin operates on different levels and in many directions. It attempts to combine scholarly activity with an aggressive program of what it likes to call "taking history to the people." The activities of the library and research divisions are predominantly on the scholarly side; those of the museum division, school services, sites and markers on the other. Publications share aspects of both. The book list includes such works of serious history as Professor Hesseltine's admirable biography of Draper; Dr. Alice E. Smith's *James Duane Doty: Frontier Promoter*; Robert S. Maxwell's *La Follette and the Rise of the Progressives in Wisconsin*; Robert Fries's *Empire in Pine: The Story of Lumbering in Wisconsin, 1830–1900*; such works of reference as *Guide to Wisconsin Newspapers, 1833–1957* and the recently published *Dictionary of Wisconsin Biography*. At the other extreme are such juvenile titles as *A Merry Briton in Pioneer Wisconsin*; *It Happened Here: Stories of Wisconsin*; and *Side Roads: Excursions into Wisconsin's Past* in which Fred Holmes, "one of Wisconsin's favorite storytellers spins tales of nostalgia about his native state's ice cream parlors, barbershops, country stores, German beer gardens, and Christmas customs at the turn of the century." This nostalgic aspect of Wisconsin's not very distant past is also often emphasized in museum displays, by the reconstruction of a drugstore, or the display of a model T Ford, barber shop mugs, or other objects certain to give any citizen of Wisconsin who happens in a pleasing shock of recognition. The museum, however, also maintains iconographic and other collections that are of a serious nature.

The *Wisconsin Magazine of History*, in its forty-fourth volume in 1960, combines aspects of a scholarly journal and popular magazine. It often has serious articles and excellent reviews of books on historical subjects; it also has features entitled "Sincerely Yours" and "Readers Choice." With changes in staff, the number of features has been reduced, for Mr. McNeil's "The Circuit Rider" no longer appears. Although I believe Dr. Fishel uses tobacco, he has not perpetuated a director's column which was once headed by a likeness of Dr. Lord, the smoke from whose pipe ingeniously formed the title "Smoke Rings." "A Soviet View of the American Past: A Translation of the Section on U. S. History in the Great Soviet Encyclopedia" that appeared, with a preface by Adlai E. Stevenson, in the autumn 1959 issue is a conspicuous example of imaginative editing that combines serious and popular interest.

Three other periodicals are completely popular in character: the monthly *Wisconsin Now and Then* is aimed at adult readers; *Badger History* at 19,877 children who are enrolled in 1,144 junior historian chapters in elementary schools; *30th Star* at high school students. An intricate series of regional conventions, awards, and other activities is maintained to provide "fun for junior historians." *Badger History* is written partly by the society's staff and partly by its readers. It may therefore contain such verse as

> I heard the deep woods calling me,
> As I lay in idle slumber,
> I heard the tone, the demanding tone,
> Of tons of ageless lumber.

or the following bit of historical anecdote:

On a hunting trip our great-grandfather, Foster Livermore, met a bear. As the animal attacked him, he shot it, but before he could reload his gun, the bear ran after one of his dogs. Great-grandfather then took out his hunting knife and with the help of his two dogs killed the bear.

Our grandparents still have the bear's claws. These people live on the farm where the bear was killed, about four and a half miles south of Augusta.

A Historymobile carried popular museum exhibitions 4,302 miles in 1958–59; visited 191 towns, and was inspected by 59,246 adults and 93,232 children, a total of 152,478.

Field Services publishes, in co-operation with the museum, *Exchange*, a quarterly newsletter for county and local historical societies and museums. It conducts an Annual Institute of Local History at which the Reuben Gold Thwaites trophy is presented to the local historical society that has had the year's most outstanding program of activities. Its staff makes numerous field trips in search of accessions for the library and museums.

The society's sites and markers staff mark historic sites throughout the State, operate the Villa Louis and Brisbois House at Prairie du

Chien; the Old Wade House, a stagecoach inn at Greenbush, restored by the Kohler Foundation; and Stonefield, a State farm and craft museum at Cassville, where a village of the 1890s is being assembled. The Circus World Museum at Baraboo—"no one can afford to miss it—it is worth driving 2000 miles to see" say the announcements—first opened in 1959, was augmented in 1960 by the Circus Sideshow of the Nineteenth Century, a reconstruction undertaken by a veteran showman and vaudeville performer, Colonel Joe Mercedes, replete with life-size models of sideshow characters. This will be operated by Colonel Mercedes for five years, at the end of which he will give it to the State Historical Society. Elephant rides, cotton candy, pink lemonade are to be had, and, among other delights offered by the society's flyer:

You can have yourself photographed in a cage with a living, roaring, black maned African lion assuring you and your children a triumph of indescribable sensations and novel photographs.

When I was in Madison in April 1960 I was assured that these modern Daniels would be well protected by invisible glass from the living, roaring animal into whose cage, for a consideration, they would be permitted to enter.

In continuation of Draper's practice, a Public Contacts staff of two interprets and publicizes the society's activities by supplying material to newspapers and TV newscasters, commentators, and special program directors. In the year 1958–59 more than half the local daily and weekly papers of Wisconsin carried releases from the society.

Rivalry in size of membership often occurs in the larger state-supported historical societies of the Mississippi valley. The 1953 report of the State Historical Society of Iowa proudly included comparative figures as evidence of its accomplishment over the preceding six years.

Historical Society	1947	1953	Yearly Dues	1950 Population
Missouri	4,312	6,300	$1.00	3,954,653
Wisconsin	2,343	3,413	$3.50	3,434,575

Illinois	1,682	3,574	$2.00	8,712,176
Minnesota	1,674	2,662	$4.00	2,982,483
Iowa	1,121	4,452	$3.00	2,621,073

The State Historical Society of Missouri, thanks, one suspects, to dues of $1, reached first place in size in 1934-35 and has held it without challenge since 1937. In 1954 Wisconsin introduced a special promotional $1 membership (without a subscription to the *Wisconsin Magazine of History*) and inaugurated a membership caravan of staff members traveling through the State, describing the society's work and selling memberships. While Dr. Lord observed that, thanks to these efforts, the membership of the State Historical Society of Wisconsin in 1956 exceeded 5,000 for the first time in its history, Iowa in 1957 claimed second place to Missouri with 5,250. Wisconsin in 1958 had dropped to 4,260. In January 1960 the Wisconsin figure was 4,153, of which 2,110 were regular ($5) members; 1,309 were special ($1) members; the balance includes 122 persons or organizations at more than $5; 447 life members, and 164 complimentary or exchange memberships. Junior membership in Wisconsin, by which school children organized into chapters pay 50c per year for the *Badger Historian*, stood at 19,872 in 1956. In 1957 and 1958 it rose to over 22,000, but in 1959 had fallen to 19,866. In these terms membership is regarded as a device for "taking history to the people" rather than an element of financial support, for each annual ($5) membership costs the Historical Society $8.61, and each special ($1) membership costs $2.30. The excellent books on Wisconsin history issued by the State Historical Society are presented in an attractive format that rivals the offerings of commercial firms. The fact that they are published in an edition of less than 1,000 copies, suggests that the large membership of the society represents a negligible market for worth-while publications. The fluctuations in membership also suggest the impermanence of gains in numbers obtained from popular campaigns.

The dual nature of the State Historical Society of Wisconsin inspires different reactions among different groups. Mr. McNeil in the 1958–59 report, in commenting on Dr. Lord's effort to give the society a broad base of popular support, well said:

In so doing, he appealed to a wide audience never before exposed to the Society or to history. In the process the Society has been criticized by scholars for over-emphasizing "popular" history, for "diluting" history, for propagandizing instead of teaching. On the other hand, many of our friends and supporters around the State contend that the Society is still much too academic, too involved with pedantry, didacticism, and erudition. To some critics the Historymobile, the museum exhibits, the brochures and the TV shows, the roadside markers, the historic sites—all seem to be so much "fluff." Others feel the scholarly publications, the library, the manuscript collections, and the research program have too limited an appeal, that they are maintained solely for the enjoyment of the scholarly elite. Why not take the Historymobile money and put it into books? ask some. You've got enough books to last anyone several lifetimes, others answer.

As the debate continues, the State Historical Society of Wisconsin attempts, by drawing to its staff able people of very different talents and by the use of both public and private funds, to ride both horses. With a large building, recently modernized, a staff of about 125, and an income of roughly $635,000 a year, it continues to claim, with justice, that it is crowded and shorthanded. If accessions and activities continue to multiply at the pace of the past fifteen years, those difficulties will become accentuated, for it is far simpler and quicker to obtain a carton of manuscripts than to place it in usable order. Operation on so many levels would be beyond the predictable resources of an independent historical society, yet one might also observe that such societies are not under the necessity of making the attempt, for much of the appeal "to a wide audience never before exposed to the Society or to history" is, consciously or otherwise, a confirmation of Reuben Gold Thwaites's remark of 1909 that "legislatures and the public at large that they represent, require coddling if their support is to be obtained."[9]

9. "The Legislators, bemused and delighted with a flood of letters from our junior members telling them about the program, generously voted a major increase in the state appropriation for this project, relieving our private funds of the serious, and almost disastrous, strain to which this healthy youngster has subjected them each of the last four years" (*Proceedings: One Hundred and Fifth Annual Business Meeting of the State Historical Society of Wisconsin held at Green Lake, June 1, 1951*, p. 18).

Chapter XII

EARLY STATE-SUPPORTED
HISTORICAL SOCIETIES

At least in some portions of the country, particularly in the Central West, state historical societies seem to have passed through stages similar to those marking the history of public schools, libraries, and museums; their useful functions have been recognized as worthy of state support, thus relieving them of their dependence upon private endowment. —JULIAN P. BOYD, 1934

THE first ten chapters of this book have dealt in some detail with the major independent State historical societies, all but two of which—Delaware and California—were established in their present forms before the outbreak of the Civil War. Down to 1860 these societies carried the burden of collecting, preserving, and publishing the sources of American history. In the century that has followed they have been joined in this effort by publicly supported historical societies and a host of other institutions. Wisconsin, as the prototype of the society deriving the majority of its support from public funds, has been treated in some detail. The chapters that follow will describe some of these newer allies of the past century in briefer and more selective manner. Not all the institutions of any one type, nor all phases of their activities, are mentioned. Only those are included that have some relation to, or some possible suggestion for the improvement of, the research and publication functions and the financial future of the independent historical societies.

Whether support comes from private citizens or Legislatures, State historical societies develop their own different approaches and characteristics. These depend in part upon location, the relative age of the State, the nature of its inhabitants, and the extent of their resources; they depend also to a considerable degree upon the personal interests and abilities of the individuals who have shaped them in critical periods of their careers. The large, useful, and prosperous societies that are mentioned in this chapter follow no rigid pattern. Each has its own character and its own particular merits; the common denominator is that all have been generously supported by public appropriations.

MINNESOTA

The first book published in Minnesota was the *Annals of the Minnesota Historical Society*, printed at Saint Paul in 1850 by James M. Goodhue, which bore on its title page this quotation:

To gather from still living witnesses and preserve for the future annalist, the important records of the teeming and romantic past—to seize while yet warm and glowing, and inscribe upon the page which shall be sought hereafter, the bright visions of song and fair images of story, that gild the gloom and lighten the sorrows of the ever fleeting present—to search all history with a steady eye—sound all philosophy with a careful hand—question all experience with a fearless tongue, and thence draw lessons to fit us for, and light to guide us through the shadowed, but unknown future.

The society[1] that published this pioneer effort had been incorporated the previous year, just seven and a half months after the establishment of Minnesota Territory. The Legislature of 1856, which revised and expanded the society's charter, passed a joint resolution for an annual grant toward its support. Steady growth began with the appointment as secretary in 1867 of J. Fletcher Williams, who worked

---

1. Mary Wheelhouse Berthel and Harold Dean Cater, "The Minnesota Historical Society: Highlights of a Century," *Minnesota History* XXX (1949), 293–330; Russell W. Fridley, "The Minnesota Historical Society," *Gopher Historian* XII, 2 (1957–58), pp. 2–4.

for two years as a volunteer whenever his duties as a newspaper reporter permitted. Rooms in the basement of the capitol were provided in 1868, while the following year the Legislature passed an act establishing the society as a free public library and appropriating $2,000 for its "better support and usefulness." With this increased income, the society provided a salary for Williams, who became its full-time librarian, a post that he filled without assistance of any kind until 1888. While J. F. Williams's chief interest was in the collection and preservation of books, manuscripts, and newspapers, a catalogue of the library and six volumes of the *Minnesota Historical Collections*, the fourth of which was his own *History of the city of St. Paul*, were published before his retirement in 1893.

Warren Upham, a geologist who was regarded as one of the State's most distinguished scientists, served as secretary and librarian from 1895 to 1914, and as archaeologist—a field to which his geological studies had led him—from 1914 to 1933. During his regime the library grew from 56,537 volumes to nearly double that number; the staff increased to ten persons; and legislative appropriations were raised from $6,000 to $20,000 annually. Upham was the author of of the two most useful volumes in the *Collections*: *Minnesota Biographies, 1655–1912* and *Minnesota Geographic Names*, which were characterized by William W. Folwell, author of a four-volume *History of Minnesota* published by the society between 1921 and 1930, as "an admirable and convenient Minnesota 'Who's Who' " and "an equally admirable 'There's where'."

Early in the twentieth century grandchildren of the Minnesota pioneers began to show an enthusiastic if somewhat undiscriminating interest in genealogy, antiques, daguerreotypes, old newspapers, and other evidences of the beginnings of the State. With the thought of canalizing this enthusiasm into useful channels, Guy Stanton Ford, soon after he became professor of history and dean of the Graduate School at the University of Minnesota, suggested that the Minnesota Historical Society needed a young and vigorous man with professional training in history to direct its activities into an organized program. So it came about that in the autumn of 1914 Solon J. Buck, then a thirty-year-old assistant professor of history at the University of Minnesota and later Archivist of the United States, became director of the society on a half-time basis.

During the seventeen years of his directorship Dr. Buck emphasized comprehensive but discriminating collecting, high standards of scholarly accuracy in the cataloguing of collections and in publications, the formation of a historical museum, the dissemination of information about Minnesota history through greater use of the society's collections by the public, and the building up of a professionally competent staff. In 1915 he inaugurated the quarterly *Minnesota History Bulletin*, which since 1925 has been known as *Minnesota History*. In the same year the Legislature appropriated $500,000 for a fireproof building for the society near the capitol in Saint Paul, which was completed and occupied in 1917. In the 1920s Dr. Buck inspired the founding of county historical societies,[2] initiated annual summer meetings in various parts of the State, and encouraged the teaching of Minnesota history in the schools. While he was active in bringing "the gospel of salvation through a knowledge of the past to all who are capable of receiving it," he was equally concerned with the accuracy and appropriateness of what was transmitted. From 1922 he had the assistance, also on a half-time basis, of Professor Theodore C. Blegen, later dean of the Graduate School

2. Several of these have assembled noteworthy collections of books and manuscripts. The Minnesota Historical Society calls particular attention to the Saint Louis County Historical Society, Duluth, whose manuscript collection is strong on iron mining and the Saint Lawrence Seaway, and which possesses a museum and pictures; the Brown County Historical Society, New Ulm, whose manuscripts, pictures, and museum are especially relevant to the Sioux War of 1862; the Hennepin County Historical Society, Minneapolis, and the Olmsted County Historical Society, Rochester, with manuscripts, library, museum, and pictures; the Ramsay County Historical Society, Saint Paul, with manuscripts, library, and museum; the Winona County Historical Society, Winona, with manuscripts, museum, and pictures; and the Pope County Historical Society, Glenwood, which has an unusually fine county genealogical collection. It should be noted that county societies exist not only in regions remote from the capital, but even in Saint Paul and Minneapolis under the very nose of the Minnesota Historical Society.

of the University of Minnesota, who became his successor in 1931. As annual appropriations increased from $20,000 to $53,100, the staff was augmented by professionally trained librarians, curators, and editors.

Dr. Blegen through the 1930s directed the popular and scholarly activities of the Minnesota Historical Society with great energy. He introduced broadcasts on Minnesota history over the University of Minnesota radio station, encouraged popular observances of historical anniversaries, made effective use of WPA projects in archival surveys, while adding luster to the society's scholarly reputation not only through editing its publications but by his own writing. In 1939 he resigned so that he might devote more time to the completion of his great *Norwegian Migration to America*.

The Minnesota Historical Society today, under the direction of Mr. Russell W. Fridley, continues vigorously along the course charted by Dr. Buck and Dean Blegen. Its library contains over 200,000 books, pamphlets, and periodicals, most of which have to do with Minnesota and the upper Midwest. A separate department cares for some 25,000 bound volumes of Minnesota newspapers and more than half a million unbound issues, which include most of the papers published in the territory and the State from the first issue of the *Minnesota Pioneer*, published on 28 April 1849. Some 540 Minnesota newspapers are currently added to the collection each week, although since 1948 microfilming is being used extensively. Both the library and newspaper collection are rich in material relating to the Scandinavian elements in the United States. The society's extensive holdings of Minnesota paintings, photographs, prints, and daguerreotypes are made widely available by a photographic service offered in the picture department.

Access to the manuscript collection, which contains an estimated 4,000,000 items, is facilitated by a *Guide to the Personal Papers in the Manuscript Collections of the Minnesota Historical Society*, compiled in 1935 by Grace Lee Nute and Gertrude W. Ackermann, which lists 455 collections, and the 1955 *Manuscript Collections of the Minnesota*

Historical Society Guide Number 2, by Lucile M. Kane, the present curator of manuscripts, and Kathryn A. Johnson, which describes 1,190 additional groups of papers alike of individuals, organizations, and business firms. The discriminating principles followed in the assembly of this great body of sources will best be appreciated by reading Miss Kane's "Collecting Policies of the Minnesota Historical Society; 1849–1852," which was published in the April 1953 issue of *The American Archivist*.[3] This perceptive and realistic appraisal, which emphasizes the change that has taken place in the nature of manuscripts during the past hundred years, deserves careful study by other institutions. Miss Kane succinctly traces the evolution from the period when "manuscripts were treasured simply because they were manuscripts rather than for specific qualities or content"— "presented because someone thought they were worth saving, they were accepted because freely given"—to the present attitude that "since the society cannot collect everything, we have felt it imperative to acquire only the best manuscripts available."

The first and second floors and the basement of the 1917 building house the books, manuscripts, and pictures appropriately. The third floor does less well for the historical museum, partly because it requires a long climb by visitors and partly because the galleries of buildings approaching the half-century mark do not easily lend themselves to flexible exhibition techniques. It is hoped that eventually a more accessible wing may be added at the rear of the building for this department. In addition to its museum in Saint Paul, the society owns two historic sites elsewhere in the State, the General William G. Le Duc House in Hastings, acquired in 1958, and the Mille Lacs Indian Museum at Vineland, which was given in 1959 by Mr. and Mrs. Harry Ayer, who had long owned and operated an Indian trading post there.[4] Through the peripatetic activities of Mr. Arch Grahn, Field Director, the Minnesota Historical Society keeps in close touch with county historical societies.

3. *The American Archivist* XVI (1953), 127–136.
4. "Society Acquires Indian Museum," *Minnesota History News* I, 1 (August 1959), pp. 1–2.

Publications, which follow a pattern that has had Dean Blegen's continued interest, range from those designed for school use, through books for the general public, to scholarly editions of sources, studies in social and cultural history, and technical aids. In addition to *Minnesota History*, there are three numbers a year of the *Gopher Historian*, a self-supporting magazine for young people, with popular articles by staff members and teachers, which is used widely in the schools of the State, and, since 1959, the bimonthly four-page *Minnesota History News*. It is worth noting that *Gopher Historian*, although designed for young people, contains informative articles that can be read without disgust by adults; it is free from that chatty "togetherness" that make some efforts to attract young readers singularly unpleasant. Dr. Grace Lee Nute's *The Voyageur* (first published commercially in 1931 and reprinted by the society in 1955), *The Voyageur's Highway: Minnesota's Border Lake Land* (1941), and *Rainy River Country: A Brief History of the Region Bordering Minnesota and Ontario* (1950) are admirable examples of history that is at once sound, readable, and saleable.

The preparation of studies in social and industrial history has been aided by private funds on several occasions. The writing and publication of Professor Philip D. Jordan's *The People's Health: A History of Public Health in Minnesota to 1948* (1953) was made possible by a gift of $25,000 from the Mayo Properties Association in Rochester. The Forest Products History Foundation, which has now been expanded into a separate national research and publishing body, the Forest History Foundation, Inc.,[5] began with a gift of $50,000 to the Minnesota Historical Society in 1946 from the Weyerhauser and Denkmann families, long identified with the lumber industry. Gifts of smaller sums from the Oliver Mining Company and the Minnesota and Ontario Paper Company assisted in the publication of Dr. Nute's *Mesabi Pioneer: Reminiscences of Edmund J. Longyear* and *Rainy River Country*.

5. One useful product of this foundation is Clodaugh M. Neiderheiser's *Forest History Sources of the United States and Canada, A compilation of the manuscript sources of forestry, forest industry, and conservation history* (Saint Paul, 1956), which surveys the manuscript holdings of institutions throughout the country on that theme.

About 90% of the income of the Minnesota Historical Society is derived from legislative appropriations, the current annual level of which is $230,595. For the year ending 30 June 1959, there were in addition $46,794.25 of private revenue, of which $8,785.30 were income from an endowment of $211,682.15, $11,214.89 were received from members' dues, and the remainder from sales of publications, contributions, and the like. In 1959 there were 2,774 members, at minimum dues of $4. In the six months following the establishment of company membership, with annual dues of $100, eighteen firms joined.

IOWA

The State Historical Society of Iowa was organized in February 1857, along lines indicated by Lyman C. Draper's experience in Wisconsin,[6] as a result of an annual appropriation of $250 voted by the General Assembly the previous month. It has always been located in Iowa City, in close proximity to the State university. Although an act of 1872 reorganized it as a State institution in the fullest sense of the term, it has no connection with the Iowa State Department of History and Archives (organized in 1892 as the State Historical Department) at the capital, Des Moines, which deals with the public records of Iowa. From 1901 to 1960 the State Historical Society occupied rooms in the university's Hall of Liberal Arts. It has very recently moved into its own building near the campus, constructed by means of $285,000 provided by the General Assembly and $165,000 of private funds, chiefly raised through the energy of Dr. William J. Petersen, who has been superintendent of the society since 1941.

While the State Historical Society of Iowa has assembled a useful library, it has not sought manuscripts with the avidity of Wisconsin or the discrimination of Minnesota, nor, because of its long residence in a university building, has it ventured into the museum field. Its

6. William B. Hesseltine, *Pioneer's Progress*, pp. 147, 162, 227–228, 248, mentions Lyman C. Draper's influence on the foundation of the Iowa and Kansas societies.

great distinction lies in its publications, which far outnumber those of any other society in the Mississippi valley. Between 1863 and 1874 twelve volumes of *Annals of Iowa* were published as a historical quarterly. After a break of eight years, three volumes of a second series were published in 1882, 1883, and 1884, as a personal venture of Samuel Storrs Howe, who had once been librarian of the society. The State Historical Society in 1885 resumed the publication of a quarterly, this time entitled *Iowa Historical Record*, and of this eighteen volumes appeared between that date and 1902. *Annals of Iowa* was revived at Des Moines in 1893 by the Historical Department of Iowa in a third series that continues to the present; this, however, represents the activity of another State agency at the capital, which is not in any way related to the State Historical Society at Iowa City.

In 1903 Benjamin Franklin Shambaugh (1871–1940), a graduate of the State University of Iowa who had returned to its faculty after taking a doctorate in political science at the University of Pennsylvania in 1895, transformed the *Iowa Historical Record* into a new periodical, *The Iowa Journal of History and Politics*. The name implies the preoccupation of the political scientist, who is having no truck with the "old pioneer" tradition that had led to the founding of the society four decades earlier, or with genealogically minded antiquarianism. The *Journal*'s handsome and dignified format, an older cousin of the one later adopted by *Foreign Affairs*, marked it as a professional effort that was intended to do credit both to the society and the university in academic circles. Professor Shambaugh undertook the editorship while a member of the board of curators of the State Historical Society. Although he became the society's superintendent and editor in 1907, he continued as head of the Department of Political Science at the State University until his death in 1940. He stated his conception of the society's role unequivocally in an information pamphlet of 1912:[7]

Responding to the progress that has been made in recent years in the application of scientific methods in nearly every sphere of human interest and activity and dom-

7. *Some Information: The State Historical Society of Iowa* (Iowa City, 1912), pp. 9–11.

inated by the spirits and standards of modern scholarship, The State Historical Society of Iowa has come to make historical research its chief function. Indeed in this respect The State Historical Society of Iowa is almost unique, its financial resources and its administrative efforts being directed largely in the channels of scientific research and critical publication.

It is true that heretofore in most States the principal function of the State historical society (as well as of the private historical society) seems to have been that of collection, preservation, and exhibition—leaving historical research, for the most part to individual initiative. But with The State Historical Society of Iowa, on the other hand, historical research and publication have become the dominant activity. Through its organization and institutional activities the materials of State and local history are discovered, critically investigated by specialists, compiled, edited, and published.

Thus, instead of simply attempting to make the largest possible collection of historical materials in one place (namely, in the Society's library), this Society endeavors to compile, publish, and distribute the greatest amount of accurate, scientific historical literature. Instead of simply hoarding books and manuscripts for the use of the few, the Society aims to make the history of the State accessible to the many.

In 1934, Julian P. Boyd calculated that during Professor Shambaugh's regime, which still had another six years to go, the State Historical Society of Iowa had employed some twenty-six trained persons to do research and had issued 720 publications totaling 75,111 pages! "It is doubtful," he remarked, "if the political and constitutional history of any commonwealth has been so thoroughly documented."[8]

Professor Shambaugh's very comprehensive publication plans involved a series of documents from the State archives, a biographical series, an economic history series, an applied history series, and popular bulletins of information. Applied history Shambaugh defined "as the use of the scientific knowledge of history and experience in efforts to solve present problems of human betterment"; the applied historian "views the past as a vast social laboratory in which experiments in politics and human welfare are daily being set and tested on

8. Julian P. Boyd, "State and Local Historical Societies in the United States," *American Historical Review* XL (1934–35), 31.

a most elaborate scale."[9] The seven volumes of the Iowa Applied History Series represent an attempt to make history useful to contemporary legislators and administrators by analyzing among other things such controversial topics as regulation of utilities, workmen's compensation, removal of public officials, and public welfare. As Julian Boyd has remarked:

> Here history is raised to the dignity of a coördinate agency of government assisting through historical scholarship to throw light upon vexing present day questions. James I might dissolve the Society of Antiquaries of London because of a fear of their peering too closely into the arcana of government, but here in a modern commonwealth we find a legislature making liberal appropriations to enable scholars to investigate its most recent activities and to broadcast their findings among 190 libraries and hundreds of members.

A monthly popular magazine in pocket-size format, *The Palimpsest*, was inaugurated in 1920; a monthly *News for Members* and *Iowa History News Flashes*, a monthly release to Iowa newspapers, began in 1947. The name of the scholarly quarterly was in 1949 simplified to *Iowa Journal of History* when a fresh typographical design was adopted. Dr. Petersen, who became superintendent in 1941, a year after Professor Shambaugh's death, shares his predecessor's energetic passion for diffusing history by means of publications. Not only is his *Iowa History Reference Guide* (1952) much used in libraries, but schools and study clubs turn frequently to the four-page *Selected Readings on Iowa History* prepared by him. In the past decade he has devoted great effort to increasing membership, chiefly as a means of diffusing history through publications. In 1903, when the *Iowa Journal of History and Politics* was founded, there were 60 members; in 1920, when *The Palimpsest* began to appear, there were 978; in 1940 the number had risen to 1,560. In 1959 the score stood at 6,067, placing the State Historical Society of Iowa second only to the Missouri State Historical Society. In 1947 approximately $2,000 was received from dues and sales of publications; in 1959 that sum had increased to $20,000, which covers the entire cost of *The Palimpsest*

9. *Iowa Applied History Series* (Iowa City, 1912), I, vii.

and much of the expense of the *Iowa Journal of History*. All other publications, like the general expenses of the society, are met from the legislative appropriation. As society publications are given to the 160 college and tax-supported libraries in Iowa, they are available to all citizens whether members or not. Anyone who chooses to join for $3, or become a life member for $100, gets his fill of good reading matter, for he receives periodicals and books costing approximately $12 a year. *The Palimpsest* is frequently printed in larger numbers than are required for the membership, due to demands from schools and study clubs that use it as a source of information for discussions.

Dr. Petersen's interest in steamboats has been shown not only by his books *Steamboating on the Upper Mississippi* (1937) and *Iowa: The Rivers of Her Valleys* (1941) but by the series of Mississippi River steamboat excursions that he has annually organized since 1948. Overland tours to the Amana colonies and other historic areas of Iowa are frequently arranged by the society.

KANSAS

A historical society chartered in 1855, less than a year after the organization of Kansas Territory, proved unfruitful, as did other attempts of 1859 and 1867. Today's Kansas State Historical Society, established in 1875, profited by Lyman Draper's experience of administration and legislative appropriations in Wisconsin. As its founders were the newspaper editors and publishers of the State, it is appropriate that the society today should have one of the largest newspaper collections in the country, comprising some 69,534 bound volumes, of which 57,551 are from Kansas presses and have been contributed by their editors. From 1877, when a legislative appropriation was granted, the society has been recognized as a necessary adjunct of the State government; since 1905 it has been the official custodian of the State archives. Its collections were housed in various rooms, always crowded, in the capitol, until a Memorial Building in Topeka was constructed for the society by the Legislature with funds voted by Congress to repay the State of Kansas for equipping troops in the Civil War. This substantial and attractive building, completed in 1914, houses the society's library, the State archives, and a historical museum.

The library, specializing in Kansas, western, and Indian history, and genealogy, attempts to secure every book, pamphlet, or magazine article written about Kansas or by a Kansan. In 1958 it had 100,307 books, 141,859 pamphlets, and 8,725 reels of microfilm. It has 5,366 Kansas maps and atlases; 33,037 photographs; and, in addition to the great newspaper collection which is its most remarkable possession, it maintains a large and well-indexed file of newspaper clippings.

Among the holdings in the manuscript collection are the records of the Saint Louis Superintendency of Indian Affairs under General William Clark; the journals and correspondence of Isaac McCoy, pioneer surveyor and Indian missionary; the journals of the missionary Jotham Meeker who was the first printer in Kansas; records of the New England Emigrant Aid Society, which helped populate the territory with Free-State settlers; and the papers of Governors Charles Robinson and Alfred M. Landon. Microfilm equipment purchased in 1946 has been extensively used to safeguard material and conserve space both in the archives and newspaper departments. Manuscripts, including public archives and private papers, occupy 5,750 cubic feet.

In addition to a well-arranged museum of Kansas history on the top floor of the Memorial Building, the society maintains and operates the restored first territorial capitol of 1855 on the Fort Riley reservation, the Kaw Methodist Mission of 1850 at Council Grove, the Shawnee Methodist Mission of 1839 in Fairway, a suburb of Kansas City, Kansas, and the boyhood home of General Frederick Funston, near Iola in Allen County.

The Kansas Historical Quarterly, edited by Kirke Mechem, was in its twenty-sixth year in 1960. This well-edited and well-printed journal, which now consists of 128 pages to an issue, contains a good variety of scholarly articles and documents on Kansas history. *The Historical Society Mirror*, a four-page bimonthly newsletter, has been published since 1955. Items from the Kansas press of 100 years ago are sent to newspaper editors in the form of monthly news releases, while the two volumes of *Annals of Kansas, 1886–1925,* which continues a previous publication begun by Daniel Webster Wilder, an early-day Kansas editor, provide a fully indexed day-by-day account of the State's development in those years. The society has recently issued *Kansas Imprints, 1854–1876* and a *Comprehensive Index to Publications, 1875–1930. Kansas—A Pictorial History,* a 300-page book, is a recent joint publication with the Kansas Centennial Commission.

With the assistance of the Baughman Foundation, the society is preparing a listing of all Kansas post offices and postmasters, past and present, which involves the rediscovery of numerous ghost towns, as well as a detailed calendar of all maps relating to Kansas and its political subdivisions. Robert W. Baughman's *Kansas in Maps,* which will contain the reproduction of many of these, is scheduled for publication in the near future by the Baughman Foundation, through the Kansas State Historical Society.

All administrative and operating expenses are met by legislative appropriation; in 1960 the sum was $272,379. Private funds consist only of $13,000 in United States bonds, the income from which can be used for the purchase of manuscripts, and $1,575 from membership fees. All 1,828 members receive the *Quarterly* and the *Mirror,* but as the State furnishes the printing, dues have been kept very low. The former rates of $2 for annual membership and $10 for life have been raised to $3 and $20, with a new class of sustaining annual members at $10. Membership is therefore a means of disseminating historical information rather than a source of support.

The Kansas State Historical Society attends to its affairs in a workmanlike and realistic manner, with a delightful freedom from boastfulness or portentous solemnity. Its secretary, Dr. Nyle H. Miller, and its editor, Mr. Kirke Mechem, are learned and literate individuals, blessed with a sense of humor. Dr. Miller recently pointed out, with documentary chapter and verse, the disparity between the actual careers of certain early western law enforcement officers and their posthumous recreation as television "heroes."[10] Mr. Mechem's account of the mythical Kansas jayhawk[11] delighted many thousands of readers, among them H. L. Mencken. The sprightly and well-balanced approach of these historians to some aspects of frontier history might fittingly be emulated elsewhere.

OHIO

The Indian mounds of Ohio, ranking among the more spectacular archaeological monuments of the United States, have long fascinated scholars. It will be recalled that Christopher Columbus Baldwin, librarian of the American Antiquarian Society, was killed on a journey to visit them; he was preceded and followed by many other students who returned home safely. Created in response to this archaeological interest, the Ohio Historical Society, with headquarters at Columbus and fifty-seven ramifications throughout the State, today controls over 4,000 acres of land and 150 buildings. After being established on 12 March 1885 as the Ohio State Archaeological and Historical Society—a name only simplified to its present form in 1954—with the broad purpose of "promoting a knowledge of Archaeology and History, especially of Ohio," it undertook to develop a library, a public museum for the preservation of prehistoric, historic, and natural history specimens, to provide lecture courses, and issue publications. In 1891 the society became the agent of the State to care for Fort Ancient, the first of Ohio's State memorials; it has in the subsequent seven decades become responsible for fifty-six others, including museums, historic houses, sites, and monuments, archaeological sites, reproductions, and natural history areas.

From quarters in the State House at Columbus, the society moved to the campus of Ohio State University, where it has occupied since

10. Nyle H. Miller, *Some Widely Publicized Western Police Officers* (Lincoln, Nebr., 1958), reprinted from *Nebraska History*, December 1958.

11. Kirke Mechem, *The Mythical Jayhawk* (Topeka, 1956), originally published in the February 1944 issue of the *Kansas Historical Quarterly*.

1913 a substantial combined library and museum building. From small and essentially archaeological beginnings, it has evolved into a state-wide organization with semigovernmental status, which serves as the official custodian of Ohio's history. The purposes of the society today are to collect and preserve the materials, sites, and data from which can be compiled the history of Ohio—interpreting history in the broad sense of including all the experience and knowledge of man—and to make these collections and the resultant history available to the people of the State. The society endeavors to achieve its aims through an extensive specialized public library, the State archives, a large State museum, the fifty-seven State memorials, research programs in Ohio history, archaeology, and natural history, and exhibits, publications, and educational programs.

The Ohio Historical Society is a very large enterprise as one might judge from its using a total staff of 174 and State appropriations for the fiscal year ending 30 June 1959 of $515,800. Eighty-seven staff members are on a full-time basis, twenty-three are seasonal, and sixty-four are part-time employees. Its work is apportioned to six divisions: history and science, library, education and public relations, business management, properties, and archives. The present director, Mr. Edwin C. Zepp, a landscape architect, was formerly the head of the properties division. Dr. James H. Rodabaugh, head of the history and science division, who has been with the society since 1944, is responsible for the Departments of Archaeology, History, Natural History, and Publications.

Since for over fifty years the primary interest of the society was archaeology, its first collections consisted of artifacts excavated from prehistoric earthworks and village sites. Thus the Ohio State Museum, which the society administers, has the finest collection in existence of Ohio prehistoric Indian materials of the Adena, Hopewell, Fort Ancient, and other cultures. The society also takes care of fifteen prehistoric Indian sites, including the celebrated Serpent Mound in Adams County, Fort Ancient in Warren County, Fort Hill in Highland County, and the Great Circle and Octagon Earthworks at

Newark. No other historical society in the United States has comparable holdings on the prehistory of its State. These possessions are treated at the highest professional level, and the curator of archaeology gives courses in archaeology and physical anthropology at Ohio State University.

Natural history, early prominent among the aspirations of many independent historical societies, in all other cases was soon abandoned or else transferred to a specialized scientific institution. The Ohio Historical Society is unique in having within the past forty years established a Natural History Department, which incorporates the former collections of Ohio State University and serves as a natural history museum for that university. This is no haphazard assortment of dusty, moth-eaten stuffed birds, such as one finds lingering occasionally in the showcases of unreformed institutions. It is a systematic scientific collection, cared for by a professional staff of three, with two student assistants. The university pays the salary of the society's curator of invertebrate collections. Portions of the natural history collections are also made attractive in an imaginative way to the great number of visitors to the Ohio State Museum. A new bird room installed in 1960, which is an example of the most subtle and ingenious exhibition techniques, with full use of sound effects, represents skillful collaboration between curators, technicians, and craftsmen of the building staff. The society also administers five natural history areas in different parts of the State.

Unique in respect to its archaeological and natural history collections, the Ohio Historical Society proves to be exceptional also in administering historic properties of surprising variety. Adena, the home of Thomas Worthington, completed in 1807 on a hill overlooking Chilicothe; the birthplace of Ulysses S. Grant at Point Pleasant; the Rutherford B. Hayes Home at Fremont; Glendower, a fine Greek revival house at Lebanon; the buildings of the German pietistic sect at Zoar; the home of Paul Laurence Dunbar, America's most famous Negro poet, in Dayton—all these exemplify the catholicity of its holdings.

The Ohio Historical Society's library in Columbus, although its additions have come slower than the archaeological materials, has assembled excellent specialized research works on Ohio history, archaeology, and natural history. It contains more than 70,000 books, 40,000 volumes and 16,000 rolls of microfilm of Ohio newspapers, 3,000 maps, 500 broadsides, and 12,000 photographs. The manuscript section contains over 1,100 collections, numbering about one million pieces, consisting of papers from 1750 to the present relating chiefly to Ohio, but including some of national interest. These are listed in Elizabeth C. Biggert's *Guide to the Manuscript Collections in the Library of the Ohio State Archaeological and Historical Society* (1953). The Rutherford B. Hayes Library at Fremont, which the society administers with the co-operation of a family foundation, contains over 50,000 volumes, including the President's personal library, and over half a million manuscripts, among which are the Hayes diaries and correspondence.

For many years the society has been concerned over the preservation of governmental records, having made numerous attempts to prevent the destruction of historical material. In 1959 it was named the archival agency of the State and is now working officially with State departments and municipal officials to this end.

When Dr. Rodabaugh came to the society in 1944, he was the only member of the staff engaged in historical research. Now in his division there are, in addition to the Departments of Archaeology and Natural History, a curator of history, two assistant curators, and two research associates, besides an associate editor and an assistant editor in the Department of Publications. The library division employs a curator of manuscripts in addition to the usual library staff.

In the past decade much effort has been spent on reorganizing the historical exhibits in the Ohio State Museum to offer popular interpretations of the domestic life, work, and cultural and political development of the people of Ohio. Along with these a carefully planned policy of collecting examples of Ohio glass, pottery, furniture, and other crafts and industries of the State has led to the acquisition of substantial holdings in local nineteenth-century decorative arts. The museum is visited by hordes of children and, on account of their importance in the society's educational program, its settings are constantly being improved. A technical staff of four in the Department of Art and Design, assisted by a skilled carpenter and other members of the building crew, are transforming major parts of the building to provide improved exhibition rooms.

The *Ohio Historical Quarterly*, which began in 1887 as *Ohio Archaeological and Historical Publications*, served a distinguished and useful scholarly purpose for more than seventy years. The announcement of a change of policy at the end of 1961 caused great regret among scholarly readers of the *Quarterly*. The January 1962 issue is in a new illustrated format, with footnotes inconveniently relegated to the rear. Happily the quality of the articles remains unchanged. It appears, as one reviewer put it, that the new "*Ohio History* is the same old vehicle, but with 'fins' added."[12] The society has long issued a popular eight-page monthly, *Museum Echoes*, volume XXXIII of which appeared in 1960.

The society's numerous publications in archaeology and Ohio history are addressed to all levels of interest. They range from popular leaflets distributed by the thousands, to such reference work as Richard G. Morgan and James H. Rodabaugh's *Bibliography of Ohio Archaeology* and William C. Mills's *Archaeological Atlas of Ohio*. Five volumes of the *Diary and Letters of Rutherford B. Hayes* were issued between 1922 and 1926. A six-volume *History of the State of Ohio* appeared between 1941 and 1944, and a one-volume illustrated State history by Eugene H. Roseboom and Francis P. Weisenburger—both of whom wrote volumes in the larger work—has gone through four printings. *Ohio Newspapers, A Living Record*, edited in 1950 by Robert C. Wheeler, then newspaper librarian of the society, presents Ohio history through 126 full-page facsimile reproductions of news-

12. Dr. Louis L. Tucker, director of the Historical and Philosophical Society of Ohio, in *History News* XVII, 10 (August 1962), p. 154. See further discussion of this change in chapter XXIII.

papers, with 100 pages of historical commentary; the result is a book at once fascinating to the casual reader and highly useful for classes in history and journalism. The society's list offers a rich variety of works of high quality on all phases of the State's history.

The Ohio Historical Society does not attempt to attract a large membership for the sake of statistics. Its activities are addressed to the eight million citizens of Ohio, who are free to benefit, if they wish, from its museums and publications. Effort is made to maintain a small membership of persons who are vitally interested in the history of the State, the activities and collections of the society, the properties it administers, and county and local historical work. As of June 1960 there was a total of 862 members; 453 participating annual at $5, 79 supporting annual at $10, 7 supporting contributors at $30, 139 life members who had paid $150, 30 honorary life members, 96 joint members with the Ohio Academy of History, 45 joint members with the Ohio Academy of Medical History, and 13 affiliate members of county societies. The total subscription list for the *Ohio Historical Quarterly*, including the 862 members, is 1,796. Through the generosity of the Legislature, which pays the entire publication cost of the society's periodicals, they are sent free to 288 public libraries, 50 Ohio college libraries, 35 Ohio newspapers, 171 legislators, and 151 institutions on exchange. The receipts of $4,381.85 from membership in 1959 are financially irrelevant in a budget involving $515,800 of public funds and approximately $80,000 from private sources. The membership, however, has an opportunity to influence the policies of the society, for it elects nine of the seventeen members of the board of trustees. The governor appoints six other members, and he with the State director of education belong *ex officiis*.

There is much to admire in the work of the Ohio Historical Society, but little, except perhaps in publications such as Wheeler's, mentioned above, that could be emulated by independent societies, whose resources are smaller. The best accomplishments of the Ohio State Museum arise from the size and variety of its staff, which make possible a fruitful collaboration between scholars who know the facts that an exhibit must convey, and technicians and craftsmen able to devise the means of presentation. This is something that can only be achieved in a large institution, with a wide variety of talents under one roof. It is significant that out of a personal services appropriation of $403,239.46 more than one half is devoted to the properties division. About 13% goes to the history and science division, approximately 7½% to the library, about 9¼% to the education and public relations division, and a little over 4% to the archives.

Chapter XIII

LATER STATE-SUPPORTED
HISTORICAL SOCIETIES

Equally divergent viewpoints may be adopted toward the work of
state and local historical societies; one may measure it by high standards of scholarship and find much of it defective, or one may compare it with a void and be grateful that so much has been done.
—JULIAN P. BOYD, 1934

THE oldest and largest of the publicly supported State historical societies have been described in the two preceding
chapters. The present concerns institutions, dating from the
last quarter of the nineteenth century, that depend in great part if
not entirely upon legislative appropriations. The Illinois State Historical Society and the State Historical Society of Missouri illustrate
in their foundation the desire to have a historical organization at the
capital in states where independent societies of earlier date were in
useful existence at the principal cities. The Nebraska, Colorado,
South Dakota, Montana, Utah, New Mexico, Nevada, Oregon, and
Washington societies represent the first significant historical activity
in those states. These eleven institutions exemplify the diversity of
activity that prevails even among historical societies that are supported
publicly.

ILLINOIS

The Illinois State Historical Society, organized on 19 May 1899 at
the University of Illinois at Urbana, differs markedly from the

societies described in the preceding chapter, for it has no collections.[1] It holds two meetings a year and publishes. While it is regarded as a quasi-public organization, its expenses are met, not by direct legislative appropriation, but by funds voted to another State agency. After three years of dependence upon dues of members, it became obvious that the objectives of the founders could not be carried out with the small amount of money received from that source. Consequently the General Assembly by act of 16 May 1903 made the society a department of the Illinois State Historical Library which had been established at Springfield in 1889, and authorized the trustees of that institution to use library funds to defray the incidental expenses of the society. Thus Dr. Clyde C. Walton, State Historian of Illinois since 1956, who is an executive officer of the Illinois State Historical Library, serves also as executive director of the Illinois State Historical Society, and as editor of its *Journal*.

The society meets twice a year for two days in different parts of the State; at the spring tour in May and the annual meeting in October, addresses by historians are combined with visits to sites of historic interest. It has published since April 1908 a well-printed and well-illustrated quarterly *Journal* that contains scholarly articles on all aspects of Illinois history, on Lincoln, and on the Civil War. A 714-page index to the first twenty-five volumes was issued in 1950. Since 1958 it has also published a quarterly four-page *Dispatch* that prints news and maintains contact with local historical societies throughout the State.

The objectives of the society were defined in 1941 as:

1) The encouragement of research and writing in Illinois history, to the end that the whole history of the state, and the record of the lives of the men and women who have contributed to its greatness, may be readily available.

2) The stimulation of interest in Illinois history among the youth of the state, and, specifically, the organization of courses in Illinois history and the formation of history clubs in all schools and colleges.

1. A brief historical sketch is in *Journal of the Illinois State Historical Society* LI (1958), 417–430.

3) The stimulation of interest in Illinois history on the part of the general public. To this end, the Society will use not only its own publications and meetings, but will utilize the newspapers, the radio, public lectures and forums, and other modern mediums as fully as its resources.

This statement of policy concludes with two admirable sentences that are worthy of especial remembrance wherever anyone undertakes to diffuse history:

In its efforts to attain these objectives the Society will continue to adhere to the strictest standards of scholarship. It believes, however, that accuracy need not mean dullness, and that there can be popular appeal without vulgarization.

Although the beliefs expressed in the final sentence are demonstrably true, yet how seldom is either ideal attained!

The society has today about 2,600 members, whose annual dues of $3 do not quite pay the printing costs of the *Journal*, wherein the editors aim at the first objective. The deficit, like other expenses of the society, is met by the Illinois State Historical Library out of a State appropriation of $206,000. To achieve the second objective, the society sponsors and the library publishes *Illinois History, A Magazine for Young People*, which appears monthly during the school year from October to May. This publication was the creation in 1948 of the late John H. Hauberg, a former president of the society, and Professor O. Fritiof Ander of Augustana College, Rock Island. Each issue is devoted to a theme announced well in advance—Illinois newspapers, Indians, senators, women, mining, or rivers, for example—and contains a mixture of articles by competent authorities and pieces submitted on those themes by school children. The subscription rate of $1.25 is reduced to 75c when ten or more copies are mailed to one address, while the magazine since the autumn of 1958 has been supplied free on request to all schools and public libraries in the State. Similarly quantities of a pamphlet series, *Stories from Illinois History*, for classroom use in junior high schools, are given away to school groups. In 1943 the society published *A Handbook of Illinois History, a Topical Survey with References for Teachers and Students*, by Paul M. Angle and Richard L. Beyer.

For thirty years the *Transactions* of the Illinois State Historical Society, as well as the *Illinois Historical Collections*, which included important material from the French and British eras of the Mississippi valley, were edited at Urbana by the University of Illinois faculty, although printed with State funds furnished by the library. During Paul M. Angle's years as State Historian (1932–45), the editing of publications shifted to Springfield, so that today the activities of the society and the Illinois State Historical Library are completely merged in everything except name and theory. The *Transactions* were altered in 1936 to *Papers in Illinois History*; then in 1947 their title was changed to *Occasional Publications*. A two-volume index to the first fifty volumes of this series was published in 1953. Recent titles have been *The Civil War Diary of James T. Ayers* (1947), edited by Professor John Hope Franklin, John Drury's *Old Illinois Houses* (1949), and Howard L. Scamehorn's *Balloons to Jets* (1957). As part of the society's fiftieth anniversary celebration in 1949, a revised edition of Theodore C. Pease's *Story of Illinois* and Jay Monaghan's pictorial history *This is Illinois* were published.

The Illinois State Historical Library, housed in part of a public building opposite the capitol in Springfield, has approximately 100,000 bound volumes and more than a million manuscripts,[2] relating to Illinois history, Lincolniana and the Civil War, genealogy, and the Mormons at Nauvoo. The newspaper collection, which is richer than any other in nineteenth-century Illinois papers, contains over 10,000 bound volumes and 9,000 reels of microfilm. At the present time thirty-nine daily and eighteen weekly or semiweekly papers from forty-eight Illinois counties are received, thirty-eight out of the fifty-seven on microfilm. Files of eight newspapers extend over 100 years, while there are runs of twenty-three others that exceed fifty years in length.

The Illinois State Historical Library ranks among the top six insti-

2. For a summary, see Clyde C. Walton, "Manuscripts in The Illinois State Historical Library," *Illinois Libraries* XL (1958), 305–313.

tutions of the country in its holdings of Lincolniana.[3] The more than 1,200 Lincoln manuscripts include some of his finest letters, and there are besides over 6,000 books and pamphlets relating to Lincoln, many of them given in 1940 by Governor Henry Horner. Among the thirty-three volumes of the *Illinois Historical Collections*, published under the direction of the library, is Jay Monaghan's Lincoln bibliography. The Alfred Whittal Stern Civil War Collection[4] of more than 10,000 books is, like the Horner Collection, housed in a separate room.

The overshadowing presence of Abraham Lincoln in Springfield is at once Illinois history's greatest glory and its hardest obstacle. In a city where he lived for nearly a quarter of a century, where his house is admirably preserved, and where his tomb has become one of the great goals of national pilgrimage, it is easy to understand how history and Lincoln have become synonymous. Yet so completely does Lincoln dominate the scene, he blocks all roads. Human and natural though it may be to neglect most other aspects of Illinois history, it is the more regrettable because research into every aspect of Lincoln's life has already been carried to microscopic detail unequaled save in some aspects of Biblical study.[5] With centennial reminders multiplying by the day and week, the years 1961 to 1965 are unlikely to see any diminution of this overpowering interest.

MISSOURI

In addition to the privately supported Missouri Historical Society at Saint Louis, there is also a younger State Historical Society of Missouri,[6] based at the capital, Columbia. The formation of the latter

3. Paul M. Angle, *The Lincoln Collection of the Illinois State Historical Library* (Springfield, 1940).

4. Donald J. Berthrong, *The Civil War Collection of the Illinois State Historical Library* (Springfield, 1949).

5. I was told at the University of Illinois that a Lincoln enthusiast had even carried pious investigation so far as to analyze a pertinent privy vault.

6. *Twenty-ninth Biennial Report of the Executive Committee of the State Historical Society of Missouri, July 1957—June 1959* (Columbia, 1959), pp. 9–29, contains a

organization, proposed at a meeting of the Missouri Press Association in Kansas City in January 1898, was completed the following May with the approval of a constitution and the election of E. W. Stephens, publisher of the *Columbia Herald*, as president. The General Assembly in 1899 made the new society "the trustee of this State" as the custodian of historical records, and from 1901 onwards has appropriated funds for its support.

For the nucleus of a library, Francis Asbury Sampson, secretary of the society from 1901 to 1915, turned over his personal collection of 1,886 books and 14,820 pamphlets on Missouri history, while Missouri editors contributed newspapers and periodicals from ninety-one counties. In 1915 the society moved to quarters in the new library building of the University of Missouri at Columbia, while Floyd C. Shoemaker began his forty-five-year career as secretary, librarian, and editor.

The library contains 141,843 books, pamphlets, bound volumes of newspapers and magazine, which, with 179,611 Missouri official publications, make a total of 321,454 items, exclusive of the J. Christian Bay collection of 4,241 items of early and fundamental works on the history and literature of the middle western states. In addition to 24,140 bound volumes, the newspaper collection contains over nine million pages of positive microfilm. The manuscript collection consists of 229,300 pages of original material, 1,284,936 pages of microfilm copies, 120,771 items of State archives, 67,501 letters and records of World War I, and 2,066 letters of World War II.

The State Historical Society of Missouri is proud of having the largest adult membership of any State historical society in the United States, for Mr. Shoemaker during his long years of service always paid great attention to increases in number. It reached second rank in 1920–21 and first in 1934–35. It has continued in first place without interruption since 1937 and has today some 12,000 members, of

------

summary history; Floyd C. Shoemaker, "Forty-five years as editor and author of Missouri History," *Missouri Historical Review* LIV (1960), 225–230.

which all but 2,200 are residents of Missouri. The long-standing policy of fixing annual dues at $1 and life membership at $20 has been helpful in achieving this record. Membership is actually an excellent bargain, for it brings with it a subscription to the *Missouri Historical Review*, published quarterly since 1907, which, even with the economies possible in an edition of 12,500 copies, costs about $1.35 per subscriber to produce. The society's income is derived from an annual State appropriation that averages $100,000.

Mr. Shoemaker in the society's publications has long made extensive use of the great collection of Missouri newspapers. A section in the *Missouri Historical Review* entitled "Missouri History not found in Textbooks" consists of newspaper quotations, ancient and modern, while the two volumes of his *Missouri Day by Day*, published in 1942–43, offer biographies and bits of State history, often derived from newspapers, arranged according to the months of the year in the manner of a birthday book. The society's chief documentary publications are the eighteen-volume *Messages and Proclamations of the Governors of the State of Missouri*, extending from 1820 to 1957, and the fourteen volumes of the journal and debates of the Missouri Constitutional Convention of 1875.

From a national point of view the most fascinating publication of the State Historical Society of Missouri is the four-volume *Ozark Folksongs*, collected and edited by Vance Randolph, which appeared between 1946 and 1950. This great compendium of 1,700 texts and 828 melodies represents some twenty years of difficult collecting in backwoods areas where old "residenters" had not yet succumbed to the blandishments of canned music. The volumes contain British ballads, songs of the south and west, humorous and religious songs— a remarkable assortment ranging from the Elizabethans to the suffragettes by way of the Chisholm Trail and the "brush arbor" music of camp meetings. These well-printed volumes, illustrated with photographs of the singers, and end papers by Thomas Hart Benton, are unique among the publications of American historical societies. They are also an excellent bargain at $15.80 for the set.

NEBRASKA

The Nebraska State Historical Society,[7] organized at Lincoln, the capital, in 1878, was designated a State institution and given its first legislative appropriation in 1883. It held, from the beginning, annual meetings at the University of Nebraska at which territorial pioneers reminisced and distinguished citizens of the State read papers upon aspects of Nebraska history of which they had firsthand knowledge. Publication began in 1885 with a volume of *Transactions and Reports*. Under various titles—*Proceedings and Collections, Collections*, and, since 1917, *Publications*—twenty-three volumes have since been issued in this series. While most volumes contained a miscellany of historical papers, a few were devoted to single works, such as Senator Thomas W. Tipton's *Forty Years of Nebraska at Home and in Congress*, Dr. Addison E. Sheldon's *Land Systems and Land Policies in Nebraska*, and three volumes of the debates and proceedings of the Nebraska Constitutional Convention of 1871. A quarterly magazine, now known as *Nebraska History*, was inaugurated in 1918; its forty-first volume appeared in 1960.

While the society has no formal ties with the University of Nebraska, it has long had a close and profitable association. In 1885 Dr. George E. Howard, who after graduate study in Europe had been appointed the first professor of history at the university, became its secretary and superintendent. Thus from its first decade the Nebraska State Historical Society was guided by one of the new European-trained professional historians. When in 1891 Professor Howard left Nebraska to become one of the original faculty of the new Stanford University, he was succeeded as head of the History Department at the University and as secretary of the society by Professor Howard W. Caldwell, who had done graduate work at Johns Hopkins. During Professor Caldwell's tenure, which extended until 1907, it became

7. James C. Olson, "The Nebraska State Historical Society in 1953 (With a Glance Backward to 1878)," *Nebraska History* XXXIV (1953), 289–310; William D. Aeschbacher, "The Nebraska State Historical Society," *Museum News* XXXVIII (September 1959), 10–11.

possible, through increased appropriations, to develop a permanent staff and to undertake research in local archaeology. Archaeology has remained a continuing interest of the society.

Clarence S. Paine, who directed the work of the society for the decade beginning in 1907, in his first year called a meeting at Lincoln of fellow historians from the middle west that led to the formation of the Mississippi Valley Historical Association, of which he served as secretary-treasurer until his death in 1917. There has long been a close tie between the Nebraska society and this larger professional body. In 1953 Dr. James C. Olson, then superintendent of the society, became secretary-treasurer of the Mississippi Valley Historical Association, a post that is held today by the present director, Dr. William D. Aeschbacher.

For many years the Nebraska State Historical Society's collections were accommodated partly in the State capitol and partly in the university. In 1953 it finally obtained its own building at 1500 R Street in Lincoln on the edge of the University of Nebraska campus, facing the capitol, which is seven blocks away. With these new quarters it has been able to develop an excellent historical museum devoted to interpreting the story of man in Nebraska and in the plains environment. Of this phase of the society's work, Dr. Aeschbacher has recently written:

Our exhibition policy is based on the belief that we can most effectively develop our museum by settting up limited objectives—namely, to tell the story of man in a limited geographical area, and to stick to these objectives, no matter how tempting opportunities may be to display exhibitions and objects that do not fit that policy. Such a limiting purpose, giving direction to collecting and to display, seems necessary to most historical museums.

In addition to its headquarters in Lincoln, the society operates a branch museum at Fort Robinson, 440 miles to the northwest, and maintains an exhibit at the State Fair grounds. During 1959 forty display units were exchanged among these three locations. The museum in Lincoln was visited by 80,952 persons, 16,998 saw the Fort Robinson exhibits, and 32,775 were counted at the State Fair displays.

The library, which emphasizes materials pertaining to Nebraska and the plains region of which the State is a part, contains some 41,000 volumes, representing about 17,000 titles, about 19,000 bound volumes of newspapers, 5,700 reels of microfilm chiefly of Nebraska newspapers, 1,200 maps, 64,000 pictures, and miscellaneous broadsides and charts. Nebraska imprints and authors are collected, as are books such as school texts, church hymnals and manuals, giftbooks, and the like, which are chiefly of value to illustrate various phases of the culture of the past. It has a number of books in the Czech, Danish, Norwegian, and Dakota languages.

The society is the official archival agency for the State of Nebraska. In addition to receiving public records in that capacity, it makes a systematic effort to collect the personal papers of outstanding Nebraskans, and to encourage organizations of all kinds to deposit records of permanent value. There are some 2,000 collections in the archives and manuscripts. Three quarters of these are small, consisting usually of a single folder or envelope. The other 500 contain one or more manuscript boxes, totaling 3,400 manuscript and letter boxes, 534 cases and cartons, 400 packages, and 5,500 letterbooks, recordbooks, or scrapbooks. The records of the United States Land Office in Nebraska, 1854–1933, run to 512 volumes; those of the Lincoln Police Department, 1871–1939, to 331; and of the Farmer's Alliance, 1885–96, to 2,000 volumes.

The Nebraska State Historical Society currently receives an annual State appropriation of $135,000. Its income from close to 2,000 annual members, paying $2 a year, was in 1959 $3,973.50. Although it is planned that membership fees shall cover the printing costs for material supplied members, these fees are not expected to produce a source of operating income.

The society considers that its two major functions are the maintenance of its historical research library and the dissemination of information collected. The latter is accomplished through the quarterly *Nebraska History*, a monthly *News Letter*, mimeographed educational pamphlets, guided tours of the museum, participation in radio and television programs, and a weekly historical column sent to all Nebraska newspapers. In a section "Looking to the Future" at the conclusion of his 1959 report, Dr. Aeschbacher remarked of these varied activities:

Mark Twain once said, "Sometimes you have to run as fast as you can to keep from falling behind." In many ways this has been the situation of the Society throughout the year just passed. In almost every area we have felt it necessary to become involved in additional activities that seriously threaten permanently planned programs. . . .

The Society knew that increased functions and responsibilities were inevitable when it occupied its new quarters in 1953 and it made a constructive effort to meet this need from 1950-1954. In the intervening years the functions and responsibilities have developed as anticipated, but the additional staff to meet these responsibilities has not been made available. The energies of the Society in the next few years must be turned more directly to the problems of gaining increased financial support and recruiting competent personnel to meet the demands currently being made on the Society.[8]

COLORADO

"Whereas, the history of Colorado, being as yet unwritten, and existing now only in tradition or fragmentary manuscripts of private individuals and of the public press," the Legislature passed in February 1879 an act "to encourage the formation and establishment of a State Historical and Natural History Society,"[9] making an appropriation of $500 to further the organization. From 1886 the society occupied the fourth floor of the Denver Chamber of Commerce, together with the Mercantile Library, the forerunner of the Denver Public Library. State appropriations, which were small in early years, were used for the accumulation of natural history specimens and Indian artifacts. In 1895 the society moved to rooms in the new State capitol, where it remained until the present State Museum was

8. *Nebraska History* XL (1959), 305–306. The society endeavors to keep high professional standards in recruiting its staff. In September 1960 there were three PH.DS, four Masters, a librarian's degree, and one vacancy in a staff of ten.

9. Le Roy R. Hafen, "History of the State Historical Society of Colorado," *The Colorado Magazine* XXX (1953), 161–185, 283–310; XXXI (1954), 37–68.

ready for occupancy in the winter of 1914–15. With the appointment of a paid curator in 1896 an educational program for the Denver schools was launched and a historical library was begun with a campaign for the systematic collection of Colorado newspapers.

Interest in natural history predominated at the turn of the century. The Natural History Department of the society, organized in 1897, changed its name in 1900 to the Colorado Academy of Science and embarked on the active solicitation of zoological and botanical specimens, but within a decade there came a noticeable shift to historical activity. State appropriations had never been markedly generous so long as there had remained uncertainty and controversy as to whether the society was a private corporation or an official State agency. This question was settled by an act of 1915, which declared the society "to be one of the educational institutions of the State of Colorado." In 1927 another act changed the name of the society to the State Historical Society of Colorado and authorized the discontinuance of the natural history collections.

In 1920 interest veered to archaeology and ethnology, although in 1924 the society engaged its first professional historian when Dr. LeRoy R. Hafen, a student of Professor Herbert E. Bolton's, became curator of history. Although the depression of the 1930s drastically curtailed expenditures, Dr. Hafen promptly turned the relief agencies of the New Deal to work on historical projects. The State Historical Society of Colorado was the first to propose a plan and establish a program for employment in historical work. From late 1933 until 1941 an average of thirty-five employees were regularly engaged with Federal funds on a variety of C.W.A., F.E.R.A., and W.P.A. projects which resulted in great benefit to the society and the State Museum. Among the results of this relief activity were the construction of fifty-one dioramas and models portraying phases of Colorado history, the binding of books and newspapers, the interviewing of pioneers in thirty-three counties, and much classifying and indexing of historical data from manuscripts and newspapers.

In 1943 a State archival division was created within the society, and by legislation of 1951 was expanded into a division of State archives and public records. In 1959 this archival agency was amicably separated from the State Historical Society and made an independent agency in the Executive Department of the State government. Mrs. Dolores C. Renze, who as State Archivist and Public Records Administrator heads this division, is secretary of the Society of American Archivists and an able ally of historians.

Its museum is the most striking feature of the State Historical Society of Colorado today, for in addition to the numerous dioramas constructed during the 1930s, a highly skilled artist and a technician, working under the direction of the curator, constantly add to and improve the quality of exhibits. These set out to explain the history of Colorado and its people to the general visitors and school groups that flock in constantly. An extensive collection of Colorado minerals, long maintained on the second floor of the State Museum by the State Bureau of Mines, was in 1959 transferred to the society, which will make it the basis of an improved exhibition on the history of Colorado mining. The society maintains five regional museums outside Denver; the most recent, the adobe ranch house at Trinidad, built by Don Felipe Baca in 1869, was acquired in 1960. The others are the Healy House and Dexter Cabin at Leadville; the Fort Garland Historical Monument; the Ute Indian Museum at Montrose; and El Pueblo State Museum at Pueblo.

The library, besides the usual reference works and volumes on local history, contains over 10,000 pamphlets dealing with many aspects of the history of the State and complete files of many Colorado newspapers, including the *Denver Post* and *Rocky Mountain News*. There are runs of papers from every part of the State from 1859 to date, and over 3,000 rolls of microfilm. Current files are kept for seventy-eight weekly and twenty-two daily Colorado newspapers.

In addition to over 100,000 items of manuscript, chiefly relating to Colorado and the West from 1805 to date, an extensive railroad collection has been gathered that includes 200,000 pieces from the archives of the Denver and Rio Grande Railroad from 1869 to

1952. Among the 25,000 pictures of Colorado are 7,000 glass plate negatives of the remarkable western photographs of William H. Jackson.

It should be noted that the Western History Department of the Denver Public Library contains first-rate research material on Colorado history, gathered in the 1930s and 1940s through the energy and imagination of Dr. Malcolm G. Wyer, who was its librarian for a quarter of a century. This is one of the most distinguished collections of historical sources owned by a city public library; it is delightfully housed on an upper floor of the new library building that dominates the southern side of the Denver Civic Center. The casual traveler of 1960, unacquainted with the intricacies of the local scene, can only assume that much of this material might at one time have been available to the State Historical Society of Colorado.

The Colorado Magazine has been the chief publication of the Society since 1923. Originally appearing at irregular intervals, it became a bimonthly in 1929 and so continued until the end of 1948, when it became a quarterly of more substantial dimensions. It is edited today by the State Historian, Mrs. Agnes Wright Spring. While it often contains such well-documented studies as those of Professor Robert G. Athearn of the University of Colorado on local railroad history,[10] many of its issues are strongly flavored with personal reminiscence and information about the society.[11] The July 1960 number, for example, contains "Forty Years in Colorado Mining Camps" from the experience of Charles McClung Leonard (1860–1951); an account of the Ouray town hall which burned in 1950; nostalgic reminiscences of dances in Cotillion Hall, Denver, conducted by an English dancing master and his widow from 1894

10. "The Origins of the Royal Gorge War" and "Captivity of the Denver and Rio Grande," *The Colorado Magazine* XXXVI (1959), 37–57; XXXVII (1960), 39–58.

11. *The Colorado Magazine* XXXVII (1960), 59–60, describes a visit from Miss Delores Marie Racine, Queen Sic-ca-pi-na-kee ("Black Eyes"), Miss Indian America VI, an attractive nineteen-year-old sophomore at Sheridan Junior College, Sheridan, Wyoming, who stopped in Denver in December 1959, while returning from the annual convention of the National Congress of Indians held in Phoenix, Arizona.

to 1922; an account of the gift of the 1908 Boettcher Mansion to the State for use as an executive residence; and some good letters reprinted from the Baptist *Michigan Christian Herald* of 1878 describing the pleasure that an unidentified correspondent had from a trip to Colorado. Other publications during the past fifteen years have been rather slight booklets, with the exception of a volume *When Grass was King* which the University of Colorado Press issued for the society in 1956. This book is the result of a research grant of $64,500 from the Rockfeller Foundation for a five-year study of the development of the range cattle industry in the Rocky Mountain region from 1850 to 1900. Although the early work was done by Herbert O. Brayer, the State Archivist from 1943 to 1949, the study was completed by Mr. Maurice Frink, a journalist who since 1954 has been executive director of the society, in collaboration with Turrentine Jackson, and Mrs. Spring. Since 1958 the society has published several issues of *The Gold Nugget*, a leaflet distributed to junior chapters of the society in schools. There are now twelve such chapters and others may be organized by five or more boys or girls in any Colorado school.

The State Historical Society of Colorado offers four classes of membership, all available either annually or by a single payment of a larger sum. Thus regular members pay $4 a year or $50 once for life membership; supporting $10 or $100; sustaining $25 or $250; and patrons $100 or $1,000. In 1960 there were 1,187 members, including all life members. For the fiscal year beginning 1 July 1960, the society received a legislative appropriation of $145,146, with an additional $26,500 for capital construction to be used in the expansion of the regional museums.

SOUTH DAKOTA

The first territorial Legislature of South Dakota in 1861 organized a historical society whose activities were sporadic. Forty years later, in 1901, the South Dakota State Historical Society was established in its present form and was placed in charge of a newly created State agency, the South Dakota Department of History. One of its founders, Mr. Doane Robinson, who had for some years previously published a historical magazine, the *Monthly South Dakotan*, was its first secretary, holding that post for twenty-five years. His son, Mr. Will G. Robinson, is the society's secretary today.

The *South Dakota Historical Collections*, a series of bound volumes of 500 to 600 pages which appear biennially, have been the society's chief vehicle of publication since 1902. A thirtieth volume is now in press. A *Monthly Bulletin* is in its fourteenth year, but a quarterly which appeared for a few years was given up because of expense and the restrictive limitation of its form. The society has preferred to concentrate upon the substantial volumes of its *Historical Collections*, although it has assisted in the publication of a number of other books, including local histories.

The society's library, housed in the Memorial Building at Pierre, contains approximately 50,000 volumes, which include books about the State and area, writings of past and present residents, genealogies, publications of other historical societies, and at least 95% of the newspapers published in the region since 1861, either in originals or on microfilm. In addition to noncurrent official records, held by it as the archival agency of the State, the society has private papers of individuals in Dakota Territory and South Dakota, school records, letters of Indian agents and other papers relating to Indians, diaries of South Dakota pioneers, Civil War soldiers, and others.

The State appropriation of $23,750 for the Department of History is supplemented by about $1,500 received annually from membership fees, donations, and sales of publications. Annual dues are $2.50; life membership is set at $20.

MONTANA

The Historical Society of Montana,[12] organized in 1865 at Virginia

12. *Montana Heritage* (Helena, 1955), no. 1; Vivian A. Paladin, "The Historical Society of Montana." *The People's Voice* [Helena, Montana] XXI, 34 (29 July 1960) and 35 (5 August 1960).

City, had the misfortune to lose its earliest possessions in an 1874 fire that destroyed the greater part of Helena. A new collection was begun, which in 1887 was moved to the Lewis and Clark courthouse; in 1902 larger quarters were provided on the ground floor of the capitol at Helena. The Legislature, which had made the society a department of the State library, designated it in 1895 the Historical and Miscellaneous Library, a sobriquet that lasted for twenty-eight years until the 1923 Legislature restored the original name. For half a century the society remained with a small library staff in the capitol, dependent entirely upon State appropriations. A 357-page first volume of *Collections* appeared in 1876, although a second was not published for twenty years. Others were issued in 1900, 1903, and 1904.

Within the past decade the Historical Society of Montana has expanded its activities in many directions. A new Veterans and Pioneers Memorial building, completed at a cost of $800,000 in 1953, on land to the east of the capitol given by the Sons and Daughters of Montana Pioneers and the Montana Pioneers' Society, provides spacious quarters for the library and ample space for museum development. The library, on the second floor, contains reference and research collections on frontier history, particularly relating to Montana and the Great Plains region, photographs, and 6,500 bound volumes of newspapers beginning in 1864. As archival agency for the State, the society has territorial and State records; the papers of James S. Brisbin, Samuel T. Hauser, and Martin Maginnis; journals and diaries of early immigrants and explorers; the records of a post trader at Fort Shaw, 1871–97; of a stage-line company, 1878–79; of a mercantile and cattle company, 1905–18; and of a banking company.

On the first floor is what is called the Formal Museum which depicts the history of Montana through six stages: the period of exploration, and the successive fur trading, mining, cattleman's, homesteader's, and industrial frontiers. "The Museum on the ground floor," according to the latest circular of information, "is called Informal because flexibility, quick visual impact, and a preponderance of guns, and the actual objects of history are the keynoting feature." The guns, over 400 in number, were collected by the late E. S. Johns of Kalispell and given recently by his son, Mr. S. Douglas Johns.

The dichotomy of formal and informal exhibition is carried into the galleries devoted to the work of Charles Marion Russell, the Montana cowboy artist. Forty-one pieces from the Malcolm S. Mackay collection were purchased in 1952 for $59,000 through an intensive state-wide fund-raising campaign. This proved the nucleus of a much larger display of Russell's work, for the society now owns some 130 pieces and often has as many as fifty more on exhibition that are lent by other owners.[13] In addition the paintings, numerous photographs, letters, and personal memorabilia are shown that convey an impression of the artist as a man.

Galleries of western art and contemporary art exhibit early paintings of the "Old West" as well as the work of modern artists, usually residents of Montana. The society undertakes to encourage local artists and craftsmen by providing space to show their work and handling the sales of works exhibited, just as it endeavors to advertise Montana by attracting visitors to its new quarters. In a statement "What does your State Historical Society do for you as a Montanan?" Dr. K. Ross Toole, who, as director from 1951 to 1958, played a large role in the recent development, thus expressed his theory of the value of the museum:

One picture is worth ten thousand words and one museum is worth a dozen text books in its capacity to teach while it entertains. These museums will not only give our own children a sense of their own heritage, they will serve the same purpose for adults—and they will be seen by some 200,000 non-Montanans a year. What better way to point out to tourists that Montana has a rich past and a great future?

The last sentence echoes the spirit of evangelical promotion of a State that was characteristic of one side of Lyman C. Draper's activities a century ago.

Montana, The Magazine of Western History, which first appeared in

13. A number of the society's pictures appear in Harold McCracken, *The Charles M. Russell Book* (Garden City, 1957).

1951, is governed by the theories that "historical articles, although accurate, need never be dull, stodgy, or too heavily documented, . . . that authentic photographs and colorful illustrations are as essential as well-written and exciting narrative, . . . that the most dramatic events of Montana history are the essence of the whole frontier West." A $4 subscription to this lively quarterly carries with it membership in the Historical Society of Montana. As it has a wide circulation beyond the borders of the State, it pays its own way. The society's last published financial statement, for the year 1957, showed total expenditures (including editorial salaries, printing, mailing, and office expenses) of $39,209.22 and receipts of $40,515.77.

Mr. Michael S. Kennedy, the present director, tells me that the current financial situation of the society is approximately the same as depicted in the 1957 report. This is extraordinarily interesting for the large amount of private support that is received to augment the legislative appropriation. In the year 1957 the Historical Society of Montana had a total revenue of $155,118.01, of which $63,106.17 was appropriated and $92,011.84 was received from private sources. Of the private funds, 44% were received from the sales of the magazine; 29% ($26,971.40) from an active gift shop and sales counter, which offers books, numerous reproductions of Charles M. Russell's paintings, Indian arts and crafts, and "authentic and unusual Treasure State novelty objects"; 13% ($11,509.85) from book and other publishing ventures; and 14% ($13,014.82) from other sources. Just as *Montana, The Magazine of Western History* showed a net profit of $1,306.55 in this year, so the sales counter, after deducting salaries, purchases of stock, and expenses of $23,145.01, produced a net gain of $3,826.39. Thus, as the introduction to the 1957 financial report indicates, the Historical Society of Montana "operates as a business within the context of government while still rendering the services of a public cultural institution." It proposes to operate on the "basis of developing every possible source of private revenue consistent with the functions and services we perform, while asking the legislature to provide us only with the appropriated base which enables us to expand and grow on our own." This ideal requires the expenditure of considerable effort in matters peripheral to history, to judge by the mention of fund raising, planning and promotion, personnel management, public relations, and publications as the five major functions of the administrative officers of the society.

UTAH

The Utah State Historical Society[14] was founded at Salt Lake City on 22 July 1897 during the semicentennial celebrations of the settlement of the region. For twenty years it did little more than meet annually. Although recognized by the Legislature in 1917 as a State institution, eleven years went by before it was granted a modest appropriation that permitted the publishing of the *Utah Historical Quarterly*, under the editorship of J. Cecil Alter. This was supended in 1933 for want of funds. With an appropriation in 1937 of $4,500 for the biennium, publication was resumed and a full-time secretary employed. The society roosted in small quarters in the State capitol, with such books as it owned uncatalogued, until it was more than fifty years old.

The present health and vitality of the Utah State Historical Society is a development of the past decade. It began in 1950 with the appointment of a professional historian as director. Dr. A. Russell Mortensen, a native of Salt Lake City whose graduate work was done at the University of California, Los Angeles, has in a remarkably short time led the society out of the wilderness. During this decade, the legislative appropriation increased from $20,000 to $125,000 a year. In 1951, when the Legislature created a division of State archives, the society was made responsible for all noncurrent public records;[15] three years later Dr. Everett L. Cooley was appointed State Archivist. With the appointment as librarian in 1952 of Mr. John James Jr., who

14. *Utah State Historical Society, Sixty Years of Organized History* (Salt Lake City, 1957), reprinted from *Utah Historical Quarterly* xxv (July 1957).

15. The Utah State Historical Society and Utah State Archives Act of 1957 further defined and reinforced the functions of the division of the Utah State archives within the society.

had majored in history and done graduate work in library science at the University of Utah, systematic cataloguing began. Finally in 1957 the society secured possession of its present quarters, the great house at 603 East South Temple built by Senator Thomas Kearns, an Irishman who had come to Utah in the 1880s as a prospector, to display the prosperity that he had acquired through silver mining. This showy residence, profusely ornamented with the elaborately carved rare woods that were, at the turn of the century, the final symbol of the change from rags to riches, was given to the State by Mrs. Kearns in 1937 for the use of the governor. Although it did not prove congenial as an executive mansion, the Kearns House offered excellent lodging for the Utah State Historical Society. This use also assures the preservation of a building, representing the architectural taste and domestic aspirations of a Utah miner who made good, that otherwise might have fallen before wreckers.

Under Dr. Mortensen's editorship, the *Utah Historical Quarterly*, which had earlier relapsed into annual appearance, has been published regularly in an attractive format. In recent years special summer issues, liberally illustrated in color, have had a wide public sale. Although the normal edition of the *Quarterly* (which is sent to 1,800 members who pay annual dues of $3) is 2,000, 25,000 copies of the July 1958 issue (vol. XXVI, no. 3) describing Utah's parks and scenic wonders were printed. The following summer with an issue devoted to the valley of the Great Salt Lake that quantity was doubled. The highly readable and informative anthology *Among the Mormons: Historic Accounts by Contemporary Observers*, edited by Dr. Mortensen and Professor William Mulder, that Alfred A. Knopf published in 1958, has brought many aspects of Utah history to a national audience.

The research library, which is the heart of the Utah State Historical Society's activities and functions, contains some 5,000 books, 3,000 pamphlets, 5,000 photographs, and 6,000 issues of periodicals. The Utah and western history sections are pleasantly housed on open shelves in reading rooms on the second floor of the building; other classifications are kept like the State archives, in the spacious basement.

Among the more than 100 periodicals received regularly are all the historical publications of the western states and of the Church of Jesus Christ of Latter-day Saints. Among important items in the manuscript collection are the John M. Bernhisel papers, the William Clayton letter books, the Francis M. Bishop diaries, and the Hosea Stout journals.

Microfilms of printed and manuscript material relating to Utah history have been procured from the Bancroft and Huntington libraries, the Library of Congress and National Archives, the New York Public Library, the Harvard and Yale libraries, the Missouri Historical Society, and other major depositories of western and Mormon sources. Working from material turned over to the society in 1951 by Mr. Dale E. Morgan, the library is constantly adding to a Union Catalogue of published works pertaining to Mormons and Mormonism, which it is hoped may be printed in the predictable future.

The private collection of Nicholas Grosbeck Morgan Sr., given to the Utah State Historical Society when it moved into its present headquarters, contains important runs of Mormon periodicals. Among these are complete sets of the *Latter Day Saints Messenger and Advocate* (Kirtland, Ohio, 1830); *The Evening and Morning Star* (Far West, Missouri, 1832); *Times and Seasons* and the *Saints Herald* from the Nauvoo, Illinois, era; the *Millenial Star* and *Journal of Discourses*, published in England at Liverpool; and Salt Lake City imprints: the *Juvenile Instructor*, *The Contributor*, *Improvement Era*, and *The Young Ladies Journal*. In addition to Mormon literature, often in association copies once owned by significant figures in church and western history, the Morgan collection contains numerous maps, early views of Salt Lake City, of Nauvoo and other historic sites along the migration route to Utah. Mr. Morgan, who has actively promoted the gas and oil resources of Utah, has also given the Utah State Historical Society lands that may eventually augment its income. In addition to collecting, Mr. Morgan has energetically financed and promoted the creation of historic commemorative statues within and beyond the bounds of Utah. He has, for example, presented a statue of Abraham Lincoln to the State of Illinois for the New Salem Park and has even sent sculpture to Greece in the form of a monument to Lycurgus, given to Sparta.

The society does not maintain a museum, although the ballroom on the top floor of its house—which in itself represents a significant piece of historical preservation—provides space for temporary exhibitions of pictures. Dr. Mortensen, as its director, is concerned with the policies of the State park system, and of the State Library.

The Utah State Historical Society concentrates its efforts on a research, publication, and archival program. The substantial progress that it has made in the past decade affords a significant example of what can be accomplished in a short period of time by intelligent and energetic planning through State support, augmented by the interest of a historically-minded private collector.

NEW MEXICO

The considerable variety that exists in State historical societies has already been demonstrated in earlier chapters. New Mexico offers still another form, evolved somewhat by accident through local conditions. The Historical Society of New Mexico, organized at Santa Fe the day after Christmas in 1859 by United States Army officers, who were then the most literate English-speaking persons in the region, adjourned *sine die* in 1863 when the professional services of its founders were in demand elsewhere. Re-established late in 1880 as a private venture, supported by the contributions of its members, it was given by statute the right to use the eastern half of the adobe Palace of the Governors in Santa Fe. As squatters were eased out of this venerable but unpretentious building, the society gained more space. Governor L. Bradford Prince, who became its president in 1883, secured a small public grant that assisted in its support.

The Museum of New Mexico, established in 1909 as a State institution and lodged in the other end of the Palace of the Governors, engaged energetically in archaeological research. While the Historical Society of New Mexico continued to occupy the eastern end of the Palace, with its officers attending voluntarily to its day-to-day work, the museum had a professional staff and public funds. As it was under the same roof it gradually and imperceptibly became more and more involved in the management of the historical society, although it had no particular interest in history. This accidental piece of caretaking reduced the incentive that might otherwise have existed to recruit new and active working members for the society as old ones died. *Old Santa Fe*, a quarterly inaugurated in 1913, died in 1916 after its twelfth issue. By the 1920s the museum and the historical society had become practically one, with relatively little attention being paid to history until 1926 when the *New Mexico Historical Review* was founded. Since 1929 this quarterly has been a joint publication with the University of New Mexico at Albuquerque, supported in part by State funds and in part by the dues of members. The Historical Society of New Mexico thus has today a somewhat ghostlike quality, for the *Review* is handled at Albuquerque by members of the university faculty, while its possessions and exhibits at Santa Fe are cared for as an orphan cousin to the archaeological and anthropological specialties of the Museum of New Mexico.

The most readily visible interest of the Historical Society of New Mexico is the series of rooms containing historical exhibits and examples of Spanish Colonial arts and handicrafts in the eastern end of the Palace of the Governors. Part of the society's modest income is allocated for museum purposes, for the building of cases, and the acquisition and preservation of objects. The excellent and attractive library, in a wing of the palace added in 1931 which is in the charge of Miss Gertrude Hill, is chiefly a Museum of New Mexico responsibility, although theoretically the society is involved in its maintenance.

By a State law of 1927 the Historical Society of New Mexico was made the official custodian of all noncurrent State records, but without being given space, equipment, or funds for their care. These were, for want of anything better, trucked from the capitol and stowed in the boiler room of the Art Gallery and in odd nooks and crannies. As State agencies continued to dump records upon the society, in the course of three decades, matters became acute. Thus the archival affairs of New Mexico moldered until 1959, when at least theoretical relief was achieved by the passage of a law establishing a State Commission of Public Records, which was to appoint a State Commissioner who would function independently of the Historical Society of New Mexico.

Although the territorial and State archives of the past century have been inaccessibly and unsuitably lodged, the earlier Spanish archives (reaching back to 1693) that were found in the Palace of the Governors in Santa Fe when the Americans took over New Mexico in 1846 have been more fortunate.[16] When all land records were segregated and taken into Federal custody in 1855, the Spanish military and civil records were left in the palace. There they remained until early in this century, when, upon an outcry from the Library of Congress, they were sent to Washington. After twenty years they were, however, returned to the Historical Society of New Mexico, where they are today extensively used for research. Thanks to a curator, to whose salary a substantial part of the society's income is devoted, they are well arranged and in good condition. It is hoped that the land records, for some years in the custody of the Federal Bureau of Land Management in Santa Fe, may eventually rejoin the collection from which they were removed in 1855.[17]

The *New Mexico Historical Review*, which is edited at Albuquerque by Professor Frank D. Reeve, is, after printing, sent to Santa Fe for distribution. This is the most substantial of the society's publications, for the more than forty numbered *Papers* that have been issued

16. They are described in Ralph E. Twitchell's two-volume work, *The Spanish Archives of New Mexico* (Cedar Rapids, Iowa, 1913).

17. In the fall of 1955 the land records were sent to the University of New Mexico for microfilming. Some Spanish records, stolen from the palace in the 1880s and 1890s, have found safe homes in the Huntington and Bancroft libraries; others may still be adrift.

between 1881 and the present are chiefly thin pamphlets, often containing only the biennial report. The fifteen numbered volumes of *Publications in History* that have appeared since 1926 consist of indexed reprints of studies that have appeared serially in the *Review*, sometimes with additional material.

The Historical Society of New Mexico now receives a State appropriation of $10,000. The remainder of its present budget of $14,000 is derived from dues and the sales of publications, for its only endowment is two $1,000 bonds. Membership has fluctuated over the years between 200 and 600; in 1960 it was 550. Annual dues, which include a subscription to the *Review*, were raised in 1959 to $5, for at the former rate of $3 every member added increased the deficit. Even at $5, the dues are far from meeting the expenses of the *Review*, whose annual printing costs are close to $5,000. The society's affairs are chiefly handled by its corresponding secretary, Mr. Bruce T. Ellis, a member of the staff of the Museum of New Mexico. In this, as in many other respects, the museum provides many hidden elements of support, without which the society could hardly continue even its present modest scale of operation.

These close ties with both museum and university have aided the scholarly quality of what the society has been able to do, although such intimate tutelage has also hindered any conscious development of the society as such. The election as president of Mr. Calvin Horn, an Albuquerque businessman, in 1959, upon the retirement of Mr. Paul A. F. Walter, who had held that office since 1926, introduces a lay interest in history into what had formerly been an academic enclave. When I was in Santa Fe in March 1960 there was talk of promoting local historical societies throughout New Mexico with a view to increasing popular interest. Change was in the wind; whether for better or worse remains to be seen.[18]

18. In the two years that have passed since my visit, Dr. K. Ross Toole, onetime director of the Montana Historical Society and, more briefly, of the Museum of the City of New York, has been appointed director of the Museum of New Mexico, has come, and has resigned. Hence change is quite as much in the wind as it was in 1960.

NEVADA

The Nevada Historical Society was founded at Reno in 1904 by a group of university professors led by Dr. Jeanne Elizabeth Wier, head of the History Department of the University of Nevada. Dr. Wier served as director until her death ten years ago when she was succeeded by the present incumbent, Mrs. Clara S. Beatty. The *Nevada Society Quarterly*, now edited by Dr. William Miller of the university's English Department, was also for many years a responsibility of Dr. Wier, who played a large part in gathering the society's collection of Nevadana.

The society as the archival agency of the State is supported chiefly by funds appropriated by the Legislature. For the biennium 1957–59 its budget was reported to the Society of American Archivists as $49,070, of which $7,000 was for renovation and the purchase of equipment. Normal annual expenditure would therefore appear to be in the neighborhood of $21,000 from public funds. Among its holdings are manuscripts relating to settlement, mining and other businesses, political activities, and the woman-suffrage movement in Nevada. There are various personal papers, the business records of a creamery, a bank, a salt works, the discontinued Nevada Central Railroad, and account books of mercantile and mining companies.

OREGON

The nine societies mentioned thus far in this chapter are located at the capitals of their states; the Oregon Historical Society is based neither at the capital nor at the seat of the university, but in the principal city, Portland. Established in 1898 as a private nonprofit institution to collect, preserve, and publish material relating to the history of Oregon and the Pacific Northwest, its original interest was focused on the early period of exploration, for the now defunct Oregon Pioneer Association, going back to the 1870s, was then publishing numerous documents on the era of pioneer settlement in its *Transactions*.

The *Oregon Historical Quarterly*, promptly inaugurated in 1900, has published for the past sixty years a great variety of valuable studies in the history of the region.[19] In addition the Oregon Historical Society has a good record of book publication, including such documents as *The Oregon Constitution and Proceedings and Debates of the Constitutional Convention of 1857*, edited by Charles Henry Carey (1925); letters (1948) and financial papers (1949) of Dr. John McLoughlin, chief factor of the Hudson's Bay Company; and *Notices and Voyages of the Famed Quebec Mission to the Pacific Northwest* (1956), translated by Carl Landerholm. The 720-page *The Doctor in Oregon: A Medical History*, by O. Larsell, appeared in 1947 as did Howard McKinley Corning's *Willamette Landings: Ghost Towns of the River*; a third edition of L. A. McArthur's *Oregon Geographic Names* in 1952; while in 1958 the society published, as the first of a series of county histories, Giles French's *The Golden Land: A History of Sherman County, Oregon*, and *Woods Words: A Comprehensive Dictionary of Logger's Terms*, by Walter F. McCulloch. The latter work, by the dean of the School of Forestry at Oregon State College, is an admirable effort to rescue and record the language of the western woods while there is still time. It is a valuable footnote to the vocabulary of the American language.

The society is abominably housed in a portion of the Public Auditorium at 225 S. W. Market Street, Portland. Its belongings have long since overflowed available space. Shelves have been improvised on stairways; through similar subterfuges a great deal has been jammed in, although at the cost of major inconvenience to the staff. This confusion will not, however, be permanent, for the society already owns the site for a new building and has well-advanced plans for improved quarters.

The library, which concentrates on the history of Oregon, on voyages and western exploration, contains some 45,000 volumes.

19. Some recent issues have been of remarkable interest to the architectural historian. That of March 1956 was devoted to Marion D. Ross's well-illustrated survey, "Architecture in Oregon, 1845–1895"; that of June 1960 to Lee H. Nelson's "A century of Oregon Covered Bridges, 1851–1952."

Twenty-three daily and 86 weekly newspapers, as well as 445 periodicals, are received currently. The manuscript collection, mostly relating to Oregon and the Pacific Northwest from 1792 to the present, contains over 100,000 items. Several very large collections of papers received during the past year are not as yet available for use because of the stringent limitations of working space. The 4,200 maps are at present being recatalogued, mounted, and repaired. One of the outstanding resources of the society is its collection of approximately 250,000 photographs and negatives, from 1855 to the present. Although overcrowding hampers museum activities, some admirable photographic exhibitions that give a vivid picture of life in Oregon have been contrived in limited space.

It should be noted that, although the Oregon Historical Society received a State appropriation of $99,550 for the 1959–61 biennium, its total income of $226,371 for this period included $64,000 of private gifts and donations, $2,421 income from endowment, $25,000 from membership dues, and $26,000 from sales and historical publications. Therefore, unlike the other societies (save for Montana) described in this chapter, it received more from private sources than from legislative appropriation. Splitting the biennial figure, its latest annual income is now $113,185.50, a very considerable improvement on the figure of $30,000 that prevailed only a few years ago, or the $8,701 receipts of 1933, which, nevertheless, supported four substantial issues of the *Oregon Historical Quarterly*.

The Oregon Historical Society relies considerably upon private assistance for the provision of its future quarters. Meanwhile its energetic director and editor, Mr. Thomas Vaughan, trained by the United States Marine Corps and the Wisconsin History Department, makes the best of the present shambles and builds a professional staff for the future. The society has recently acquired a well-qualified chief librarian and a chief museum curator. It has also an associate editor; catalogue, pictorial, and manuscript librarians; an office manager and assistant, a registrar, a bookkeeper, a public service representative, and a field representative.

There are in the vicinity of 2,200 members, with normal annual dues of $5, although there are the usual higher brackets, as well as a teacher and student membership at $2.50. Although the $5 membership covers the cost of supplying the *Oregon Historical Quarterly*, a loss is incurred on each $2.50 member. Local unions of carpenters, communication workers, moving picture projectionists, wood and steel workers, as well as the Oregon Fuchsia Society, Inc., have appeared in the membership list. Reports of the activities of affiliated county historical societies are published in the *Oregon Historical Quarterly*, while excursion meetings are held in various parts of the State. The July 1960 gathering at Medford, although similar in spirit to what California designates a *romería*, becomes further north the Fourth Annual Trappers' Rendezvous.

WASHINGTON

The Washington State Historical Society was organized in 1891, only two years after Washington Territory became a State, and incorporated in 1897. Its building at 315 North Stadium Way, which commands a striking view of the Tacoma waterfront, contains a number of museum galleries in addition to the good working library. The society's interests range from artifacts of Northwest Coast Indians to scrapbooks of Harry Hopkins and papers of Ralph Chaplin, "poet laureate" of the I.W.W. The latter cover much of the early labor history of the Pacific Northwest.

Its members, the majority of whom pay annual dues of $4, receive the *Pacific Northwest Quarterly* published by the University of Washington at Seattle. John A. Hussey's detailed study *The History of Fort Vancouver and its physical structure*, prepared by the National Park Service, which appeared in 1957, is the most ambitious publication of the Washington State Historical Society. Mr. Bruce Le Roy, who became director in 1959, has a pamphlet series in preparation that will include accounts of the guns of the Lewis and Clark expedition, ships that made local history, and the significance of the sea otter to the Pacific Northwest.

While the Washington State Historical Society has good books, manuscripts, and photographs relating to the history of the State, it has been shorthanded for some time. It has also been somewhat overshadowed by the energetic activities of the History Department and library of the University of Washington. Professor Edmond S. Meany, who founded the *Pacific Northwest Quarterly* under its earlier name of the *Washington Historical Quarterly*[20] in 1910, enjoyed such a position both within and without the university that a hotel in Seattle has been named for him—an uncommon tribute to American history.[21] With the University of Washington library engaged most aggressively in the acquisition of historical manuscripts for its Pacific Northwest collections,[22] and with Professors Charles M. Gates and Robert E. Burke of the History Department editing the *Quarterly*, much of the scholarly activity that in some states centers around the historical society has in Washington migrated to the university at Seattle. The society, however, sponsors the Pacific Northwest History Conference, concerned with the region of Washington, Oregon, Idaho, Montana, and British Columbia, which meets annually in the spring. The twelfth conference, in April 1959, was held at Portland with the Oregon Historical Society as host; the thirteenth, in April 1960, at Seattle, with the University of Washington, Seattle University, Seattle Pacific College, and the Seattle Historical Society as joint sponsors.

The Washington State Historical Society is at the present time making efforts to increase its membership and extend its influence more widely in popular directions. While doing so, it is not neglect-

20. The present name was adopted with volume xxxvii (1936). A double column illustrated format was adopted with volume xliv (1953). Notwithstanding its present tabloidish appearance, the scholarly character of the *Pacific Northwest Quarterly* remains unchanged.

21. Is it possible to imagine a Hotel Edward Channing in Cambridge or a Hotel Charles M. Andrews in New Haven?

22. See the introduction by J. Ronald Todd, Chief Reference Librarian, to *The Stevens Collection* (Seattle, 1958), which is the first of a *Manuscript Series*. Number two, *The Erastus Brainard Papers, 1880–1919*, appeared in 1959, and number three, *The Thomas Burke Papers, 1875–1925*, in 1960.

ing the growth of its research holdings, for whenever possible it adds to its manuscripts. Recent accessions include, for example, the papers of William Burr, a nineteenth-century inventor of an ironclad ship, submarine, and floating drydock, and those of William Hunter, Assistant Secretary of State in nine administrations. Hunter, who spent fifty-seven years in government service, received letters from Presidents of the United States from Van Buren to Cleveland; he was himself Acting President for a day, when after Lincoln's assassination Andrew Johnson was not sober enough to take the oath of office and Secretary of State Seward had been wounded and was unable to serve.[23]

23. Bruce Le Roy, "Washington State Historical Society Acquisitions," *Pacific Northwest Quarterly* L (1959), 172.

Chapter XIV

THE HISTORICAL
ASSOCIATIONS

For nearly a century before the founding of the American Historical
Association these state and local societies provided almost the sole
channels for effective promotion of historical study in the United
States; they received the support of such leading historians as Bancroft, Sparks, Motley, Parkman, and others; and it was one of the
unfortunate consequences of the founding of the national body that
much of the best talent in the subordinate groups transferred its
allegiance to the larger association of scholars.

—JULIAN P. BOYD, 1934

J FRANKLIN JAMESON, reminiscing on the fiftieth anniversary of the American Historical Association, recalled not only
the state of history but the general condition of American scholarship at the time of the foundation of that body in 1884.[1] In
commenting on the development of historical studies that began in
the 1880s and 1890s, he said:

The causes of this advance were various. The most fundamental, no doubt, was the
heightened sense of national importance and unity that followed upon the period
of Civil War and Reconstruction. Not a little of the impulse, however, came from
Germany—that old Germany of disinterested scholarship and quaint, unworldly
professors which seems to have disappeared, but to which in the seventies and
eighties the élite of American students flocked in impressive numbers, and from
which they returned with eager ambition to raise American scholarship to higher
levels.

With all this went an impulse toward the formation of national societies of
specialists. A dozen such—of chemists, archaeologists, engineers, students of mod-

1. J. Franklin Jameson, "Early Days of the American Historical Association, 1884–
1895," *American Historical Review* XL (1934), 1–9.

ern languages, of history, of economics, of geology, of mathematics—came into existence between 1876 and 1888. Their growth and flourishing have made an immense difference in American scholarship and science. Men of learning and of science are now grouped in definite professions, with the influence and encouragement that come from such combination, where fifty years ago they were isolated.

A man fighting his way through a mob in a hotel lobby during Christmas week at the annual meeting of one of these professional societies sometimes thinks with longing of the older isolation, when men of learning and science were less formally grouped in definite professions. Many of these bodies have now become so large that their members attend out of a sense of duty rather than for the anticipation of pleasure. Their number constantly increases by the formation of more specialized splinter groups. Overwhelmed with numbers and bored by uninteresting programs in the large association, its members of congenial interests cohere like amoebae. They decide to form a new organization, usually with brave professions that there are to be no rules, no officers, no dues.[2] If the splinter group survives, sooner or later it acquires all these vices and, finally, the ultimate one of a permanent paid secretariat. At this point dissident members begin to complain about size, lack of cohesiveness and interest, while some of them begin to talk of splitting off like a group of amoebae with no rules, no officers, no dues. Thus organizations multiply. Their specialization has become so acute that collective bodies like the American Council of Learned Societies and the Social Science Research Council have been created in an effort to break down the barriers, while, in similar direction, universities and foundations lovingly nurture what are fashionably called interdisciplinary studies. Thus meetings multiply in size and scale, and life becomes more complicated by the year, in strict compliance with Parkinson's Law.

2. Julian P. Boyd, whose *Papers of Thomas Jefferson* have inspired so many similar editorial projects, remarked in "'God's Altar Needs Not Our Pollishings,'" *New York History* xxxix (1958), 5–6, that "we may even be approaching that dangerous extremity when someone will arise and suggest that we form an association or found a journal to provide a forum for discussion of our common problems."

This phenomenon is not a peculiarity of learned professions. It is a national pastime of an exhausting sort, which reaches its highest perfection in Washington. In 1945, when joint and allied military and naval operations had brought to a conclusion the greatest war hitherto known to man, there was an immediate outcry for the unification of the armed forces. To eliminate the duplication inherent in separate War and Navy Departments, a third Department of the Air Force was created from the Army, like Eve from the rib of Adam, while a fourth Department of Defense was established to co-ordinate the other three. Thus two hierarchies became four, with a flowering of papers that makes the life of a vice-admiral in the Pentagon today considerably more harassing than that of a commander twenty years ago.

These are reflections of hindsight, for in the late 1880s the American Historical Association offered so clear an opportunity for the encouragement of history and the conquering of the old isolation that it rapidly became a truly national organization. As indicated in the quotation at the head of this chapter, "much of the best talent in the subordinate groups transferred its allegiance to the larger association of scholars."[3] Thus the new professionals and the old amateurs tended to congregate in separate camps, which regarded each other with some degree of suspicion. Those in one group looked down their noses at anyone who was so bold as to write history without a PH.D., preferably from a German university; those in the other regarded a Doctor of Philosophy as guilty until proved innocent.[4]

3. Julian P. Boyd, "State and Local Historical Societies in the United States," *American Historical Review* XL (1934), 11.

4. Some of this state of mind, engendered late in the nineteenth century, could still be seen in Massachusetts within the past decade through the outspoken opinions of the Phillips brothers, who were unreconstructed Federalists from Salem. Stephen Willard Phillips, president of the Essex Institute and a distinguished collector of Pacific voyages, and James Duncan Phillips, an officer of Houghton Mifflin Company and the author of a three-volume history of his beloved Salem, seldom failed at a meeting of the Massachusetts Historical Society or the Colonial Society of Massachusetts, where professionals and amateurs have long been blended harmoniously, to express their low opinion of the degree of Doctor of Philosophy. To these vigorous spiritual des-

When professionalism had the charm of novelty, when science was unquestionably about to regenerate and improve all aspects of the universe, including history, a man had to be wholeheartedly for or against the new gospel. Today few scholars look down their noses at palatable and literate presentation of historical research, although not many can write as skillfully as Samuel Eliot Morison, whose *History as a Literary Art* is the ideal statement of that principle. And at the 1959 meeting of the American Historical Association, Sir Isaiah Berlin in his paper "The Concept of Scientific History" effectively demonstrated, with the skill of an Oxford philosopher, the incompatibility between the techniques of history and the sciences, and concluded that "the attempt to construct a discipline which stands to concrete history as pure to applied, is not a hope for something beyond human powers, so much as a chimaera, born of a profound incapacity to grasp the nature of natural science, or of history, or of both."[5]

Sixty or seventy years ago the lines between the older historical societies and the American Historical Association were more clearly drawn than they are today. Consequently it is easy to see why, in various states, groups of university professors and other teachers of history organized regional bodies on the pattern of the American Historical Association that were distinct from previously existing State historical societies. In chapter VIII, when treating of Georgia and South Carolina, I ventured the suggestion that there was a

---

cendants of the Essex Junto, whose lungs demanded salt air that had gained fragrance by blowing across clam flats, a "freshwater college Ph.D." was anathema. Although Harvard graduates themselves, they regarded even holders of the Harvard doctorate with suspicion, for Edmund S. Morgan could never, in his younger days, read a paper at the Colonial Society without causing Stephen W. Phillips to comment vociferously upon "the profundity of his research and the absurdity of his conclusions." At this point Samuel Eliot Morison would, equally invariably, blow Mr. Phillips out of the water by a brilliant counterattack with shells of decisive caliber. There were few occasions when one of these fine survivors of the amateur tradition failed to express some derogation of the then not-so-new professionals. These outbursts, of which I received my fair share, furnished a good deal of innocent amusement at the time; they have often been affectionately recalled since the deaths of their perpetrators.

5. *History and Theory*, (1960), 1–31.

semantic distinction between the terms "society" and "association"; that the latter might convey the idea of a professional group, meeting perhaps annually, with publications but without collections—in short a regional emulation of the American Historical Association. The Texas State Historical Association is the outstanding example of such an academically inspired organization. It will be recalled that the Georgia Historical Association, founded at Athens by faculty members anxious to disturb the somnolence of Savannah, soon merged with the Georgia Historical Society, but that the South Carolina Historical Association, composed of history teachers throughout the State, continues as an independent group. The Arkansas Historical Association,[6] a similar body organized in 1941, has as its principal activity the publication of the *Arkansas Historical Quarterly*, which has appeared continuously since March 1942. As it has neither a library nor a museum, it advises and urges owners of books and manuscripts of historical interest to give them to a local library, to the Arkansas History Commission Library and Museum at Little Rock, or to the University of Arkansas Library at Fayetteville. The association is an independent organization, which depends upon the dues paid by its 1,500 members, upon donations, and sales of the *Quarterly* for funds. Its annual income of about $4,500 is spent entirely upon publications and postage, for Professor Walter L. Brown of the History Department of the University of Arkansas serves as secretary-treasurer of the association and as editor of the *Quarterly*. The university reduces Professor Brown's teaching load

6. Leslie W. Dunlap mentioned an Antiquarian and Natural History Society of the State of Arkansas, incorporated in 1837, that gave up the ghost soon after 1842. The Arkansas History Commission, a State agency, was established in 1905. An act of 1909 enlarged the commission, provided for an executive secretary, and appropriated money for the printing of the *Publications of the Arkansas Historical Association*. Although four of these volumes were printed at Fayetteville in 1906, 1908, 1911, and 1917, this association became defunct sometime after World War I and the History Commission ceased to issue the *Publications*. The Arkansas Historical Commission has from time to time since 1941 made a small annual gift to the present Arkansas Historical Association, in return for the right to publish material in the *Arkansas Historical Quarterly*.

to half time and furnishes him a student assistant to help with the association's work.

The term "historical association" does not, however, invariably imply an organization of the type formed in Texas, Georgia, South Carolina, and Arkansas, for the New York State Historical Association, although it long devoted its efforts entirely to an annual meeting and to publications, was originally an "up country" group led by amateurs rather than by professional historians. In Louisiana the name was in 1889 appropriated by a body of Confederate veterans who established a museum in New Orleans.

The Texas State Historical Association and the New York State Historical Association, both established before the turn of the century although for somewhat different reasons, have acquired premises and important collections that warrant detailed description, while the very recent transformation of the Louisiana Historical Association raises points worthy of mention. This chapter will therefore be concerned chiefly with these three organizations.

TEXAS

The Texas State Historical Association,[7] the oldest learned society in the State, was founded at the University of Texas at Austin in 1897 through the efforts of Professor George P. Garrison, head of the History Department, who evolved the idea following a summer visit to the University of Wisconsin. In this, as in other respects, Texas worked out its own pattern. Following a preliminary gathering of ten men on 13 February, some 250 Texans were invited to a meeting on the State's independence day, 2 March, at which a constitution was adopted. The objects of the association were to be "in general, the promotion of historical studies; and in particular, the discovery, collection, preservation, and publication of historical material, especially such as relates to Texas." Membership was divided into four

---

7. H. Bailey Carroll, "A Half-Century of the Texas State Historical Association," *Southwestern Historical Quarterly*, extra number (1 February 1947), pp. 9–17.

classes: members, unlimited in number; fellows, limited to fifty "who show, by published work, special aptitude for historical investigation"; life members, who pay $50 (later raised to $100) or give "an equivalent in books, MSS., or other acceptable matter"; and honorary life members "who rendered eminent service to Texas previous to annexation." By these categories the association thus sought to attract persons, academic or lay, with an interest in Texas history, to segregate as fellows productive historians, and to honor venerable worthies who had made history. While men prominent in State history and politics, from Oran M. Roberts onward, have held the presidency, the management of the association was from the beginning firmly in academic hands. Dr. Garrison was elected recording secretary and librarian. In July 1897, only five months after the initial move, he brought out the first number of the *Quarterly of the Texas State Historical Association*, which he continued to edit until his death in 1910.

This scholarly journal, the earliest as well as the most important undertaking of the association, adopted in 1912–13 its present name of the *Southwestern Historical Quarterly*. For more than sixty years it has maintained high standards of careful editing and authenticated research, thanks to a series of members of the university faculty. Professor Eugene C. Barker, who took over upon Dr. Garrison's death, continued for twenty-seven years, with Professors Walter Prescott Webb, Charles W. Hackett, and Rudolph L. Biesele as a committee of editors. Thus distinguished members of the History Department were closely involved in the affairs of the *Quarterly*. Professor Webb in 1939 became its managing editor and director of the Texas State Historical Association and was succeeded in those posts by Dr. H. Bailey Carroll, the present incumbent, who is also a professor of history at the university.

Although the association collected independently for a short time, all books and manuscripts that it has received for many years have become a part of the University of Texas Library or Archives. In 1945 the Board of Regents of the university created the Eugene C.

Barker Texas History Center and, after the completion of the present skyscraper library, installed the Center in the former library building on the university campus. By this means the Texas State Historical Association is attractively housed under the same roof as the Texas collection, the archives, and the newspaper collection of the university library.

The association receives no direct State appropriation. The $5 annual dues of its 2,275 members cover the printing bill of the *Southwestern Historical Quarterly*, but as the salaries of the director and the staff of the Eugene C. Barker Texas History Center are paid by the university, the State (through the university) subsidizes the association, whose annual expenses are in the vicinity of $50,000.

Professor Webb in 1940 laid plans for the compilation and publication of an encyclopedia of Texas history and biography to consist of some 15,000 articles, written by a variety of hands. The purpose was "to assemble in one usable, practical, ready-reference work the most significant information about the widest possible range of Texas topics." Twelve years and the work of a thousand individuals, under the direction of Professor Carroll as managing editor, were required to bring this great project to completion. Although the war caused inevitable delays, subjects were established and assigned by 1945. The two massive volumes of *The Handbook of Texas*—a unique and wholly admirable reference work—were published in 1952 in an edition of 6,000 copies, priced at $30. Thus the Texas State Historical Association provided a model solution for the difficult task of making accurate historical information widely available to anyone who may have need for it. The *Handbook* is an invaluable tool for the scholar, the journalist, or anyone else who seeks information about Texas; one hopes that its successful completion will inspire similar ventures in co-operative scholarship in other states.

The expense of its preparation—in the vicinity of $100,000—was met by the University of Texas and by a grant from the Rockefeller Foundation. Receipts from sales of the *Handbook*, of which only 1,000 sets remain, and returns from other books have been placed in a revolving publication fund, which now amounts to over $100,000. This makes possible the association's book publishing program, which began in 1943 with Dr. Carroll's *Texas County Histories: A Bibliography*. The series has included such biographies as Duncan W. Robinson's *Judge Robert McAlpin Williamson: Texas' Three-Legged Willie* and Professor Barker's *The Life of Stephen F. Austin: Founder of Texas*;[8] such reference works as Ernest W. Winkler's *Check List of Texas Imprints, 1846–1860* and a cumulative index to the first forty volumes of the *Southwestern Historical Quarterly*; Barnes F. Lathrop's *Migration into East Texas, 1835–1860*; Wallace Hawkins' *El Sal del Rey*, a history of Texas mineral law; and histories of Post City and Collin, Western Falls, and Young counties. Manuscripts of other county histories are awaiting publication, for Professor Carroll's ideal would be to publish scholarly volumes on all 254 counties of the State. Dr. Llerena B. Friend, the able librarian of the Eugene C. Barker Texas History Center, has in preparation a manuscript continuing Winkler's *Texas Imprints* through the year 1876.

Beginning in 1923 the Texas State Historical Association has encouraged and aided the organization of county and local historical societies throughout the State. In 1939 Professor Webb inaugurated a series of regional meetings, in addition to the April annual meeting at Austin, and a project for encouraging high school students to develop an interest in local history, through the formation of a junior branch of the association. Of this J. Frank Dobie remarked: "I don't know but that when Webb gets to St. Peter, he may not have more credit there for the Junior Historians of Texas than he will for the books he has written." This movement in the public schools, which has been well described by Professor Carroll[9] who has been in charge of it since 1940, was designed to encourage members of local and almost autonomous clubs, to engage in small pieces of genuine

---

8. The publication of this edition of a standard work was aided by Mr. Karl Hoblitzelle and the Hoblitzelle Foundation of Dallas, Texas.

9. H. Bailey Carroll, "The Junior Historian Movement in the Public Schools," *Bulletins of the American Association for State and Local History* 1, 12 (February 1947).

research into local aspects of Texas history. The original concept was that, by interviewing parents and early settlers and by engaging in serious investigation of local events, high school students might, within their limitations, turn up some useful sources, while gaining for themselves valuable practice in the technique of research. There are now 120 chapters in the State. *The Junior Historian*, which Professor Carroll has edited since January 1941, publishes the results of their investigations, and very nearly finances its six issues a year on a subscription fee of $1.50. Unlike the children's publications of some other organizations, the intention was not to provide popular history watered down for the young, but to offer a vehicle for printing small pieces of serious investigation carried out by students behaving like adults. Professor Carroll requires high standards, is more interested in quality than quantity, and has no sympathy with the practice later developed in other states of lowering the age level to a point where fun rather than work is emphasized.

The Texas State Historical Association has no museum functions or responsibilities for public archives, both of which are dealt with by other State agencies in Austin. It continues to keep its sights on scholarly production. One might define its present role as one of serving scholarship and increasing communication between the History Department of the University of Texas and residents of the State of all ages.

NEW YORK

The New York State Historical Association, organized in 1899, is *sui generis*. It belies the ordinary connotations of its name by owning elegant premises and extensive collections. It is located neither at the capital, near a university, or even in a major city, but in bucolic surroundings on the shores of Lake Otsego, just outside the village of Cooperstown. It devotes a larger share of its efforts to museum exhibition than any organization previously described in this book. Although it receives no public funds of any kind, it carries on extensive popular educational programs, both for adults and children, that are closer in spirit to the activities of the large middle western publicly supported State historical societies than to those of its eastern neighbors. It offers yet another proof that, while no two historical organizations are alike, some are less alike than others.

Unlike Texas, and contrary to the implications of its name, the New York State Historical Association was not founded by an academic group. Its original centre of operations was at Caldwell on Lake George. Although it received a charter from the regents of the State University of New York and announced its purpose as the promotion and encouragement of original historical research, of lectures and publication, the marking of historic sites and the acquisition of historic properties, unsympathetic observers characterized it as an outing club. For eight years its annual meetings were held around Lake George, then a pleasanter part of the State than it is now; the ninth was held at Buffalo, and thereafter meetings were arranged in different localities.

Beginning in 1901, the New York State Historical Association published *Proceedings*, containing papers read at its annual meetings. The first five volumes were slim, but the sixth, which contained E. M. Ruttenber's extended study *Indian Geographical Names*, marked the start of more substantial publication. In 1920 the *Proceedings* were succeeded by a *Quarterly Journal* that, with a change of name to *New York History* in the early 1930s, has continued its scholarly career to the present without popularization either of contents or format.

In 1926 Horace A. Moses of the Strathmore Paper Company, who had been born in Ticonderoga, New York, provided in his native town a headquarters for the New York State Historical Association. This building, a replica of the destroyed John Hancock House in Boston,[10] furnished with copies of eighteenth-century pieces in the new

---

10. This anticipates the notion, which reached its full flowering in the present building of the Chicago Historical Society, that American history should be presented in copies of colonial buildings having some connection with the origins of the American Revolution.

American Wing of the Metropolitan Museum made under the direction of R. T. H. Halsey, excited great enthusiasm at the time. In a speech of acceptance at the dedication, Alexander C. Flick, State Historian of New York and corresponding secretary of the association, exulted:

In the olden times, when the children of Israel were homeless wanderers, Moses led them from the Promised Land and gave them the world's greatest constitution, the Ten Commandments. His renown has covered the world. In these modern days the sons and daughters of Clio, also homeless wanderers, have been led by another Moses to the Promised Land. An endowment of 10 $10,000 bonds has brought a new freedom and a new opportunity. His renown will go down in our annals as a benefactor of the human race.[11]

Although the association, equipped with premises, entered the library and museum business, meetings and publications continued to be its major interest.

A remarkable era in the life of the New York State Historical Association began when Professor Dixon Ryan Fox of Columbia University was elected its president in 1929. Although the first professional historian to hold the presidency, his interests were less confined by academic barriers than were those of many of his colleagues. As a conspicuous exponent of the then "new" social history, he was disposed to investigate nooks and crannies that had previously been ignored. With contagious enthusiasm he inspired the support of everyone in the association. Of him a former director of the association[12] recently wrote me:

The institution was galvanized by Dixon Ryan Fox. He was the perpetual president, re-elected by acclamation each year, and no one would have thought of exchanging

11. *Proceedings of the New York State Historical Association* XXIV (1926), 269.

12. Directors of the New York State Historical Association in the 1930s were more than once called away to larger responsibilities elsewhere. Edward P. Alexander, now a vice-president of Colonial Williamsburg, who took over when Julian P. Boyd (whose letter I quote above) went to the Historical Society of Pennsylvania, became director of the State Historical Society of Wisconsin in 1941, while Clifford L. Lord, now a Columbia dean, followed Dr. Alexander both in New York State and Wisconsin. Louis C. Jones, *Cooperstown* (Cooperstown, 1949).

him for another. He attended every meeting, inspired everyone with his zeal, wrote endless letters in indecipherable script about the most minute details of the Association, and literally wore himself out in promoting its endeavors. Those endeavors, as he demonstrated on every level of activity, might be as full of gossip and fun as a family reunion (which in many respects the annual meetings resembled), but could be justified only as they deepened and extended the understanding of New York history. In brief, while everybody, high and low, had a thoroughly good time, *scholarship* was the keynote. The annual meetings were three day affairs and they brought together some of the country's most distinguished historians, local antiquarians, patricians of the Hudson Valley, old New Yorkers, and so on and so on. There were no cocktail parties but Fox made everyone feel intoxicated with his own enthusiasm for scholarship. He was a remarkable leader.

By the contagion of his enthusiasm for scholarship, Fox broke down the barriers between professionals and amateurs, persuading the historians at Columbia and many other institutions to work cordially and effectively with local antiquarians when something useful was involved. Franklin D. Roosevelt, who was a loyal supporter of Fox's crusade for historical scholarship, was proud to be the town historian of Hyde Park. Unlike Talleyrand, who only became Mayor of Valençay in retirement, he retained that office at the same time that he was President of the United States.

Within three years, the results of Dixon Ryan Fox's influence became apparent in a remarkable series of publications. Between 1932 and 1938 volumes of the New York State Historical Association series, published by the Columbia University Press, crowded upon one another. E. Wilder Spaulding's *New York in the Critical Period, 1783–1789* appeared in 1932; Howard Swiggett's *War Out of Niagara, Walter Butler and the Tory Rangers* in 1933; Herbert Barber Howe's *Jedediah Barber, 1787–1876* in 1934; Arthur C. Parker's *A Manual for History Museums* in 1935; Milton W. Hamilton's *The Country Printer: New York State, 1785–1830* in 1936; S. G. Nissenson's *The Patroons' Domain*, Edward P. Alexander's *A Revolutionary Conservative: James Duane of New York*, and Ralph Foster Weld's *Brooklyn Village, 1816–1834* in 1938. And between 1933 and 1937 Columbia also published in the series the ten-volume *History of the*

State of New York, edited by Alexander C. Flick, the ninety-nine chapters of which were written by about seventy authors.

Although Dixon Ryan Fox became president of Union College in Schenectady in 1933, he continued as president of the association until his death in 1945. His hand was in everything. Each issue of *New York History* opened with "The President's Page" in which he set the tone for the coming quarter. In the January 1941 issue, for example, he remarked:

The New York State Historical Association, in contrast with many learned bodies, has always sought to make history a popular interest. As between the professional historian and the "ordinary layman", we have generally voted for the latter, and professionals among us, when gathering for Association enterprises, have left high hats at home.

His tone was invariably disarming. While he had unrivaled gifts as a promoter, he never confused the means with the end, or allowed anyone to be deluded into thinking that the association had any other purpose than the advancement of historical scholarship.

President Fox's death marked the end of an era in the New York State Historical Association. It is typical, however, that a casual visit that he made to Cooperstown in 1938, seeking endowment for a new professorship at Union College, caused the association to move its headquarters there the following year and to embark upon its present program.

Cooperstown, settled after the Revolution by the efforts of Judge William Cooper, father of the novelist, is set in a scene of great natural beauty. As it was bypassed both by canal and railroad, its rural attractiveness has survived to this day. Fortunately soon after the death in 1851 of James Fenimore Cooper, who was long its most distinguished inhabitant, much of the village and the surrounding lands became the property of another family that cared deeply for it. Edward Clark, the partner of Isaac M. Singer in the manufacture of sewing machines, bought a place in Cooperstown in 1854 for summer use; in succeeding years members of his family came to have a deep interest in the region. One of his grandsons, Edward Severin Clark, a bachelor, indulged in a passion for large buildings by constructing the vast Otesaga Hotel, giving a gymnasium and hospital to the village, by building himself in 1918 a great stone "cow palace," which was one of the largest barns in New York State, and in 1930 a brick Georgian residence, of comparable dimensions, known as Fenimore House. After the death of Edward S. Clark in 1933, his brother, Stephen C. Clark, sought an appropriate use for these large buildings that would contribute to the stability and prosperity of Cooperstown. Thus the New York State Historical Association came to occupy Fenimore House as its headquarters and as a museum, and to establish its admirable Farmers' Museum in the "cow palace."

The present large-scale museum and educational activities of the association have developed since the move to Cooperstown and represent a rationalization of the new surroundings and the personal interests and generosity of their donor. Just as the greater part of the endowment of the Virginia Historical Society is due to the bequest of Mr. and Mrs. Alexander W. Weddell, so the premises and much of the collections of the New York State Historical Asssociation today are due to the continuing interest of Mr. Stephen C. Clark, the chairman of its board until his death in September 1960. Dr. Louis C. Jones, the present director, in *A Decade of History, 1947–1956*[13]— a ten-year report in which he summarizes the growth of the association—is explicit upon this point.

The blue print of what has been accomplished over these years is his. I recall— always with pleasure—a long conversation with Mr. Clark in the summer of 1946 when he was discussing with me the possibility of my coming to Cooperstown. We sat that early August morning on the back porch of the Hotel Otesaga with the Lake lying before us. As he talked of the Association and the future he saw for it, I began to see his vision of a historical society which would reach out to all our fellow citizens—men, women, and children—and give them a sense of their inheritance as Americans. His concept of a cultural center on the shores of this lake, his conviction that a museum should be alive, not sacrosanct and stuffy, most of all his

13. (Cooperstown, 1957). Later reports are published in the January issues of *New York History*.

faith in our countrymen and our country moved me. The philosophy behind everything we have done since, he enunciated that morning.

Beginning with the presidency of Dixon Ryan Fox, the Association had been concentrating less on political and military history and increasingly on social history. Mr. Clark's leadership encouraged an advance in this direction over a broad front. The Association became less of a society and more of an educational force, seeking to tell the story of Everyman as he labored, built, played, thought and created. We no longer could think in terms of a few hundred members, but in terms of hundreds of thousands of citizens previously unreached. We set out to tell the story of our inheritance to children, to college students, to specialists and scholars and to a general public however well or ill informed about our history.

The vehicles for this widespread effort are Fenimore House and the Farmers' Museum. These two adjacent museums in Cooperstown are so much the heart of the present association that its activities cannot be understood without a brief consideration of them. Although the association and the Farmers' Museum are separate legal entities, their operations are so closely intertwined that in any realistic study of their support and use they must be regarded as an entity. The two museums are, as Dr. Jones points out, "very different, yet they are bound together by a common emphasis on New York's social history. At Fenimore House it is primarily through the artist that we see the progress of social and cultural history: at The Farmer's Museum that history is presented three-dimensionally with the visitor in intimate contact with the scene."

When the New York State Historical Association first moved to Cooperstown, its earlier library and the majority of its possessions were left at Ticonderoga.[14] The present collections have mostly been assembled since the move. By 1947 Mr. Stephen C. Clark had acquired numerous paintings relating to New York State—landscapes of the Hudson River School; genre paintings by W. S. Mount, Eastman Johnson, Edward Lamson Henry, Thomas Waterman Wood, Tompkins H. Matteson, James F. Pringle, and others;

14. This first headquarters was maintained as a branch library and museum until 1958, when it was turned over to the Fort Ticonderoga Association and all activities again became centered in one place.

portraits by Benjamin West, Gilbert Stuart, Samuel F. B. Morse, Ezra Ames, and Ralph Earl—and the remarkable collection of life masks by John H. I. Browere that had recently been rediscovered after a century of obscurity in storage. These were installed on the first and second floors of Fenimore House, with material relating to James Fenimore Cooper, lent by Dr. Henry Fenimore Cooper and Mr. Paul Fenimore Cooper. In 1948 Mr. Clark gave the house to the association. In the same year an exhibition of American folk art, arranged by the staff, caught the imagination of Mr. Clark, who then in subsequent years purchased various collections to augment it. The April 1950 issue of *Art in America* describes and illustrates the varied works of art exhibited in Fenimore House at that time. Since then, in the folk art field alone, Mr. Clark added the extensive collections of Jean and Howard Lipman and of Mr. and Mrs. William J. Gunn. Fenimore House has today much to offer the student of American arts and crafts, while the many genre paintings give a vivid reminder of lost aspects of American life. Mount's *Eel Spearing at Setauket*, Matteson's *The Turkey Shoot*, Pringle's view of the Smith and Dimon shipyard on the East River in 1833, to mention only three of many, are documents of a high order for the social historian.

The Farmers' Museum seeks to show how the pioneer farmer or craftsman and his family lived and worked in a recently settled land, both by the display and the demonstration of tools and implements of agriculture and related trades. Unlike museums containing breakable or irreplaceable objects, this one encourages visitors to touch, to turn cranks, and heft implements. Edward S. Clark's great stone barn provided an admirable setting for such exhibits, which extend into the Village Crossroads, a synthetic village composed of buildings brought from their original sites and reconstructed in plausible relation to one another. A schoolhouse, country store, drug shop, tavern, blacksmith shop, offices of doctor, lawyer, and printer furnish a realistic background for the exhibition of objects associated with them. These buildings, which have been given to the association by friendly individuals and institutions, have homogeneity, for they date from the period between the end of the Revolution and the 1840s, and come from an area of the State west of the Hudson, south of the Mohawk River, north of the Pennsylvania border, and east of a line dropped between Syracuse and Binghamton. With crops growing in the fields, suitable animals about, weaving, candle-making, and cooking going on, the Farmers' Museum and the Village Crossroads have a considerable air of verisimilitude.

Each year they attract visitors in steadily increasing numbers. In 1946, 8,913 persons visited the Farmer's Museum and 5,559 Fenimore House. In 1960, 111,489 came to the former and 52,542 to the latter, making a total of 164,031 visitors, a remarkable number in view of the relative inaccessibility of Cooperstown. These figures, although 11,312 below the 1959 attendance, represent a year of prosperity, leisure, and mobility for many Americans who in earlier times stayed at home, yet a questionnaire filled out by visitors in the late summer of 1957 indicated that a large proportion came from the immediate area. Sixty-two per cent reported that they were on a day's excursion; 85% did not expect to be away from home for more than three days, while 95% expected to be away from home less than a week. The reported causes of the visits were even more significant. Thirty-four per cent had been told about the museums by friends, 21% had been there before, and 25% had been influenced by leaflets that the association distributes in large numbers. The remaining 20% were divided as follows: newspapers 6, magazine articles 4, road signs 4, radio 2, "just passing by" 4. That only 12% were due to the influence of the self-vaunted mass media is worthy of note.

The library in Fenimore House was described in 1956 as having 11,000 catalogued books, pamphlets, and bound periodicals on open shelves in the reading room, and others stored elsewhere. It concentrates on the history and life of people living in upstate New York. Close to 10,000 titles were added by gift and purchase in the years 1948–59. The manuscript collection, dealing chiefly with upstate New York between 1750 and 1850, had at the end of 1959 approximately 2,000 bound volumes and 109,000 separate pieces. Among these are some 500 account books of farmers, weavers, blacksmiths, and general storekeepers. In 1960, 809 visitors used the library, with genealogy as their primary interest. The library since 1955 has been in the charge of Miss Dorothy C. Barck, former librarian of the New-York Historical Society, who also edits *New York History*. Although the museum exhibitions were a major preoccupation of the association during its first decade in Cooperstown, effort is today increasingly concentrated on the library as the indispensable first step in any research program. At the December 1961 meeting of the American Historical Association, Dr. Jones announced the purchase of the extensive library of Americana collected by Roger Butterfield, author of *The American Past* and long a member of the staff of *Life*.

This adds 100,000 American newspapers, 50,000 issues of periodicals, over 10,000 books and serials, 5000 pamphlets and several thousand ephemeral items such as broadsides, almanacs, song books, cartoons and posters, and important collections relating to the development of American farm implements. The new library will give us complete runs of all the earliest pictorial news weeklies such as *Ballou's*, *Harper's*, *Leslie's*, and others. The sale was made at considerable personal sacrifice to Mr. Butterfield because he wanted these materials, so lovingly gathered, to remain in Otsego County, a part of the world to which he hopes to return, and in which his family history goes back 160 years. This important addition to our thriving library makes it possible for us to look forward to a much greater usefulness, not only to the research workers on our own staff but to scholars everywhere.[15]

A requirement in the syllabus for the social studies in New York State schools that State and local history be taught in the seventh and eighth grades, combined with the desire for wide dissemination of history that followed the move to Cooperstown, led the New York State Historical Association in 1942 to establish a junior membership for school children up to the age of eighteen. Miss Mary E. Cunningham was responsible for this program for fifteen years until, in 1957, she left the association to become Deputy Director of State Publicity for the New York State Department of Commerce; Mr.

15. Louis C. Jones, "The Trapper's Cabin and the Ivory Tower," *Museum News* XL, 7 (March 1962), pp. 11–17.

Frederick L. Rath Jr., vice-director of the association, was until recently in sole charge of the "Yorkers," as these junior members are called. He is now assisted in this work by Mr. Milo Stewart, who was in February 1961 appointed associate in education. From ten chapters with 147 members in the beginning, their number grew to 207 chapters with over 7,000 members in 1959. In addition to *The Yorker* magazine, numerous attractions are offered, such as membership pins, felt emblems for T-shirt or sweater, regional jamborees, pen pal correspondence, "Yorker-Corker" dances, state-wide contests, awards and trophies, and an annual meeting. These activities have not, however, led any great number of Yorkers to progress to the adult activities of the association in later years. Miss Cunningham in 1957 noted:

We have from the first regarded Yorkers as potential Association members, yet how to sustain their interest in New York State history in the crowded years after leaving high school when young people are attending college, starting their first jobs, getting married and beginning families, has always proved to be an insoluble problem.

In addition to the Yorker program, the association encourages the visits of school groups to the Cooperstown museums. In 1951—the first year for which accurate figures were kept—165 groups, containing 6,553 children came. That number has increased steadily to the 1959 figure of 379 groups of 18,000 children. The association endeavors to provide teachers with material that will elucidate the meaning of a visit to Cooperstown. On this point Dr. Jones observed in the July 1962 issue of *New York History*:

I am well aware of the pressures on teachers, the great number of subjects they are expected to cram into the little heads in front of them: I am also aware of the fact that a visit to our Museums, in fact to any museum, without adequate preparation is little more than a day out of school. Frankly, this Association is not particularly interested in school holidays. Our Education Department, under the direction of Mr. Stewart, has been publishing a series of prefatory memoranda covering various aspects of the class visit and more of these are in preparation, so that we will have an increasing volume of material, certain sections of which will be selected for teachers at different grade levels.

The problem of school groups visiting the Museums in the spring has become increasingly acute. We are having many, many more applications than we can handle and this year we probably turned down nearly 50% as many as we have accepted. On top of these maximum crowds have come school groups whose teachers either refused to accept "no" for an answer or who didn't notify us of their coming in any way whatsoever. The confusion and unusual pressures that this kind of inconsiderateness creates we have tried to meet as best we could. About all we can do is to proceed steadily on our way, doing our best to make clear in every place possible that ours are teaching museums, that we are only interested in the school group visitation for which there has been adequate preparation.

These organized programs are more difficult to maintain at the college level. Dr. Jones observed in 1957:

The pattern of our relations with the colleges is varied, indeed almost haphazard, resulting from the interest or initiative of some individual professor or administrator rather than from any planned policy of ours such as we administer for school children. College administrators are not so mobile-minded as principals of central schools who have a fleet of buses at hand and who are oriented to class trips of various kinds. The collegians stay put.

The lack of interest in state and local history among academic historians is certainly a factor in the relatively small number of college classes that come to Cooperstown, but we have not done our share in making clear to teachers of art, anthropology, literature, sociology, economics how much we have to offer in their fields.

Early in the 1950s the association conducted a college essay contest for the best pieces of research in New York State history and folklore, but, because of the meagre response, abandoned it as unproductive. More recently two-day autumn local history workshops have been tried; one was held in September 1958 at Union College, another a year later, in conjunction with a meeting of the Conference on Early American History, at the State University Teachers College at New Paltz, and a third at Oswego in September 1960.[16]

16. This workshop on "New York State and the Civil War," breezily reported in the 12 September 1960 issue of the association's biweekly bulletin under the title "Oswego So Goes the Nation," had as one highlight of its program "Joe Thatcher's final appearance as a member of the staff; dressed in his Civil War blues with all the equipment, he demonstrated the shooting of a musket, nearly blowing the sides out of the auditorium."

The annual seminars on American culture, held for a fortnight every July since 1948 for adults not connected with universities, have proved an extremely attractive feature of the association's program. Courses in various aspects of social and cultural history are offered by the association's staff, by visiting members of university faculties, private scholars like Mrs. Bertram K. Little, literary men like Henry Beston and Carl Carmer, and by Dr. Albert B. Corey, State Historian of New York. Between the 180 persons that attended the first seminar in 1948 and the 238 that were present in 1959, attendance has fluctuated between a low of 107 and a high of 355, depending upon the course offerings of particular years. Of the attendance, Dr. Jones wrote in 1957:

As for the students, there are certain constants: one-third will be repeaters, one third will be teachers (with considerable overlapping in those two thirds). Beyond that nothing is predictable. They are lawyers, doctors, collectors, local historians, therapists, housewives, mail carriers, farmers, business men, librarians, museum workers, writers, photographers, dealers, tea bag inspectors, and representatives of any number of other occupations.

They have come to us from all over the continent. While 79% of the 1813 students are residents of New York State, the other 21% (382) have come from twenty-nine states, the District of Columbia and three provinces of Canada. Pennsylvania (67), New Jersey (65), Massachusetts (50) and Connecticut (45) have led the states, but every year sees every section represented. We send out 35,000 to 40,000 descriptive folders each spring and it is my feeling that there are great values to the Association in getting the story of Seminars across the country. It has broadcast our concept of a historical society as an educational center as nothing else could do.

On a more specialized level was "Historic-House Keeping: A Short Course," which was offered in 1955, 1956, and 1957, with the support of the National Trust for Historic Preservation and of Mr. Stephen C. Clark, to provide professional guidance for those concerned with the preservation, interpretation, and administration of historic properties. "Conversation Week Ends," held in January for art historians, beginning in 1958, were an effort to bring specialists and scholars together at Cooperstown.

The attractiveness of Cooperstown, combined with the varied and imaginative offerings of the museums and seminars, have greatly enlarged the parish boundaries of the New York State Historical Association. Once a visitor has seen the place, he has a natural desire to return. There is, however, a considerable amount of labor and expense involved in passing the word about an institution that is off the beaten track. This keeps the two staff members concerned with public relations fully occupied. By distributing 100,000 to 125,000 leaflets a year, maintaining seventy-eight road signs and two 14′ × 50′ billboards, by arranging (in co-operation with local hotels) Country Holiday, a party for the press, by a maple festival, the annual Farmers' Museum junior livestock show, and other means the net is widely spread. The Public Relations Department also distributes numerous stories about the museums to the press. During a six-month period in 1959, for example, 1,079 different stories about the New York State Historical Association appeared in 283 newspapers in New York State. Most of these originated in the association's public relations office, although "129 came . . . gratuitously on the basis of our past reputation."

Despite the necessity of these excursions into mass communications, the association has carefully attempted to maintain clear boundaries between its offerings to the public and to the scholar. Dr. Jones notes that there has been no profound change in the character of *New York History* over the years.

About 1953 there came before the Trustees a plan to popularize the magazine, radically change the format, greatly increase the number of pictures, aim at a wider, less scholarly readership. Their response was unqualified rejection and they were wise in this. We have a primary responsibility to the scholars in the field which is best met in the way we are meeting it.

After the death of Dixon Ryan Fox in 1945 a fund of $10,000 was raised in his memory to support the publication of books about New York State. Conceived as a revolving fund, grants have been made to aid in the preparation and publication of worth-while historical books. A new edition of *The Golden Age of Homespun*, by Jared van

Wagenen Jr., issued by the Cornell University Press in 1953, quickly brought back the subsidy provided for it by the fund. Another useful product of the Fox Fellowship is *A Short History of New York State* by David M. Ellis, James A. Frost, Harold C. Syrett, and Henry J. Carman, published by Cornell in co-operation with the association in 1957.

In 1961 the New York State Historical Association had a membership in excess of 10,000, of which 2,100 were annual individual members paying $5 a year and 8,516 were junior members at $1.50. Membership dues, however, represented only 6% of an annual income of approximately $340,000, the second largest of any privately supported historical society in the United States. Fees paid for seminars account for another 4%, and admission fees to the Farmers' Museum and Fenimore House for 30%. The remaining 60% is derived from endowment and current gifts and grants. The personal generosity of the late Stephen C. Clark played a great role not only in the provision of buildings and collections for the New York State Historical Association, but in the support of its current operations, for his will included the bequest of an endowment fund of $2,000,000 to the association.[17]

Being in the country, with space to maneuver, the New York State Historical Association has had freedom to develop its museum far more extensively and satisfactorily than is possible in a city. Good exhibiting takes space.[18] Moreover, most organizations in cities that place emphasis on their museums are restricted by the nature of their buildings, which were generally designed at an earlier period for other uses. But the natural beauty of Cooperstown, which plays a part in attracting the annual thousands of visitors, is not readily equaled elsewhere, nor do other places of extraordinary beauty necessarily come equipped with generous and devoted benefactors

17. This bequest made permanent approximately the amount of income for current operations that he had been accustomed to provide during his lifetime.

18. It also takes men of uncommon skill, like Per E. Guldbeck, Research Associate, whose imaginative hand has guided the exhibits of the Farmers' Museum.

whose interests turn to the popularization of history. The preceding chapter offered, in the case of the Utah State Historical Society, a striking example of how much can be accomplished in a few years by well-directed public support. The experience of the New York Historical Association in the past two decades indicates that great transformations may still be achieved by generous private support. It does not necessarily follow, however, that the methods that have proved successful at Cooperstown are of universal application elsewhere, for they have developed largely in response to particular surroundings and personal support. Indeed so individual are its circumstances that very few of the recent developments of the New York State Historical Association have pertinence to the future activities of the older independent historical Societies.

LOUISIANA

A Historical Society of the State of Louisiana, organized at New Orleans on 15 January 1836, suspended activities after a few meetings, but was revived ten years later under the name of Louisiana Historical Society. The society went into a coma in 1851, was resuscitated in 1859, incorporated in 1860, and reincorporated in 1877. The Sala capitular of the Cabildo in New Orleans, in which took place the transfer of Louisiana from Spain to France on 30 November 1803 and the transfer from France to the United States on 20 December 1803, bears a tablet stating that it was dedicated to the perpetual use of the Louisiana Historical Society by the City Council of New Orleans on 30 June 1908. In 1917 the society began publication of the *Louisiana Historical Quarterly*, which was until recent years supported by a State appropriation of $7,500.

The late Edward Alexander Parsons, its perennial president, informed me in February 1960 that the Louisiana Historical Society had no endowment; that its membership fees were $5 per year; that a State appropriation of $10,000 per year for its support, as well as $7,500 for the *Quarterly*, had been discontinued; and that its library, which contained the best run of *Le Courrier de la Louisiane* and copies of records from the French archives, was housed with the library of the State Museum. With the discontinuance of State support, the *Louisiana Historical Quarterly*, of which Dr. Joseph G. Tregle Jr., now dean at Louisiana State University, New Orleans, was the last editor, ceased to appear.

A Louisiana Historical Association,[19] founded on 11 April 1889 by groups of veterans, was concerned entirely with Confederate matters,[20] although its announced purpose included the collection and preservation of material concerning the Louisiana territory at all periods. Two years later it had achieved a Memorial Hall at 929 Camp Street, New Orleans, built for it in the Romanesque style by its president, Frank T. Howard, adjoining the Howard Library on Lee Circle. In this hall, which was devoted to a museum of Confederate relics, the body of Jefferson Davis lay in state on 27 May 1893, when en route from a temporary tomb in Metairie Cemetery to Richmond. For twenty years the association flourished, for its museum, like Battle Abbey in Richmond, had rich meaning for war veterans. As their number diminished, the support of the association declined, for there were no younger members to carry on. For forty years it remained in a state of complacent inertia, until in 1956 Mr. Kenneth Trist Urquhart, an instructor in history at St. Mary's Dominican College took the presidency with a laudable ambition to bring it back to life.

In the spring of 1958 a group of professional historians from most of Louisiana's universities and colleges, and other interested persons, feeling that no existing group was serving the functions of an active state-wide historical society, met in Pineville at Louisiana College,

19. Kenneth Trist Urquhart, "Seventy Years of the Louisiana Historical Association," *Louisiana History* I (1960), 5–23.

20. Membership was open to "white persons of good moral character, who were in the service of the Southern Confederacy, and of their white descendants of good moral character, and also of white persons of good moral character who were not in such service, but who have been citizens of Louisiana for more than five years previous to their application for membership." This alone would make clear that the name "historical association" was chosen without any thought of suggesting kinship with the American Historical Association.

at the call of Professor Edwin A. Davis, head of the History Department of Louisiana State University, to organize such a body. To this meeting, which represented the typical method of founding a professionally-oriented historical association, Mr. Urquhart made a proposal. The existing Louisiana Historical Association, to which he was applying artificial respiration, had, in addition to a charter, a building, and a bank account of $10,000, a name that appropriately represented the purposes of the proposed new body. He suggested that the group assembled at Pineville join the 1889 association, reorganize it, and convert it into an active historical society for the entire State.

This plan met with approval. On 6 June 1958, at a meeting in Memorial Hall, a revised charter of the Louisiana Historical Association was adopted; Professor Davis was elected president, Mr. Urquhart vice-president, and Mr. John C. L. Andreassen, director of the State Archives and Records Commission, became secretary and treasurer. The following month a pamphlet entitled *An Invitation to Join the Louisiana Historical Association*[21] was widely distributed to obtain members. By the end of 1959, 400 had joined; in September 1960 the number had risen to 678. Thus a historical association, strongly supported by professional groups, had begun to make its way in Louisiana.

To tide over the period of reorganization, Mr. Andreassen issued a monthly mimeographed *News Letter*, containing much information about current historical activities and publications within and beyond the boundaries of Louisiana. In January 1960 the first number of *Louisiana History*, a ninety-six-page illustrated quarterly, edited by Professor Davis, was published. The association promptly launched this scholarly journal, in co-operation with Louisiana State University, from its own limited funds, with the hope of obtaining a legislative appropriation that would assure its permanence. The summary dismissal of Mr. Andreassen from the directorship of the State Archives and Records Commission in the late summer of 1960 and his

21. This pamphlet contains details on the transformation of the association.

replacement by a successor of political rather than archival qualifications deprived the new association of one of its mainstays. What future it will have remains to be seen.[22]

22. I have had no direct news of the association since the autumn of 1960. The subsequent death of Mr. Parsons, whose long-continued presidency of the Louisiana Historical Society was one of the contributing causes for the establishment of the association, eliminates one reason for the maintenance of two organizations in the State.

Chapter XV

LOCAL HISTORICAL SOCIETIES

Great fleas have little fleas upon their backs to bite 'em,
And little fleas have lesser fleas, and so *ad infinitum*.
And the great fleas themselves, in turn, have greater fleas to go on;
While those again have greater still, and greater still, and so on.
—AUGUSTUS DE MORGAN, 1872

THE principle of voluntary association for the common good that inspired the Reverend Jeremy Belknap and his friends in 1791 has led to the organization of more local historical societies than can accurately be counted. Sometimes they were due to the friendly association, through drink and talk, of professional men with an amateur interest in history similar to Dr. Belknap's circle; in other instances teachers of history, librarians, and archivists have provided the impetus. Frequently, in New England at least, a single determined lady, who might pull poison ivy from colonial gravestones with her own hands until the selectmen were shamed into taking better care of the town cemetery, would badger her neighbors into the preservation of a local building and thus initiate both a society and a collection. Although in recent years certain of the larger publicly supported State historical societies, of which Minnesota is the most conspicuous example, have systematically inspired the organization of county counterparts which receive some assistance from taxes, the greater part of local historical societies owe their origin to the interest and devotion of people on the spot who genuinely care for the characteristics of their region.

349

In the first half of the nineteenth century, even though State historical societies often had difficult sledding, numerous local groups were founded. Leslie W. Dunlap, in his listing of the sixty-five societies established before 1860, reports nine in Ohio, seven each in Massachusetts and New York, three each in Illinois, Indiana, Pennsylvania, and Vermont, two each in Connecticut, Iowa, Rhode Island, and Virginia. The 1961 edition of the American Association for State and Local History *Directory of Historical Societies and Agencies* lists some two thousand! One should not conclude from these figures that historical societies have multiplied thirtyfold in the past century, for the *Directory* includes a considerable number of institutions like the National Archives, the Smithsonian Institution, the Winterthur Museum, the Boston Athenæum, and the Civil War Centennial Commission that, while concerned with American history in one way or another, could not by any possible stretch of the imagination be considered as historical societies. These brief listings indicate whether an organization has a museum, a library, manuscripts, archives, newspaper collections, or issues publications; they do not attempt, wisely, to give any suggestion of the extent of its resources. Of the 2,000 organizations listed, only a little over one third report their ownership of libraries.[1] As any extensive research and publication activity by a society normally, although not invariably, presupposes its possession of a library,[2] it is apparent that these functions are less widespread than the considerable number of organizations listed in the *Directory* might, at first glance, suggest.

Another approach is to examine the number of county and local historical societies throughout the United States that reported their

---

1. This differentiation was first pointed out by Mrs. Alice Palo Hook, librarian of the Historical and Philosophical Society of Ohio, in "The Historical Society Library," *Special Libraries* L (1959), 114–118.

2. The Colonial Society of Massachusetts, which from 1892 to 1955 had its only office in its editor's hat, has inspired considerable research and issued forty-one substantial volumes of *Publications*. The Cambridge Historical Society, described later in this chapter, has also, without premises or a library, produced thirty-seven volumes of *Publications*.

holdings to the National Historical Publications Commission *Guide to Archives and Manuscripts in the United States*. They number 209, of which thirty-seven were in New York State, thirty-six in Pennsylvania, thirty in Massachusetts, nineteen in Minnesota, twelve in Wisconsin, ten in New Jersey, nine in Connecticut, and six in Illinois. Two states had five societies represented; five states had four; one had three; three had two; eleven had one. Twenty states were without any local historical society reporting to the compilers of the *Guide*. Incidentally six of the thirty local Massachusetts societies that appeared in the *Guide* were not included in the 1961 edition of the American Association of State and Local History *Directory*. The most that one deduces with certainty from the perusal of these two publications is that there are today a few hundred State and local historical societies with resources useful for scholarly research in American history.

Unfortunately no general listing will ever give the full picture of the scattered documents that have found safe homes in unlikely places. Take, for example, the Massachusetts instance of the South Natick Historical, Natural History and Library Society—open, according to the *Directory*, on Wednesdays and Saturdays from 2:30 to 5:00—whose holdings are thus described in the *Guide*:

A few pieces dated from 1652, relating chiefly to the village and its vicinity. Included are photostatic copies of letters of John Eliot (Mass.; Congregational clergyman, missionary to the Indians, translator, author), 1652–57; and scattered letters of several persons of national importance.

The last clause, although strictly in accordance with the rules of the *Guide* limiting the naming of individuals to instances when the quantity of their papers amounts to more than fifty items, is a masterly understatement, according to Dr. Ralph L. Ketcham, who furnished me with this account of a visit that he paid there:

Miss Mabel A. Parmenter, the curator of the South Natick (Massachusetts) Historical, Natural History and Library Society, informed us, in response to a general inquiry, that the Society had a Madison letter. When I went to the Society (open on Wednesday and Saturday afternoons), Miss Parmenter conducted me to the basement where she said the Madison letter was inserted in a volume of Civil War newspapers "to keep it safe and flat." As I turned the pages of the volume, I found not one but two Madison letters, two Jefferson, two John Adams and three or four John Quincy Adams letters, all of which I copied and sent to the appropriate editors. Where the Society got the letters or how long they had been there I do not know; but they were preserved and made available to scholarly use.

Visits like Dr. Ketcham's to South Natick are a delightful and profitable way of passing the time. Whenever, over the past twenty-five years, I have spoken to a country historical society in New England, I have invariably met pleasant people, enjoyed the sound of their voices, and learned something useful. I wish that in the course of this study I had had the time to visit more of the small local societies in other parts of the country. Had I done so, my travels would have consumed two years rather than one, without commensurate advantage, for research and publications activities, which were my chief concern, thrive more readily in State than in local societies. Moreover, the American Association for State and Local History announced in May 1960 its intention of conducting a nationwide survey that would involve personal visits to "a select sampling of the smaller local groups" and the mailing of a questionnaire to "all of the 1,900 or so local societies." As this book goes to press the results of that study have not yet been published. The present chapter is therefore confined to the consideration of thirteen county and local historical societies in various states with which I have some personal acquaintance, chosen partly to illustrate instances of the combination of regional piety with research and publication interests of broader significance, but chiefly to indicate their diversity.

Among county historical societies in the United States, the Essex Institute in Salem, Massachusetts, unquestionably takes first place for the extent and richness of its library and manuscripts and its century-long record of continuous scholarly publication. Although its field is Essex County, many of its possessions, particularly in manuscripts[3] and unique broadsides, are of national significance, while its collections, endowment, and publications considerably surpass those of

3. *A Guide to Archives and Manuscripts in the United States*, pp. 275–276.

many State historical societies. Its field is rich and varied, for the settlement of Essex County goes back to the 1620s. By the end of the seventeenth century the majority of its present-day towns were recognizable communities. Its maritime accomplishments, particularly in the half century following the close of the American Revolution, were remarkable. Its industrial development, although substantial, and at times prosperous, never completely altered the face of the county, which still retains some surprisingly rural aspects. Although several Essex County tribes, like Cabots, Lowells, Jacksons, Higginsons, Peabodys, and Gardners, migrated to Boston to fill the shoes of Loyalists who had decamped during the Revolution, the North Shore and the inland towns of Hamilton and Wenham became in more recent times a favorite choice for the country houses not only of Bostonians but of winter residents of more distant cities. Thus, while descendants of Essex County men are found all through the west, the county has never become depopulated in the manner of many areas in northern New England.

The richness of the Essex Institute's historical sources is due not only to the variety of history that the county affords, but to the acquisitiveness that has long charcterized persons living within striking distance of Boston. L. H. Butterfield began an address before the 1960 annual meeting of the Society of American Archivists[4] with a pertinent observation:

The two-legged pack rat has been a common species in Boston and its neighborhood since the seventeenth century. Thanks to his activity the archival and manuscript resources concentrated in the Boston area, if we extend it slightly north to include Salem and slightly west to include Worcester, are so rich and diverse as to be *almost* beyond the dreams of avarice. Not quite, of course, because Boston institutions and the super-pack rats who direct them are still eager to add to their resources of this kind, and constantly do.

The Essex Institute was organized in 1848 through the amalgamation of the Essex Historical Society of 1821 and the Essex County Natural History Society of 1833. As the Reverend William Bentley

4. *The American Archivist* XXIV (1961), 141–159.

(1759–1819), one of the most diligent Salem pack rats, died before any of these organizations were founded, his papers found their way to the American Antiquarian Society in Worcester. But Dr. Edward Augustus Holyoke, a medical version of the species, although born in 1728 lived until 1829 and so became the first president of the Essex Historical Society. Consequently his accumulations remained in Salem, as did those of Dr. Henry Wheatland (1812–93), founder of the Essex County Natural History Society and long secretary of the Essex Institute. The race survived into the present century in the persons of such officers of the institute as George Francis Dow, Lawrence Waters Jenkins, and the brothers Stephen Willard and James Duncan Phillips.

The Essex Institute is a historical society with open membership. Although it has no formal connection with its near neighbor, the Peabody Museum of Salem (established in 1799 by the Salem East India Marine Society), the two institutions long ago hit upon a reasonable division of labor and fields, with resulting mutual exchanges of material. The Peabody Museum, which is managed by a self-perpetuating board of nine trustees, concerns itself with maritime history, with the ethnology of the Pacific and the Far East, and with the natural history of Essex County; the Essex Institute concentrates upon the architecture, decorative arts, and the history—political, social, literary, and family—of the county. Or, as it was explained to Dean A. Fales Jr. when he came from Winterthur in 1959 to become director of the Essex Institute, the collections of the Peabody Museum consist of "boats, birds, botany, and Buddhas, while the Institute has everything else."[5]

The library and museum of the Essex Institute, located on Essex Street, Salem, are housed in an amalgamation of Plummer Hall,

5. This is the definition of Miss Huldah M. Smith, curator of the institute's museum, quoted in Essex Institute, *Annual Report 1959–60* (Salem, 1960), p. 8. The only point subject to clarification concerns books and manuscripts in maritime history. Down to the mid-thirties, although all ship pictures, models, and objects relating to the sea were concentrated in the Peabody Museum, library and archival material in that field was housed at the institute because it had a fireproof bookstack and a library staff.

built in 1857 for institutional uses, and of a vast brick dwelling house, built in 1851 for the merchant Tucker Daland. To these were added in 1906 a fireproof bookstack. The grounds of the institute have gradually been expanded to include the contiguous Pingree House,[6] built by Samuel McIntire in 1804 for Captain John Gardner, and the slightly later and even larger Andrew-Safford House, facing Washington Square. Into this enclave have been moved the John Ward House, dating in part from the late seventeenth century, the Crowninshield-Bentley House of 1727, and a variety of architectural fragments salvaged from destroyed buildings. All are open to visitors, save the Andrew-Safford House in which the director lives. The institute also owns and exhibits the Peirce-Nichols House,[7] built by McIntire in 1782, which is on its original site at 80 Federal Street in another part of the city. It should be noted that the Pingree and Peirce-Nichols Houses are included in Ralph E. Carpenter's *The Fifty Best Historic American Houses Colonial and Federal Now Furnished and Open to the Public*,[8] published in 1955, and that the Crowinshield-Bentley House, whose restoration was completed in 1960, is of comparable quality.

Although the 1906 bookstack accommodates 300,000 volumes, it has long since bulged at the seams, for manuscripts and books arrive at the Essex Institute faster than they can be comfortably assimilated, and until very recently nothing was ever disposed of. With very limited funds—twenty-five years ago the total annual expenses were under $20,000—the institute has always been shorthanded. Nevertheless, Miss Harriet Silvester Tapley, a staff member since 1902,

---

As that stack became crowded and that staff inundated, the Peabody Museum began to retain under its own roof maritime books and manuscripts, rather than sending them across the street. The addition of a reading room and a three-story bookstack to the Peabody Museum in 1960 would suggest the logic of concentrating the research material in maritime history there in close proximity to the objects. The Peabody Museum of Salem will be described in the next chapter.

6. Fiske Kimball, *Mr. Samuel McIntire, Carver, The Architect of Salem* (Salem, 1940), p. 107.

7. *Ibid.*, pp. 58–59.

8. (New York, 1955), pp. 40–41, 44–45.

who, in addition to running the library, edited the quarterly *Historical Collections* from 1920 until 1955, knew what she had, made scholars feel at home, spurred on Harvard graduate students who found their way to Salem, and did a remarkable amount of scholarly work herself. Her 512-page *Salem Imprints 1768–1825, A History of the First Fifty Years of Printing in Salem, Massachusetts With Some Account of the Bookshops, Booksellers, Bookbinders and the Private Libraries* does great credit to her and to the institute, which published it in 1927.

The *Essex Institute Historical Collections*, published quarterly since April 1859, are a mine of well-indexed monographs and documents on all phases of Essex County history. On Miss Tapley's retirement, Dr. Benjamin W. Labaree of the Harvard history department became managing editor, with a distinguished board of editors from neighboring institutions consisting of Robert G. Albion, Lyman H. Butterfield, Douglas S. Byers, Abbott L. Cummings, Kenneth B. Murdock, Mrs. Lovell Thompson, and Philip S. Weld.[9] With the January 1956 issue the *Historical Collections* appeared in a new format designed by Rudolph Ruzicka. These changes are indicative of an awareness, which was first shown during the directorship of Dr. Walter M. Merrill (1955–59), that the institute must appeal not only to Salem but to a wider audience. When Dr. Labaree's duties as senior tutor of Winthrop House at Harvard made it impossible for him to continue as managing editor of the *Historical Collections*, Mr. Fales, the present director, assumed that additional responsibility.

The volume and quality of documentary publication achieved during the first half of the twentieth century by George Francis Dow[10] and by Miss Tapley is stupendous. The four volumes of *The*

9. The place of Mr. Weld, who is at present living in France, is now filled by Professor Norman Holmes Pearson of Yale University.

10. Secretary of the Essex Institute, 1898–1918, and director of the Museum and editor of the Society for the Preservation of New England Antiquities from 1919 until his death in 1936, George Francis Dow was a self-made scholar of extraordinary energy and imagination, who was responsible for the restoration and preservation of many historic houses as well as the publication of an amazing number of documents.

Diary of William Bentley, D.D.—one of the most fascinating personal records of the young republic—issued between 1905 and 1914, the eight volumes of the records of the Quarterly Courts of Essex County, 1636–83, the three volumes of Essex probate records, 1635–81, the seventy volumes of vital records of Massachusetts towns, the ship registers of Salem and Beverly, Gloucester, and Newburyport, are, with the *Historical Collections,* the most conspicuous products, but a recent twenty-four-page catalogue offers an extraordinary variety of studies in local biography, history, and genealogy that are still available at reasonable prices. Alas, the stock of Fiske Kimball's *Mr. Samuel McIntire, Carver, The Architect of Salem,* printed by the Anthoensen Press in 1940 and the handsomest book the institute ever did, has been long since exhausted.

The museum of the Essex Institute, which contains fine furniture, portraits, and examples of the decorative arts in great quantity, has long suffered from overcrowding. Early in the century George Francis Dow arranged in three alcoves of the museum hall a Salem kitchen of 1750 and a bedroom and parlor of 1800, thus anticipating considerably the exhibition techniques that were later to flower in the American Wing of the Metropolitan Museum and to reach their height at Winterthur. But as more objects arrived, more cases were stuffed into every available vacant space. The high (or perhaps the low) point was reached with the exhibition of costumes in double-decker cases whose upper sections could only be seen from the gallery. These have now been removed.

Although by the 1930s the museum galleries were checkmated, the Peirce-Nichols House and the Pingree House—two of McIntire's handsomest buildings—were, with the aid of Mrs. Francis B. Crowninshield and other friends, beautifully furnished. Indeed until

---

He initiated new techniques of museum display and created the Pioneer Village at Salem—an outdoor reconstruction of seventeenth-century houses—in connection with the Massachusetts Bay Tercentenary. A good deal of a promoter, he sometimes mixed history and personal profit, as in the publications of the seemingly disinterested Marine Research Society, which he organized in 1922, and which was in fact a shrewd commercial operation.

very recent times the institute's chief interest has been the embellishment of these fine houses, to the relative neglect of the museum galleries and the library, which, in the opinion of at least some of the officers, were at once sacrosanct and "untouchable." The preservation and exhibition of these houses was a highly useful service to a city whose amenities were slowly but inexorably deteriorating. They unquestionably brought new friends to the institute, but the emphasis upon them tended to make the great needs of the library secondary.

The Essex Institute's most distinguished recent accomplishment sprang from an emergency in historic preservation. In 1959 the house at 106 Essex Street, built about 1727 by John Crowninshield, in which the diarist Dr. Bentley boarded from 1791 until his death in 1819, was about to be demolished to create a parking lot. Through the energetic efforts of Frederick J. Bradlee of Boston, over $42,000 was raised to move the house to a corner of the Essex Institute grounds at 126 Essex Street and to restore and furnish it as a memorial to Mrs. Francis B. Crowninshield (1877–1958), who had been so generous a friend of the Peirce-Nichols and Pingree Houses. This major effort is described and illustrated in the April 1961 issue of the *Historical Collections.*

While these houses remain the show pieces of the Essex Institute, Mr. Fales and Miss Huldah M. Smith, the curator, are bringing order into the museum collections, and it is hoped that before long there may be additional hands to help cope with the library. The chief problems of the Essex Institute are a fondness of Salem residents for the established order, be it good or bad; the rich accumulations of past collectors; and shortage of money to enlarge the staff to a size commensurate with the work to be done. On 31 March 1962 the endowment funds, carried at a book value of $1,044,622.37, had a market value of $1,842,922.50. The income for the fiscal year ending on that day was $81,620.60, of which $64,384.05 was the income from endowment and $7,030 the receipts from membership dues. The year's operating expenses were $69,350.36. This represents a substantial improvement over the past twenty-five years, but there is still a long way to go. There is also a firm foundation to build upon once the plan is set and the remaining debris cleared away.

Essex is not a large county. It contains 355,840 acres. After deducting tidal marsh, ponds, rivers, and swamps, it has only 299,551 acres useful for tillage, woodlands, and the sites of its thirty-four cities and towns,[11] yet it has a preoccupation with history that is out of all proportion to its size. In addition to the Essex Institute, twenty-three Essex County cities and towns have local historical societies that are currently members of the Bay State Historical League. These are Andover, Beverly, Boxford, Danvers, Essex, Gloucester (Cape Ann Scientific, Literary and Historical Association), Haverhill, Newburyport (Historical Society of Old Newbury), Ipswich, Lynn, Lynnfield, Manchester, Marblehead, Middleton, North Andover, Peabody, Rockport (Sandy Bay Historical Society and Museum, Inc.), Rowley, Saugus, Swampscott, Topsfield, Wenham, and West Newbury. The Essex Institute informs me that there are historical societies in Amesbury and Newbury that are not members of the Bay State Historical League, and one in course of formation in Georgetown. Thus Essex County has a historical society for every 11,095 acres of land! Only seven towns out of thirty-four are without one.[12] In addition, the First Ironworks Association in Saugus—distinct from the Saugus Historical Society—operates a major reconstruction of the seventeenth-century ironworks,[13] the Society for the Preserva-

11. Walter Muir Whitehill, "The Topography of Essex County in 1859," *Essex Institute Historical Collections* xcv (1959), 69–81.

12. Methuen, one of the seven, once had a society whose publications around the turn of the century were listed in Appleton P. C. Griffin, "Bibliography of American Historical Societies," *Annual Report of the American Historical Association for the Year 1905* (Washington, 1907), II, 441–442. Griffin also listed (p. 382) publications of an Amesbury Historical Society or Amesbury Improvement Historical Association that does not seem to exist today. The Whittier Home Association, which maintains John Greenleaf Whittier's home in Amesbury, seemingly considers itself the historical society of the town. In Newbury there is a Sons and Daughters of First Settlers of Newbury. Neither it nor the Whittier Home Association belongs to the Bay State Historical League.

13. E. N. Hartley, *Iron works on the Saugus* (Norman, 1957).

tion of New England Antiquities maintains three historic houses each in Ipswich and Newbury, two in Danvers, one each in Gloucester, Rowley, and Saugus, and the Rocky Hill Meeting House of 1785 in Amesbury, while the birthplace of John Greenleaf Whittier in Haverhill and his home in Amesbury are exhibited by separate charitable corporations organized for that express purpose. Indeed the multiplicity of historical organizations within this small area is reminiscent of Augustus De Morgan's inelegant jingle: "And little fleas have lesser fleas, and so *ad infinitum*" quoted at the head of this chapter.

The collective property of the twenty-three local historical societies of Essex County is impressive. The Ipswich Historical Society's John Whipple House of 1640 and the Jeremiah Lee Mansion of 1768, owned by the Marblehead Historical Society since 1909, are two of Ralph Carpenter's "fifty best historic American houses"; indeed eight of his fifty are in this single county, and all but one of these eight have been preserved through voluntary private association.[14] Other houses, too numerous to mention in passing, owe their preservation and continued maintenance to the local societies, many of which have developed around a landmark that might otherwise have disappeared. Most of the societies have museums, which range from the orderly and instructive to the "grandma's attic" variety. Some have libraries and issue publications, although only a few maintain their sources for research in an orderly manner or are open at hours that would permit a visiting scholar to drop in without prearrangement. Very few employ professionally trained persons full time. Some benefit from the assistance of professionally competent residents of the town who give their services in leisure moments.

14. In addition to these two, and the Essex Institute's pair, he chooses the King Hooper Mansion of 1728, owned by the Marblehead Art Association; the House of Seven Gables in Salem, preserved since 1910 by the House of Seven Gables Settlement Association; the Old Iron Master's House of 1640 at Saugus; and the Richard Derby House (1761–62), which forms part of the Salem Maritime National Historic Site, administered by the National Park Service.

Many have resident curators or caretakers who, although lacking a broad acquaintance with history, have acquired, through long familiarity with the region, a knowledge of the local scene that could not be found in books.

These societies are intensely local; Andover and North Andover, parts of the same town until 1855, each have their own. They are on good terms, however, and occasionally share an officer. Nine societies were founded in the last quarter of the nineteenth century; the rest are twentieth-century creations that have, almost without exception, developed within the community. The considerable services of George Francis Dow to the Topsfield Historical Society and of Miss Harriet S. Tapley to the Danvers Historical Society were rendered by them as residents of those towns, rather than as officers of the Essex Institute. Summer residents and those who work in Boston but sleep in Essex County are tolerated more readily in some societies than others. When Mrs. Francis B. Crowninshield first suggested restoring and refurnishing the Lee Mansion (at her expense), the Marblehead Historical Society was not sure about wanting "summer people" mixing in their affairs. Crowninshields had, after all, only *summered* at Peach's Point for three quarters of a century, and Marblehead is a deeply conservative place where, until modern times, boys might throw rocks at any Salemite, or other stranger, who appeared in its streets. In the end, Mrs. Crowninshield's tact surmounted even the New England aversion to "rusticators."

Most towns have had, and many still have, one or more persons who are walking repositories of local information and mainstays of the local historical society. Such a man was the late Amos Everett Jewett, once the express agent and later the antiquarian bookseller of Rowley. This town, settled in 1639, remains one of the least spoiled rural areas in the county. Its population in 1860 was less than it had been in 1790; it has not succumbed to an industrial boom, and it is mercifully too far from Boston to have been tarred with the brush of suburbia. The Rowley Historical Society, organized in 1918, purchased and restored the Platts-Bradstreet House, begun in the seventeenth century and enlarged in the eighteenth. If, during a meeting in the house, some captious member inquired about an unlabeled cornet that he had seen upstairs, "Deacon" Jewett would rise and provide a full account of who had played the instrument, when, and in what band. In 1948 he and his wife published for the Jewett Family Association a well-documented and praiseworthy town history: *Rowley, Massachusetts, "Mr Ezechi Rogers Plantation" 1639–1850*.[15] In the same year he wrote two of the three articles in *Publications of the Rowley Historical Society No. 3* and, anonymously, paid the entire printing bill. The treasurer's report for 1948 indicated receipts of $369—dues $202, rummage sale $110.13, admissions to Platts-Bradstreet House $10, gift $8—and expenses of $236.32, with assets in the bank of $1,574.20. This is a characteristic example of a local society that, with purely local support and interest and with no concern with either the tourist trade or the academic world, has accomplished a great deal with limited resources in preserving a segment of local history.

Wenham was known far outside New England for the ice from its lake that Frederic Tudor of Boston began to ship to the West Indies early in the nineteenth century. By 1833 he had developed the technique to a point that permitted the extension of his operations to Calcutta, thus accounting for the adjutant bird in Kipling's *Second Jungle Book* who swallowed "a seven pound lump of Wenham Lake ice, off an American ice ship," thrown at him from a boat in the Ganges. Wenham, like Rowley, is still a remarkably beautiful rural community, but nearer Boston, and with large country houses interpersed among the original farms. For the first half of the present century Mrs. Edward B. Cole (1865–1959) had a decisive hand in almost everything that concerned the town, including its history. From 1896 she was a mainstay of the Wenham Village Improvement Society, and in 1921 she persuaded that body to buy the

15. I am proud to have had a hand in persuading "Deacon" Jewett to write his "The Tidal Marshes of Rowley and Vicinity with an Account of the Old-Time Methods of 'Marshing'," *Essex Institute Historical Collections* LXXXV (1949), 272–291.

Claflin-Richards House, whose construction had been begun in 1664 by Robert Macklauflin. A historical committee of the society not only restored and furnished the house, but transcribed and printed the town records from 1643 onward. Mrs. Cole's *Notes on Wenham History* appeared in 1943, and in 1951, aged eighty-six, she published *Notes on the Collection of Dolls and Figurines in the Wenham Museum*, a collection for which she was herself largely responsible. In the winter of 1951–52, coincident with the building of a museum, designed by Nelson W. Aldrich, adjoining the Claflin-Richards House, the Wenham Historical Association and Museum, Inc., was incorporated as a separate organization.

The expenses for operating the Wenham Historical Association and Museum in 1960 were $14,552.56. The parent Village Improvement Society, which operates the Wenham Tea Room and Exchange, continues to provide some $6,000 a year toward the support of the historical association. Nearly another $6,000 was earned by a concert, an auction, rummage sales, and other community enterprises. Dues produced $907. The operation of the museum depends almost entirely upon current gifts and activities, for endowment funds total less than $10,000.

The museum, a skillful and unobtrusive piece of contemporary design built around a central court, provides both permanent lodging for the doll collection and space for rotating exhibitions. It is open regularly five afternoons a week. Beyond it is Burnham Hall, used not only by both societies but for all kinds of community purposes, including wedding receptions and private parties. The Massachusetts Society for Promoting Agriculture, founded in 1792, whose secretary, James R. Reynolds, assistant to the president of Harvard University, has a farm in the town, has added a wing to the museum to accommodate their library and records.[16] This also provides library space for the historical association. A nineteenth-century cobbler's shop

16. *Massachusetts Society for Promoting Agriculture 1792–1961* (Wenham, 1961), reprinted from *Food Marketing in New England* [First National Stores], spring 1961 issue.

has been moved into the yard. It is hoped that eventually a building may be added to house the now-stored collections of farming and ice-cutting tools.

During her long lifetime Mrs. Cole had a strong personal influence upon everything that the organization did. Although the museum has employed a full-time director in recent years, the custom, on which she insisted, of active hard work by members of the board has continued. Mrs. Edward H. Osgood, who succeeded her as president, and her fellow trustees take a far more energetic part in the week-to-week operation of the museum than is usual elsewhere, for it has become quite as much a community centre as a historical society. Consequently loan exhibitions may include collections of Oriental art or other fields entirely unrelated to local history that happen to be of interest to Wenham residents. While the museum caters primarily to the local community, the doll collection attracts a considerable number of antique collectors from a distance.

Most of the Essex County local historical societies are more concerned with the remote than with the immediate past, with the attractive or decorative aspects of history rather than its economic and technological manifestations. The North Andover Historical Society is a conspicuous exception to this rule.[17] The town has a Jekyll-Hyde character. At one end, where it adjoins Middleton and Boxford, it presents the aspect of a farming community. At the other, an industrial area merges imperceptibly with South Lawrence. Between these two opposites lies North Andover Centre, whose common, until recently shaded by great elms, retains the aspect of a village green. For a century and a half the chief industry has been the manufacture of woolen textiles, begun in 1813 by Nathaniel Stevens and continued by M. T. Stevens and Company, although recently a Western Electric plant has been built in the northern part of the town.

The Stevens family, fond of the town's past, have done much to

17. Another is the Waltham Historical Society, which in 1957 published Edmund L. Sanderson, *Waltham Industries. A Collection of Sketches of Early Firms and Founders,* a useful and informative book that is admirably printed and illustrated.

preserve its traditional amenities and to prevent the thoughtless vulgarization that often occurs in an industrial community. Thus the late Mr. and Mrs. Samuel Dale Stevens in 1913 founded the North Andover Historical Society, to which they gave some fine examples of local seventeenth- and eighteenth-century furniture and decorative arts which they had personally collected. Soon after its organization, the society obtained possession of a white wooden cottage facing the common at North Andover Centre. After two decades the cottage barn was replaced by a brick museum building.

In 1950 the society bought the house in Osgood Street long believed to be the home of the poetess Anne Bradstreet, and thought to have been built soon after 1666. In preparation for its restoration, Abbott Lowell Cummings made in 1956 an intensive study of the building and of its deeds. This led him to the conclusion that the tradition was quite wrong; that the building had instead been built about 1715, more than a quarter of a century after Anne Bradstreet's death, by the Reverend Thomas Barnard (1658–1718), minister of the north parish of Andover. Although this investigation destroyed a cherished literary association, memorialized widely, the house was as good an architectural monument as ever; indeed, a better one, for something precise was known about its history. The North Andover Historical Society promptly accepted Mr. Cummings's conclusions, renamed the building the Parson Barnard House, and proceeded with a thorough and conscientious restoration and refurnishing of it for exhibition.[18] The society also in the late 1950s took custody of two landmarks adjacent to the common: the white wooden hay scales, built in 1818 and subsequently maintained by the Proprietors of the Hay Scales in Andover North Parish,[19] and the brick general store, constructed in 1828 by the Brick Store Company in Andover North Parish.

18. Abbott Lowell Cummings, "The Parson Barnard House," *Old-Time New England* XLVII (1956–57), 28–40; Horatio Rogers, M.D., *Early Owners of the Parson Barnard House and Their Times* (North Andover, 1958).

19. Walter Muir Whitehill, "The North Andover Hay Scales," *Old-Time New England* XXXIX (1948–49), 34–37.

Although most of the visible activities of the society for its first forty-five years had been concerned with the remote past, with architecture and the decorative arts, its founder Samuel D. Stevens had assembled an extensive collection of early spinning wheels, looms, and other artifacts relating to the woolen textile industry. These, although given to the society, had for many years been stored for want of suitable exhibition space. Since 1813 when Nathaniel Stevens had embarked on the manufacture of woolen goods, the textile industry had been a decisive element in the economy of the town, as well as the mainstay of neighboring industrial cities along the Merrimack River. It therefore seemed reasonable that the society should concentrate its efforts upon this aspect of local history rather than diffusing them upon others which were repetitively dealt with in many other places.

Through the energetic efforts of Mrs. Horatio Rogers, president of the North Andover Historical Society and a daughter of its founder, the Merrimack Valley Textile Museum, Inc., was incorporated in 1960. Its purposes went far beyond exhibiting the stored artifacts relating to the handicraft period, for they included assembling material that would illustrate the wool industry in America after the impact of the Industrial Revolution, and developing a library and archives that would become a centre of scholarly research in the history of the wool industry. Through generous gifts from the Nathaniel and Elizabeth P. Stevens Foundation, the Quaker Hill Foundation, and from friends connected with the textile industry, totaling close to half a million dollars, the construction of a spacious building costing $300,000 was begun in September 1960 on land adjacent to the historical society. This will provide adequate space for the exhibition and storage of objects, and well-designed quarters for the research library and archives. The trustees of the museum include not only certain officers of the North Andover Historical Society, but Professor Ralph W. Hidy of the Graduate School of Business Administration, Harvard University. Among its constant advisers is Mr. Robert W. Lovett, head of the manuscript division and archives of the Baker Library. The planning of this new institution is therefore proceeding in harmony and co-operation with the principal centre of research in business history in New England. Mr. Bruce Sinclair, a former Hagley-Eleutherian Mills Fellow at the University of Delaware who became director of the North Andover Historical Society in 1959, has been appointed director of the museum. In July 1961 Mr. Rex D. Parady, formerly of the Chapin Library, Williams College, joined the museum staff as librarian. Although the building was completed in the summer of 1961, it is still not open to visitors, for efforts are being concentrated on archival work and the planning of exhibitions that will show the development of techniques from antiquity through the homespun methods to the dramatic changes introduced by power machinery.

In 1960 the North Andover Historical Society, through a committee headed by Mr. S. Forbes Rockwell Jr., and the Andover Historical Society, through the late Henry Stevenson, microfilmed many thousands of pages of the principal town and parish records of Andover. Xerox enlargements have been made of certain of the more important volumes, and positive microfilms are available for consultation at the North Andover Historical Society and the Andover Public Library. This enterprise brings together for ready reference a sizable body of documents, beginning in the seventeenth century, that have hitherto been divided between the vaults of two town clerks and other inaccessible places. In 1959 the two societies joined in publishing Claude M. Fuess's *Andover: Symbol of New England, The Evolution of a Town*, a popular narrative projected in 1946 in connection with the Andover tercentenary, but only completed some thirteen years later. Exclusive of the cost of printing this book and of sums devoted to the textile museum, the operating expenses of the North Andover Historical Society for the year ending 30 August 1960 were in the vicinity of $17,000. The society has 247 members, paying annual dues of $3, and endowment funds (in addition to those of the museum) of $164,103.

The present activities of the society fully represent the dual nature of the town. On the one hand it preserves for local interest aspects of a typical New England farming town; on the other it is pioneering, with professional competence, in an area of industrial and technological history that extends well beyond the town boundaries. In this last respect it differs from its neighbors, but it strongly resembles the other local historical societies of Essex County in being completely the product of local initiative and private support.

There is no set formula for the privately supported local historical society. Everything depends upon the combination of historical material, people, and financial resources that happen to be present in a given area. The three local societies just described are not presented as typical, but as examples of the different ways in which intelligent and devoted individuals have inspired the preservation of the historical record of three Essex County towns. And I have chosen Essex County as a microcosm not because it is either typical or better than other parts of New England, but solely because I happen to have known it rather intimately for a quarter of a century and watched its historical societies develop long before this study was even thought of. There are dozens of local historical societies in New England, particularly in Massachusetts and Connecticut, whose activities would repay consideration, if space and time permitted. Once one leaves New England the county, rather than the town, becomes the more normal unit of measurement, but wherever one goes, and whatever the unit, an independent historical society usually represents the work of some inspired person or persons whose motives would have gladdened the heart of Jeremy Belknap, John Pintard, or Isaiah Thomas.

The Connecticut valley frontier town of Deerfield, Massachusetts, has benefited by a remarkable combination of such people, male and female, during the past hundred years. George Sheldon, born in 1818 in the Deerfield house that had been the home of his family since 1708, became in his early fifties seized with a desire to perpetuate the memory of those who had suffered in the Indian attack of 29 February 1704 that was the bloodiest and most spectacular event in the early history of the town. Until the age of thirty-five he had stayed on his family farm.[20] After five years in a cotton factory down the valley, he sensibly returned home; during the second half of his long life he devoted his efforts to preserving the record of the history of Deerfield. In May 1870 he procured a charter for the Pocumtuck Valley Memorial Association, organized

for the purpose of collecting and preserving such memorials, books, records, papers and curiosities as may tend to illustrate and perpetuate the history of the early settlers of this region, and of the race which vanished before them.

The association met annually in Deerfield and held field meetings at various historic sites in the Connecticut valley. Within a decade, to house its growing collections, it took over the three-story 1799 brick building, formerly occupied by Deerfield Academy. Memorial Hall, as it was renamed, was dedicated on 8 September 1880.

Having set out to establish a memorial, the farmer George Sheldon became a scholar in the process. While his most conspicuous work was his two-volume *History of Deerfield*—924 pages of history, 407 pages of genealogy—his hand was for forty-six years in everything that the Pocumtuck Valley Memorial Association collected, did, or published. In 1890 he instigated the printing of the 510-page first volume of *History and Proceedings of the Pocumtuck Valley Memorial Association*, covering the years 1870–79. Four similar volumes, each larger than its predecessor, carrying the record through 1911, appeared in his lifetime.[21] When in 1897, as a widower of seventy-eight, he married the forty-five-year-old Miss Jennie Maria Arms, a teacher at Mrs. Shaw's school in Boston, he acquired not only a devoted wife but an indefatigable coadjutor in his historical interests. For the time she had received exceptional training, having been an

20. His autobiographical paper "'Tis Sixty Years Since, The Passing of the Stall-Fed Ox and the Farm Boy," *History and Proceedings of the Pocumtuck Valley Memorial Association* III (1890–98), 472–490, is as fine a document on one phase of Connecticut valley farm life in the 1830s as could be found.

21. Seven clothbound volumes, ranging from 510 to 685 pages, appeared between 1890 and 1929. A briefer volume VIII, covering the years 1930–38, was published in 1950. Proceedings for 1939–42 appeared annually in paper wrappers as parts of volume IX. The association hopes soon to bring the *Proceedings* up to date.

early student at the Massachusetts Institute of Technology and the Boston Society of Natural History.[22] In 1912 Mrs. Sheldon became curator of the Pocumtuck Valley Memorial Association, a post that her husband had combined with the presidency since 1870.

Although Professor Albert Bushnell Hart in 1911 described George Sheldon as "the dean of historical scholars and the doge of the republic of Deerfield,"[23] that compliment did not cause its ninety-two-year-old subject, who was even more patriarchally bearded than Hart, to rest on his oars. Three years later he gave a spirited defense of Captain James Lawrence at the annual meeting of the association, of which he continued to be president until his death in 1916 in his ninety-ninth year. In the last year of his life he added to Memorial Hall a three-story brick wing, fifty feet by twenty-nine feet in size, which provided fireproof housing on the first floor for the best seventeenth- and eighteenth-century furniture, a library on the second floor, and a manuscript and map room on the third. After his death, his personal working library of historical books and manuscripts was added to the material that he had assembled for the association. Altogether Sheldons presided over the organization for sixty-eight years, for George was succeeded by his son John (1848–1929) and by his widow, who continued as president and curator until her death in 1938.

Another spunky schoolteacher of Deerfield origins, Miss C. Alice Baker (1833–1909) of Cambridge, was a valued ally of George Sheldon's in the early years of the association. Deeply interested in the Deerfield captives, she traced their later lives in Canada. In addition to contributing twenty-one papers to the *Proceedings*, she bought in 1890 the late seventeenth-century Frary House, the oldest extant building in Deerfield, put it in order, lived in it in the summers, and

22. The "Autobiographical Sketch of Jennie Maria Arms Sheldon," published posthumously in *History and Proceedings of the Pocumtuck Valley Memorial Association* VIII (1930–38), 148–158, is a charmingly modest account of an intelligent and spunky Connecticut valley bluestocking in the Boston of the last third of the nineteenth century.

23. *History and Proceedings* V (1905–11), 519.

bequeathed it to the association.[24] Her housewarming of 1892, with John Putnam, the colored fiddler of Greenfield, calling off square dances, was so long remembered that a villager once remarked to a stranger:

You don't know Miss Baker; never heard of her ball? Why they came from Boston and New York, Hartford, Springfield and the Adirondacks; they had hair-dressers and costumers and they danced the mignonette![25]

In 1939, after the death of friends to whom Miss Baker left life interests, the Pocumtuck Valley Memorial Association obtained occupancy of the Frary House, which is now open to visitors as a supplement to the exhibitions and research material in Memorial Hall.

The Pocumtuck Valley Memorial Association in the course of ninety-two years has collected and published an enormous amount. It runs in a modest way. Its expenses in 1961 were $11,424.10; its receipts $10,846.90, of which $6,039.85 came from admissions to Memorial Hall and the Frary House. Its exhibits attracted 12,203 visitors in that year. Yet few local societies can offer the scholar more agreeable surroundings in which to investigate a regional scene than the library and manuscript room on the upper floors of the Sheldon wing of Memorial Hall.

Two other organizations unobtrusively help to make Deerfield one of the most attractive towns in New England. Over the past sixty years, Dr. Frank L. Boyden, who has made Deerfield Academy a school of national reputation, has had a deep affection for the character of the town. One of the academy trustees, Henry N. Flynt of Greenwich, Connecticut, with his wife, has greatly aided Dr. Boy-

24. J. M. Arms Sheldon, "Tribute to C. Alice Baker," *History and Proceedings* v (1905–11), 352–364. Miss Baker's researches on New England captives in Canada, first published in *History and Proceedings*, were reprinted as *True Stories of New England Captives Carried to Canada During the Old French and Indian Wars* (Cambridge, 1897). Subsequently her friend Miss Emma Lewis Coleman, who had accompanied her on her first research expedition to the Quebec archives in 1888, amplified the record in a two-volume work, *New England Captives Carried to Canada Between 1677 and 1760 During the French and Indian Wars* (Portland, 1925).

25. *History and Proceedings* ix (1940 Annual), 81.

den's efforts. Mr. and Mrs. Flynt, with characteristic understatement, have thus described their share in the undertaking:[26]

For almost a quarter of a century we have cherished our close relationship with Frank Boyden, the Academy's renowned headmaster, and his wife, Helen Childs Boyden, herself an extraordinary teacher. Our common interest in preserving the village has strengthened this friendship and one project has led to another. For instance, the Deerfield Inn was thoroughly inadequate, so its purchase and renovation was our first effort. Then, as the Academy housing problems became acute, we realized that preserving some of the eighteenth century houses could accomplish two things: maintain the buildings for museum purposes and provide better living conditions for Deerfield's fine faculty.

After mentioning the work of the Pocumtuck Valley Memorial Association, although not the fact that Mr. Flynt is president of that organization, they continue:

To insure the continuation of our efforts, the Heritage Foundation was established in 1952. The purposes of the Foundation are "to promote the cause of education in and appreciation of the rich heritage of the early Colonies . . . to stimulate and promote in any manner an interest in and a desire to preserve the principles of our early settlers and the standards which have made this country great . . . to receive gifts of money or tangible personal property, the income or principal of which may be used for any of the purposes of the Foundation."

The work proceeds slowly because of inadequate funds, although the Foundation has received over the last few years some greatly appreciated gifts for endowment, general expense, scholarship, building, and other purposes. The Heritage Foundation already owns several of the old houses, a good deal of furniture, and other decorative art items.[27] In addition it started in 1956 an eight-week summer course

26. In their foreword to the Deerfield section of Alice Winchester, ed., *The Antiques Treasury of Furniture and Other Decorative Arts* (New York, 1959), pp. 233–278, where examples of the furniture, ceramics, textiles, glass, silver, pewter, treenware, portraits, and prints are reproduced. See also Samuel Chamberlain and Henry N. Flynt, *Frontier of Freedom, The Soul and Substance of America Portrayed in one Extraordinary Village, Old Deerfield, Massachusetts* (New York, 1957).

27. The Ashley, Sheldon-Hawks, Stebbins, and Dwight-Barnard Houses, owned by the foundation, are open to visitors, as are the Hall Tavern and the Wilson Printing House, which are owned by Mr. and Mrs. Flynt. The Dwight-Barnard House was moved to Deerfield from Springfield and the Hall Tavern from Charlemont to insure their preservation.

for unmarried college undergraduates, to encourage the younger generation to enter the museum and American studies fields.[28]

The result is a town in which people live, teach, and learn, where the best of the past is enhanced by thoughtful improvements and additions. Half a dozen houses are open to visitors; the rest are occupied by the academy and townspeople. As Deerfield Academy has required new buildings, these have been designed to blend unobtrusively into the scene. The Heritage Foundation has bought a number of houses, some of which are admirably furnished as exhibits, while others are rented to provide living space and to help support the museum houses. The trappings of the tourist trade are completely and mercifully absent, for the Heritage Foundation recognizes that no venture of this kind can be made self-supporting.[29] The remarkable thing about Deerfield is that one can never tell at a glance whether an agreeable feature is due to Deerfield Academy, the Heritage Foundation, the Pocumtuck Valley Memorial Association as institutions, or to Dr. and Mrs. Boyden or Mr. and Mrs. Flynt or other residents as individuals, for institutions and individuals alike work together for Deerfield with uncommon skill, taste, generosity, and reticence.

The societies thus far described have been the chief centres of historical activity in their communities. On occasion, however, the old amateur spirit of learning in history still survives, sometimes with sociable or social ramifications, in the shadow of universities. The Cambridge Historical Society, founded in 1905, has had a respect-

28. This admirable course, directed by Mr. Jere Daniell, tutor in history at Harvard College, is now in its seventh year. It brings to Deerfield each summer six undergraduates, who in addition to receiving instruction in museum techniques and local history, have an opportunity to visit Winterthur, Sturbridge, and institutions in Boston and New York. It is completely free from "vocational recruiting," being designed simply to show promising students the interest of this field of history at an impressionable time in their careers.

29. Less than one seventh of the annual operating expenses of the Heritage Foundation come from the admission fees of visitors. The long-range objectives of the foundation envision an endowment of $2,500,000, approximately one fifth of which is already in hand. Meanwhile current gifts from trustees and a few friends supplement the endowment already received.

able sprinkling of the Harvard faculty among its members. They are there, however, as individuals rather than *ex-officiis*. Membership is limited to 225. Although by bequest of Dean and Mrs. William Emerson the society recently became the owner of one of the handsomest "Tory Row" house in Brattle Street, for more than half a century it had no quarters of any kind and devoted its efforts chiefly to reading and publishing papers on the history of Cambridge. During its meetings, which were held regularly at members' houses, one often had the illusion that Cambridge was still a nineteenth-century town, for the turn of mind and the voices of many of the members could have been duplicated in Rowley or in Vermont.

Although the thirty-seven volumes of Cambridge Historical Society *Publications*—well-edited and admirably printed—contain a good deal of personal reminiscence of local life, the articles are so generally the thoughtful recollections of literate people that the series constitutes a valuable historical source. The emphasis is chiefly on institutions, people, ideas, and, to a lesser extent, buildings. Nobody cares about genealogy, or if he does he conceals it. Before the acquisition of the Emerson House, the society's chief income was $1,000 to $1,200 of annual dues, and its only major expenditure was was for the printing of its *Publications*, which might cost $1,000 a volume.

The New Haven Colony Historical Society by contrast has a large and handsome building in New Haven, Connecticut, in which it maintains a museum and a library of 6,000 volumes with emphasis on local history and genealogy within the bounds of the ancient New Haven Colony. For the first fifty years after its foundation in 1862, the society was dominated by local "first families" and was highly social. In its second half century a gradual liberalization has taken place, although its members today are predominantly of middle age or older. There are today some 550 members in various classes, with $10 as the minimum annual dues. These represent a blending of town and gown. At present James T. Babb and Alexander O. Vietor of the Yale University Library and Professors Leonard W. Labaree and

Edmund S. Morgan of the Yale history department are among its officers. The society occupies a large and handsome building at 114 Whitney Avenue, New Haven, built in the late 1920s to house its library and museum. This is open regularly six days a week. It is staffed by a part-time curator and librarian, Mr. Ralph W. Thomas, a full-time and a part-time secretary, and a part-time janitor, all of whom work for low pay, as the annual income from all sources— dues and endowment—is barely $15,000. The Old Morris Mansion, a typical late eighteenth-century house on the east side of New Haven harbor, bequeathed with its own endowment to the society, and open to the public for six months of the year, is self-supporting.

The New Haven Colony Historical Society offers its members eight good and serious lectures a year, all issues of a quarterly *Journal*, and a copy of occasional publications, as well as the use of its library. The sixteen pages of an issue of the *Journal* contain a good deal of current "news," as well as articles such as the one in the September 1959 issue describing the discovery in a storeroom of an original model of Ely Whitney's cotton gin. In addition to a ten-volume series of *Papers*, begun in 1865, the society has published a number of volumes of colonial New Haven town and court records, as well as several genealogies and studies of local history.

In Charlottesville the ties between town and gown are closer than in Cambridge and New Haven, for the Albemarle County Historical Society, from its foundation in 1940, has placed all historical material that it has collected in the Rare Books and Manuscript Room of the Alderman Library of the University of Virginia. Members of the staff of the Alderman Library have always taken an active part in the affairs of the society, which meets quarterly, usually in the Albemarle County Court House. Its modest income, derived chiefly from dues—originally $1, raised to $2 in 1953—, is chiefly devoted to publication. Volume I of the *Papers of the Albemarle County Historical Society* appeared in March 1941; in 1952 the title was changed to *The Magazine of Albemarle County History*, although the form—a fifty- to sixty-page pamphlet appearing at most annually—was little altered.

A stranger exploring New York City for the first time might be forgiven if he failed to realize how completely self-sufficient a community Brooklyn had been in the nineteenth century. The magnitude of the Metropolitan Museum would hardly suggest the existence of the Brooklyn Museum, nor would he expect, while visiting the New-York Historical Society, that at 128 Pierrepont Street, Brooklyn Heights, the Long Island Historical Society[30] maintained substantial premises of its own. This organization, which takes as its special field the four counties comprising Long Island, was founded in 1863, when Brooklyn still maintained its own institutions, with James Carson Brevoort as president and Dr. Henry R. Stiles—historian, among other things, of bundling—as librarian. In its early years it sponsored lectures, maintained medical and natural history departments, and cheerfully embraced gifts to its library of books and manuscripts having no relation to the locality. Its first fund—$2,000 received in 1865—was from two spinsters for the formation of a collection of books relating to the history of Egypt, the Holy Land, and Greece, as a memorial to their brother. The S. B. Duryea bequest of 1892 included, for example, incunabula, Latin choir books, and books of hours.[31] Even within American history, the society gladly accepted gifts of manuscripts unrelated to New York, such as 123 Washington letters (collected by Edward Everett) concerning the management of Mount Vernon, and a large collection of letters of Henry Laurens of South Carolina, president of the Continental Congress, and of his son Colonel John Laurens, once owned by William Gilmore Simms. In both instances, Dr. Brevoort, president of the society from 1863 to 1873, was instrumental in acquiring these important manuscripts.

Between 1867 and 1889 the Long Island Historical Society published four substantial volumes, the 1679–80 travel journal of Jasper Dankers and Peter Sluyter, books on the Battle of Long Island and

---

30. *The Long Island Historical Society, 1863–1938, A Record in commemoration of the seventy-fifth anniversary of the founding of the Society in 1863* (Brooklyn, 1938).

31. *The Manuscripts and Early Printed Books Bequeathed to the Long Island Historical Society by Samuel Bowne Duryea* (Brooklyn, 1898).

the Campaign of 1776, and the texts of its Washington letters. A printed catalogue of the library, then containing over 50,000 volumes, was issued in 1893.

A sizable four-story building at the corner of Pierrepont and Clinton Streets, designed by George B. Post, was begun in 1878 and formally opened in January 1881. It contained an auditorium on the ground floor, a two-story library of considerable architectural distinction, and a museum on the fourth floor. Although somewhat shabby, it is today an attractive building of real interest that excites the enthusiasm of architectural historians.

In the nineteenth-century heyday of Brooklyn, the Long Island Historical Society flourished. In the twentieth century its fortunes have declined. As lectures were gradually given up after 1898, the auditorium was first given to the Red Cross and finally in 1926 remodeled into rentable space, today occupied by the *Brooklyn Eagle*. At the same time, to provide for expansion of the library, ethnological and natural history objects were lent to other institutions and the museum floor mainly converted to newspaper storage. A few weapons, spinning wheels, and the like still nestle in corners.

With the growth of the Brooklyn Mercantile Library and the establishment of the Brooklyn Public Library, the society gradually limited itself to history, biography, and genealogy. The heavy emphasis on the latter field was seemingly due to the interests of Miss Emma Toedteberg, librarian from 1890 to 1936,[32] her successor Miss Edna Huntington, who retired in 1959, and the majority of readers who frequented the library during the past seventy years. While particularly concerned with Brooklyn and Long Island data, the collections of family and local histories and the genealogical tools include materials from the New England states and the eastern seaboard, and even, in decreasing quantity, from more remote parts of the country. Miss Toedteberg built up extensive files of census

32. As Miss Toedteberg had already been employed by the society for twenty-one years when she was made librarian in 1890, her total service extended over sixty-seven years.

records, typed copies of cemetery inscriptions, and other forms of personal vital records. In 1955 the society published a catalogue of its genealogies, which it considered comparable in importance to the collection of the New England Historic Genealogical Society.

With this genealogical emphasis, there was little continuation of the interest in the broader aspects of American history that had marked the society's early years. The library was still handsome, but its collections chiefly attracted persons of somewhat parochial outlook. Meanwhile membership decreased and money became tighter.[33] In 1958 the society engaged as assistant librarian a recent graduate of the Pratt Institute Library School, who was the first person of professional training to be employed in the library. On Miss Huntington's retirement, she was succeeded as librarian on 1 September 1959 by Miss Helen P. Bolman, formerly of the Brooklyn Public Library, an alert and experienced professional librarian with good interest in local history. Miss Bolman and her assistant are seriously attempting, with limited funds and inadequate staff, to put their house in order.

The Long Island Historical Society is highly organized in accordance with Parkinson's Law. The 675 members elect twenty-five directors, who in turn choose seven officers and twenty councilors. This hierarchy, with, until Miss Bolman's recent arrival, only an elderly genealogist to advise them, made laudable efforts to dispose of books unrelated to history. They sensibly sold an elephant folio of Audubon, a Shakespeare collection, and a good deal of general literature. They also, to the consternation of scholars and editors in many parts of the country, sold in 1959 to an antiquarian bookseller the Laurens papers, which had given the Long Island Historical Society greater distinction as a place for research in American history than any other of its possessions.[34] There have been no publica-

33. The seventy-fifth anniversary volume of 1938 reported 230 annual and 86 life members, and a general endowment fund of only $190,000. In 1882 there was a peak membership of 1,600, which had declined to less than 1,000 in 1898. In 1960 it had climbed back to 675.

34. Although the Laurens papers are of national and of South Carolina significance, their presence in the Long Island Historical Society for nearly a century had been so

tions in recent years. To an outsider the society appears to be lost in the forest of its own possessions, which are also its chief asset and reason for existence. The officers and staff are now endeavoring to chop paths through the underbrush. While it is not easy to make an accurate map of the forest while engaged in such operations, it is necessary to have one before the goal of a future journey can be set.

Local historical societies in New England are concerned with a tradition of British settlement. Various organizations in Florida and California deal with the Spanish background of those regions by similar means. Few small American cities offer as rich a field for a local historical society at Saint Augustine, Florida. Founded in 1565 by Pedro Menéndez de Avilés, it remained Spanish until 1763 when Florida was ceded to England. After twenty years of English rule, Saint Augustine became Spanish once again and so remained until the annexation of Florida by the United States in 1819. The Saint Augustine Historical Society has evolved from an organization founded in 1883 that was originally primarily concerned with archaeology and natural history.[35] Its books and manuscripts concerning local history were originally housed in the Saint Augustine Public Library, and its museum collection in space provided by Henry M. Flagler in the Alcazar Hotel. After the museum, which was in 1913 moved to a historic house on the bay front, was destroyed in the great fire of the following year, the War Department permitted the society to occupy the Castillo de San Marcos, then known as Fort Marion. This great fort, begun in 1672 to protect the northernmost Spanish settlement from English encroachment from the Carolinas, remained in the care of the society until 1935, when the

---

well known to scholars that it was assumed that nothing short of a fire or the dissolution of the society would disturb them. Their private sale to a dealer, without giving interested institutions an opportunity to bid, raised fears that the collection might be dispersed in the autograph market or, if kept as a whole, pass into the inaccessibility of a private collection.

35. The Saint Augustine Institute of Science was reorganized in 1898 as the Saint Augustine Institute of Science and Historical Society. In 1918 it was rechartered as the Saint Augustine Historical Society and Institute of Science, and in 1953 the name was shortened to its present form.

National Park Service took over its administration. In 1918 the society purchased the so-called "Oldest House" at 14 Saint Francis Street, parts of which, it has claimed, go back to the sixteenth century. To this was added in 1923 the Webb Memorial Building to house the library and museum.

The Saint Augustine Historical Society has at present about 350 members at $2 per year. It has never received large private gifts or any public funds. With admission fees from the Oldest House and from the Castillo de San Marcos, however, the society was frugally able over the years to buy and restore for rental three historic houses, to build up a good working library, achieve a very presentable narrative museum, and set aside a reserve fund in excess of $100,000, mostly invested in government bonds. As income from the Oldest House has dropped considerably in the past few years while expenses have been increasing, there is at present little margin for expansion. Nevertheless the society in the past decade has issued half a dozen useful publications in co-operation with the University of Florida Press, the University of Miami Press, and the *Florida Historical Quarterly*. The most important of these is *Barcia's Chronological History of the Continent of Florida*, translated under the society's sponsorship by Anthony Kerrigan and published, with a foreword by Professor Herbert E. Bolton, in a handsome limited edition by the University of Florida Press in 1951. Charles W. Arnade's 1959 monographs, *Florida on Trial, 1593–1602* and *The Siege of St. Augustine, 1702*, should be noted, as well as the *Saint Augustine Historical Society Microfilm Calendar* of Spanish records pertaining to Florida, 1512–1764, in various other collections.

While Saint Augustine is nearly four centuries old, the history of Spanish settlement in California goes back only half as far. George Wharton James began his account of the California missions with this observation:

Perhaps nowhere in the history of the world is there to be found a clearer example of the nothingness of Time and Place when man is absent than is presented in the history of California. It was the same California that it is now long centuries before

Cabrillo first discovered it. It was still the same in the ages that it remained practically undisturbed after Cabrillo, until the time of Serra.[36]

Although things moved slowly enough for the first eighty years after Fray Junipero Serra and his brown-robed Franciscans arrived on the scene, the rate of change in California since the middle of the nineteenth century has accelerated to the speed of chain lightning. Gold rushes, booms, seekers of winter climate, and, more recently, off-shore oil have inflated villages into cities and obliterated much of the past with surprising efficiency. But as vestiges of the past disappear, someone always attempts to save the remnants.

Santa Barbara, where a presidio was founded in 1782 and a Franciscan mission begun in 1787, remained pastoral until the 1840s. As a Spanish town it probably never had more than 500 inhabitants, yet for the past century and a quarter seafaring men from New England, "mountain men" in buckskins, and a variety of more elegant types have been settling there. While it has kept its amenities better than most cities, the gulf between its idyllic past and the present widens at an alarming rate. Consequently in 1932 a Santa Barbara Historical Society was organized. This remained inactive until 1954, when through the kindness of the Franciscan Fathers it had the opportunity to occupy several rooms on the ground floor of the Old Mission for a ten-year period. For the past seven years it has been usefully employed in historic preservation and in collecting a research library on the city and county of Santa Barbara. One of the directors of the society, Mr. W. Edwin Gledhill, a retired photographer, serves as museum director, and his wife as curator. Another director, Mr. Edward Selden Spaulding, acts as editor of *Noticias*, the society's quarterly bulletin. As the society operates on an annual budget of $4,500, derived almost entirely from the dues ($5 minimum) of its 500 members, almost everything has to be accomplished by volunteer work at the present time, but promised legacies amounting to several hundred thousand dollars will eventually be of assistance.

The rooms presently occupied in the Old Mission contain some

36. *In and Out of the Old Missions of California* (Boston, 1907), p. 1.

objects from the Spanish period, works of such Santa Barbara painters as Carl Oscar Borg, Clarence Mattei, and William Louis Otie, and a working library of local history and genealogy. The society has the original records of the 1870 census of Santa Barbara and microfilms of other locally useful censuses, as well as genealogical records, compiled by Thomas Workman Temple II from material in the Bancroft Library, of 280 Spanish and Mexican families of California. From the Mexican period there are manuscripts of José Maria Covarrubias, Secretary of State under Pio Pico, of the trader Alpheus Basil Thompson, who came to Santa Barbara in 1834; from the American period are papers of Colonel W. W. Hollister, a pioneer in the 1860s and 1870s.

Through the leadership of the society, the mayor and council approved in 1959 a resolution designating the original site of Santa Barbara as Pueblo Viejo and providing that "primary consideration to the preservation of the atmosphere of our California Spanish historic heritage" be given in this area of sixteen blocks. The intent is that surviving buildings of the Spanish period be respected and that new construction be in harmonizing adobe. This was implemented by the passage of an El Pueblo Viejo Ordinance on 8 March 1960. In less than two years, business concerns have become so eager for sites in the area that land values have risen, with consequent danger that private individuals occupying historic houses in the Pueblo Viejo may be taxed out of their ownership. The Santa Barbara Historical Society, in co-operation with other groups throughout the State, is actively pressing for the adoption of Senate Constitutional Amendment No. 11 at the November 1962 election. If adopted, this would permit tax relief to historic buildings in private hands. The society is thus energetically engaged in historic preservation along lines inspired by Mr. Jacob H. Morrison's work on preservation laws in New Orleans and the success of the Vieux Carré Commission there. The society owns through the bequest of Mrs. John Russell Hastings a remarkable little Cape Cod cottage at 412 West Montecito Street, built in the local adobe in 1854 by Captain Horatio Trussell, a New England shipmaster, which was dedicated as State Historic Landmark 559 on 12 October 1957. It is attempting to preserve in an adjacent area fronting on Montecito and Castillo Streets various examples of nineteenth-century architecture from the American period. To this area in 1959 the society moved the home of the late Judge Charles Fernald, as a desirable example of the Victorian wooden pretentiousness that was characteristic of the 1860s. By the end of 1959 nearly $6,000 had been contributed toward the moving and restoration, with Mr. Elmer H. Whittaker, one of the directors, not only overseeing the operation but generously advancing the difference between funds in hand and an anticipated expense of some $21,000. The Fernald House on its new site adjoins the Hunt-Stambach House, designed in the 1870s by the architect Peter J. Barber and now owned by the Assistance League, which moved it to that site in 1955 under Mr. Whittaker's skillful supervision.

An issue of the sixteen-page *San Diego Historical Society Quarterly* looks very much like *Noticias*, the Santa Barbara Historical Society periodical, but the similarities between these two California coastal county societies end there. In Santa Barbara a group with a specific program of historical collecting and preservation has proceeded from one step to the next with small private funds. In San Diego a single private individual, with monumental and commemorative purposes, created a society and a building that has since been supported by public funds.

San Diego, where Fray Junipero Serra founded the first Californian mission in 1769, had 650 inhabitants in 1850. In 1920 their number had grown to 74,683; in 1950 to 334,387. Heaven knows what the population may be by the time this book appears—certainly enough to have obliterated anything that is not well protected. Through the earlier stages of the transformation from village to city, George White Marston (1850–1946), a New Englander out of Wisconsin who had come to San Diego in 1870, ran a department store that prospered as the place grew. Among other good works, he was long a trustee of Pomona College at Claremont. Although a faithful member of the Congregational Church and a devoted supporter of the YMCA, George Marston was deeply moved by the memory of the founding Franciscans. Regarding Presidio Hill, on which Father Serra first raised the Cross on 16 July 1769, as the birthplace of European civilization on the Pacific coast and as a site comparable in interest to Plymouth Rock, Marston began buying land there in 1907.[37] Eventually he acquired some twenty acres, which he considered as held in trust for the city. In 1927 he began developing the hill as a park.[38] The following year he instigated the founding of the San Diego Historical Society, incorporated 14 December 1928, of which he became the first president. The next step was the construction of a building, architecturally inspired by the early missions, that would serve as a memorial to Father Serra, as the crowning feature of the landscape, and as a home for the historical society. It is dramatically located. From below it looms handsomely against the sky; its arcades and terraces command magnificent views up the valley to the mountains and over Mission Bay and San Diego Bay to to the Pacific. To furnish it, fifteenth-, sixteenth-, and seventeenth-century furniture was brought from Spain, on the theory that these were articles that early Californians might have known in their native land. Presidio Park was dedicated on 16 July 1929, the 160th anniversary of the founding of the San Diego Mission, with a solemn high mass celebrated on the terrace by the Provincial of the Franciscan Order, with naval bands, a pageant, addresses by the Governor of California, the mayor, the Spanish ambassador, the president of Claremont Colleges, and by Mr. Marston himself. Although the City Council accepted Presidio Park for the city the following week, Mr. Marston personally supervised and paid for its continued embellishment and maintenance until 1940. He went

37. Mary Gilman Marston, *George White Marston, A Family Chronicle* (Los Angeles, 1956), II, 140–166, 304.
38. Mr. Marston also sold lots in a Presidio Hills subdivision on the edge of the park; *ibid.*, II, 143.

there nearly every day and knew every tree and most of its shrubs and plants by heart.

Today the City of San Diego allots about $19,000 annually for the salaries, utilities, and supplies for operating the Junipero Serra Museum, while the County of San Diego provides $7,500 annually for a tape-recorded interviewing of early settlers. Income from membership ($3 minimum) produces about $2,000 a year, most of which goes into the *Quarterly*. The society has a small and considerably used reference library of California historical material, with special emphasis on the local area, which includes some manuscripts, an incomplete file of local newspapers back to 1868, and the Kerr collection of California land titles. An average of 3,500 school children are given personally conducted tours of the museum during the year.

The director, Mr. Jerry Mac Mullen, a former newspaper man, is the author of *Paddle-wheel Days in California* and other valuable books and articles on maritime history. He chooses his staff on personality, interest in and knowledge of local history, as well as ability to meet and handle the public. They are, in his words,

Curator a retired officer of the local fire department, assistant curator a former insurance investigator and hotel man, all with a particular aptitude for the work. Maintenance man is another retired fire captain, clerk is a former Navy yeoman now employed as an accountant; last two are one day a week only.

The monumental character of the Junipero Serra Museum does not make it easy to arrange temporary exhibitions of an instructive sort. There are too many refectory tables and *fraileros* in the way, and *braseros* to stumble over. It is a romantic reconstruction, very beautiful, and hard to do anything with. However impractical for current use, this touching tribute from a New England Congregationalist to the valor of Catholic missionaries is in itself a document of American social history. Its construction is a conspicuous example of private generosity to history, even though on its monumental fringes. It further represents the romanticizing and idealization of the

Spanish tradition,[39] a process that in California today often leads descendants of Mexican foot soldiers on garrison duty to regard themselves as *hijos de los conquistadores*.[40]

At the other extreme of the Pacific coast, the Seattle Historical Society has in the past decade pursued an energetic course in popularizing history that is quite unlike anything previously mentioned in this chapter. The society was founded on 13 November 1911, the sixtieth anniversary of the debarkation from the schooner *Exact* of the pioneer founders of Seattle, "to preserve the history of the City of Seattle and King County and the history and biography of those identified with its progress." Mrs. Morgan J. Carkeek, at whose home the organizational meeting was held, remained president until her death in 1926. For the first thirty years the society's chief adherents were ladies of the "costumes and old lace" school of thought. Monthly meetings were held, and through fund-raising efforts some $14,000 had been accumulated towards a museum by the early 1940s.

In 1945 the Boeing Airplane Company pledged $50,000 for an

39. This is not without its practical aspects. Mr. Marston's daughter writes in the memoir (II, 162–163): "In the rejuvenation of the Old Town [below Presidio Park] father's most important contributions were the building of the golf course, his assistance to the Cardwells in building the Pico Motel, and his help in making possible the Old San Diego Community Church. He was more than compensated for the financial vicissitudes of the 'Presidio Hills Golf Club, Ltd.,' which he started during the depression by the satisfaction he got from it. [It was sold to the city in 1944.] The charming Casa de Pico was father's conception of the type of modern architecture that is appropriate to the traditions of Old San Diego. Father chose Richard S. Requa as architect and Kenneth Cardwell as proprietor and eventual owner. The motel was such an immediate success that the money he had advanced came back to him quickly."

40. The romanticists who regard all western sheriffs as heroes and dub all white Virginians "Cavaliers" tend to consider all Spaniards in Mexico as "Conquistadors." The word is consequently creeping into the vocabulary of press agents and journalists. See, for example, "A Blonde Called Me-Me-Oh, Yvette Mimieux starts road to film fame," *Life*, 9 May 1960, where an eighteen-year-old cover girl, a "warmly wistful starlet"—"a home-town girl, born and brought up in Hollywood, but her father is French and her mother is Mexican"—is shown on a rock above the Pacific "like her conquistador forebears," gazing "dreamily into a golden future." The story states that her ancestors "include the conquistador who founded Monterrey, Mexico. Her managers have also discovered a Spanish king among her forebears and hint of a mystical kinship with Quetzalcoatl, an Aztec god."

aviation wing as a memorial to its former officer, Philip G. Johnson, on condition that the projected museum must cost at least $250,000 and that ground be broken within five years. This conditional gift inspired a popular fund drive, involving professional money-raisers and businessmen, for the creation of a Museum of History and Industry. By agreement between the city and the Seattle Historical Society, a site on the edge of the University of Washington Arboretum was agreed upon, and there was built a modern two-story concrete structure, including the Johnson aviation wing, which was opened to the public and presented to the City of Seattle on 15 February 1952.

As the museum welcomes models and exhibits from industrial firms, gladly accepts bulky artifacts like cable cars, and stresses the policy that "no historical item is too small to be of interest," space will always be at a premium. In 1957 a financial drive for a maritime wing was opened, in co-operation with the Puget Sound Maritime Historical Society. Through the gifts of 119 individuals and business corporations, $140,000 was raised. On 9 June 1959 the Joshua Green-Dwight Merrill Maritime Wing, named in honor of two of the principal donors, was opened.

John Jewett was master of ceremonies for the dramatic program, which carried out many Pacific Northwest traditions. A color guard from the United States Marine Reserve presented the colors at the entrance of the wing, to martial music by the 13th Naval District Band. Historical Society President McCurdy presented a deed-of-gift for the new wing to Mayor Clinton. Five-year-old Herbert Henry Gowen, great grandson of Mr. Green, smashed a bottle of spruce beer over an old ship's binnacle to "christen the ship." Flower girl was five-year-old Merrill Wright, great granddaughter of Mr. Merrill. The beer was brewed to the receipe used by Captain George Vancouver on his voyage to Puget Sound in 1792. President James Vallentyne of the Puget Sound Maritime Historical Society signalled for a series of triumphant shrieks from the steam whistle of the old Russian trading vessel, *Politkofsky*. Another historical milestone was achieved by the Society.[41]

The result is a handsome setting for figureheads, ship models, and

---

41. *Progress Report, The Seattle Historical Society and The Museum of History and Industry, 1959–1960.* (Seattle, 1960), pp. 5–6.

the like. Contemplated projects "to enable the Museum to serve the community more efficiently" include transportation, Alaskan, and lumber wings, as well as an auditorium.

The all-embracing nature of the collection will be seen from the account of acquisitions in the 1959–60 report, where it is stated:

> An increasing number of individuals is becoming aware that by donating memorabilia of the past to the Museum they will share beloved items in perpetuity with the thousands who visit the Museum.
>
> A shoemaker's chest, donated by Mrs. Meal Nichols and Mrs. L. E. Wolcott, and two coffee cans from Louch-Augustine & Co., Grocers, donated by O. E. Kahan, are typical of small items that help create accurate scenes of life in the past. A saloon door from Billy's Mug, circa 1898, donated by James E. Ray, typifies items used to add interest to displays.
>
> In addition, an increasing number of individuals is recognizing the value of the Museum of History and Industry as a worthwhile repository for rare and unusual artifacts. These gifts make possible an expansion of the Historical Society's educational and historical services. But whatever the acquisition—from ethnographic to industrial, from householder's memento to hobby material—all accessions are important and appreciated.

Recent acquisitions have included walnut parlor furniture of the 1880s, a hunting wagon, Eskimo artifacts, early miner's equipment, jewelry, gas street lamps, early experimental aviation models, historical office equipment, early picnicking and camping gear, pioneer art, and the cornerstone and furniture from a destroyed United States post office. Such variety attracts children of all ages in large numbers.

In 1958, 98,066 persons visited the museum, and 109,493 in the first nine months of 1959.

The director of the Museum of History and Industry, Mrs. Sutton Gustison, and her staff, consisting of a curator, a design consultant, an educational director, a secretary, one person for publicity, two handicraft teachers, and two hostesses, keep a great number of balls in the air at once, with the help of numerous volunteers organized by the Women's Museum League. Changing exhibits, lectures on Northwest history for fourth grade schoolteachers, guided tours of the museum for school children, handicraft classes during the school year, summer industrial tours for children, and "Christmas Around the World" programs involving fourteen nationality groups, take organizing. So does the administration of a society with eleven officers—six of them vice-presidents—, sixty-nine trustees, twenty honorary trustees, and an executive committee of twenty-four. It is apparently a hard core of four or five members of the board who meet every Saturday morning at 7:30 a.m. that keeps things straight.

The Seattle Park Department maintains the building and grounds, while the King County Board of Commissioners raised its annual appropriation of $5,000 for the museum to $10,000 in 1959. The Seattle Historical Society's disbursements for the year 1958, the last report to be published, were $25,868.50, which were met by receipts of $26,436—$17,372 from membership dues,[42] the $5,000 county appropriation, $2,982.71 from projects, $781.29 shop profit from sales, and a $300 contribution. The souvenir shop sells post cards, books, colored slides, as well as Mohai (Museum of History and Industry) "do-it-yourself" kits "to make models of two old-time Cable Cars, a Stone-tower Lighthouse and silk-screen designs!" in a "Fun with Pacific Northwest History for boys and girls 8 to 12 years" program sponsored by the Women's Museum League. The circular of the Mohai kits announces that

Every owner of a Mohai set is automatically a member of the Mohai Club. Mohai—the gift horse of the Museum of History and Industry—sends a membership button with the first kit in the set. He also signs each membership card for members' wallets.

The Mohai project also has won national honors from the American Association for State and Local History.

42. There are some 1,300 individual members, in five classes, ranging from annual at $5 to life with one payment of $1,000. Those whose families came to Washington Territory before 1889 are eligible for Pioneer Life Membership at the reduced rate of $500. There are also five classes of business firm membership. The Boeing Airplane Company and the Port of Seattle are benefactor members at $1,000 a year. Over one hundred co-operative members pay $100 a year; fifteen contributing members pay $25; one sustaining member pays $10, and thirty-two less benevolent business firms pay $5. Various parent-teacher associations, labor organizations, and clubs participate in a club group membership at $25 with the privilege of using the museum facilities once a year without additional charge.

Although there is on the ground floor a library of Northwest Americana, a picture collection of 7,000 items and 1,500 slides, the atmosphere of the Museum of History and Industry is more conducive to popular activity than to investigation. The museum's exhibitions are tastefully and skillfully arranged, but, at least on the occasion of my visit in 1960, they seemed better calculated to evoke wonder and amazement in the young and nostalgia in their elders than to convey much serious information about American history. The Seattle Historical Society has made a real place for itself in the community by general activity that appeals to the eye rather than the mind; the organization and constant effort needed to retain this popular interest hinders rather than promotes serious historical investigation. Having embarked upon coddling the public to raise the large sum of money necessary to build the Museum of History and Industry, the society has now become chiefly an instrument to assist in the support of its creation. It is so deeply involved in artifacts and popular education that any thought of research and publication has been lost on the way. The latter functions thrive, however, in the not-far-distant University of Washington Library, where, in co-operation with the history department, a vigorous amount of manuscript collecting, research, editing, and publishing goes on constantly.

The thirteen county or local societies described in this chapter represent a remarkable diversity in date of origin, resources, and purpose. In fact the only thing that they have in common is that all thirteen were founded without public funds or official encouragement, and that eleven of them have continued to operate on that principle. Their chief virtue is that they not only collect and preserve much that might otherwise be lost, but that they serve as a rallying point for an immense variety of studies of local themes, great and small, that help collectively to make up the mosaic that is our record of the American past. Thus one can be grateful that the historical society, like the flea, progresses not only from great to little to lesser "and so *ad infinitum*," but from great to greater to "greater still, and greater still, and so on."

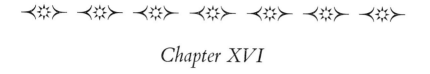

Chapter XVI

THE TOMBSTONE WITH
A FOOTNOTE

I know not by what fate it comes to pass, that historians, who give immortality to others, are so ill requited by posterity, that their actions and their fortunes are usually forgotten; neither themselves encouraged while they live, nor their memory preserved entire to future ages. It is the ingratitude of mankind to their greatest benefactors, that they who teach us wisdom by the surest ways . . . should generally live poor and unregarded; as if they were born only for the public, and had no interest in their own well-being, but were to be lighted up like tapers, and to waste themselves for the benefit of others. —JOHN DRYDEN, 1683

IN the Moravian Cemetery at Bethlehem, Pennsylvania, where orderly files of graves are marked by uniform stones lying flat on the ground, is an inscription remarkable for its historical conscientiousness. Marking the grave of an Indian convert, it reads:

No. 52
ISAAC
OTAPAWANAMEN
of Shecomeco
a Wompanosh Ind^{n}
Bap. a. 1742
in Oley
Dep. Aug. 2nd 1746

see Losk . hist. 2nd part
pag. 21 & 94

The reference is to Georg Heinrick Loskiel, *History of the Mission of the United Brethren among the Indians* (London, 1794), translated by Christian Ignatius La Trobe from the German original, *Geschichte der Mission der evangelischen Brüder unter den Indianern in Nordamerika* of 1789, where an account of the conversion and edifying life of Isaac may be found by anyone requiring such information. This tombstone with a footnote typified the respect, indeed the holy zeal, of the Moravian Church for sound and adequate documentation. In 1957 this small Protestant fellowship, known officially as the Unitas Fratrum, celebrated the quincentennial anniversary of its founding by followers of John Hus, the Bohemian reformer. Although virtually annihilated by the Thirty Years' War, the Moravian Church was restored in 1722 by a small group of its members who found shelter on the Saxon estate of Nicholas Louis Count Zinzendorf. There a community called Herrnhut developed, which was to be both "unter des Herrn Hut" [under the Lord's watch] and "auf des Herrn Hut" [on the watch for the Lord]. In this place developed a zeal for spreading the Gospel that brought Moravian missionaries to Georgia in 1735, and led them to establish on the Lehigh River in Pennsylvania a settlement that was, on Christmas Eve 1741, named Bethlehem. For a century this settlement remained a closed community restricted to bona fide members of the Moravian Church. Today it is an industrial city, the seat of the great steel company that bears its name and of Lehigh University. It remains, notwithstanding these changes, the centre of the Northern Province of the American Moravian Church. There, cheek by jowl with the steel works, stand the eighteenth-century buildings that are so moving a reminder of a religious community in the wilderness. There too is Moravian College and the Moravian Archives, in which are preserved with scrupulous care the records of the Northern Province of the Church. The Moravian Archives, although established and preserved for the use of the Church, contain much that is of value for other aspects of American history. They will thus be considered in this chapter as one of four institutions—two of eighteenth-century and two of twentieth-century foundation—widely different in location and subject matter, that preserve or publish significant sources of American history. Their only common ground is that they are all the result of voluntary association, all privately supported, all skillful in making good use of their relatively modest funds. This common ground makes their problems essentially identical to those of most independent historical societies.

THE MORAVIAN ARCHIVES

The spirit that inspired the placing of an accurate footnote on the tombstone of Isaac the Indian grew from Count Zinzendorf's requirement that his widely scattered brethren should forward to him detailed accounts of their activities overseas. Of this practice the Right Reverend Kenneth G. Hamilton has written:[1]

As a result, our Archives contain many specimens of the diaries kept during the eighteenth century by Moravians in America. Usually one of the local ministers served as diarist. The events he recorded included not merely those relating to strictly ecclesiastical matters, but all important happenings that affected the community life of these church settlements—and many unimportant ones as well. Thus the Bethlehem Diary, to provide a single example, contains a long account of how John Paul Jones, on a visit to Bethlehem in 1783,[2] took a lead in dealing with suspicious characters at the Crown Inn, who were reported to have assaulted a traveler and to have taken forcible possession of the place. In the event they proved to be innkeepers from further down the Philadelphia-Bethlehem Road.

The Bethlehem Diary unquestionably constitutes our most important single holding. Recently the first fifty manuscript volumes of this record were micro-

1. The career of Bishop Hamilton, who has been president of the executive board of the Moravian Church, North, since 1956, is an example of the combination of learning and missionary zeal that is found in this Church, which has some 300,000 members in the world, of which over 50,000 are in the United States and Canada. After serving as a missionary in Nicaragua from 1919 to 1937, he became a professor at Moravian College in Bethlehem and assistant archivist; and took a PH.D. in history at Columbia in 1941 before being consecrated bishop in 1947. See his "The Resources of the Moravian Church Archives," *Pennsylvania History* XXVII (1960), 263–272.

2. Samuel Eliot Morison, *John Paul Jones, A Sailor's Biography* (Boston, 1959), p. 333, explains that Jones spent the late summer of 1783 at the Moravian sanitarium in Bethlehem taking the "cold bath" treatment for an intermittent fever—perhaps malaria—that he had picked up in the Caribbean. He left thoroughly cured. John Adams and so many other distinguished figures passed through Bethlehem during the American Revolution that this period of the diary would doubtless repay careful examination.

filmed in preparation for rebinding. This required 16,676 exposures, each reproducing two manuscript pages.

The Bethlehem Diary, however, cannot compare for extensiveness with another series of 162 bound volumes. They are in German script (as are all but the last of the 50 microfilmed volumes of the Bethlehem Diary). This series represents extracts taken from the diaries of Moravian congregations all over the world and transcribed in Germany for the benefit of Moraviandom everywhere. Our Bethlehem set covers the years 1747 to 1818 inclusive, and contains approximately 93,500 pages.

The records of the "period of the Economy," the first twenty years of the life of Bethlehem, when the town operated as a community in which everyone worked for the Church receiving in return food and shelter, which contain over 312,000 pages of manuscript, are rich in the details of social and economic life, as are later records of congregations and the many autobiographies prepared by individual Church members to be read at their own funerals. Personal reports from traveling evangelists telling of their conversations and interviews are a rich mine of information about eighteenth-century American life, while the records of Moravian missionaries to the Indians are comparable to the Jesuit relation as sources. Maps, architects' drawings, town plans, musical scores, designs for machinery, portraits abound.

The oldest records were originally deposited in the Gemeinhaus of 1741 on Church Street,[3] that was long the centre of community life in Bethlehem. In the nineteenth century they were accommodated in the Central Church, but in 1930 they were transferred to a separate fireproof building, specially built for them at Main and Elizabeth Avenues, Bethlehem, adjacent to Moravian College. Bishop Hamilton, the head of the Northern Province, serves as archivist, assisted by various clergymen and members of the faculty of Moravian College who give what time they can spare to the care of the records. The present building was, for example, achieved by the efforts of the late Reverend William N. Schwarze, professor at Moravian College and ultimately its president, who served as archivist from 1906 until his

3. Kenneth G. Hamilton, *Church Street in Old Bethlehem* (Bethlehem, 1942).

death in 1948. His successor, the Right Reverend S. H. Gapp, translated Georg Neisser's manuscript treatises and printed them in 1955 under the title *A History of the Beginnings of Moravian Work in America*, as *Publications* No. 1 of The Archives of the Moravian Church. The Reverend John Fliegel has spent years preparing a detailed card index to over 50,000 pages of manuscript relating to the Moravian ministry among American Indians. Seldom have I encountered such an admirable atmosphere of intelligent, useful, energetic, and unremunerated devotion to learning.

The National Historical Publications Commission *Guide* reports for the Moravian Archives:

7,300 vols. and 58,000 pieces, 1457 to date, consisting of letters, reports, diaries, and other papers relating chiefly to the Moravian Church in the Western Hemisphere, particularly in North America. A great deal of the material relates to activities in Pennsylvania, but importantly represented also are church organizations in Canada, Connecticut, Illinois, Iowa, Kansas, Maryland, New Jersey, New York, North Carolina, Ohio, and Rhode Island. Papers of individuals include extensive quantities of papers of John Ettwein (N.C., Pa.; Moravian missionary to the Indians, bishop), 1772–97; John Gottlieb Ernestus Heckewelder (Pa., Ohio; Moravian missionary to the Indians, author), 1765–1823; Augustus Gottlieb Spangenberg (Pa., N.C.; Moravian bishop, overseer of the Bethlehem settlement of Moravians, missionary) 1744–60; and David Zeisberger (Pa., Ohio; Moravian missionary to the Indians, author), 1745–98. There is much material relating to Indians and Indian missions, including a large number of papers of the Society for Propagating the Gospel Among the Heathen, 1735–1811. Included also are manuscripts of religious music, 1710–1850 (900 pieces); and archives of the Moravian College, Bethlehem, 1840 to date.

Now this mass of material is safely housed in an appropriate building and lovingly cared for by learned men. It is ideally suited for investigation in Moravian history, for it is arranged by the organization of the Church, and much of it is in the neat parcels in which it was placed soon after receipt. But a colossal amount of calendaring, indexing, and, in some cases, transcription and translation must be accomplished before its immensely varied resources become readily usable for other aspects of American history. The sociologist, the architectural or economic historian, the student of Indian linguistics, all of whom would find great riches here, are unlikely to be sufficiently versed in eighteenth-century German script and Moravian history to find their way unaided through the maze. The reconstruction of the Schoenbrunn Village State Memorial, begun by the Ohio Historical Society in 1923, was made possible only by the records and maps preserved at Bethlehem.[4] Here the problem was relatively simple, for Schoenbrunn, the first town built in Ohio by Christian Indians, was inspired by Moravian missionaries. In other instances useful material would come less readily to hand. One cannot reasonably expect the Moravian Church to spend substantial sums of money to make its records more easily available to the great variety of scholars in secular fields who would profit by them if they knew what was there. The Church has admirably done its part in creating, preserving, and safely housing the archives; it needs help to carry out the next step, which is, in the words of Worthington C. Ford, "to encourage the investigator and writer of history by offering these records in a form fitted for his purpose."[5]

PEABODY MUSEUM OF SALEM

The Salem East India Marine Society, organized in 1799, had three purposes: the relief of widows and children of deceased members, the collection of "such facts and observations as may tend to the improvement and security of navigation," and the formation of a "museum of natural and artificial curiosities, particularly such as are to be found beyond the Cape of Good Hope and Cape Horn." The second object produced a collection of journals of voyages; the third

4. James H. and Mary Jane Rodabaugh, *Schoenbrunn and the Moravian Missions in Ohio* (Columbus, 1956), p. 3.

5. On 7 and 8 May 1959 a conference of fourteen historians and archivists was held at Bethlehem on the invitation of Bishop Hamilton to consider the problems of the Moravian Archives. This group, which was greatly impressed by the richness of the collection and its usefulness to American historians, ethnologists, sociologists, and other scholars, felt strongly that outside financial support was urgently needed to carry out the needed calendaring and arrangement of the papers.

a remarkable museum illustrating the native cultures of Polynesia, Micronesia, and Melanesia, as well as the maritime activity that took Salem shipmasters to the Pacific. This was housed in East India Marine Hall in Essex Street, Salem, dedicated in 1825 with the assistance of President John Quincy Adams and of enough liquor to permit the drinking of no less than fifty toasts.

As membership in the Salem East India Marine Society was restricted to shipmasters "who have navigated those Seas at or beyond the Cape of Good Hope," the decline of Salem trade in the middle of the nineteenth century so seriously reduced the number of eligible candidates that the future of the museum became dim. At this point the philanthropist George Peabody of London founded what is now the Peabody Museum of Salem by giving to a board of nine self-perpetuating trustees funds for the purchase of the building and collections of the East India Marine Society, and the endowment of the new institution thus created.[6]

The Peabody Museum of Salem is concerned today with three fields: the maritime history of New England, Pacific and Japanese ethnology, and the natural history of Essex County. It has a library covering these fields, including photographs, and a manuscript collection of 2,300 volumes and 1,900 boxes of logbooks, journals, account books, and miscellaneous papers relating to maritime history, shipbuilding, and trade with the Far East, Africa, and the Pacific Islands. To East India Marine Hall, now devoted entirely to

6. The corporate name Peabody Academy of Science adopted in 1868 was legally changed to Peabody Museum of Salem in 1915. For the detailed history of the institution, see Walter Muir Whitehill, *The East India Marine Society and the Peabody Museum of Salem, A Sesquicentennial History* (Salem, 1949). For a general description see Ernest S. Dodge and Charles H. P. Copeland, *Handbook to the Collections of the Peabody Museum of Salem* (Salem, 1949). Among detailed catalogues of the permanent collections are Ernest S. Dodge's *The Hervey Island Adzes* (1937), *The Marquesas Islands Collection* (1939), *The New Zealand Maori Collection* (1941), and *George Crowninshield's Yacht* Cleopatra's Barge by *Walter Muir Whitehill and a Catalogue of the Francis B. Crowninshield Gallery* (1959). There are also numerous illustrated catalogues recording temporary exhibitions in maritime history. Mr. Dodge's published reports, issued annually since 1950, describe a remarkable record of accomplishment and are delightful reading as well.

maritime history, were added East Hall (1889) for Pacific ethnology, Weld Hall (1907) for Japanese ethnology, the Francis B. Crowninshield Galleries (1953), a bookstack and reading room (1960), and a meeting room (1961). These latest additions, which were the gift of Messrs. Stephen Phillips, Mrs. Richard M. Saltonstall, Henry Belin du Pont and other friends, have, for the first time in fifty years, equipped the museum with adequate space for its exhibition, storage, and research functions.

The exhibition rooms are open free seven days a week, in return for which the City of Salem has long supplied a police constable. Otherwise the museum has operated entirely on private funds, which were until recent years in the form of income from endowment. Within the past decade this has been supplemented by a number of private gifts and foundation grants for special research projects, some of which have involved expeditions to Polynesia. In 1960, for example, when operating expenses totaled $93,075.52, $84,655.26 of this sum was met by income from invested funds, and the remainder from current gifts.

Although responsibility for the museum rests entirely in the board of trustees, there are three organizations with members that assist in various ways. The Peabody Museum Marine Associates, a group of men all of whom have some special knowledge of maritime history, was organized in 1939. Having neither bylaws, officers, or dues, it has flourished pleasantly ever since as a means of exchanging information. Every so often the curator of maritime history sends the notice of a meeting to the membership list and someone reads a paper. Once a year there is a "Dutch-treat" dinner at the Boston Yacht Club. At its meetings one often finds a combination of historians, yachtsmen, lawyers, and tattooed seamen and the owners of the steamships in which they once served. While the Marine Associates exist merely for the interchange of useful knowledge, the Fellows and Friends of the Peabody Museum, organized in 1951, provide financial support that has been helpful in acquiring special collections. Fellows give $50 or more annually; Friends $10 or more.

In 1960 the subscriptions of 116 Fellows and over 350 Friends totaled $11,284.75. At least one meeting a year is held for them, and they receive certain publications from time to time.

The director, Ernest S. Dodge, and the assistant director, M. V. Brewington, have both recently held Guggenheim Fellowships, the former for an investigation of Polynesian ethnological specimens in European collections brought back by Captain James Cook, the latter for the preparation of a dictionary of marine artists and ship portraitists. Although they, with Miss Dorothy E. Snyder, curator of natural history, and eight others, constitute the paid staff, the Peabody Museum has a large number of honorary curators and volunteer associates who work regularly on different aspects of the collections. Colonel George Lamberton Smith, honorary curator of anthropology, has, since his retirement from the army at the end of World War II, been indistinguishable from a professional curator save that he generously contributes his services. Two of the trustees, Francis B. Lothrop and Oliver Wolcott, are regularly at the museum at fixed times, engaged respectively in curatorial work on the print and ethnology collections. That these, and more than twenty other volunteers, assist regularly in curatorial work is a tribute to the atmosphere of scholarly industry that Mr. Dodge inspires. Save in the Harvard Museum of Comparative Zoology in the era of the late Thomas Barbour, I have seen no other instance in which so many volunteers work so professionally and so consistently in curatorial tasks.

The research projects and expeditions in Polynesian ethnology and linguistics sponsored by the museum are beyond the scope of this study. Its comparable activities in American maritime history are, however, pertinent. The library and the photograph and manuscript collections of the Peabody Museum of Salem constantly attract a large number of scholars, professional and amateur, in this field. The museum has in the past twenty-five years published a number of books, including such contemporary narratives as the late Judge F. W. Howay's edition of *The Voyage of the* New Hazard *to the*

Northwest Coast, Hawaii and China, 1810–1813, by Stephen Reynolds, *a member of the crew*; my *New England Blockaded in 1814, The Journal of Henry Edward Napier, Lieutenant in H. M. S.* Nymphe; and *The New Zealand Journal 1842–1844 of John B. Williams of Salem, Massachusetts,* edited by Dean Robert W. Kenny of Brown University. Other journals of the China trade and Pacific voyages, and the papers of the naval constructor Josiah Fox, have been transcribed and will be published as time for editing and funds permit. Such monographs as Charles Edey Fay's *Mary Celeste, The Odyssey of an Abandoned Ship,* Frederic A. Eustis's *Augustus Hemenway 1805–1876 Builder of the United States Trade with the West Coast of South America,* and my sesquicentennial history of the museum have been published in similar format.

The American Neptune, A Quarterly Journal of Maritime History, which has been published regularly since 1941, evolved from the Peabody Museum Marine Associates. As it was designed to be national in scope—an American counterpart of *The Mariner's Mirror* —a separate Massachusetts nonprofit corporation, The American Neptune, Incorporated, was organized for its publication, to avoid any suggestion that the journal was a house-organ of the Peabody Museum. Its editorial board has always contained representatives of universities and libraries throughout the country, as well as a number of private scholars. From 1941 through 1950 I edited the journal from, successively, the museum, the Navy Department, and the Boston Athenæum. Since 1951, when Ernest S. Dodge took over the editorship, the *Neptune* has returned to Salem.

The Carnegie Corporation of New York in 1940, through the efforts of Waldo G. Leland, made a grant of $1,500 to subsidize the cost of a prospectus and the printing of the first number. Editors and contributors are unpaid. The Peabody Museum amiably provides some clerical and bookkeeping assistance. Otherwise the *Neptune* has depended entirely upon the income from subscriptions—originally $5, now $10 a year—for its support. The journal has regularly appeared quarterly since January 1941 in issues of eighty to ninety-six pages, liberally illustrated in collotype. Thanks to the services freely given by its editors, and the helpfulness of its printers, The Anthoensen Press of Portland, Maine, who have extended credit in lean periods, *The American Neptune* has survived as a self-supporting scholarly journal for two decades. Although its nose has always remained above water, it has, at times, seemed in peril of drowning, for during and since the war printing costs have spiraled, and there never are quite enough subscribers for comfort. Recruits to the subscription list, which seldom exceeds 1,000, have to come chiefly from word of mouth and personal contact, for none of the editors has time to spare for organized promotion. Indeed with a journal in so specialized a field, the cost of any conventional publicity would be self-defeating.[7] As the size of issues has to be kept within limits imposed by the revenue from subscriptions, many worth-while articles have to be refused for want of space and some of those accepted are longer delayed in publication than is desirable. There is at present sufficient accepted material on hand to publish *The American Neptune* for two years. A modest but dependable subsidy would permit an increase in the number of pages in each issue, thus accelerating the speed of appearance of articles and greatly enlarging the scholarly usefulness of *The American Neptune* without the slightest increase in overhead. Good material arrives constantly; at present there is not space to print enough of it.

The Peabody Museum of Salem today offers a striking example of an old independent institution that has in recent years rationalized and organized the rich accumulations of more than 160 years, without change in its fundamental aims or its means of support. Its buildings and equipment are now adequate for convenient contemporary use, for it has had the assistance of a group of devoted supporters,

7. Several years ago two friendly commercial publishers in the maritime field allowed the editors of *The American Neptune* to circularize their large mailing lists. One hundred new subscriptions resulted, but the printing and mailing expense of the circularization exactly equaled the first year's revenue from these. At the same time a devoted subscriber wrote personal letters to thirty friends, using his own paper and stamps, and scared up twenty-five new subscriptions at no expense to the *Neptune*.

many of whom are outside New England, who have been attracted by the serious aspects of its historical and ethnological activities. Although some 49,600 visitors trooped through its exhibition galleries in the year 1960, they represent an expense rather than a source of support. Within the limit of its resources, the museum attempts gladly to meet all legitimate requests from the local and traveling public. It was visited in 1960 by 289 school classes and other organized groups. It does not, however, artificially seek to inspire or increase attendance, for its trustees, staff, and supporters are more concerned with the advancement of knowledge than with its popular dissemination. Of its future, Mr. Dodge wrote in his 1960 report:

Our only remaining need is substantially increased endowment; at least fifty per cent of what we have now, or roughly a million dollars. This will be the fuel to put our ship into orbit. But while money is an institution's fuel, spirit is the catalyst that makes it burn efficiently. The combination is necessary—spirit alone cannot do it, for after years it gets wrecked on the rocks of frustration. Adequate finances alone will not do it, for without the spirit an air of comfortable complacency enshrouds a place and sluggards in sinecures beget themselves endlessly. But the two together, properly mixed, will cause an institution to glow and be seen and used as a beacon that will call the humble, the wise, and the discriminating from far corners of the earth. They will gather like moths around a light. The museum will be a better mouse trap.

NORWEGIAN-AMERICAN HISTORICAL ASSOCIATION

In 1925, 100 years after the little sloop *Restauration* arrived in New York from Stavanger with the first group of Norwegian emigrants to the United States, the Norwegian-American Historical Association[8] was formed at St. Olaf College, Northfield, Minnesota. Its general purpose, according to the certificate of incorporation was "to seek and gather information about the people in the United States of Norwegian birth and descent and to preserve the same in

8. *A Review And A Challenge*, a 33-page mimeographed document published by the association in 1938, gives an admirable analysis of activities to that date. The occasional *News Letter* supplies later information.

appropriate form as historic records." Specifically it was proposed through voluntary contributions and membership dues to develop a historical archive at St. Olaf College; to assist in the support of the Norwegian-American Historical Museum already in existence at Luther College, Decorah, Iowa; to encourage historical research and literary effort; and to publish monographs and other works dealing with Norwegian-American history, literature, art, and culture. The association was under literate and distinguished professional guidance from the beginning, for its first secretary was the novelist O. E. Rölvaag, professor at St. Olaf College, while its managing editor was Dr. Theodore C. Blegen, who was later to become Dean of the Graduate School of the University of Minnesota.

The association has from the beginning made it clear "that quality rather than quantity was to be the yardstick for measuring the worth of publications." While adhering to that standard, it has, neverthe-less, with limited resources issued a truly phenomenal number of books. The presence on its board of editors of men like Dean Blegen, the late Marcus L. Hansen, Professor Einar Haugen of the University of Wisconsin, Professor Carlton C. Qualey of Carleton College, and Professor Kenneth O. Bjork, the present managing editor, has assured a high standard of scholarship by men trained in the writing of history, careful selection of materials, and scrupulous care in editing. The tie with St. Olaf College has continued to be a close one. On the death of Dr. Rölvaag in 1931, Dr. J. Jörgen Thompson, long dean of men at the college, became secretary of the Norwegian-American Historical Association and held that post until 1958, when he was succeeded by Professor Lloyd Hustvedt. The college pro-

---

When the study of independent historical societies was first announced in 1959, the late Carl L. Lokke of the National Archives wrote to call my attention to the association. He concluded: "For your study you will have to draw the line somewhere. When you draw it, I hope the Norwegian-American Historical Association will land within it." A visit to Northfield in March 1960, under the guidance of Mr. Arch Grahn of the Minnesota Historical Society, amply confirmed everything that the late Dr. Lokke had told me about the association. As I was never able to thank him in person for this suggestion, I can only record my gratitude to him here.

vides space on the seventh floor of its library and, since 1959, has taken over the care of the manuscripts collected by the association.[9]

The professional standards of the editors have not led to narrowly specialized interests. On the contrary Dr. Blegen in 1930 insisted the association should strike the "note of tolerance and breadth of interest." Among subjects for possible investigation he outlined the following:

We are interested in ski runners who have brought northern sports into American vogue. We are interested in men and women who have pioneered on America's far-flung frontiers—and in their children and children's children. We are interested in the work of businessmen, professional men, artisans, laborers. We are interested in sailors who have gone down to the sea in ships, in soldiers who have followed the flag, in politics and parties and leaders, conservative, liberal, or radical. We are interested in the church and every denomination. We are interested in those who have not been identified with the church or have been hostile to it. We are interested in music, art, literature, the press, periodicals, scholarship. We are interested in the organizations that have been active among the Norwegian-Americans. We are interested in schools and colleges, their principles, methods, teachers and achievements. We are interested in the tangled problems involved in the adjustment of people to the new environment. History must lift the curtain on a thousand varied activities, on men and women of all classes, on people in every section, helping us to understand the onward march of human forces, with all their baffling interrelationships. Our interest in the human contingent that followed the trails of Cleng Peerson and Ole Rynning, that came out of the rock-bound land of the North and sought its destiny in the New World, is one with an interest in this American civilization of which we are a part and into the building of which have gone the varied cultural impulses of peoples drawn from all parts of the world, impulses modified by the contact of these peoples with one another, given new directions by the forces of the American environment, and working themselves out on the loom of time, one generation after another, with adaptation and conservation both playing into the weave.

9. The *Guide* lists "8 filing cases and 120 pieces, 1856–1925, relating chiefly to Norwegian pioneers in Minnesota and other States, Norwegian Lutheran Church history, and St. Olaf College. " Although the collecting of sources has always been secondary to research and publication, the association's manuscript collection is considerably larger than this entry indicates. It is now being organized for more convenient use, and a guide prepared. Reports on the progress of this work have been published in the *News Letter* from March 1961 onward.

The forty-three substantial books published by the association in less than that many years give evidence that the goals set by Dr. Blegen have been more fully achieved than is usual in programs of such breadth. There are first of all twenty-one volumes of *Studies and Records*, containing historical monographs, translated documents, and bibliographies of recent publications relating to Norwegian-American history. These have long been favorably noted by the *American Historical Review*, the *Mississippi Valley Historical Review*, and other periodicals. The six volumes of the Travel and Description Series include translations of Ole Rynning's and Peter Testman's accounts of America, published in Norway in the 1830s, which influenced emigration; the 1847–48 letters of Ole Munch Raeder, a Norwegian scholar sent to America by his government to make a study of the jury system; letters from a Wisconsin parsonage, 1855–58, by Olaus Frederik Duus, from Gro Svendsen, a frontier mother, 1861–80; and from Elise Wærenskjold in Texas, 1851–95. Among the special publications are the two parts of Dean Blegen's *Norwegian Migration to America*, Carlton C. Qualey's *Norwegian Settlement in the United States*, Kenneth O. Bjork's *West of the Great Divide: Norwegian Migration to the Pacific Coast, 1847–1893*, Knut Gjerset's *Norwegian Sailors on the Great Lakes* and *Norwegian Sailors in American Waters: A Study in the History of Maritime Activity on the Eastern Seaboard*. Other volumes deal with Norwegian engineers, journalists, scholars, and farmers.

Admiration for the variety of subject, the quality of research, editing, and book production involved in this remarkable series can only be exceeded by amazement that so much has been accomplished with such limited financial resources. The chief source of revenue has always been members' dues. Associate membership is $5, sustaining $20, patron $25 or more per year. Life membership payments of $100 have been placed in a permanent endowment fund, which now totals $22,000. The membership has only once exceeded 1,000, and in most years is below that figure. Like *The American Neptune*, the Norwegian-American Historical Association depends entirely upon the unpaid but considerable services of its officers and editors, all of whom have many other things to do. The secretary has some part-time salaried clerical assistance; otherwise all time is donated, while St. Olaf College provides housing. Thus all dues and any gifts and bequests are promptly plowed back into more research and more publication.

Sometimes, as with *The American Neptune*, the outlook becomes cloudy. The December 1949 *News Letter* contained the report of an engaging conversation between two veterans of the executive committee, Treasurer Birger Osland and Secretary J. Jörgen Thompson.

Sitting under a fig tree in the garden of President [Olaf] Halvorson after the executive meeting in Huntington Park [California], Thompson remarked: "You look gloomy, Birger, what is up?"

"Well, Jörgen, do you realize that, at this meeting, we have authorized publications and research work which is likely to cost us every dollar we now have in the treasury?

"What bothers me is, that I feel I am getting too old for my job. Formerly, I could go to my friends for a lift when we needed it, to Magnus Swenson in Madison; to O. M. Oleson in Fort Dodge or to Arthur Andersen in Chicago. They understood, they could do it, and they were willing. They have all passed away.

"At my age of eighty one does not readily acquire new friends. I am too old for the job of treasurer."

A fig dropped from the tree in Osland's lap. Thompson grabbed it and held it up .

"Birger," said he, "that is the way it may happen."

As eleven volumes have appeared since that conversation, the parable of the fig tree was clearly heeded.

Again, as with *The American Neptune*, there is always difficulty in locating interested possible members and in selling the stock of publications that remains after the initial distribution. Scholarly books of this kind should be printed in editions large enough to meet all possible needs over a period of years. Advertising is too expensive to be considered, and trade channels are of little help. As the word sometimes passes slowly, stock accumulates. The December 1958 *News Letter* included an inventory of books on hand, with the comment:

If the retail price of the above inventory be used, the stock totals over $39,000. If the 25% discount allowed to members be the basis, then the figure reaches something more than $29,000. Because a free copy is always given to each new member (now *West of the Great Divide*) no accurate estimate can ever be reached. However, the inventory does suggest several things. First, OUR BOOKS SHOULD BE OUT AMONG THE PEOPLE, NOT ON OUR SHELVES. Second, the income from the sale of these books would go far to finance future publications, and also to pay for second and third printings of some books, should the demand be great enough.

Professor Franklin D. Scott of Northwestern University described the Norwegian-American Historical Association as "a prototype for other groups who would search the past to gain understanding of themselves, and of the America they have helped to build." Its importance, however, goes beyond the emigrant groups, for the intelligent, generous, and single-minded devotion of those who have created and maintained it should serve as an inspiration to any society concerned with any aspect of American history. It is a model of what scholars with a plan can accomplish.

MUSEUM OF NAVAJO CEREMONIAL ART

The preceding paragraphs have described the efforts of a group of professional scholars to study and describe all possible aspects of one national group in the United States. Those that follow concern the effort of an amateur, equally remarkable in its way, to record and preserve what would otherwise have been lost of a single central aspect of a very different group. The Museum of Navajo Ceremonial Art in Santa Fe, New Mexico, incorporated in 1937 to perpetuate the myths, music, poetry, sacred lore and objects connected with the Navajo religion for the general public, for research students, and for the Indians themselves, was the creation of one Boston woman, Miss Mary Cabot Wheelwright (1878–1958). This institution is a striking instance of what Lyman Butterfield would call "the Boston pack rat tradition," transplanted to the southwest and applied to a primitive people whose history was unwritten.

Miss Wheelwright was the only child of a pair of Bostonians who were not young when she was born.[10] The first half of her life was conventionally enough limited to Mount Vernon Street and Northeast Harbor, Maine, but even there she showed energy and imagination in pursuing her interests. She loved music and founded The Carry-On Shops, which sold handicrafts in Boston and Northeast Harbor, to raise money for the South End Music School. In a substantial converted pilot boat, she cruised the Maine and Nova Scotia coasts. She collected ship pictures and New England folk art and handicrafts long before they became popular. When Phillips Barry, Fannie Hardy Eckstorm, and Mary Winslow Smyth had in 1928 nearly completed their *British Ballads from Maine*, Miss Wheelwright forcibly assured them that texts without airs left much to be desired. Because of publication arrangements with the Yale University Press, there was only a month to spare. Nevertheless Miss Wheelwright— "as clear-sighted and practical as she is enthusiastic" was the way the editors described her—conjured up by telegram from an Indian reservation in South Dakota an expert in musical notation, transported him to Maine, and financed his work in securing tunes from the singers who had previously provided texts. Thus when the 535-page *British Ballads from Maine* was published in 1929, it was the richer for Miss Wheelwright's intelligent and decisive intervention.

After her parents' deaths, Boston saw little of her, for she divided her time between three widely scattered houses, each one a remarkable example of its kind: a Mediterranean villa in the hills above Palma de Mallorca, a fisherman's cottage on Sutton's Island, Maine, named, from the way it sat on the ground, "The White Hen," and

10. Her father, Andrew Cunningham Wheelwright, a member of the Harvard Class of 1847, performed a valued service to historic preservation in Boston some seventy years ago. When in 1892 the West Church, whose pulpit had been occupied by Jonathan Mayhew, went the way of many city churches, Mr. Wheelwright bought its dignified meetinghouse at the corner of Cambridge and Lynde Streets and held it until in 1894 the City of Boston had the wit to convert the building into a branch library. Thus a fine building, designed by Asher Benjamin in 1806, has survived as one of the few amenities of that part of the city. See Walter Muir Whitehill, *Boston Public Library, A Centennial History* (Cambridge, 1956), pp. 125–126.

Los Luceros, an ancient Spanish ranch in Alcalde, New Mexico. Although easily identifiable as a Bostonian at any range within sight or sound,[11] Miss Wheelwright had great curiosity about the most unlikely things and instinctive sympathy with distant surroundings. In New Mexico, despite the barrier of language, she won the friendship of Hasteen Klah, then the most famous of all Navajo medicine men, whom she first met when snowbound on the Navajo Reservation. Through him she gained entrance to rites and ceremonies never before witnessed by white visitors. With his help she learned to appreciate the Navajo religion, began to collect the record of its innumerable ceremonies, and in the end established the Museum of Navajo Ceremonial Art to ensure their safe preservation.

Oliver La Farge, who came to know Miss Wheelwright about 1930 through their common Navajo interests and who is now president of the museum's trustees, has recently written:

Materially, Navajo culture was, and still is, simple, with a Spartan lack of physical comforts. Yet in this culture flourish famous arts of weaving and silver-smithing and a religion that includes a noble philosophy, great prose, great poetry, beautiful rites, and, perhaps best known of all, the highly sophisticated symbolic art of the sand-paintings and dry-paintings.

Everything that a traditional Navajo family possessed, if we except their live-stock and the great riches they carried within their own minds, could be loaded in a single wagon to be drawn by two horses, yet out of what that wagon carried and out of themselves they could produce religious and secular beauty that have won admiration throughout the world. At the heart of these riches is the Navajo religion with its attendant ceremonials, and the religion also embraces them all. If one knows the whole of Navajo religion, one knows, in effect, the whole of Navajo culture.

Few people, probably no non-Navajos, know the whole of Navajo religion. For centuries it was perfected and elaborated by thinkers and artists, although

11. I first met her in 1933 in the Estación de Francia in Barcelona, when she and a mutual friend were coming to join my wife and me in a month's journey along the pilgrimage road to Santiago de Compostela. Long before I sighted her tall tweed-coated person, I heard, above the commotion of porters and passengers debarking from the Paris night express, an unmistakably New England voice calling repeatedly and with authority for Thomas Cook's representative. Immediately I knew that Miss Wheelwright must be in the offing.

those whom we would call artists certainly never so considered themselves. They were merely men who had a drive to make the myths more beautiful, the designs more perfectly expressive. Rites were devised for every possible need or occasion; religion came to permeate every part of daily life. Each rite carried with it its symbols and its highly poetic prayers, was supported by a prose myth rich in imagination and color, and usually involved a greater or smaller number of sand-paintings. The most learned Navajo priests or "singers" felt qualified to be in charge of only a portion of the total.

For several generations the civilized world, with its countless hordes of people, its machine culture has exerted almost unbearable pressure upon the Navajos. . . . Under the circumstances small wonder that the great complex of religion, art, literature, and ceremonial has fallen away. Already there are major rites and groups of rites that are forgotten—except that they are preserved, in writing and in reproduction, in the Museum of Navajo Ceremonial Art.

Mr. La Farge notes that the museum's approach was "most unusual in that it involved not only the technical, scientific recording of what is usually meant by 'ceremonial', but also the capturing of the spirit and quality of a religion that the museum's founder and her co-workers regarded with profound respect." He continues:

A major result of this approach, as well as of the great confidence Miss Wheelwright herself inspired in devout Navajos, has been that the "singers" themselves have increasingly joined in the effort to cause the whole religious heritage to be recorded in all its ramifications. Again and again material has been supplied by old men who found no acolyte to study under them and knew that, with their death, their knowledge would be lost unless given to this institution. The museum now possesses a mass of written records, graphic reproductions, collection of actual ceremonial objects, and sound recordings that is unequalled—and the work is still incomplete.

The beautiful and symbolical paintings in colored sands that are an essential element of Navajo ceremonies are rubbed away at the conclusion of the rite of which they form a part. The designs and their meaning thus remain only in the medicine man's head. To insure the preservation of some of the most important, Hasteen Klah learned to weave—normally woman's work—and, with his nieces, wove thirteen blankets, in sizes ranging from four feet square to eight by nine feet, to perpetuate certain of his sand-painting designs from the

Night Chant and the Hail Chant. These are in the museum, with 559 water-color copies of sand-paintings from a great variety of ceremonies, and 65 cassein copies of others, eight feet square, made for exhibition. There are manuscripts of 16 chants and ceremonies, usually in several versions, as given by different medicine men and collected by various recorders, 1,500 sound recordings of chants, as well as an extensive collection of Navajo ceremonial objects—masks, prayer sticks and bundles, rattles, herbs—and similar artifacts from other Indian tribes and pueblos, and from Tibet, China, Japan, India, New Zealand, and prehistoric Europe for comparative purposes. There is also a good working library of books and journals in the field.

The Museum of Navajo Ceremonial Art is located on the Camino Lejo, near the Old Pecos Road, two miles southeast of the Santa Fe plaza. Its striking site, comprising ten acres in the foothills of the Sangre de Cristo mountains, was the gift of Miss A. E. White. The building, designed as an interpretation in modern form of a Navajo ceremonial *Hoghan*, contains on its upper level an impressive gallery for the rotating exhibition of the large cassein copies of sand-paintings. On the ground floor are smaller exhibition rooms, storage space, the library, offices, and living quarters for the director, Mr. Kenneth E. Foster. The large upper gallery, with its cribbed log roof, single skylight, and octagonal sides, effectively carries the visitor into another world. The lower floor offers a convenient and agreeable area for research.

The museum has published seven bulletins (at 25c each) containing the abbreviated form of myths upon which the sand-paintings are based, and four sumptuous volumes (at $20 each) in the Navajo Religion Series, with full texts, illustrated by silk screen plates. The latter are Miss Wheelwright's *Navajo Creation Myth* (1942), *Water and Hail Chants* (1946), *Great Star Chant and Prayers*, and *Coyote Chant* (1957), and the *Emergence Myth According to the Hanethnlaye or Upward-Reaching Rite* (1949), recorded by Father Berard-Haile, o.f.m., and revised by her. Father Berard-Haile's *Star Lore Among the*

Navajos and *The Four Directions of Time*, a paper by C. A. Burland of the British Museum on similarities between Mexican and Navajo conceptions of religion, have also been issued by the museum. The Peabody Museum, Harvard University, published as volume xxxii, no. 3 (1956) of its *Papers*, *A Study of Navajo Symbolism*, by Franc J. Newcomb, S. A. Fishler, and Miss Wheelwright, as well as an album of *Navajo Creation Chants* on five double-faced records of sixteen songs, originally sung by Hasteen Klah.

Although the Museum of Navajo Ceremonial Art was organized as a nonprofit corporation under the laws of New Mexico, with a board of trustees[12] and several classes of membership (annual from $5 to $100, life $1,000), Miss Wheelwright during her lifetime furnished the lion's share of its support. She created it, oversaw most of its work, and contributed the $8,500 a year that were its normal operating expenses. Because of the old Boston theory that money should be kept in the family and that daughters could not safely be trusted with it, most of her income came from life trusts, the principal of which was outside her control. In her later seventies, being acutely aware that she could not bequeath a capital sum that would compensate for the loss of her current annual gifts, she began a strenuous effort to build up an endowment fund. At the time of her death on 29 July 1958 this was barely under way. In December 1959, Oliver La Farge, who had succeeded to the presidency of the board, made an appeal for gifts to the Mary Cabot Wheelwright Memorial Fund, in which he stated that $15,000 was on hand and $135,000 expected on the final settlement of her estate. As a minimum of $225,000 was considered necessary to ensure the museum's continuance "as anything more than a mere warehouse," the difference of $75,000 was urgently needed. In April 1960 he reported that the "gap now to be closed stands at slightly over $50,000." This was still

12. They are today Oliver La Farge, president; Kenneth E. Foster, secretary-treasurer; John Otis Brew, Robert Euler, Miss Alice Marriott, Oliver Seth, Mrs. McIntosh Buell, John Y. Gannaway, David P. McAllester, Fowler McCormick, Mrs. Hoyne Wells, and Leland C. Wyman.

further reduced later in the year by a grant of $25,000 from the Bollingen Foundation. In January 1962 he passed along the encouraging news that the minimum goal of $225,000 had been achieved.

The museum runs in a modest and unbureaucratic way. Over 8,000 visitors come each year, adults paying 50c, children 25c, school groups, members, and Indians free. The membership, which is unlikely ever to be large because of the nature of the institution, supplies a couple of thousand dollars in dues, and sometimes considerably more in contributions. It is fortunate that the director, Mr. Kenneth E. Foster, had worked closely with Miss Wheelwright for a number of years; that he is devoted to the subject; that he works energetically and imaginatively; and that his personal wants are modest. A former college teacher of fine arts, with a special interest in the far east, he travels and lectures extensively. In the winter of 1959–60 after a brief vacation in Japan, he continued around the world at the request of the State Department, lecturing on the museum and its collections in Japan, Hong Kong, Thailand, Burma, India, Nepal, Greece, Italy, Sweden, England, and France. While part of his expenses were paid by the State Department, the greater share came out of his own pocket.

The most touching tribute to the value of the Museum of Navajo Ceremonial Art comes from the Navajos themselves. In 1956, on the occasion of the museum's twentieth anniversary and the Blessing Chant which was given to celebrate it, the chairman of the Navajo Tribal Council sent the following message:[13]

Hasteen Klah, who had such a large part in bringing this Museum into being, was my clan uncle. Therefore, I have the honor to pay homage to this great spiritual leader of the Navajo people and also to give thanks to Miss Mary Cabot Wheelwright for her vision and generosity in establishing this unique museum.

At the time she began her study of the religion of the Navajo people, few indeed were the non-Navajos who tried to understand the religious heritage of our people.

Because of her interest and philanthropy there has been created in Santa Fe a most unusual living tribute to our religion. We owe a great deal to her profound

13. Published in *The New Mexican*, 4 December 1956.

and sympathetic understanding in preserving the most sacred thinkings of our way of life in an atmosphere of great reverence and beauty.

Originally this museum was blessed by Hasteen Klah himself, before it was opened to the public. It is my understanding that already it has become a sort of religious shrine which religious students from all over the world have visited. Yet it is more than that, for it is also a repository of a great wealth of information which will be kept safe for future generations of all those who are interested in studying the great beliefs and the rituals of my people.

It is to her credit that Miss Wheelwright, Mr. [Kenneth] Foster and the staff of this institution have not regarded this knowledge and these sacred objects as mere curiosities, but have preserved them in a form which perpetuates the significant vitality of what we Navajo people still consider the source of our strength and beauty of our way of life.

The Museum of Navajo Ceremonial Art has captured the harmonious interweaving of religion, art, and the literature of the Navajo people and has accomplished this in a manner which is pleasing to us and in which we can ourselves take great pride.

The religious ceremonies, the prayers, and the rituals, the sand paintings, and the myths can be so easily misinterpreted or misunderstood. If, through the preservation of these things in the beautifully proportioned Hogan of the museum the visitor can capture the feeling of harmony between deity, man, and nature, then he will have glimpsed that element of piety which is so characteristic of the spiritual life of individual Navajos.

It is certainly most unusual and difficult for a museum to achieve the purpose of keeping alive something of the spirit of the religion of a people who never had a written language. Yet I have the feeling that in this place the beliefs of our religious heritage will be kept alive for future generations to know.

On behalf of the Navajo people I wish to express our thanks to Miss Wheelwright for undertaking with courage what could only be accomplished in the most intangible awareness of spiritual tranquility and symbolic beauty. She has accomplished this, and she has done it well. The Navajo people will be forever grateful to her for this achievement of building the things of the spirit into visible and physical form in the Museum of Navajo Ceremonial Art.

(*Signed*) Mr. Paul Jones, Chairman
Navajo Tribal Council,
The Navajo Tribe
Window Rock, Arizona
December 1, 1956

Chapter XVII

THE SHINTO TEMPLE

One lady had a lot to tell about her family in a rather high-pitched voice. I did not prolong my intrusion. I felt bewildered. I said to myself that I came from a country whose ancestor worship is world-renowned, yet I had never seen so much reverence for ancestors anywhere in China as I saw in Boston.　　—CHIANG YEE, 1959

IN an address before the Virginia Historical Society in May 1960, I quoted with singular pleasure a flight of fancy of J. Franklin Jameson which I had only recently discovered. This came from his article on "The Future Uses of History," first published in 1912 and reprinted in the October 1959 issue of the *American Historical Review* "not only in recognition of the centenary of Jameson's birth, but as an illustration of his vision." In this Jameson wrote:

In the field of history, indeed, the advancement of learning may be likened to the advance of an army. The workers in organized institutions of research must go before, like pickets or scouting parties making a reconnaissance. Then, after some interval, comes the light cavalry of makers of doctoral dissertations, then, the heavy artillery of writers of maturer monographs, both of them heavily encumbered with ammunition trains of bibliography and footnotes. Then come the multitudinous infantry of readers and college students and school children, and finally, like sutlers and contractors hovering in the rear, the horde of those that make textbooks. . . . At all events, the conductor of the reconnaissance must have his eye on the future, rather than the immediate, needs of his profession, and must constantly make such forecast of them as he can.

I then attempted to extend the analogy to take cognizance of developments of the past half century in the following paragraphs:

When this image was created in 1912, the lowest form of animal life in the historical profession was the maker of textbooks. Jameson had not encountered the present-day horde of those that vulgarize and pervert history—riggers of television quizzes, promotional types who manufacture pseudo-historic monuments to catch the tourist dollar, eager "salesmen of history" who pander rather than elevate the public taste by emphasizing what is trivial in the past, publishers who regard four-color illustrations on slick paper as acceptable substitutes for thought or style, and their kindred. These contemporary nuisances are, to expand Jameson's image, the camp followers who come along, in the train of the army, corrupting, undermining health and spirit and diverting those who engage in dalliance with them into abandoning their primary duty in an act of prostitution.

If the pickets or scouting parties, in which the historical societies are enlisted, turn back to see how the infantry is progressing, pause to have a friendly beer with the sutlers and contractors, or sneak off in the bushes with the camp followers, their reconnaissance is bound to suffer.

When the reprint of this address, entitled "Cerebration Versus Celebration,"[1] reached the librarian of an eastern independent historical society, he wrote me as follows:

Your comments about "camp followers" make me wonder if some place in the T/O could not be found for the genealogists. My own inclination, at least some of the time, is to classify them as partisans, guerrillas, maquis, or what have you—occasionally useful in reconnaissance where they are familiar with the terrain but too often overly involved in operations against objectives of limited tactical value and no strategic use; ever ready to call on the scholars of the regular advance troops to dig them out of a hole but often inclined to be slightly derisive of historians (read "West P'inters") who do not share their enthusiasms. But then maybe I'm prejudiced.

One morning in 1960 when I arrived at a historical society west of the Mississippi, its able and scholarly librarian greeted me with the annoyed remark: "I'm running a Shinto temple instead of a library this morning!" The ground of annoyance was that four genealogists had arrived simultaneously to pre-empt, and quarrel over, the library's two microfilm readers.

In a number of the historical societies that I visited, both publicly and privately supported, a considerable amount of the library traffic

1. *Virginia Magazine of History and Biography* LXVIII (July 1960), 259–270.

came from genealogists. The amateurs and professionals of this discipline are sometimes snappish about historians and *vice versa*. Too often one finds the same unthinking and emotional hostility that divided the older amateur and the newer professional historians. This is undesirable, for both are enlisted in the same army. While each has developed his special tactics, both draw upon a common store of ammunition. It is not the basic disciplines that are incompatible, but rather the lack of imagination and experience of some practitioners of both. Just as history today frequently suffers from the antics of illiterate enthusiasts who confuse the wearing of hoop skirts and whiskers with a knowledge of the past, so genealogy often gets a bad name from the scalp-hunting of persons who attempt to reinforce their self-esteem, or bring a touch of romance into otherwise machinemade lives, by boasting of their descent from one or more distinguished individuals, while ignoring, or conveniently forgetting, a great number of other ancestors who formed an equal part of their inheritance. This is where trouble starts.

In the chapter of the *Oxford History of the United States*[2] devoted to social evolution from 1870 to 1900, Samuel Eliot Morison provides a section entitled "Joining and other Sport." In commenting on the fact that "despite his racial heterogeneity the average American was becoming urban in his environment, and uniform in his appearance, manners, and thought," Mr. Morison wrote:

The American "joiner" was a creation of this period. A reflex desire for distinction in a country of growing uniformity, a human craving for fellowship among urban masses who missed their old village and neighborhood associations, drew the descendants of stern anti-masons into secret societies and fraternal orders. Freemasons and Oddfellows, both of English origin, proved too exclusive to contain would-be members; the Elks, Woodmen, Royal Arcanum, Moose, and so forth, were founded between 1868 and 1888. The Catholic Church, wisely embracing a movement that it could not exclude, created the Knights of Columbus for its increasing membership; even the Southern freedmen had their United Order of African Ladies and Gentlemen, and Brothers and Sisters of Pleasure and Prosperity. This, the first form of the joining movement, brought people of different classes together; the second,

2. (London, 1927), II, 376–377.

based on race and ancestry, kept them apart. The Sons and Daughters of the American Revolution, Colonial Dames, Mayflower Descendants, Daughters of the Confederacy, and the like, were essentially a drawing together of the older American stock against their polyglot competitors.[3] Much they have done to preserve historical landmarks, records, and traditions; too often have they interpreted these traditions in a narrow and provincial spirit.

Although Mr. Morison does not mention it, some of the real "joiners" have succumbed to the temptation of hereditary organizations based on descent from signers of Magna Charta or William the Conqueror's Norman barons. A simple arithmetical calculation shows the slight nature of the common bond involved in such association. We are nearly 900 years, or thirty generations, away from 1066. In thirty generations, provided no inter-marriage among one's forebears occurred, one accumulates one billion, seventy-three million, seven hundred and forty-one thousand, eight hundred and twenty-four ancestors. I did not spend time doing this arithmetic, but found it conveniently tabulated in one of the meticulous publications of the Genealogical Society of the Church of Jesus Christ of Latter-day Saints.[4] It suggests that, even with due allowance for ancestors who, for want of anyone more exciting, married their cousins, the blood of Norman barons has become somewhat diluted after 900 years.

It is the "joiners" who raise the blood pressure of librarians of historical societies, primarily because they go to sources and return— in the words of Edward P. Cheyney—"not, like reapers, loaded with heavy sheaves of historical knowledge, but, like gleaners, with only a scanty store of names and dates and relationships."[5] In a per-

3. Another aspect of this drawing together—the agitation for immigration restriction—is well sketched by Barbara Miller Solomon, *Ancestors and Immigrants, A Changing New England Tradition* (Cambridge, 1956).

4. Archibald F. Bennett, *A Guide for Genealogical Research* (Salt Lake City, 1956), p. 22.

5. See Edward P. Cheyney, "Thomas Cheyney, A Chester County Squire: His Lesson for Genealogists," *Pennsylvania Magazine of History and Biography* LX (July 1936), 209–228. This address, delivered at the annual meeting of the Historical Society of Pennsylvania on 11 May 1936, could be read with profit by anyone considering the relationship between history and genealogy.

ceptive address before the National Genealogical Society in 1955,[6] Dr. Lester J. Cappon, director of the Institute of Early American History and Culture at Williamsburg, explained how "the growth of nationalism and the trend toward academic specialization . . . alienated the historian and the genealogist and made them suspicious of each other. . . . In the America of the early nineteenth century, the genealogist was not distinguishable from the typical historian who himself was frequently an antiquarian and a compiler of annals." He points out how even a century ago "there was no thought of separating historical and genealogical activities"; how "genealogy as the handmaid of history benefited from the close kinship between them," and how "the historian, for his own purposes, could hardly overlook the value of personal and family records so close at hand." In discussing the founders of the New England Historic Genealogical Society, organized in Boston in 1845, he observes that

In the period antedating professional historians and genealogists, these men and other members of the Society mixed their abiding interest in the past with the diversified activities of every-day life. Their stated objectives precluded a narrow, circumscribed program: "Whatever serves to influence or illustrate New England life and character, in what has been written, in what has been said, or in what has been done, whether by direct influence or remotely by contrast, comes of necessity within the scope of our design."

In the last third of the nineteenth century, as hereditary societies based on race or ancestry came into being "as exponents of so-called Americanism and defenders of the old against the new" and as the academic historians were developing, through the American Historical Association, new standards of professionalism, the roads of the genealogist and the historian began to diverge. As Dr. Cappon puts it,

Of all the factors contributing toward the estrangement of genealogy and history none was more virulent than the chauvinism of the latter nineteenth century which prescribed American patriotism in narrow terms incompatible with a democratic

---

6. "Genealogy, Handmaid of History," *National Genealogical Society Quarterly* XLV (March 1957), 1–9; reprinted as Special Publication No. 17.

society and proscribed those persons who could not qualify for lack of proper ancestral credentials. . . . Americans began to search the past for a venerable and glorified ancestry. If genealogy had ceased to be the handmaid of history, she had become the indentured servant of neo-patriotism.

As the "joiners" grew in number and vociferousness, genealogy became increasingly distasteful to librarians and historians. Prior to their advent genealogical information was often considered a desirable element in the publications of historical societies. Gradually that has ceased to be the case. With the third series of the *William and Mary Quarterly*, initiated in 1944 under the auspices of the Institute of Early American History and Culture, genealogical contributions disappeared. The New Jersey Historical Society, whose *Proceedings* go back to 1845, discontinued genealogical information after 1951; so in 1955 did the *Essex Institute Historical Collections*, begun in 1859.

In spite of this rising divorce rate, there are still a good number of historians and genealogists who understand and respect each other's activities. Witness the fact that Dr. Cappon, a historian, archivist, and editor of wide experience, not only delivered his "Genealogy, Handmaid of History" at the annual dinner of the National Genealogical Society, but has this year prepared for the New York Public Library *American Genealogical Periodicals, A Bibliography with a Chronological Finding-List*. And one has only to look at such recent works as Bernard Bailyn's *The New England Merchants in the Seventeenth Century*,[7] John A. Munroe's *Federalist Delaware, 1775–1815*,[8] or Miss Mildred Campbell's essay "Social Origins of Some Early Americans"[9] to see how essential a knowledge of family history and the intertwinings of kinship is to a broader consideration of colonial history. Similarly a perusal of *English Genealogy*,[10] by Sir Anthony

---

7. (Cambridge, 1955).

8. (New Brunswick, 1954).

9. In James Morton Smith, ed., *Seventeenth-Century America, Essays in Colonial History* (Chapel Hill, 1959), pp. 63–89.

10. Although an abridged version, with the title of *English Ancestry*, is available as number 25 of the Oxford Paperbacks, the full version of this work by Garter King of Arms is preferable because of its wealth of diverting and instructive illustrative detail.

Wagner, Garter King of Arms, recently published by the Clarendon Press, will show how rich a harvest may be reaped by a genealogist who approaches his subject with impersonal motives. Early in the second chapter, he likens English society to "a lofty structure with many shallow steps by which the skilful and persistent might climb, while some others slipped down and many more kept the framework solid by standing still." But, he adds, "even those who stood still might find that the ground had moved under them." He gives vivid illustrations of such movement in the chapter on "The Rise and Fall of Families," where the family of Jane Austen is described, and the pedigrees of three successful shopkeeping families in the London area are presented as patterns of social movement. In such works, genealogy proves itself to be not only handmaid of history, but a very comely and able one.

Although a consideration of genealogical societies as a group is beyond the scope of this study, mention must be made of the New England Historic Genealogical Society[11] in Boston, not only because of its antiquity but because its problems today are identical with those of the older independent historical societies. Incorporated by a special act of the Massachusetts General Court on 18 March 1845, its stated object is "to collect, preserve, and publish historical, biographical, and genealogical data, and, through its Library and its publications, to make such records available to members and the public." Its library of some 220,000 volumes has for nearly fifty years been housed in a fireproof building at 9 Ashburton Place, Boston, a stone's throw away from the Massachusetts Archives in the State House and from the valuable records in the Suffolk County Court House. It is freely open to the public. That is how Mr. Chiang Yee, while writing *The Silent Traveller in Boston*, chanced to make the observation quoted at the head of this chapter. Members of the society have the additional convenience of access to the stacks and the

11. See William Carroll Hill, *A Century of Genealogical Progress Being a History of the New England Historic Genealogical Society 1845–1945* (Boston, 1945); George G. Wolkins, "The Prince Society," M.H.S. *Proceedings* LXVI (1936–41), 223–254.

right to borrow books by mail. Since 1847 it has published quarterly the *New England Historical and Genealogical Register*, now under the editorship of the Reverend Gilbert H. Doane.[12] This is not only the oldest, but continues to be the most consistent and distinguished, periodical in its field in the country.

The society is privately supported from the income of endowment and dues of its 3,008 members. As of 30 March 1962 its investments, whose book value was $632,706, had a market value of $892,418. There are three classes of membership: annual at $15, life at $150, and colonial at $300. The latter class carries the privilege of transferring the membership in perpetuity without further payment. Membership receipts cover at least half of the annual operating expense, which is in the vicinity of $60,000. Although the fees for life memberships are low, the annual rate is realistic, for the cost of publishing the *Register*, which is sent to all members, is more than covered by dues and subscriptions. The possibility of borrowing books by mail leads many persons in distant parts of the country to become members.

In recent years the society has succeeded in balancing its budget chiefly by paying extremely modest salaries to its staff and relying upon scholars already retired from other posts to fill its chief administrative positions. In 1951 the Reverend Arthur Adams, F.S.A., an eminent genealogist and herald who had retired from the faculty of Trinity College, Hartford, became librarian. Although his knowledge of the field was unequaled, his age and infirmities made it difficult for him to carry out the duties of his office as energetically as would have been desirable. In 1959 he became librarian emeritus. At this point Dr. Doane, although still based in Wisconsin with other duties, became editor of the *Register*. He comes to Boston for a fortnight four times a year. The day-by-day work of the *Register* and much of the administrative detail of the society is carried on by Miss

12. Formerly director of libraries and now archivist of the University of Wisconsin, a Fellow of the American Society of Genealogists, and author of *Searching for Your Ancestors, The How and Why of Genealogy* (3rd ed., Minneapolis, 1960).

Elsie McCormack, associate editor and assistant secretary, who has been for forty-three years on the staff of the society. Miss Pauline King, with thirty-two years of service, administers the library with the title of acting librarian. These ladies and their assistants attend to the daily routine of the society in an efficient and workmanlike manner, but their days are too fully occupied to permit them to give much attention to the problems presented by the future of the society in a rapidly changing world. Thus through the lack of a general administrative officer,[13] and through the illness and death of the last president, the society has appeared, at least in the eyes of its neighbors, to have been somewhat adrift so far as future policies are concerned. The most unhappy consequence has been the seizure of the society's convenient headquarters in Ashburton Place by the commission charged with the construction of a new State office building. Thus in the near future new quarters must be found. This is particularly regrettable, for, not to mention the expense and upheaval involved in moving, no situation could be as advantageously equidistant between the two sources of records pertinent to the society's interests as the present one. Moreover there is the haunting feeling that with energetic political action the whole situation might never have arisen.

The future of the New England Historic Genealogical Society will depend entirely upon the imagination and energy that its officers and staff show in the next two or three years. New quarters in an appropriate location must be found, as well as increased support. With Charles Moorfield Storey as president and Frederick M. Kimball as treasurer, the wind is beginning to blow from a favorable quarter. Very recently the salaries of the staff have been increased to a more suitable level, and steps are being taken to raise new funds. Fortunately the society is national rather than purely local in its

---

13. On 1 August 1962, while this book was in press, Dr. Edgar P. Dean took over this post. A Harvard PH.D. in history with considerable administrative experience in foundations and in the armed forces, he gives every sign of being unusually well qualified to steer a correct course for the society.

appeal, for its services extend wherever the mails go, and there are descendants of New Englanders scattered throughout the other forty-four states.

The most energetic and worldwide collecting project of genealogical sources in the United States is being carried out not for historical but for religious motives. This is the work of the Church of Jesus Christ of Latter-day Saints; the results are assembled in its Genealogical Society in Salt Lake City. This mighty effort implements the doctrine of salvation for the dead (derived from 1 *Corinthians* 15:29) thus enunciated by the Prophet Joseph Smith on 3 October 1841:

The doctrine presents in a clear light the wisdom and mercy of God in preparing an ordinance for the salvation of the dead being baptized by proxy, their names recorded in heaven and they judged according to the deeds done in the body. This doctrine was the burden of the scriptures. Those saints who neglect it on behalf of their deceased relatives, do so at the peril of their own salvation.[14]

Joseph Fielding Smith, president of the Council of the Twelve Apostles, in an article on "Salvation for the Dead" written for the August 1959 issue of the *Millennial Star*,[15] the official publication of the Church in Great Britain, observed in amplification:

Since the coming of Elijah the work of genealogical research has taken hold of the people in lands all over the earth. The children are turning to their fathers and seeking out their genealogical records preparatory to having the necessary work done for them in the temple by which the dead, who died without a knowledge of the Gospel, are able to receive the blessings of salvation through the ordinances vicariously performed. Moreover it is the duty of the children to see that the records are gathered and compiled preparatory to the performing of the ordinances vicariously for the worthy dead.

As the compilation required for the performance of temple work consists of

an accurate and complete record of our own family group, of the families of all

14. *The Millennial Star* CXXI (August 1959), 298. I owe this publication and other helpful information to Messrs. G. Wesley Johnson Jr. and Paul G. Salisbury.

15. CXXI (August 1959), 300.

who are descended from us, and of the families for every marriage of every pro-
genitor (or direct ancestor) through whom our own life came[16]

and as these must be traced back as far as possible,[17] it will be readily
seen that European records are quite as essential as American ones.
With the purpose of assisting in such work the Genealogical Society
of Utah was incorporated in 1894 by a group of members of the
Church. Fifty years later, in 1944, it was reincorporated under the
title of the Genealogical Society of The Church of Jesus Christ of
Latter-day Saints, directly under the Church authorities, without
paid membership, and with its facilities "available to all of the public
who are of *good moral standing*, without regard to race, color or
creed."[18] The library of the Genealogical Society during 1938 began
using microfilm to obtain copies of birth, marriage, death, and census
records. In 1941 microfilming began in the British Isles and has since
spread to many parts of the world. As of 1 January 1960 there were
assembled in the library at Salt Lake City the following number of
100-foot rolls of film:

1. Sweden	50,936
2. Great Britain	26,115
3. The Netherlands	24,246
4. Denmark	23,227
5. Mexico	17,149
6. Germany	13,890
7. Finland	13,318
8. Canada	4,699
9. Belgium	4,077
10. Norway	3,665
11. Switzerland	897
12. France	797
13. Iceland	763
14. Australia	152

16. Archibald F. Bennett, *A Guide for Genealogical Research*, p. 16.
17. Bennett, *op. cit.*, p. 25, mentions "in the Genealogical Library a pedigree chart
running back from President George Albert Smith for fifty-two generations, to about
the year 480 A.D., and to a Frankish King of Cologne."
18. *Handbook for Genealogy and Temple Work* (Salt Lake City, 1956), pp. 8–12.

15. Italy	72	
16. New Zealand	70	
17. Miscellaneous foreign countries	560	
Total foreign microfilms		194,633
Total American microfilms		52,205
Total rolls to 1 January 1960		246,838

At this time microfilming had been generally completed in Connecticut, Delaware, Maine, Maryland, New Hampshire, North Carolina, Vermont, and Virginia, and was underway although not completed in twenty-one other states. It was estimated that 361,999,200 pages were included in these films.[19] This stupendous work, accomplished on a budget from the Church by sixty cameras and cameramen operating simultaneously in different parts of the world will go on indefinitely everywhere that the workers can get access to records. It is an awesome sight to see a room with 150 microfilm readers, every one in use, and, besides, students of printed books filling every available desk in a large building and spilling over onto stairs and into corridors. In the research department are forty genealogists, who, for coping with written inquiries, charge $2 an hour, which is less than the society pays them. These specialists have more orders than they can keep up with. While the majority of readers are members of the Church engaged in their religious duties, the library of the Genealogical Society may be used freely by anyone who turns up and who can find place to sit down in this beehive of activity. It is doubtful if any other privately supported group has ever spread so wide a net in the collecting of microcopies of historical sources, let it down so often, and hauled ashore so much material. Consequently the Genealogical Society of the Church of Jesus Christ of Latter-day Saints deserves special mention in this study even though the material that it films is, by virtue of the purpose that it serves, restricted to records of genealogical interest.

19. The number has undoubtedly greatly increased since. I quote from figures given me during a visit in the spring of 1960 by Mr. Archibald F. Bennett, secretary and librarian of the Genealogical Society.

Chapter XVIII

A CLOUD OF WITNESSES

The historian has been successful in gaining to a remarkable extent what he most needed—something both costly in money and trying on the nerves of many groups—that is, access to the records of the past. Here the appetite of the scholar has been insatiable. Catering to his needs (real or fancied) is like throwing peanuts to pigeons, or shoveling corn to swine. There was a time when the historian had to collect his own material.   —PAUL H. BUCK, 1961

D URING the first half of the nineteenth century the preservation of manuscript sources of American history was the almost unaided responsibility of privately supported historical societies. In the latter half of the century State legislatures, mostly west of the Alleghanies, began appropriating sums for the support of newer State historical societies that supplemented and extended the efforts of the older independent bodies. In the twentieth century a great variety of institutions, public and private, became active collectors of manuscripts and other historical sources. New federal and State agencies appeared upon the scene; long-established colleges and universities developed new interests; private collectors converted their libraries into public institutions. The January 1957 issue of *Library Trends*, devoted to "Manuscripts and Archives," discusses many phases of this evolution.

Historians exploring a new line of thought often turned up large bodies of papers which, for convenience in use, they induced their university librarians to house. Sometimes institutions sheltered the homeless by accepting groups of manuscripts which they did not need and to which they could give little care. This they did solely from historic conscience and the realization that these papers, obviously too good to throw away, had to be housed somewhere. Now and then, ignoring the fact that with manuscripts, as with Black Angus beef, there is a distinction between the fillet and the tail, an institution on the make would gloatingly assemble great quantities of papers because they were impressive in bulk and were to be had for the asking. Indeed a phenomenal respect for manuscripts as such developed in some institutions, despite the sobering reality that more trash has been written than ever has been printed. Then too documents assembled by private collectors have sometimes found their way to libraries frequented by scholars, but in other instances have been given, for reasons that seemed excellent to their owners, to town libraries, country historical societies, and schools and colleges where no one would expect to find them.

Since its reorganization in 1950, the National Historical Publications Commission has performed many services to learning, but the most welcome is *A Guide to Archives and Manuscripts in the United States*, published in January 1961 by the Yale University Press. This, like Virgil's appearance to Dante in the *selva oscura*, will lead many a perplexed wanderer through the maze of institutions that possess manuscripts today. The executive director of the commission, Dr. Philip M. Hamer, had the extraordinary kindness to allow me to examine a carbon copy of the *Guide* while it was still in press, thus saving me mountainous correspondence in attempting to discover who has what today.

The 775 pages of the *Guide* are full of surprises. How otherwise would one learn that a medieval cartulary of Ipswich Abbey is in the Lexington [Kentucky] Public Library, or notarial records of the monastery of San Lorenzo, Venice, 1478–1520, in the Public Library of Davenport, Iowa? And how would any one in need of Italian sources find his way to the

19 parchments, chiefly papal documents, 1550–1800; a few unpublished letters dealing with the Napoleonic wars; and several passports, hunting licenses, and the like, 1840–1860

reported—with some amused pleasure, one suspects—by the reverend librarian of St. Benedict's College, Atchison, Kansas. Although
there are Swinburne letters in New Brunswick, New Jersey, and
Browning manuscripts in Waco, Texas, it is American historical
manuscripts that all but fill the pages of the *Guide*.

A little imaginative ratiocination might lead someone seeking
letters of the Marquis de Lafayette to Lafayette College at Easton,
Pennsylvania, which possesses 200, mostly to George Washington.
The other holdings of that college are a few medieval manuscripts,
an autograph collection of English literary figures, and the records of
a late nineteenth-century local slate industry. But a student of the
Confederate States of America might easily be excused if he had not
thought to look for 3,015 letters of its vice-president Alexander H.
Stephens, exchanged with his brother Linton between 1834 and
1872, in the Manhattanville College of the Sacred Heart Library at
Purchase, New York, or for a few papers relating to Confederate
Army equipment and supplies in the Deschutes County Library at
Bend, Oregon. A detective or a poet could have a great deal of
diversion from themes inspired by leafing through the *Guide*, but the
student of American history will be even more grateful to the
National Historical Publications Commission for this remarkable
work, which is the first to provide adequate indication of where
his materials may be hiding.

For this study it has provided valuable information about several
institutions with whose collections I had no previous acquaintance.
It has also furnished a sense of relative scale for the holdings of many
familiar libraries, even with due allowance for the tendency of
harrassed curators to report in even hundreds of thousands or even
millions. The 996,992 pieces reported by the South Caroliniana Library in Columbia carry a greater ring of conviction than a figure
neatly ending in zeros. Several years ago I noted with surprise that a
neighboring Massachusetts library stated that it had 750,000 books,
while the Boston Athenæum, according to its latest report, claimed
a ragged figure that was just under 400,000. As the building of the

library in question would have fitted into that of the Boston Athenæum several times over, leaving room for a bowling alley and a skating rink, I was puzzled. Was I guilty of the New England passion for understatement, or had my neighbor indulged in wishful thinking? Over the next few months one of the Athenæum staff, to whom I had confided my perplexity, amused herself with our shelf list and an adding machine and found that our reputed holdings were correct. I have had some slight suspicion of neatly rounded numbers ever since, but nevertheless I am most grateful for any figures that appear in the *Guide*, rounded or otherwise. I have quoted many in these pages.

The *Guide* contains valuable information on the manuscript holdings of the historical societies described in preceding chapters. It also indicates how many university, public, and private libraries have acquired substantial groups of papers bearing upon American history. Sometimes these collections are directly related to the region in which they are housed. The earliest and most conspicuous example of this was the purchase by the University of California in 1905 of the library that, as the basis of his far-flung writing and publishing activities in western history, Hubert Howe Bancroft (1832–1918) had assembled.[1] Under the guidance of Henry Morse Stephens, Herbert E. Bolton, Herbert I. Priestley, and now George P. Hammond, the Bancroft Library at Berkeley has steadily grown in relationship to the university's historical research and teaching. It reported to the *Guide* "3,500,000 items, 1500–1955, relating chiefly to western North America and especially to California and Mexico." To bring together sources on the European background of the history of the Pacific Coast, including Central America and Mexico, the Bancroft Library Foreign Microfilm Project, begun in 1948, has yielded nearly three million frames of microfilmed materials from British, French, Dutch, Portuguese, Spanish, and Mexican archives.

As I mentioned in chapter XIII, the University of Washington

1. John Walton Caughey, *Hubert Howe Bancroft Historian of the West* (Berkeley, 1946), pp. 185–190, 351–355, 358–363, 391–407.

library has recently taken an active interest in adding manuscripts to its Pacific Northwest collection. At Seattle the specter of national competition has inspired renewed efforts to prevent papers of regional interest from migrating elsewhere. The University of Washington is currently developing imaginative plans for assembling trained groups that, during summer vacations, will go to smaller libraries in the Pacific Northwest to arrange and microfilm their manuscripts. Thus sources now widely scattered among institutions that have few facilities for coping with them will become readily available for interlibrary loan in a series of films modeled on the *Presidential Papers* of the Library of Congress. This is an example of the intelligent co-ordination of the varied talents and interests of librarians and of teachers and students of history.

The University of Virginia Library at Charlottesville reported to the *Guide*:

5,000,000 items, dated from the 13th century to the present and embracing primarily (1) papers relating to the history of Virginia and the southeastern United States, (2) papers on American literature and, to a lesser degree, English literature, and (3) the deposited archives of the University of Virginia and of several other institutions.

The present distinction of this library as an instrument of learning is due to its former librarian Harry Clemons and to two younger disciples, John Cook Wyllie and Francis L. Berkeley Jr., whom he established as curators, respectively, of rare books and of manuscripts. Mr. Wyllie has succeeded Mr. Clemons as librarian. Mr. Berkeley continues not only to guide the manuscript division, but to play a vital role in the affairs of the Virginia Historical Society, of the project for microfilming Virginia materials overseas, and of most scholarly enterprises that concern Virginia history. Few men are as widely beloved as he for their unobtrusive and disinterested service to learning. In 1950 he and Mrs. Constance E. Thurlow published a calendar of *The Jefferson Papers of the University of Virginia*[2] containing

2. (Charlottesville, 1950), number 8 of University of Virginia Bibliographical Series.

2,341 entries. The library in addition maintains a Jefferson check list, a chronological card file of some 60,000 of Jefferson's manuscripts, and letters to and from him, in various libraries. This was begun more than twenty-five years ago by Mr. Wyllie and expanded by many hands. Messrs. Wyllie and Berkeley also undertook a similar inventory of the writings of James Madison, which was the first step toward *The Papers of James Madison*, now being edited and published as a joint project by the Universities of Chicago and Virginia. By these and similar undertakings, the University of Virginia Library has become not only a custodian of sources for the history of Virginia but an active partner in projects for their use extending far beyond Charlottesville.

In the same State one should remember that Dr. E. G. Swem, long librarian of the College of William and Mary, not only developed there a manuscript collection—reported to the *Guide* as "450,000 pieces relating chiefly to Virginia and the South"—but compiled singlehanded the mammoth two-volume *Virginia Historical Index* that is an indispensable tool for anyone working in Virginia history.

These are but a few of the instances in which the librarians and faculties have contributed substantially to the history of the regions in which their universities are situated. With the development of American history as an academic discipline, it was, however, inevitable that professors should attempt to attract to the libraries that they daily used, sources that would be conveniently accessible for their own research. While the nineteenth-century antiquarian naturally concentrated on his own locality, it by no means followed that the twentieth-century professor had any especial interest in the region in which he was teaching. Moreover professors moved from one university to another, carrying their interests with them. Soon after Frederick Jackson Turner migrated from the University of Wisconsin to Harvard in 1910, the Harvard Commission on Western History[3] began the active assembly in the Harvard College Library of

3. An effort that sprang largely from Turner's friendship with Mrs. William

the kind of sources that interested Turner. These would hardly have been the object of intensive collecting in Cambridge before his arrival. In other instances the interests of alumni and friends have caused universities to specialize in fields of American history far removed from their doorsteps. The Western Americana manuscripts in the Yale University Library reflect the enthusiasm of William Robertson Coe, who in 1910 bought Buffalo Bill's Wyoming ranch, and of Winlock W. Miller Jr., a Yale alumnus from Seattle.[4] One should not underestimate the fact that Yale's librarian, James T. Babb, hails from Idaho. Between faculty, alumni, and librarians who relish the joys of the chase, the rare book and manuscript rooms of great American universities may contain almost anything.

Colleges and universities often seek to attract to their libraries the papers of distinguished graduates or of eminent figures from their region. Thus the Dartmouth College Library has 1,500 Daniel Webster manuscripts, even though the *Guide* reports other major bodies of Webster papers in the Library of Congress, the Massachusetts Historical Society, the Houghton Library at Harvard, and the New Hampshire Historical Society, with smaller caches at Phillips Exeter Academy, the Columbia University Library, and the University of Virginia. Thus the Houghton Library has papers of Charles Sumner, Jared Sparks, Theodore Roosevelt, William Cameron Forbes, and Joseph C. Grew; Yale papers of Henry L. Stimson, Robert A. Taft, and Wilbur L. Cross; Princeton James V. Forrestal and John Foster Dulles; Virginia Thomas Jefferson, Carter Glass, and Claude A. Swanson; Kentucky Alben W. Barkley; Alabama Surgeon General William C. Gorgas and Senator James T. Heflin;

Hooper, a Bostonian who had grown up in Burlington, Iowa, where her father, Charles Elliott Perkins, was president of the Chicago, Burlington and Quincy Railroad. The correspondence in the Huntington Library between Turner and Mrs. Hooper which Professor Ray A. Billington and I are editing for publication, throws light on the commission's activities. This is a diverting and classic example of the effect of an individual's interest, backed by private funds, upon university policy.

4. Mary C. Withington, *A Catalogue of Manuscripts in the Collection of Western Americana founded by William Robertson Coe Yale University Library* (New Haven, 1952).

Chicago Stephen A. Douglas, Governor Frank O. Lowden, and Julius Rosenwald.

Sometimes manuscripts that would be appreciated in several regions come to roost in one, to the sorrow of others. That is the case with Miles Poindexter, whose papers are at the University of Virginia, the State in which he spent his earlier and later life, although he was for thirteen years Senator from Washington. Sometimes the spirit of the stadium causes neighboring institutions to compete for material in what seems to be the same field. This would appear to be the case with the Southern historical collection[5] of the University of North Carolina at Chapel Hill and the Duke University Libraries a few miles away at Durham. The former reported to the *Guide*:

3,200,200 pieces, 1588–1955, relating chiefly to North Carolina and the other Southern States, particularly valuable for ante bellum political history, the plantation system and slavery, and military and civilian aspects of the Confederacy.

The latter reported:

Thousands of volumes of diaries, journals, account books, letterpress books, and other bound manuscripts and 2,650,000 items, dating from the 10th to the 20th centuries but mainly from the American Revolution to recent years, and relating chiefly to the Southern States. Of first importance are papers pertaining to the Civil War, including official records of the Confederate and State governments, papers of many military and naval officers, and letters and diaries of soldiers and civilians (in over 500 collections) for the war and reconstruction period.

Such developments only bear out Jeremy Belknap's remark of 1795 that "there is nothing like having a *good depository*, and keeping a *good lookout*," for many manuscripts have wandered far from home solely because of the lack of these essentials. Many of the papers from Virginia, the Carolinas, Kentucky, and Tennessee that Lyman C. Draper collected might have been lost had he not carried them to Madison. Whenever the Parthenon marbles become the subject of international agitation, one wonders what would have happened to them had Lord Elgin left them in Athens. And architectural sculpture survives longer than letters.

5. Begun by Dr. J. G. de Roulhac Hamilton.

Once a library contains an important body of material on any subject however geographically remote—like the Boston Athenæum's notable collection of Confederate imprints[6]—people keep on adding to it. To have research material where it is safe and likely to be used is of greater importance than considerations of regional piety. Nevertheless anyone who cares deeply for a locality whose records have wandered far afield cannot avoid regretting the failure of earlier natives to act like Jeremy Belknap. The late J. Harold Easterby's comment[7] on the dispersal of South Carolina manuscripts to North Carolina, Wisconsin, the District of Columbia, and Pennsylvania has already been quoted in chapter VIII.[8]

The creation of a new field of academic investigation sometimes leads to the assembly of large numbers of manuscripts. Thus the foundation early in this century of the Graduate School of Business Administration of Harvard University eventually caused the collecting of the great body of business records now in the Baker Library ("41,000 vols., 4,000 boxes, and 200 crates, 1200–1955, but largely of the 18th and 19th centuries, relating chiefly to business history in the United States"). To a librarian, crates as a unit of measure has an ominous sound, suggesting almost limitless future work and expense. But, as Paul H. Buck, director of the Harvard University Library, suggested in the paragraph quoted at the head of this chapter, the appetite of the scholar *is* insatiable.[9]

6. See my introduction to Marjorie Lyle Crandall, *Confederate Imprints, A Check List Based Principally on the Collection of the Boston Athenæum* (Boston, 1955), I, xi–xxviii, and reference to the library later in this chapter.

7. *The Study of South Carolina History* (Columbia, 1951), p. 18.

8. Dr. Easterby remarked: "In some instances the owners of these papers are not without blame; cases might be cited in which local repositories were looked on with contempt, and it was thought a distinction to have one's family records in an institution of national renown." A similar instance was the gift to the Smithsonian Institution by Miss Mary Louisa Adams Clement in 1950 of memorabilia of the Adams family, including portraits, china, glass, books, and family letters; see *The Opening of the Adams-Clement Collection, Exercises Held in the Arts and Industries Building, Smithsonian Institution, on the Afternoon of April 18, 1951* (Washington, 1951). There are, for comparable reasons, a good number of portraits of Bostonians, not always national figures, in the American painting rooms of the National Gallery.

9. In his address "The Historian, The Librarian and the Businessman," *Eleutherian*

As one leafs through the *Guide* one can readily appreciate the extent and variety of manuscripts preserved in university libraries. Any attempt to summarize further these already laconic entries would result in meaningless confusion. I can only note that the descriptions of the holdings of Columbia, Cornell, Rochester, Syracuse, Rutgers, Haverford, Swarthmore, Georgia, Louisiana, Texas, Indiana, Michigan, Iowa, and Missouri—to pick a few universities not already mentioned—include in considerable quantity manuscripts identical in character to those preserved in historical societies. So do the manuscript division of the Library of Congress (with more than 15,600,000 items relating to the history of the United States) and the New York Public Library (with 9,000,000 pieces in the manuscript division proper). Their interests are of national scope. Much of regional importance is preserved in public libraries, notably in the Burton historical collection in Detroit, in the McClung historical collection in Knoxville, Tennessee, in the Western History Department of the Denver Public Library, and the Boston Public Library. Although the Cleveland Public Library reports only "letters and other documents relating to Cleveland," members of its staff sponsored the establishment of the Great Lakes Historical Society, which has since 1945 published the quarterly *Inland Seas*.

Not only universities, the Federal Government, and cities have taken an active part in the collection and preservation of historical sources. So have the institutions founded by great private collectors. While the John Carter Brown and William L. Clements libraries are attached to universities, the Henry E. Huntington and Pierpont Morgan libraries, having grown up in the shadow of their founders' homes, operate completely independently of other institutions. The quality of collections of all four and the nature of their use warrant special mention of these libraries.

The Providence merchant John Carter Brown (1808–74) began in 1846 the large-scale acquisition of Americana from the era of dis-

---

Mills Historical Library, A Record of its Dedication on 7 October 1961 (Greenville, Delaware, 1961), pp. 9–14.

covery through the year 1800. Through extensive purchases in London, made on his behalf by the Vermonter Henry Stevens, he obtained in a quarter of a century of collecting a phenomenal library of the earliest printed sources on the history of the Americas.[10] After John Carter Brown's death, his books received devoted attention from his family. A printed catalogue containing some 7,000 titles of books published before 1801, prepared by John Russell Bartlett, was published in the years 1875–82. In 1895 George Parker Winship became librarian. Three years later, when Mrs. John Carter Brown gave the library to her son, John Nicholas Brown, the new owner took prompt steps to organize it as a public institution of scholarly usefulness. Although he died before his generous intentions could be carried out, he left the books, an endowment fund of $500,000, and a building fund of $150,000 to trustees who in 1901 gave them to Brown University. In accordance with John Nicholas Brown's instructions, his father's collection was to be housed in a separate building with its own staff and administered by a committee of management appointed by the corporation of Brown University. Thus the John Carter Brown Library, as a semiautonomous institution under the wing of the university, was opened for scholarly use on 17 May 1904.

The library has grown both judiciously and extensively over the past fifty-eight years, but as the terminal date of 1800 has been maintained for its collecting, it has remained compact, intelligible, and (thanks to recent skillful alteration) within the walls of its 1904 building. It has today some 25,000 rare books and 6,500 supporting bibliographical reference books. It has also had, throughout its existence, the inestimable benefit of being directed by librarians of learning and imagination. By the time Winship resigned in 1914 to go to Harvard, his intelligent collecting had more than doubled the size of the library. For half a dozen years thereafter Worthington C. Ford served as acting librarian, completing and publishing four

10. Lawrence C. Wroth, *The First Century of the John Carter Brown Library, A History with a Guide to the Collections* (Providence, 1946).

parts of a new printed catalogue and bringing the John Carter Brown Library into active co-operation with the Massachusetts Historical Society (of which he was editor) in the publication of its Photostat Americana series. From 1923 until his retirement in 1957 the librarian of the John Carter Brown Library, Lawrence C. Wroth, and the institution that he directed with consummate skill were synonymous. His successor, Thomas R. Adams, wrote of Mr. Wroth: "For many years a part of the Library's eminence has rested on the fact that people all over the world turned to its librarian for counsel." A typical instance is Mr. Wroth's analysis of the collecting policies of the New-York Historical Society, mentioned in chapter II. The imaginative variety of his collecting in Providence is best seen by the catalogue of a retrospective exhibition[11] held in 1949, in which were shown 113 of the 5,500 books, maps, engravings, or manuscripts of American history prior to 1801 which he had acquired for the library in the previous twenty-six years. There were works on geography, voyages and travels, cartography, science, the Indian, Mexico, Peru, the Spanish Southeast and Southwest, the English colonies, New France, the American Revolution, the western expansion, and American political, religious, social, and cultural history. Mr. Wroth not only bought books but he read them; by his writing and by the exhibitions that he arranged he opened new vistas to other historians and to scholars in varied fields. The annual reports of the library were far more than a record of acquisitions, for in reporting a purchase or gift he would describe it and analyze its significance for the period. Thus his reports were read not only for delight as they appeared, but treasured for future reference. In such books as *The Colonial Printer*;[12] *The Way of a Ship, An Essay on the*

11. *In Retrospect, 1923–1949. An Exhibition commemorating twenty-six years of service to The John Carter Brown Library by Lawrence C. Wroth, Librarian* (Providence, 1949). This illustrated catalogue was the gift of the craftsmen who printed it: the Anthoensen Press and John W. Marchi of Portland, Maine, and the Meriden Gravure Company.

12. First printed for the Grolier Club by the Merrymount Press in 1931, a revised and enlarged second edition was published by the Southworth-Anthoensen Press in 1938.

Literature of Navigation Science;[13] and *The Cartography of the Pacific*[14] he made significant contributions to history as well as bibliography, while the exhibitions arranged for the annual meetings of the Associates of the John Carter Brown Library—for which catalogues were often published[15]—not only evoked the admiration and envy of fellow collectors, but frequently brought to the attention of scholars useful sources that, because of their rarity, they had never realized existed.

The John Carter Brown Library never blew its own horn stridently. It aimed its activities at serious scholars and collectors who knew what they were about, for it had neither the space, the staff, nor the desire to attract crowds. When in 1944 it was found "in common with most institutions dependent upon endowment,[16] . . . that for several years past the increase in the cost of books and maintenance has paralleled a shrinkage in income," the Associates of the John Carter Brown Library were organized. This group of well-wishers, composed of scholars, collectors, printers, and booksellers from many parts of the country, which now has more than 600 members, has by annual gifts of from $7,000 to $13,000 made possible many of the recent acquisitions that fill out chinks in the collection. The growth of the Associates reflects the respect and affection with which Messrs. Wroth and Adams are held in many parts of the country and the unremitting personal efforts that they both make to draw like-minded people to the library. A sincere admiration for the library, and what its librarians, with modest staff and resources, try to do with it, is the motive that brings the Associates together.

13. (Portland, Maine, 1937).

14. *Papers of the Bibliographical Society of America* XXXVIII, 2 (1944).

15. Such as Lawrence C. Wroth and Marion W. Adams, *American Woodcuts and Engravings, 1670–1800* (Providence, 1946); *The Colonial Scene* (Worcester, 1950); *The American Tradition* (Providence, 1955).

16. The initial gift of the elder John Nicholas Brown long remained the sole fixed source of income. In 1953 this was transferred to the Consolidated Fund of Brown University (at a figure of $507,637.24) in order to gain the advantage of participation in a larger and more widely diversified list of investments. See *Annual Report 1952–1953*, pp. 67–68.

In the autumn of 1959 the committee on management adopted a program, proposed by Mr. Adams, for the future growth of the John Carter Brown Library, which included the development of new bibliographical reference aids to the printed literature on the early history of the Americas, the preparation of a new catalogue, and the creation of fellowships. During the following year Brown University made possible needed renovation of the building. In November 1960 a conference on the early history of the Americas was held at the library in which some fifty scholars in the fields of history, literature, art, and anthropology participated. Subsequently published were papers by Robert E. Spiller of the University of Pennsylvania on "The Use of Old Sources in New Ways," by Lewis U. Hanke of the University of Texas on "Early American History as a Part of the History of Western Civilization," and by Durand Echevarria of the Brown faculty on the use of the library in fields other than history.[17] One of the first fruits of the conference was the establishment in 1962 of a twelve-month fellowship of $4,000 for an advanced graduate student and a limited number of post-doctoral fellowships of $500–$600 per month for shorter periods of time. These were made possible by a gift of the chairman of the Associates, Mr. Clifton Waller Barrett, and a Ford Foundation grant. By these recent developments the John Carter Brown Library widens its influence while maintaining its traditional objectives and character.

The creation of the William L. Clements Library of Americana at the University of Michigan offers certain parallels to the history of the institution just described. William Lawrence Clements (1861–1934), a Michigan industrialist specializing in the manufacture of heavy cranes for railway use, began early in the twentieth century the serious collecting of printed books relating to American history before 1800. He was aided in this by his friendship with Worthing-

17. *The John Carter Brown Library Conference, A report of the meeting held in the Library at Brown University on the Early History of the Americas* (Providence, 1961), which contains (pp. 7–13) the program for future growth and (pp. 14–18) a summary of the strength of the library in various fields.

ton C. Ford and George Parker Winship, and by such antiquarian booksellers as Lathrop C. Harper of New York and Henry N. Stevens of London, whose father had been instrumental in augmenting John Carter Brown's collecting in the same field half a century earlier. Mr. Clements's warm friendship with the head of the History Department of the University of Michigan, Professor Claude H. Van Tyne, whose interests lay in the colonial and Revolutionary periods, furnished further stimulus for collecting in those fields. In 1922–23 Mr. Clements gave his library to the University of Michigan, as well as a separate building in which to house it. Thereafter, under the joint influence of Professor Van Tyne and Worthington C. Ford, he began to collect British manuscripts of the Revolutionary period, acquiring for gift to the university the papers of the second Earl of Shelburne, of Sir Henry Clinton, of Lord George Germain, and of General Thomas Gage. The formation of the library thus represents the generous activity of a private collector working in a friendly and intelligent relationship with historians and bibliographers and with the university of which he was both a graduate and a regent.[18] It is an instance of a private library being turned to general scholarly use during the lifetime and with the assistance of the man who began to assemble it.

While the John Carter Brown and William L. Clements libraries are specifically devoted to early American history, that field is only a single facet of the Pierpont Morgan Library. Its founder, the elder John Pierpont Morgan (1837–1913), gathered works of art, books, and manuscripts of every kind in the manner of a Renaissance prince.[19] The private library at 33 East 36th Street, which he built from designs of Charles Follen McKim, adjoined his New York

18. *The William L. Clements Library of Americana at the University of Michigan* (Ann Arbor, 1923). *Dictionary of American Biography*, Supplement One, pp. 179–181, contains a sketch of Mr. Clements by Randolph G. Adams, director of the library until his death in 1951. The present director, Howard H. Peckham—a historian like his predecessor—was formerly director of the Indiana Historical Bureau.

19. Francis Henry Taylor, *Pierpont Morgan as Collector and Patron, 1837–1913* (New York, 1957).

house and was, as Francis Henry Taylor put it, "one of the Seven Wonders of the Edwardian World." Within it were housed the finest medieval illuminated manuscripts in the United States, Mesopotamian cuneiform tablets, Egyptian, Greek, and Coptic papyri, books from the beginning of printing, drawings, paintings, tapestries, Rembrandt etchings, and, incidentally, among authors' autograph manuscripts and letters from the sixteenth to the twentieth centuries, much that is of value to the American historian. In 1924 John Pierpont Morgan (1867–1943), who had inherited the library on his father's death in 1913, created a board of trustees, to whom he conveyed the library buildings, land, and contents with an endowment of $1,500,000 "freely dedicated . . . to the purposes of scholarship." In 1927 he added an annex to the library containing reading rooms and work rooms, and increased the endowment. For the first twenty-five years of its life as a public institution, the Pierpont Morgan Library had as its director the late Belle da Costa Greene, who had become Mr. Morgan's librarian in 1905. This vivid, whimsical, and inspired lady, who concealed great qualities of knowledge and judgment under an assumed capriciousness, was a perceptive and daring collector. She knew chalk from cheese and could distinguish a scholar from a pedant or a phony at a distance of 2,000 yards. If a scholar knew what he wanted, and the Morgan Library had it, as it generally did, Miss Greene gave him free rein with a magnanimity and generosity in keeping with the atmosphere of the place.

Even the passage of thirty-eight years as a public institution has not dulled the unique character of the Pierpont Morgan Library. It is still a breath-taking place, for, as Frederick B. Adams Jr., its present director, has defined it:

It is the Library's function to assemble, organize, exhibit, and preserve the intimate achievements of the creators of western culture. Not the panoramic arts—sculpture, painting, architecture—but the less clamorous and often more significant creations that communicate privately, like music in a darkened room.[20]

20. *Fourth Annual Report to the Fellows of the Pierpont Morgan Library* (New York, 1953), p. 7.

In an essay contributed to a volume in memory of Miss Greene, Lawrence C. Wroth[21] summarized the resources available to the historian in the Pierpont Morgan Library. In American terms these begin with atlases, globes, and narratives of the voyages of exploration and discovery, printed tracts of the colonization period, and continue through some 300 letters, documents, and maps, relating to the Yorktown campaign of 1781, 173 letters from Thomas Jefferson to his daughter Martha, and nearly 2,000 letters and documents by or pertaining to 169 bishops of the Protestant Episcopal Church. Mr. Wroth observed:

> Americana has not been specifically a Morgan field, but those who built the Library were men proud of their American heritage. Throughout their collecting of the materials of world history, letters, and art—their principal concern—they could not resist buying from time to time the great American books we have mentioned, and many others, even though they had no idea of trying to rival the notable collections of Americana formed by certain bookmen of another generation. The result of this departure from a main purpose, the personal indulgence, we may call it, is that the Americanist finds in the library they built much material of the sort that brings him close to the current doing and thinking of the colonial period of the United States and Canada.

Since the "personal indulgences" include 114 letters of George Washington, 17 of John Adams, 36 of Abraham Lincoln, and like manuscripts, the American historian may well find sources of great value to him even though these represent a "departure from the main purpose" of the library.

As the Pierpont Morgan Library is an entirely independent institution without university affiliation, it has since 1949 developed its own "alumni" through a nationwide organization of Fellows, with a minimum annual subscription of $100. From 218 in the first year, the number increased within a decade to 461 annual and 15 life Fellows. Over this period annual gifts in cash have ranged between $31,475 in 1950–51 and $96,705.49 in 1958–59. In the same years Fellows have also annually given books and objects valued between $6,445 and

21. In Dorothy Miner, ed., *Studies in Art and Literature for Belle da Costa Greene* (Princeton, 1954), pp. 10–22.

$51,340. The organization has thus materially increased the collecting potentiality of the library, for from its gifts $98,362.18 were spent in 1959 for medieval and Renaissance manuscripts, early printed books, examples of binding, autograph manuscripts and letters, drawings, and publications.

Henry Edwards Huntington (1850–1927), a nephew of the pioneer railway builder Collis P. Huntington, came to San Franciso in 1891 to represent the family interests in California.[22] Soon after his uncle's death in 1900 he shifted his activities to southern California, where he bought great holdings of land and developed the Pacific Electric Railway into an extensive interurban system. When at the age of sixty he retired partially by transferring the Pacific Electric system to the Southern Pacific Company, he devoted the energies previously spent on business to the acquisition of paintings, books, and manuscripts on a hitherto unprecedented scale. Starting late in life and feeling that time was short he bought where possible complete libraries or as large groups of any objects that interested him as could be obtained in single transactions. By buying the entire collection of E. Dwight Church, who died in 1908, and important sections from the Hoe, Huth, Britwell Court, and Beverly Chew libraries, Henry Huntington soon established himself as a book collector on a scale scarcely known before or since, while in pictures—where his taste leaned towards the English eighteenth century—he acquired a remarkable number of portraits by Reynolds, Gainsborough, Romney, and Lawrence.[23] Although his library was initially housed in New York City, he ultimately moved it to San Marino, California, eleven miles from Los Angeles, where he had since 1902 owned a 550-acre ranch. There he had built a house in 1910 and established a botanical garden with a remarkable collection of cycads and a fifteen-acre garden of cactus and other succulents. By the summer of

22. Robert O. Schad, *Henry Edwards Huntington, The Founder and the Library* (San Marino, 1952).

23. *Henry E. Huntington Library & Art Gallery. Handbook of Art Collections Illustrated* (San Marino, 1956).

1919 he had determined to perpetuate his collection in an independent institution to be known as the Henry E. Huntington Library and Art Gallery, and for that purpose began the construction of a library building at San Marino about 200 feet east of his house. The books were transferred there in 1920. The remaining years of Mr. Huntington's life were devoted to adding to the collection. After his death in 1927, when the control of the institution passed to a small board of trustees, the library began to draw scholars to San Marino and to acquire the reference books that were essential for the use of the portentous quantity of original sources that Mr. Huntington had assembled in seventeen years of collecting.

As San Marino is off the beat of most scholars, means had to be found of attracting them there. To accomplish this Dr. Max Farrand, formerly professor of American history at Yale, was asked to come to the library as director of research and to devise plans for converting it from a gigantic private collection into a research institution in the study of English and American civilization. This was accomplished by inviting to the permanent research staff historians of the caliber of Godfrey Davies, Robert G. Cleland, Louis B. Wright, and (now currently) Allan Nevins, while providing assistance to scholars from other institutions to work at the library for shorter periods. Since 1951 the director has been the historian John E. Pomfret, formerly president of the College of William and Mary. As the collections are unsurpassed and as San Marino is an uncommonly pleasant place, particularly when the camellias are in bloom, the mountain has indeed come to Mahomet. Any sensible person with a piece of research in English or American history or literature welcomes an excuse to complete it at the Huntington Library. In addition thousands of more casual visitors greatly enjoy the pictures and the gardens without hindering the peace of the scholars who are hidden away in the working areas of the library. It was estimated that in the first twenty-five years of its existence 6,000 scholars had used the library and that the museum had had 3,300,000 visitors.

The Huntington Library has approximately 1,000,000 manuscripts, 250,000 rare books, and 250,000 reference books, about one fifth of which are concerned with American history. The leading collections in this field deal with the colonial and Revolutionary periods, the Civil War, Mormons, the Southwest, Californiana, and westward expansion. The annual budget of approximately $1,000,000 is met chiefly from endowment, now about $25,000,000, left by Mr. Huntington. Other relatively small sources of income include the $10 annual membership fees paid by some 1,700 Friends of the Huntington Library. In addition to a library staff of fifty, including three photographers and three binders, the library usually has as permanent residents three or four research associates, who are senior scholars representing its major fields of interest, and it spends in the vicinity of $25,000 each year on fellowships ($4,000 per year) and grants-in-aid ($500–$1,000 each) to aid academic applicants to work for shorter periods.

The Huntington Library is a happy exception to the rule that it is appropriate to subsidize research but not the publication of its results. It has since its establishment published over seventy books by scholars who have at some time worked at the library as grantees or readers. Thus, as the majority of the authors are "first-book men," the publication program represents a form of aid to promising younger scholars. During the directorship of Dr. Pomfret the publication program has been accelerated to the point where $20,000 to $25,000 is annually budgeted and four to six books are published each year. The fields covered are American history and literature, California and the Southwest, English history, literature, and art, bibliography, and horticulture. The library publishes about one fourth of the manuscripts submitted to it, but those chosen have included fewer "salesless wonders" than most institutional lists. Of forty books published during a ten-year period, three lost heavily,[24] but several have gone

24. Dr. Pomfret writes me on 6 July 1960: "In our bookkeeping we spread the costs of a scholarly publication over seven years and those of a semi-popular nature over three years. Thus, unlike commercial publishers, costs can be spread over a period of more than one fiscal year. (We publish neither fictions nor textbooks). Nevertheless in the last ten years the Publications Department has never shown a yearly deficit."

into third printings. Thus with a substantial back list still in print, gross sales come to more than $40,000 a year. Any surplus above maintenance and printing costs is applied to printing additional books. Two factors are involved: the books are attractively designed and well printed, in accordance with the best California standards, and the library approaches their publication with optimism rather than the usual heavy heart. The *Huntington Library Quarterly*, with about 800 paid subscriptions at $5, normally loses $1,000 to $1,500, a sum cheerfully anticipated as one of the institution's contributions to scholarship.

Another example of the evolution of a public institution of national scholarly usefulness from a private collection in the home of its owner is the Henry Francis du Pont Winterthur Museum at Winterthur, Delaware. Like the Huntington Library, it is supported by the generosity of its collector. Close to forty years ago, Mr. du Pont began buying American furniture.[25] His interests soon expanded to include the paneling of entire American rooms from the seventeenth to the early nineteenth century, and everything that appropriately belonged in them, whether made by American craftsmen or imported from Europe and Asia. Soon after inheriting in 1927 Winterthur, a family house set in singularly beautiful rolling country five miles northwest of Wilmington, he began to enlarge it to accommodate his growing collection. Eventually the house grew to 80 rooms and 45 alcoves and corridors in which were installed woodwork from houses ranging from New Hampshire to North Carolina, each of which contained contemporary furnishings of the highest quality and appropriateness. In 1951, when the collection had become in the words of the late Joseph Downs, "the largest and richest assemblage of American decorative arts ever brought together,"[26] Mr. du Pont

25. Joseph Downs, *American Furniture, Queen Anne and Chippendale Periods in the Henry Francis du Pont Winterthur Museum* (New York, 1952), is the first of a series of detailed catalogues. For a general account see Alice Winchester *et al.*, *The Antiques Treasury of Furniture and other Decorative Arts at Winterthur, Williamsburg, Sturbridge, Ford Museum, Cooperstown, Deerfield, Shelburne* (New York, 1959), pp. 7–56.

26. Mr. Downs left the curatorship of the American wing of the Metropolitan Museum in 1949 for a similar post at Winterthur. On his death in 1954, Charles F.

moved to a smaller house nearby and opened Winterthur as a public museum. The transformation from a private house to a functioning institution was achieved by the assembly of a curatorial and research staff, the addition of a five-story wing for library and offices at the south end of the building, and the development of a teaching centre for graduate students and a research centre for advanced scholars. The Winterthur library concentrates on American architecture and decorative arts, with special emphasis on sources of design and the technical analysis of production. It includes the Joseph Downs manuscript collection (specializing in household inventories and craftsmen's inventories, bills, trade cards, advertisements, account and letter books), the Waldron Phoenix Belknap Jr. Research Library of American Painting,[27] the Decorative Arts Reference Library (photographs of documented American decorative arts objects in public and private collections), and the Index of American Culture.[28]

In 1952 the museum established, jointly with the nearby University of Delaware, the two-year Winterthur Program in Early American Culture,[29] leading to the degree of Master of Arts. Prior to this time, research in the American decorative arts seldom employed the critical techiques that are taken for granted by the historian. Museum curators were often tasteful persons who relied unduly upon aesthetic considerations and who accepted dates and attributions furnished by

Montgomery became director of the Winterthur Museum. In 1961 Mr. Montgomery voluntarily retired from the directorship to give full time to research and teaching and was succeeded by Dr. Edgar P. Richardson, formerly director of the Detroit Institute of Arts. See Henry Francis du Pont, *Joseph Downs An Appreciation and A Bibliography of His Publications* (Winterthur, n.d., reprinted from the 1954 Walpole Society Note Book).

27. See *Waldron Phoenix Belknap, Jr. whose ideals of scholarship are perpetuated in The Belknap Press at Harvard University, Cambridge, Massachusetts and the Establishment of a Research Library of American Painting bearing his name at The Henry Francis du Pont Winterthur Museum, Winterthur, Delaware* (Cambridge, 1956).

28. An accumulation of primary sources bearing on American culture filed according to the principles of the Human Relations Area File located at Yale University.

29. E. McClung Fleming, "The Winterthur Program in Early American Culture," *American Studies* IV, 4 (July 1959), pp. 1–5.

collectors and dealers without sufficient recourse to documents. The Winterthur program has done much to improve this situation by relating to objects the evidence of books and manuscripts; by encouraging suspended belief in supposedly acceptable theories until documentary corroboration can be found; by applying, whenever possible, the critical methods of history and archaeology to the study of the decorative arts. While the program was primarily designed to produce museum curators, Winterthur has proved a valuable training ground for editorial and administrative work in historical societies.[30]

Winterthur is one of three neighboring public institutions that owe their origin to members of the du Pont family. In the field of horticulture the Longwood Gardens at Kennett Square, Pennsylvania, the creation of the late Pierre S. du Pont, are as imaginative, extensive, and perfectly achieved as the Winterthur Museum is in the decorative arts. The Eleutherian Mills-Hagley Foundation, Inc., at Greenville, Delaware, maintains the Hagley Museum, which portrays the industrial history of the Brandywine valley, and the Eleutherian Mills Historical Library. The museum[31] conducts, jointly with the University of Delaware, a two-year graduate training course similar to the Winterthur program, but with emphasis on the industrial development of America rather than on the decorative arts.[32] The library houses and makes available to scholars the personal and business papers of the du Pont family,[33] 1780–1954, the

30. Of the thirty-three Fellows who comprised the first eight classes, five remained at Winterthur, four are on the staff of the Smithsonian Institution, eight are employed by other museums, two are National Park Service curators, and two curators in restorations on historic sites. Others are engaged in further graduate study. Wendell D. Garrett, assistant editor of *The Adams Papers* at the Massachusetts Historical Society, was a Winterthur Fellow and Dean A. Fales Jr., director of the Essex Institute, Salem, went there from the Winterthur staff. Mrs. Fales, author of *American Silver in the Henry Francis du Pont Museum*, was a Winterthur Fellow.

31. *The Hagley Museum, A Story of Early Industry On the Brandywine* (Greenville, Delaware, 1957).

32. John A. Munroe, "The Hagley Program," *American Studies* IV, 4 (July 1959), pp. 5–6.

33. The library's first publication, edited by its first director, Dr. Charles W. David, was Victor Marie du Pont, *Journey to France and Spain 1801* (Ithaca, 1961).

records of E. I. du Pont de Nemours & Co., 1802–1902, and regional sources relating to Delaware and Pennsylvania.

At the dedication of the Eleutherian Mills Historical Library on 7 October 1961, Professor Paul H. Buck considered the relationship of such institutions to the great research libraries. Pointing out that in half a century the New York Public Library had grown from 2,000,000 to 7,000,000 volumes, the Library of Congress from 1,800,000 to 12,000,000, the Harvard University Library from 1,400,000 to 6,697,111, he concluded:

We have obviously reached a point where new concepts and methods must be used in the handling of this continuing process of accelerating growth.... The idea that any one library, however great, affluent, or wisely managed, can cover all aspects of learning is outmoded. There comes a time when sheer size in one establishment becomes fatiguing to administration, bankruptive of resources, and inhumane to the user. The alternative is the concept of co-ordinated decentralization.

Consider what has already happened in the handling of the papers of the presidents of the United States. A generation ago the then Curator of Manuscripts of the Library of Congress was following the policy of centralizing in the Library of Congress the papers of all the presidents. This concept shortly collapsed. The enormously increasing quantity of these collections made it impossible to house them all in one center. The mass would be so Himalayan in proportion[34] as to dehumanize and render inefficient scholarly activity, defeat the efforts at management of even a staff as large and able as that of the Library of Congress, and exhaust even the budget of a department of the federal government.

A wise solution to the problem was achieved by an act of Congress which permits a degree of decentralization mildly and sensibly co-ordinated by the National Archivist. Under this the Roosevelt Library at Hyde Park and the Truman Library at Independence have already been established, and plans are under way for the establishment of a Hoover Library and an Eisenhower Library.[35] Recent as has been this development, several observations can be made. First, the participants and friends of each administration derive much greater pleasure in building and supporting an identifiable collection than in burying themselves in the vast, cavernous

34. There are few things more discouraging than to visit a State archives and observe that the papers of a single recent governor often fill more sections than those of all his predecessors from the beginning of the republic to the advent of the mimeograph machine.

35. Since this address, plans have been laid for an eventual Kennedy Library in proximity to Harvard University.

and anonymous reaches of Washington. Second, a presidential administration in itself is significant enough to justify a separate collection and the cost and effort of its maintenance. Decentralization could be carried to an absurdity if each cabinet officer, congressman and senator sought to establish a library of his own. Ideally each administration should be a unit. Third, the wise provision of the act of Congress and the sensible administration by the National Archivist permit just the necessary degree of gentle guidance from the center to guarantee high standards of administration. Finally, the scholars who have used the libraries thus far established are enthusiastic in praise of the service they received.[36]

The foregoing paragraphs, although written to explain the rationale of regional libraries, are quoted here because they indicate the background of the presidential libraries which involve both public and private elements in their origin and support. Dr. Waldo G. Leland in "The Creation of the Franklin D. Roosevelt Library: A Personal Narrative"[37] tells how President Roosevelt on 10 December 1938 outlined to White House luncheon guests "a long-cherished plan to present to the United States his already vast accumulation of correspondence and other papers, documents, books, pamphlets, pictures, and objects of personal or historic interest" to be placed in a building to be erected at private cost on land to be given to the United States from his mother's estate at Hyde Park, New York.

The ostensible purpose of the luncheon was to obtain the advice and approval of representative historians and other scholars respecting the President's proposal, and this advice was reported to be entirely favorable and the approval unanimous. (But had it been otherwise I do not think it would have made any difference.)

Less than a fortnight later the Franklin D. Roosevelt Library, Inc., filed a certificate of incorporation in the State of New York. This corporation, of which Samuel Eliot Morison, Randolph G. Adams, Dr. Leland, Frank C. Walker, and Basil O'Connor were the first trustees, raised $400,000 from private sources to build the library. Legislation approved on 18 July 1939 authorized the Archivist of the United States to accept title to the Hyde Park land to be used as the site, to permit the private corporation to construct the building,

36. *Eleutherian Mills Historical Library, A Record of its Dedication on 7 October 1961*, pp. 11–12.

37. *The American Archivist* XVIII (January 1955), 11–29.

to accept the historical materials offered by President Roosevelt, and acquire other contemporary or relevant historical materials by gift, purchase, or loan. The building was dedicated and the exhibit rooms opened to the public on 30 June 1941. The war, and the third and fourth terms, kept the president from enjoying the leisurely retirement among his papers that he had contemplated when the creation of the library was proposed. President Roosevelt had been dead for over a year before his papers were finally transferred there and the search room opened to investigators on 1 May 1946. Although some hundreds of miles from Washington and built with private funds, the Franklin D. Roosevelt Library is a division of the National Archives and Records Service.

The Harry S. Truman Library in Independence, Missouri, has a similar history. Built and furnished without cost to the government from funds privately collected by the Harry S. Truman Library, Inc., it was dedicated on 6 July 1957. Happily it still enjoys the continuing presence and interest of the man whose papers it was created to house. When I first visited it in January 1960 and was received by President Truman, was presented to Mrs. Truman who was pinch-hitting for an absent mail clerk, and saw Thomas Hart Benton high on a scaffold completing a mural, the virtues of a presidential library were at once apparent. Simultaneously it provides an ex-president with an appropriate base of operations and furnishes scholars using the library with a means of access to the man whose personal knowledge might contribute to the solution of problems they encounter. Mr. Truman's historical interest in the nature and function of the presidency is reflected in the museum exhibits and in the collecting policies of the library, which seeks to acquire not only the papers of members of his administration, but published works bearing on the office of President of the United States at all periods, and on the history of American foreign policy and diplomatic relations, with emphasis on the first half of the twentieth century.

The Harry S. Truman Library Institute for National and International Affairs, a nonprofit corporation organized under the laws of

Missouri in 1957 with a number of distinguished historians among
its directors, aims to encourage and assist the growth of the library as
a national centre for study and research. It secured in 1958 a grant of
$48,700 from the Rockefeller Foundation for the purchase of books
and microfilms relating to the history and nature of the presidency,
the Truman administration, and United States foreign relations.
The institute has also established a program of grants-in-aid to provide scholars with travel and living expenses for short periods of
work at the library.

Like Janus, presidential libraries have two very different faces;
a research area appealing to a small number of qualified scholars, and
a museum attractive to the general public, including the idly curious.
In his recollections of the creation of the Franklin D. Roosevelt
Library, Dr. Leland recalls his concern over the space allotted to the
exhibition of gifts, junk, and gadgets, and the president's bland reply:
"Well, you know, if people have to pay a quarter to get into the library they will want to see something interesting inside." Dr. Leland
continues:

More than two million persons have paid their quarters, and they have certainly
seen much that is interesting and some things that are strange as well. . . . The
visitor is immediately impressed and perhaps a little overcome by the great variety
of objects on display and by the immense number of them. Gifts from the governments and peoples of all countries, many of them of great splendor and beauty,
illustrate more vividly than written documents the central place that the President
of the United States holds in the world of today. A big room in the basement is
filled with every sort and description of the little things that are sent to the President by thousands of people. The room is appropriately called the "oddities room."
Cigarette holders, donkeys and figurines abound. . . .

Nearby, in the "carriage room" are family vehicles, including a sleigh, said to
have belonged to Napoleon III, a family carriage of the tycoon era, and two ice-
boats; one of which the President sailed on the frozen Hudson in the winters of his
youth. Part of the wall of the building had to be taken down to make possible the
entrance of the other iceboat, a 48-footer that belonged to the President's uncle. It
was with such objects in mind that Samuel Morison, in the address that he delivered
at the library in 1941, on the occasion of its dedication, appealed to the friends and
neighbors of the President not to donate their hair-trunks or similar family relics to

the Franklin D. Roosevelt Library. I heard that the President was slightly irked by this admonition, but it had my complete approval. I understand that now the specially equipped Ford which the President drove has been added to the collections.

The museum objects are displayed in rotation, for it would be impossible to exhibit them all at the same time. They constitute a real problem and make the functioning of the library as a research center more difficult. But the entrance fees of the museum have contributed something like $425,000 after tax deduction to a special income account that is drawn upon heavily each year for the work of the library. On June 30, 1953, the balance of this account was $199,000, after expenditures during the fiscal year of $37,400.

At the Truman Library the research and museum areas are judiciously separated, each with its own entrance. The exhibits are instructively arranged to explain to the casual visitor the nature and history of the presidency, with only a modest amount of space devoted to "oddities" and gifts, which are reduced to typical examples rather than proliferated to encourage vulgar curiosity. A reproduction of the president's office in the west wing of the White House contains many of the pictures and furnishings of his administration, including the small desk-reminder that reads "THE BUCK STOPS HERE." The research room is open "to qualified persons on application in advance to the Director," Dr. Philip C. Brooks. The offices and Mr. Truman's suite are not open to the public at any time, but on payment of an admission fee of 50c the museum may be visited daily, save for Thanksgiving, Christmas, and New Year's Day. Organized school groups, persons in the care of charitable institutions, and uniformed members of the Armed Forces are admitted free. Visitors come in very considerable numbers, for some $50,000 a year are normally received from admissions, which considerably more than cover the annual cost of exhibits and other services to the general public. Dr. Robert H. Bahmer of the National Archives has very kindly furnished me with certain figures concerning the cost of operating these two presidential libraries. On an average over the past several years the archival and research activities of the Truman Library cost $110,000 annually, of which $75,000 is appropriated and $35,000 comes from trust funds, while the exhibits cost $25,000, of which $15,000 is appropriated and $10,000 is derived from trust funds. Of the $50,000 received in admission fees, $35,000 is normally applied to archival and research functions and $7,000 to exhibits and public services. The pattern of the Roosevelt Library is similar. Archival and research functions annually require $115,000 ($75,000 appropriated, $40,000 from trust funds) and the exhibits and public services $20,000 ($15,000 appropriated, $5,000 from trust funds). Of the annual receipts from admissions of $45,000, $40,000 are applied to archival and research functions and $5,000 to exhibits and public services. Thus in these two institutions the casual visitor not only pays his way, but contributes very respectably to the maintenance of scholarly activities. Such is the magnetism of the presidency. No independent historical society has or is likely to have a legitimate popular attraction as potent as the memory of Franklin D. Roosevelt or the living presence of Harry S. Truman.

Returning from the presidential libraries to institutions that are entirely private in their support, brief mention must be made of a few eighteenth- and nineteenth-century libraries that possess substantial sources of American history, whether printed or in manuscript. The largest of these is the Newberry Library in Chicago, founded in 1887. It derives its name from Walter Loomis Newberry (1804–1868), who came to Chicago in 1833, engaged in the commission business, later went into banking, and consistently invested his profits in Chicago real estate. The *Dictionary of American Biography*[38] notes that "what he bought by the acre he sold later by the front foot." In 1841 he was a founder and first president of the Young Men's Library Association; in 1857 he joined the recently formed Chicago Historical Society, of which he was president from 1860 until his death. As both his sons died in infancy, and both his daughters died young unmarried—Julia, whose diary[39] was published

38. Sketch by George B. Utley, XIII, 447–448.
39. Margaret Ayer Barnes and Janet Ayer Fairbank, *Julia Newberry's Diary* (New York, 1933) and Tracy D. Mygatt, *Julia Newberry's Sketch Book* (New York, 1936), are touching reminders of a young girl who died in Rome in 1876, discovered and published more than fifty years after her death.

thirty years ago, was one of them—he had no descendants who long survived him. Thus, as the result of a contingent provision in his will, half his estate, or about $2,100,000, went to establish the reference library that bears his name. As much of the property that he bequeathed was in undeveloped real estate, which later increased in value, and as substantial gifts from other sources have been added to the original bequest, the Newberry Library has acquired rich holdings in literature, history, genealogy, philology, music, and the graphic arts. While it has always been freely open to the public, and at times overrun and abused by it, the control and support of the library is in the hands of a board of private trustees. Unlike the Brown, Clements, Morgan, and Huntington libraries, the Newberry is not built around the personal collecting of its benefactor— any books he owned burned in the Chicago Fire—but represents instead systematic purchasing over seventy-five years not only of great rarities but of whatever would serve scholars in the humanities. As its librarian for the past two decades has been a historian, Dr. Stanley Pargellis,[40] who is a shrewd and energetic collector, much material of value for historical research is constantly being added.

The Newberry Library owns some 800,000 books as well as manuscripts occupying 4,300 feet of shelf space. The Edward E. Ayer collection, relating to the archaeology and ethnology of Indians in North and South America, to their relations with white men, and to voyages of discovery, exploration, and frontier history, has over 80,000 volumes. The genealogical and local history stacks house some 50,000 volumes. A rough estimate would suggest that perhaps a quarter of the total holdings of printed books have to do with American history. The library holds papers of many midwestern authors and publishers, as well as the very bulky records of the Chicago, Burlington and Quincy Railroad Company and the Illinois Central Railroad. It publishes numerous check list and bibliographical records of its holdings as well as a semiannual *Bulletin*. By confer-

---

40. On his retirement later this year, Dr. Pargellis will be succeeded by Lawrence W. Towner, editor of the *William and Mary Quarterly*.

ences and fellowships it actively seeks to attract scholars from all parts of the world to use its resources.

Several of the older proprietary libraries, by virtue of standing their ground and guarding their early acquisitions, have preserved unique holdings of historical sources. The Charleston Library Society in Charleston, South Carolina, founded in 1748, continues after two centuries as a private subscription library without other support than it receives from its members. It has today some 71,100 volumes, chiefly for general reading, and a small group of manuscripts relating to South Carolina. Its great resource to the historian is its files of early Charleston newspapers. Of these the late J. Harold Easterby wrote:

Such scholars as Charles M. Andrews were unstinted in their praise of the resources of the Charleston Library Society, especially its files of early South Carolina newspapers. Its policy was to encourage gifts from the rich resources of Charleston private collections, and its capable librarian, Ellen M. FitzSimons, never missed an opportunity to make her collections available to serious scholars.[41]

One can say the same of her successor, Miss Virginia Rugheimer, one of whose recent accomplishments has been the completion of the microfilming of *The Charleston Daily Courier* from 1852 through 1873 in thirty-seven reels, each 100 feet long. The cost of filming was underwritten by the Post and Courier Company; ownership of the negatives remains with the Library Society, which offers positive films for sale at $370 a set; within the first year the sale of sixteen complete sets and several individual reels for $6,117.50 more than paid for the filming. Profits from any future sales will be used for further microfilming.

An undertaking of this sort does great credit to the library and aids learning. It does not, however, benefit the almost insoluble financial problem in a period of rising costs of an old institution which receives no public support. The expenditures of the library for the year 1961 were $27,976.56. While two thirds of this sum came from endowment, the only current income is derived from the dues of the

41. *The Study of Carolina History*, p. 17.

society's 1,337 members. In 1961 annual dues were raised from $6 to $8 for adults and from $2 to $3 for junior members. At the same time a class of sustaining memberships at $25 per year and one of life members at $200 were instituted. Greater use is not the answer, for, as President Albert Simons pointed out in his 1961 report:

> The dues paid in membership cover only a fraction of the cost of the services received. A sudden increase in membership would therefore throw a heavier work load on the staff without providing sufficient funds to employ additional assistants.

Here then is the familiar problem of many an independent historical society, which is echoed in Mr. Simons's remark:

> Our book shelves have now become completely filled, and the ingenuity of the staff cannot solve this problem much longer, even by placing shelves in toilet rooms. More land and the enlargement of our building will before long become imperative.

The Charleston Library Society's building is of the present century. The only one of the eighteenth-century proprietary libraries that has remained in its original quarters is the Redwood Library and Athenæum at Newport, Rhode Island, which still retains the accumulations of two centuries in the enchanting Palladian structure designed by Peter Harrison in 1749.[42] The New York Society Library, incorporated in 1754, in the course of several northward moves up Manhattan Island to its present house at 53 East 79th Street has become chiefly a circulating library for general reading. The most venerable of all such institutions, the Library Company of Philadelphia, is, after the many vicissitudes and Phoenix-like revival described in chapter v, in the process of casting off the general reader and becoming purely a research library.

The Boston Athenæum, founded in 1807, is the only one of the proprietary libraries that has steadily grown to sizable dimensions, without change of course or major vicissitudes. It is equally concerned with the needs of the scholar and the general reader. For the former it keeps what it has acquired over 155 years and buys the

42. Carl Bridenbaugh, *Peter Harrison, First American Architect* (Chapel Hill, 1949), pp. 45–53, 183–186.

best serious current works that it can find in its fields whether they seem likely to be wanted day after tomorrow or not; for the latter it buys what is currently in demand, with the comforting thought that ephemeral books when they fall to pieces need not be replaced. It has today 422,351 volumes, pleasantly housed in a building of 1847, so skillfully enlarged (and made fireproof) by vertical expansion in 1913–14 that it has not yet burst its seams.

The Boston Athenæum has its share of great rarities,[43] many of them in the collection of tens of thousands of pamphlets and tracts so largely due to the squirrel-like qualities of William Smith Shaw, librarian from 1807 to 1822 and the real founder of the library. It has the parochial library sent to King's Chapel in Boston in 1698 through the efforts of Prebendary Bray,[44] substantial portions of the libraries of George Washington[45] and John Quincy Adams,[46] great runs of newspapers, and, unlikely as it seems, more Confederate imprints[47] than exist together elsewhere. But its greatest usefulness to the scholar lies in thousands of less spectacular books that are not to be found in newer collections. They are all in place; one finds them if one looks

43. For a sample see Walter Muir Whitehill, *A Boston Athenæum Miscellany, Catalogue of an Exhibition in Honor of the Visit of the Grolier Club on February 11, 1950* (Boston, 1950). Although the Athenæum has some manuscripts (listed in the *Guide*), most of them have some special reason for being there. The library in its present collecting policy fully respects the primacy of the Massachusetts Historical Society as the proper depository of historical manuscripts.

44. Walter Muir Whitehill, "The King's Chapel Library," *Publications of the Colonial Society of Massachusetts* XXXVIII, 274–289.

45. Appleton P. C. Griffin and William Coolidge Lane, *A Catalogue of the Washington Collection in the Boston Athenæum* (Boston, 1897).

46. Worthington C. Ford and Henry Adams, *A Catalogue of the Books of John Quincy Adams Deposited in the Boston Athenæum* (Boston, 1938).

47. Marjorie Lyle Cranfall, *Confederate Imprints*, published in 1955 in two volumes, listed not only the Athenæum collection but all Confederate imprints in the Union Catalogue and those reported to the Athenæum by Duke and Emory universities, the universities of Virginia and North Carolina, the Virginia State Library, the Massachusetts Historical Society, and the Huntington Library. A particularly appreciated example of co-operation between Massachusetts and Virginia was the publication by the Virginia State Library of Richard B. Harwell's *More Confederate Imprints*, a first supplement, which followed the typography and numbering system of Miss Crandall's work.

in the catalogue under author, title, or subject, but with the best will in the world too few of them have been reported to the Union Catalogue of the Library of Congress,[48] save in answer to weekly want lists. The Athenæum has published a dozen books in the present century, but its chief service to scholarship is in making available what it has to any serious inquirer who appears in person or writes an intelligible letter.

The Athenæum receives no public support. All but some $30,000[49] of its 1961 expenses of $167,614.27 were met from the income of investments having a book value of $2,307,365.03 and (on 30 November 1961) a market value of $5,479,250. Funds restricted to the purchase of books have remained adequate; the $36,401.89 spent from these during 1961 met all current needs acceptably. Unrestricted income has always been tight, with consequent difficulty in paying adequate salaries and coping with housekeeping. Consequently a great effort has been made in recent years to increase unrestricted endowment. The 1961 figures quoted above, when compared with those of a decade earlier, show improvement, for in 1951 the book value of the investments was $1,299,599 and the market $1,897,268.45. Yet the increase in income has barely kept up with rising costs. After a decade on this treadmill we have lost no ground, which in these days is a great deal, but we have not gained as much as is desirable.

48. From sheer lack of hands to check the printed Library of Congress catalogue against our cards, we are still disgracefully early in the alphabet.

49. Received by current payments of the 1,049 proprietors for the right to take out books and for tickets supplied to other readers.

Chapter XIX

THE SHIP OF THESEUS

The combination of entertainment and uplift, of the relaxed mood
of tourism and the satisfaction of learning about the American past,
is a powerful one and has paid off. In short, historic preservation and
restoration have become big business. —L. H. BUTTERFIELD, 1961

IN Plutarch's life of Theseus it is stated that "The ship wherein
Theseus and the youth of Athens returned [from their celebrated
voyage to Crete] had thirty oars, and was preserved by the
Athenians down even to the time of Demetrius Phalereus, for
they took away the old planks as they decayed, putting in new and
stronger timber in their place, insomuch that this ship became a
standing example among the philosophers, for the logical question
as to things that grow; one side holding that the ship remained the
same, and the other contending that it was not the same." Arthur
Hugh Clough helpfully notes that the "logical question" was "the
problem called Auxanomĕnos, the grower, like the more famous one
called Pseudomĕnos, the liar."[1] The Greek philosophers, were they
able to visit the United States today, would have happy fodder for
extended dispute, for the problems raised by historic preservation,
restoration, and reconstruction far exceed those posed by the ship of
Theseus.

A certain number of old buildings—mostly churches and dwelling
houses—are still used for their original purposes on their original

1. A. H. Clough, *Plutarch's Lives. The Translation called Dryden's* (Boston, 1874),
I, 21.

sites, yet most, like the ship, have their share of new timber. Not long ago my dining room ceiling, after having resisted the law of gravity since 1826, fell on our heads during lunch. It was soon replaced, at the cost of some hundreds of dollars and considerable dust. The room is the same as to use and arrangement, but the new plaster clings to wire lath, for that is the only way my Italian neighbor would now dream of plastering a ceiling. Few are the buildings that have not at least been modified by the installation of heat, light, and water, but those that continue to serve the purpose for which they were originally constructed hold first place in the categories of historic preservation. Such, for example, in Boston terms,[2] are King's Chapel of 1750 and the superb Bulfinch House of 1800 at 85 Mount Vernon Street occupied by Miss Evelyn Sears.

In the next category come those buildings that are preserved on their original sites, through private or public piety, as memorials to distinguished occupants or as examples of architecture. The homes of the first three presidents are the supreme examples: Mount Vernon and Monticello, purchased by private organizations founded for the purpose, and the Adams Mansion in Quincy, given to the National Park Service by the family. Throughout the country are hundreds of less widely known buildings in this category, open regularly to visitors as historic monuments through the activities of the National Trust for Historic Preservation, the Society for the Preservation of New England Antiquities, and a myriad of historical societies and State agencies.

Moving through the spectrum, one enters the area where houses remaining on their original sites have been converted to new uses, where, in their transformation to apartments, schools, clubs, or offices, the exteriors, and sometimes a number of the interior features, have remained unchanged. The West Church in Boston, built by Asher Benjamin in 1806, after eighty-six years in its original use and more than sixty as a branch library, seems about to turn

2. For Boston examples cited, see my *Boston A Topographical History* (Cambridge, 1959), particularly pp. 201–206.

church again. It and the neighboring brick mansion designed by Charles Bulfinch in 1796 for Harrison Gray Otis, now the headquarters of the Society for the Preservation of New England Antiquities, are the sole survivors of a region of Boston lately bulldozed for redevelopment.

Williamsburg, the most extensive and distinguished effort in historic preservation undertaken in the United States, combines examples of all the preceding categories, with a totally new element, that of reconstruction. There an entire community has been turned back to the eighteenth century. Between 1927 and 1941, 591 modern buildings were torn down or moved from the restoration areas. Eighty-three buildings that survived from the eighteenth century were restored to their original appearance.[3] To create the illusion of the colonial capital, other important buildings were entirely rebuilt on their original foundations. So carefully and so soundly has it all been done that the town carries conviction. The visitor has to consult his guide book to be certain where restoration stops and reconstruction begins. Bruton Church, like King's Chapel, has always continued in its original use. George Wythe's house, looking as he would have enjoyed seeing it both inside and out, is exhibited to visitors rather than occupied as a dwelling. Other eighteenth-century buildings, not open to visitors, have been converted within to new purposes. The kitchens and outbuildings of houses have been transformed into living quarters for restoration employees, and much else of a practical nature accomplished, yet the exteriors appear unchanged as part of the eighteenth-century scene. But as the capitol and the Governor's Palace had perished, what the visitor enjoys today are, like the Raleigh Tavern where Jefferson danced in the Apollo Room, modern reconstructions, built upon the original foundations after meticulous archaeological and historical investigation.

Many buildings have survived at the cost of being trundled off to

---

3. Rutherford Goodwin, *A Brief & True Report Concerning Williamsburg in Virginia* (Williamsburg, 1941), pp. 96–125; *Colonial Williamsburg Official Guidebook* (Williamsburg, 1960), pp. xvii–xix.

new sites. The Shirley-Eustis House in Roxbury, Massachusetts, built in the middle of the eighteenth century by Governor William Shirley, was in 1867 moved thirty feet to make room for a new street in a land development that effectively ruined the attraction of its once magnificent surroundings. This great house survives, although unfurnished and a ghost of its former self.[4] Other ancient buildings, jostled by housing developments, new highways, or parking lots, have found shelter in the lee of friendly institutions. Early in this century the Essex Institute in Salem began gathering architectural flotsam in its back garden; very recently the Crowninshield-Bentley House of 1727 has found a new home on a corner of the institute's grounds. Other organizations, like the Santa Barbara Historical Society, have preserved threatened houses by moving them intact to a nearby site. Still others have been saved by being dismantled and moved to distant locations, sometimes at astronomical expense. A recent instance is Boscobel, a great manor house in the Adam style, begun by Staats Morris Dyckman in 1804 at Crugers in Westchester County, New York. Demolished in 1955 after being sold to a housewrecker for $35, the building has been reassembled on a new site overlooking the Hudson fifteen miles away at Garrison-on-Hudson, at a reported cost of $1,250,000. When dedicated by Governor Rockefeller on 21 May 1961, Boscobel was safely settled on a thirtysix-acre plot, with the same relation to the Hudson as its original site and with a $500,000 endowment fund provided by the Reader's Digest Foundation, headed by Mr. and Mrs. DeWitt Wallace.[5]

4. *Final Report of the Boston National Historic Sites Commission*, 87th Congress, 1st Session, House Document No. 107 (Washington, 1961), pp. 181–186. The Shirley-Eustis House Association, organized in 1911, has preserved the house from destruction for half a century, but has been unable to attempt its restoration and furnishing. The commission recommends that the United States accept the house from the association for preservation by the National Park Service and that a proper setting be re-created for it as part of the planning for urban renewal in Roxbury.

5. Merrill Folsom, "Hudson Mansion Lives Again," *New York Times*, Sunday, 21 May 1961, p. xx3, reports that the principal contributors at the start were Mr. and Mrs. DeWitt Wallace, co-publishers of *The Reader's Digest*. Mrs. Wallace gave $750,000, while she and her husband, through The Reader's Digest Foundation, set up a trust fund of $500,000 to keep the restored property open to the public in per-

Many smaller buildings, hitherto unrelated to one another, have been transported to new surroundings and resettled in what their admirers resent having called "synthetic villages." At Cooperstown during the past fifteen years, the New York State Historical Association has collected from various localities a school, country store, tavern, and small offices and shops to form a "Village Crossroads"as an adjunct to its Farmers' Museum. In 1941 the Marine Historical Association, Inc., brought to Mystic, Connecticut, the New Bedford whale ship *Charles W. Morgan*. Six years later it began to assemble buildings for the creation of a Seaport Street. Today it has brought together numerous ships and craft, as well as buildings from Hoboken, Plymouth, and intervening points.[6]

While the Village Crossroads and the Mystic Seaport are the creation of organizations founded with quite different purposes,[7] other assemblies of old buildings have sprung from the indefatigable activities of private collectors. The caprice of collecting buildings and carting them about on a wholesale scale is part of our heritage from

---

petuity. "Other contributions have been received and pledged for the restoration. The total sum required, apart from the trust fund, was set at $1,250,000." See also "Boscobel, Garrison-on-Hudson," *Historic Preservation* XIII (1961), 70–72.

6. One finds, for example, the square-rigger *Joseph Conrad*, built at Copenhagen in 1882, the ferry boat *Brinckerhoff* which once plied the Hudson River between Poughkeepsie and Highland, an 1824 rope walk once belonging to the Plymouth Cordage Company, and the Gothic revival Station Ten clubhouse of the New York Yacht Club, built in 1845 at Hoboken, New Jersey, in a region improbably designated the Elysian Fields. See Samuel Chamberlain, *Mystic Seaport, A Camera Impression* (New York, 1959).

7. For the New York State Historical Association, see chapter XIV. The Marine Historical Association, Inc., was founded at Mystic in 1929 by Carl C. Cutler, author of *Greyhounds of the Sea, The Story of the American Clipper Ship*, and by Edward E. Bradley and Charles K. Stillman. Into some old mill buildings on the Mystic riverfront, these three friends installed their own collections of half-models and other maritime possessions. For the first dozen years things were very simple, with most work donated and an emphasis on research and publication. In 1940 there were two small buildings, one full-time employee, 225 members, and a budget of $3,000. But as Carl Cutler was an able scholar, with firsthand experience at sea, those in need of guidance in maritime history often found their way to his door. The acquisition of the *Charles W. Morgan* in 1941, which sparked the growth and expansion of the association, also changed its character. In 1960 it owned 20 acres of land, 40 buildings, 5 historic ships,

Henry Ford's energetic but ill-considered efforts to repair some of the damage created in the United States by his product. In spite of his earlier aspersions upon history,[8] Ford in the 1920s fell victim to a sentimental nostalgia for the scenes of his youth, which caused him to purchase the Wayside Inn in Sudbury, Massachusetts, take up square dancing, promote the "McGuffey type" education of children (in air-conditioned log cabins with indirect electric cove lighting), and to transport to the Edison Institute Museum and Greenfield Village in Dearborn, Michigan, an incredible quantity of artifacts and buildings, related to one another only in his own mind. The theory behind this he expressed in 1926 in his *Today and Tomorrow*:

> I deeply admire the men who founded this country and I think we ought to know more about them and how they lived and the force and courage they had. Of course, we can read about them, but . . . the only way to show how our forefathers lived and to bring to mind the kind of people they were is to reconstruct, as nearly as possible, the exact conditions under which they lived.

Acting upon this notion of keeping the gains and repairing some of the losses of modern industry, he hauled to Dearborn a jittery miscellany of buildings that included the brick shed in which he built the first Ford car, a Cotswold stone cottage, a Cape Cod windmill, a courthouse where Lincoln practiced law, the early laboratories of his hero Edison, and heaven knows what else.[9]

---

more than 100 small craft, had 6,500 members, investments for endowment of $1,242,307 (market value $1,753,053), and 76 full-time employees (who, alas, no longer included Carl Cutler). It had become so large an enterprise, depending so much upon the traveling public ($289,523, or 59%, of its 1960 income came from admissions) that the greater part of its vastly augmented revenues had to be devoted to the care of property and visitors. The 1960 treasurer's report breaks down the year's expenses of $490,843 thus: salaries, wages, and annuities, $342,802 (69.8%); maintenance, $51,463 (10.5%); supplies, $28,583 (5.8%); utilities, $23,360 (4.7%); insurance and taxes, $24,996 (5.1%); professional services and special events, $16,091 (3.3%); and, last and least, library and exhibit material and appropriations, $3,548 (.8%).

8. See Allan Nevins and Frank Ernest Hill, *Ford Expansion and Challenge 1915–1933* (New York, 1957), p. 138.

9. Nevins and Hill, *op. cit.*, pp. 498–506; Keith Sward, *The Legend of Henry Ford* (New York, 1948), pp. 259–275; William Adams Simonds, *Henry Ford and Greenfield Village* (New York, 1938); *The Book of Greenfield Village* (Dearborn, 1961).

Two assemblies of old buildings in New England—Old Sturbridge Village at Sturbridge, Massachusetts, and the Shelburne Museum at Shelburne, Vermont—developed from the enthusiastic acquisitiveness of private collectors. In 1936 Albert B. and J. Cheney Wells of Southbridge, Massachusetts, who were being driven out of house and home by the extent of their American antique collecting, bought a 250-acre tract of land in Sturbridge and moved buildings to it for the accommodation of their numerous possessions. Ten years later Old Sturbridge Village, established as a private nonprofit educational institution, was opened to the public.[10] Eighteenth- and early nineteenth-century buildings of many types have been brought here from considerable distances and arranged in the form of a typical New England village. As the topographical character of the land was carefully considered, the area chosen includes fields, woodland, a stream and millpond, hills, rocks, and ravines. Into this appropriate setting, the transplanted buildings merge with unobtrusive felicity. The place *looks* like a New England village. Houses sit well on the ground; brooks spring up opportunely; rubbish is skillfully accumulated in likely places; the ox driver knows how to drive oxen.

At Shelburne[11] the illusion is less complete, for the site chosen for the museum, although blessed with a stupendous view of the Adirondacks and Green Mountains, has none of the topographical character of a village. It is simply a fine field in which buildings from various parts of Vermont and New Hampshire have been reassembled after moving, with the primary purpose of housing the vast antique collection of the late Mrs. J. Watson Webb, who created the museum. Although nobody beside Henry Ford has had the funds to assemble an *omnium gatherum* on the scale of Greenfield Village, Mrs. Webb did the best she could along this line. A 168-foot covered bridge that once spanned the Lamoille River at Cambridge, Ver-

10. See Catherine Fennelly, "Foreword," in Samuel Chamberlain, *A Tour of Old Sturbridge Village* (New York, 1957), pp. 3–6.
11. Ralph Nading Hill and Lilian Baker Carlisle, *The Story of The Shelburne Museum* (Shelburne, 1955).

mont, was dismantled and brought to Shelburne, even though no stream required its services there. With incredible difficulty the 892-ton side-wheel steamboat *Ticonderoga* was moved overland from Lake Champlain. Similarly the Colchester lighthouse, which once marked a treacherous reef near the middle of the lake, has in retirement come ashore to loom over the houses from various parts of Vermont and New Hampshire that were reassembled after moving, with the primary purpose of providing exhibition space for Mrs. Webb's immensely varied collections of china, glass, dolls, paintings, prints, primitives, decoys, textiles, hardware, and carriages. The element of personal whim predominates even in the architecture at the Shelburne Museum. Consider, for example, what is called the Vermont House. This began as an early nineteenth-century wooden cottage in another part of the town. As its interior had been gutted and its clapboards were decayed, it was, after moving, encased in weathered stone appropriated from a neighboring gristmill. The paneling installed in one room comes from Connecticut; the eighteenth-century Queen Anne and Chippendale furniture from southern New England. The whole is, according to the museum handbook,

conceived as having been owned by a retired Captain—a man of some wealth who had ranged the seven seas, had gathered his possessions over the decades of his travels, and built himself a fine house in which to place them.

This very personal, romantic, and improbable concept is calculated to confuse rather than instruct the visitor. The assembly and preservation of the buildings at the Shelburne Museum is a tribute to Mrs. Webb's indefatigable and very personal collecting; they do not fit together with the plausibility of Old Sturbridge Village.

Passing further in the spectrum of historic preservation, from the ship that remains the same to the one that does not, one leaves restoration and enters reconstruction. Here again there are degrees and variations, depending upon the amount of data available, the care given to research, and the skill of architect and craftsman. But even the finest reconstruction is quite another matter from an actual building that has simply been repaired and stripped of later additions. When Governor William Tryon's palace in New Bern, North Carolina, burned in 1798, only the separate west wing survived. Soon less distinguished houses rose on its site. Nearly a century and a half later, Mrs. James Edwin Latham of Greensboro led a movement for the reconstruction of the palace, which she reinforced by personal gifts and a bequest of more than $1,500,000. With these and other private funds, and with State appropriations, the Tryon Palace Commission re-created the building at a cost of just under $3,000,000. It was opened to visitors in the spring of 1959.[12] Fortunately, in addition to the foundations and the west wing, John Hawks's elevation and plan of the building survived in the Public Record Office in London; equally fortunately the architects, Perry, Shaw, Hepburn and Dean, had not only a wealth of experience from their work at Williamsburg but clients who were perfectionists. Thus with great care and vast expense was, in the words of Professor John Coolidge, "a modern dream of the past made concrete."[13]

When the First Iron Works Association, Inc., was organized at Saugus, Massachusetts, in the early 1940s, all that remained from the Hammersmith iron works of 1646–53 was the fine Ironmaster's House[14] and a slag pile overgrown with trees. The house had been bought for Henry Ford's Greenfield Village at Dearborn, Michigan, but as there was strong local sentiment against its removal, the association was formed to attempt to keep it on its original site. With $4,000 appropriated by the Commonwealth of Massachusetts, a similar sum by the town, and $9,000 raised privately, the association secured title to the Ironmaster's House and adjacent land. Excavations in

12. "Tryon Palace," *Twenty-eighth Biennial Report of the North Carolina Department of Archives and History, 1958–1960* (Raleigh, N. C., 1960), pp. 79–82; Alonzo Thomas Dill, *Governor Tryon and his Palace* (Chapel Hill, 1955).

13. *Historic Preservation* X (1958), 84. In addressing the Rhode Island Preservation Seminar on 10 May 1958, Professor Coolidge questioned the wisdom of diverting vast sums, as at Williamsburg, to "these romantic reconstructions of the past," and inquired: "Which is more important, a genuine old building saved, or a modern dream of the past made concrete?"

14. *Final Report of the Boston National Historic Sites Commission*, pp. 230–232.

1948 uncovered evidence of the seventeenth-century blast furnace. Historical and archival research over the next five years,[15] supplementing the archaeological evidence, made possible a full-fledged replica of the seventeenth-century Hammersmith works in the series of buildings, waterwheels, and machinery that are to be seen today at the Saugus Ironworks Restoration. Perry, Shaw, Hepburn and Dean were again the architects of the reconstruction, which was dedicated in 1954. The cost of $2,350,000 was borne by the American Iron and Steel Institute of New York. As the institute in the summer of 1961 announced its intention of terminating its annual contribution of $25,000, which covered the maintenance and operating costs, the future of this Saugus reconstruction is, at the time of writing, in doubt.[16]

Tryon Palace and the Saugus Ironworks, like many less ambitious ventures in reconstruction, have the merit of standing upon the actual sites of the buildings that they re-create. There is, however, still another category to be considered: out-and-out reconstructions of early buildings, for which there is only fragmentary evidence, built for commemorative celebrations or for supposedly educational purposes in public parks or upon other sites than the structures whose memory they evoke once stood. Sometimes they are designed by learned men after careful research. Even so, they are so far removed from their originals that even the most contentious of the Greek philosophers would hardly argue that they *were* the same ship in which Theseus journeyed to Crete.

15. The chief results were published in *Ironworks on the Saugus, The Lynn and Braintree Ventures of the Company of Undertakers of the Ironworks in New England* (Norman, 1957), by Professor E. N. Hartley of the Massachusetts Institute of Technology, who served as research historian of the project from 1949 to 1954.

16. Mr. J. Sanger Atwill, president of the First Iron Works Association, Inc., tells me that between 12,000 and 17,000 visitors a year come. Although there is a 50c admission fee for the works, and 50c for the Ironmaster's House, this income is far from meeting operating expenses, particularly as children are admitted free. In a region where there are many demands for the preservation of authentic ancient buildings, it will not be easy to find private support for this great reconstruction, good as it is.

The Pioneers' Village in Forest River Park, Salem, Massachusetts, was built in 1930 to mark the Massachusetts Bay Tercentenary.[17] It served as the background for a pageant commemorating the arrival of Governor Winthrop in the ship *Arbella* on 12 June 1630. Unlike the *Arbella*, which was nothing more than the respectable 1870 Maine coasting schooner *Lavolta* made ridiculous by the addition of a supposedly seventeenth-century superstructure,[18] the Pioneers' Village was a serious piece of reconstruction by George Francis Dow, with landscaping by Harlan P. Kelsey. It realistically represented the rude houses, huts and dugouts, and wigwams that sheltered the first settlers. Since the tercentenary it has been maintained in decent manner by the Salem Park Commissioners. The thatch is getting thin. Here and there plaster has fallen away from a chimney, revealing wire lath. Trees and shrubs have obscured the original pattern, but as commemorative efforts go it deserves a better mark than most.

In the Jamestown celebrations of 1957, the fort of 1607, the glasshouse, and other reconstructions for the benefit of visitors to the Jamestown Festival, were intentionally placed on other than the original sites in order not to jeopardize the archaeological evidence of foundations on Jamestown Island.[19] At Plymouth, Massachusetts, the modern town is built upon the site of the original settlement. Consequently the Pilgrim Village of 1627 and the Fort Meeting-

17. *A Reference Guide to Salem, 1630, Forest River Park, Salem, Massachusetts* (Salem, 1959).

18. See Ernest Stanley Dodge, "The Last Days of Coasting on Union River Bay," *The American Neptune* IX (1949), 169–179. Mr. Dodge observes: "If, after the celebration, she had been scuttled or beached somewhere all would have ended well. But unfortunately three years after the tercentenary *Lavolta* became the property of the city of Salem. Reconditioned and rerigged in a sad, imaginary, and incorrect sort of way, she was placed on exhibition at the Salem Willows pier during July and August 1937. From the Willows she was taken to the Pioneers' Village at Forest River Park and horsed into a hole in the ground. Gradually disintegrating, the venerable old vessel has become the greatest unintentional historical hoax of the region as each summer wide-eyed midwesterners marvel that a ship could be so well preserved for three hundred years." That was 1949; mercifully she is no longer there.

19. Jamestown-Williamsburg-Yorktown Celebration Commission, *The 350th Anniversary of Jamestown 1607–1957, Final Report to the President and Congress* (Washington, 1958), pp. 17–18.

house reconstructions undertaken in the past decade by Plimoth Plantation[20] are on an entirely unrelated site at Eel River, two miles south. On the Plymouth waterfront is exhibited *Mayflower II*,[21] the replica of the Pilgrim vessel, designed by the American naval architect William A. Baker, built in England and sailed across the Atlantic in 1957 under command of Captain Alan Villiers. The aim of this reconstruction is to have Plimoth Plantation today "look as much like the original Plantation as historical and archaeological research can make it." The research has been careful, yet the reconstruction that results has much of the unconvincing impermanence of pageantry about it.

The preceding pages have, I hope, indicated that the gamut of historic preservation in the United States—from buildings still used for their original purposes on their original sites to out-and-out reconstructions built elsewhere—makes the ship of Theseus look like a simple problem. The early history of all this has been perceptively studied by Dr. Charles B. Hosmer Jr. in *Old Houses in America. The Preservation Movement to 1926*, a 1961 Columbia dissertation[22] that will, I hope, soon be published in enlarged form by the National Trust for Historic Preservation. The motives behind these multifarious efforts in preservation are as disparate as the buildings themselves. One can find instances of disinterested devotion to history and architecture, of regional or individual pride, patriotism, education, personal vanity, muddled thinking, and downright commercialism. For the purposes of this study, the matter to be considered is the extent to which efforts in historic preservation have contributed to research and publication in American history.

20. A nonprofit educational organization formed, according to its circular of information, "to tell the story of the Pilgrims."

21. William A. Baker, *The New* Mayflower, *Her Design and Construction* (Barre, Mass., 1958); Warwick Charlton, *The Second* Mayflower *Adventure* (Boston, 1957); Alan Villiers, *Wild Ocean* (New York, 1957), pp. 156–168.

22. Available on microfilm (61–3435) from University Microfilms, Inc., Ann Arbor, Michigan. This carefully organized and delightfully written work neatly disproves the popular belief that a doctoral dissertation *must*, by its nature, be dull or insignificant.

Behind all serious attempts at historic preservation there must be thorough and meticulous research. This was strongly emphasized at a session on American outdoor museums at the December 1961 meeting of the American Historical Association by Carlisle H. Humelsine, president of Colonial Williamsburg, and by Louis C. Jones,[23] director of the New York State Historical Association. Edward P. Alexander of Colonial Williamsburg several years ago remarked that "it is all-important that historical restorations be created in the spirit of historical accuracy, especially since three-dimensional history is so believable." Mr. Alexander went on to point out that

Visitors are accustomed to exercise scepticism toward the printed word, but they are not so ready to argue with brick and mortar or furniture and furnishings. History in the round has blandishments that can easily mislead all but the most expert. . . . The restoration that loses its regard for authenticity is committing its own destruction. Experts will observe unreasonable lapses and uncorrected mistakes, and the word will spread to the public. Without a basic devotion to truth, a restoration can easily degenerate into a tourist trap.[24]

During the past thirty-five years a tremendous amount of research in architectural and social history has been carried on at Williamsburg. Most of it, however, has been used for some immediate purpose of restoration or reconstruction, and the evidence consigned to filing drawers, the existence of which is apt to be unknown to scholars beyond the Colonial Williamsburg staff. Since Mr. Humelsine became president in 1958, there has been increased emphasis upon making this valuable material generally available. Two volumes by Marcus Whiffen opened a new series of Williamsburg Architectural Studies: *The Public Buildings of Williamsburg, Colonial Capital of Virginia, An Architectural History* appeared in 1958 and *The Eighteenth-Century Houses of Williamsburg, A Study of Architecture and Building in the Colonial Capital of Virginia* in 1960. The Williamsburg Architectural Studies were undertaken to make available material gathered

23. Published as "The Trapper's Cabin and the Ivory Tower," *Museum News* XL, 7 (March 1962), pp. 11–16.
24. Edward P. Alexander, "Historical Restorations," *In Support of Clio, Essays in Memory of Herbert A. Kellar* (Madison, 1958), pp. 208–209.

from widely scattered sources in the course of restoration, unlike the Williamsburg Restoration Historical Studies[25] of the 1940s, which consisted of new editions of books and documents on colonial life in Virginia, or the Williamsburg in America Series,[26] begun in 1950 to provide popular histories of Tidewater Virginia in the eighteenth century.

The greatest service that Williamsburg has rendered to historical scholarship has been through the Institute of Early American History and Culture,[27] organized in 1943 under the joint sponsorship of the College of William and Mary and Colonial Williamsburg for "the furtherance of study, research, and publications bearing upon American history approximately to the year 1815." In January 1944 a third series of the *William and Mary Quarterly*, with its scope broadened to include the whole field of early American history, was inaugurated.[28] Under the editorship successively of Richard L. Morton, Douglass Adair, Lester J. Cappon, and Lawrence W. Towner, the *William and Mary Quarterly* has achieved high rank among scholarly periodicals.

The three directors of the institute—Carl Bridenbaugh (1945–50), L. H. Butterfield (1951–54), and Lester J. Cappon (1955–)—have been singularly productive scholars, who have made the place attractive to colonial historians, old and young, from all parts of the country. The May meetings of the Institute Council, which consists of fifteen scholars from other institutions plus the presidents of Colonial Williamsburg and the College of William and Mary, have become a delightful rallying point for colonial historians. The fel-

25. The first of these, published in 1940 under the editorship of Hunter Dickinson Farish, was a new edition of the 1727 pamphlet *The Present State of Virginia, and the College*, by Henry Hartwell, James Blair, and Edward Chilton. The third and last was Farish's edition (1945) of the journal and letters of Philip Vickers Fithian.

26. This series consists of Carl Bridenbaugh's *Seat of Empire, The Political Role of Eighteenth-Century America*, Edmund S. Morgan's *Virginians at Home, Family Life in the Eighteenth Century*, Earl Schenck Miers's *Blood of Freedom*, and Robert S. Rutland's *Reluctant Statesman*.

27. See *Handbook* of 1957.

28. Published since 1892 as a magazine of Virginia history.

lowships, awarded to promising young scholars on a three-year postdoctoral appointment, provide time for study and writing, combined with some teaching at the college, at the moment when it is most needed.

Under the editorship of Lester J. Cappon for ten years, and of James Morton Smith from 1955 to the present, the institute has published chiefly through the University of North Carolina Press thirty-nine scholarly books—monographs, biographies, documentary materials from original manuscripts, new editions of books long out of print, and bibliographical essays and compilations. The Lilly Endowment, Inc., of Indianapolis in 1957 granted the institute $60,000 to promote the expansion of its book publication program. The seven titles of the 1961–62 season will indicate the variety of subjects embraced by the institute: Jackson Turner Main's *The Anti-federalists: Critics of the Constitution, 1781–1788*, Benjamin Quarles's *The Negro in the American Revolution*, John A. Schutz's *William Shirley: King's Governor of Massachusetts*, Don Higginbotham's *Daniel Morgan: Revolutionary Rifleman*, Louis Leonard Tucker's *Puritan Protagonist: Thomas Clap of Yale College*, Edmund S. Morgan's *The Gentle Puritan: A Life of Ezra Stiles, 1727–1795*, and Lynn Turner's *William Plumer of New Hampshire*. With the blessing of the National Historical Publications Commission, the institute and the College of William and Mary are jointly laying plans for an edition of the papers of John Marshall, to be edited by James Morton Smith. Planning is also progressing rapidly for an *Atlas of Early American History*. The institute manuscript award of $1,000 in 1962 was won by Howard C. Rice's edition of the travels of the Marquis de Chastellux, which will be published by the University of North Carolina Press in 1963.

The institute has endeavored to stimulate study in special fields as yet only slightly exploited or in need of a fresh approach by arranging conferences and publishing their results. The first of these, convened by Mr. Butterfield in 1952, led to the publication of *Early American Science, Needs and Opportunities for Study* by Whitfield J.

Bell Jr., with a provocative bibliography. Similar conferences have been held on Indian-White relations to 1830, early American law, early American education,[29] early American architecture, and the seventeenth century. A conference on early American decorative arts, jointly sponsored with the Henry Francis du Pont Winterthur Museum and the Smithsonian Institution, is planned for the coming year.

Like most scholarly organizations, devoted purely to research and publication, the Institute of Early American History and Culture accomplishes a great deal on a relatively small amount of money. Its 1962–63 budget—as large as it has ever had—of $84,385 is provided in equal shares by the College of William and Mary and Colonial Williamsburg. Thus, although it is in the lee of a great project in historic preservation whose annual income and expenses in coping with the public run into millions, the institute operates in the same frugal and efficient manner as the independent historical societies that are the subject of this study. It is beyond question the most valuable asset to general American history contributed by the field of historic preservation.

The publications of most organizations concerned with historic preservation are in the nature of guides or catalogues, locally focused. A happy exception is the *Bulletin* of the Society for the Preservation of New England Antiquities, founded by William Sumner Appleton in 1910, which since its eleventh volume in 1920 has borne the title of *Old-Time New England*. Now in its fifty-second volume, it has always been more than a house organ of the society that publishes it. Two books published by the society should also be noted as

29. Professor Bernard Bailyn's *Education in the Forming of American Society* (1960) has just been reissued as a paperback by Vintage Books (v–509). In 1962 Collier Books has reprinted the late Charles S. Sydnor's *Gentlemen Freeholders* (1952) under the new title *American Revolutionaries in the Making* (AS140) and Robert Allen Rutland's *The Birth of the Bill of Rights* (1955) as AS134. Last year the late Joseph Charles's *The Origins of the American Party System* (1956) was in Harper Torchbooks (TB 1049). To have one tenth of the entire institute list appear in paperbacks in less than two years is a significant indication of interest in serious works that would have been viewed dimly by commercial publishers a few years ago.

studies in social history: George Francis Dow's *Every Day Life in the Massachusetts Bay Colony* (1935) and Abbott Lowell Cummings's *Bed Hangings, A Treatise on Fabrics and Styles in the Curtaining of Beds, 1650–1850.*

The Old Sturbridge Village Booklet Series, edited (and sometimes written) by Catherine Fennelly, is an outstanding example of first-rate popularization. Although intended chiefly for visitors to the village, these picture books are more widely useful because of the excellence of their illustrations and the texts that accompany them. Abbott Lowell Cummings's *Architecture in Early New England*, for example, in thirty-two pages provides a summary of accurate information not readily found elsewhere in so convenient a form. Designed by John O. C. McCrillis of Yale University Press and printed by the Meriden Gravure Company, this series, like the picture books of the Boston Museum of Fine Arts and the Massachusetts Historical Society, makes graphic material available at very reasonable cost through the economies of sizable editions in offset. *The New-England Galaxy*, the village's little popular quarterly of New England life, manners, and social history, is equally attractive because of its literacy and excellent format.

Wormsloe plantation, on the Isle of Hope near Savannah, is a remarkable example of a coastal Georgia plantation that has remained in one family since Noble Jones first leased it from James Oglethorpe in 1736. It has also an extraordinary tie with historical sources and research. There in 1847 George Wymberley Jones De Renne, great-grandson of Noble Jones, began the publication of the Wormsloe Quartos—reprints of scarce sources on the history of Georgia, previously mentioned in chapter VIII. Both he and his wife gathered remarkable historical libraries. Their son Wymberley Jones De Renne (1853–1916) continued his father's devotion to the Georgia Historical Society, endowed for a time a chair in State history at the University of Georgia, and gathered at Wormsloe a significant library of sources on Georgia history. This collection, for which a library was built in 1907 under the live oaks on the plantation, has now passed to the

University of Georgia at Athens. In 1931 W. J. De Renne's daughter, Mrs. Craig Barrow, became the twelfth master of Wormsloe. The Wormsloe Foundation which she established in 1951 has thus far produced four excellent historical publications, distributed by the University of Georgia Press. E. Merton Coulter's *Wormsloe, Two Centuries of a Georgia Family* appeared in 1955. Professor Coulter then edited two volumes of the journal of William Stephens, secretary of the province of Georgia, covering the years 1741–45. In 1960 Professor Clarence L. Versteeg of Northwestern University edited the unique copy, owned by the John Carter Brown Library, of Patrick Tailfer's *A True and Historical Narrative of the Colony of Georgia*, with comments by the Earl of Egmont. The Wormsloe plantation is a remarkable survival, of great beauty. The Wormsloe Foundation publications carry on a distinguished historical tradition in a manner highly useful to present and future scholars.

I cannot leave the coast of Georgia and the subject of historic preservation without a tribute to the memory of Mrs. Margaret Davis Cate of St. Simons Island, who died on 29 November 1961. The widow of a Brunswick physician, she became the energetic and highly professional historian of the colonial era of coastal Georgia. Fort Frederica on St. Simons Island is her monument, for besides much else she was the moving spirit of its preservation. The Fort Frederica Association, organized in 1941, in which Mrs. Cate was staunchly supported by Mr. Alfred W. Jones of Sea Island, raised nearly $100,000 to buy and preserve the site. After the association turned the property over to the Federal government for maintenance by the National Park Service as the Fort Frederica National Monument, Mrs. Cate continued her exhaustive research upon the history of this site, built in 1736 under Oglethorpe's direction as the chief British outpost against Spaniards in Florida. Her book *Early Days in Coastal Georgia*, published in 1955 by the Fort Frederica Association and the University of Georgia Press, gives, with Dr. Orrin Sage Wightman's fine photographs, a vivid picture of the region. But one had to sit in Mrs. Cate's small living room, among the orderly piles of photostats and boxes of microfilm from American and foreign archives, to realize the widespread nature of her investigations and the profundity of her research. Margaret Davis Cate's work at Fort Frederica was living proof that the investigation of a local site need not be restricting, for the study of this frontier fort led her into the far-flung complexities of the politics and strategy of England and the continent. Here was a spiritual descendant of Jeremy Belknap who never grumbled over using a microfilm reader. Here was a woman of modest means, whose triumphant vitality transported her beyond her local scene to the limitless realm of sound but imaginative scholarship.

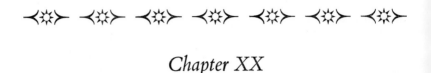

Chapter XX

STATE ARCHIVAL AGENCIES

The ultimate purpose of the preservation and efficient administration of the public records . . . is to make it possible for our present generation to have enduring and dependable knowledge of its past, and for future generations to have such knowledge of their past, of which our present is a part.   —WALDO G. LELAND, 1950

D URING the nineteenth century, public records in the United States, save for those that had a continuing official use, were consistently neglected. Sometimes, as in Maryland and New Hampshire, early and important segments of State records might be deposited in a historical society, but bulkier and less attractive groups might well be stowed in any available cellar or attic, where they were both inaccessible and combustible. Indeed enough records were destroyed by fire to supply indolent clerks, unwilling to explore those that survived, with a plausible excuse for their failure to produce specific documents. A public archives commission, appointed by the American Historical Association in 1899, undertook methodical investigation of the records of the states.[1] Within a decade it had issued forty-one reports on State and municipal archives, and, in response to this stimulus, half the states passed laws relating to the preservation and custody of their records. J. Franklin Jameson, for many years editor of the *American Historical Review*, and Waldo G. Leland, his younger colleague in the Depart-

1. The annual reports of the American Historical Association from 1900 show the progressive activities of this commission.

ment of Historical Research of the Carnegie Institution, led in the development of an archival consciousness that eventually brought about the establishment of the National Archives, greatly improved conditions in many states, and, in 1936, the formation of the Society of American Archivists.[2]

The National Historical Publications Commission *Guide* indicates that many State archival agencies, in addition to the official records that are their chief responsibility, possess substantial quantities of private papers and business records. More than passing reference to the important work of these agencies would be beyond the scope of this study of independent historical societies. It would be uselessly repetitive because of the studies sponsored by the Society of American Archivists. The extensive mimeographed *1957 Comparative Study of State and U. S. Territorial Laws Governing Archives*, compiled for that society by Mrs. Mary Givens Bryan, then chairman of its State Records Committee and in 1959–60 its president, makes valuable comparative information readily available. Moreover Dr. Ernst Posner is now engaged in a nationwide study of State archives, based upon personal visits, for the society.

The diversity of organization is considerable. Mrs. Bryan reported seven states with independent history, archives, or records commissions: Arkansas, Delaware, Maryland, Michigan, Minnesota, Pennsylvania, and Vermont. Seven others have separate departments of archives and history or archives departments: Alabama, Iowa, Mississippi, North Carolina, South Carolina, West Virginia, and Wyoming. Nine states operate archival programs under the State library or library and archives: Arizona, Connecticut, Florida, Indiana, Oklahoma, Oregon, Tennessee, Texas, and Virginia. Others have placed their archives under the administration of the Secretary of State or the department of education, while ten states in 1957 had

2. See the excellent summary by G. Philip Bauer, "Public Archives in the United States," in William B. Hesseltine and Donald R. McNeil, ed., *In Support of Clio: Essays in Memory of Herbert A. Kellar* (Madison, 1958), pp. 49–76; also T. R. Schellenberg, *Modern Archives, Principles and Techniques* (Chicago, 1956).

their archival programs integrated with their State historical societies. Mrs. Bryan observes that

Archival and records management programs to be most effective need to be *integrated*, not *separated*. The most effective programs where the two are integrated are organized as independent agencies or commissions, or under the Secretary of State, or wherever they serve close to top administration. . . . It is evident from all surveys that archives operating under state historical societies are rather buried unless a separate division is established like those in Colorado and Utah, with their own appropriation for archives and records work.[3] State historical societies are found to be more closely allied to the museum and history fields than archives.

State libraries, historical commissions, and departments of archives and history often perform valuable services to history, extending far beyond the care of public records and the official purposes for which they primarily exist. In New York, Pennsylvania, and Virginia, for example, where major independent historical societies have long existed, State agencies carry on important projects in the preservation of historical sources, and in research, editing, and publication, that valuably supplement and enlarge the work of the older private organizations. I regret that limitations of space and the purpose of this book prevent any account of them. The organizations treated in chapters XI, XII, and XIII have been described in some detail only to indicate how the State historical society as an institution evolves when it relies upon public rather than private support. The present chapter is concerned only with State agencies that were established at the instigation of historical societies that lacked the resources to develop as independent organizations, and with instances where previously founded State agencies have begotten and nurtured satellite historical societies as a means of fostering public interest. A few of these will now be briefly mentioned, although with the repeated warning that I make no attempt to consider the work of State archival agencies save in this peripheral connection.

3. This was written in 1957. Readers of chapter XIII may recall that in 1959 the archival agency of Colorado was amicably separated from the State historical society and made an independent agency in the Executive Department of the State government.

ALABAMA

In some parts of the south, a department of archives and history, created as an integral agency of the State government, assumed the functions elsewhere carried out by State historical societies.[4] This development, which began in Alabama[5] soon after the turn of the century, occurred in regions where earlier historical societies had failed to secure adequate private gifts or public appropriations. Reflecting the American Historical Association's concern over archival matters, it represented a joint effort by professional historians and the older amateur groups to secure public backing for a carefully planned historical department involving the custody of public archives, the assembly of unofficial sources, and the issuing of publications.

An Alabama Historical Society, organized in 1850 at Tuscaloosa, was a war casualty. Revived in 1874 and again in 1898, its activities consisted chiefly of an annual meeting, for it had no staff, building, library, manuscripts, newspapers, nor museum. In 1898 it received its first annual State appropriation of $1,000, and the following year issued a volume of *Transactions*. In 1900 it moved to Birmingham.

The present Alabama Department of Archives and History, a State institution located at the capital, Montgomery, was founded by a legislative act, approved 27 February 1901, to care for official archives and to collect and publish material bearing on the history of the State. In addition to maintaining a library, manuscript collection, museum, and historic sites, the department has encouraged and aided research not only in history but in anthropology and archaeology. Its founder and first director, Dr. Thomas McAdory Owen, regarded

4. Thomas McAdory Owen, "State Departments of Archives and History," *Annual Report of the American Historical Association for the Year 1904* (Washington, 1905), pp. 237–257.

5. Professor Charles G. Summersell, chairman of the History Department of the University of Alabama, very kindly gathered information for me on historical societies in his own State and in Mississippi. On three occasions when I have visited the University of Alabama, he has proved an invaluable guide to the history, life, and architectural monuments of Alabama.

it as a rallying point for local historical work. The Alabama Historical Society moved from Birmingham to Montgomery in the course of 1901, and within a few years its activities were entirely taken over by the department. Mrs. Owen, who succeeded her husband, and Mr. Peter A. Brannon, the present director, have continued the tradition of contact with local historical groups throughout the State. The State appropriation for all functions of the department in 1959 was $91,040.

In addition to noncurrent official records, the department has a sizable collection of personal papers of political and other figures, including various members of the Bankhead family, Jabez Lamar Monroe Curry (2,500 pieces), Jefferson Davis (a large group), Andrew Jackson (200 pieces relating to East Florida), Senator Oscar W. Underwood (20 drawers), William L. Yancey (1,000 pieces), and numerous other individuals. It has records of the Alabama Anthropological Society, the Alabama Historical Society, numerous church groups, as well as diaries, scrapbooks, and maps.

MISSISSIPPI

In Mississippi the pattern was similar. After a brief and inglorious attempt in 1858, a Mississippi Historical Society was successfully brought into being in 1898 through the able leadership of Professor Franklin L. Riley of the University of Mississippi, who was responsible for the editing of fourteen substantial volumes of *Publications*. The society led in the establishment of the Mississippi Department of Archives and History at the capital, Jackson, in 1902, to which it turned over its collection of manuscripts and relics.

Mr. Dunbar Rowland, the first director of the department, took an active part in historical and archival developments. He was, for example, in 1907 appointed chairman of the American Historical Association's very distinguished Committee on Co-operation of Historical Departments and Societies, which developed the project, carried out by Waldo G. Leland, through which historical agencies of the Mississippi valley united in supporting a catalogue of documents in French archives relating to the history of their region.[6]

William D. McCain, Mr. Rowland's successor in the department, began the publication of *The Journal of Mississippi History* in 1939 as a quarterly organ of the Mississippi Historical Society. The present director of the department, Miss Charlotte Capers, serves as editor of the *Journal* and secretary-treasurer of the society. Although the Mississippi Historical Society has had periods of quiescence, it has been increasingly active since 1953. At the present time it has upwards of 600 members, paying annual dues of $4, which are its main source of revenue. It holds an annual two-day meeting; seeks to promote interest and research in Mississippi history, to assist in the collection and preservation by the department of source materials, and to encourage county historical societies.

The present manuscript holdings of the Mississippi Department of Archives and History, official and personal, are 5,000 volumes and 2,750,000 pieces. Jefferson Davis is here represented by seven volumes and 557 other items. There are large and varied groups of personal papers; records of numerous fraternal and religious organizations; plantation journals; accounts of commission merchants at Natchez dating back to 1779; records of railroads from 1852; papers of other business firms; and the extensive transcripts from foreign archives that derived from Dr. Leland's co-operative investigation prior to World War I. The State appropriation in 1959 for all functions of the department, including archives, museum, historical markers, reference library, and publications, was $47,582.

6. Dunbar Rowland, "The Cooperation of State Historical Societies in the Gathering of Material in Foreign Archives," *Annual Report of the American Historical Association for the Year 1907* (Washington, 1908), I, 57–62; "Report of Committee on Cooperation of Historical Societies and Departments to the Conference of State and Local Historical Societies of the American Historical Association," *Annual Report . . . for the Year 1908* (Washington, 1909), I, 149–153; similar report in *Annual Report . . . for the Year 1909* (Washington, 1911), pp. 289–292; Waldo G. Leland, "Report on Work of the Catalogue of Documents in French Archives relating to the History of the Mississippi Valley," *Annual Report . . . for the Year 1911* (Washington, 1913), I, 252–253.

NORTH CAROLINA

The North Carolina Department of Archives and History was created in 1903 under the name of the North Carolina Historical Commission.[7] Seventy years earlier, in 1833, the General Assembly had granted, without immediate visible consequences, a charter for a North Carolina Historical Society to nine incorporators, one of whom was Governor David Lowry Swain. Through the efforts of Swain, who had become president of the University of North Carolina in 1835, a Historical Society of the University of North Carolina was organized at Chapel Hill in 1844. Although this society assembled a considerable body of historical documents, it did not long survive its founder, who died in 1868.[8] In 1900 the North Carolina Literary and Historical Association was founded. This body in 1903 successfully urged the General Assembly to create the North Carolina Historical Commission. Although the association has no collections or other visible and tangible assets, it meets from time to time. The director of the commission (later known as the Department of History and Archives) acts as its secretary, and its members receive, in return for their $5 dues, a subscription to the *North Carolina Historical Review*, a scholarly quarterly, edited until his recent retirement by Mr. D. L. Corbitt, and published by the department since 1924.[9]

7. [R. D. W. Connor,] *The North Carolina Historical Commission, Forty Years of Public Service, 1903–1943* (Raleigh, 1943), issued as the commission's Bulletin No. 43, gives a very full historical summary of the first forty years. Later years are treated in similar detail in the biennial reports of the North Carolina Department of Archives and History. The change of name, without change of function, occurred in the early 1940s.

8. Some of its papers went to the University of North Carolina; others long afterwards were given to the North Carolina Historical Commission. Some twenty years ago this defunct society was revived, on a state-wide basis, with the name of Historical Society of North Carolina. Membership, at first limited to fifty, has been raised to seventy-five. It meets twice a year for the reading of papers, but has no collections or premises. Its president is Mr. D. L. Corbitt, until recently head of the division of publications in the North Carolina Department of Archives and History.

9. Half of the dues of each member go to the department in return for the subscription to the review.

From modest beginnings, the North Carolina Department of Archives and History has become one of the largest and most liberally supported State organizations in the country. When R. D. W. Connor, later Archivist of the United States, became its full-time secretary in 1907, he was its only employee. Dr. Connor guided the affairs of the department until 1921. The present director, Dr. Charles Christopher Crittenden, has been in charge since 1935. The State appropriation in 1903 was $500. It increased to $5,000 in 1907 and had reached $30,865 by 1930. Over the next fourteen years it relapsed, dropping to $11,315 in 1934, but from 1945, when $45,290 was appropriated, increases have been not only steady but spectacular, for the 1959 figure was $435,867. This large sum supports varied activities on both scholarly and popular levels.

The department reported to the *Guide* the possession of 5,070 cubic feet of manuscripts, of which 4,285 were State archives and 785 were unofficial manuscripts relating primarily to North Carolina, but including much of interest at the national level. *A Guide to Manuscript Collections in the Archives of the North Carolina Historical Commission*, published in 1942, listed the 815 personal collections that were owned at that time. Appendix III to *The North Carolina Historical Commission, Forty Years of Public Service, 1903–1943* provides a useful summary of all types of holdings, while the three volumes of *The Historical Records of North Carolina*, edited by C. C. Crittenden and Dan Lacy in 1938–39, describe county records in detail. In the 1920s extensive copying of manuscripts relating to North Carolina in British and Spanish archives was undertaken. An effort was made to secure either an original, a photostat, or a microfilm copy of every newspaper published in North Carolina before 1801, and other steps taken to assemble in the department all possible sources for research in North Carolina history. Since 1939 the department has occupied part of a State office building adjacent to the capitol in Raleigh. The staff has risen from one in 1907 to forty-two in 1957 and to sixty in 1959.

The work of the department is divided into four divisions: archives and manuscripts, including a records management program, historic sites, museums, and publications. The first of these, in addition to serving the State, makes a major effort to encourage private historical and genealogical research; the second administers six historic sites in various parts of North Carolina, co-operates in others, including the Tryon Palace restoration at New Bern, and has a hand in a historical highway marker program. The division of museums is responsible for the Hall of History, a historical museum springing from a collection begun in the 1880s by Colonel Fred A. Olds, c.s.a., and for the department's educational program. Dr. Crittenden, in a recent discussion of the role of the historical society in modern America, stated, on behalf of his department, that "we believe in using every trick in the bag, in not pulling our punches, in bringing out every weapon in the arsenal, in order to sell our state's history to our people."[10] The museum consequently encourages group visits by schools, provides a traveling exhibit for school extension work, and conducts a class for eighth graders interested in early crafts practiced in North Carolina. In the school year 1956–57, 899 groups, totaling 37,808 children, visited the museum; in 1957–58 the number, although smaller, was still substantial—761 groups, bringing 33,639 children. For want of a full-time staff member, the Tarheel Junior Historian Association had in 1957–58 only twenty-nine clubs with a total membership of 1,261, although the 1956–58 biennial report states that "with adequate supervision the Association should have at least seven or eight hundred clubs within the State."

The Division of Publications is very productive both on the scholarly and popular levels. Since 1903, between documentary volumes, pamphlets, leaflets, maps, and charts, it has issued more than 400 items. *The North Carolina Historical Review*, both in contents and dress, continues on its original course as a serious scholarly quarterly, while a four-page bimonthly newssheet, *Carolina Comments*, begun in 1952, is aimed at a wider audience. The division has published

---

10. Quoted in *In Support of Clio: Essays in Memory of Herbert A. Kellar*, p. 147.

multivolume editions of the papers of a number of distinguished figures in the State, as well as eight volumes of *Records of the Moravians in North Carolina*, edited by Adelaide L. Fries between 1922 and 1954, and volumes of the addresses, letters, and papers of recent governors. On the school level it publishes numerous popular pamphlets on North Carolina history that are sold in large numbers in kits for educational use. Between these clear-cut types there are intermediate publications like William S. Powell's *The Carolina Charter of 1663*, containing the text of that document (owned by the department) with brief sketches of the eight Lords Proprietors to whom Charles II granted Carolina, and a facsimile edition of Lemuel Sawyer's four-act comedy *Blackbeard* of 1824.

The North Carolina Department of History and Archives maintains close and friendly relations with some sixty local historical societies in the State, using its informal ties with the North Carolina Literary and Historical Association as a means of wide public contact. Once a year, during "Culture Week," a vast network of meetings of friendly organizations is held. This observance began in 1913, when the North Carolina Folklore Society joined with the Literary and Historical Association in holding their meetings concurrently. In recent years the Roanoke Island Historical Association, the North Carolina Federation of Music Clubs, the North Carolina State Art Society, the North Carolina Society for the Preservation of Antiquities, the North Carolina Symphony Society, the Historical Book Club of North Carolina, Inc., the Society of Mayflower Descendants, the North Carolina Society of County and Local Historians—a "grass roots" body organized in the late 1930s by Paul Green that conducts Sunday tours—and the North Carolina Poetry Society have joined the original sponsors to achieve a Tuesday through Saturday program.[11]

11. "Culture Week," *Carolina Comments* VII, 4–5 (November 1958–January 1959), pp. 2–3. The program of these joint meetings held at Raleigh on 2–6 December 1958 contained membership lists of the participating societies. One of the incidental delights of a visit to Raleigh in November 1959 came from Dr. Crittenden's urging me to explore the North Carolina Museum of Art. This admirable collection, beautifully

SOUTH CAROLINA

The South Carolina Archives Department at Columbia, which derives from a historical commission appointed by the State in 1891, has already been mentioned in the account of the South Carolina Historical Society in chapter VIII. Unlike its neighbor to the north, this department confines its activities to public archives and to a distinguished series of publications of colonial and State records. It has no museum and undertakes no program of popularization. It maintains no great body of private manuscripts, for it works in close and harmonious relationship with the neighboring South Caroliniana Library of the University of South Carolina and with the South Carolina Historical Society in Charleston, both of which specialize in such material. Although the department officially limits its areas of operation to archival matters, Dr. J. Harold Easterby, who was its director from 1949 until his untimely death on 29 December 1960, had a beneficent and decisive personal tie with every worthwhile historical effort in the State. As his colleague W. Edwin Hemphill pointed out in a memorial for the Society of American Archivists,[12]

Harold Easterby was a historian first, an archivist second. Few members of the Society have ever found these careers more logically united, so beneficial mutually. As a historian, he demonstrated the instincts of an archivist; and when he became an archivist he remained an historian. By living observantly and by learning both formally and informally, he became preeminent in his understanding of his native South Carolina's development.

---

installed, is a striking example of what can be accomplished in a short time by well-directed State support. The museum is full of surprises. It is one thing to meet a Copley of the Pepperrell family and a portrait of Flora Macdonald. It is another to go on to Boucher and Nattier, to van Dyck's Mary Duchess of Lennox, Sebastiano Ricci, country after country, school after school, and to find not just names on labels but fascinating and unknown pictures, chosen with catholic and cultivated taste. The installation is subtly understated, in pleasing contrast to the ostentatious showmanship that now afflicts some of our older institutions that should know better. This is an achievement of which the State of North Carolina may be justly proud.

12. W. Edwin Hemphill, "James Harold Easterby, 1898–1960," *The American Archivist* XXIV (1961), 160–161.

Dr. Easterby established a standard that is, fortunately for the future, fully appreciated by his successor, Charles E. Lee, who became director of the South Carolina Archives Department on 15 July 1961.

The new archives building, opened in the spring of 1960, will greatly facilitate the work of the department. The 1959 appropriation for the department was $82,185, of which $9,070 was provided for the editing and printing of *The Papers of John C. Calhoun*.

GEORGIA

While the Alabama, Mississippi, North and South Carolina departments are separate State agencies, the Department of Archives and History at Atlanta is under the Secretary of State of Georgia. The *Guide* reports 90,000 volumes and 4,000,000 pieces of manuscript from 1732 to the present. Although the greater part are noncurrent official records, the department possesses certain papers of James Oglethorpe, founder of Georgia, of Harman Verelst, secretary to the trustees of the colony, of nineteenth-century governors Joseph E. Brown and Howell Cobb, of General James Longstreet, of Lucian Lamar Knight, State Historian and organizer of the department, as well as records of churches, educational institutions, and some local historical societies.

The department has a Barrow Laminator and does a great deal of microfilming. Thus it has rescued from damage or destruction many county and local records, as well as important holdings of private organizations. Its director, Mrs. Mary Givens Bryan, who was president of the Society of American Archivists in 1960, is of imaginative assistance to local groups throughout the State and to the Georgia Historical Society in Savannah. For a number of years Mrs. Bryan has carried on an admirable archival program under grievous limitations of space. The recent decision of the Georgia Legislature to follow the example of South Carolina and provide an adequate building for its Department of Archives and History is a cause of great rejoicing. The 1959 appropriation was $150,000, of which two thirds was for the archives and the remainder for the microfilm department and records centre.

WEST VIRGINIA

The West Virginia Department of Archives and History, with offices, library, and museum in the capitol at Charleston, was organized in 1905. Its manuscripts consist of State archives, the personal papers of four nineteenth-century governors, the records of a temperance society, 1839–41, and those of several Baptist and Methodist churches. It maintains a historical library and newspaper collection and, in the capitol basement, an unreformed historical museum in which stuffed birds jostle the household gear of pioneers. Objects are frequently added, but from want of space little has been possible in the way of systematic arrangement. A leaf from a tree overhanging the grave of Jefferson Davis is exhibited, as is an assortment of ammunition bearing the plaintive label:

Note: These bullets, grapeshot, minnie balls, cartridges, etc. have been moved so many times that they are separated from their correct papers of information. Here are some of the interesting sources from which they have been collected . . . .
   Most interesting if you use your imagination.

Hope is held out that a new building may permit improvement.

The West Virginia Historical Society, which has published the quarterly *West Virginia History* since its organization in 1939, holds an annual meeting in October in different parts of the State. It has 375 members who pay annual dues of $4, raised from $3 in 1959. Mr. Kyle McCormick, a former journalist who became director of the Department of Archives and History in 1957, serves also as executive secretary of the society. The society pays a part-time editor of *West Virginia History* from its dues, while the department bears the cost of printing the quarterly. Articles are contributed, usually by PH.D. candidates and others outside the State.

The State appropriation for all department expenses in 1960 was $44,000. Lack of funds and of space prevent any active collecting of private papers in competition with the efforts of the West Virginia University Library at Morgantown, which reported to the *Guide* the possession of 2,500,000 items, 1736–1954, relating chiefly to West Virginia and the upper Ohio valley.

IOWA

At the American Historical Association meeting of 1904, Professor Franklin L. Riley of Mississippi spoke of the desirability of having in all states both a historical society and a department of archives and history—"two co-ordinated State supported agencies, one with headquarters at the State University, the other with headquarters at the State Capital, and both of them working successfully and harmoniously in their respective fields."[13] Doubtless he had Iowa in mind, for, although the State Historical Society of Iowa—patterned upon Wisconsin and receiving public support—had been in operation at the State university at Iowa City since 1857, a State department of History and Archives was established in 1892 at the capital, Des Moines, with a separate appropriation. This is the body that in 1893 began publishing the third series of *Annals of Iowa*, which still continues. The department built up a library, newspaper collection, museum of archaeology and natural history, a portrait gallery, and encouraged anthropological and archaeological field work in the exploration of mounds and ancient graves in Iowa.

It reported to the *Guide* "an unknown quantity" of State archives, as well as personal papers. The largest of the latter category are the 200,000 pieces of Senator William B. Allison, but there are 23,200 items of the jurist Horace R. Deemer, 455 volumes of the papers of Grenville M. Dodge, some of which relate to the Union Pacific Railroad, smaller quantities of the papers of eleven other individuals, as well as records of the Iowa Equal Suffrage Association and other woman suffrage groups, 1854–1919, correspondence of the Union

13. *Annual Report of the American Historical Association for the Year 1904* (Washington, 1905), pp. 229–232.

League of America, and several large collections pertaining to the Civil War. Of a total appropriation of $92,500 in 1959, $29,112 was devoted to archives and records management, and $30,000 to microfilming, including newspapers.

WYOMING

The Wyoming State Archives and Historical Department, with headquarters in the State Office Building at Cheyenne, reported to the *Guide* 300 cubic feet of manuscripts, including State archives, and diaries and narratives of pioneers, collections of private papers, and letters of public officials and private citizens relating to Wyoming and the west, 1869–1955, as well as microfilm copies of State records not in its possession, some county records, and numerous collections of manuscripts in private hands. It maintains a historical library and a museum, publishes *Annals of Wyoming*, and is responsible for historic sites and markers. The 1959 State appropriation for the department was $139,216, of which $77,500 was devoted to archives and records management.

The Wyoming State Historical Society, founded in 1952, is an independent organization closely allied with the department, whose director, Miss Lola M. Homsher, serves as executive secretary of the society. Single membership is $3.50 a year or $50 for life; joint membership $5 and $75. The seventh annual meeting was held at Buffalo on 24–25 September 1960, offering a choice of guided historical tours to the Petrified Forest, Lake De Smet, Fort McKinney, and the sites of the TA Ranch and Wagon Box Fights and the Fetterman Massacre. Members receive copies of *Annals of Wyoming* that the society purchases from the department, as well as a mimeographed bimonthly *History News*. A note in the September 1960 issue of the latter indicates that the Wyoming State Historical Society shares the disgust of its colleagues in Kansas for the perversions of history dished up currently on television programs.

For those who have long ceased to enjoy the distortion of western American history, *The Wild, Wild West* by Peter Lyon, published in the *American Heritage*, comes as a refreshing interlude. The writer neatly states his thesis: "Thousands of books have been written about it (i. e. the west) many of them purporting to be history or biography; all but a few are fiction, and rubbish to boot." With a sharp, keen wit, Mr. Lyon exposes five paragons of the Wild, Wild West who rest in the "Valhalla of the comic, movie and TV." They are Billy the Kid, Jesse James, Wild Bill Hickok, Bat Masterson, and Wyatt Earp.

Peter Lyon follows up his thesis of the "Wild, Wild West," in "Reading, Writing, and History," in the same issue. This article "offers assistance in telling where fact leaves off and fiction begins." ...

Both of these articles should provoke comment and possibly argument by readers, but they point to the day when we may see on TV and in Western magazines the homesteader grubbing his land for a living or the cowboy facing the dangers of a stampede instead of the hired gun slinger playing poker in some gambling hell.

INDIANA

An Indiana Historical Society, organized at Indianapolis in 1830 and incorporated on 10 January 1831, had its ups and downs for fifty-five years, with long periods of inactivity. Reorganized on a more stable basis in 1886, it began a series of *Publications* in 1897, of which volume XIX was issued in 1957. The *Indiana Magazine of History*, which first appeared in 1905 under the society's auspices, was later transferred to Indiana University at Bloomington, where it is owned and edited by the history department. Members of the Indiana Historical Society receive the *Magazine* as one of the benefits from their annual dues of $5. The society pays the university a flat mass rate for these subscriptions, and there is a mutual agreement against memberships that do not include the *Magazine*, or subscriptions that do not include membership in the Indiana Historical Society. In 1960 there were 2,425 members, who received, in addition to the quarterly *Magazine* and the monthly *Indiana History Bulletin*, one or more publications each year. The latter have included the two-volume work by R. Carlyle Bailey, *The Old Northwest: Pioneer Period, 1815–1840*, which won a Pulitzer Prize in 1950, Louis A. Warren's *Lincoln's Youth:*

Indiana Years (1959), and volumes in the *Indiana Bibliography Series* and the *Prehistory Research Series* supported by the Lilly Endowment, Incorporated.

Although the Indiana Historical Society is a private corporation receiving no direct legislative appropriation, it benefits indirectly from public support. Its collections are housed rent-free in the State Library and Historical Building in Indianapolis, and the director of the Indiana Historical Bureau—now Hubert H. Hawkins, who succeeded Howard H. Peckham in 1953—serves as the secretary and principal administrative officer of the society. It procures the *Indiana Magazine of History* on favorable terms from the State university. Thus from its annual income of some $15,000, less than $4,000 has to be expended for salaries and none for housing.

The Indiana Historical Commission, created in 1915 as a State agency, was superseded in 1925 by the Indiana Historical Bureau, which is supported from the State Library appropriation. The bureau publishes annual volumes of *Indiana Historical Collections* and the monthly *Indiana History Bulletin*. It has in preparation a five-volume history of the State by John D. Barnhart, Emma Lou Thornbrough, Donald Carmony, and Clifton J. Phillips to be issued as part of Indiana's sesquicentennial celebration. Under way are a literary history of Indiana by Arthur Shumaker of de Pauw university, a documentary volume on the Indian agency at Fort Wayne, 1809–1815, an account of the Indianapolis sojourn of the archaeologist Heinrich Schliemann, and a volume on the domestic architecture of Indiana by Wilbur Peat.

The National Historical Publications Commission *Guide* reports three manuscript collections in the Indiana State Library building: the archives division of official records, the Indiana division of private and business papers, and the Indiana Historical Society's holdings of "25,000 pieces, 1741–1850, relating chiefly to Indiana and the Old Northwest," including papers of William Henry Harrison, Robert Dale Owen, and Lew Wallace. Both the Indiana division of the State Library and the Indiana Historical Society, which are in the same building although separately housed and administered, actively collect manuscript material. Concerning the division of fields, Mr. Hawkins has written me:

They are in a degree in competition with each other. In the past there has been a tendency for the Society to emphasize pre-Civil War material but this line of demarcation has been increasingly blurred in recent years. A very happy spirit of cooperation has existed between these two agencies and it has usually been possible to avoid competitive bidding at auction sales.

TENNESSEE

The Tennessee Historical Commission established in 1919 to collect information on the State's participation in World War 1 became dormant after a few years, but was revived in 1941 with the responsibility of stimulating a greater interest in Tennessee history throughout the State. Financed entirely from State funds, its major work is in the fields of historic sites, historical markers, and publications. It has published a number of historical and biographical works, *A Guide to the Study and Reading of Tennessee History*, by William T. Alderson, executive secretary of the commission, and Robert H. White, State Historian, and four volumes of *Messages of the Governors of Tennessee*, edited by Mr. White, which carry a projected ten-volume series through 1857. With the Tennessee Historical Society, which was simultaneously resuscitated in 1941, the commission has published the *Tennessee Historical Quarterly*.

The society, founded at Nashville in 1849, suffered from the recurring attacks of sleeping sickness with which we have become so familiar in other states. In 1902 it joined with the Peabody Normal School in publishing volume VII of *The American Historical Magazine and Tennessee Historical Quarterly* in continuation of a magazine previously sponsored by the school alone. This died with volume IX in 1904. The society eventually turned over its possessions in trust to the State, the objects being placed in the State Museum and the books and manuscripts in the archives division of the State Library and

Archives. The director of the archives division has for many years served as recording secretary of the Tennesseee Historical Society, while for the past dozen years Daniel M. Robison, State Librarian and Archivist, and William T. Alderson, executive secretary of the Commission, have edited the *Quarterly*.

Under the initial agreement between the commission and the society, the commission paid two thirds of the publication cost of the *Tennessee Historical Quarterly*, while all receipts from subscriptions and memberships, as well as publications received in exchange, went to the society.

The commission's aim in its publications program is to make possible the printing of sound historical works that, because of limited market, would not be attractive to a commercial publisher. It gives copies of each of its publications to every high school, college, university, and public library in the State.

Chapter XXI

THE ORGANIZATION MEN

> Were these bodies consolidated into a single organization, which would work along lines systematically planned by historical experts, there would undoubtedly be a marked increase in the extent and importance of activities. But such a consolidation is impracticable, even undesirable. Over-organization is a danger to be shunned; individuality should be developed. —WALDO G. LELAND, 1909

IN 1876 as part of its contribution to the Centennial Exhibition in Philadelphia, the Bureau of Education of the Department of the Interior published a special report on *Public Libraries in the United States of America, Their History, Condition, and Management.*[1] The subject was a timely one, for in October of that year the American Library Association was organized. Its first president, Justin Winsor, was superintendent of the Boston Public Library, the earliest significant institution of the kind in the United States, which had been opened for public use only in 1854. Chapter XIII of the Bureau of Education report was entitled "Historical Societies in the United States."[2] As its compilers, Henry A. Homes of the New York State Library and W. I. Fletcher of the Watkinson Library, Hartford, stated:

In the attempt to collect the most recent statistics which should exhibit the intellectual condition of the United States, it was impossible to overlook so important an illustration of the subject as would be afforded by a view of its historical societies.

From information gathered by questionnaire, the compilers fur-

1. (Washington, 1876).
2. Pp. 312–377.

nished accounts of seventy-eight historical societies with a total of 27,244 members and libraries containing 482,041 volumes, 568,801 pamphlets, and 88,771 pieces besides 1,361 volumes of manuscripts.

The desire to take stock of national resources was an aspect of the new professionalism that developed in the last quarter of the nineteenth century. Although the American Historical Association created its Historical Manuscripts Commission in 1894 and its Public Archives Commission in 1899, it did not systematically pay much attention to the historical societies until 1904. At the annual meeting in Chicago in the latter year, Professor Henry E. Bourne of Western Reserve delivered a paper on "The work of American historical societies,"[3] in which he analyzed their resources and activities. "Historical societies," he found, "are, broadly speaking, of two types, illustrated by the Massachusetts and the Wisconsin." The Massachusetts Historical Society "is a characteristic product of a period and of a state in which higher education and similar scientific activities were, and still are, left mainly to private initiative and generosity. The Wisconsin Historical Society, on the other hand, is a State institution, palatially housed and generously supported by the State." Bourne pointed out that local societies in New England were generally town organizations, while south and west of the Hudson they represented a county or a district, and that there were 400 to 500 of them throughout the country.

The work any society can undertake is quite as often dependent upon the size and stability of its income as upon the other circumstances to which reference has been made.

The largest private societies were those of Massachusetts, with an income of $18,000, New York ($12,000), and Pennsylvania ($24,000), but "west of the Alleghanies only a few States ... do not grant liberal subsidies to the State historical society." Here he cited Wisconsin's $43,000, Iowa's $17,500, Minnesota's $15,000, Kansas's and Ohio's $7,000–$8,000, and Nebraska's $5,000. Asking "Is it possible to

3. *Annual Report of the American Historical Association for the Year 1904* (Washington, 1905), pp. 115–127.

increase the co-operation between the societies as a whole?", Professor Bourne observed that most of them were members of the American Library Association or the American Historical Association. He recalled the beneficial work of the Comité des travaux historiques in France, and concluded:

If some common direction is needed in a highly centralized country like France, where the intellectual life centers in Paris, it is much more necessary here. The necessity is present; the materials are at hand. The question is, What shall be done?

That question still echoes after fifty-eight years.

At the 1904 meeting the first Conference of State and Local Historical Societies was held, with Reuben Gold Thwaites of Wisconsin in the chair.[4] Discussion, which was restricted to the two points: "the best methods of organizing State historical work and the possibilities of co-operation between societies," came chiefly from scholars active in western and southern states. Thomas M. Owen of Alabama spoke on archives; B. F. Shambaugh of Iowa proposed the affiliation of local with State societies; Franklin L. Riley of Mississippi suggested two co-ordinated societies in each State, one at the university, the other at the capital. Professor Riley observed that "it was quite evident that among the earliest needs was the publication of calendars of each other's manuscript collections, on some well-accepted plan." He suggested that sectional or neighborhood co-operation was highly desirable; that the Louisiana Purchase states as one group, or those on the Pacific coast as another, might get together and discuss sources of documents. It was voted to establish a similar conference the following year,[5] and the council of the association designated Thwaites, Shambaugh, and Riley as a subcommittee to report in detail on the theme of the first conference.

Thus at the Baltimore meeting of the American Historical Association in December 1905 there was more evidence on hand, although

4. *Ibid.*, pp. 219–234.
5. Limited largely to southern and western societies on the unsound theory that the older eastern societies "were not as a rule confronted by the questions which troubled those of the newer States."

it added little, save in bulk, to what Professor Bourne had presented the year before. The subcommittee had in February 1905 sent a detailed questionnaire, which, while not universally welcomed or promptly answered, produced "a body of useful, although quite unequal, data" from 223 societies, which was duly tabulated and published.[6] On organization Thwaites, Shambaugh, and Riley found:

Each historical society is in large measure the product of local conditions and opportunities. But back of these, molding conditions and taking advantages of opportunities, are needed individuals imbued with genuine and self-sacrificing enthusiasm for the work. However, enthusiasm will not alone suffice, for the promoters of such enterprises should by their erudition and technical skill command the attention and respect of scholars, while by display of practical common sense, business ability, energy, and convincing arguments they are at the same time winning the confidence of hard-headed men of affairs. Very likely this is an unusual combination of qualities, and an ideal seldom, if ever, realized, for historical societies can not pay large salaries. Certain it is, however, that even when liberally endowed no society has attained its full usefulness without some such personality dominating its affairs. Institutions dependent upon State aid are particularly in need of this vigorous personal management. The lack of it has been the undoing of a goodly share of the wrecked or moribund societies—wherein everybody's business was nobody's concern—that strew the pathway of our recent investigation.

The Massachusetts and Pennsylvania societies are prototypes of the privately endowed organizations of the Eastern States, which without official patronage have attained strength, dignity, and a high degree of usefulness; while Wisconsin, Minnesota, Iowa, and Kansas similarly stand for the State supported institutions of the West.

Of recent years there has appeared in several Commonwealths the "State Department of Archives and History". This is an official bureau of the Commonwealth, obtaining the essential personal touch through maintenance of close relations with the State historical society, whose duties, under such conditions, are chiefly literary and advisory. Alabama and Mississippi are the typical examples; but in Iowa the State society, at the seat of the State university, retains a strong individuality in all lines of activity despite a liberally supported historical department at the capital; in Kansas, the society has charge of the department.

As to which method is best for new Commonwealths—that of the Alabama type, that of the Wisconsin, that of the Iowa compromise, or that of the Kansas union—

6. *Annual Report of the American Historical Association for the Year 1905* (Washington, 1906), I, 249–325.

your committee will not venture an opinion. Each has certain merits, largely dependent on conditions of environment. . . .

After all, the principal desideratum is, as we have indicated, the personality back of the work, rather than the form of organization. . . . Logically, there is no reason why the work of collecting and disseminating historical material should not be quite as much a public charge as that of the public library or of the public museum. But the fact that historical work appears to be best prosecuted by individual enthusiasm seems to render advisable the society organization.

At the conference Reuben G. Thwaites presented a report, "Publishing Activities of the Historical Societies of the Old Northwest," and Ulrich B. Phillips, also from Wisconsin, "Documentary Collections and Publications in the Older States of the South."[7] Perhaps the most useful part of the conference was a statement by J. Franklin Jameson that he had obtained for 1906 "a definite appropriation for furthering projects of co-operation with historical societies." He also stated his desire to place at the service of these societies the Carnegie Institution of Washington's information on the location of documentary material, whether in this country or in Europe.[8] Moreover, the American Historical Association paid its respects to these component groups by publishing as part II of its 1905 *Annual Report* a "Bibliography of American Historical Societies" compiled by Appleton P. C. Griffin. Unhappily, the 1,374 pages of this work were called by Worthington C. Ford "as cheerful reading as a cemetery list."[9]

The third conference of 1906 produced little of moment. At the fourth in 1907 Professor Evarts B. Greene observed:

This general survey of the work done in the various States of the Union gives reasonable ground for encouragement, though in some of the States the conditions are evidently less satisfactory. Prosperity, however, brings some dangers of its own which need to be carefully considered. Large sums have been appropriated by many of the State legislatures, often with the expectation of definite returns in a comparatively short time. It is, of course, always important to show tangible

7. *Ibid.*, I, 188–204.
8. *Ibid.*, I, 209–210.
9. *Annual Report of the American Historical Association for the Year 1909* (Washington, 1911), p. 305.

results from the expenditure of public funds; but there is some danger that departments and societies, in their desire to show these tangible results, may occasionally be led into hasty action.

At this meeting, held in Madison, Wisconsin, a Committee on Co-operation of Historical Societies and Departments was appointed, consisting of Dunbar Rowland chairman, J. Franklin Jameson, Worthington C. Ford, Reuben G. Thwaites, Evarts B. Greene, Thomas M. Owen, and B. F. Shambaugh. This able group for the first time included a representative of one of the older independent societies, namely Ford from the Massachusetts Historical Society. Meeting at the Carnegie Institution in Washington on 16 April 1908, they suggested co-operation in five particulars: searches of foreign archives to produce a full descriptive calendar of documents relating to American history, copying, securing photographic reproductions, publishing documentary history common to a group of states, and periodical publications. Having observed that many states of the Mississippi valley were vitally concerned in the archives of France, the committee recommended that the historical agencies of that region join in a co-operative search of French archives for pertinent historical material, that a calendar be prepared and published, and that money be raised by voluntary contributions from interested societies. This admirable proposal, bearing the Jameson touch, was presented at the fifth conference at Richmond in 1908, where Waldo G. Leland gave a paper on "The Application of Photography to Archive and Historical Work."[10]

"In December 1909," as Dr. Leland recalled forty years later, "the American Historical Association celebrated the 25th anniversary of its founding, with some pomp and considerable circumstance."[11] To this meeting came George W. Prothero from England, H. T. Colen-

10. *Annual Report of the American Historical Association for the Year 1908* (Washington, 1909), I, 145–167.

11. In a diverting paper, "The First Conference of Archivists, December 1909: The Beginnings of a Profession read at a luncheon of the American Historical Association and the Society of American Archivists" at Boston on 29 December 1949, published in *The American Archivist* XIII (1950), 109–120.

brander from the Netherlands, Camille Enlart from France, and Rafael Altamira from Spain to read papers on the work of historical societies in their countries. At the sixth Conference of Historical Societies,[12] St. George L. Sioussat summed up the activities of the preceding five years, and Bourne, Ford, and Thwaites read papers. The most significant feature was Dunbar Rowland's report for the Committee on Co-operation, which indicated that $1,800 had been raised between ten Mississippi valley institutions for the proposed calendar of documents concerning their region in French archives, and that Dr. Leland had agreed to undertake it.[13] Detailed reports of progress of this work were presented to the 1912 and 1913 conferences.[14] Although at the outbreak of war in 1914 research in France necessarily came to a halt, all the notes reached the Carnegie Institution in safety.[15]

The Conference of Historical Societies continued to be an element of the annual meetings of the American Historical Association for more than thirty years. Its efforts, like most cases of unreciprocated affection, do not at this distance of time seem to have accomplished much. Digests of the holdings and activities of historical societies were diligently compiled and published as an appendix to its proceedings, but as less than one fifth of those to whom questionnaires were sent troubled to return them, the results could hardly be called representative or significant.[16]

12. *Annual Report of the American Historical Association for the Year 1909* (Washington, 1911) contains (pp. 281–322) the proceedings of the sixth conference and (pp. 229–277) the papers on European historical societies.

13. He was then engaged in preparing the Carnegie Institution's general guide to sources of American history in the French archives and undertook the direction of this additional specific task as a labor of love.

14. *Annual Report of the American Historical Association for the Year 1912* (Washington, 1914), pp. 202–205; *Annual Report . . . for the Year 1913* (Washington, 1915), I, 211–215. As the work took far longer than had been originally anticipated, the subscribing institutions had to raise additional money to pay the French researchers working under Dr. Leland's direction.

15. *Annual Report of the American Historical Association for the Year 1914* (Washington, 1916), I, 301–304.

16. In 1913 of 500 blanks sent out, only 90 were returned; *Annual Report of the American Historical Association for the Year 1913*, p. 207. The reports for that year (pp.

Meanwhile the one significant occupation of the conference, that is the search among the foreign sources of American history, proceeded without particular reference to the conference or to the historical societies that it had ineffectually sought to harness. This was undertaken by other hands, chiefly those of J. Franklin Jameson. The Carnegie Institution, between 1907 and 1943, published guides to manuscripts in England, France, Spain, Italy, Switzerland, Germany, Austria, Russia, Canada, and Mexico, most of which had been completed before 1928 when Jameson left the institution to become chief of the manuscript division in the Library of Congress.

Herbert Putnam, soon after he was appointed Librarian of Congress in 1899, became deeply concerned with the need of American scholars for manuscript sources of our early history. He thus caused the manuscript division of the Library of Congress to commission handwritten transcripts of documents in foreign archives. This work was eventually greatly enlarged through the receipt in 1925 of an endowment fund from James B. Wilbur of Vermont and a gift from John D. Rockefeller Jr. in 1927 to support an extensive copying program in Europe and America over a five-year period. By this time photostats or microfilms were substituted for transcripts. Some two million manuscript pages had been copied by 1933, while since then nearly a million more have been added, chiefly through the income of the Wilbur Fund. Thus countless reproductions, subject to interlibrary loan, have been obtained for the Library of Congress not only from the countries covered by the Carnegie Institution guides but from Scotland, Ireland, Wales, Holland, Denmark, Norway, Sweden, Czechoslovakia, Argentina, Chile, and Yucatán. The Library of Congress also has, in separate collections, extensive microfilms made in England and Wales between 1941 and 1945 for the American Council of Learned Societies. In the spring of 1961 the present Librarian of Congress, Dr. L. Quincy Mumford, assembled a

---

225–236) included 14 from Massachusetts, 9 from New York, and 13 from Pennsylvania, but none from the Massachusetts Historical Society, the New-York Historical Society, or the Historical Society of Pennsylvania.

group of scholars from both universities and historical societies to discuss a further expansion of the copying program. Under the intelligent guidance of Messrs. David C. Mearns and Daniel J. Reed of the manuscript division, plans are now being developed that will greatly increase this aspect of the usefulness of the Library of Congress.[17]

So far as American sources were concerned, the most heroic effort at co-ordination was attempted by the Historical Records Survey.[18] Sponsored as a relief measure by the Works Progress Administration between 1935 and 1942, under the direction of Dr. Luther H. Evans, later Librarian of Congress, the survey undertook a nationwide listing of public records and manuscripts in each State. This led to such useful ramifications as Douglas C. McMurtrie's *Early American Imprints*, inventories of portraits and church records, the Historical American Buildings Survey, and the Historical American Merchant Marine Survey. By 1942 the survey had published, usually in mimeographed form in small editions, more than 1,700 inventories, guides, and check lists of historical sources. Few libraries have more than a regional scattering of these volumes. Their quality is necessarily uneven, but, after the passage of twenty years, they often still represent the best, if not the only, source of information about the material treated. The sterotype of the W.P.A. worker leaning on a shovel with which he is not digging a useless ditch is more than eclipsed by the concept and accomplishment of the Historical Records Survey. Quickly improvised in an emergency, it represents a type of effort that might reasonably have been expected to emerge from the well-ordered deliberations of the Conference on Historical Societies, and did not.

Summing up the situation on the fiftieth anniversary of the American Historical Association in 1934, Julian P. Boyd wrote:

17. Another important activity of the manuscript division is the Presidential Papers project which will be discussed in a later chapter.

18. See the excellent summary by David L. Smiley, "The W.P.A. Historical Records Survey" in Hesseltine and McNeil, ed., *In Support of Clio, Essays in Memory of Herbert A. Kellar* (Madison, 1958), pp. 3–28.

From 1904, when the American Historical Association first began to pay serious attention to the problem of coöperation among these bodies, until 1914, the proceedings of the annual conference were reported in some detail in the *Annual Reports*; papers read at the meetings were usually printed in full, and some of them were highly useful. Since 1914, however, the conference has made no appreciable progress in furthering the primary object for which it was established. Tacked on usually at the end of the annual meetings of the American Historical Association, its sessions sparsely attended, its papers scarcely ever printed, and its officers and policies constantly changing, the conference has succeeded chiefly in enlisting the support of the Central West and of those chiefly allied with universities. For, although the conference invariably voiced the best standards of scholarship and coöperation, its voice was that of the parent body and not the joint product of those actively in charge of the administration of the historical agencies of the country. The difficult problems of organizing state historical work and of effecting intersociety coöperation either remain largely in the status they were in when the conference first addressed itself to them, or else have been modified largely by the initiative of state and regional societies.[19]

Mr. Boyd concluded his article on "State and Local Historical Societies in the United States" with the sentence:

We have returned to the question put by Dr. Bourne in 1904: "The necessity is present.... The question is, What shall be done?"

Six years later in New York, on 27 December 1940, the American Association for State and Local History was founded at the thirty-sixth conference of State and Local Historical Societies.[20] The new body was the creation of a policy committee, appointed at the 1939 conference, under the chairmanship of Dr. C. C. Crittenden of the North Carolina Historical Commission, which included among its fifteen members Dr. Edward P. Alexander of the New York State Historical Association, Dr. Herbert A. Kellar of the McCormick Historical Association, Mr. Ronald F. Lee of the National Park Service, and Dr. Jean Stephenson of the Daughters of the American Revolution. While the organization meeting was held at the New-York Historical Society, whose director Alexander J. Wall and li-

19. *American Historical Review* XL (1934–35), 29.
20. *Annual Report of the American Historical Association for the Year 1940* (Washington, 1941), pp. 95–109.

brarian Miss Dorothy C. Barck supported the plan with enthusiasm, none of the other older independent historical societies were represented, or indeed interested. Like the conference which gave it birth, the new association was chiefly manned from State agencies and small local societies. The report of the policy committee indicated the services that it was hoped the new association might render, first of which was publicity.

> Certain phases of historical work have tended to become too highly professionalized, and this tendency now needs to be corrected and better contacts with the masses of the people need to be established. There are opportunities for promoting such a broad popular program of which full advantage has never been taken in North America.

Note the complete *volte-face* from the original purpose of the parent conference, which had been to inculcate the professional standards of the American Historical Association in societies essentially controlled by amateurs. Other projected services included co-operation with the National Park Service, Federal relief agencies, "patriotic"[21] and other organizations, the promotion of historical programs for adults, the encouragement of the writing of high-standard State and and local histories as well as of adequate historical courses in the schools, the compilation of lists of local historians and genealogists, the promotion of closer co-ordination between State and local historical organizations, publications, and conferences. It was considered that the most important service would be the establishment of "a permanent secretariat which would serve as a clearing house" for information on the organization of local historical groups, the "most successful methods of securing increased contributions or appropriations," suitable types of buildings, collecting and publication programs, "the planning and conduct of historical celebrations, plays, and pageants," and much else.

Dr. Kellar explained that two suggestions had been made at Policy Committee meetings; that the older and more affluent societies form an association and operate it, gradually spreading out and taking in more members;[22] and the second, that the

21. The patronizing use of quotation marks occurs in the original report.
22. Essentially the principle of the American Council of Learned Societies, which

beginning be made with local societies, on a national basis, including those with an amateur interest in local history, and working up a strong national society. The organization actually proposed by the Committee embraces both these ideas in a middle-of-the-road program.

In the discussion that followed, Mr. Alexander J. Wall observed that

The world is now struggling for democracy. Unless we can show what democracy has done, how can we save ourselves? Historical societies, without funds have gathered and preserved tremendous collections of manuscripts, books, and newspapers. Now their collections should be interpreted and used in telling the story of democracy. The man in the street is interested in local happenings and everyone loves his own community. The visitor to an historical museum must be interested not only in the history of his own locality, but means should be used to lead him also to an interest in national history. Interest can be stimulated by pointing out the history of each visitor's own line.

The late William G. Roelker, a retired businessman who had recently become librarian of the Rhode Island Historical Society, pointed out proudly that "he had increased its membership 27 percent in 60 days."

His invitation to join the society had brought one immediate acceptance with the comment that the new member had not, in 25 years, been asked to join. The society was now placing emphasis on the collection of ephemeral material on current events such as the hurricane of 1938 and the election of 1940. Members were given the task of collecting material on some specific happening, locality, club, or racial group, and individual responsibility had been found of the greatest appeal to new members.

The report of the policy committee and the constitution of the American Association of State and Local History were duly adopted. Dr. Crittenden was elected president and Dr. Alexander vice-president of the new organization. The Conference of State and Local Historical Societies then disbanded. The cast remained the same, although they now had a new play in which to exercise their talents.

The purpose of the new association was, it seemed, more popular

---

admits, only after careful investigation, organizations of proven seriousness and accomplishment.

than professional, but popularization was much in the air at the time. It was no monopoly of historical societies; many of the most distinguished professional historians were intrigued by it. The Society of American Historians, embracing many of the most productive scholars in the country,[23] was formed in 1938 and incorporated the following year "to promote a wider knowledge and keener appreciation of both American and world history, and to lend support to the magazine which was to be the principal instrumentality of this effort." In 1941 there appeared a pretentious, plush, *Fortune*-like prospectus,[24] printed at the Condé Nast Press, of *Horizons, The Magazine of American and World History*, whose cover was adorned with a color reproduction of "The Signing of the Declaration is Announced," by Arthur Crisp, N.A. Copyrighted by the History Publishers Foundation, Washington, D. C., and edited by Allan Nevins and Henry F. Pringle, this projected magazine had the backing of the Society of American Historians. An announcement stated that

Founded on the conviction of historians and experienced publishers, that there is a growing need among our 90 million [including 8,098,579 Full-Time High School and College Students] newspaper and magazine readers for an approved popular monthly publication of American and World history, this magazine *Horizons* has been developed to fill the need and to stimulate further American historical interest and learning.

The leading article by Pringle, entitled "Today is Tomorrow's History," included, among other sententious and Messianic observations,

There might have been no Treaty of Versailles had there been better historians and had they been listened to. There might have been no Mussolini and no Hitler and no Stalin.

as well as the question:

23. President Douglas Southall Freeman, vice-president Carl Becker, secretary John A. Krout, treasurer Julian P. Boyd; councillors Conyers Read, Henry F. Pringle, William L. Langer, Marquis James, Allan Nevins, and Carl Van Doren.
24. Given by the late Mark Antony de Wolfe Howe on 21 January 1944 to the Boston Athenæum, where it is preserved with the remains of other periodicals that never reached birth or died young.

Who would say, for instance, that a recent book by David L. Cohn, *The Good Old Days*, is less a history than some volume on the Supreme Court? Mr. Cohn did a prodigious amount of research. He examined all the catalogues of Sears, Roebuck & Company from 1886, when their publication began, to 1939. Few bearded scholars[25] have examined so many pages.

Specimen articles included Allan Nevins, "John D. Rockefeller at Forty"; Marquis James, "A Stolen Railroad Train"; Henry F. Pringle, "A Beloved Master of the Law" [William Howard Taft]; Seth E. Frazier, "Heraldry of the Cow Country"; Van Wyck Brooks, "Restless Henry Adams"; Carl Bridenbaugh, "Colonial Newport, 1760-1775"; Thomas Craven, "Eight American Paintings" in full-page color, ranging from J. S. Copley to George Bellows; and others—an all-star cast, running to 140 pages. *Horizons* never to my knowledge progressed beyond the prospectus, although one heard whispers about such a beatific undertaking for the next decade.

The American Association for State and Local History began more modestly with a series of occasional "how-to-do-it" bulletins and a four-page monthly newsletter, *History News*, published wherever the secretary or editor of the moment happened to be based. *History News* in its early years was clearly aimed at establishing "better contacts with the masses of the people." Not only did it emphasize programs of popularization; it even carried for a time a feature entitled "The Lighter Side," devoted to such jokes as the following:

First farmer: "What was that explosion over at Zeke's place yesterday?"
Second farmer: "Oh, Zeke started feeding his hens some of that 'Lay or Bust' and one of 'em was a rooster."[26]

First Eskimo: "I think I'll marry that cute little Eskisquaw over there in the mink parka."

25. One wonders what beards have to do with research. Today beatniks wearing beards are sometimes not only dirty and pretentious, but lazy. Did it follow, in the pre-beatnik era, that a beard indicated laziness? Or was "bearded," to the popularizer, an adjective that had as inevitably to be coupled with the noun "scholar" as "musty" with "archives"?
26. *History News* VII, 7 (May 1952), p. 26.

Second Eskimo: "Don't rush things. Wait six months and see how she looks in the daylight."[27]

"See," said the mother, pointing to a picture, "the Pilgrims went to church every Sunday."

"Sure," replied her young son, pointing to the guns on the men's shoulders. "I'd go to church, too, if I could shoot Indians on the way."[28]

This section, strangely resembling "Corn Crib Cracks" in the bimonthly *Barn-E-Gram*,[29] published by Allied Mills, Inc., of Fort Wayne, Indiana, ceased with the August 1952 issue. On a more serious level, the *Nassau County (New York) Historical Journal* was commended for an "unusually interesting story of the Long Island clam in fact, fable, and fiction,"[30] and the advice given by Mr. Earle W. Newton, long an officer of the association, to the 131st annual meeting of the Rhode Island Historical Society, urging historical societies "to expand their bases of operation to reach and to include large segments of the general public" was reported. The item continued:

The real value of history lies in its usefulness as a social tool which tells us certain things we need to know in a democracy. It helps us gain perspective in the face of change.

Newton suggested that the Society take $10,000 of its capital funds to underwrite an expanded program to include the dissemination of information through newspapers, radio, TV, magazines, and films.[31]

In the "Shop Talk" section, Herbert Fisher, preparator in the Detroit Historical Museum, discussed "The Exhibit and how *not* to avoid the public."

We must at all times satisfy our public *first*, and then the donors, the society members, the "professional" historians and, of course, the many back seat drivers.

In describing "copy," Mr. Fisher offered the following admonitions:

27. *History News* VII, 9 (July 1952), p. 34.
28. *History News* VII, 10 (August 1952), p. 38.
29. Which reaches me occasionally, unsolicited, addressed to "Boxholder, R.F.D. #1, Starksboro, Vt." through the courtesy of the Wayne Feed Supply Co., Inc., of Middlebury, Vermont.
30. *History News* VII, 8 (June 1952), pp. 29.
31. *History News* VIII, 1 (November 1952), p. 1.

WRITE YOUR COPY IN TERMS OF *YOU* (the reader) . . .

WRITE LIKE PEOPLE TALK

> Stay away from the Harvardese, a form of looking down the nose at the reader. Maintaining the ordinary guy's conversational tone will help hold the reader's interest.

FORGET YOU'RE A GRAMMARIAN

> If the split infinitive sounds more natural—why go ahead and split it! If a proposition wants to dangle let'er dangle.[32]

With volume XI, number 1, in November 1955 *History News* was enlarged from four to eight pages a month. In this issue "The Children's Corner" section opened with the assertion: "History can be fun. We think so and we'd like to prove it to you." On a different level the December 1955 issue began the serial publication of the excellent "Guide for Collectors of Manuscripts," by Lucile M. Kane of the Minnesota Historical Society, one of the ablest curators in that field in the country. In short, the newsletter in its early years offered something for almost everyone, except the historian.

In 1947 the association began the publication of *American Heritage* as a magazine for teachers, designed to promote and broadcast work in local history. After a couple of years it changed both policy and format, becoming instead a popular magazine of American history liberally illustrated with four-color plates, that sometimes did double-duty in commercial advertising. In this manifestation *American Heritage*, in paper covers, was a poor man's version of the sumptuous *Horizons*, proposed earlier by the Society of American Historians. In 1954 *American Heritage* passed into the hands of the American Heritage Publishing Company, founded in New York by James Parton and others, who energetically developed it as a commercial venture. Although the American Association for State and Local History and the Society of American Historians appear as sponsoring societies and are paid certain royalties[33] for their previous labors in

---

32. *History News* X, 11 (September 1955), p. 43.

33. *History News* IX, 10 (August 1954), p. 37, stated: "We will be paid a substantial 15% royalty on income from the magazine." X, 1 (November 1954), contains the statement of President Howard H. Peckham that the association must pay a large bill for the summer 1954 issue of *American Heritage* out of next year's royalties.

the vineyard, *American Heritage* has become a regular commercial enterprise, entirely controlled by its common stockholders.[34] The December 1954 issue of *History News* informed the association that

The editorial policy of *American Heritage* will be "to lift the fascinating story of America from its musty archives and make it live again, that Americans may better sense their past and understand their present." To quote the editor, Bruce Catton: "It is our belief that history can be the most fascinating subject in the world if properly presented. *American Heritage* will tell the story of the American people as human beings—doing, thinking, hoping and dreaming."

Under its new ownership *American Heritage* was immediately placed in an inexpensive hard cover binding, thus giving the illusion that each issue was a book, and incidentally justifying a price more suitable for a book than a magazine. The device worked, for there was an initial sale of 80,000 copies, which considerably exceeded a break-even point estimated at 55,000.[35] In August 1960, when Mr. Oliver Jensen very kindly gave me figures, the circulation was conservatively estimated at 325,000. The American Heritage Publishing Company also publishes annually a large, staff-prepared book, based on original material not taken from the magazine, whose sales also run in the hundreds of thousands. Great Historic Places (1957), the Revolution (1958), the Pioneer Spirit (1959), the Civil War (1960), the American Indian (1961), the Flight (1962) have been treated in this manner, while an American Heritage Junior Library, aimed at young teenagers, puts out every two months a single-subject book on a part-subscription, part-bookstore basis. In September 1958 a subsidiary corporation began the publication of *Horizon, A Magazine of the Arts*, like *American Heritage* a lavishly illustrated bimonthly in hard covers, and without advertising. The corporation has since extended its activities into publishing books, such as the volume on the Renaissance that appeared in 1961.

The *American Heritage* formula has been an extraordinary com-

---

34. I am grateful to Mr. Oliver Jensen of *American Heritage* for clarifying the relationship between publisher and sponsors and giving me figures of circulation.
35. *History News* x, 2 (December 1954), p. 5.

mercial success. Perhaps the attempts to imitate it—like *Eros, A New Quarterly on the Art of Love* whose prospectus flooded the mails last spring—are the sincerest tribute to the selling power of the booklike magazine. Nevertheless, the volume in memory of Herbert A. Kellar, who did so much to set the American Association for State and Local History on its present course, says unsympathetically that

the magazine turned into a money-making proposition, and nothing remains of its original purpose. Now the *American Heritage*, in hard covers, has as its mission the popularization of national history among the *Fortune, Vogue,* and *Better Homes and Gardens* clientele.[36]

The loss of *American Heritage* and the corresponding increase in revenue from royalties paid by its successful new owners caused the association to take stock of its situation. A Committee on Long-Range Planning, headed by Christopher Crittenden, recommended in 1957 the establishment of a paid secretariat and the professionalization of the organization.[37] He noted that

Throughout the country there are tens and even hundreds [of] thousands of persons who are interested in state and local history, but we have brought in only very few of them. Now that it is possible to subscribe to *American Heritage* without joining our Association, we may have lost our great drawing card for the masses. . . .

We cannot now use this magazine to build up membership in our Association. And what else do we now have to offer the general public?

In view of this situation, it is recommended that we recognize that in the future, as in the past, our membership will probably consist mainly of professionals (while at the same time not barring but actually welcoming any interested layman who may wish to join us).

So between 1940 and 1957 a full circle was completed.

To achieve the paid secretariat that had been recommended, Dr. Clement L. Silvestro was brought to Madison in the spring of 1957. He was needed to assist Dr. Clifford L. Lord, who was serving in a dual capacity as president of the association and director of the State Historical Society of Wisconsin. Subsequently, in April 1959, Dr. Silvestro was appointed to the new post of director of the association.

36. *In Support of Clio,* p. 138.
37. *History News* XIII, 5 (March 1957), pp. 35–38.

Under his editorship, *History News* appeared in a new and enlarged format in November 1957. Its standards were to be reportorial rather than critical, according to the statement of policy in volume XIII, number 1.

Our major objective is to give you the story behind the successful programs conducted by the many local and state historical societies in the country—what makes these programs click, and the planning and preparation that helped put them over. An idea used in one locality does not always assure success in another. We will leave it to individual members to evaluate what his neighbor has done or is doing, and to adopt as much or as little of the program that can be applied to his own particular institution.

Thus one finds, without comment, such news items as:

Although the Manistee County (Michigan) Historical Society asserts that it is not acting as county scavenger, on occasion it might welcome the appointment. Recently it rescued, from a pile of refuse near the museum, one drinking fountain formerly located at the corner of Fifth Avenue and Washington street in Manistee, and one out-moded fire hydrant (former location unknown). Since these articles belong to the city, the society is considering them as a permanent loan. They will be placed on exhibit next spring.[38]

Although most things are reported with this noncommittal desire to encourage everybody and offend no one, the periodical now contains a good deal of news from all parts of the country, as well as a book review section.

Sometimes it seems that the American Association for State and Local History has been more concerned with the ambitions of institutions, and the individuals that serve them, than with the broader problems of history. It has been at times greatly preoccupied with competition in collecting. In 1956 it addressed a communication to the Librarian of Congress stating that it "views with anxiety and dismay the active solicitation by the Library of Congress in procuring family papers in those states that have respectable local repositories for manuscripts."[39] In the same year, some eight months

38. *History News* XV, 2 (December 1959), p. 16.
39. Published, with Mr. Mumford's reply and a statement of the Library of Congress acquisition policy, in *History News* XI, 11 (September 1956), pp. 81–84.

after the Presidential Libraries bill had been enacted into law, is protested the act as "preempting the entire field of manuscript collecting," and inquired: "What is left for historical societies to collect free from Government competition?"[40] Similarly a passage in a report of its committee on Professional Standards[41] smacks of collective bargaining.

It is therefore recommended that salaries of directors of societies or agencies with broad programs and large responsibilities should range between $10,000 and $15,000, comparable to at least the more poorly paid deans of large universities and the presidents of small colleges.

It is obvious that the hiring of top-flight directors is apt to result in a closer approach to fulfillment of the potentialities of the organization. It is undeniable that in general a good salary will prove a powerful inducement to a good man to enter and stick with historical society or agency administration. It is therefore recommended that salarywise the less pecunious organization may make its best investment in compensation adequate to attract and hold an able administrator, of deanly or presidential calibre.

The recruiting pamphlet *Your Job Opportunities with a Historical Agency*, gaudily designed in promotional manner, strikes a related chord of personal interest. By contrast, the summer Seminars for Historical Administrators, held at Williamsburg each year, in which the association is joint sponsor with the National Trust for Historic Preservation, Colonial Williamsburg, and the American Association of Museums, are useful and sober affairs that attract a good quality of graduate student.

Such ambivalence runs through the activities of the American Association for State and Local History because, I suspect, the association clings to a desire to be all things to all men. It has not been willing entirely to renounce the hot-gospel tent and fairgrounds techniques along with, as might be said, an "assist" from the lucrative

40. See the papers "Acquisition Policies of Presidential Libraries," by Herman Kahn and David C. Mearns, read at the 1957 annual meeting of the association, in James H. Rodabaugh, ed., *The Present World of History, A conference on certain problems in historical agency work in the United States* (Madison, 1959), pp. 34–62.

41. Published in *History News* XI, 4 (February 1956), pp. 27–28; XII, 3 (January 1957), pp. 19–22. The committee consisted of Clifford L. Lord chairman, Donald R. McNeil, R. W. G. Vail, Louis C. Jones, and K. Ross Toole.

devices of national advertising. Still, there are among its members those who recognize that the finding of historical facts and their interpretation and presentation to the public is a matter of devoted, persistent labor. Such labor is most usually unregarded while it is in progress and inadequately rewarded after it has been done. As examples, the association in May 1959 joined with Broadcast Music, Inc., in sponsoring a national competition for the two best 1,500-word essays on "Reflections While Standing Before the Lincoln Memorial," with awards of $500 each to the best professional and nonprofessional writer.[42] In February 1962 it awarded grants-in-aid to ten academic historians for research projects in local history, on the recommendation of a committee of distinguished historians. *Ideas in Conflict, A Colloquium on Certain Problems in Historical Society Work in the United States and Canada,*[43] which is the record of the discussion at the 1954 annual meeting, deals with subjects of limited interest in a tone of hearty, jovial bonhomie, half Boy Scout, half Rotary Club. On the other hand, the comparable record for the 1957 meeting, *The Present World of History*, offers subjects of far broader scope, delivered with literacy and scholarly civility.

The association's best publications are its recent technical manuals in the *Bulletin* series, such as Carl E. Guthe's *The Management of Small History Museums* (II, 10, 1959) and Lucile M. Kane's *A Guide to the Care and Administration of Manuscripts* (II, 11, 1960). Such distillations of long experience in specialized fields cannot fail to be useful. These, and the recent grants-in-aid, represent a more intelligible approach to co-operation than the earlier evangelistic salesmanship of history. At the December 1961 meeting of the American Historical Association, both speakers at the joint session with the American Association for State and Local History—Carlisle H. Humelsine, president of Colonial Williamsburg, and Louis C. Jones,[44] director

42. *History News* XIV, 7 (May 1959), p. 57.
43. Edited by Clifford L. Lord (Harrisburg, 1958).
44. Published as "The Trapper's Cabin and the Ivory Tower,"*Museum News* XL, 7 (March 1962), pp. 11–16.

of the New York State Historical Association—strongly emphasized the need of sound professional research as the foundation of all activities in outdoor museums. On this occasion the members of the parent and daughter associations were speaking the same language and understanding one another. This suggested that the twenty-first birthday of the American Association for State and Local History represented not only the technical attainment of legal majority but the actual arrival at years of discretion; that the adolescent strivings of its early teens were, hopefully, a thing of the past. What it will be able to achieve as an adult remains to be seen. It has thus far come no nearer a definitive answer to Professor Bourne's question of 1904— "What shall be done?"—than its predecessor, the Conference of State and Local Historical Societies. The individuality of hundreds of historical societies is so distinct, and desirably so, that no ready formula is any more likely to be found than a structure that will embrace the humanities and the natural sciences. But, as the physicist Gerald Holton remarked[45] on the latter subject,

As a consequence the need is greater than ever to recognize how small one's own portion of the world is, to view from one's own narrow platform the search of others with interest and sympathy, and so to re-establish a learned community on the recognition that what binds us together is mainly, and perhaps only, the integrity of our individual concerns.

45. *Dædalus* LXXXVII, I (1958), p. 6.

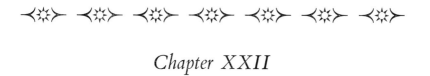

Chapter XXII

THE VIRTUOSO'S COLLECTION

> The documentary sources of American history are so voluminous that it is easy to overlook the data afforded by physical survivals and objects of material culture. Yet such vestiges of the past may be quite as revealing as written records.
> —*Harvard Guide to American History*, 1955

NATHANIEL HAWTHORNE 120 years ago poked fun at collectors and the museums they assemble in a story entitled "A Virtuoso's Collection," first published in *The Boston Miscellany of Literature and Fashion* for May 1842 and later printed in *Mosses from an Old Manse.* In this he described a museum whose stuffed animals included the wolf that ate Little Red Riding-Hood, Argus, Cerberus, Dr. Johnson's cat Hodge, the favorite cats of Mahomet, Gray, Walter Scott, as well as Shelley's sky-lark, Bryant's waterfowl, and "Coleridge's albatross, transfixed with the Ancient Mariner's crossbow shaft." Among "antiquarian rarities" to be admired were "Charlemagne's sheepskin cloak, the flowing wig of Louis Quatorze," "the robe that smothered Agamemnon, Nero's fiddle, the Czar Peter's brandy-bottle," Arthur's sword Excalibur, Peter Stuyvesant's wooden leg, a remnant of the Golden Fleece, the chisel of Phidias, the shirt of Nessus, Joseph's coat of many colors, President Jefferson's scarlet breeches, and other objects of value and curiosity.

Now, as the late Charles E. Goodspeed pointed out in a delightful little book,[1] the model that inspired Hawthorne's flight of fancy was

---

1. First published as "Nathaniel Hawthorne and the Museum of the East India

the museum of the Salem East India Marine Society, founded in 1799 by a group of shipmasters who lovingly assembled in their fine hall such natural and artificial curiosities as they encountered in their voyages to Europe, Africa, the Pacific, and the Orient. This collection, which happily contained not only the junk that Hawthorne satirized but unique Polynesian objects and a remarkable record of Salem shipping, today forms part of the Peabody Museum of Salem, which is, by virtue of this inheritance, the oldest museum in continuous operation in the United States.[2] I have already indicated in chapter XVI the present state of this institution. Its exhibits no longer bear any resemblance to those that Hawthorne satirized.

Like many a museum and historical society curator since, Hawthorne's virtuoso thought chiefly of acquisition. He loved the chase. The competitive spirit was in his blood. His ideal was to procure as many rare and curious objects as his time and purse permitted. The more he had the happier he was. Thus having filled his premises to capacity, or emptied his purse, he could bask in the admiration of the wondering and amazed visitor. Although the virtuoso's practice has not completely vanished from the earth, it is generally felt today to represent an inadequate and not very inspired ideal. Mere pride of possession, arousing wonder in the uninformed, is no longer enough. The possessor should know accurately what he has, and why it is important, for motives above and beyond personal gratification, for him to have it. He should have his possessions in such order that they will survive into an unpredictable future and will be currently accessible to those who have serious need of using them. Moreover when he exhibits anything he should do so in a manner that will instruct

---

Marine Society," *The American Neptune* v (October 1945), 266–285; reprinted in 1946 with illustrations and a facsimile of the *Boston Miscellany* publication of Hawthorne's story by the Peabody Museum of Salem as *Nathaniel Hawthorne and the Museum of the Salem East India Marine Society or The Gathering of a Virtuoso's Collection*, and by the Club of Odd Volumes, Boston, in a limited edition of 99 copies (with still more illustrations) as *Nathaniel Hawthorne and the Marine Museum of the Salem East India Marine Society or The Gathering of a Virtuoso's Collection*.

2. Walter Muir Whitehill, *The East India Marine Society and the Peabody Museum of Salem. A Sesquicentennial History* (Salem, 1949).

the visitor, that will convey the meaning and significance of the object shown, and that will go beyond the satisfaction of idle and purposeless curiosity.

No one will question that the preservation of historic buildings and the exhibition of objects lends color and vividness to history. To look out of George Washington's bedroom window on a crisp October day and see the Potomac framed in the red and yellow foliage of autumn is not only a memorable experience but a useful one, for it explains in a flash the owner's deep affection for Mount Vernon. An afternoon at Monticello tells a great deal about the mind of Thomas Jefferson. I have returned there repeatedly for thirty-two years in all seasons and never tire of it. On a windy day, when the first shoots of spring bulbs are showing and the leafless trees permit a more generous view of the Blue Ridge than in summer, or on a snowy Christmas morning, the house and its surroundings speak eloquently of its builder. Four generations of Adamses become more readily intelligible in the old house and stone library at Quincy, preserved, as Brooks Adams left them, by the National Park Service.

Houses of this kind have the strongest power to evoke the past, yet the best museums play their part effectively. Winterthur recreates the urban elegance of the eighteenth century as vividly as the Farmers' Museum and the hunter's cabin at Cooperstown do the rural life of upstate New York in the next century. In museums like these the objects, whether elegant or rustic, are carefully chosen for a specific purpose by people who know their meaning and understand what to do with them. They are not the random accumulation of a public attic or the result of indiscriminate pursuit of the rare and curious. At many of its visitors' centres the National Park Service, with only a few original objects, has, by appreciation of what is historically significant about the site and by skillful use of maps, photographs, and captions, created exhibits of remarkable value.

By contrast, haphazard collecting of historical artifacts without adequate interpretation can be downright misleading. Extremely large objects, because of their very bulk, assume an importance that is sometimes out of all relation to their historical significance. A single carriage, of whatever origin, crowded into a museum gallery distracts the visitor from what may be more to his lasting instruction, whereas the hundred or so carriages in the great barn at the Shelburne Museum[3] present a reasonable picture of elegant horse-drawn vehicles in the nineteenth and twentieth centuries, because they are by themselves with room to be seen, and there are enough of them to be adequately representative.[4] Because an object is large, rare, expensive, curious, or has some personal association does not mean that it is worth showing. Carl E. Guthe gives a delightful list of typical objects that might once have found their way into museums,

from the desire to attract visitors through their interest in strange, unusual, or grotesque things—the river pebble shaped like a foot, the model church built of burnt matchsticks, the piece of marble chipped from an ancient Greek temple, the two-headed calf, the ashes from a cigar smoked by Teddy Roosevelt, the tree trunk with a cannon ball embedded in it, the crocheted American flag. None of these are truly typical, documented objects, nor do they have intrinsic aesthetic, historic, or scientific value. They belong in amusement arcades or in fair midways, certainly not in museums.[5]

The argument that something unsuitable should be given house room because "people like to look at it" will not hold water. A display of French pornographic post cards would doubtless attract a large audience.

A good museum is not a simple or a static thing. It requires first of all a good bit of space, not only for exhibition but for storage. It requires objects of a wide diversity and a staff who know not only what these objects mean but who have the ingenuity and dexterity to exhibit them intelligently and attractively. Once an exhibition is installed, it is good for only a relatively short period. In a few years

3. Lilian Baker Carlisle, *The Carriages at Shelburne Museum* (Shelburne, 1956).

4. The same could be said of many of the specialized collections at the Shelburne Museum, which are admirably exhibited, often in buildings by themselves. It is in matters of architecture and the decoration of "period rooms" that the element of caprice enters, to the confusion of history.

5. *So You Want a Good Museum. A Guide to the Management of Small Museums* (Washington, 1957), p. 2.

it begins to be shabby and requires titivation if not replacement. Such an institution does not stay clean any more readily than the grass in its front yard stays cut. And there is no more Sisyphean task than offering really good public instruction. Just as there is more of an iceberg below water than above, so the well-run museum has extensive ramifications that do not appear on the surface. A good library is a prerequisite. There must be curators who know what the collections mean and technicians skilled in installing and presenting them. Last, but not least, all of this takes a considerable amount of money, which has to come from somewhere.

So many varied talents are required in a museum that size is a positive advantage. A curator who knows the facts, an artist who is able to present them skillfully, carpenters, painters, electricians to carry out the presentation, and (if the museum yearns for organized popular education) someone who is skilled in teaching are all essential. Some of these people can be hired in for a specific purpose, but it is far more economical to have them permanently on the spot.[6] This all costs more than can be afforded in most places. The single-handed genius who combines the talents of scholar, carpenter, and teacher is too rare[7] to make the very small museum, running on a shoestring, a generally useful institution.

A century ago, when people stayed put, there was something to be said for the general museum collection, however shallow it might be. Today when Americans are increasingly mobile, or were until the recent unpleasantness in the stock market, there is little justification for attempting to have something of everything everywhere. Today a plow, a wing chair, a flax spinning wheel, a lustre tea set, somebody's wedding dress, and a Dutch oven, jumbled together in the ell of a historic house, only spell confusion. An intelligent and

6. In 1960 when I was in Columbus, the Ohio Historical Society was rigging a remarkable ornithological exhibit. The cost was considerable, but the presence of scholars, skilled technicians, and craftsmen on the permanent staff made it far lower than it would have been by outside contract.

7. E. Milby Burton, director of the Charleston Museum, is one of the most remarkable examples of this.

discriminating specialization, by which institutions choose to do certain things really well, is preferable to interminable duplication in which everything is done everywhere badly. There is no merit in attempting to repeat locally, on a smaller scale and with inadequate resources, what is done supremely well elsewhere.

It will be alleged that every region is different and that there is, in consequence, a justification for historical museums that will portray the particular characteristics of the locality in which they are. Sometimes, when by a happy accident adequate funds are available, such museums develop through the generous enthusiasm of individuals for regions in which they summer. The Fruitlands Museum at Harvard, Massachusetts, which was in the vanguard of outdoor museum development, evolved from such a circumstance. In 1914 Miss Clara Endicott Sears (1863–1960) of Boston bought the wooden farmhouse called Fruitlands, in which Bronson Alcott and other high-minded and impractical Transcendentalists had attempted in 1843 to create a "New Eden." This venture in community living soon collapsed, but the memory of it remained among the disciples of the Concord group. Miss Sears had built a summer house on the crest of Prospect Hill in Harvard, from which one has a breath-taking view across the Nashaway valley towards Mount Wachusett. Fruitlands stood, neglected, lower down the hill. In everything save its association with Alcott's community it was just another Massachusetts farmhouse, but the Transcendentalists who had so briefly lived in it struck Miss Sears's imagination. As she explained in the introduction to her book *Bronson Alcott's Fruitlands*:

> As I looked down on it from my terrace on the hill, pitying its infinite loneliness, the thought came to me that I must save it. If for a time it had borne the semblance of a New Eden, then that time must be honored, and not forgotten. I longed to see it smiling again upon the valley in its glowing coat of ochre-red.[8]

So she bought and restored Fruitlands, filling it with furniture, portraits, and manuscripts of the Transcendentalists, and opening it to visitors in the summer months. She also made friends with the

8. (Boston, 1915), p. xvi.

eldresses of the dwindling Shaker Society at Harvard, publishing in 1916 *Gleanings from Old Shaker Journals.*[9] When that community came to an end, Miss Sears bought a 1794 wooden house from the deserted Shaker Village and moved it to her own property. Re-settled on the hill a little above Fruitlands, this house was opened in 1922 to exhibit a collection that she had formed illustrative of Shaker life and industries. Although the museum was incorporated in 1930, with a board of trustees, Miss Sears continued for many years per-sonally and singlehandedly to buy and arrange the collections, write books about them, hire the help needed to receive visitors, and pay the bills. In 1930 she built a brick museum to house a collection that she had assembled dealing with local Indians, to which she added a wing in 1932. A brick picture gallery containing portraits by itiner-ant painters was built in 1940 and enlarged in 1947 to provide space for a collection of nineteenth-century landscapes. Thus over thirty-three years the Fruitlands Museum grew to contain four units, each housed in its own building,[10] which admirably illuminated the past of a small but singularly beautiful stretch of Massachusetts country-side. Only in her eighty-sixth year did Miss Sears give up single-handed responsibility for the institution. In 1949 she engaged as director William Henry Harrison, who has during the past thirteen years made skillful and subtle improvements in the exhibitions and has brought the museum into close and friendly relationship with other historical institutions in eastern Massachusetts.[11] When Clara Endicott Sears died in her ninety-seventh year, her will provided the

9. (Boston, 1916). Miss Sears's developing interest in the history, literature, and art of the region led her to collect and write on themes that eventually were treated in the museum. Thus she later published *Some American Primitives: A Study of New England Faces and Folk Portraits* and *High Lights Among the Hudson River Painters*, whose landscapes often strikingly approach in spirit the view from Prospect Hill.

10. Harriet E. O'Brien, *Lost Utopias, A brief description for three quests for happiness, Alcott's Fruitlands, Old Shaker Museum, and American Indian Museum Rescued from obliv-ion, recorded and preserved by Clara Endicott Sears on Prospect Hill in the old township of Harvard Massachusetts* (Harvard, Mass., 1947).

11. The trustees include the present directors of the American Antiquarian Society, the Society for the Preservation of New England Antiquities, the Boston Athenæum, and the Peabody Museum, Harvard University.

trustees with an endowment completely adequate for the future maintenance and growth of the Fruitlands Museums. Dr. Charles B. Hosmer Jr.,[12] in his unpublished history of the preservation movement, quotes a statement by Miss Sears:

> This must always be a place where thinkers can come and find an atmosphere that is appealing to them. . . . There are public parks given over to recreation. This place is not meant for recreation. It is meant for inspiration. The surrounding view lends itself to it. The history of Fruitlands and the Shaker house and the Indian Museum with its historic lore and the whole breadth of the Nashaway Valley are both conducive to it. It must always remain more or less like a poem.

and remarks that "Fruitlands stands almost alone in the history of the preservation movement as a house saved purely for the inspiration of contemplative thinkers."

Fort Ticonderoga on Lake Champlain is, like the Fruitlands Museum, set in a scene of great natural beauty. It is, however, so enthusiastically visited by the traveling public that "contemplative thinkers," if they went there, would be in danger of being trampled under foot by a herd of wild tourists. Nevertheless the preservation of Fort Ticonderoga and its development as a military and historical museum is due to the personal effort of a family that summered beneath its walls. Early in the nineteenth century, William Ferris Pell, a New Yorker whose business took him to Burlington, Vermont, while passing up and down Lake Champlain, was struck by the beauty of the site and the romantic interest of the ruins of the fort, which then belonged jointly to Columbia and Union colleges.[13] In 1816 he leased and in 1820 bought the fort, building below it a summer house and attempting to prevent the deterioration of the fortifications. The death of a son, killed in 1838 by the explosion of a cannon that he was firing as a salute to his father who was coming up the lake, caused William Ferris Pell to abandon his visits to Ticon-

12. *Old Houses in America: The Preservation Movement to 1926* (Ann Arbor, 1961), pp. 126–127.

13. As part of lands, deeded as a contribution to education, by the State of New York in 1790. See "The Restoration of Fort Ticonderoga," by John H. G. Pell, in S. P. P. Pell, *Fort Ticonderoga, A Short History* (Ticonderoga, 1954), pp. 93–111.

deroga. Although "The Pavilion," as his house was called, was rented for many years and operated as a hotel, the property remained in the Pell family.

Late in the nineteenth century, Stephen Hyatt Pelham Pell, as a small boy of eight, became fascinated by Fort Ticonderoga. In 1908, having grown up and married, he and his wife determined to rehabilitate "The Pavilion" and to spend their summers there so that he might undertake the restoration of the fort. This was a large order, involving initially the acquisition of the property from seventeen scattered heirs within the Pell family as well as from interlopers who had acquired squatter's rights in part of it. Fort Ticonderoga was the passion of Stephen Pell's life; its restoration and the assembly of its collections are due solely to his tireless enthusiasm. The wing containing the officer's mess and quarters had just been completed when he went overseas during World War I. During his absence in France, so many visitors came seeking admittance that Mrs. Pell, who spent her summers superintending the work, hired a full-time guide and charged sight-seers a small sum to pay the man's salary. Thus the fort, although still private property, was first opened to the public. In 1931 Mr. and Mrs. Pell established the Fort Ticonderoga Association, a nonprofit educational corporation[14] whose objects are the preservation and future restoration of the fort and its presentation to the public. Stephen Pell remained its president until his death in 1950 when he was succeeded by his son, John H. G. Pell.

The South Barracks contain exhibitions concerning the history of the fort and region, as well as Indian artifacts and a varied collection of articles and tools used by later settlers. On the ground floor of the West Barracks is the Armory with an extensive gun collection; above is a very complete military library of the colonial and revolutionary period, including manuscripts, as well as a considerable amount of material on the general area. These sources, although little used, are available to qualified scholars. Certain of them have

14. The association has a very small membership, chiefly members of the Pell family.

been printed in issues of the *Bulletin of the Fort Ticonderoga Museum*. The fort's earlier publications had the air of publicity for a tourist attraction. *Lake Champlain and the Upper Hudson Valley*, by Edward P. Hamilton,[15] who became director of the museum in 1957, represents an admirable change of course. This beautifully printed little book,[16] containing historical maps explaining the geographical significance of the Lake Champlain-Hudson River route between Montreal and New York, is a fine example of soundly based historical popularization.

The Fort Ticonderoga Museum, although coping with an immense number of annual visitors, receives no public support. The preservation of the site over a century and a half was due to a single family; its restoration and conversion into a museum was the work of one devoted member of that family, aided only by friends and relatives. It has, however, no endowment and so must make the best it can of admission fees and of the profits (if any) from sales of the type of souvenirs dear to the traveling public that are displayed in large quantities in a pseudo-log cabin at the entrance to the fort. Consequently the mood is considerably different from that inspired by the Fruitlands Museum.

The Adirondack Museum at Blue Mountain Lake, New York, owes its origin to the interest and affection for the region of a summer resident. At Fruitlands and Ticonderoga a museum developed from the preservation of a building; at Blue Mountain Lake one evolved from a remarkable book entitled *Township 34, A History with Digressions on an Adirondack Township in Hamilton County in the State of New York*, privately printed in 1952 by its author, Harold K.

15. Colonel Hamilton, an officer of the Massachusetts Historical Society, exemplifies the tradition of research and writing of professional quality by nonacademic historians long fostered by that society. While still engaged in business in Boston he came to know more than anyone else about early water-powered mills and windmills and published a stimulating and lively *History of Milton* (Milton, 1957). Since retiring from business and becoming director of Ticonderoga, he has published *The French and Indian Wars* (Garden City, 1962) in the *Mainstream of America* series. The royalties of the latter book he has generously given to the Massachusetts Historical Society.

16. Published in 1959.

Hochschild, honorary chairman of the American Metal Company, Ltd., and a director of numerous mining companies. His acquaintance with the region went back to his childhood, for in 1904 his father, Berthold Hochschild, with two friends, Henry Morgenthau Sr. and Ernst Ehrmann, had bought a large tract of Adirondack land at Blue Mountain Lake.[17] In addition to its scenic beauty, this Eagle Nest property offered possibilities for deer hunting, duck and partridge shooting, fishing, golf, and farming. In the year of his father's death, 1928, Harold Hochschild wrote a sketch for members of his family, chiefly of recollections of his own summers in the neighborhood, beginning in 1904. During the next twenty-four years these informal reminiscences developed into a 612-page volume, carefully documented and profusely illustrated. *Township 34* is an admirable and remarkable piece of local history. No comparable area of American wilderness has ever had such a historian, whose interests reached into every possible aspect of the region over centuries. Indians, land titles, early settlers, mines, lumbering, forestry, Ned Buntline, summer hotels, railroads, steamboats, country clubs, local eccentrics, energetic promoters, and visiting capitalists all figure in the pages of this exhaustive and delightfully written book.

In the nineteenth century, collectors sometimes "extra-illustrated" books by the insertion of prints and of original manuscripts and drawings. The Adirondack Museum is essentially an extra-illustration of *Township 34* in three-dimensional terms, not only with dioramas, but with original objects as large as an 1890 private railroad car. It is a nonprofit educational institution operated by the Adirondack Historical Association, whose board of trustees includes members and friends of the Hochschild family.[18] Normally a

17. Ehrmann died in 1909. The elder Morgenthau, who was Wilson's Ambassador to Turkey from 1913 to 1916, came only infrequently to Blue Mountain Lake after 1912. Berthold Hochschild, however, remained constant in his affection for the region until his death in 1928, as his children have since.

18. Originally organized in 1948 by year-round residents, the association lay fallow for several years. The development of the museum, for which plans were laid in 1954, is chiefly due to the energy and generosity of the trustees.

regional museum accumulates over many years a number of objects and then has to determine what they are and how, if at all, they may be used to elucidate local history, about which too little of a precise sort is usually known. Here the process was reversed. The history was already written. One therefore knew what was wanted, and for what purpose. It was possible to plan a museum and then seek the objects that were needed for its exhibits. Unlike Fruitlands and Ticonderoga, where the devoted founders worked for many years by their instincts before obtaining professional assistance, this institution had from the beginning a director, the anthropologist Dr. Robert Bruce Inverarity, who was fully conversant with current scholarly and museum techniques.

The Adirondack Museum opened in 1957. Its main building—whose portico with columns of gigantic tree trunks so startlingly recalls the primitive origins of the Doric temple—was still under construction when gifts of objects began to come in from a radius of a hundred miles. Others were bought, and a number of dioramas were constructed. Whatever was acquired by whatever means was useful in illustrating the theme of the museum—the relationship of man to the Adirondacks. In the entrance hall is a great relief map of the area, on which, by pushing buttons, the visitor may turn on lights that indicate the location of towns, villages, rivers, mountains, and lakes. To the left a gallery contains photographs, drawings, and paintings, arranged to illuminate the history of the Adirondacks; to the right thirteen dioramas illustrate early logging techniques, historical events, and ways of life in the region. The visitor then goes out of doors and proceeds to a dozen other areas where camps, trains, boats, vehicles, logging equipment, and the living fish of the Adirondacks may be seen. Behind the scenes is an admirably equipped research library and laboratory for the treatment and preservation of museum objects.

In five years the Adirondack Museum has issued twelve publications. Seven are revisions of portions of Mr. Hochschild's *Township 34*, which thus becomes available for general distribution. Dr. Inverarity's *Winslow Homer in the Adirondacks* grew out of an exhibition of Homer's Adirondack work held in 1959. Other volumes, like the *Journal of a Hunting Excursion to Louis Lake, 1851*, and *The Adirondack Letters of George Washington Sears. Whose Pen Name was "Nessmuk,"* make available unpublished or little-known accounts of life in the region.

Although the museum is open to visitors only from 15 June to 15 October, as one might expect in a mountain region, Dr. Inverarity carries on its scholarly activities throughout the year. Visitors come, in considerable numbers for so remote a place, but there is no illusion that the museum will become self-supporting from admission fees.[19] The purchase of land and the construction of buildings and exhibits, with necessary equipment, has already involved private gifts of over $1,000,000. Less than a third of the annual operating expense of over $100,000 is met by the fees paid by visitors; the remainder comes from current gifts of a small group of private supporters, which it is anticipated will eventually be reinforced by bequests to endowment.

Fruitlands, Fort Ticonderoga, and the Adirondack Museum all show, in different forms, what private individuals can accomplish through personal generosity in elucidating the history of regions in which they have a particular interest.[20] Considerable amounts of money are involved in the creation and maintenance of such museums. Most independent historical societies simply do not have the means to attempt such things, without detracting from their three primary duties of assembling, ordering, and publishing the source materials of American history to serve the scholar.

Nearly all of the older societies began with "cabinets," some of which contained objects as strange as those cherished by Hawthorne's virtuoso. In the earlier chapters I have indicated how many of these have been eliminated. The Massachusetts Historical Society, the American Antiquarian Society, and the Historical Society of

19. One dollar for adults and fifty cents for children.
20. It should be noted, however, that only the Adirondack Museum has any broadly planned program of research and publication.

Pennsylvania now maintain no museums, although all three buildings are rich in portraits, prints, furniture, and historic objects that, treated as household effects, are, like their libraries, available to and intended for the serious investigator. This is the result of a deliberate decision to concentrate their resources on their main purpose, and to try to do that well, rather than to scatter their shot and do several things inadequately. At Battle Abbey the Virginia Historical Society's fine gallery of Virginia portraits and the two Confederate memorial rooms attract numerous casual visitors, although the sole purpose of the recent addition is to facilitate research. Virginia House, it will be recalled, was a concomitant of the Weddell bequest, which contributes the lion's share of the Virginia Historical Society's general endowment. The New-York Historical Society and the New York State Historical Association[21] maintain excellent museums with able specialized staffs, but they are among the three best-endowed independent historical societies in the country. The third, the Chicago Historical Society, also maintains an excellent museum, but at the expense, as I indicated in chapter IX, of its research and publication functions. In small societies the attempt, in limited space and with few hands, to serve the scholar and attract the public often leads to confusion and the satisfaction of neither.[22]

State-supported historical societies, whose incomes greatly exceed those of most independent societies, place substantial emphasis upon their museums. This is reasonable in their situation, for an attractive museum, however costly it may be to operate, draws large numbers of people,[23] which are an essential ingredient in justifying public

21. It will be recalled, from chapter XIV, that the museum collections and buildings at Cooperstown are almost entirely due to the personal generosity of Stephen C. Clark.

22. In one society that I visited, cartons of tea cups and other caterer's gear, required for the opening of an exhibition, effectively blocked the way to the safe containing the best manuscripts and the rarest books.

23. Note the remark of Dr. K. Ross Toole, then director of the Historical Society of Montana, at the 1954 annual meeting of the American Association for State and Local History: "Interest, as far as I'm concerned, is absolutely paramount, because until you get that you haven't got anything. And if I have to import can-can girls, which

appropriations. One cannot deny that even the most important manuscripts do not readily strike the eye of the uninformed observer. The papers of John Winthrop, William Penn, Benjamin Franklin, George Washington, or Abraham Lincoln, when housed in gray cardboard manuscript boxes on shelves in a vault, are less dramatic than a cigar-store Indian or a bit of gaudy carving from a steamboat. Thus, when one attempts to attract the widest audience, the museum becomes an essential instrument, notwithstanding the risk of emphasizing the spectacular at the expense of the significant or of giving space to pots and pans, barbershop mugs of the 1890s, or other trivialities, for no more elevated purpose than providing the pleasurable "shock of recognition" to the most uninformed visitor.

In Ohio, Wisconsin, Minnesota, Kansas, and Colorado in particular, State historical societies have applied much thought, expense, and technical skill to their museums. Yet even in their large buildings and with their substantial budgets, space is often inadequate for a balanced presentation of the history of the region. For that matter, the United States National Museum until very recently, in spite of the erudition concentrated backstage, gave the impression of a virtuoso's collection through its startling juxtaposition of airplanes, French china, costumes, cable cars, ship models, stuffed dogs, and postage stamps. This was due solely to the necessity of ramming important objects into crowded halls, with outsize items placed out of sequence where they would fit, sometimes hanging from the ceiling. To visit its recent installations of American history and decorative arts is like passing into another world. The building now under construction in Constitution Avenue for the Museum of History and Technology will permit American history to be as superbly presented as the arts are in the National Gallery. Nevertheless the perennial problem of space in cities suggests that some physical aspects of American history are likely always to be best presented in

_____

I once did in Montana, I'll do it in order to get people into my place in the first place." *Ideas in Conflict* (Harrisburg, 1958), p. 149.

the country, at places like Williamsburg, Cooperstown, and Sturbridge, where there is room to swing a cat.

A good museum cannot exist without a library to furnish the information requisite for the development and presentation of its exhibits. The reverse is not true. A good research library has no necessary need for space to display objects. A library attracts a small number of workers whose chief demands are a place to sit and to work quietly with sources made available to them. A museum attracts a considerable number of visitors who mill about, whether proceeding independently or in convoy. The two can be accommodated harmoniously under one roof, as in the Truman Library, where each activity has its separate entrance, but there is no essential connection between them. Appropriate quarters for chamber music and for Wagnerian opera could conceivably be provided in a single building, but normally one would not attempt to do so, so different are the requirements in setting and seating. As the heart of an independent historical society is its library, one readily understands why Massachusetts, Pennsylvania, and the American Antiquarian Society, among others, have forsworn museums in order to concentrate their resources upon their primary responsibilities. This aspect of American history can best be left to publicly supported institutions to whom it has essential usefulness, and to the devoted private individuals whose imagination is fired by some scene that is particularly appealing to them. We are constantly told that times are changing; that the days of great gifts, in the Huntington, Morgan, and Rockefeller manner, are over; that one must, in the familiar platitude, "broaden the base of support" by increasing the number of small gifts. When public support is a factor, this is all very well, for every display of interest, however small, indicates a potential vote. What has happened in the past two decades at the Virginia Historical Society and the New York State Historical Association, at Winterthur, Deerfield, Tryon Palace, and Boscobel, as well as the Fruitlands and Adirondack Museums, indicates that, when private support is the basis, more has been accomplished by a small number of large gifts than by a great number of small ones. A few years ago I took Miss Mary Cabot Wheelwright, founder of the Museum of Navajo Ceremonial Art described in chapter XVI, to see the Fruitlands Museum. She and Miss Clara Endicott Sears, then ninety, readily agreed[24] that the most certain formula for good health and a long life was to found a museum and to wear warm stockings.

24. Although both Bostonians they were not well acquainted, for Miss Wheelwright not only was fifteen years younger than Miss Sears, but wintered in Alcalde, New Mexico.

Chapter XXIII

TOGETHERNESS

And I said unto them, If ye think good, give me my price; and if not, forbear. So they weighed for my price thirty pieces of silver.
—*Zechariah* 11:12

OVER the bar of the Omaha airport in the spring of 1960 my wife and I saw, among the bottles, an advertising poster of the Joslyn Art Museum, offering "family membership" at $10 a year, inviting the reader to "visit your museum soon," and describing the institution as

THE PLACE TO GO
AND GROW
TOGETHER.

Our plane for Minneapolis arrived too soon to permit us to exchange the bar for the art museum; even without a visit it was apparent that a full-blown case of the new "togetherness" had developed in Omaha. The symptoms of this disease in American art museums are easily recognized, for they are nothing more than the application to the arts of the flattering advertising methods designed to sell breakfast food or cigarettes, crossed with the tear-jerking and repetitious techniques of the professional fund-raiser. The postal meter used to cancel direct-mail appeals will bear such slogans as

VISIT   ENJOY   JOIN!
SUPPORT   ITS
YOUR ART MUSEUM   *YOUR* MUSEUM

while the literature contained in these envelopes abounds in mass-produced "personalizations." Typical is a recent Boston offering whose cover is equally divided between the title "Your Museum of Fine Arts" and a photograph of young mother holding up little daughter to admire a diminutive ivory and gold Minoan snake goddess of 2000 B.C. On page 2 comes the assertion:

> THIS IS
> . . . a recreation center
> . . . a place to learn
> . . . a collector's paradise
> . . . a research laboratory
> . . . a craftsman's mecca
> . . . a "World's Fair" of art
> THIS is YOUR family's PERSONAL Museum
> of Fine Arts

on page 3 the listing of the classes of membership by which the recipient may make it HIS or HER family's PERSONAL museum. The inducements offered include free admission to paid exhibitions, invitations to previews, programs for children, concerts, tours and lectures, discounts on publications and art classes, and "use of attractive New MEMBERS' ROOM." Similar appeals pour from many art museums throughout the United States; even across the border in the province of Quebec, where bilingual appeals are necessary, the style and typography are familiar. One side of a leaflet asserts:

> The
> Montreal
> Museum of . . . this is YOUR museum
> Fine Arts are YOU a member?

and the other:

> Le Musée
> des
> Beaux-Arts . . . est VOTRE musée
> de Montréal en ÊTES-VOUS membre?

Such appeals are often supported by painted thermometers or graphs demonstrating spectacular increases in membership. They lead to previews in which so many people, eager to demonstrate their status as members, crowd into galleries that it is virtually impossible to derive either artistic enlightenment or social pleasure from the occasion. While gatherings of this sort often resemble rush hour in the subway, they provide the "togetherness" that many art museum directors seek today. James Johnson Sweeney, in describing the Guggenheim Museum,[1] appraised its "great-room character," "which permits the accommodation of 1,200 to 1,500 visitors at once under, as it were, a single ceiling" as "the most individual and gratifying feature of this building as an art museum."

And its effect on the public is immediately noticeable. There is no sense of cloistered contemplation. There is a sociability in participation evident on all sides among the spectators.

Some of this springs simply from natural gregariousness and from the American passion for the bigger and better elephant. We have in this country a touching national belief that the more people one can induce to mill about in a limited space the better. Thus many organizations in need of financial support, art museums and historical societies included, embrace the simple faith that a substantial increase in membership will solve all their problems. If one's aim is simply to spread the gospel, which has recently become the central purpose of most art museum directors, the more the merrier. But if the object is to any considerable extent the financial support of an institution, the costs of such activity in money, staff, and wear and tear must be carefully weighed against the returns. The attraction of large numbers of people requires outlay for exhibitions, publications, publicity, and that universal common denominator, food and drink. Once attracted, members must be held. This requires not only more of the same, but the novelty of frequent change.

In seven years, from 1954 to 1961, the Museum of Fine Arts in Boston has, by unremitting work on the part of its director, Perry T. Rathbone, and a large and energetic Ladies' Committee, raised the

1. "Chambered Nautilus on Fifth Avenue," *Museum News* XXXVIII, 5 (January 1960), pp. 14–15.

number of its members from 2,152 to 10,612 and the receipts from this source from $38,289 to $160,183. This institution, incorporated in 1870 as an outgrowth of the Boston Athenæum gallery, is, and always has been, supported wholly by private gifts. To quadruple the income from membership in seven years is a notable performance.[2] Yet without an annual income from endowment[3] of over $1,500,000, one may reasonably wonder whether—short of sacrificing most scholarly functions—it would have been possible to provide the remarkable variety of temporary exhibitions, concerts, lectures, and television programs, that have been a powerful inducement in attracting these thousands of new members.

The economies of production resulting from great volume and the assembly line are an article of faith of American industry. Only in a very few respects does this principle affect historical activity. A book that can be sold in an edition of 10,000 copies obviously has greater possibility of financial self-sufficiency, or even profit, than one with a market of a few hundred. Unfortunately economies possible with inanimate objects do not extend to human beings. Colonial Williamsburg is the largest and most richly endowed historical institution in the country.[4] It draws myriads of visitors from all over the world who annually leave there millions of dollars.[5] Yet even there

2. Five times as many members have produced four times as much income from that source. Mr. Rathbone notes with pride in his 1961 report that in these years "the Boston Museum in respect to annual dues-paying membership has risen from one of the lowest figures per capita in the country to one of the highest, if not actually the highest."

3. Book value of $31,901,469 and market value on 31 December 1961 of $48,835,-604.

4. The 1960 report showed endowment funds with a cost or book value of $47,236,-177.

5. During 1960 Colonial Williamsburg, Incorporated (the nonprofit corporation which carries out the historical and educational purposes of the restoration), had operating income of $2,068,273.43. The business corporation, Williamsburg Restoration, Incorporated, which operates or leases the inns, restaurants, and similar necessary properties, received gross income in the same year of $7,493,843.02. The number of visitors required to produce such sums explains the remark attributed to an elderly resident of Williamsburg (not connected with the restoration) that she wished "the tourists would stay at home and simply *send* their money."

numbers do not bring profit, or even economic self-sufficiency. Mr. Carlisle H. Humelsine, president of Colonial Williamsburg, was within the past year explicit on this point:[6]

The generosity of the late Mr. John D. Rockefeller, Jr., made possible the high standards Williamsburg enjoys today—but increasingly we find ourselves in the common plight of many endowed institutions, including the larger universities. The public supposes that we are rolling in money, but the truth of the matter is that no matter how large the gifts bestowed upon us, we are always in need, for a very simple reason.

The more successful we are, the more money we must spend to keep up our standards. And today we are forced to subsidize our regular program by over $1,000,000 a year. This is in addition to our capital expenditures for restoration, reconstruction, buying antique furniture and other valuable and expensive items for our collections. This need was put clearly not long ago by Clarence B. Randall who pointed out that some kind of subsidy must aid every cultural and educational enterprise in our country. Even such heavily-endowed schools as Harvard, Wesleyan, Beloit and the University of Chicago have found that "the actual cost of the education offered is on the average twice the amount of payments made on behalf of the student." The Williamsburg visitor, going through the Governor's Palace or the Public Gaol, may not imagine that this is the case with his visit, but I can assure you that it is. *Rather than profiting from the increased flow of visitors, we have reached the point where greater volume means only greater costs,* if we are to maintain our standards of interpretation and our general program, which we are determined to do.

The phrases that I have italicized in this authoritative testimony should serve as a timely warning that increases in numbers will not alone solve the problems of any historical institution. It is true that Mount Vernon and Monticello, admirably preserved by private organizations, are maintained from the fees of their very numerous visitors, and that the Thomas Jefferson Memorial Foundation not only maintains Monticello from that source but makes annual gifts to Mr. Jefferson's University of Virginia for a professorship, graduate fellowships, and the purchase of Jeffersonian books for the library. However, by virtue of their original inhabitants, these houses are unique instances. Moreover both the Mount Vernon Ladies Associa-

6. At the December 1961 meeting of the American Historical Association.

tion and the Thomas Jefferson Memorial Foundation had an extended uphill struggle of national fund-raising to purchase the properties and achieve their preservation and furnishing. Their early trials and tribulations are graphically described in Dr. Charles B. Hosmer's forthcoming book on the early preservation movement. He cites the instances of many other historic buildings that were confidently expected, during the initial attempts at preservation, to become a "Mecca" for visitors, and concludes that "within a few years of the purchase of a historic house, a preservation group usually found it necessary to campaign for some form of endowment that would close the gap that existed between admission fees and running expenses."[7]

If numbers do not necessarily bring financial self-sufficiency, one may well question the value of "togetherness" in an independent historical society. In such an organization it is the workers, rather than the visitors, that count, a corollary of which is that it is ultimately more significant to wrestle with ideas than to gape at objects.[8] There is every reason why people should use their eyes, particularly if they are looking at something pleasant, provided they do not permit their wits to be atrophied by relapsing into the passive role of onlookers who are incapable of thought, imagination, or literary expression. The number of people who make full use of their minds has always been small; it may be doubted if it is in any way increased by the brightly colored illustrations, the television programs, and the so-called "visual aids to learning" that are currently so much the fad. Most statistics proudly displayed to prove "growth" or "progress" are open to question where matters of the mind are concerned. In a library, circulation figures have no usefulness other than to impress politicians responsible for appropriations, who are blissfully unaware of their true irrelevance. All that really matters in a library is bringing the right book to the right mind at

---

7. *Old Houses in America: The Preservation Movement to 1926*, p. 408.
8. At the Shelburne Museum last summer I overheard a mother remark with awe to her child: "Look! It's like in *TV*!"

the right time. So with historical societies the quality rather than the quantity of use matters.

Organized effort to increase the quantity of use may stimulate current gifts for a time. By following this line an organization may vastly increase its annual budget. Its income may multiply many times over, but the point to watch is the nature of the expenditure. If increased income be dissipated in the building of parking lots, public toilets, and the maintenance of a bureaucracy developed according to Parkinson's Law, "the last state of that man is worse than the first." Only if the income available for the primary purposes of the society be materially increased at the same time is this kind of hurly-burly justified. I have yet to see it proved in an independent historical society.

In the accounts of societies in earlier chapters I endeavored where possible to give specific figures of returns from membership dues in relation to the cost of publications furnished in exchange. The desire to keep dues low is understandable. Where things of the mind are concerned, barriers imposed by money, or the lack of it, are to be deplored. Yet, as privately supported organizations have to make ends meet or perish, there must be a realistic accounting of costs. Such a review in Richmond three years ago indicated that every member added to the Virginia Historical Society increased the drain upon endowment income by a sum roughly equivalent to the dues that he paid. Thus the lowest annual dues were raised from $5 to $10. Most societies are acutely aware of this problem, for it is only a singularly well-endowed organization that can afford the luxury of "togetherness" without detriment to its primary purposes. With costs as they are today, $10 appears to be the lowest annual fee that will produce any appreciable operating income, while $15—as charged by the California Historical Society and the New England Historic Genealogical Society—is even more realistic.[9] To avoid

9. The Museum of Modern Art in New York City, which has only recently been seeking endowment on a large scale, charges a minimum of $15 for nonresident and $18 for resident and suburban members. Mrs. Harry A. Woodruff, director of

hardship upon devoted members of long standing, any considerable increase in dues might well be accompanied by a provision that anyone who has paid dues for twenty-five years or has reached the age of 65, whichever is earlier, may *upon request* be exempted from further payment.

In the preceding chapter I endeavored to show that, because of the variety of specialized talent required, a large museum was apt to be able to accomplish its objectives more skillfully than a small one. The same situation exists in regard to educational activities. Few independent historical societies have space or equipment for popular instruction comparable to those of schools, public libraries, or some art museums, or are able to employ persons specially skilled in the art of teaching. Auditoriums and classrooms are singularly uneconomical unless used constantly to good purpose. There is no virtue in attempting to duplicate in a historical society, for occasional use, space that is available elsewhere in the vicinity. Realistically the society should regard itself as a source of information to be disseminated by those teachers whose duty it is to instruct the young, rather than to set up in that business itself with inadequate space and amateur staff. The production in other states of encyclopedic works modeled on the *Handbook of Texas* would be a boon to librarians, teachers, and journalists, who by their activities profoundly influence the great majority of their fellow countrymen. Such research projects could have greater lasting influence than attempts in small-scale retail education. At a more modest level, a proliferation of offset picture books of the type published by Old Sturbridge Village and the Massachusetts Historical Society would put much historical evidence in the hands of teachers at reasonable cost.

------

membership, tells me that the expenses involved in their membership of 30,000 amount to slightly less than 60% of the dues received. But even beyond the sum of money realized is the relation of the membership program to publications. As Mrs. Woodruff points out, "An annual distribution of 30,000 means that the unit cost of a book can be brought way down which, in turn, permits us to sell the book to the public at a lower rate than if we did not have any members."

The difference in outlook regarding popularization between independent and state-supported historical societies was crystallized last winter over the question of serial publications. In the first three quarters of the nineteenth century the pattern of *Collections* or *Transactions* or *Papers*, issued at irregular intervals, was general. In 1877, however, the Historical Society of Pennsylvania began the publication of *The Pennsylvania Magazine of History and Biography*, an admirable quarterly periodical that during the past eighty-five years has been widely emulated. A decade later appeared the *Ohio Archaeological and Historical Publications*, which became *The Ohio Historical Quarterly*. The Virginia Historical Society inaugurated the *Virginia Magazine of History and Biography* in 1893. Upon its foundation in 1897, the Texas State Historical Association began the publication of a quarterly that has been known since the 1912–13 volume as the *Southwestern Historical Quarterly*. At the turn of the century the South Carolina Historical Society began publishing a quarterly. Professor B. F. Shambaugh launched the *Iowa Journal of History and Politics* (now the *Iowa Journal of History*) in 1903 for the State Historical Society of Iowa, while Professor Edmond S. Meany in Seattle began publishing in 1909 the *Washington Historical Quarterly*, known since 1936 as the *Pacific Northwest Quarterly*. From the decade of 1910–20 date the *Georgia Historical Quarterly*, the *Wisconsin Magazine of History*, and the *New-York Historical Society Quarterly*; from the 1920s the *North Carolina Historical Review*, *New York History* of the New York State Historical Association, *Minnesota History*, and the *California Historical Society Quarterly*; from the 1930s the *Utah Historical Quarterly* and the *Kansas Historical Quarterly*. Originally nearly all these periodicals bore a family resemblance; seeing them on a table one would not have necessarily known which came from an independent and which from a publicly supported organization. In relatively recent times that has changed. *Minnesota History*, the *Wisconsin Magazine of History*, and the *Pacific Northwest Quarterly* have attempted to disguise the seriousness of their purpose by a two-column illustrated format on slick paper. The recent decision of the Ohio

Historical Society to explore a similar path inspired vigorous statements of dissent from two of the older independent societies.

The January 1962 issue of *The Pennsylvania Magazine of History and Biography* opened with an affirmation of faith by its editor, Miss Lois V. Given. In "Upholding A Tradition," Miss Given explained, with dignity, authority, and force, that "from its outset the *Pennsylvania Magazine* has been essentially a scholarly publication"; that "as it has evolved over more than three quarters of a century, it has become a valued research instrument."

Our ambition is to see it grow ever richer as a fundamental source for Pennsylvania history. To foster this ideal, all its pages are devoted to the task, for it is in no sense to be considered a house organ for the Society. True, in days gone by, it did contain obituaries of officers, the treasurer's annual report, and allied matters, but such information is now carried elsewhere. Thus, to its maximum ability, the *Pennsylvania Magazine* reflects the scholarly, research interests of its publisher.

Recently, we learned of the death of an old, respected historical society journal similar to ours. While the reasons for this sad demise have not been entirely clarified, it would seem that support was withdrawn in order that a more popularized approach to history might be followed. Fortunately, neither the Publications Committee nor the Council of our Society desires to change the mission of *The Pennsylvania Magazine of History and Biography*. Styles in presentation may come and go, but the route charted for the *Magazine*—the publication of scholarly articles on our state's history—is a true course. There is, and will continue to be, a need for such periodicals as ours.

Mr. Charles E. Baker, editor of the New-York Historical Society, treated the same theme in that society's annual report for 1961. He began:

For some years now historical-society journals, one after another, have been undergoing a transformation of format, style, and content into imitation popular magazines. This phenomenon was punctuated in 1961 by an abrupt termination of the vigorous 70-year-old *Ohio Historical Quarterly* to provide for another increment of periodical quasi-history—and this despite the unanimous protest of the Ohio Academy of History and published regrets (which this editor shares) in sister quarterlies. Such sacrifice of scholarship to a supposed popular predilection for costume-ball history reverses the long process by which historical-society journals, including our own, achieved their proper sphere of usefulness and influence. Why?

He then explains clearly the manner in which the *Quarterly* that he edits, begun originally as "a self-advertising staff-written 'house organ'," transformed itself into a scholarly journal useful to the professional historian.

Trying to do this in such manner that professional historians might rely upon the findings, be led to the sources, and take over the uncultivated areas where our tiny pioneer clearings lay, we tried also to sustain nonprofessional interest through clarity of presentation, with sufficient interpretation and background to make the immediate subject matter significant in its broader context and with pictorial illustrations chosen to enrich the textual content imaginatively but accurately. It is therefore gratifying that our nonspecialized readers, without a single dissent, also voiced greater interest and pleasure than before. And this, I gather, has been—or once was—the experience of most historical-society quarterlies in passing through similar developments to scholarly usefulness.

Why, then, in so many instances, the aforementioned reversal of this salutary trend? Every one of the journals so far noted as having succumbed to the pressures toward "popularization" now relies for a major part of its yearly income upon appropriations by State legislation. A magazine looking as if the "average voter" might possibly read it and even take part in the society activities therein reported— perhaps as one of the tourist millions clocked in at a series of historic-site markers and frontier-village restorations or as one of the parents of school children numbering in hundreds of thousands guided each year through the society's satellite museums—such a magazine seemingly supports the statistical argument for large State subsidies more successfully than a two-thousand-copy quarterly addressed to the needs of scholars and research librarians, many of whom even reside outside the State. This fact of political life is only one of the not-unmixed blessings of State support.

We are indeed fortunate that a well-invested endowment, steadily increasing over the years through wise management and through generous gifts, has enabled this Society, as reflected in the character of its *Quarterly*, to minimize its former antiquarian and peripheral interests (which, providentially, other metropolitan organizations have arisen to satisfy) in order to foster increasingly useful service to scholars and serious readers of history. We are fortunate, too in having officers and trustees who, knowing that in the course of time sound historical work will proliferate and endure long after the costume-ball has been forgotten, provide the incentive and direction for continual improvement. The *Quarterly*, no less than our other publications, therefore strives to become progressively better not only in the quality and specific gravity of its contributions, but also in its attractiveness and readability, for there is no inherent reason why the two goals should not move forward together.

These forthright statements by the editors of two of the most respected and useful independent historical societies represent the opinion of the great majority of such organizations that learning is to be preferred to "togetherness." Unlike the Guggenheim Museum, they are not afraid of "cloistered contemplation." And they put no store in "sociability in participation" when it is, as usually happens, at the expense of scholarship.

Chapter XXIV

MAMMON AND MONUMENTS

So are the ways of every one that is greedy of gain.—*Proverbs* 1:19

UILDINGS in America have always been imperiled by
those who covet the land upon which they stand. In 1808,
when the First Church of Boston, during the pastorate of
Ralph Waldo Emerson's father, sold its "Old Brick" meetinghouse
of 1713 in Washington Street to move to Chauncy Place, the following lamentation appeared in the *Independent Chronicle*:

> If a proposition had been made in London, Paris, or Amsterdam to the society
> owning the First Church of either of those respectable Cities, to sell (on a principle
> of speculation) their ancient edifice, it would have been spurned with indigna
> tion—the trifling profit anticipated by the sale would never have led the proprie
> tors to have razed a house of worship so well repaired as the Old Brick to gratify
> the rapacity of a few men who trouble society both in Church and State. After the
> demolition of the Old Brick, there is scarcely a vestige of antiquity in the town.
> We hope "Old South" will maintain its original ground. Even the British troops,
> though they attacked other places of worship never dared meddle with the Old
> Brick—for Chauncy was there.[1]

Nevertheless the Old Brick came down, and sixty-eight years later
the Old South of 1729, a few blocks down Washington Street, came
within an ace of doing so. That congregation, unable to resist

1. Quoted by the Reverend Richard D. Pierce in the preface to his recent and
monumental edition of *The Records of the First Church in Boston, 1630–1868; Publications of the Colonial Society of Massachusetts* XXXIX, xlvii. This instance of protest over
the demolition of a historic building in Boston is earlier than any I have previously
encountered.

$400,000 offered them, also sold their meetinghouse for demolition. This time there was a clamor too great to withstand. The Boston Tea Party had been brewed in the Old South Meeting House; the anniversary orations commemorating the Boston Massacre were delivered there. Poets and orators mounted the stump to such purpose that the Old South Association in Boston was formed to preserve the building as a historic monument. This was the first instance in Boston—and, indeed, the first of such magnitude in the United States—where respect for the historical and architectural heritage of the city triumphed over considerations of profit, expediency, laziness, and vulgar convenience.[2]

In chapter xix I indicated the extent to which historic preservation has progressed in the years since 1876, when the Old South was saved. Now we have gone so far in that direction that new dangers arise. Those who are "greedy of gain" today not only covet the land upon which historic buildings stand. They also seek to exploit and pervert history, or invent pseudo-history, to suit their own purposes.

When history becomes "good business," the genuine article may be imperiled by the imitation. A special report by Stanley M. Elliott, "Historic Buildings Exposed to Confiscatory Tax Danger" in the 18 February 1962 issue of the *Santa Barbara News-Press*, discusses a specific Californian instance.

In May 1960 the Santa Barbara City Council enacted an ordinance to preserve historic structures in the "old town" area, and to require the architectural conformation of new buildings erected in what was designated as El Pueblo Viejo.

Now, less than two years later, two unanticipated effects have become apparent:

1. Business concerns are willing to pay high prices for sites *within this premium zone, where they have the assurance of quality environment in the future.* [The italics are mine] A lot in the Pueblo Viejo section is reported to have sold for $250,000 recently.

2. Because of this rise in values, the historic landmarks themselves are threatened with being taxed out of their ownership. It is a privilege and a distinction to

2. *Freedom and the Old South Meeting House*, Old South Leaflet number 201; L. H. Butterfield, "Bostonians and Their Neighbors as Pack Rats," *The American Archivist* XXIV, 2 (April 1961), pp. 147–148.

possess an adobe constructed more than a century ago,[3] but there is a limit to what even the proudest possessor can tolerate on his assessment bill.

In chapter xv I mentioned the part played by the Santa Barbara Historical Society in obtaining the ordinance, and the efforts that it is now making to protect the area. The El Pueblo Viejo Ordinance provides that within a stated area in the centre of Santa Barbara

No present existing building of adobe structure or of special historic or aesthetic interest or value situated within the area . . . shall be torn down, demolished or otherwise destroyed.[4]

It further provides that any buildings thereafter constructed or altered must conform in their exterior appearance to the "California Adobe" type, the "Monterey type," or "to the type of architecture generally known as 'Spanish' or 'Spanish Colonial'." Thus, if El Pueblo Viejo has become—in the horrid phrase of the real estate world—a "premium zone," with lots selling at a quarter of a million dollars, it can only be because it is thought that "Spanish Colonial" surroundings will seriously promote the prosperity of any business that settles there by providing "the assurance of a quality environment for the future." Just what relevance adobe construction may have to the sale of hardware, whiskey, or insurance, to banking, or to the filling of teeth, is not clear, but the scramble for sites in El Pueblo Viejo indicates that the Santa Barbara business community thinks there is some. Thus, with spiraling values, the genuine elements of the region are reported to be endangered.

In a Chicago suburb a luxurious eight-room ranch house in the "Williamsburg Colonial style," with "unusual 'windowpane and shutter' doors so the garage looks like a wing of the home instead of a garage," is a harmless although confusing flight of fancy.[5] Clearly

3. On the relative value of antiquities in different regions, see my " 'In My Father's House Are Many Mansions'," *The American Archivist* XXIV, 2 (April 1961), pp. 137–138.

4. The last clause is prudent, for I am told that a little determined work with a fire hose will dissolve an adobe pretty rapidly.

5. Caroline Lewis, "Here's Williamsburg!", *Chicago Daily Tribune*, 16 December 1961, H, part I, 17, describing a house recently built in Oakbrook.

it has nothing to do with the past of Illinois, but the comfortable "Gothic" houses of the last century, complete with coal grates, porches, and rocking chairs, had no understandable relation to the history of the Hudson River. The principle of free enterprise has always supported the theory: "Is it not lawful for me to do what I will with mine own?" It is to be profoundly regretted when private owners, disregarding all protests, tear down India Wharf on the Boston waterfront to make way for another parking lot.[6] It would be a national disgrace to allow public or private action to befoul the present unspoiled view of the Maryland shore of the Potomac River opposite Mount Vernon.[7] Such threats to historic buildings, like the poor, we have always with us. It is ironical that they are now being augmented by threats springing from an imperfect understanding of the popularization of history. A straw in the wind a couple of years ago was the proposal to remodel a respectable Georgetown house of the Federal period, lowering its roof and putting a new brick façade over the present one "along the line of Williamsburg architecture."[8] If a rash of colonial imitations, whether of English or Spanish inspiration, covers the United States, the promoters thereof are likely, from confused motives or inadequate knowledge, to do almost as much harm as those who destroy through simple greed.

It is needless to point out that the tourist trade is going great guns. Chambers of commerce, automobile manufacturers, and oil companies gloat over the spiraling statistics. The National Geographic Society's recent four-pound extravaganza *America's Historylands, Landmarks of Liberty*—"676 illustrations, 463 in breathtaking color"—offers "vacation ideas for years to come." Peanut

6. Abbott Lowell Cummings, "The Beginnings of India Wharf," *Proceedings* of The Bostonian Society, (1962), pp. 17–24, indicates the importance of this Bulfinch building which was demolished in the late spring of 1962, irrespective of any opinion save that of the present owners.

7. Speech of Hon. Frances P. Bolton of Ohio in the House of Representatives, 18 April 1962, reprinted from the *Congressional Record*.

8. Jack Eisen, "Georgetown Preservationists Object to Wheeler's 'Williamsburg' façade," *The Washington Post*, 25 January 1960, concerning the old Beall's Express building at 1522 Wisconsin Avenue, N.W.

stands, wax works, reptile farms, and gift shops stand ready and eager to benefit from the passing millions; so do almost as many sites claiming the mantle of history. Their variety is extraordinary. A rack of flyers in a Florida motel office may invite the traveler to include in his itinerary Thomas A. Edison's winter home in Fort Myers, "Florida's Shrine of Science," or to "Step Back Into Time 800 Years" by visiting the "Ancient Spanish Monastery, Oldest Building in the Western Hemisphere," which is "only minutes away from almost any place in Greater Miami." This monastery from Sacremenia in the province of Segovia is, I suspect, one of the buildings dismantled by the Spanish art dealers, Mr. and Mrs. Arthur Byne, for William Randolph Hearst that never reached San Simeon.[9] At any rate, the flyer states:

It is not a reproduction nor a copy. It is the original monastery itself. You have probably seen it on television, heard about it on radio, read about it in national magazines, newspapers, and foreign publications.[10]

Although this monastery is indeed neither "a reproduction nor a copy," a great many things offered the traveling public are. Where buildings thought to be of some interest have vanished, steps are often taken to reconstruct them. Sir John Summerson, in appraising suitable subjects for historic preservation, expressed satisfaction that in Great Britain, excluding Scotland, "we have never given way to the craze for preserving birthplaces, usually the least significant structures in any man's life." He continued:

I believe we should preserve the houses of great men only when architecture comes into the picture *as* architecture; and chiefly when this architecture is itself eloquent of the mind which inhabited it. Abbotsford: yes. Garrick's Villa at Hampton: yes. Scott's birthplace: no. Garrick's birthplace: no.[11]

9. For some of the things that did get reconstructed there, see Oscar Lewis, *Fabulous San Simeon* (San Francisco, 1958).

10. Directly opposite Abraham Lincoln's house in Springfield, Illinois, is an establishment offering "Rest Rooms—Air-Conditioned—Bookshop—Gifts," whose sign admonishes: "Don't come this far and fail to go through the Museum whose displays have been praised by the New York Times and featured in other newspapers and magazines from coast to coast."

11. *Heavenly Mansions and Other Essays on Architecture* (London, 1949), pp. 225–226.

Nevertheless a generation ago George Washington and Theodore Roosevelt, whose birthplaces had vanished, were posthumously furnished with reconstructions thereof. In spite of the preservation of Monticello, a stone's throw away, certain residents of Charlottesville have recently supplied Thomas Jefferson with a superfluous reconstructed birthplace at Shadwell. On a humbler level, the New Orleans *Times-Picayune* for 23 February 1960 reported:

"Uncle Tom's Cabin," built of cypress logs chinked with clay, has been restored near Natchitoches, where the legendary "Uncle Tom" may have lived.

"Uncle Tom" was the central character of Harriet Beecher Stowe's novel, "Uncle Tom's Cabin."

Owners of the site recently reconstructed the cabin. They have offered to turn the site over to the state parks and recreation commission.[12]

The spectacle of a demagogue who interlards his purple passages with supporting quotations from Washington, Jefferson, or Lincoln—almost invariably taken out of context—is unedifying. So, when it cloaks itself in the disguise of something superior, is the ignoble activity of touting goods to indifferent buyers. Julian P. Boyd has pointed out "the obvious dangers in our preoccupation with the American past" that

In much of it there is the base alloy of commerce which becomes at its worst an exploitation of history, keeping one eye on a handful of patriotic shibboleths and the other on the balance sheet.[13]

The advertising profession too frequently exploits history in this way. A single example will suffice. In the summer of 1959 members of the American Historical Association received from an oil company proofs of a full-page ad appearing in *Time*, *Newsweek*, the *Saturday Review*, and the *National Geographic Magazine*, urging

12. Although the report stated that the owners "have restored ₁read "reconstructed"₁ the cabin to resemble an original building taken to the Chicago World's Fair in 1893" and that "the new cabin has persimmon-wood hinges on the door and shingles just like the original," "authorities said proof is lacking that the site is authentic."

13. *1958 Proceedings of the Wyoming Commemorative Association* (Wilkes-Barre, 1958), pp. 8–9.

tourists to "Visit Kings Mountain—where the mountainmen made you free." Above, in full color, mother, dad, and the kiddies are admiring a young man disguised as a Revolutionary soldier in Kings Mountain National Military Park, South Carolina. Below is the pitch:

Out of the mountains they came with hunting knives, Kentucky rifles and *freedom blazing white-hot in their eyes.* And waiting for them on Kings Mountain was a superior force of Redcoats and Tories under the redoubtable Major Ferguson who boasted that "all the rebels outside of——couldn't drive him from the mountain." In one short, volcanic hour the untrained mountainmen won a crucial victory that fired up the Colonies and led to Yorktown and independence.

Today, Kings Mountain slumbers in the heart of one of the South's most scenic vacationlands where you can swim, fish, ride . . . visit historic sites and stately country homes. At Kings Mountain, now carefully preserved, you can browse through the museum . . . recreate the action on a self-guided tour . . . and pause at the grave of the doughty Pat Ferguson who, true to his boast, is still there.

And you can muse for a moment on the unlettered backwoodsmen *who wrote a shining page in freedom's book.* The handwriting might be crude—but the message was unmistakably clear . . . *no mountain is too high for men to scale when freedom waits at the top.*

Below are the addresses that will supply free tour information and maps. In the margin the advertiser "salutes the American Historical Association," which is, with unhistorical inaccuracy, stated to have been chartered in 1896. The whole is typical of the corporate mind at work when it enlists the services of Madison Avenue to enable it to pay a heavy-handed pseudo-tribute to a cultural institution. A covering letter from the chairman of the board concludes with the immortal sentences:

We believe that the American people are indeed fortunate that the Association has existed since 1884 to promote the study of history (and not, as inadvertently shown in our salute in several publications merely since 1896!). It is our hope that this advertisement will bring added attention to the many distinguished historians who contribute so ably to the understanding and continuity of the American civilization.

The advertisement attempts, rather crudely, to present "history" as an unholy alliance between a learned historical association on the one hand and a great body of tourists on the other, whose main object is to "swim, fish, ride . . . visit historic sites and stately country homes" —an alliance manufactured by a great corporation whose only aim is to increase gasoline sales. Such instances give force to Adlai Stevenson's inquiry:

With the supermarket as our temple[14] and the singing commercial as our litany, are we likely to fire the world with an irresistible vision of America's exalted purposes and inspiring way of life?[15]

It is not necessary to take to the road to find examples of the misuses of history. Every local newspaper has its quota of the per-versions that all too readily spawn in the heads of politicians, public relations men, advertising types, and other promoters. The *Boston Herald* of 30 September 1959 showed a group of women in fancy dress with the caption:

James Frazier, chairman of the Plymouth board of selectmen, shows an engraved certificate to townsfolk in Puritan [sic] dress announcing the award of a Federal grant of $1,027,873 for a 30 acre urban renewal project at Plymouth.

A fortnight later the *Herald*'s readers were treated to a view of a bus collision on the upper level of the Mystic River Bridge in which twelve persons were injured. These unfortunate victims were mem-bers of the American Association of State Highway Officials in an eleven-bus caravan inspecting the new Massachusetts expressway systems. They were at the time "en route to a reenactment of the Mayflower Compact signing." It is not clear why they were being treated on 14 October 1959 to the re-enactment of an event that took place on 11 November 1620, or, indeed, what possible relation the Mayflower Compact has to highway officials and new expressways. But apparently it is always a good thing to pull in the Pilgrims some-how.

The celebration of anniversaries often furnishes the opportunity

14. Which may well sport a "colonial" (English or Spanish) façade.
15. *Life*, 30 May 1960, p. 97.

for commercialism to disguise itself in sheep's clothing. Mr. Robert T. Taylor's study of the Jamestown Tercentennial Exposition of 1907 in the April 1957 issue of the *Virginia Magazine of History and Biography* furnishes a beautifully documented and dispassionately presented case history of how a supposedly historical celebration can get out of hand when it falls into the grip of promoters. This deserves careful study. In May 1960, when the Civil War Centennial was still a year in the future, I warned the Virginia Historical Society that

unless Virginians and New Englanders band together to laugh at the commercial perversions of history that will be offered us in increasing quantity, the years from 1961 to 1965 are going to be very unpleasant indeed.

The *Richmond Times-Dispatch*, supporting my view in an editorial of 7 May 1960 entitled "Against Hawkers and Hucksters," pointed out in reinforcement:

The sort of crudity against which Dr. Whitehill warned has popped up already in New Jersey—as a dismaying editorial on this page from the Newport News *Daily Press* shows. Special cigars, rum drinks and hats are being created for sale at a race track there—all of them tied up in some remote and ridiculous way with the Civil War anniversary (which actually occurs four years hence, in that particular instance).

The year 1961 provided its quota of *opéra bouffe*, including the event satirized "by a Combat Artist of The *Washington Post*" in its issue of 24 July 1961. A cartoon entitled "Survivors fleeing the Battle of 3d Manassas (1961)" shows a job-lot of dusty tourists with thermos bottles, lunch baskets, and squalling children, leaving the hot sun of the battlefield in the company of individuals disguised as soldiers, who are refreshing themselves after combat with soft drinks.

The appointment late in 1961 of Professor Allan Nevins as chairman of the Civil War Centennial Commission gave promise of hope, particularly when he stated on 31 January 1962 that

If we confine ourselves to battles and campaigns, the sigh of relief that went up over the real Appomattox in 1865 may conceivably be nothing to the national sigh of relief that will go up over the commemorated Appomattox of 1965.

He announced that the commission planned a series of thirteen scholarly volumes concerning the impact of the war in such areas as agriculture, poverty, crime, charities, and literature, to be written by competent historians and published by Alfred A. Knopf. His promise that "The National Commission would re-enact a battle only over my dead body"[16] gave great relief to many. This statement was made just twenty-four hours too late, for, on the very day that Dr. Nevins was addressing the Civil War Centennial Commission in Washington, the attempt to fire a cannon in the driveway of the Museum of Fine Arts in Boston to celebrate the opening of an exhibition, "The Civil War, The Artist's Record," only succeeded in breaking numerous windows in neighboring apartment houses. Then, alas, on 7 May 1962 the *New York Times* reported that, because of President Kennedy's remark: "I like sham battles," the Civil War Centennial Commission had bowed to superior force and now planned to re-create Antietam in September 1962. Thus we may apparently expect to have hostilities break out at any time through April 1965.

While national celebrations offer the richest field for commercial exploitation, even the mildest local anniversary furnishes an opportunity for someone to dress up and make a fool of himself. A well-organized event causes beards to be grown (by "brothers of the brush") and hoopskirts to be worn (by "sisters of the swish") in quantity. Hawkers and hucksters swarm to it like flies to honey.

It would be charitable to assume that many organized celebrations spring from legitimate motives and that commercial exploitation of history only slips into them by the way. Such an assumption cannot apply to "Freedomland U.S.A." in the Bronx, which opened in June 1960. Notwithstanding Governor Nelson A. Rockefeller's misleading endorsement:

Freedomland is the ultimate expression of the effort to dramatize our history and to bring it home vividly to everyone who sees it—an effort which, incidentally, originated on a far smaller scale in the Lake George area of upstate New York, with the reconstruction of Fort Ticonderoga and Lake George Village.[17]

16. *The Washington Post*, 1 February 1962, p. D 1.
17. On the second page of a twenty-page advertising section of the *New York*

Freedomland, for all its veneer of pseudo-history, was from the outset a commercial effort of Mr. William Zeckendorf's firm, Webb and Knapp.[18] It was simply an amusement park, charging admission at the gate, plus fees for the "attractions" within. Moreover the Freedomland Inn, a Zeckendorf hotel, provided

gracious dining in a unique restaurant and a convenient coffee shop. 400 rooms with air-conditioning, TV and radio. There's an Olympic-size swimming pool for your pleasure, and a separate wading pool and play area to delight the children. Tree-lined promenades, feathery fountains, central gardens . . . .

This inn was at hand not only to house those who came intentionally to Freedomland but to pick up transients from the Hutchinson River Parkway and the New England Thruway, who might, after a night's lodging, choose to break their journey in order to explore "the biggest Disneyland-type playground of them all."

Freedomland, according to its Texas-born engineer-showman creator, C. V. Wood Jr., was to offer its visitors "a giant slate of assorted wholesome fun, integrated around a theme." Of his profession Mr. Wood observed:

I view it as an imaginative combination of big business, show business, design creativity and mass education through entertainment. What more could a person want?

Of this particular instance, he explained:

In building this world's champion outdoor entertainment park, I told my design staff I wanted to tell the whole American story in one vast area shaped like the nation's map and segmented into regions. We came up with 500 thrilling American themes, discussed and discarded until we had the top 14 major stories now in

Times of 19 June 1960 entitled: "Our Whole, Wide, Wonderful FREEDOMLAND Comes to Life in New York City. World's Largest Entertainment Center." Joining Governor Rockefeller in testimonials, Mayor Wagner mentioned "wholesome, leisure-time entertainment," while Milton T. Raynor, president of Freedomland, promised "not only to provide the maximum of fun for every member of the family, but also the utmost in convenience and service."

18. See Edward Sorel and Paul Davis, "A Modern Bestiary, Two naturalists identify some fauna from current mythology," _Horizon_ IV, 6 (July 1962), pp. 120 ff., which includes "The Sand Hog, or Badger (_Zechendorfus barbarus_)" among other contemporary caricatures.

the park, some of them with four or five separate attractions. This is our way of dramatizing the American heritage.

The *Times*, in a pre-opening description, reported on 12 June 1960 that

the theme being America's history, the new kind of showmanship is able to offer many of the thrills of the old carnival-type rides by overlaying its "new" rides with a veneer of history. Thus the "Dragon Ride" in the New Orleans enclave is presented as part of that city's Mardi Gras. Many an old-timer will recognize in it the basic philosophy of the old-style tunnels of love, as the dragon snakes its way, puffing and blowing, with people inside it, through the streets of New Orleans.

Other attractions included a "Continental Tour" on the Santa Fé,

buckskin-clad riders of the Pony Express, red-shirted firemen who will strive every twenty minutes (with the help of any volunteer patrons who want to pump the old-fashioned fire engines) to put out the Chicago Fire of 1871; camps of authentic Red Indians from seven tribes, some of whom with gun and tomahawk will be raiding the Santa Fé express as it crosses the Great Plains.

Having been able to resist a personal visit, I have learned of subsequent developments only through the press. *Time* on 26 September 1960 reported "Trouble in Freedomland." According to this account there had been preliminary difficulty in the financing; on the opening day, when things were not completed, 60,000 people—twice the anticipated number—appeared and complained; three hoodlums, unobserved in the flurry of frontier life, later robbed the office of $28,836; construction bills were unpaid; stock issued at $17.50 had dropped to $6.25; and so on. *Time* reported the proposed solution:

In a characteristically complicated financing plan, Webb & Knapp will buy $11.5 million in convertible debentures from International Recreation [the operating corporation], which will use $3,000,000 of this sum to pay off its construction bills, use the remaining $8,500,000 to buy the leases of Webb & Knapp's Astor, Manhattan, and Commodore Hotels, thus returning the cash to Webb & Knapp. With the purchase of the debentures, Webb & Knapp will have further control over Freedomland and an $18.5 million stake in it. The park will be run by officials appointed by the real estate firm. By taking over the midtown Manhattan hotels, Freedomland will have a year-round income, hopes to be able to offset hotel profits with playground losses.

From time to time during the summer of 1961 I heard, unwillingly, an FM radio commercial, extolling Freedomland as "a world of fun and adventure where you can ride high in the sky in an open ore-basket"; "also there is dancing to big-name bands." The announced addition of a Roman chariot race, King Arthur's knights, the Three Musketeers, the charge of the Light Brigade, and the Bengal Lancers indicated that the theme had been expanded beyond American history. I do not know what has happened in 1962. It is clear, however, that from the start Freedomland was using American history for purely commercial ends.[19]

A major misfortune of such abuses of history is that they may mislead the uninformed. A seventy-two-view, brightly colored souvenir booklet *The Adirondacks, The World's Largest Park*, widely offered to tourists in upper New York State, illustrates on terms of absolute equality with the basically genuine Fort Ticonderoga, the reconstructed Fort William Henry at Lake George, and a variety of purely commercial attractions, such as Storytown U.S.A.,—"where your favorite nursery rhymes come to life" plus outlaws and jungle safaris —Gaslight Village, a reconstruction of the "Gay Nineties" with dancing in a beer garden, the imported "Wild West" Frontier Town, the Land of Makebelieve, and Santa's Workshop at North Pole, New York.

As commercialism seeks to cloak itself in history, it becomes absolutely essential for legitimate historic houses, restorations, and outdoor museums to avoid even the appearance of evil in their actions. If they disfigure the highways with billboards identical to those of commercial "attractions"; if they offer tawdry "souvenirs," banners, and penny-catchers in their shops; if they affix bumper placards to visitors' automobiles; if, from whatever motives, they embrace commercial tactics to increase attendance, how in God's

19. The *New York Times* of 12 June 1960 reported: "Freedomland seems to have been conceived as the East Coast's answer to the West Coast's Disneyland. Some comparisons are in order. Disneyland's original cost was $17,000,000. By this month, its investment will be $32,500,000. Freedomland's investors announce that its investment at present is $65,000,000."

name can the average man distinguish between the popularization of history and its commercial exploitation? Freedomland indicates that there must be an insurmountable wall between history and the entertainment business, or indeed any other form of commercialism. If historical organizations cannot survive without resorting to such tactics, it is time they died.

Chapter XXV

WHAT SHALL BE DONE?

The necessity is present; the materials are at hand. The question is,
What shall be done?   —HENRY E. BOURNE, 1904

FIFTY-EIGHT years ago Professor Bourne, in reporting to the American Historical Association, found that historical societies were, "broadly speaking, of two types, illustrated by the Massachusetts and the Wisconsin." They still are, as I have tried to demonstrate in the preceding chapters of this study. During the years that have elapsed, societies of both types have grown very considerably in resources and usefulness, but the division by type remains as clear as it was in 1904. This is due to a difference of objectives. The independent society is primarily concerned with the advancement of learning; the publicly-supported society not only with its advancement but its wide dissemination. Both seek to serve the scholar, but the former reaches a wide audience only indirectly through the work of others, while the latter seeks direct contact with large numbers of people. Both types have their place. Both have developed through the activities of inspired individuals, no two of whom have been exactly alike, and through the particular circumstances of their regions. No common pattern of organization can be devised that will fit both. Nothing would be gained by the reincarnation of Procrustes.

At the ceremony at the Massachusetts Historical Society last year commemorating the publication of the first four volumes of *The*

Adams Papers, Professor Paul H. Buck described the evolution of the Harvard University Press over half a century. He concluded his address thus:

In recent years both historical societies and university presses have been exposed to criticism and have been required to justify their right to exist and to solicit support. I submit that the publication of *The Adams Papers* is the final answer to such criticisms.

Who but a University and a historical society dedicated to scholarship could have conceived of so vast a project on so non-commercial a basis? Who but these in partnership could have commanded the respect, understanding, and support of alumni to finance the project? Who but these could command the interest and advice of scholars to guarantee the highest standards of editorial competency?

The answers to these questions must be "None." And in that affirmation of the uniqueness of this partnership we see the ultimate justification for both the Massachusetts Historical Society and of the Harvard University Press.[1]

Although *The Adams Papers* are the most conspicuous recent example of the work of an independent historical society, so much is being accomplished in so many quarters by societies of this type that there can be no doubt that they serve a valuable purpose in the United States. My study has led me to the conviction that their organization and method of operation are fundamentally sound, that nothing would be gained, so far as their basic function of serving the scholar is concerned, by seeking legislative funds for their general support[2] or by attempting to expand their activities into the museum field or the cause of popular education. Nearly all of them need more money, which must, if they are to prosper and develop, come from

1. *The Adams Papers, A Ceremony Held at the Massachusetts Historical Society on September 22, 1961 Marking the Publication of the* Diary and Autobiography of John Adams (Boston, 1962), p. 13.

2. Public assistance in specific projects of scholarly utility, such as microfilming newspapers and local records, for example, could be both appropriate and helpful. Independent historical societies should enter wholeheartedly into any co-operative projects emanating from the Library of Congress, the National Archives, and the National Historical Publications Commission that fall within their field. It is chiefly in the local area, where conditions of reciprocal back-scratching by voters and legislators might affect the general policies of a society, that public support has its perils.

private individuals and foundations. The independent historical society is as reliable and suitable a recipient of such funds as a university or a laboratory. It can be as great a credit to a community as an art museum, an orchestra, a hospital, or a charitable institution. It should be supported by many of the same persons who give generously to those, even though the results of its work, like those of any institution devoted to basic research, are seldom spectacular and not always immediately apparent.

The majority of the independent historical societies are already closely tied to one another, and to related institutions, through an informal and intimate network of friendships between scholars and collectors. Between the meetings of countless learned and professional societies, of the Institute of Early American History and Culture, of the Grolier Club and the Club of Odd Volumes, and the activities of the great editorial projects, information usually reaches those who need it with creditable speed. Internecine warfare and empire building are conspicuously absent. Most societies are realistically limiting their fields in order to make the best use of their resources. Limitations of space, staff, time, and money are a powerful inducement to intelligent co-operation and the avoidance of useless duplication. The personal visits and correspondence essential in the collecting stages of the Jefferson, Franklin, Adams, and other editorial projects have informally helped to co-ordinate some of the scattered sources of American history. An editor looking for one thing incidentally finds another and passes the word to the appropriate quarter. Every new bibliography locates something previously unknown or unappreciated.

Isaiah Thomas in 1814 remarked that

Any to whom the Library and Cabinet of [the American Antiquarian] Society may be useful, will not greatly regret the distance which separates them from the objects of their pursuit, if they can but eventually obtain in one place, what, otherwise, they would have to seek in many.

The hope of achieving completeness *in one place* on even limited subjects has gone the way of the dodo. Even when not accidentally scattered, material is frequently deliberately decentralized. But as the hope of completeness has faded, the development of microform has provided new methods of bringing together what the scholar needs. With thoughtful planning, even a single institution of modest resources can achieve by this means "such a multiplication of copies as shall place" important books and manuscripts "beyond the reach of accident" and within the reach of scholars. The Massachusetts Historical Society's microfilm edition of the Adams papers paid its own way through subscriptions. So has the American Antiquarian Society's microprint *Early American Imprints, 1693–1800,* which, incidentally, reproduces books from many other libraries than that of the sponsoring society. These two undertakings required several years of effort and large sums of money; their subscription prices of $4,500 and $8,000, respectively, place them beyond the reach of individuals. *Early American Imprints, 1693–1800* reproduces every extant book, pamphlet, and broadside printed in what is now the United States, but not newspapers. On a less gigantic scale, *Early American Newspapers in Microprint* produces microcards that can be afforded by individuals as well as libraries. Editing in installments for the American Antiquarian Society, Ebenezer Gay, executive officer of the Boston Athenæum, issues small segments of colonial newspapers at reasonable prices, as time and funds permit. In addition to its remarkable newspaper files, the American Antiquarian Society as sponsor provides quarters and encouragement. In what time he can spare from his normal duties at the Boston Athenæum, Mr. Gay assembles, collates, and prepares for filming the required papers. The Massachusetts, Connecticut, New-York, and Wisconsin historical societies, the Boston Public Library, the Boston Athenæum, the Harvard College Library, and the Library of Congress have lent originals, or furnished photographic copies, of newspapers needed to complete runs. Mr. Gay and his associates have formed the Micro-Research Corporation to handle the details of printing and distributing the microcards. The Franklins' *New-England Courant* (1721–27) and *The Weekly Rehearsal* (1731–35) are available at

$12.50; three papers covering the critical period preceding the Revolution, *The Massachusetts Spy* (1770–75), *The Boston Chronicle* (1767–70), and *The Censor* (1771–72) at $19.95; from New York *Rivington's Royal Gazette* (1773–83) at $37.55. The most expensive series reproduced thus far is *The Boston News-Letter* (1704–76), which sells for $99. A number of other papers are available, or in preparation. This principle of microprint publication in segments of manageable size is of broad application.[3]

It is one thing, with the aid of Charles Evans's *American Bibliography*, Clarence S. Brigham's *History and Bibliography of American Newspapers*, and the *Union List of Newspapers*, to track down for reproduction early American newspapers and imprints. These often exist in multiple copies; even if one is well hidden another may come readily to light. With manuscripts, the situation is many times more complicated. While a number of historical societies and other libraries have issued guides to their collections, these are of necessity summary in their descriptions. Many important groups were first recorded in the National Historical Publications Commission *Guide* of 1961 that has been so frequently mentioned in the preceding chapters. This guide was a milestone of outstanding significance and utility, but its makers fully recognized that it marked only the first mile of a long journey. A second step in the same direction was the action of the Council on Library Resources, Inc., in November 1958 of granting $200,000 to the Library of Congress for the creation of a National Union Catalog of Manuscript Collections. Planning for this had begun as early as 1951. The money was made available for gathering and editing the essential data from the many diverse types of manuscript repositories, preparing cards for these, furnishing each participating institution with the printed cards for its reported collections, and establishing in the Library of Congress a national union catalogue in dictionary form of all such collections. As part of

3. The Micro-Research Corporation is prepared to consider the microprint publication of historical sources other than newspapers for which there might be a minimum demand of a hundred copies.

its existing series of published catalogues, the Library of Congress is preparing to print these cards in book form, with a subject index and an extensive index of names. The first volume, containing 7,300 entries, is now in press.

The project began operation in April 1959 under the direction of Dr. Lester K. Born, head, manuscripts section, descriptive cataloguing division. The first cards were printed the following June, while in the first year of the project some 2,000 collections were fully catalogued and about 750 cards printed. Dr. Born visited many libraries throughout the United States, seeking their co-operation in reporting their holdings. Almost without exception, the plan was enthusiastically welcomed, for the obvious utility of the National Union Catalog of Manuscript Collections to scholars, librarians, and archivists is self-evident. Many institutions are already co-operating to the limit of their abilities. The rub comes from the fact that, with the best will in the world and full appreciation of the importance of the project, many others are too shorthanded to be able to report details in the predictable future.

The testimony of "a law professor recently engaged in historical research" is helpful, for it emphasizes the reaction of a scholar who approaches historical manuscripts from another field. Professor Gerald Gunther of Columbia University School of Law, who is engaged in preparing a history of the United States Supreme Court, observes that

> To a lawyer accustomed to the probably excessive array of indexes, digests, citations, and services available for legal research, the difficulty of locating scattered manuscript records of American history is astounding.

It is less astounding to the historian, who has grown up with the situation. It has never occurred to him that his sources would be "packaged," like Bartlett's *Familiar Quotations*, which, though a useful work of ready reference, seldom inspires profound thought. He has expected to have to quarry. He has never enjoyed the "probably excessive" array of lawyer's tools of trade. Nevertheless there are few historians who would not regretfully confirm Professor Gunther's complaint that there are too few milestones along the road:

Nor can the researcher expect to find adequate cataloguing and indexing at most of the depositories he chooses to visit. Chronic staff and fund shortages have prevented most manuscript custodians from acquiring detailed knowledge about their own holdings. A listing of the sender and recipient of most letters in a collection, as at the Historical Society of Pennsylvania, is rare indeed; a detailed catalogue only intermittently maintained, as at the Library of Congress, is frustratingly inadequate, and poorly organized and incomplete descriptions are all too common even in the most important depositories, such as the New York Public Library. Staff deficiencies often affect the care of manuscripts as well; threatening the preservation of existing holdings and delaying for years the organization of new acquisitions.[4]

The explanation will be evident to anyone who has read this book. Most independent historical societies are too shorthanded to attempt the kind of detailed arrangement and indexing of their manuscripts that they would be the first to desire. They obtain material and place it under such controls as their time and resources permit. These are generally sufficient to enable the librarian, or a scholar thoroughly familiar with the field, to find what he wants in a reasonable length of time. Twenty-five years ago at the Peabody Museum of Salem I was confronted by some dozens of sea chests containing papers of their shipmaster owners. Their quantity was too great to permit any detailed indexing of individual documents. But by placing the papers of each shipmaster in manuscript boxes, arranged by the vessels commanded and then chronologically by complete voyages, with a brief inventory typed and pasted on the outside of each box, this mass of manuscripts came under reasonable control for the maritime historian. Similar procedures have been followed in many historical societies with generally satisfactory results. But when a lawyer, or someone engaged in a study peripheral to the main interest of the collection, asks if there are particular letters from a given person, or information on a certain subject, a great deal of time is lost in the search. This is the dilemma faced by the architectural historian or the

4. *Harvard Law Review* LXXV (June 1962), 1669–1670.

student of Indian linguistics who approaches the Moravian Archives, which are, as I pointed out earlier, admirably arranged for the study of Moravian history which is their reason for being.

Few historical societies have a curator who is able to give constant and undivided attention to the arrangement and indexing of manuscripts. Few days pass when that curator is not helping a visiting scholar or engaged in some similar worth-while interruption. In many societies the possibility of making prompt and full reports to the National Union Catalog of Manuscript Collections is non-existent. Yet if the National Union Catalog does not include the holdings of all important libraries, its usefulness will be jeopardized.

The first obvious answer to the question "What shall be done?" is the solution of this problem. My formula would be the provision by a foundation of a sum of money large enough to permit at least a dozen independent historical societies to add to their staffs for a period of years one or more competent scholars whose sole duty would be the arrangement and calendaring of manuscript collections, with the object of expediting reports to the National Union Catalog. This would break the log jam and be of immeasurable service to the societies, to the Library of Congress, and to historians as individuals. I cannot think of a better use for several hundred thousand dollars, for if carried out the plan would be not only of national scholarly usefulness, but would incidentally raise the spirits of the participating societies. When a devoted person works singlehandedly, or with inadequate assistance, the arrival of like-minded company can prove a powerful stimulus. The Massachusetts Historical Society was greatly enlivened, and its general purposes strengthened, when L. H. Butterfield came in 1954 to begin the editing of the Adams papers. A similar enlargement of staff would set off a chain reaction in some other institutions. The prompt and thorough organization of manuscript collections, which cannot be done rapidly enough from existing resources, is the essential first step.

Once that is accomplished, and the National Union Catalog of Manuscript Collections lives up to its name and promise, the obvious second step is to establish a microcopying program that would lead to a permanent pool of manuscript resources on negative microfilm that (on positive film or in Xerox prints) would be readily and inexpensively available for purchase or on interlibrary loan. This has been repeatedly urged by L. H. Butterfield, with whose thoughts on the subject I am in hearty accord. The National Archives' microfilm publications program and the Library of Congress's Presidential papers series[5] are obvious models for such action. They are, however, like the Massachusetts Historical Society's Adams microfilms, simply the microcopying of what exists in one depository. The proposed program should extend to collaborative efforts between institutions, so as to bring together in microform the two sides of a correspondence, or other essentially related documents that are now widely scattered. The full development of this step would presuppose the achievement of the first. Nevertheless it is not too soon to attempt to establish standards for the editorial preparation of manuscript materials thus to be copied, to devise a code that would govern their use, with due respect for the owning institution's rights,[6] and to undertake a few simple experimental projects with manuscripts whose locations are already adequately known. It is obvious that the proper physical arrangement of large masses of manuscripts, preparatory for publication on microfilm, is an exacting, slow, and costly operation. Most societies cannot undertake this without added support.

Wide availability of manuscript sources in microform would not only ease the path of the scholar but safeguard the originals. "A

5. See *List of National Archives Microfilm Publications 1961* (Washington, 1961); also *Microfilming Presidential Papers*, Hearing before the Subcommittee on the Library of the Committee on House Administration House of Representatives *Eighty-Fifth Congress First Session on H. R. 7813* (Washington, 1957). A printed index to each group of presidential papers thus far published is sold by the Superintendent of Documents for a small sum. Positive copies of the microfilms may be purchased from the photoduplication service of the Library of Congress or borrowed on interlibrary loan from its loan division.

6. Howard H. Peckham discusses this in "Policies Regarding the Use of Manuscripts," *Library Trends* v, 3 (January 1957), pp. 361–368.

multiplication of copies" provides not only against sudden and complete loss by fire but gradual destruction through needless repeated handling and copying. When every man does his own hunting individually, a great number of unique originals are microfilmed over and over again in piecemeal fashion on demand. This is needlessly costly, and harmful to the documents. Moreover, availability in microform would satisfy all needs for some types of manuscripts. With figures like Thomas Jefferson and Benjamin Franklin, it is desirable that all of their writings be available in printed form with full critical annotation. The printed edition of *The Adams Papers*, however, will be selective rather than complete. It would be impracticable to print *all* the papers of four generations of so articulate a family, even if one were so misguided as to wish to do so. The 608 reels of microfilm, now available to scholars in more than forty libraries, are all the publication likely to be required of John Quincy Adams's epic poems, his metrical translations of the Psalms, and his addresses to small-town fire departments. Thus the meticulously edited volumes of *The Adams Papers* will contain only a careful selection of those manuscripts that genuinely deserve printing in the noble format provided by the Belknap Press of Harvard University Press.

Some of the independent historical societies are intimately concerned with the future of the great editorial projects embraced in the current program of the National Historical Publications Commission. With a magnanimity that is heartening to historical scholarship, university presses have shown a generous willingness to assume the heavy and protracted burden of printing and publishing costs. Custodians of documents gladly make them available. Devoted and inspired editors willingly subordinate their personal interests and isolate themselves in undertakings that often cannot possibly be completed within their lifetimes. These three groups have played their parts more generously than, with exceptions, the philanthropic foundations, for both in universities and historical societies the continued support of the necessary editorial work has been, and still is, the major obstacle. The *New York Times* and Time, Inc., generously provided for the launching and initial voyages of the editorial offices of the Jefferson and the Adams papers, yet both projects now face crises in providing for their continued operation during the long years required for completion. The $25,000 annually paid the Massachusetts Historical Society for a ten-year period by Time, Inc., will not carry the editing of *The Adams Papers* beyond 1964. In the year that has elapsed since his retirement as executive director of the National Historical Publications Commission, Dr. Philip M. Hamer has not yet been able to secure funds for the editing of the Henry Laurens papers—a project in which the South Carolina Historical Society has a considerable interest. The John Marshall papers, a joint enterprise of the College of William and Mary and the Institute of Early American History and Culture, heartily approved by the commission, is still seeking editorial funds although an able editor and publisher are already enlisted. The National Historical Publications Commission is currently considering this dilemma in its broadest aspects. By the time this book appears, I trust that its members will have evolved some concrete proposals for its solution.

To turn from wholesale to retail problems of publication, I have been struck in my travels by the need of some co-operative means of distributing existing publications of independent historical societies. Even for the smallest and most straitened society it is very often possible to find the means of printing a worth-while monograph or collection of documents. The trouble begins when the stock is bound and delivered. Too often, after the initial local distribution, the stock remains encumbering shelves, for possible buyers at a distance have no way of knowing that the book exists. A fair supply of the late Christopher L. Ward's *The Delaware Continentals 1776–1783*, which now and then turns up in booksellers' catalogues as "out of print" at $10, is still available from the Historical Society of Delaware at the 1941 published price of $3.75. Similar instances could be multiplied, for the expense involved in individual advertising would be unreasonable. Moreover, in few such organizations does anyone have the time required to devise plans for getting into useful circulation such books as are of too specialized interest for the commercial market. The annual preparation of a co-operative catalogue, modeled in simplified form on the joint listings of university press books, of the current stocks of a few dozen historical societies, libraries, and museums, if sent by each to its own mailing list, would offer a means of getting such books distributed at small cost to the participating institutions. A further step in this direction might be the establishment, in some rural region where overhead would be low, of a common warehouse, where institutions could send on consignment a limited number of copies of each of their books. The Stinehour Press in Lunenburg, Vermont, the printers of this book, has expressed willingness to explore the possibilities of such an arrangement.[7] A co-operative catalogue might also usefully enlarge the subscription lists of such periodicals as the *William and Mary Quarterly*, the *New England Quarterly*, and *The American Neptune*.

Provided they can be distributed, publications offer the most useful means of making the resources of historical societies generally available. The *Handbook of Texas*, described in chapter XIV, is a model that might well be emulated in other states. This, it will be recalled, was planned by Professor Walter Prescott Webb in 1940, carried out by the Texas State Historical Association at an expense of about $100,000 provided by the University of Texas and the Rockefeller Foundation, and published in 1952 in an edition of 6,000 copies. Receipts from the substantial sales of the handbook have greatly augmented the Texas State Historical Association's revolving publication fund. This is a pattern of broad application. Even in states like Massachusetts and New York such a work of general reference would be extremely helpful. In regions where less historical writing

---

7. The book publishing activities of *The Barre Gazette* in Barre, Massachusetts, a country newspaper owned by Alden P. Johnson, corresponding secretary of the American Antiquarian Society, have led to the appearance of several useful historical works whose distribution was thought to be too limited for commercial publication.

has been done, it would be even more valuable. Such a project anywhere, if soundly planned and staffed by workers of suitable literacy and historical competence, could produce a work that would both be valuable in itself and stimulating to the historical society that undertook it.

The foregoing paragraphs concern chiefly the larger independent State historical societies that possess substantial research resources. In many parts of the country, county and town societies abound, the most extreme instance doubtless being Essex County in Massachusetts, where I estimate that there is a local historical society for every 11,095 acres of dry land. Nevertheless the snowball annually increases to a point where the American Association for State and Local History has thought it wise to issue a pamphlet of ground rules on *Organizing A Local Historical Society*. This contains much sensible advice, although it skates rapidly over the thin ice of the question of genuine need of still more organizations. The "cloud of witnesses" of many kinds is already very great. Most existing organizations have inadequate resources for their present purposes. One may thus ask whether more are required? Whether the purpose is solely the advancement of history, or whether considerations of personal aggrandizement, undirected energies, local pride, or other irrelevancies enter in? If it is solely the advancement of history, a widespread community effort is needless, for it is only the serious workers that count, and their number will always be small. Word often gets around faster by a grapevine than by blaring loudspeakers to which people are inclined not to listen.

Present-day reincarnations of Belknap, Pintard, and Thomas could profitably meet together under their own roofs for the exchange of ideas, discussion, and the reading of papers, with a complete absence of expense or formal organization. If they accumulate more worth-while books and manuscripts than their own shelves will accommodate, there is likely to be an existing institution somewhere—whether a university or public library, museum, or historical society—that will gladly assure their preservation and use. It is always preferable to concentrate resources where they are most likely to be used rather than to proliferate splinter groups for personal reasons.[8] The key to such simplicity is to avoid the temptation of becoming loaded with bulky objects, whose upkeep inevitably brings financial problems that may come to outweigh everything else. If for the appearance of a region, or important considerations of history or architecture, it is desirable to preserve a building, it is usually sounder to convert it to some self-supporting present-day use than to attempt to place it on exhibition. A handsome house, occupied by responsible tenants who care for it, is preferable to the same house as an inadequately supported "museum." So long as a group, however small, works seriously and remains unencumbered by a baggage train of belongings, the chances of it making a useful contribution to history are high.

8. The Huntington Library, although eccentrically located for personal reasons, has made sense over the years because Mr. Huntington left an endowment adequate to develop the necessary reference library, to maintain a staff of resident scholars, to bring others there for shorter periods, and to publish the results of their researches. To have established such an institution without adequate provision for its future support would have been folly. To establish one, only with endowment for maintaining the *status quo*, without provision for the growth and *use* of the collection, would be doing a disservice to learning.

INDEX